Probability

and Its Engineering Uses

PROBABILITY AND ITS ENGINEERING USES. *By* THORNTON C. FRY. Second Edition.

TRANSMISSION NETWORKS AND WAVE FILTERS. *By* T. E. SHEA.

ECONOMIC CONTROL OF QUALITY OF MANUFACTURED PRODUCT. *By* W. A. SHEWHART.

ELECTROMECHANICAL TRANSDUCERS AND WAVE FILTERS. *By* WARREN P. MASON. Second Edition.

POISSON'S EXPONENTIAL BINOMIAL LIMIT. *By* E. C. MOLINA.

ELECTROMAGNETIC WAVES. *By* S. A. SCHELKUNOFF.

NETWORK ANALYSIS AND FEEDBACK AMPLIFIER DESIGN. *By* HENDRICK W. BODE.

CAPACITORS—THEIR USE IN ELECTRONIC CIRCUITS. *By* M. BROTHERTON.

FOURIER INTEGRALS FOR PRACTICAL APPLICATIONS. *By* GEORGE A. CAMPBELL and RONALD M. FOSTER.

APPLIED MATHEMATICS FOR ENGINEERS AND SCIENTISTS. *By* S. A. SCHELKUNOFF. Second Edition.

EARTH CONDUCTION EFFECTS IN TRANSMISSION SYSTEMS. *By* ERLING D. SUNDE.

THEORY AND DESIGN OF ELECTRON BEAMS. *By* J. R. PIERCE. Second Edition.

PIEZOELECTRIC CRYSTALS AND THEIR APPLICATION TO ULTRA-SONICS. *By* WARREN P. MASON.

MICROWAVE ELECTRONICS. *By* JOHN C. SLATER.

PRINCIPLES AND APPLICATIONS OF WAVEGUIDE TRANSMISSION. *By* GEORGE C. SOUTHWORTH.

TRAVELING-WAVE TUBES. *By* J. R. PIERCE.

ELECTRONS AND HOLES IN SEMICONDUCTORS. *By* WILLIAM SHOCKLEY.

FERROMAGNETISM. *By* RICHARD M. BOZORTH.

THE DESIGN OF SWITCHING CIRCUITS. *By* WILLIAM KEISTER, ALASTAIR E. RITCHIE, and SETH H. WASHBURN.

SPEECH AND HEARING IN COMMUNICATION. *By* HARVEY FLETCHER. Second Edition.

MODULATION THEORY. *By* HAROLD S. BLACK.

SWITCHING RELAY DESIGN. *By* R. L. PEEK, JR., and H. N. WAGAR.

TRANSISTOR TECHNOLOGY, Volume I. *Edited by* H. E. BRIDGERS, J. H. SCAFF, and J. N. SHIVE.

TRANSISTOR TECHNOLOGY, Volume II. *Edited by* F. J. BIONDI.

TRANSISTOR TECHNOLOGY, Volume III. *Edited by* F. J. BIONDI.

PHYSICAL ACOUSTICS AND THE PROPERTIES OF SOLIDS. *By* WARREN P. MASON.

THE PROPERTIES, PHYSICS AND DESIGN OF SEMICONDUCTOR DEVICES. *By* J. N. SHIVE.

PRINCIPLES OF ELECTRON TUBES. *By* J. W. GEWARTOWSKI and H. A. WATSON.

Probability

and Its Engineering Uses

by

THORNTON C. FRY

Former Member of the Technical Staff
Bell Telephone Laboratories

Second Edition

D. VAN NOSTRAND COMPANY

Princeton, New Jersey

Toronto   New York   London

D. VAN NOSTRAND COMPANY, INC.
120 Alexander St., Princeton, New Jersey (*Principal office*)
24 West 40 Street, New York 18, New York

D. VAN NOSTRAND COMPANY, LTD.
358 Kensington High Street, London, W.14, England

D. VAN NOSTRAND COMPANY (Canada), LTD.
25 Hollinger Road, Toronto 16, Canada

———————

COPYRIGHT © 1928, 1965, BY
D. VAN NOSTRAND COMPANY, INC.

———————

Published simultaneously in Canada by
D. VAN NOSTRAND COMPANY (Canada), LTD.

———————

To Louise

"Coincidences, in general, are great stumbling-blocks
in the way of that class of thinkers who have been
educated to know nothing of the theory of probabilities:
that theory to which the most glorious objects of human
research are indebted for the most glorious of illustration."

— *The Murders in the Rue Morgue*

Acknowledgments

When the first edition of this book was published in 1928 I wrote:

"This textbook is the outgrowth of a set of notes originally prepared for one of the "Out-of-Hour Courses" of Bell Telephone Laboratories, and subsequently revised for use in a course of lectures delivered at the Massachusetts Institute of Technology in its Department of Electrical Engineering. I am deeply indebted to both these institutions for arrangements whereby it was possible to try out the material under actual classroom conditions — a rare opportunity for a mathematician engaged in industrial work."

My indebtedness to them is as great now as then, for without the first edition there would be no second. In addition, I must now express my pleasure and my thanks to Bell Telephone Laboratories for its decision to retain this revision in the Bell Laboratories Series, an honor which, as an employe now retired, I deeply appreciate.

I am also indebted in various ways to others, especially to the National Center for Atmospheric Research, and to its Director, Dr. Walter Orr Roberts, for placing the entire facilities of the Center at my command during the preparation of this revision.

THORNTON C. FRY

Carmel, California
February 1, 1965

Contents

Chapter I
Introduction

SECTION | PAGE

1 The Fundamental Subject Matter of Probability — 1
2 How Probability Is Measured; The Unit of Measure — 2
3 How Probability Is Measured; The Fundamental Axioms
  and Conventions — 3
4 How Probability Is Measured; The Primary Measure of Probability
  Defined — 6
5 How Probability Is Measured; Shortcomings of the Definition — 7
6 Final Remarks — 8

Chapter II
The Language of Probability

7 Chance, Random, Stochastic — 10
8 Experiments; Mathematical Models; Monte Carlo Methods — 11
9 Events — 12
10 Probability Distribution; Sample Space; Probability Density — 13
11 Sets of Points — 15
   Problems — 17
12 The Concept of a Population — 18
13 Statistics; Inference — 19
14 Chance Variables; Chance Functions — 21
15 Concluding Remarks — 22

Chapter III
Permutations and Combinations

16 Introduction — 24
17 General Laws of Composition of Events — 24
   Problems — 26
18 Definitions — 26
19 Application of the General Laws of Composition to Permutations and
   Combinations; Some Typical Examples — 28
20 Applications of the General Laws of Composition to Permutations;
   General Theorems — 29
   Problems — 31

SECTION   PAGE
21 Factorials; the Gamma Function   32
22 Restatement of General Theorems in Permutations   34
23 Application of the General Laws to Combinations   35
    Problems   37
24 Some General Properties of C_n^m; Pascal's Triangle   37
25 Some General Properties of C_n^m; The Binomial Theorem   39
26 Relations Among Binomial Coefficients   40
27 The Solution of More Complicated Problems   42
28 Symmetric Functions   44
29 A Complicated Problem in Permutations   47
    Problems   49

Chapter IV
Elementary Principles of the Theory of Probability

30 Complementary Probabilities   59
31 Unconditional Probabilities   59
    Problems   61
32 Some Sample Spaces   63
33 Random Association of Events   64
34 Conditional Probabilities   66
35 Some Instructive Illustrations; A Transition Matrix   68
    Problems   70
36 Representation of Conditional Probability in the Sample Space 71
37 Compound Probabilities   72
    Problems   74
38 Alternative Compound Probabilities   75
39 Some Instructive Illustrations; a Contingency Matrix   78
40 Some Instructive Illustrations; The Psychic Research Problem 79
41 Some Instructive Illustrations; A Generalization of the Psychic
    Research Problem   80
42 Some Instructive Illustrations; Independent Trials   81
43 Some Instructive Illustrations; A Generalization of the Problem of
    Independent Trials   83
44 Some Instructive Illustrations; A Typical Urn Problem   85
45 Some Instructive Illustrations; Another Typical Urn Problem   85
46 Particle Physics; the Bose-Einstein, Fermi-Dirac, and Maxwell-
    Boltzmann Statistics   88
47 Some Instructive Illustrations; A Problem in Matching   90
48 Some Instructive Illustrations; Another Urn Problem   92
49 Some Instructive Illustrations; Another Urn Problem   92
50 Chance Paths   94
    Problems   99

Chapter V
Probability and Experiment; Bernoulli's Theorem

SECTION		PAGE
51	Introductory Remarks	104
52	Limits and Things which Approach Them	105
53	The Upper Bound of a Set	107
54	Regarding Probability as a Limit	109
55	Regarding Repeated Independent Trials	111
56	The Limiting Condition as the Number of Trials Is Greatly Increased	113
57	Bernoulli's Theorem	116
58	Résumé	119
59	Mathematical Justification	120
60	Stirling's Formula	121
61	Another Approximate Formula	125
62	Justification of the First Half of Bernoulli's Theorem	125
63	Justification of the Second Half of Bernoulli's Theorem	127
64	Regarding the Experimental Determination of Probability	128
65	The Multiplication Theorem	129
66	Chance Paths	131
67	Random Paths	134
68	First and Subsequent Passage	137
69	First Return from a Chance State	139
	Problems	140

Chapter VI
Probability and Experiment; Bayes' Theorem

70	The "Life on Mars" Paradox	144
71	Bayes' Theorem	146
72	Some Instructive Illustrations; Bertrand's "Box Paradox"	148
73	Some Instructive Illustrations; Another Urn Problem	149
74	Some Instructive Illustrations; The Bad Penny	151
75	The Uses to which Bayes' Theorem May Be Put	152
76	Some Instructive Illustrations; An Elementary Problem in Sampling	154
	Problems	156

Chapter VII
Distribution Functions and Continuous Variables

77	Introductory Remarks	157
78	The Random Choice of a Point on a Line Segment	157
79	A Paradox Associated with the Random Choice of a Point on a Line Segment	161
80	Extension of the Significance of the Preceding Paragraphs	162
81	Distribution Functions for Continuous Variables	162

SECTION		PAGE
82	A Variable which Is Not Distributed at Random	164
83	Distribution Functions Derived Empirically	165
84	Distribution Functions in Many Variables	166
85	Change of Variable in Distribution Functions; the Jacobian	169
86	An Example of Change of Variable in Distribution Functions	175
87	Derivation of a Distribution Function for the Velocities of Gas Molecules	177
88	Some Instructive Illustrations; Change of Variable in Maxwell's Equation	179
89	Information that Can Be Derived from (87.2) and (88.2)	181
90	Hyperspherical Coordinates	183
	Problems	184

Chapter VIII
Averages

91	Definition of an Average	188
92	Mathematical Expectation	188
93	Derived Averages and Expectations	192
94	Average Values of Continuous Variables	193
95	The Median	195
96	The Deviation, Variance and Standard Deviation	197
97	Standard Form of Distribution Functions	199
98	Expectation and Variance of a Sum; Covariance	200
99	Résumé	203
100	Some Instructive Illustrations; The General Case of Independent Trials	204
101	Some Instructive Illustrations; The Expectation of the Hypergeometric Distribution	205
102	Some Instructive Illustrations; A Dice Problem	206
103	Some Instructive Illustrations; The St. Petersburg Paradox	206
104	The Expectation of a Probability	209
105	Generating Functions	211
106	Some Instructive Illustrations; First Return to Zero Score in a Coin Tossing Game	214
107	Some Instructive Illustrations; The Poisson Distribution	217
108	The Sums of Chance Integers	218
109	Convolutions	220
110	Generating Functions for Continuous Variables	221
	Problems	222

Chapter IX
The Distribution Functions Most Frequently Used in Engineering

111	Introductory Remarks	227
112	Distribution Functions for Discrete Variables; The Binomial Distribution and Various Approximations to It	229

SECTION   PAGE

113 Some Instructive Illustrations; Computation of Binomial Sums   234
114 Distribution Functions for Discrete Variables; The Poisson
       Distribution as a Limiting Case of the Binomial   236
115 Definitions of the Phrases "Individually at Random" and
       "Collectively at Random"   238
116 Second Demonstration of the Poisson Distribution   240
117 Discussion of the Poisson Distribution; Problems to which It Is
       an Appropriate Solution   243
118 Discussion of the Poisson Distribution; Variable Traffic Density in a
       Telephone Exchange   246
119 Discussion of the Poisson Distribution; The General Problem of
       β-ray Emission   249
120 An Approximation to the Poisson Distribution   251
121 Other Distribution Functions   253
122 The Normal Approximation to the Multinomial Distribution   253
       Problems   255
123 Further Remarks About the Normal Distribution   257
124 Hermite Polynomials; The Gram-Charlier Series   257
125 Gram-Charlier Approximation to the Binomial Distribution   261
126 Gram-Charlier Approximation to the Poisson Distribution   263
127 The Central Limit Theorem   264
128 Comments on the Central Limit Theorem   271
129 Empirical Families of Curves; Transformation of Variable   273
       Problems   274

Chapter X
Matrix Methods and Markov Processes

130 Introductory Remarks; Processes   276
131 Matrices   277
132 Multiplication of Matrices   279
133 The Transition Matrix as an Operator   280
134 Some Instructive Illustrations; Reconsideration of Example 35.1   281
135 Some Instructive Illustrations; A Problem in Bose-Einstein Statistics 283
136 Some Instructive Illustrations; A Waiting-Line Problem   286
137 Markov Processes   289
138 Some Instructive Illustrations; A Non-Markovian Process   291
       Problems   293

Chapter XI
The Foundations of Statistics

139 Introductory Remarks   297
140 Precision of Measurement   298
141 Estimation of Parameters   301

Contents

SECTION		PAGE
142	Precision of Measurement; Numerical Examples	304
143	Levels of Confidence; Confidence Intervals	305
144	Distribution of Variance; First Approximation	306
145	The Accepted Criterion as to Goodness of Fit	307
146	Some Instructive Illustrations; The Biased Die	309
147	Discussion of Example 145.1	312
148	Some Instructive Illustrations; Weldon's Dice Data	312
149	The Measure of the Goodness of Fit, $P(> \chi^2)$	316
150	The Solution of Examples 148.1 and 148.2	319
151	Résumé of the Test of Goodness of Fit	320
152	Null Hypothesis; Errors of Types I and II	322
153	Some Instructive Illustrations; Some Telephone Data	323
154	Dependence and Independence; Introductory Remarks	325
155	Some Instructive Illustrations; A Test of Independence	327
156	Regression	328
157	Correlation	331
158	Discussion of Regression and Correlation	333
159	Some Instructive Illustrations; An Example of Correlated Chance Variables	335
160	Rotation of Axes; Correlation Vectors	337
161	The Distribution of Statistics	339
162	The Distribution of the Mean; The Distribution of Variance, Second Approximation	340
163	The Distribution of $\bar{\delta}/s$; the t-Distribution	343
164	The Distribution of the Ratio of Two Variances	344
	Problems	346

Chapter XII
The Theory of Probability as Applied to Problems of Congestion

165	Introductory Remarks	354
166	Notation	356
167	General Assumptions	357
168	Some Problems of Lost Traffic	358
169	The Elementary Probabilities; Lost Calls Held	360
170	Introduction of the Assumption of Statistical Equilibrium; Lost Calls Held	362
171	The Probability Formulas Corresponding to Assumptions 7 and 10	365
172	The Probability Formulas Corresponding to Assumptions 8 and 10	366
173	The Probability Formulas Corresponding to Assumptions 9 and 10	367
174	The Elementary Probabilities; Lost Calls Cleared	369
175	The Probability Formulas Corresponding to Assumptions 7 and 11	369
176	The Probability Formulas Corresponding to Assumptions 8 and 11	371
177	The Probability Formulas Corresponding to Assumptions 9 and 11	372

SECTION		PAGE
178	Recapitulation of Formulas	373
179	Numerical Comparison of Formulas; The Dependence of the Probability of Loss upon the Number of Sources when the Traffic Density of the Group Is Held Constant	376
180	Numerical Comparison of Formulas; The Dependence of the Allowable Traffic Density upon the Number of Sources when the Proportion of Loss Is Fixed	378
181	Charts for Purposes of Computation	379
	Problems	383
182	Some Hunting Problems	384
183	Individual Hunting from a Normal Position	386
184	Individual Hunting with Stay-Put Switches	390
185	Group Hunting with Stay-Put Switches	390
186	The Problem of Double Connections	395
187	Delays in Awaiting Service	397
188	Calls of Equal Length at Noncooperative Channels; The Probability of Congestion j	399
189	Calls of Equal Length at Noncooperative Channels; The Expected Delay	400
190	Exponential Distribution of Holding Times; Delays at Cooperative Groups of Channels	402
191	Exponential Distribution of Holding Times; The Probability of Congestion j	404
192	Exponential Distribution of Holding Times; The Expected Delay	406
193	Exponential Distribution of Holding Times; The Probability of a Delay Exceeding the Length τ If Calls Are Served in the Order in which They Originate	407
194	Exponential Distribution of Holding Times; The Proportion of Delayed Calls	408
195	Exponential Distribution of Holding Times; The Expected Delay of Delayed Calls	409
	Problems	410

APPENDIX

I.	The Factorials of Integers	413
II.	The Logarithms of Factorials	415
III.	The Binomial Coefficients C_n^m	425
IV.	The Normal Error Function	439
V.	The Normal Law, Its Integral, and Its Derivatives up to the Sixth	442
VI.	The Poisson Formula, $^{\infty}P'(i)$	444
VII.	The Poisson Formula, $^{\infty}\Pi'_v$	449
VIII.	Pearson's Criterion of Goodness of Fit, $P(>\chi^2)$	454
IX.	Student's Test of Significance $2P\,(>|t|)$	456
	Index of Notation	457
	Index	459

Chapter I

Introduction

1. The Fundamental Subject Matter of Probability

It is the fundamental purpose of the theory of probability to answer such questions as: What is the probability of tossing an ace with a die? What is the probability that Christmas falls on Monday? What is the probability that the next child born in New York is a girl? What is the probability that Friday falls on Sunday? What is the probability that twenty sheets of paper in a package of 500 differ from the average by more than 1% in thickness?

The subject deals with other questions—about "expectation," "correlation" and the like—but they are all subordinate to the question, What is the probability of a certain phenomenon? Whatever the subject matter, the phenomenon of which the probability is sought is called an "event."

Asking for the probability of an event in itself implies some degree of doubt as to its occurrence; that is, it implies the possibility that the event may not occur. Of course, there are certain causative or controlling factors that determine whether or not the event will occur. Divine intervention is not anticipated; and with sufficient information the answer to the question would be either "It is certain to occur" or "It is certain not to occur."

Thus, in the case of Friday falling on Sunday, the answer is "It is certain not to occur," for *we know* that the thing cannot occur. Moreover, if the question, What is the probability that Christmas falls on Monday? were asked about Christmas of this year, it would be possible to look it up in a calendar and find out on what day it actually falls. As it either does or does not fall on Monday, the answer would then be a statement of fact, not of likelihood. *Unless a certain amount of ignorance exists such questions are trivial.*

However, asking for the probability of an event implies *more* than mere ignorance. It also implies that ignorance is sometimes of less consequence than at other times. Take, for example, the questions,

1

What is the probability that the next child born in New York is a girl? and What is the chance that the next ten children born in New York are all girls? The *fact* is not known in either case; but no doubt exists that ignorance is more serious in the first case than in the second. One event is less in doubt than the other. From this point of view the probability of an event evaluates the importance of our state of ignorance regarding it.

This illustration reveals two phases of the intuitive concept of probability. One is that either event *may* occur: that is, the next child *may* be a girl, or the next ten children *may* be girls. This phase is purely *qualitative*. The other is that the first event is decidedly more probable than the second. This phase is *quantitative*: some probabilities exceed others.

Consider also the matter of Christmas falling on Monday. There are seven days in the week and it is a matter of common knowledge that there is nothing in the arrangement of the calendar that tends to favor one of these days rather than another. This thought finds expression in the phrase: Christmas is "just as likely" to fall on Monday as on any of the other days. Moreover, we find it natural to say that Christmas is twice as likely to fall on either Monday or Tuesday as it is on Monday alone; and that it is three times as likely to fall on Sunday, Monday, or Tuesday, as on Monday alone.

This illustration reveals two more intuitive ideas associated with the concept of probability. One is the idea of "equally likely." The other is the idea that, under certain circumstances at least, the probability of *one or the other* of several events is the sum of their separate probabilities.

2. How Probability Is Measured; The Unit of Measure

These ideas are of a purely intuitive nature. They are merely an appraisal of that common understanding of the word "probability" which makes it an element of speech. Define it we cannot, any more than we can define "length" or "time" or "value" or other quantitative concepts; but we *can* define a method of measuring it, just as in the case of "length" or "time" or "value." And just as we are accustomed in speaking of "length" to substitute the number for the fact, so, too, we shall generally, after we have passed on to the mathematical phases of our discussion, use the word "probability" for what we should, if we were exact, speak of as the "measure of probability." For the present, however, we maintain the distinction, and, admitting our inability to define probability, seek for a method of measuring it.

Such a method flows naturally from the ideas already presented.

Using again the Christmas illustration, the numerical measure of the probability of Christmas falling on Monday may be denoted by p. The value of p is unknown, but certain relations into which it enters have already been stated. For instance, the chance of Christmas falling on Tuesday is also p, and the chance of it falling on any other day is the same. Moreover, we have said that it appears natural to say that the chance of it falling on one or the other of several days is the sum of the probabilities for the separate days; the probability of it falling on one or the other of the seven days of the week is therefore $7p$. But it is certain that Christmas falls on some day of the week: therefore $7p$ must be the number which represents certainty.

What number shall be chosen for this purpose is purely optional, although some numbers may seem more appropriate than others. For example, infinity might seem peculiarly suitable, because it seems natural to say that the event is "infinitely likely to occur." But, if infinity is chosen, the equation

$$7p = \infty$$

is obtained; and this requires that p also be infinite. Thus the choice leads to the logical absurdity that the chance of Christmas falling on Monday is represented by the same symbol as certainty, though it does not accord with the idea of certainty.

Unity is the only other number which recommends itself to denote certainty. It leads to the equation

$$7p = 1,$$

from which it is found that $p = \frac{1}{7}$. This value does not violate intuitive ideas, and is therefore more satisfactory than the other. Thus it has become customary to adopt unity as a symbol for certainty. As a consequence of this choice all probabilities are confined to the range of proper fractions, including the end points 0 and 1 which represent *impossibility*[1] and *certainty*,[1] respectively.

3. How Probability Is Measured; The Fundamental Axioms and Conventions

The above illustration contains, by implication at least, the essential ideas needed for a general definition of the measure of probability. But before proceeding to such a general definition, it is desirable to sort out and restate, as best we can, the intuitive ideas (or axioms) upon which the illustration was based. They are:

---

[1] In § 79, certain remarks are made regarding the use of these words.

AXIOM I. *The question, What is the probability that the event A occurs? has an answer.*

AXIOM II. *This answer is quantitative; that is, it can be stated in terms of a unit measure and a ratio (a pure number).*

AXIOM III. *If two events differ in no other known pertinent attribute than identity, they are equally likely.*

CONVENTION I. *The unit of measure is certainty.*

CONVENTION II. *The scale of measure is to be so chosen that the probability that either A or B happens is the sum of their separate probabilities, so long as the events A and B are mutually exclusive; that is, so long as it is impossible for both of them to happen.*

The third of these axioms requires some discussion. Since the concept of "equally likely" events is intuitive, it cannot be defined, just as other intuitive concepts, such as Time, or Sweet, or I, cannot be defined. It is possible, however, by intelligent consideration to give them a greater depth of meaning. Put it this way. Defining an expression enables one to learn *what it means*. We cannot do this with intuitive ideas; but intelligent discussion may enable us to appreciate more fully *what we mean by them*. Thus Axiom III can in no way be called a definition of "equally likely," but it is consistent with the idea which that expression conveys and may even be an aid in checking doubtful cases.

If the Christmas illustration is viewed in the light of this statement, there are seven possible events: Christmas may fall on any one of the seven days of the week. These events differ in *identity*. Otherwise they could not be thought of as distinct events at all. The days themselves differ in other known attributes: Sunday is a day when people go to church, Monday is washday, Election Day falls on Tuesday, and Saturday is (or once was) payday. Of necessity the events themselves partake to some extent of these attributes; for instance, "Christmas falls on Monday" partakes of the attribute of the day and may also be phrased "Christmas falls on washday." These attributes, however, are not *pertinent* to the question at hand: our state of ignorance would be just as important—and no more so—if they were unknown, or even untrue. If habits changed and Thursday become the conventional washday, Christmas would still be *just as likely* to fall on Monday as before *and no more so*.

There may be other attributes to these days which are pertinent, but which are unknown. For instance, if the question is directed at Christmas of this year, one of the days of the week possesses the attribute of being "the day of the week on which Christmas does fall." This is obviously an essential attribute—in fact, our state of ignorance regarding it is precisely the thing that is being appraised; but so long as it is unknown the probability that Christmas falls on Monday is unaffected.

It may be argued that Axiom III proceeds in a circle because "pertinent attributes" means merely those that influence the likelihood of the event. This is true, and it would be a valid objection to a *definition*; but it must be remembered that III is *not* a definition: it is merely an attempt to illuminate the intuitive meaning of the phrase "equally likely."

Finally, a word of caution should be said about confusing the absence of any pertinent difference between two events, with inability to evaluate the importance of known differences. I ask, If I receive just one telegram today, what is the chance that it will be between 1 and 2 o'clock in the afternoon? There are obviously 24 hours in the day, and I do not know what the probability is for any one of them. Shall I therefore assert that they are equally likely? Obviously not; there are vastly more people awake during the hour in question than between 1 and 2 in the morning, for example, and this certainly is a pertinent difference so far as the likelihood of a telegram being received is concerned. In a later section (§ 70) we shall again refer to this point, which is the fundamental error in a widely quoted paradox.[2]

Before closing this section a word should also be said about the conventions by means of which the scale of measure is defined. Regarding this scale it has already been agreed that unity shall represent certainty, and zero impossibility. The end-points of the scale are therefore fixed. The method of division is also provided for by Convention II; but it must be emphasized that this convention is limited to *mutually exclusive* events; that is, to events of which one at most can happen. Why such a limitation is necessary will become evident from a simple example. If all days but Sunday are "weekdays," the

---

[2] There were formerly two schools of thought, calling themselves "insufficient reasonists" and "cogent reasonists," both of whom accepted Probability as an *a priori* concept, but whose ways parted on the "definition" of the term "equally likely." The insufficient reasonists said, as we have done (though we do not call it a definition), that two events are equally likely if there is no reason to think them otherwise. The cogent reasonists said they are equally likely if there is a cogent reason for thinking them so.

The dispute has to a considerable degree subsided among mathematicians, but the paradox itself, which embodies the principal objection of the cogent reasonists to the other point of view, is still illuminating. The present would be the proper time to consider it, except that the paradox makes use of certain facts which will not be established until the end of Chapter V.

Insofar as one who does not regard the concept of "equally likely" as capable of definition can be said to belong to either school, I am an insufficient reasonist: to me the most "cogent" reason for thinking two things equally likely is the absence of any reason for thinking them otherwise.

probability of Christmas falling on a weekday is $\frac{6}{7}$, for it is the sum of the probability of Christmas falling on Monday, on Tuesday, and so on. But the probability of it falling "either on Monday or on a weekday" is not therefore $\frac{6}{7} + \frac{1}{7} = 1$. Such a result is absurd.

The difficulty is not peculiar to probability theory, but is a fundamental one met in all methods of measurement by direct comparison. We may say, "A rod is two units long if it contains two parts each a unit in length," but in so saying we obviously mean mutually exclusive parts. We can cut off a unit of length from either end of a bar which is only 1.1 units long, both of which are therefore contained in it; but we do not therefore conclude that its length is 2.

4. How Probability Is Measured; The Primary Measure of Probability Defined

We are now prepared to make use of these axioms and conventions in the formulation of an exact definition of the "measure of probability." We begin by noting that the argument of § 2, from which the number $\frac{1}{7}$ was derived, made use of the following facts:

1. The event for which the probability was sought (Christmas falling on Monday) is one of a group of events (corresponding to the various days of the week).
2. The events are mutually exclusive.
3. They are equally likely.
4. The group is "complete"; that is, one or the other of the events *must* happen.

These four facts made it possible to set up the equation $7p = 1$, from which the probability of the event happening was obtained in the form $p = \frac{1}{7}$.

If the complete group had contained m events, the probability of a particular one occurring would obviously have been obtained from the equation $mp = 1$ and would, therefore, have been $p = 1/m$.

To the question, What is the probability that Christmas falls either on Sunday, Monday, or Tuesday? Convention II may be applied. The answer is the sum of the probabilities of the separate events contained in this group of three. As the probability of each of these is $\frac{1}{7}$, the answer must be $\frac{3}{7}$. More generally, if there were m members in the complete group and it were required to find the probability that some one of a smaller group of n events took place, it would only be necessary to add together n fractions each of the value $1/m$. The answer is therefore n/m. This leads at once to the definition:

DEFINITION 4.1. *If a subgroup of n events is contained in a complete group of m mutually exclusive and equally likely events, the probability of some one of the subgroup occurring is measured by n/m.*[3]

5. How Probability Is Measured; Shortcomings of the Definition

This definition of the measure of probability is not without short-comings. In the first place, it virtually implies that both n and m are finite; otherwise "indeterminate forms" arise. This difficulty is a superficial one, however, for infinite quantities never have a meaning except as the result of a limiting process, and the same limiting processes are applicable to the ratio n/m as to any other number.

In the second place, a similar difficulty arises when we ask for the probability that a shot will miss its mark by a distance of between 11 and 12 feet; for distance is a continuous variable, which raises difficulties similar to those met in defining irrational numbers. We shall find, however, when the occasion arises, that we are capable of overcoming this difficulty also.

There is, however, another difficulty of a much more fundamental sort. If we ask the question, What is the probability that the next child born in New York is a girl? it is impossible to build up any group of events which satisfies the conditions of our definition, for though the group "boy, girl" is complete and though its events are mutually exclusive, they are known *not* to be equally likely. There are many examples of this type: almost everything about which "statistics" are taken would be suitable as an illustration. In fact, among the questions of doubt which arise in many fields of research and which we would like to resolve by measuring a probability, there are more by far to which this primary method cannot be applied than to which it can.[4] Hence other methods must often be used.

This need for more than one system of measurement is not unusual. We find it almost everywhere in scientific work. Take, for example, the measurement of length. Here, the intuitive concept is that of extension in space, and the primary method of measurement consists in selecting a suitable unit of length, and then laying this unit

---

[3] We have conformed to the usual custom of calling this statement a "definition." It is in fact a theorem.

[4] Because of this, many scholars have been led to seek a foundation for the whole theory of probability in the gathering of statistics, rather than in *a priori* logic. They have, in my opinion, failed. Not only are simplicity and directness replaced by complexity and devious-ness, but the logical difficulties associated with such ideas as "equally likely," "independent," and the like, remain. They must remain, because they lie at the heart of the matter.

That this is so will become clear in Chapter V. See, in this connection, footnote 5, § 54.

end-to-end, without gaps or overlaps, along the length to be measured.[5] This is the way in which carpenters measure boards, or surveyors chain a field. There are, however, other lengths which are not accessible to such measurement. The earth's diameter, the distance to a star, a wavelength of sound, and a molecular diameter are all examples. To measure these, other methods have had to be evolved progressively as our understanding of the physical universe and its interrelations has evolved. These methods are sometimes very indirect. We measure the wavelength of sound by resonance or refraction; the distance to a star by some form of triangulation, or by the red-ward shift of spectral lines.

None of these methods can be applied to all situations. A carpenter can no more measure the length of a board by the red-ward shift of light than the astronomer can find a star's distance with the carpenter's rule.

In the measurement of probability likewise various methods are needed and fortunately exist. Two of the most useful ones are the method of sampling and the method of repeated trials, which we shall discuss in due time. Such methods cannot be adopted arbitrarily, however. They must be consistent in the sense that, wherever two or more can be applied to the same experiment, they must yield the same results. Section 12 will establish that the method of sampling is consistent with the primary method, and in Chapter V we shall show that the method of repeated trials is also.

6. Final Remarks

In what follows, we shall use from time to time whatever system of measurement is most convenient. We shall adhere to the point of view however that the primary method of measurement is the standard, and that others are valid only insofar as they are consistent with it.

Since the primary method holds this central position, we stress once more the importance of the words "complete," "equally likely," and "mutually exclusive" in the definition and in Convention II; and to stress the point that human nature is prone to forget them, a mistake of a great mathematician will be used to point the remarks.

D'Alembert, when asked for the probability that "heads" will appear at least once in two throws of a penny, argued as follows: Heads appear either first, last, or not at all. There are thus three

---

[5] The analogy between the primary methods of measuring length and probability is exceedingly close. See in this connection, Fundamental Concepts in the Theory of Probability, *American Mathematical Monthly*, 1934, pp. 206–217.

events, two of which are included in the subgroup desired. Hence the chance of heads appearing during the two throws is $\frac{2}{3}$.

But if "heads first" (or last) means "heads then and tails the other time" the group is not complete, for "heads both times" is also possible; whereas if "heads first" (or last) means "heads then, no matter what appears the other time" the events are neither equally likely nor mutually exclusive: not equally likely because they differ in the *essential* attribute that two depend on the result of a single throw only, while the other combines the results of two throws; and not mutually exclusive because "heads both times" is included both in "heads first" and in "heads last." Actually, as d'Alembert thought of the problem, the question was answered if heads appeared on the first throw, and a second throw was not needed; hence to him "heads first" meant "heads first no matter what happens last"; while "heads last" meant "tails first and heads last." His group, then, was complete and mutually exclusive; but the events were not equally likely.

Fortunately a suitable group can be found. It is

heads—heads,
heads—tails,
tails —heads,
tails —tails.

As three of these events produce at least one head, the correct answer is $\frac{3}{4}$.

* * *

The foregoing discussion is far from complete and raises a number of questions of a logical nature, the attempt to answer which would be of interest if it were consistent with the main purpose of the text. These questions, however, must be passed by, and we undertake instead a connected account of some of the more important technical terms which will be met in the chapters that follow.

Chapter II*

The Language of Probability

7. Chance, Random, Stochastic

To say that something *happens by chance*, or, using the adjective, that it is *a chance occurrence*, implies, in the broadest sense, that some essential element of information, without which the event cannot be predicted, is missing. This could be because, as in the arrival of cosmic rays, the causative mechanism (if any) is beyond our understanding or control; or because, as in tossing a die[1] or making an electric lamp, we do not choose to exercise control.

By contrast, the word *random* is used only of chance occurrences that are, in some sense, equally likely. Thus, to say that a hand of cards was dealt "by chance" implies only that, because of lack of knowledge or control, the outcome was uncertain; to say that it was dealt "at random" implies that all possible selections were equally likely. Or, to say that there is a chance dispersion of hits on a target does not imply that all parts of the target are equally likely to be hit; to say the dispersion is random does have this implication.[2]

The reader should also be acquainted with another widely used adjective *stochastic*, which has a related meaning. By etymology and dictionary usage, it has a purposeful connotation: thus the ramblings of a very drunken man who is trying to go home, or the misses of a marksman who is trying to hit a target, are stochastic, whereas the

---

* This chapter brings together in one place a number of words which the reader will meet in the literature of probability and statistics. It is intended primarily for reference. It need not be read consecutively, or it may be omitted entirely at this time.

[1] A machine could, without doubt, be designed to seize and retoss a die so that the same face was always uppermost. Similarly, electric lamps and most other manufactured products could be made much more uniform. We do not do these things because, for one reason or another, they are not worth while.

[2] It is unfortunately true that some writers use the word "random" loosely, especially in the phrases "random variable" and "random walk," at the same time restricting it narrowly in other phrases such as "random choice." We shall use it consistently in the narrow sense and shall say "chance variable" or "chance walk" when a broader interpretation is allowable.

meanderings of a gas molecule, or the points of impact of cosmic rays on a photographic plate, are not. In the literature of probability, however, the word does *not* have this connotation. Instead, it sometimes carries an implication of sequential, or time-dependent, occurrence; at other times it is used about as broadly as we use "chance." We shall not need the term and will not use it.

8. Experiments; Mathematical Models; Monte Carlo Methods

Any procedure that determines whether a chance result does or does not occur is called an *experiment*. Thus, tossing a coin or a die is the experiment by means of which we determine what face appears. In this instance the word has its usual meaning.

So, also, if we ask, What is the probability that Christmas falls on Tuesday?—meaning, thereby, that it so falls in a year chosen at random—we might set up a procedure for selecting four digits at random and then, with a suitable calendar, determine the outcome. This procedure would be an experiment.

It may seem a little more unusual to call the operation of an automatic screw machine an experiment; but we shall so regard it, since it is this process which makes the next (or any other) screw either good or bad.

"Experiments" need not be, and often are not intended to be, performed. Some, in fact, would be impossible. For example, it is not possible to *perform* an experiment with a perfect die, since we cannot produce one. We would have equal difficulty in constructing a die for which the probabilities of the faces were 0.164, 0.165, 0.166, 0.167, 0.168, 0.170. We can, however, discuss imaginary experiments with either and reach interesting conclusions regarding such matters as, for example, the probability of more than 175 aces in 1000 throws. Furthermore, if we owned a die which had been acting in a peculiar way and which we suspected of being biased, we might compare its observed performance with our deductions regarding these imaginary experiments and thus confirm or deny our suspicion.

Such imaginary (or ideal, or conceptual) experiments are called *mathematical models*. They may be said to constitute the subject matter of probability theory. Sometimes they are studied for purely mathematical ends, and without much concern whether there is a parallel phenomenon in the physical world. But even when the purpose is most practical, situations are idealized either because of what we do not know about them or to simplify the discussion. Thus, to study real experiments we resort to mathematical models.

The converse is also sometimes true: when the analysis of a model becomes too involved, we may resort to a physical experiment.

For example, consider a group of, say, six pay telephones in a railway station. When all are busy a potential customer is inconvenienced, and we would like to know how often this will happen. If we assume that those who cannot be served at once leave and do not return, the answer is easily found.[3] But if we make the more reasonable assumption that some wait and others return a little later, the analysis becomes much more complex. It is then simpler to set up a controlled experiment which is so designed as to conform precisely to the mathematical model. Such methods are known as Monte Carlo procedures and can take many forms. With the advent of high-speed digital computers it has become feasible to carry out very elaborate Monte Carlo studies, and they have assumed an important role in the practice of probability.[4]

9. Events

The word *event*, which we have used frequently in the first chapter, has a very broad meaning. It embraces anything which could conceivably happen in a chance experiment.

Events are automatically associated with one another in sets by the experiments to which they relate. Thus, if a penny is tossed it may come up heads or tails, or just possibly stand on edge. Hence heads, tails (and perhaps edge) constitute the set of events appropriate to this experiment.

We have already indicated that the theory of probability is concerned with such sets and have introduced the concepts of *mutually exclusive* events and of *complete sets*. Other concepts will be of frequent use later.

First, note that to every way in which an experiment may result, there is the alternative that it may not result in this way. These are called *complementary* events. For example, if a penny is tossed, heads may appear. The complement is, heads do not appear—which in this

---

[3] See §§ 174 and 176, Chapter XII.

[4] Such procedures were used for decades, perhaps for centuries, before they acquired a catchy name and thereby attracted general attention. For example, the telephone problem referred to in the text, and others considerably more complex, were studied in this way. Some of the studies were carried out by card file methods; others by mechanisms designed for the purpose. But without the electronic computer they were always slow and onerous. These disadvantages have now largely disappeared. Monte Carlo methods are of great importance, but they will not be further referred to in this volume, since they are more properly related to numerical methods of computation than to the subject of probability itself.

instance is identical with the event "tails appear," unless we contemplate the possibility that the coin may stand on edge. Other examples are: It rains today, or it does not; a manufactured item passes inspection, or it does not.

Clearly, an event and its complement are mutually exclusive and together constitute a complete set. Such a set is called a *dichotomy*. Since there is a dichotomy corresponding to every conceivable event, the study of such sets is of special significance. Chapter V, in particular, is devoted to this subject and leads to one of the most fundamental theorems in the entire theory of probability.

If an event comprises within itself several alternatives, we say it is *composite*; otherwise, it is a *simple* (or *primary*) event. For example, if a die is tossed, either an even or an odd face may appear. These two events form a dichotomy. Neither, however, is a simple event since an even face comprises *either* a deuce, *or* four, *or* six, and an odd face means *either* an ace, *or* three, *or* five.

Whether we regard an event as simple or composite may depend upon the aspects of an experiment in which we are interested. In a sociological study, for example, a person selected for observation might be either male or female. If our interest extends no further, these are simple alternative events. But we might be interested in marital status as well, in which case we would have four simple events: single male, married male, single female, married female. In this context male would be the composite of single male and married male.

As a second example, suppose two pennies are labeled 1 and 2 and tossed together. If we denote the appearance of heads on penny 1 by H_1, etc., we have a set of four simple events: H_1H_2, H_1T_2, T_1H_2, T_1T_2. In this frame of reference H_1, the appearance of heads on penny 1, is a composite event with the alternatives H_1H_2 and H_1T_2. If we had tossed only penny 1, H_1 and T_1 would be simple events.

This does not mean that the words are ambiguous. It merely emphasizes the extent to which language is conditioned by its context—in our case by the experiment, or model, which is being discussed.

There is, however, a more fundamental difficulty associated with the idea of a primary event when the events to which an experiment may lead are not discrete. Consider, for example, the experiment of measuring an orange. Its diameter may lie in any of the ranges $< 2.0''$, $2.0''-2.5''$, $2.5''-3.0''$, $> 3.0''$, which therefore constitute a complete set of mutually exclusive events. But they are not primary events, for each range can be further subdivided, and it is easily seen that this likewise applies to any system of classification we may set up. Thus, when the result of an experiment may vary continuously, the concept of a primary event breaks down.

10. Probability Distribution; Sample Space; Probability Density

If we neglect for a moment experiments whose results are continuously distributed, we may say that every experiment has associated with it a set of primary events, which we may denote by $\{e_1, e_2, \ldots, e_n\}$, or more compactly $\{e_i\}$, and we may denote by p_i the probability that the event e_i will occur. Then

DEFINITION 10.1. *The set of numbers* $\{p_1, p_2, \ldots, p_n\}$, *or more compactly* $\{p_i\}$, *which are the probabilities of the complete set of primary events associated with an experiment, is called the probability distribution of the experiment.*

Thus, in tossing a biased penny, the probabilities p_1 of heads and p_2 of tails constitute the probability distribution; if the penny is perfect, the distribution is $\{\frac{1}{2}, \frac{1}{2}\}$.

Or, if the experiment consists in dealing five cards at poker, the distribution consists of 2,598,960 numbers, one for each of the different hands which might be dealt.[5] In the case of a random deal, all these numbers would be equal and, since their sum must be 1, would be 1/2,598,960. If the deal is not random, there are still 2,598,960 numbers in the distribution, but not all (and perhaps none) would be equal.

Such distributions may be represented graphically by selecting a suitable set of points, labeling them to correspond to the various primary events, and erecting upon each an ordinate equal to the corresponding probability.

Thus, in the case of the perfect penny, the two points 0, 1 on an axis might be chosen, labeled "heads" and "tails," and an ordinate of length $\frac{1}{2}$ erected on each.

For the poker hands we might choose the points $0, 1, \ldots, 2,598,959$ along the axis, label each to correspond with one of the possible hands, and erect suitable ordinates. Or we might do it differently. We might imagine a space of five dimensions with coordinate axes s, h, c, d, and p, the first four corresponding to spades, hearts, clubs, and diamonds, and the fifth representing probability. Along the s-axis the points $0, 1, \ldots, 2379$ could be labeled to correspond to the 2380 different groups of spades[6] which can be found in a poker hand, and the h-, c-, and d-axes could be similarly labeled. Then any possible hand would correspond to some 4-dimensional point (s, h, c, d), and an ordinate of appropriate length could be extended in the direction of the fifth, or probability, axis.

Alternatively—and this is often a useful concept—we might imagine a weight attached to each of the coordinate points, instead of erecting ordinates upon them. If these were equal to the respective probabilities,

---

[5] How this and other numbers in this chapter are derived will become clear later on. For this one, see Problem 23.3.

[6] See Problem 23.4.

the probability of any composite event would obviously be represented by the combined weight of all those primary events included in it. Thus, the probability of dealing five spades would be the combined weight of the 1287 points which correspond to the various possible combinations of five spades which can be dealt.

Clearly, there are many alternative ways in which a probability distribution may be represented graphically. However we choose to do it, it is customary to refer to the system of coordinates as a *sample space*, and to the point corresponding to a particular event as a *sample point*.

DEFINITION 10.2. *The* SAMPLE SPACE *corresponding to an experiment is the coordinate system (that is, the set of points) on which we choose to graph its probability distribution. The point which corresponds to a particular primary event is the* SAMPLE POINT *of that event. The group of sample points corresponding to a composite event is called its* SAMPLE SUBSPACE *(or its* SET, *or* SUBSET, *of points).*

What about those experiments whose results may vary continuously, which we have so far neglected? For example, what about measuring the diameter of an orange?

Clearly, to represent the possible results of such an experiment we need, not a discrete set of points on an axis, but a continuous segment of it. Also, instead of discrete ordinates to represent discrete probabilities, we need to construct a curve $p(D)$ such that, in any interval (D_1, D_2) the area $\int_{D_1}^{D_2} p(D)dD$ is equal to the probability of an orange having a diameter within these limits. Alternatively, we need a distributed mass—or density—$p(D)$, such that the weight of any interval is equal to the probability appropriate to this interval. Because of this analogy, we often speak of a continuous probability distribution $p(D)$ as a *probability density*.

Thus, although the concept of a primary event does not extend gracefully to experiments whose results are not limited to a discrete set of values, the concepts of a probability distribution and its associated sample space do.

11. Sets of Points

As we have seen, a sample space, together with the probability distribution which it supports, is the logical analog of an experiment. We have also seen that it is not constrained to one particular form, but that there is great freedom of choice in the disposition and labeling of the sample points. However this is done, there are certain relations among the sample points themselves which are quite independent of the geometry of the sample space. These are determined by, and characteristic of, the experiment, and hence, by virtue of the analogy, of the set of sample points also.

The mathematical Theory of Point Sets, which deals with such non-geometric properties, is for this reason a very powerful tool in the Theory of Probability, since any theorem that applies to sets of points in general must of necessity apply to sample spaces, and hence also to the experiments they portray. Its most important uses, however, come at a more advanced level than that of this book, and for that reason we shall have little occasion to refer to it. There are, however, a few simple relations, and two symbols, which we shall use and which will serve the general reader as an introduction to the character of this nongeometric logic.

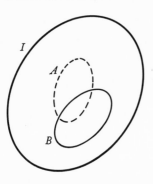

FIG. 11.1

Consider, then, a set of points I which, for purposes of visualization, we shall suppose to lie within the largest curve of Fig. 11.1. I might, for example, be the sample space for the diameter and weight of oranges, in which case it would be a continuous two-dimensional area; or the sample space for the diameters only, in which case it would be a line segment. It could be six discrete points, as in tossing a die, or only two, as in tossing a coin.

Any group consisting of one or more of these points is called a *subset*. In the figure, for example, the points of set I which lie within the dotted curve can be called the subset A, and those within the other small curve, subset B, as indicated by the notation on the curves.

The points of I which are *not* included in A also constitute a subset. This is known as the *complement* of A, or *not-A*, and denoted by A'.[7]

A pair of sets such as A and B automatically define two related sets. One of these is the set of all points which lie in the overlapping region; that is, which belong to *both A and B*. This is called the *intersection* of A and B and is denoted by $A \cap B$. The other is the set of all the points which occur in *either A or B or both*. (Points which occur in both are counted only once.) This is called the *union* of A and B and is denoted by $A \cup B$. By contrast, when the notation $A + B$ is used, the points common to both are counted twice. This leads at once to the relation

$$A \cup B = A + B - A \cap B. \qquad (11.1)$$

Finally, if there are no points whatever within a set A, it is said to be *empty* or a *null-set*. This is indicated by writing $A = 0$.

We may now note some interesting relations among these various sets. First, if the points of the set I are identified with all possible primary events that can occur in an experiment, any event to which this experiment may lead, either primary or composite, will be represented by some subset A. The complementary set A' will, therefore, represent every possible outcome of the experiment other than event A.

We may also note that, if the experiment can result in only a finite number of ways, all of which are equally likely, the probability of the event A is just

---

[7] To avoid possible ambiguity, it is necessary to make clear whether points on the curve A itself are regarded as being in A or in A'. For our purposes (but not for some others) either convention is satisfactory.

the ratio of the number of points in A to the number of points in I. This is merely a restatement of the final paragraph of § 4. When the primary events are not equally likely, the probability of the event A is the sum of the masses associated with the points of A. This is a restatement of Convention II.

The intersection (overlap) $A \cap B$ clearly implies that both A and B occur. The union $A \cup B$ implies that either A or B, or both occur.

If A and B are mutually exclusive, they cannot both occur; there is no overlap; the intersection $A \cap B$ is empty. Thus

$$A \cap B = 0, \tag{11.2}$$

and, by (11.1),

$$A \cup B = A + B, \tag{11.3}$$

if A and B are mutually exclusive. This is Convention II stated in yet another form.

A set A and its complement A' are particularly interesting since they correspond to a dichotomy. Between them they include every point of the set I and they have no common points; that is,

$$A \cup A' = I, \tag{11.4}$$

and

$$A \cap A' = 0. \tag{11.5}$$

There are many other relations which can be established by similar reasoning, or by use of one or more of the relations (11.1) to (11.5). The reader may be interested in verifying a few of these which are set forth in the following problems.

Problems

1. If the set B is entirely included in A, what are $A \cap B$; $A \cup B$; $A + B$?

2. Show that $A \cup A' = A + A'$.

3. Recognizing that A is clearly included in itself, what are $A \cap A$, $A \cup A$, $A + A$?

4. If the set B is empty, what are $A \cap B$, $A \cup B$, $A + B$?

5. What is $(A')'$?

6. By reasoning from Fig. 11.1, show that $(A \cup B)' \neq A' \cup B'$.

7. By reasoning from Fig. 11.1, show that $A' \cup B' = (A \cap B)'$.

8. By merely renaming the sets, so that complements are interchanged, Problem 7 should lead to $A \cup B = (A' \cap B')'$. Show by direct reasoning from Fig. 11.1 that this is so.

9. Add another curve C to Fig. 11.1, and interpret the symbols $A \cap B \cap C$ and $A \cup B \cup C$.

10. Show that $(A \cup B) \cup C = A \cup (B \cup C)$.

11. Show that $A \cup B = B \cup A$.

12. Using Problems 10 and 11, show that $(A \cup B) \cup (A \cup C) = A \cup B \cup C$.

[Answers to problems are given at chapter ends.]

12. The Concept of a Population

When a biologist, an actuary, or a market analyst sets out to study problems associated with his particular field of endeavor, he seeks first to determine the proportion of individuals, among all those with whom he is concerned, who have blue eyes, or who will live to age seventy, or who might be induced to buy a color television set. *He can then assert that this proportion is the probability that an individual, selected at random, will possess this characteristic.*

This assertion is made possible by the primary definition of probability. To see this, we note that the events with which we are concerned are the choosing of one individual or another. These events are mutually exclusive, since the selection of one individual excludes all others; the group is complete, since selection of any one else is not permitted; the events are "equally likely" because that is the meaning of "selected at random." If, then, there are n individuals in the population and n_b have blue eyes, the primary definition gives $p(b) = n_b/n$, which is just the proportion in question.

The group of individuals involved in such a study is sometimes the entire population of the world; sometimes the population of a country or a city. It is quite natural to call such groups *populations*. It was with such a *real* population that the preceding paragraph dealt.

But it takes only a flight of fancy to create an *imaginary* population, corresponding to any conceivable experiment. All that is necessary is to endow this population *by hypothesis* with the property that it contains individuals, or objects, labeled to correspond with every conceivable result of the experiment, and that their numbers be in proportion to the probabilities (whether to us known or unknown) that the experiment will so result.

Suppose, for example, that our experiment is to be the toss of a die. Our population will consist of many "individuals" each labeled ace, deuce, etc. If the die is perfect, these classes will be equally numerous. If the die is biased, their numbers will be unequal, and we may not know them. Indeed, in many important applications we do not know them. But *by hypothesis* their numbers are proportional to the probabilities that the various faces will appear. Unless the probabilities are rational numbers, this requires that the total population be infinite. Even when the corresponding probabilities are simple fractions, the number of individuals in a population is usually, though not always, thought of as infinite, or at least very large.

Clearly, in this imaginary population, the "individuals" are unimportant. We are concerned only with the events which their labels identify. Hence, by another flight of fancy, we can replace the individuals by their corresponding events, thus arriving at a *population of events*. Having done so, we can say that "the probability of an event occurring is the proportion of that event in the population." Or we can say it is the proportion of individuals so labeled. Or we can say it is the probability of selecting such an individual, or such an event, from the population by random choice.

We shall not attempt to extend the population concept to continuous distributions, partly because of the logical questions involved, but more particularly because such questions are always circumvented in statistical practice by a process of *classification*. Thus, the ages of a real population are not recorded to the microsecond, but often only to the year, or even a longer period. Oranges would not be given infinitely fine gradations of size, but instead would be divided into a relatively few "grades." So, in general, for statistical purposes, a continuous distribution is always replaced by a discrete set of compound events, each representing an interval, or sample subspace, of the parent distribution. In this process, a new mathematical model is produced for which the concept of a discrete population is adequate.

13. Statistics; Inference

Broadly speaking, probability and statistics deal with questions of precisely opposite character. Both deal with the probabilities underlying an experiment, and the various ways it may turn out. But the theory of probability starts with the probabilities and attempts to answer questions about the results. Statistics, by contrast, starts with a known result, and seeks to answer questions about the probabilities. Or, in the language of § 12, the theory of probability starts with a population, and seeks information about a sample drawn from it, whereas statistics asks what we can infer about a population from the characteristics of a sample.

Such questions-in-reverse are inherently difficult, precisely because, as everybody knows, a sample may now and then not resemble the population at all. Thus, if the population had just two kinds of events in equal numbers (e.g., the population of heads and tails corresponding to a perfect coin) and a sample of ten were chosen (i.e., the coin was tossed ten times), there would be only one chance in four of it fairly representing the population (i.e., having just five heads and five tails), and there would be almost one chance in ten of getting either eight heads or eight tails![8] Clearly, there are dangers in drawing inferences from statistical data.

The central concern of statistics is precisely this: to determine what degree of confidence may be placed in such inferences. And the central word in that statement is *confidence*. It has a precise meaning which will be explained in greater detail in Chapter XI, but which may be illustrated by an example here.

Suppose that, over a considerable length of time, 96.5% of a factory product has met inspection standards and it is the intention of management to maintain that level. Suppose today, in a sample of 50 pieces, 5 were found defective. Should we infer that the process is below the intended standard?

We cannot give a positive answer to this question, for even if 99% of today's product is good, we might by chance get 5 defectives in a sample of 50. Or, at the other extreme, if 50% of today's product were bad, we might still by chance get 45 good pieces in a sample of 50. *But either of these would be unlikely to happen*, and this fact is the clue to our puzzle.

If we make a number of different hypotheses regarding the real proportion of defectives in the day's production, we may ask in turn how likely the observed result would be if each hypothesis were true. We will thus find that when a day's production is more than 98% good, the probability of getting 5 defectives in a sample of 50 is less than 0.001. Similarly, if less than 71% of the product is good, the chance of getting 5 defectives in a sample of 50 is less than 0.001. Hence, the experimental result does not support either the hypothesis of a going rate greater than 98% or less than 71%, and we may state with very great confidence that today's operation was within these limits.

Indeed, the negligible plausibility of such hypotheses is indicated in a general way by the small upper limit, 0.001, for the probability which was used in the argument. That probability and the two limits 98% and 71% to which it led are set down in the first line of Table 13.1.

TABLE 13.1

Level of Plausibility	Confidence Limits	Confidence Level %
0.001	98–71	99.9
0.01	97–78	99
0.1	96–83	90

We can narrow down the limits by using a different probability. For example, as the second line shows, the chance of 5 defectives in the sample would be less than 0.01 if the day's product was above 97% or below 78% good. And, as the third line shows, the chance is less than 0.1 if the day's product is outside the limits 83% to 96%.

---

[8] See § 42.

We can therefore say with very great confidence that the operation is within the top set of limits, and with progressively less confidence that it is within the middle or lower limits.

These intervals $(71, 98)$, $(78, 97)$, $(83, 96)$ are called *confidence intervals*; and their end-points, *confidence limits*. Likewise, the complement of what we have called the plausibility is known as the *confidence level*. Using these terms we would say, "At the 90% level of confidence, the going rate is between 83% and 96%." We would also say, "The hypothesis that the process is normal is *rejected at the 90% level*," meaning that the normal 96.5% lies outside the confidence limits for the plausibility index 0.10; but we say, "It is *not rejected at the 99% level*," meaning that 96.5% lies within the confidence limits for 0.01.

The question asked above was: "Should we infer that the process is below the intended standard?" The factory manager would no doubt like an answer, yes or no, and the reader may feel that the answers we have given, are indirect, iffy, and involved.

As a matter of fact, we cannot answer yes or no, for the observed sample could have been obtained in either case. But in spite of the complexity we have accomplished something, for the word *confidence* has been given a meaning which, however involved it may appear, is nevertheless precise and quantitative, thus enabling us to distinguish between the various levels of assurance with which inferences may be drawn.

14. Chance Variables; Chance Functions

It is customary, particularly when using the language of sample space, to think of the result of an experiment as a variable which can wander over the set of sample points. It is thus a variable whose value is *determined by* the experiment. We shall call it a *chance function* of the experiment. Thus the number of defective parts in § 13, or the face which appears when a die is tossed, or the measured diameter of an orange, are chance functions of their respective experiments.

DEFINITION 14.1. *Anything that is unambiguously determined by the chance results of an experiment is called a* CHANCE FUNCTION[9] *of the experiment.*

Oranges, however, vary not only in size, but also in value. If we assume, for the sake of argument, that value is determined by size alone, the experiment that determines the size of the orange will simultaneously determine its price. Thus price, like size, is also a chance function of the experiment.

---

[9] The term more commonly used is *random variable*. It is not a good one: First, because the word *random* is not used in the sense of equal probability of occurrence, for which it should be reserved. Second, because the word *variable* does not imply dependence (upon the experimental outcome), which is an essential part of the meaning. The inappropriateness of the term has long been recognized by those who use it, but it has nevertheless persisted. It is hoped that *chance function*, which is an innovation, may gain favorable reception.

Of course, since functions are also variables, we shall not hesitate to use *chance variable* also.

We may interpret this in terms of the corresponding sample space (which, as we saw in § 10, may be taken as a line segment) by saying that to each point of the line there correspond two well-defined quantities, size and price, each of which is a chance function of the experiment.[10]

As a second example, consider the Brownian motion of a gas molecule. At an instant of observation it would be found to have a precise velocity, the magnitude and direction of which can be represented by a point in three-dimensional space. All magnitudes and all directions are possible; therefore the sample space is continuous and infinite in all three dimensions, and the observed velocity is a *chance function* of the experiment, which is defined over this infinite sample space. But the energy of the molecule, which is proportional to the square of its speed, is also well defined at every sample point. Energy is, in other words, also a chance function of the experiment.

Not all chance functions are numerical. Many are concerned with decision making processes. Consider, in this connection, the problem of quality control discussed in § 13. The sample space for this experiment contains fifty-one discrete events corresponding to $0, 1, 2, \ldots, 50$ defectives in the sample. The action taken by management varies from point to point in this sample space. If only a few defectives occur, say four or less, no action is required. If 5, 6, or 7 occur, it may be concluded that a tool is worn and should be replaced. More than 8 might lead to stopping production until the trouble could be located. This set of well-defined decisions, each determined by the outcome of the experiment, is also a chance function.

Finally, consider the probability itself. This is also clearly well defined at each point of sample space, either in the form of the associated mass if the sample points are distinct, or by means of the density function if the sample space is continuous. Hence the set of probabilities associated with a given experiment also constitute a chance function.

15. Concluding Remarks

The concepts of sample space and population have much in common. This is necessarily so, since both provide a language and a pictorial background for the discussion of chance experiments. But the full extent of the resemblance is somewhat obscured by the fact that the words "space" and "point" evoke a geometrical image, as does also the phrase "coordinate system" which we used in defining a sample space; whereas "population," "individual" and "sample" do not.

Actually, the concept of sample space is also nongeometric, however

---

[10] We have visualized the sample points as labeled to represent size. Thus, if L is the label on the sample point, S is size, and P is price, we would have $S = L$, but P would generally be a step-function, constant over each of the grades into which the oranges are classified.

helpful it may be from time to time to think of lines or areas or volumes. We attempted to make this clear in § 10, when we considered the sample points for a poker hand to be either distributed along a line or in four-dimensional space. It is the set of events (mirrored by the sample points) and their probabilities (mirrored by the weight associated with each) that are essential, and these imply no geometry.

Realizing this, it is easily seen that both the population and the sample space are peopled by fictitious objects which, in both instances, mirror certain aspects of a chance experiment. Both demand the same unambiguous specification of the events to which this experiment may lead, and of an unambiguous (though perhaps to us unknown) probability for each. The difference between them lies principally in the fact that, if the object corresponding to one event is Mr. Jones, and that corresponding to a less likely event is Mr. Smith, there will be in the *sample space* one fat Mr. Jones and one lean Mr. Smith, while the members of the *population* will be equally well-fed, but there will be more Messrs. Jones than Messrs. Smith.

Both concepts are important. There is great economy of thought and language in speaking of very diverse situations simply in terms of "individuals," "populations," and "samples"—or in terms of "sample points," "sample spaces," and "distributions." The choice between them is largely a matter of convenience, the concept of sample space being especially useful in discussing abstract mathematical relations, especially in the more advanced parts of probability theory, and the population concept in the theory and practice of statistics.

In what follows we shall from time to time use both systems of speech as they happen to serve our purpose. But, since we wish to keep the relationship of mathematics to reality constantly in mind, we shall more often speak directly in terms of the experiment, without recourse to either of its mirror images.

After all, without the experiment—either a real one or a mathematical model—there would be no reason for a theory of probability.

Answers to Problems at end of § 11

1. B; A; $A + B$. **3.** A; A; $2A$. **4.** 0; A; A. **5.** A.

Chapter III

Permutations and Combinations

16. Introduction

In order to measure a probability by the primary method explained in §§ 2 to 4, one must enumerate both the complete group of possible events and the desired subgroup. For example, if one asks for the probability of getting 5 spades in a hand at bridge, one must determine how many different hands are possible, and how many of them have 5 spades.

It is the purpose of the present chapter to review certain algebraic laws that will frequently be needed in such problems of enumeration.

17. General Laws of Composition of Events

The study of permutations and combinations rests upon two general laws regarding the composition of events.

FIRST LAW OF COMPOSITION. *If an event A can happen in m ways and an event B can happen in n other ways, "either A or B" can happen in m + n ways.*

This law is so simple that it scarcely requires proof. A few illustrations will serve to establish its validity. Suppose there are three ways of going from New York to Philadelphia and two ways of going from New York to Boston. Then the number of ways of going *either* to Philadelphia *or* to Boston is obviously 3 + 2 or 5. This is in agreement with the law, but it does not indicate why the ways in which the event *B* happens must be different from the ways in which *A* happens, as is implied by the word "other." A second illustration will make this point clear.

Suppose there are three routes to Philadelphia, one of which leads through Princeton, and that there is no *other* route to Princeton. Then although there are three routes to Philadelphia and one to Princeton the number of ways of going "either to Philadelphia or to

24

Princeton" is not four, but three. It is evident that the word "other" is an essential part of the law.

SECOND LAW OF COMPOSITION. *If an event A can happen in m ways and thereafter an event B can happen in n ways, "both A and B" can happen in this order in mn ways.*

If a penny is tossed it may fall in two ways, heads or tails. If a die is thrown it may fall in any one of six ways. Hence, according to the second law, the number of results which can be obtained by tossing first the penny and then the die is $2 \cdot 6 = 12$. This result can be checked by listing the separate possibilities. They are

1. heads and ace	7. tails and ace
2. heads and deuce	8. tails and deuce
3. heads and three	9. tails and three
4. heads and four	10. tails and four
5. heads and five	11. tails and five
6. heads and six	12. tails and six

As a second illustration, consider the modified checkerboard shown in Fig. 17.1, and ask: In how many ways can a man be moved from the top row, and thereafter a man from the middle row? It is immediately obvious that every man in the top row has two possible moves, which makes a total of 8 ways of moving a man in the top row. After moving the man in the top row there are always two moves possible from the middle row. Hence, the number of possible combinations of moves is $8 \cdot 2 = 16$. Again the combinations of moves can be listed and will be found to check this result.

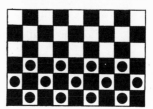

FIG. 17.1

Both these illustrations agree with the second law. There are, however, two essential differences between them. In the first illustration the result was obtained by multiplying the total number of possible ways in which a penny may fall by the total number of ways in which a die may fall. In the second illustration, on the other hand, the total number of different moves which are possible from the middle row is 8, one for each of the end men and two for the others; but the correct answer is not obtained by multiplying this number by the 8 possible moves in the top row.

The second difference lies in the fact that in tossing a die and a penny it makes no difference which one is tossed first. The number of possible combinations is the same in either case. In the checkerboard problem the number of ways in which a man can be moved from the middle row and thereafter a man from the top row is zero, since a man cannot be moved from the middle row at all until a space is opened up for him.

The cause of these differences lies in the fact that the events which take place in the first illustration are *independent*, whereas those which take place in the second illustration are not. The way a penny falls exerts no conceivable influence over what the die may do; but the way in which the man is moved from the first row determines which men are released in the second row and what moves they may make. The necessity of taking account of such dependence reveals itself in the presence of the words "thereafter" and "in this order" in the statement of the second law.

Problems

1. Three people enter a room in which there are seven chairs. In how many ways can they be seated?

2. A dish contains one piece of each of seven kinds of candy. In how many ways can three people be served?

3. A dish contains four pieces of each of seven kinds of candy. In how many ways can three people be served?

4. In how may different *orders* can six people pass through a turnstile?

5. Regarding the alphabet as consisting of 21 consonants and 5 vowels, how many distinct five-letter words are possible, each having three consonants and two vowels alternated?

6. In how many of the words of Problem 5 does no letter occur more than once.

7. For purposes of cable code, where a different charge is made according as the combinations of letters are pronounceable or unpronounceable, it might be desirable to obtain a very large number of words of the type mentioned in Problem 5. How many vowels should an alphabet of 26 letters have, to be most suitable for this purpose?

8. The Greek alphabet has only 24 letters: 17 consonants and 7 vowels. Is it better or worse than the English for the purpose of Problem 7?

9. If numbers such as 000 and 069 are included, there are 1000 three-digit numbers in the decimal system. In how many are all three digits different? In how many are all adjacent digits different?

10. If only numbers between 100 and 999 are included in Problem 9, what are the answers?

18. Definitions

From the standpoint of the study of permutations and combinations, a group of objects has three characteristics: the kinds of objects included in the group, the number of objects of each kind, and the way in which they are arranged. Thus in the group of letters

$$\mathbf{a\ b\ a\ a,}$$

the fact that there are two kinds of objects, that there are three of one kind and one of the other, and the way in which these are arranged in the group would be the pertinent information.

DEFINITION 18.1. *Two groups of objects are said to form different "combinations" if they differ in the number of any kind of object included.*

Thus the combination

$$\mathbf{a\ b\ a\ a}$$

differs from the combination

$$\mathbf{a\ b\ a,}$$

because the number of **a**'s is not the same as before. It also differs from the combination

$$\mathbf{a\ b\ a\ b}$$

for the same reason, although the total number of objects in the group in this case is left unchanged.

On the other hand, the combinations

$$\mathbf{a\ b\ a\ a,}$$
$$\mathbf{a\ a\ b\ a,}$$
$$\mathbf{b\ a\ a\ a,}$$
$$\mathbf{a\ a\ a\ b,}$$

are all the same, since the number of **a**'s and the number of **b**'s is the same in each case.

DEFINITION 18.2. *Two groups of objects are said to form different "permutations" in either of two cases: (a) if they form different combinations; (b) if they form identical combinations but differ in arrangement.*

Thus

$$\mathbf{a\ b\ c\ d,}$$
$$\mathbf{a\ b\ d\ c,}$$
$$\mathbf{d\ c\ a\ b,}$$

are identical combinations because each of them has one **a**, one **b**, one **c**, and one **d**. They are all different permutations, however, because the arrangement of the letters is different in each group.

The groups

$$\mathbf{a\ b\ c\ d,}$$
$$\mathbf{a\ b\ d,}$$

are different combinations because they have different numbers of **c**'s. They are therefore also different permutations. As another illustration

a b c d,

a b c e,

are different combinations and therefore also different permutations.

The above definitions apply to objects of any kind. The following relates only to positive integers:

DEFINITION 18.3. *Any set of positive integers, including 0, which has the sum n is called a "partition" of n.*

Thus, 6, 2, 0, 1 and 2, 4, 2, 1 are *partitions of 9 into 4 parts;* 3, 3, 1, 1, 1 and 9, 0, 0, 0, 0 are *partitions of 9 into 5 parts.*

19. Application of the General Laws of Composition to Permutations and Combinations; Some Typical Examples

The two general laws stated in § 17 make possible the solution of many of the problems of permutations and combinations. A few examples will illustrate the method of procedure.

EXAMPLE 19.1.—*How many permutations of three letters each can be formed from the letters* **a b c d***?*

The answer to this question may be obtained by thinking of the process involved in writing down the various permutations. In writing down any permutation there are just four ways in which the first letter can occur. After this event has taken place there are three ways of writing

TABLE 19.1

PERMUTATIONS OF FOUR LETTERS THREE AT A TIME

a	b	c	b	a	c	c	a	b	d	a	b
a	b	d	b	a	d	c	a	d	d	a	c
a	c	b	b	c	a	c	b	a	d	b	a
a	c	d	b	c	d	c	b	d	d	b	c
a	d	b	b	d	a	c	d	a	d	c	a
a	d	c	b	d	c	c	d	b	d	c	b

the second letter. Finally, the third letter can be written in only two ways. Hence the number of ways of writing three letters is $4 \cdot 3 \cdot 2 = 24$. There is no other conceivable way of putting the letters together. Hence there are just 24 permutations of four letters three at a time.

Table 19.1 shows these permutations arranged in the order in which they were supposed to be obtained. The four ways of writing the first letter correspond to the four vertical columns. In each of these columns there are three pairs corresponding to the three ways of choosing the second letter. Finally, the two members of each pair correspond to the two ways in which the last letter may appear.

EXAMPLE 19.2.—*How many combinations of three letters each can be formed of the letters* **a b c d**?

Because of the simple numbers involved the easiest way of getting the answer to this problem does not involve the two general laws at all. Whenever a group of three is chosen from four letters, one is left; and it is evident that there will be as many different combinations of *three* letters as there are different ways of having *one* letter left over; that is, four.

Unfortunately, most problems cannot be so easily solved. To illustrate the general process the same answer will be obtained in a less direct way.

Two permutations differ (*a*) when they are different combinations and (*b*) when they are different arrangements (i.e., permutations) of the same combination. This is a matter of definition. Suppose x is the number of combinations of four things three at a time. Each of these combinations is a group of three and is capable of a certain number of different arrangements. Call this number y. Every other combination is also capable of y permutations, thus making xy in all. Clearly, no two of these are identical and, since every permutation must be an arrangement of some combination, xy must be the total number of permutations, which is already known to be 24. Hence

$$xy = 24. \tag{19.1}$$

As for y itself: The first letter of a group of three can be chosen in three ways, the second in two, and the third in one. Hence $y = 3 \cdot 2 \cdot 1 = 6$. Substituting this value in (19.1) it is found that $x = 4$. This is the same result as before.

20. Applications of the General Laws of Composition to Permutations; General Theorems

The processes used in Examples 19.1 and 19.2 are perfectly general and make it possible to obtain general formulas for the permutations and combinations of groups of objects.

First consider a group of m different objects, and attempt to find the number of permutations of n objects each that can be made from this group of m.

Since the objects are all distinct, the first one in order can be chosen in m ways. Thereafter the second can be chosen in $m - 1$ ways, the third in $m - 2$ ways and so on. In general the number of ways of choosing an object is m minus the number of objects already chosen. When the choice of the last, or n'th, object is reached, $n - 1$ will already have been chosen, and therefore the last choice can take place in $m - n + 1$ ways. The entire group of possible choices therefore numbers

$$m(m - 1)(m - 2) \ldots (m - n + 1). \qquad (20.1)$$

This is the general formula. If $m = 4$ and $n = 3$, the problem treated in Example 19.1 is obtained. In this case $m - n + 1$ is 2 and the answer is the product of all the integers from 2 to 4 inclusive. This, of course, is the same result as before.

An important special case of (20.1) is that in which m and n are equal. In this case $m - n + 1 = 1$ and (20.1) becomes

$$m(m-1) \ldots 3 \cdot 2 \cdot 1. \qquad (20.2)$$

This is the number of different ways in which a group of m unlike objects can be arranged, or, in technical terms, "the number of permutations of m things m at a time."

A slightly more general problem is:

EXAMPLE 20.1.—*A group contains "a" kinds of objects. There are m_1 of the first kind, m_2 of the second kind, and so on, the total number of objects being $m = m_1 + m_2 + \ldots + m_a$. In how many distinct ways can they be arranged?*

What is meant by saying that m_1 objects are "of the same kind" is that interchanging two of these objects makes no difference in the arrangement of the group. For instance, **a a b b** is a certain group: it may be thought of as a row of alphabet blocks. If the blocks containing the **a**'s are interchanged, the group is still **a a b b** and is unaltered.

Suppose the answer to the problem is x. Let one of these x permutations be chosen, and the objects of like kind be tagged to establish their identity. By this means all the objects are rendered distinct. Then the m_1 objects of the first kind will be capable of $m_1(m_1 - 1) \ldots 2 \cdot 1$ permutations among themselves, none of which, however, would have been different from the one chosen if the objects had not been tagged. Those of the second kind will likewise be capable of $m_2(m_2 - 1) \ldots 2 \cdot 1$ permutations among themselves, any of which may be associated with any of the permutations of the objects of the first kind without altering the original permutation of the untagged objects. A similar statement can obviously be made for each of the a kinds of objects. Hence for each of the original permutations there is now a total of

$$(1 \cdot 2 \ldots m_1)(1 \cdot 2 \ldots m_2)(1 \cdot 2 \ldots m_3) \ldots (1 \cdot 2 \ldots m_a)$$

permutations, all of which were made possible by tagging the objects. This makes a total of

$$(1 \cdot 2 \ldots m_1)(1 \cdot 2 \ldots m_2)(1 \cdot 2 \ldots m_3) \ldots (1 \cdot 2 \ldots m_a)x. \quad (20.3)$$

It must now be noted that every possible permutation of the $m = m_1 + m_2 + \ldots + m_a$ tagged objects is included in this way: for if there were another one, and if the objects were arranged in this permutation and the tags taken off, the result would of necessity be one of the untagged permutations. All possible arrangements which can be made from these, however, have already been provided for in (20.3). Hence this "other one" must be identical with one of those already provided for.

Finally, it is already known from (20.2) that the number of permutations of the tagged objects is

$$1 \cdot 2 \cdot 3 \ldots m. \quad (20.3)$$

Hence, from (20.3)

$$x = \frac{1 \cdot 2 \cdot 3 \ldots m}{(1 \cdot 2 \ldots m_1)(1 \cdot 2 \ldots m_2) \ldots (1 \cdot 2 \ldots m_a)}. \quad (20.4)$$

Problems

1. How many permutations of the letters of the word "concatenation" are possible?

2. A firm has four positions available and a list of eleven applicants. How many possible ways are there of filling them?

3. A horseshoe contains eight nails. In how many different orders may they be driven? If enough horses are to be provided so that one shoe may be attached in every possible way, how many miles of four-foot stalls would be required to accommodate them?

4. How many different permutations of six letters each can be made from the vowels **a e i o u**, if each can be used as often as desired?

5. How many permutations of n objects each can be made of a kinds of objects if the supply of each kind is unlimited?

6. A freight train carries 14 cars of which 6, 3, 4, and 1 are to be dropped at four different points. In how many ways can they be arranged so that the cars to be dropped at each point are always on the rear of the train?

7. Four men and four women are shipwrecked on a tropical island. In how many ways could they be paired in marriage?

[Think of the men arranged in alphabetical order, and permute the women.]

8. A boy has ten marbles: 4 red, 4 blue, and 2 green. They are otherwise indistinguishable. In how many different orders may they be laid in a row?

9. A ribbon is to be woven in five parallel stripes, all of different colors. There are eight colors of silk available. How many distinct patterns could be made?

10. If, instead of all stripes different, only *adjacent* stripes are different, what is the answer to Problem 9?

11. If, instead of having all stripes different, the patterns of Problem 9 are to be symmetrical, how many patterns are possible?

12. A seamstress would regard two ribbons as identical if they were alike after one had been turned end-to-end. How many of the patterns of Problem 9 would she regard as distinct? Of Problem 10?

13. How many of the ribbons of Problem 11 would a seamstress regard as distinct?

21. Factorials; the Gamma Function

The combination of numbers which presents itself in (20.2) is a very common one in more than one branch of mathematics, so much so that it has been given a name and a shorthand symbol. It is called "factorial *m*" and is usually written *m*! That is,

$$m! = m(m - 1) \ldots 2 \cdot 1. \tag{21.1}$$

When defined in this way, $m!$ has no meaning unless m itself is a positive integer; but, as the following paragraphs will show, this limitation can easily be removed by certain artifices.

In the first place, it is easily shown by direct integration that when m is an integer

$$\int_0^\infty x^m e^{-x} \, dx = m!. \tag{21.2}$$

If, then, we adopt (21.2) instead of (20.2) as the *definition* of $m!$, the symbol will have the same significance as before for integers, and it will also have a meaning for fractions. This is the definition usually adopted.[1]

But even this definition applies only when $m > -1$, for the integral does not have a value for other values of m. However, it is immediately obvious from (21.1) that

$$m! = m \cdot (m - 1)! \tag{21.3}$$

when m is an integer, and by integration by parts it can readily be shown that (21.2) also obeys this law. If, then, we take (21.3) as a universal property of $m!$, it may be used to define the function even when m is negative.

---

[1] A much more complicated definition is sometimes given for purely mathematical purposes in order to overcome the limitation to which the next paragraph of text calls attention. For our purposes, however, the definition (21.2) is entirely satisfactory, and the reader will not be misled by it.

For instance: it is known[2] that $\frac{1}{2}! = \frac{1}{2}\sqrt{\pi}$. By setting $m = \frac{1}{2}$ in (21.3), and inserting this known value, it is found that

$$\frac{1}{2}\sqrt{\pi} = \frac{1}{2}(-\frac{1}{2})!$$

or

$$(-\frac{1}{2})! = \sqrt{\pi}.$$

Similarly, by putting $m = -\frac{1}{2}$ in (21.3), we get

$$\sqrt{\pi} = -\frac{1}{2}(-\frac{3}{2})!$$

or

$$(-\frac{3}{2})! = -2\sqrt{\pi}.$$

By starting from a suitable positive factorial and using this device it is possible to obtain the factorial of any negative number whatever.

The factorials of negative integers are particularly interesting. It is obvious that $1! = 1$. Setting $m = 1$ in (21.3) it is found that $0!$ also equals unity. Then putting $m = 0$ in (21.3)

$$0! = 0(-1)!$$

or

$$(-1)! = \frac{1}{0} = \infty.$$

By the same process:

$$(-2)! = \frac{(-1)!}{-1} = \infty,$$

and so on. Since infinity divided by any succession of finite quantities is still infinite, it follows that *the factorial of any negative integer is infinite.*

---

[2] By definition

$$\frac{1}{2}! = \int_0^\infty e^{-x} x^{\frac{1}{2}} \, dx.$$

Replace x by y^2. Then

$$\frac{1}{2}! = 2 \int_0^\infty e^{-y^2} y^2 \, dy.$$

But it makes no difference whether the variable is y or z. Hence

$$\frac{1}{2}! = 2 \int_0^\infty e^{-z^2} z^2 \, dz.$$

Now, multiply these equations member by member and place the z's under the sign of y-integration, with respect to which they are constant.

$$(\tfrac{1}{2}!)^2 = 4 \int_0^\infty \int_0^\infty e^{-(y^2+z^2)} y^2 z^2 \, dy \, dz.$$

This integral extends over the entire first quadrant in the yz-plane. Rewriting it in polar coordinates, we have

$$(\tfrac{1}{2}!)^2 = 4 \int_0^\infty dr \int_0^{\pi/2} d\theta \, r^5 e^{-r^2} \cos^2\theta \sin^2\theta.$$

In this form both the θ integral and the r integral are easily evaluated, giving $\pi/16$ and 1, respectively. Hence $\frac{1}{2}! = \frac{1}{2}\sqrt{\pi}$.

The behavior of the function will be made clearer by reference to Fig. 21.1, in which the factorials of numbers between −6 and +3 are plotted.

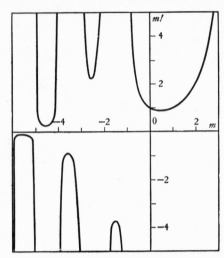

FIG. 21.1 THE FACTORIAL

From the foregoing discussion the student should retain the following facts:

(a) Factorial m, when m is an integer, means the product of the integers from 1 to m. It is written $m!$.

(b) The symbol has a meaning for other numbers than integers. Its value may be found tabulated, just as logarithms are.

(c) The factorial of zero is equal to unity. [$0! = 1.$]

(d) The factorial of a negative integer is infinite. [$(-j)! = \infty$ if $j > 0.$]

(e) The factorials of negative *fractional* numbers are not infinite.

There will be many occasions to use factorials in what follows, but they will generally be the factorials of integers. To simplify numerical calculations, the values of the factorials of integers up to 200 are listed in Appendix I. As many of the numbers are inconceivably large, only a few significant figures are written, followed by the power of ten by which they must be multiplied. Thus 20! is given as 2.4329020^{18} which means

$$2.432\ 9020 \cdot 10^{18} = 2,432,902,000,000,000,000.$$

Appendix II contains the logarithms of the factorials up to 1200.

For completeness one more fact should be mentioned. The symbol $m!$ and word "factorial" are often restricted to positive integral values of m, and another symbol $\Gamma(m)$, called the "gamma-function," is used for the more general case. The two are related by the law

$$\Gamma(m) = (m - 1)!.$$

Thus $\Gamma(3) = 2! = 2$; and $\Gamma(0) = (-1)! = \infty$.

As the multiplication of names and symbols serves no useful purpose, all such numbers will be called "factorials" in what follows.

22. Restatement of General Theorems in Permutations

Let the symbol P_n^m stand for the number of permutations of m things n at a time. Then (20.1) may be rewritten as

$$P_n^m = m(m - 1) \ldots (m - n + 1)$$

$$= \frac{m(m - 1) \ldots (m - n + 1)(m - n)(m - n - 1) \ldots 2 \cdot 1}{(m - n)(m - n - 1) \ldots 2 \cdot 1},$$

or, in factorial notation,

$$P_n^m = \frac{m!}{(m - n)!}. \tag{22.1}$$

Similarly (20.2), which represents the number of permutations of m objects m at a time, becomes

$$P_m^m = m!. \tag{22.2}$$

Likewise, the number of possible arrangements of a group composed of a kinds of objects, m_1 of the first kind, m_2 of the second, and so on, may be denoted by $P_{m_1, m_2, \ldots, m_a}^{m_1, m_2, \ldots, m_a}$. Then (20.4) becomes

$$P_{m_1, m_2, \ldots, m_a}^{m_1, m_2, \ldots, m_a} = \frac{m!}{m_1! m_2! \ldots m_a!}, \tag{22.3}$$

where $\Sigma m_i = m$.

Sometimes, especially in algebraic manipulation, the "objects" which are being permuted are letters $j_1, j_2, \ldots, j_m$ which represent integers. Examples of this will be found in §§ 28 and 29, and in Problem 29.62. When these j's are allowed to range over a succession of values, two or more of them may at times be equal and at other times not. Under such circumstances neither the number of different integers, which is the a of (22.3), nor their multiplicities m_i are fixed. It is then necessary to use, in place of the symbol $P_{m_1, m_2, \ldots, m_a}^{m_1, m_2, \ldots, m_a}$, another which displays the objects (i.e., the integers j_i) explicitly. For this we shall use the symbol $\pi(j_1, j_2, \ldots, j_m)$.

For example, $\pi(1, 1, 1, 0, 0, 4, 7)$ means the number of permutations of three 1's, two 0's, a 4 and a 7, which is, of course, $P_{3,2,1,1}^{3,2,1,1}$.

In general, $\pi(j_1, j_2, \ldots, j_m)$ is $m!$ divided by 2! for every pair of equal j's, 3! for every triplet, etc.

When known integers are written explicitly (i.e., not represented by letters), the notation may be further simplified by using exponents to indicate the multiplicities. Thus $\pi(1, 1, 1, 0, 0, 4, 7)$ would become $\pi(1^3, 0^2, 4, 7)$.

23. Application of the General Laws to Combinations

A formula for the number of combinations of m things taken n at a time can be derived by the line of argument used in Example 19.2. Each combination is capable of $n!$ permutations within itself. If, therefore, the number of combinations is denoted[3] by C_n^m, the total

---

[3] A widely used symbol for this number is $\binom{m}{n}$. We shall consistently use C_n^m instead, both because of its mnemonic value and for typographic reasons.

number of permutations will be

$$P_n^m = C_n^m n!.$$

The value of P_n, however, is known from (22.1). Hence

$$C_n^m = \frac{m!}{n!(m - n)!}. \tag{23.1}$$

This is the general formula for the number of combinations of m things taken n at a time. In particular, for the case considered in Example 19.2, we may set $m = 4$ and $n = 3$ and obtain

$$\frac{4!}{3!1!} = \frac{4 \cdot 3 \cdot 2 \cdot 1}{3 \cdot 2 \cdot 1 \cdot 1} = 4,$$

as before.

Some further examples may be given.

EXAMPLE 23.1.—*How many straight lines can be drawn through five points in such a way that each line contains two points?*

A straight line can be drawn through any pair of points whatever. There will therefore be as many straight lines as there are pairs of points. The only question that remains for consideration is whether the pairs $p_1 p_2$ and $p_2 p_1$ are to be considered identical or distinct.

For the purposes of this example we shall regard them as identical. The problem then becomes one of combinations, and the solution is[4]

$$C_2^5 = \frac{5!}{2!3!} = 10.$$

If we had chosen to regard $p_1 p_2$ and $p_2 p_1$ as distinct, the problem would be one of permutations, and we would find that the number of *directed* lines (vectors) is $P_2^5 = 20$.

EXAMPLE 23.2.—*How many distinct hands of 13 cards can be dealt from a full pack without a joker?*

This is obviously a question of combinations since the order in which the cards are dealt is immaterial. The answer is

$$C_{13}^{52} = \frac{52!}{13!39!} = 635,013,559,600.$$

---

[4] There are exceptions to this answer. For instance, if all five points are collinear, there is only one possible line. In obtaining the answer above it is tacitly assumed that no three points are collinear.

Problems

1. How many possible stacks of 7 dominoes can be dealt from a set of 28?

2. There are 11 candidates from among whom 200 electors are to choose a board of directors. Half of the electors have two votes each to one each for the rest. The board is to consist of five members. On each ballot the lowest man is discarded, until only five remain. How many boards are possible?

3. How many different poker hands (5 cards) can be dealt from a full pack without a joker (52 cards)?

4. How many different combinations of spades can there be in the poker hands of Problem 3?

5. How many distinct groups of 3 red and 4 black cards can be dealt from 26 red and 26 black?

6. If the order of appearance is taken into account, in how many ways can the 3 red and 4 black cards of Problem 5 be dealt?

7. How many distinct groups of 3 *a*'s and 4 *b*'s can be made from 26 *indistinguishable a*'s and 26 *indistinguishable b*'s? How many permutations?

8. How many distinct groups of n_1 men and n_2 women can be formed from m_1 men and m_2 women?

9. Prove that

$$\sum_{j=0}^{n} C_j^{m_1} C_{n-j}^{m_2} = C_n^{m_1+m_2}. \tag{23.2}$$

[If *n* persons are chosen from m_1 men and m_2 women, *j* of them must be men. Compare this proof with the derivation in Problem 29.38.]

10. How many different sets of three initials each might a Chicago child have? Are they equally likely? Do they constitute a complete set?

11. The Greek alphabet contains 24 letters. How many more sets of three initials are available to a child in Chicago than in Athens?

12. There are available m_1 objects of one kind, m_2 of another, and so on. How many possible permutations can be built up using n_1 of the first kind, n_2 of the second kind, and so on? It is assumed that each *m* is at least as big as the corresponding *n*.

13. What is the answer to Problem 12 if one *n*, say, n_1, exceeds the corresponding *m*?

24. Some General Properties of C_n^m; Pascal's Triangle

The first solution of Example 19.2 was obtained by noting that whenever a different combination of three letters was taken out of the four supplied, a different combination of one was left. A little reflection shows that this is a general law: whenever a different combination of n things is taken from a group of m a different combination of $m - n$ things remains. There must therefore be at least as many distinct combinations of $m - n$ as there are of n, and, since this rule works backward just as well as forward, the distinct groups of n must be at least as numerous as the distinct groups of $m - n$. Thus[5]

$$C_n^m = C_{m-n}^m. \tag{24.1}$$

Appendix III contains the values of C_n^m for groups not larger than 100. It uses the same notation as Appendix I. The size of the table has been reduced by making use of the property (24.1), according to which the numbers in any column repeat themselves in the inverse order after the center of the column is passed. For instance, C_{31}^{50} is not given in the table, since by (24.1) $C_{31}^{50} = C_{19}^{50}$, which is given as 3.0405943^{13}.

Another general property of the quantities C_n^m can be obtained from the identity

$$(m - n)(m - 1)! + n(m - 1)! \equiv m!. \tag{24.2}$$

If this is divided through by both $n!$ and $(m - n)!$ and a few obvious cancellations are made, it reduces to

$$C_n^{m-1} + C_{n-1}^{m-1} = C_n^m. \tag{24.3}$$

This equation belongs to the class known as "recursion formulas." That is, once we know the combinations that can be made from a

TABLE 24.1

VALUES OF C_n^m

n	$m = 5$	$m = 6$	$m = 7$
0........	1	1	1
1........	5	6	7
2........	10	15	21
3........	10	20	35
4........	5	15	35
5........	1	6	21
6........	0	1	7
7........	0	0	1

group of $m - 1$ things, it enables us to find the combinations that can be made from m things. For instance, in Table 24.1,[6] the column

---

[5] This rule can also be derived directly from (23.1). The argument in the text makes it possible to "see why" the answer is correct.

[6] The number 1 opposite the marginal number 0 is the value taken by (23.1) when $n = 0$, regardless of the value of m. Of course, this does not make sense when phrased as "the number of different groups of no things each which can be formed from a group of m things"; it must be regarded as an extension of the meaning of symbol C_n^m by definition. It is required for the general validity of (24.1) and (24.3).

for $m = 6$ can be obtained from the column for $m = 5$ by the use of (24.3); for, upon putting m equal to 6, (24.3) becomes

$$C_n^6 = C_n^5 + C_{n-1}^5,$$

which says that each entry in the column headed 6 is the sum of the adjoining number in the 5 column, and the number next above the latter. Thus C_1^6 is the sum of 5 and 1, C_2^6 is the sum of 10 and 5, and so on.

The 7 column can be obtained in the same way from the 6 column.

25. Some General Properties of C_n^m; the Binomial Theorem

The rule for algebraic multiplication is that every term of the one factor of the product is to be multiplied by every term of the other factor of the product, and all of these partial products are then to be added together. This is the "distributive law of multiplication." It can also be phrased in the following words: "The product of two polynomials is the sum of the partial products of all possible combinations of terms obtained by taking one term from each of the factors."

Suppose a product of two factors has been obtained in this way and that this product is then multiplied by a third polynomial. The product thus obtained contains the sum of all possible partial products of three terms each which can be formed by taking one term from each of the three polynomials.

In general, when m factors are involved the product must contain the sum of every possible partial product which can be formed by taking one term from each of the m polynomials.

Suppose now that each of the m factors is the same binomial $x + y$. The product will then be $(x + y)^m$. Since there are only two possible terms, x and y, every partial product must be a power of x multiplied by a power of y. Furthermore, since one term must be taken from each factor, the sum of the two powers must always be m. In other words, the product, when it has been completely worked out, must take the form

$$c_0 x^m + c_1 x^{m-1} y + c_2 x^{m-2} y^2 + \ldots + c_m y^m, \qquad (25.1)$$

where the values of the c's are as yet unknown.

It is not difficult to determine the c's. The complete product must contain just as many partial products of the form $x^n y^{m-n}$ as there are different ways of choosing x's from n different factors, the order of choice being immaterial; in other words, the coefficient of x^n in the binomial expansion of $(x + y)^m$ is C_n^m. The y's of course, come from the remaining $m - n$ factors.

Substituting this for c_n in (25.1), we get

$$C_0^m x^m + C_1^m x^{m-1}y + C_2^m x^{m-2}y^2 + \ldots + C_m^m y^m,$$

or in shorthand notation

$$(x + y)^m = \sum_{n=0}^{m} C_n^m x^{m-n} y^n. \tag{25.2}$$

Referring to Appendix III, the reader will at once recognize the sequences of numbers

$$1,\ 1$$
$$1,\ 2,\ 1$$
$$1,\ 3,\ 3,\ 1$$

as belonging to the well-known binomial expansions for $(x + y)^1$, $(x + y)^2$, and $(x + y)^3$. Even the integer 1 standing alone under the heading $m = 0$ fits into this arrangement, because $(x + y)^0 = 1$.

26. Relations Among Binomial Coefficients

In dealing with groups of discrete objects, as we have done in the sections above, we are necessarily dealing with positive integers. Hence the m and n in C_n^m have so far been restricted in this way. But the equation

$$C_n^m = \frac{m!}{n!(m-n)!} \tag{23.1}$$

may be considered simply as defining a function of the two variables m and n, without regard for its origin, and since $m!$ was given a meaning in § 21 for all values of m, (23.1) can also be evaluated for all values of m and n.[7] When C_n^m is defined in this way, (24.1) and (24.3) are still valid. In fact, (24.1) depends only upon the symmetry of (23.1), and (24.3) upon the identity (24.2), which is true for all values of m and n.[8]

---

[7] The function C_n^m can also be defined without explicit reference to the factorial by means of the integral

$$B(m - n, n) = \int_0^1 x^{m-n}(1 - x)^n \, dx.$$

This is known as the Beta-function (the B is, in fact, the capital form of β, not b), and, when $m - n$ and n are both positive integers, is equal to $(m - n)/C_n^m$. But the integral exists for fractional m and n as well, provided $m + 1 > n > -1$. Hence we may use this integral and the recursion formula (24.3) to *define* C_n^m for all values of m and n, just as (21.2) and (21.3) were used in § 21 in extending the meaning of $m!$ This definition is consistent with the one used in the text.

[8] There is one curious exception. If $m = n = 0$, (24.2) becomes formally $0 \cdot \infty + 0 \cdot \infty = 1$, which is clearly without meaning. In this case (24.3) becomes $1 + 1 = 1$ and is false. In all other cases where indeterminate forms arise in (24.2), (24.3) remains valid when C_n^m is given the values defined in the text.

Equation (25.2) is not valid when m is negative or fractional, but it has a valid analog in the Taylor Series.

$$(x + y)^m = \sum_{n=0}^{\infty} C_n^m x^{m-n} y^n; \qquad (26.1)$$

and it can be shown that the coefficient of y^n is indeed the C_n^m defined by (23.1), as we have indicated. Furthermore, this reduces to the polynomial (25.2) when m is a positive integer; for in this case $(m - n)! = \infty$ and $C_n^m = 0$ for every n greater than m, and the upper limit of summation in (26.1) can be replaced by m without changing its value.

When both m and n (or m and $m - n$) are negative integers, $m!$ and $n!$ are infinite, and (23.1) appears to be indeterminate. It can, however, always be evaluated by repeated use of the equation (21.3), which we adopted as part of our definition of $m!$ Thus, for example, $C_{-2}^{-2} = (-2)!/2!(-4)!$ can be evaluated by writing $(-2)! = (-2)(-3)$ $(-4)!$, or $C_2^{-2} = 6/2 = 3$. The reader may readily verify that this is the coefficient of y^2 in Taylor's expansion of $(x + y)^{-2}$, as it should be for consistency with (26.1).

There are many other interesting relations among the binomial coefficients, some of which we shall need to refer to later. We shall demonstrate two of these relations in the paragraphs which follow and a few more as problems at the end of this chapter.

As a first example, we shall prove that

$$\sum_{j=b-a}^{c-d} C_b^{a+j} C_d^{c-j} = C_{b+d+1}^{a+c+1}. \qquad (26.2)$$

The proof will be by induction; that is, we shall first prove that if (26.2) is true for any value of a, it is necessarily true for all larger values. Then we shall show that (26.2) is true for that a which makes the two limits of summation equal. This is clearly the smallest a for which (26.2) has any meaning, so it will follow that (26.2) is true whenever it has meaning.

For brevity, call the left-hand side of (26.2) $f(a, b, c, d)$. Then, using (24.3), we may write

$$f(a, b, c, d) = \sum_{j=b-a}^{c-d} C_b^{a+j-1} C_d^{c-j} + \sum_{j=b-a}^{c-d} C_{b-1}^{a+j-1} C_d^{c-j}.$$

The second summation is clearly $f(a - 1, b - 1, c, d)$; the first would be $f(a - 1, b, c, d)$ if the lower summation limit were $b - a + 1$ instead of $b - a$. But when $j = b - a$, $C_b^{a+j-1} = C_b^{b-1} = 0$, so the extra term contributes nothing and we have

$$f(a, b, c, d) = f(a - 1, b, c, d) + f(a - 1, b - 1, c, d). \qquad (26.3)$$

If we now suppose (26.2) to be true for the value $a - 1$, we know the values of the two terms on the right of (26.3) and may write

$$f(a, b, c, d) = C_{b+d+1}^{a+c} + C_{b+d}^{a+c},$$

and by (24.3) this sum is just C_{b+d+1}^{a+c+1}. So if (26.2) is true for some integer $a - 1$ as supposed, it must also be true for the next higher integer, and hence also for the next, and so on; in other words for all integers as great as, or greater than, $a - 1$.

This completes the first part of the proof.

The second part is very simple. If a has such a value that both limits of summation are equal, there is only one term in the sum, and for that term

$$j = b - a = c - d. \tag{26.4}$$

Hence (26.2) becomes

$$C_b^b C_d^q = C_{b+d+1}^{a+c+1},$$

which reduces to a true equation $1 = 1$ when we observe that the last two members of (26.4) require that $a + c = b + d$.

Hence (26.2) is true for every a for which $b - a \leqq c - d$; that is, for $a \geqq b + d - c$.

As a second example, we shall derive the formula

$$C_n^\mu = (- 1)^n C_n^{n-\mu-1}. \tag{26.5}$$

First, we note that by using (21.3) repeatedly we get

$$\mu(\mu - 1) \ldots (\mu - n + 1) = \frac{\mu!}{(\mu - n)!}. \tag{26.6}$$

Next we change the sign of each factor on the left side of (26.6), and again make repeated use of (21.3), thus getting

$$(- 1)^n(n - \mu - 1) \ldots (1 - \mu)(- \mu) = (- 1)^n \frac{(n - \mu - 1)!}{(- \mu - 1)!}.$$

Equating this to (26.6) and dividing both sides by $n!$ we are led directly to (26.5).

27. The Solution of More Complicated Problems

There are many problems in permutations and combinations which do not fall into the simple classes dealt with above. Such problems can often be solved by the intelligent use of the general laws stated in § 17. A few examples will illustrate the general line of attack.

EXAMPLE 27.1.—*How many combinations of four letters each can be made from the word* **pepper***?*

This example is complicated by the fact that some letters are repeated. The simplest method of dealing with it is to note that there are two general classes of combinations: those that contain **r** and those that do not.

Those that contain **r** must also contain some combination of three formed from three **p**'s and two **e**'s. It is a simple matter to list these combinations, which turn out to be

$$\mathbf{p \ p \ p,}$$
$$\mathbf{p \ p \ e,}$$
$$\mathbf{p \ e \ e.}$$

Those groups that do not contain **r** must have four letters chosen from the three **p**'s and the two **e**'s. It is evident that there are only two such combinations:

$$\mathbf{p \ p \ p \ e,}$$
$$\mathbf{p \ p \ e \ e.}$$

Since the cases which contain **r** and those which do not are mutually exclusive, the first general law of composition gives the total number of combinations as five.

In solving this example it was not necessary to make use of any of the formulas that have been derived for permutations and combinations. An illustration in which those formulas are useful as an adjunct to the general laws is the following:

EXAMPLE 27.2.—*How many combinations of four letters each can be made from the letters of the word* **provocative**?

This word has eleven letters, two **o**'s, two **v**'s, and one each of the seven letters **a, c, e, i, p, r, t.**

The possible combinations of the **o**'s and **v**'s are

oovv	**oov**	**oo**	**o**
	ovv	**ov**	**v**
	vv		

The first column contains a combination of four; it is therefore one of the cases sought. The second column contains combinations of three, and by the second law of composition it is known that each of these can be combined with every possible combination of one formed from the seven distinct characters. Likewise each of the combinations in the third column can be combined with the C_2^7 combinations of 2, and each of the fourth column with the C_3^7 combinations of 3. Finally there are C_4^7 combinations of four letters containing neither **o**'s nor **v**'s. Using the first law, the total number of combinations is found to be

$$1 + 2 \cdot C^7 + 3 \cdot C_2^7 + 2 \cdot C_3^7 + C_4^7$$

This works out to be 183 combinations in all.

It is frequently necessary in considering problems in permutations and combinations to make use of artifices of this sort. In such cases the ease with which the solution is obtained depends largely upon the appropriateness of the method of attack, so that experience and that sense which we call intuition are necessary before such problems can be satisfactorily handled. We add one more example:

EXAMPLE 27.3.—*In bridge, four hands of 13 cards each are dealt from a pack of 52. In how many different ways can this be done, if neither the order of appearance of the cards, nor the player who holds a given hand, is material?*

Suppose we call the four players A, B, C, D. Then, clearly, A may hold any one of C_{13}^{52} hands, the other 39 cards being somehow distributed to B, C, and D. For each of A's possible hands, B may be dealt C_{13}^{39} different hands; the remaining 26 cards being distributed to C and D. There are therefore $C_{13}^{52}C_{13}^{39}$ distinct ways of dealing hands to A and B. Of course, these include cases which would be alike if A and B exchanged hands, contrary to the conditions of the problem, but we will take care of this later. Whatever A and B hold, C can have C_{13}^{26} possible hands; D obviously takes what is left. Hence the total possibilities thus enumerated are $C_{13}^{52}C_{13}^{39}C_{13}^{26}$. To compensate for duplications, we note that the four hands resulting from *any* deal could be permuted among the players in $P_4^4 = 24$ ways. Hence each deal which is distinct in the sense of the problem has been counted 24 times, and the desired answer is

$$\tfrac{1}{24}C_{13}^{52}C_{13}^{39}C_{13}^{26} = 2.235\cdot10^{27}.$$

28. Symmetric Functions

A function of the variables $x_1, x_2, \ldots, x_a$ is said to be *symmetric* in these variables if it remains unaltered when any two are interchanged. Thus $\sin(x_1 + x_2 + x_3)$ and $e^{-c(x_1^2 + x_2^2 + x_3^2)}$ are symmetric in the three variables x_1, x_2, x_3; $\sin(x_1 + x_2)$ and $e^{-(c_1 x_1^2 + c_2 x_2^2 + c_3 x_3^2)}$ are not. This can be verified, for example, by interchanging x_1 and x_3.

This definition can be restated as follows:

DEFINITION 28.1. *A function is symmetric in the variables $x_1, x_2, \ldots, x_a$ if it remains unchanged when these variables are permuted in all possible ways.*

By using this definition, a symmetric function can be generated from any starting function whatever. It is necessary only to permute the variables in all possible ways and add the resulting terms. For example, a function which is symmetric in the variables x_1, x_2, x_3 can be generated from $\sin(x_1 + x_2)$ by replacing x_1, x_2 by each of the other permutations x_1, x_3; x_2, x_1; x_2, x_3; x_3, x_1; x_3, x_2 and adding. The result is

$$2\sin(x_1 + x_2) + 2\sin(x_1 + x_3) + 2\sin(x_2 + x_3),$$

which clearly remains the same no matter how the variables are interchanged.

The symmetric functions of special importance in the theory of probability are those generated by such starting functions as x_1, $x_1 x_2 x_3$, $x_1 x_2^3 x_3^2$, etc., or in general $x_1^{j_1} x_2^{j_2} \ldots x_a^{j_a}$, where the j's are any positive integers, zero included. Such functions are called *elementary symmetric functions* and are said to be of *order* n if $j_1 + j_2 + \ldots + j_a = n$. They are illustrated, in the case of three variables, in Table 28.1.

Taking the group of order 4 as an example and comparing it with the general case (order n, in a variables), the following points should be noted:

1. The generators could also be written as

$$x_1^4 x_2^0 x_3^0, \qquad x_1^1 x_2^3 x_3^0, \qquad x_1^2 x_2^2 x_3^0, \qquad x_1^1 x_2^1 x_3^2,$$

thus corresponding exactly to the general term $x_1^{j_1} x_2^{j_2} \ldots x_a^{j_a}$. When so written, it is evident that each set of exponents is a partition[9] of 4. In general, each set of exponents is a partition of the order n, as indeed it must be by the definition of "order."

TABLE 28.1

Order	Generator	Symmetric Function	Symbol
1	x_1	$x_1 + x_2 + x_3$	$^3s_1$; $^3S_1$
2	x_1^2	$x_1^2 + x_2^2 + x_3^2$	$^3s_2$
	$x_1 x_2$	$x_1 x_2 + x_1 x_3 + x_2 x_3$	$^3s_{1,1}$; $^3S_2$
3	x_1^3	$x_1^3 + x_2^3 + x_3^3$	$^3s_3$
	$x_1 x_2^2$	$x_1 x_2^2 + x_1 x_3^2 + x_1^2 x_2$ $+ x_1^2 x_3 + x_2 x_3^2 + x_2^2 x_3$	$^3s_{1,2}$
	$x_1 x_2 x_3$	$x_1 x_2 x_3$	$^3s_{1,1,1}$; $^3S_3$
4	x_1^4	$x_1^4 + x_2^4 + x_3^4$	$^3s_4$
	$x_1 x_2^3$	$x_1 x_2^3 + x_1 x_3^3 + x_1^3 x_2$ $+ x_1^3 x_3 + x_2 x_3^3 + x_2^3 x_3$	$^3s_{1,3}$
	$x_1^2 x_2^2$	$x_1^2 x_2^2 + x_1^2 x_3^2 + x_2^2 x_3^2$	$^3s_{2,2}$
	$x_1 x_2 x_3^2$	$x_1 x_2 x_3^2 + x_1 x_2^2 x_3 + x_1^2 x_2 x_3$	$^3s_{1,1,2}$
n	$x_1^{j_1} x_2^{j_2} \ldots x_a^{j_a}$	$\hat{\Sigma} x_1^j x_2^{j_2} \ldots x_a^{j_a}$	$^a s_{j_1, j_2 \ldots, j_a}$

2. There is an elementary symmetric function corresponding to every partition of 4 except 1, 1, 1, 1; this would require a generator of the form $x_1 x_2 x_3 x_4$ which is not possible with three variables. In general, there is a symmetric function of order n corresponding to every partition of n which does not have more than a parts.

3. The general symbol for a symmetric function is $^a s_{j_1, j_2, \ldots, j_a}$. However, j's which are known to be zero can be omitted without ambiguity: enough 0's can always be supplied to make the number of subscripts equal to the superscript a. Thus, $^3s_4$ can be built out to $^3s_{4,0,0}$. Similarly $^5s_{3,2}$ could be built out to $^5s_{3,2,0,0,0}$, and corresponds to a generator $x_1^3 x_2^2 x_3^0 x_4^0 x_5^0 \equiv x_1^3 x_2^2$.

---

[9] See § 18 for the definition of this word.

4. When the entire group of exponents is displayed, as in paragraph (1) above or in the last line of the table, the polynomial can be written out *either* by permuting the x's with the exponents fixed, *or* by permuting the exponents with the x's fixed. Thus, the function $^3s_{1,3}$ generated by $x_1x_2{}^3 \equiv x_1{}^1x_2{}^3x_3{}^0$ can be written down by keeping the order $x_1x_2x_3$ fixed and using in succession as exponents the six permutations of $1, 3, 0$. In fact, this is the form in which the functions appear in the table. Making use of this fact, the general symmetric function can be set down as

$$ {}^a s_{j_1, j_2 \ldots j_a} = \sum^{\wedge} x_1^{j_1} x_2^{j_2} \ldots x_a^{j_a}, $$

where the symbol $\hat{\Sigma}$ is understood to mean summation over all permutations of the j's. Note that, in the notation of § 22, the number of terms in this symmetric function is $\pi(j_1, j_2, \ldots, j_a)$.

5. The symmetric functions generated by terms such as $x_1, x_1x_2, x_1x_2x_3, \ldots$ with no powers greater than 1 are of special interest and will be denoted by ^aS_n, in which the subscript denotes the number of factors in the product; this is of course the order n since each factor has exponent 1.

To illustrate the uses to which symmetric functions may be put, consider the following example:

EXAMPLE 28.1.—*How many different permutations of n things each can be made from "a" distinct kinds of things, if J of each kind are available?*

Now, though the exact makeup of any permutation is not specified, it must clearly have some number of objects of each kind, which may be denoted by $j_1, j_2, \ldots, j_a$. By the statement of the problem this must be a partition of n, and none of the j's may be greater than J.

If the "objects" are represented by the letters $x_1, x_2, \ldots, x_a$, the product

$$ x_1^{j_1} x_2^{j_2} \ldots x_a^{j_a} \qquad (28.1) $$

may represent a group of n objects, of which j_1 are x_1's, j_2 are x_2's, etc.; it is, therefore, one group of objects which must be considered. It is capable of $P^{j_1, j_2, \ldots, j_a}_{j_1, j_2, \ldots, j_a}$ permutations within itself. If, then, all such products can be exhibited, the total of the internal permutations of each will be the desired answer.

A different group is obtained, however,

(*a*) Whenever a different partition of n is used for the exponents in (28.1).

or

(*b*) Whenever the j's of a given partition are assigned to different x's; that is, permuted among themselves.

The groups produced by (*b*) are precisely the terms of the symmetric function generated by (28.1). The number of these is $\pi(j_1, j_2, \ldots, j_a)$, and since each may be permuted within itself in $P^{j_1, j_2, \ldots, j_a}_{j_1, j_2, \ldots, j_a}$ ways, the aggregate of all permutations *corresponding to the specified partition* is the product of this P and π.

To find the wanted solution it is necessary only to sum such products over all admissible partitions of n, as required by (*a*). By "admissible partitions" we mean, of course, those for which no j_i is greater than J, and with this understanding regarding the range of summation the answer is[10]

$$P_n^{J^a} = \sum P_{j_1,j_2,\ldots,j_a}^{j_1,j_2,\ldots,j_a} \cdot \pi(j_1, j_2, \ldots, j_a). \qquad (28.2)$$

The use of this formula is much simpler than its appearance would suggest. To be specific, consider 15 objects, 3 each of 5 kinds, from which permutations of 6 objects each are to be chosen. Here $a = 5$, $J = 3$, $n = 6$, and Table 28.2 gives the details of the solution. The partitions of 6 into 5 parts,

TABLE 28.2

Partitions	Generator	P	π	$P\pi$
3 3 0 0 0	$x_1^3 x_2^3$	20	10	200
3 2 1 0 0	$x_1^3 x_2^2 x_3$	60	60	3,600
3 1 1 1 0	$x_1^3 x_2 x_3 x_4$	120	20	2,400
2 2 2 0 0	$x_1^2 x_2^2 x_3^2$	90	10	900
2 2 1 1 0	$x_1^2 x_2^2 x_3 x_4$	180	30	5,400
2 1 1 1 1	$x_1^2 x_2 x_3 x_4 x_5$	360	5	1,800
				14,300

no one of which exceeds 3, are given in the first column. Each of these is a set of j's. The corresponding generators of the symmetric functions are in column 2, and the corresponding P's and π's in the third and fourth columns. The P's are computed by formula (22.3) and the π's by the rule stated in § 22.

The final column contains the separate terms of (28.2); their sum, 14,300 is the wanted answer.

29. A Complicated Problem in Permutations

In Example 28.1 the available number of each kind of object was the same. If this is not true—if instead there are J_1 objects of the first kind, J_2 of the second, and so on—the situation is much more complex. However, with some ingenuity it can usually be broken down into a set of alternatives, each of which can be evaluated by symmetric functions, just as in the simpler case of Example 28.1. Example 29.1 will illustrate this process[11]

EXAMPLE 29.1.—*There are 5 kinds of objects, which may de designated x_1, x_2, x_3, x_4, x_5, of which 3, 5, 5, 7, and 10 each are available, respectively. How many permutations are possible, each containing 12 objects?*

[10] The rather odd symbol $P_n^{J^a}$ means—as stated in the example—the number of permutations of n things each, if there are a different kinds of things available, and J of each kind. If there had been different numbers of each kind, as there are in Example 29.1, we would have written $P_n^{J_1,J_2,\ldots,J_a}$.

[11] It is possible to write an expression which, formally, is the solution for the general case. This was done in § 17 of the First Edition. Where numerical computation is involved, however, the approach here illustrated is usually better.

This can be broken down into alternatives as follows:

(a) There are either 0, 1, 2, or 3 x_1's. In each case the rest of the 12 must be x_2, x_3, x_4, or x_5, and either
(b) there are *no more than 5 of any of them,* or
(c) there are more than 5 x_4's and *no more than 5 of the other three,* or
(d) there are more than 5 x_5's and *no more than 5 of the other three,* or
(e) there are 6 each of x_5 and x_6, in which case there are certainly no others.

The italicized phrases in (b), (c), and (d) lead to subsidiary problems of the kind discussed in § 28, the solutions of which are of form (28.2). In (b) the order of the corresponding symmetric function is 4; in (c) and (d) it is 3.

To be more specific, consider those permutations not containing x_1's. The above lettered paragraphs yield:

(b) $P_{12}^{5^4}$ permutations of x_2, x_3, x_4, x_5, $[a = 4, J = 5, n = 12]$,
(c) 6 x_4's combined with $P_6^{5^3}$ permutations of x_2, x_3, x_5,
       $[a = 3, J = 5, n = 6]$,
     7 x_4's combined with $P_5^{5^3}$ permutations of x_2, x_3, x_5,
       $[a = 3, J = 5, n = 5]$,
(d) 6 x_5's combined with $P_6^{5^3}$ permutations of x_2, x_3, x_4,
       $[a = 3, J = 5, n = 6]$,
     7 x_5's combined with $P_5^{5^3}$ permutations of x_2, x_3, x_4,
       $[a = 3, J = 5, n = 5]$,
    *8 x_5's combined with $P_4^{5^3}$ permutations of x_2, x_3, x_4,
       $[a = 3, J = 5, n = 4]$,
     9 x_5's combined with $P_3^{5^3}$ permutations of x_2, x_3, x_4,
       $[a = 3, J = 5, n = 3]$,
    10 x_5's combined with $P_2^{5^3}$ permutations of x_2, x_3, x_4,
       $[a = 3, J = 5, n = 2]$,
(e) $P_{6,6}^{6,6}$ permutations of 6 x_4's and 6 x_5's.

Now consider one of these cases, say the one indicated by an asterisk, and inquire in how many ways the x_5's may be distributed among the other x's. This can readily be answered by regarding the other x's as 4 partitions separating 5 boxes; by Problem 10,[12] the x_4's can be put in these in C_8^{12} ways. Hence there are a total of $C_8^{12}P_4^{5^3}$ permutations for the starred line.

Dealing in a similar fashion with the other lines, the total number of permutations containing no x_1's is found to be

$$P_{12}^{5^4} + 2\,C_6^{12}P_6^{5^3} + 2C_7^{12}P_5^{5^3} + C_8^{12}P_4^{5^3} + C_9^{12}P_3^{5^3} + C_{10}^{12}P_2^{5^3} + P_{6,6}^{6,6}.$$

$$(29.1)$$

Turning to those permutations which have exactly 1 x_1, the same procedure can be followed, except that only 11 objects x_2, x_3, x_4, x_5 are required. It is easily seen that this leads to the same list of possibilities as above except that the subscript on each P is reduced by 1, and case (e) drops out entirely. This leads to a formula quite analogous to (29.1) for the number of ways in which the 11 objects (not including the x_1) may be permuted. The

---

[12] Following this section.

x_1 may now be combined with each of these permutations in C_1^{12} ways, as we can see by regarding the other 11 objects as partitions of boxes into which x_1 is placed. The total number of permutations containing just one x_1 is therefore

$$C_1^{12}[P_{11}^{5^4} + 2\,C_6^{11}P_5^{5^3} + 2\,C_7^{11}P_4^{5^3} + C_8^{11}P_3^{5^3} + C_9^{11}P_2^{5^3} + C_{10}^{11}P_1^{5^3}].$$

$$(29.2)$$

Similarly, the number with 2 and 3 x_1's is

$$C_2^{12}[P_{10}^{5^4} + 2\,C_6^{10}P_4^{5^3} + 2\,C_7^{10}P_3^{5^3} + C_8^{10}P_2^{5^3} + C_9^{10}P_1^{5^3} + 1], \qquad (29.3)$$

$$C_3^{12}[P_9^{5^4} + 2\,C_6^{9}P_3^{5^3} + 2\,C_7^{9}P_2^{5^3} + C_8^{9}P_1^{5^3} + 1]. \qquad (29.4)$$

The 1's in the last two brackets correspond to cases where *only* x_5's occur; obviously there is only one possible permutation when all objects are alike.

The answer to the problem is the sum of (29.1), (29.2), (29.3), and (29.4). Taking numerical values for the binomial coefficients from Appendix III, and the P's from Table 29.1, it is found to be 184,681,717.

TABLE 29.1

n	$P_n^{5^4}$	$P_n^{5^3}$	$P_n^{2^4}$	$P_n^{2^3}$
1	4	3	4	3
2	16	9	16	9
3	64	27	60	24
4	256	81	204	54
5	1,024	243	600	90
6	4,092	726	1,440	90
7	16,296	2,142	2,520	—
8	64,428	6,174	2,520	—
9	251,664	17,178	—	—
10	965,832	45,486	—	—
11	3,618,384	112,266	—	—
12	13,131,888	250,866	—	—

Problems

1. In how many ways can four cards in sequence in the same suit be chosen from a full pack if the order of choice is immaterial, so that

six	six	eight
seven	nine	six
eight	eight	seven
nine	seven	nine

are all regarded as identical?

2. If the order of choice of the cards in Problem 1 is of interest, how many ways are there?

3. In how many ways can a cribbage hand of six cards be dealt, (*a*) if the order of dealing is taken into account, so that identical hands, the cards of which appear in different orders, are regarded as different? (*b*) if the order of dealing is neglected?

4. In how many ways can seven keys be arranged on a ring?

5. Eight persons are to be seated at a circular table. How many different chair assignments are possible? In how many arrangements does at least one guest have a different neighbor?

6. A printing telegraph machine contains a number of sliding bars each capable of taking two positions in response to current pulses of two different types. When the bars have all been set, one and only one character is selected for printing. It is evident that the number of characters which the machine is capable of selecting will depend upon the number of bars. How many bars are required to handle 50 characters?

7. If in the printing telegraph of Problem 6 the bars are capable of taking three positions instead of two, how many bars are required?

8. There are a boxes and n unlike balls. In how many ways can the balls be distributed into the boxes?

9. Same as Problem 8, but no more than one ball allowed in any box.

10. Same as Problem 8, but all balls are alike.
[Imagine the boxes separated by $a - 1$ partitions, denoted by the symbol |; and denote the balls by 0. The question may then be phrased in terms of permutations of the balls and partitions.]

11. Same as Problem 10, but only one ball allowed per box.

12. The following argument professes to be a solution of Problem 10: Let the number of arrangements be x. Now imagine the balls marked for identification. Each arrangement is subject to $n!$ permutations. Hence $n!x$ must be the solution of Problem 8, that is, a^n; or $x = a^n/n!$.
This argument is not correct. What is the error?

13. In how many ways can p +'s and n −'s be placed in a row so that no two −'s come together?
[1. See Problem 11. 2. Alternatively: find the number of ways beginning with + by setting up n pairs of the form + −. Then find the number beginning with − by setting up $n − 1$ pairs of the form + −.]

14. In how many ways can n identical balls be placed in a boxes so that no box is empty?
[1. This can be deduced from Problem 11 if the role of balls and partitions is interchanged. 2. Alternatively, use an initial |0, a terminal |, and combine the remaining partitions into combinations |0.]

15. In how many different ways can the integer n be partitioned into a parts, $j_1 + j_2 + \ldots + j_a = n$, if the order in which the j's appear is taken into account, and if one or more j's may be zero?
[Count the balls in each box of Problem 10.]

16. What is the answer to Problem 15 if zeros are not permitted?
[Compare with Problem 14.]

17. How many different combinations can be made of 10 objects, 3 of which are alike and 3 others alike, the remaining 4 being different, (a) if the number of objects in a combination is not restricted; (b) if it is equal to 4?

18. How many different connections must a telephone exchange be capable of setting up if it accommodates 10,000 subscribers?

The cylinder lock illustrated in Fig. 29.1 contains five tumblers. These tumblers are in the form of pins, cut in two parts so that when forced into the proper position by the edge of the key (Fig. 29.1b) they offer no restraint to the rotation of the cylinder. The cuts may be made at any one of ten

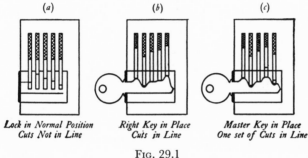

(a)   *(b)*   *(c)*

Lock in Normal Position   *Right Key in Place*   *Master Key in Place*
Cuts Not in Line   *Cuts in Line*   *One set of Cuts in Line*

FIG. 29.1

points along the pin. When the key is out, as in Fig. 29.1a, or if the wrong key is inserted, the cuts do not all coincide with the edge of the cylinder and it cannot move.

If a master key is required for a number of locks, certain tumblers may be cut in more than one place, as in Fig. 29.1c. When this is done, one set of cuts is the same on the tumblers of all locks; they can therefore all be opened by the same master key. The other set of cuts is different for every lock, so that the key corresponding to any one will not operate the rest. In Fig. 29.1c, those cuts which are not in line would be brought in line by the key shown in 29.1b. Thus this particular lock could be operated by *either* key.

The following four problems refer to locks constructed on this system:

19. How many different locks can be made without changing the keyway? (No double-cut pins.)

20. When the key of a lock is stolen and it is desired to protect the owner against possible entry, the pins are taken out and interchanged. If three of the pins happen to be cut differently, the remaining two being alike, how many times may this be done without duplication?

21. If double-cut pins are used on the first and fourth tumblers to provide for a master key, how many distinct locks will it open?

22. Each of five floors of a hotel is to have a separate and distinct master key. How many rooms may each floor have without permitting any guest's key to open any but his own room, provided (a) only one double-cut pin is used; (b) two double-cut pins; (c) three double-cut pins?

23. Four red and four black balls are to be placed in four red and four black boxes, one ball to each box. In how many ways can this be done so that there is (a) just one black ball in a red box? (b) Two black balls in red boxes? (c) Three black balls in red boxes? Consider only the final arrangement, not the order of insertion.

24. There are m red and n black boxes, and m red and n black balls. In how many ways can the balls be distributed, one to each box, so that there are just i red and j black balls in the red boxes?

25. The 13 black spades and 13 red hearts from a pack of playing cards are laid out in natural order. In how many ways can the 13 black clubs and 13 red diamonds be laid alongside, so that there are just i red pairs and i black pairs? What is the answer if the spades and hearts are not in the natural order? If they are face down and the order in unknown?

26. In a bridge game, if player A holds the following cards: Spades K, J, 9, 3, 2; hearts A, 7, 5, 3; diamonds Q, 4; clubs 10, 6, how many distinct hands may his partner C hold? What would the answer if be A held different cards?

27. Under the conditions of Problem 26, how many distinct hands might C hold with no face cards (A, K, Q, J)? With just two face cards in hearts? With the ace of spades? Would these answers be the same no matter what cards A holds?

28. If, in Problem 24, i and j are not specified, in how many distinct ways may the balls be distributed?

29. Dominoes are marked with two sets of dots, the number of dots in any set being $0, 1, \ldots, n$. The dots are so arranged that a, b and b, a are indistinguishable. How many different pieces will a complete set contain? [Consider separately the like and unlike pairs.]

30. Twelve people meet for three tables of bridge. In how many different ways may the tables be chosen?

31. How many distinct pairs of bridge partners can be chosen from twelve people? How many distinct "tables" consisting of two pairs each? Why is this not the same as Problem 30?

32. How many different groups of four can be chosen from twelve people? If two pairs of partners are chosen from each group, how many different possibilities? Compare with Problem 31.

33. Four boxes each contain three balls, one red, one white, one black. If one ball is taken from each box, there may be two of one color and two of another, or two of one color and two different, or three of one color and one different, or all alike. In how many different ways may the following selections be made: 2 red, 2 black; 4 white; 1 red, 1 white, 2 black; 3 white, 1 red?

34. In general, if each of n boxes contains a balls of different colors, and if $j_1 + j_2 + \ldots + j_a = n$, in how many ways can j_1 balls be of a stated color, j_2 of another, . . . , be chosen, one from each box?

35. Using the series for $1/(1 + y)$ and (26.1), find the value of C_n^{-1}. Show that (26.5) gives the same result.

36. By using (21.3) and the known value for $\frac{1}{2}!$, construct a table of $(j + \frac{1}{2})!$ for $-6 \leqslant j \leqslant 5$.

37. Using the results of Problem 36, find the values of $C_j^{\frac{1}{2}}$ for $0 \leqslant j \leqslant 5$. Compare with the series expansion of $(1 + y)^{\frac{1}{2}}$.

38. Prove that, when m_1 and m_2 are not integers, the analog of (23.2), Problem 23.9, is

$$\sum_{j=0}^{\infty} C_j^{m_1} C_{n-j}^{m_2} = C_n^{m_1 + m_2}. \tag{29.5}$$

[Using (26.1) multiply the two Taylor Series

$$(1 + y)^{m_1} = \sum_{i=0}^{\infty} C_i^{m_1} y^i,$$

$$(1 + y)^{m_2} = \sum_{j=0}^{\infty} C_j^{m_2} y^j,$$

and collect the terms in y^n. Equate this sum with the term for y^n in

$$(1 + y)^{m_1 + m_2} = \sum_{k=0}^{\infty} C_n^{m_1 + m_2} y^n.$$

Note that, since $C_{n-j}^{m_2} = 0$ for $j > n$, (29.5) is equivalent to (23.2).]

39. Using $m_1 = 3$ and $m_2 = 5$ and taking values from Appendix III, verify (23.2) for $n = 2$. For $n = 7$.

40. Using $m_1 = \frac{3}{2}$ and $m_2 = \frac{5}{2}$ and the results of Problem 36, verify (29.5) for $n = 2$ and $n = 7$.

41. Using (25.2) show that

$$\sum_{n=0}^{m} C_n^m = 2^m. \tag{29.6}$$

42. Show that

$$\sum_{j=0}^{n} (- 1)^j C_j^\mu = (- 1)^n C_n^{\mu - 1}.$$

[Use (24.3).]

43. Show that

$$\sum_{j=0}^{n} C_j^{\mu + j - 1} = C_n^{n + \mu}. \tag{29.7}$$

[Write (24.3) in the form $C_j^{\mu+j-1} = C_j^{\mu+j} - C_{j-1}^{\mu+j-1}$ and sum.]

44. Prove that

$$\sum_{j=r}^{x-y} 2^j \frac{j + 2y}{2x - j} C_{x+y}^{2x-j} = 2^r C_{x+y}^{2x-r}.$$ (29.8)

[Use the identities $j + 2y \equiv (x + y) - (x - j - y)$ and $C_{\beta-1}^{\alpha-1} - C_{\beta}^{\alpha-1} \equiv C_{\beta}^{\alpha} - 2C_{\beta}^{\alpha-1}$.]

45. Prove that

$$\sum_{j=0}^{x-r} \frac{r + 2j}{2x - r} C_{x+j}^{2x-1} = C_{x-1}^{2x-r-1}.$$ (29.9)

46. Under the conditions stated in Problem 15, what is the number of distinct partitions of n into not more than A parts?

[Use the result of Problem 43.]

47. Under the conditions of Problem 16, what is the number of distinct partitions of n into not more than A parts?

48. Under the conditions of Problem 16, what is the total number of distinct partitions of n?

49. Show that

$$m(m - 2) \ldots (m - 2n + 2) = 2^n (\tfrac{1}{2}m)! / (\tfrac{1}{2}m - n)!.$$

50. Using the results of Problem 49, show that

$$(2m)! = 2^{2m} m! (m - \tfrac{1}{2})! / (- \tfrac{1}{2})!.$$

51. Verify the formula

$$C_m^{2m} = 2^{2m} C_m^{m-\frac{1}{2}}.$$

52. Using (26.5) and Problem 51, show that

$$C_m^{2m} = (- 4)^m C_m^{-\frac{1}{2}}.$$

53. Using (23.2) and (24.1), prove that

$$\sum_{j=0}^{n} (C_j^n)^2 = C_n^{2n}.$$

54. What is the coefficient of $r^2 b^2$ in the expression $(r + w + b)^4$? Of $rb^2 w$?

[The four factors correspond to the boxes of Problem 33.]

55. What is the coefficient of $x_1^{j_1} x_2^{j_2} \ldots x_a^{j_a}$ in the expansion of $(x_1 + x_2 + \ldots + x_a)^n$?

56. Using (22.3) and the result of Problem 55, show that

$$(x_1 + x_2 + \ldots + x_a)^n = \sum P_{j_1, j_2, \ldots, j_a}^{j_1, j_2, \ldots, j_a} \cdot a_{s_{j_1, j_2, \ldots, j_a}},$$

where the sum is taken over all partitions of n.

57. Starting with terms of the form $x_1 x_2^2 x_3$; $x_1^7 x_2^2$; $x_1 x_2 x_3$; x_1^5, write (a) the symbol for the corresponding symmetric function; (b) the summation; (c) the polynomial for $a = 4$.

58. Prove that $^{a+1}S_n = \, ^aS_n + x_{a+1}\,^aS_{n-1}$.
[A term either contains x_{a+1} or it does not.]

59. How many terms are there in the polynomial expansion of ^aS_n? Of $^aS_{j_1, \, 2, \, \ldots, ja}$?

60. In the polynomial expansion for $(1 - x_1)(1 - x_2) \ldots (1 - x_a)$, what is the coefficient of $x_1 x_2$? Of $x_3 x_5 x_a$? Of $x_1 x_2 \ldots x_j$?

61. Using the paragraph numbered (5) in § 28 and Problem 60, show that

$$(1 - x_1)(1 - x_2) \ldots (1 - x_a) = \sum_{j=0}^{a} (-1)^j \, ^aS_j.$$

[Call $^aS_0 = 1$.]

62. Using the results of Problems 56 and 59, show that

$$\sum \pi(j_1, j_2, \ldots, j_a) \cdot P_{j_1, j_2, \ldots, j_a}^{j_1, j_2, \ldots, ja} = a^n,$$

where the sum is taken over all the partitions of n. Verify for $n = 5$, $a = 7$ and for $n = 5$, $a = 3$.

63. Using the results of Problems 59 and 61, show that

$$\sum_{j=0}^{a} (-1)^j C_j^a = 0.$$

Show that this also follows from (25.2).

64. In Example 28.1, if $J \geq n$, how many permutations of 6 objects each can be made?

65. Imagine a ribbon machine limited to supply not more than 5 colors of warp, and not more that 30 threads of any one color. These are supplied in groups of 5 adjacent threads, which can be placed in any desired position across the width of the ribbon, thus producing a stripe. How many warp designs are possible in a ribbon that is 60 threads wide?

66. How many of the designs of Problem 65 are symmetrical?

67. From the user's standpoint, two ribbons with design reversed right and left are identical, since one can be made identical with the other by turning it end to end. How many of the designs in Problem 65 are different from the user's standpoint?

68. Show that ^aS_n does not exist for $n > a$.

69. If, in Problem 65, there are 15 black threads, 25 each of yellow and red, 35 of brown, and 50 of white, how many designs are possible?
[See Example 29.1.]

70. How many of the designs in Problem 69 are symmetrical?
[Use Table 29.1.]

71. From the user's standpoint, how many of the designs of Problem 69 are distinct?

Answers to Problems at End of §17

1. $7 \cdot 6 \cdot 5 = 210$. **2.** $7 \cdot 6 \cdot 5 = 210$. **3.** $7^3 = 343$. **4.** $6 \cdot 5 \cdot 4 \cdot 3 \cdot 2 = 720$. **5.** $21^3 \cdot 5^2$. **6.** $21 \cdot 20 \cdot 19 \cdot 5 \cdot 4$. **7.** 10. **8.** Better; 240,737 vs. 231,525. **9.** 720; 810. **10.** 648; 729.

Answers to Problems at End of §20

1. 64,864,800. **2.** 7920. **3.** 40,320; 7.64. **4.** $5^6 = 15,625$. **5.** a^n. **6.** 103,680. **7.** 24. **8.** 3150. **9.** 6720. **10.** 19,208. **11.** Two answers are possible. If the center stripe must differ from the edge stripes, 336. If not, $8 \cdot 7 \cdot 7 = 392$. **12.** 3360; 9800. **13.** All.

Answers to Problems at End of §23

1. 1,184,040. **2.** $C_5^{11} = 462$. Information regarding method of selection is superfluous. **3.** $C_5^{52} = 2,598,560$. **4.** $\sum_{j=0}^{5} C_j^{13} = 2380$. **5.** $C_3^{26}C_4^{26} = 38,870,000$. **6.** $C_4^{26}C_4^{26}P_7^7 = 195,904,800,000$. **7.** 1; $P_{3,4}^{3,4} = 35$. **8.** $C_{n_1}^{m_1}C_{n_2}^{m_2}$. **10.** $26^3 = 17,576$; No, JJS is certainly more likely than QQQ; No, some people have more and some less than three initials. **11.** $26^3 - 24^3 = 3752$. **12.** Two interpretations are possible. If "objects of a kind" are indistinguishable (e.g., m_1 a's, m_2 b's, etc.) the answer is $P_{n_1,n_2,\ldots,n_a}^{n_1,n_2,\ldots,n_a}$. If distinguishable (e.g., m_1 spades, m_2 hearts, m_3 diamonds, etc.) the answer is $C_{n_1}^{m_1}C_{n_2}^{m_2}\ldots C_{n_a}^{m_a}P_n^n$, where $n = n_1 + n_2 + \ldots + n_a$. **13.** 0.

Answers to Problems at End of §29

1. 40. **2.** $40P_4^4 = 960$. **3.** $P_6^{52} = 14,658,134,400$; $C_6^{52} = 20,358,520$. **4.** $P_6^6 = 6!$ if the ring cannot be turned over; 6!/2 if it can. **5.** 8!; 7!/2. **6.** $2^n > 50$; $n = 6$. **7.** $3^n > 50$; $n = 4$. **8.** a^n. **9.** $a!/(a - n)! = P_n^a$. **10.** C_n^{a+n-1}. **11.** C_n^a. **12.** The nature of the error can be seen by considering a particular arrangement, namely, all balls in box 1. Even if balls are marked for identification, this gives only 1 arrangement in Problem 8, not $n!$. **13.** C_n^{p+1}. **14.** $P_{a-1,n-a}^{a-1,n-a} = C_{a-1}^{n-1}$. **15.** C_{a-1}^{n+a-1}. **16.** C_{a-1}^{n-1}. **17.** There can be 0, 1, 2, 3 of first kind, etc. Hence $4 \cdot 4 \cdot 2 \cdot 2 \cdot 2 \cdot 2 - 1 = 255$, excluding "no objects at all"; 46. **18.** 49,995,000. **19.** 10^5. **20.** $P_{2,1,1,1}^{2,1,1,1} - 1 = 59$. **21.** 99: not 100, because the private key to one would open all the rest. **22.** 9, 99, 999, unless a universal master key is required, in which case 1, 9, 99. Note that in the former case the floor masters may differ in the single cut pins; in the latter case all single cut pins must be alike. **23.** 16; 36; 16. **24.** $C_i^n \cdot C_j^n$. **25.** $(C_i^{13})^2$; same; same. **26.** $C_{13}^{39} = 8,122,425,444$; same. **27.** $C_{13}^{27} = 20,058,300$; $C_2^3 C_{11}^{36} = 1,802,415,888$; $C_{12}^{38} = 2,707,475,148$; no. **28.** This can be answered directly as $P_{m,n}^{m,n}$. Or, using the result of Problem 24 and noting that $i + j = m$, as $\sum_{j=0}^{n} C_{m-j}^m C_j^n$. By (23.2) this is C_m^{m+n}. The two results are identical. **29.** $C_2^{n+1} + C_1^{n+1} = C_2^{n+2}$. **30.** There are two possible solutions: without giving attention to partners, $C_4^{12}C_4^8C_4^4/P_3^3 = |34,650;|$ with| attention to partners, multiply by $3^3 = 27$. **31.** $C_2^{12} = 66$; $C_2^{12}C_2^{10}/P_2^2 = 1485$; many of the arrangements in Problem 30 would have the same pair of partners at one table, but the other tables would be different. **32.** $C_4^{12} = 495$; $C_4^{12}C_2^4/P_2^2 = 1485$.

33. $\dfrac{4!}{2!2!} = 6;\qquad \dfrac{4!}{4!} = 1;\qquad \dfrac{4!}{2!1!1!} = 12;\qquad \dfrac{4!}{3!1!} = 4.$

34. $P^{j_1,j_2,\ldots,j_a}_{j_1,j_2,\ldots,j_a}.$ **35.** $(-1)^n.$

36.

$j + \tfrac{1}{2}$	$-\tfrac{11}{2}$	$-\tfrac{9}{2}$	$-\tfrac{7}{2}$	$-\tfrac{5}{2}$	$-\tfrac{3}{2}$	$-\tfrac{1}{2}$
$\dfrac{(j+\tfrac{1}{2})!}{\sqrt{\pi}}$	$-\dfrac{32}{3\cdot5\cdot7\cdot9}$	$\dfrac{16}{3\cdot5\cdot7}$	$-\dfrac{8}{3\cdot5}$	$\dfrac{4}{3}$	-2	1

$j + \tfrac{1}{2}$	$\tfrac{1}{2}$	$\tfrac{3}{2}$	$\tfrac{5}{2}$	$\tfrac{7}{2}$	$\tfrac{9}{2}$	$\tfrac{11}{2}$
$\dfrac{(j+\tfrac{1}{2})!}{\sqrt{\pi}}$	$\dfrac{1}{2}$	$\dfrac{3}{4}$	$\dfrac{3\cdot5}{8}$	$\dfrac{3\cdot5\cdot7}{16}$	$\dfrac{3\cdot5\cdot7\cdot9}{32}$	$\dfrac{3\cdot5\cdot7\cdot9\cdot11}{64}$

37. $1,\ \tfrac{3}{2},\ \tfrac{3}{8},\ -\tfrac{1}{16},\ \tfrac{3}{128},\ -\tfrac{3}{256}.$ **46.** $C^{A+n}_{A-1}.$ Note that partitions such as $n, 0$; $n, 0, 0, 0$, which differ only in the number of zeros, are counted as distinct in this answer. **47.** $\displaystyle\sum_{j=0}^{A-1} C^{n-1}_j.$ **48.** $\displaystyle\sum_{j=0}^{n-1} C^{n-1}_j = 2^{n-1}.$ **54.** 6; 12. **55.** $P^{j_1,j_2,\ldots,j_a}_{j_1,j_2,\ldots,j_a}.$

57. $^aS_{1,2,1},\qquad ^aS_{7,2},\qquad ^aS_{1,1,1} \equiv\ ^aS_3,\qquad ^aS_5;$

$$\hat{\sum} x_1^{\ 1}x_2^{\ 2}x_3^{\ 1}x_4^{\ 0}\ldots x_a^{\ 0},\qquad \hat{\sum} x_1^{\ 7}x_2^{\ 2}x_3^{\ 0}\ldots x_a^{\ 0},$$

$$\hat{\sum} x_1^{\ 1}x_2^{\ 1}x_3^{\ 1}x_4^{\ 0}\ldots x_a^{\ 0},\qquad \sum_{i=1}^{a} x_i^{\ 5};$$

$$x_1x_2x_3^{\ 2} + x_1x_2x_4^{\ 2} + x_1x_2^{\ 2}x_3 + x_1x_2^{\ 2}x_4 + x_1x_3x_4^{\ 2} + x_1x_3^{\ 2}x_4$$
$$+\ x_2x_3x_4^{\ 2} + x_2x_3^{\ 2}x_4 + x_2^{\ 2}x_3x_4 + x_1^{\ 2}x_2x_3 + x_1^{\ 2}x_2x_4 + x_1^{\ 2}x_3x_4,$$
$$x_1^{\ 7}x_2^{\ 2} + x_1^{\ 7}x_3^{\ 2} + x_1^{\ 7}x_4^{\ 2} + x_1^{\ 2}x_2^{\ 7} + x_1^{\ 2}x_3^{\ 7} + x_1^{\ 2}x_4^{\ 7} + x_2^{\ 7}x_3^{\ 2}$$
$$+\ x_2^{\ 7}x_4^{\ 2} + x_2^{\ 2}x_3^{\ 7} + x_2^{\ 2}x_4^{\ 7} + x_3^{\ 2}x_4^{\ 7} + x_3^{\ 7}x_4^{\ 2},$$
$$x_1x_2x_3 + x_1x_2x_4 + x_1x_3x_4 + x_2x_3x_4,\qquad x_1^{\ 5} + x_2^{\ 5} + x_3^{\ 5} + x_4^{\ 5}.$$

59. $P^{n,a-n}_{n,a-n} = C^a_n;\ \pi(j_1,j_2,\ldots,j_a).$ **60.** 1; -1; $(-1)^j.$
62. The partitions of n and the corresponding values of π and P are: for $a = 7,$

Partition	π	P	πP
5 0 0 0 0 0 0	7	1	7
4 1 0 0 0 0 0	42	5	210
3 2 0 0 0 0 0	42	10	420
3 1 1 0 0 0 0	105	20	2100
2 2 1 0 0 0 0	105	30	3150
2 1 1 1 0 0 0	140	60	8400
1 1 1 1 1 0 0	21	120	2520

$$16,807 = 7^5;$$

for $a = 3$,

Partition	π	P	πP
5 0 0	3	1	3
4 1 0	6	5	30
3 2 0	6	10	60
3 1 1	3	20	60
2 2 1	3	30	90

$$243 = 3^5.$$

64. a^6. Cf. Problem 20.4. **65.** As set up on the machine, 239,376,060. This is computed from (28.2) with $a = 5$, $J = 6$, $n = 12$. **66.** 14,300. See Example 28.1. **67.** $\frac{1}{2}$(239,376,060 + 14,300) = 119,695,180. **69.** 182,943,684 if the limitation to 30 threads of one color is retained; or 184,681,717 if it is not. **70.** 7080; or 7329. **71.** 91,475,382; or 92,344,523.

Chapter IV

Elementary Principles of the Theory of Probability

30. Complementary Probabilities

The events "A happens" and "A does not happen" are mutually exclusive. Hence, by Convention II, § 3, the probability that "either A happens or A does not happen" is the sum of their separate probabilities. But one or the other of these two events is certain to occur, and therefore the sum must by unity. Hence, if the probability that A happens is denoted by $P(A)$ and the probability that A does not happen by $P(A')$, it follows that

$$P(A) + P(A') = 1,$$

or

$$P(A) = 1 - P(A').$$

The numbers $P(A)$ and $P(A')$, which represent the probability of an event taking place and the probability of it not taking place, are known as "complementary probabilities."

31. Unconditional Probabilities

The simplest type of problems in the theory of probability are known as "problems in unconditional probability." Their principal characteristic is the assurance with which the conditions surrounding them can be stated. It is impossible to describe them more exactly, as their classification is of a vague and somewhat illogical nature, but the implication of the name, which is a very useful one, will become clear in the course of a few sections. They can frequently be solved by the direct application of the fundamental definition of probability. A few examples will illustrate this type of problem.

EXAMPLE 31.1.—*What is the probability of throwing an ace with a die?*

There are six faces to the die, only one of which may appear. In an actual die they are not equally likely to appear, for the die is certainly unsymmetrical to a greater or lesser degeee. The nature of this

59

asymmetry is unknown, however, and therefore plays no part in the problem. There are other known characteristics of the faces, such as the number and arrangement of the dots, but these characteristics are not pertinent except insofar as they affect the symmetry of the die, and their effect in this respect is unknown. Hence it must be concluded that each of the six faces is "equally likely" to appear. Of this complete group of six faces only one is an ace. Hence, by definition, the chance of an ace appearing is $\frac{1}{6}$.

EXAMPLE 31.2.—*The letters of the word* **tailor** *are written on cards. The cards having been thoroughly shuffled, four are drawn in order. What is the probability that the result is* **oral**?

The number of permutations of six distinct things four at a time is $6!/2! = 360$. These permutations differ in no known pertinent respect except their identity. Hence they form a complete group of equally likely events. Only one of these events, however, is the word "oral." Hence the answer to the question is $\frac{1}{360}$.

EXAMPLE 31.3.—*The letters of the word* **pepper** *are written on cards. The cards having been thoroughly shuffled, four are drawn in order. What is the chance that the result is* **peep**?

In this case a distinction must be made between *cards* and *letters*. The permutations of the *cards* are all equally likely. The permutations of the *letters* need not be. The permutations of the cards form a complete group of 360 events of which a certain subgroup gives the desired word. The problem is to find the number of permutations in the subgroup.

To do this, we note that two cards can be selected from the three which bear **p**'s in $C_2^3 = 3$ ways, and that each of these can be combined with the cards bearing **e**'s to form a combination **p e e p**. Having arranged them in this order, we can permute the cards bearing **p**'s in $P_2^2 = 2$ ways; and each of these can be combined with $P_2^2 = 2$ permutations of the cards bearing **e**'s. Hence the desired subgroup of permutations is $C_2^3 \, P_2^2 \, P_2^2 = 12$, and the answer is $\frac{12}{360} = \frac{1}{30}$.

EXAMPLE 31.4.—*First Appearance of the Psychic Research Problem.*[1]—*A*

---

[1] This example, which recurs in various forms, has the following interesting history: A certain pseudo-medical hoax, of which the problem is a disguised formulation, was under investigation by a friend of mine. He was anxious to formulate the number of "reds" and "blacks," and other features of the experimental procedure, so as to make the chance of an *accidental* high score, and particularly of ambiguous scores which the "medium" would undoubtedly regard as favorable, as small as possible. It was necessary to have a reasonable proportion of "reds"; and the number of "cards" which the "medium" would consent to handle was limited. We finally arrived at a setup which, although none too satisfactory, was the best we could get; and with fear and trepidation my friend conducted the experiment. The outcome justified his fears—one of the least probable results occurred. The "medium" got the lowest possible score.

spiritualistic medium claims to be able to tell the color of a playing card without seeing it. In order to test her claims an experiment is conducted with four red and four black cards. These cards are thoroughly shuffled and placed face down on the table. The medium is told that there are four red and four black cards, but presumably knows nothing as to their arrangement. The experimenter picks up a card and without either looking at it himself or showing it to the medium asks its color. If she answers "red," he places it at one side of the table. If she answers "black," he places it on the other side of the table. This process is repeated until all cards are exhausted.

If the medium does not have the ability which she claims to possess, what is the chance that there will be just one black card in the pile that should be red?

The order in which the medium will call her "reds" and "blacks" is, of course, unknown; but if she has no power of detecting the nature of the cards, the order of calling will be quite independent of that in which the cards actually appear. Her chance of success would, in fact, be just the same if she were to state the order in which she expected the cards to appear before they were dealt—that is, if she claimed the gift of "prophecy" instead of "occult understanding." Suppose, then, that we think of this order in which she calls the cards, whatever it is, as a "standard order," and ask for the chance that the cards are so dealt as to match this standard order to just the extent prescribed by the statement of the problem.

It is asserted that the medium knows that there are just four red and four black cards. It may therefore be accepted as a fact that she will call red and black exactly four times each; that is, the standard order contains four reds and four blacks.

Now turning attention to the order in which the cards appear, it is at once obvious that the $P^{4,4}_{4,4} = 70$ possible permutations constitute a complete group of equally likely and mutually exclusive events. Among these there is a certain subgroup which matches the standard order in exactly three reds. If the number of events contained in this subgroup can be found, the problem will have been solved.

There is, however, a precise analogy between this situation and Problem 29.23, the balls corresponding to the cards and the boxes to the called order. There it was found that there were 16 ways of placing the balls, so that just one red box contained a black ball. Hence the required probability is $\frac{8}{35}$.

Problems

1. Three pennies are tossed. What is the chance that just two come up heads?

2. A penny is tossed three times. What is the chance that: (*a*) Heads comes up the first two times? (*b*) Heads comes up the first two times only? (*c*) Heads comes up exactly two times? (*d*) Heads comes up at least two times?

3. If it is assumed that births are uniformly·distributed throughout the year (which is not quite true) and that a year consists of 365 days (which also is not quite true), what is the probability that the birthday of a person chosen at random will be: (*a*) July 4? (*b*) In January? (*c*) On Easter Sunday? (*d*) Before May 1?

4. A connector switch in a step-by-step exchange reaches ten subscribers on each of ten levels—100 subscribers in all. Every subscriber is represented on such a switch. What is the chance that Mr. A's line appears on the third level?

5. Assume that the various operations of a connector switch consume time as follows:

(*a*)	First vertical step	0.15 sec.
(*b*)	Succeeding vertical steps	0.10 sec.
(*c*)	First horizontal step	0.25 sec.
(*d*)	Succeeding horizontal steps	0.10 sec.

An observer visiting the exchange watches a connector until it operates, and notes the operating time. What is the probability that it is less than 0.66 second? What is the probability that it lies between 0.66 and 1.51? What is the probability that it exceeds 4 seconds?

6. Mr. A makes two calls during an hour and is twice called by other subscribers, of whom one is Mr. B. The calling subscribers, in case they find Mr. A busy, repeat their calls. Each call occupies one of the 60 minutes of the hour. What is the chance that Mr. B is successful on his first attempt to call?

7. In the psychic research experiment of Example 31.4, what is the chance of the medium scoring 100%.

8. If, in the psychic research experiment of Example 31.4, six red cards and two black cards are used, what is the chance of the medium scoring 100%?

9. If, in the psychic research experiment of Example 31.4, six red cards and two black cards are used, what is the chance that the medium places just one wrong in each color?

10. Each of two groups of cards contains four red and four black cards. Group I is laid out in order. Group II is thoroughly shuffled and dealt on the cards of Group I. What is the chance of just six matched pairs?

11. A milkman starts on his route with ten dozen quarts of fresh milk, together with five dozen quarts left over from the preceding day. Having delivered 125 quarts, he arrives at the home of Mrs. A, who receives one quart. What is the chance that it is stale?

12. A batch of one thousand lamps is 5% bad. If five are tested, what is the chance no defectives will appear? What is the chance the test batch will be 40% defective?

13. If a die is tossed, what is the probability that the face which appears is: (*a*) Even? (*b*) Greater than 3? (*c*) Not greater than 5?

14. What is the chance of throwing an ace with an unsymmetrical die, if the ace is 5% more likely than the adjacent sides, and the six 10% less likely?

15. In Example 31.3, what is the probability of the word **peer**?

16. Two dice are thrown. What is the probability that the larger number is j?

17. If the digits of a five-digit number are selected at random and zero is acceptable as a first digit, what is the chance that even and odd digits alternate?

18. If, in Problem 20.9, the colors are chosen at random, what is the chance that all stripes will be different colors? That no two adjacent stripes will be the same color? That adjacent stripes will not be the same color, and the ribbon will not be reversible?

[The answers to Problems 20.9, 20.10, and 20.11 will be helpful.]

19. Two players A and B agree to risk $1 a throw on the toss of a penny. Player A, who has just $2 in his purse, takes heads, and player B, who has $3, takes tails. After three throws, what is $P(j)$, the probability that player A has j dollars?

[Assume that the play will cease, or at all events no money will change hands, after a player has lost his last dollar.]

20. Under the conditions of Problem 19, what is $P(j)$ after the first throw? After the second?

32. Some Sample Spaces

Sample spaces can easily be constructed for the examples of § 31. That corresponding to the die of Example 31.1 consists of 6 points of equal weight.

For Example 31.2, it is simplest to think of the various permutations of the cards as the primary events. This leads to a sample space of 360 points, each corresponding to one of the four-letter "words" which these permutations spell out. Again, all are equally likely, so each point must be assigned a weight $\frac{1}{360}$. The subgroup that satisfies the conditions of the problem is a single point.

Example 31.3 can be interpreted in this same sample space, but in this instance the subgroup that satisfies the condition of the problem contains 12 sample points. Alternatively, we may regard the permutations of the *letters* as primary events. This leads to a different sample space (though of course not to a different answer). To construct it, consider the 5 possible *combinations* of letters which have already been noted in § 27. These are set down below, together with the number of *permutations* that can occur within each combination. Since each permutation is clearly a different "word" the total number of words that can be formed is 38. If these are the primary events, we must have a sample space of 38 points.

Combination	Permutations	Relative Weight	Weight
p p p e 4		12	1/30
p p p r 4		6	1/60
p p e e 6		12	1/30
p p e r 12		12	1/30
p e e r 12		6	1/60

In this sample space the points do not have equal weight. We have seen in Example 31.3 that 12 equally likely permutations of cards would fall in order so as to spell out **p e e p**, and the argument there used would apply equally well to any other arrangement of these four letters. But an analogous argument (Problem 31.15) shows that only 6 permutations of cards would spell out **p e e r**. We conclude, therefore, that if the cards are selected at random, the sample point for **p e e p** would have twice the weight of the sample point for **p e e r**. If each sample point is considered separately in this way, their relative weights come out as shown in the third column. Thus 16 of the 38 points are of relative weight 6, and 22 of relative weight 12. To reduce them to the proper unit of measure they must be divided by 360, which leads to the weights in column 4.

Finally, consider Example 31.4. Here the primary events are the 70 different orders in which the cards may fall. Each of these has equal weight $\frac{1}{70}$, and 16 are included in the desired subspace. In this case also a different sample space could be constructed by calling the degree of mismatch the primary event. Clearly this mismatch must be in either 0, 2, 4, 6, or 8 cards, thus leading to a space of only 5 sample points. From the results of Problem 29.23, these must be assigned relative weights of 1, 16, 36, 16, and 1, respectively, or, when these are adjusted to proper unit of measure, $\frac{1}{70}, \frac{8}{35}, \frac{18}{35}, \frac{8}{35}, \frac{1}{70}$.

The reader may feel that these constructions have added nothing to our understanding. In a sense this is true, for the sample space is only a pictorial representation of the basic facts: in concrete numerical situations like the above it merely restates what is already known.

The value of the concept lies principally in providing a precise and universal language for theoretical studies.

33. Random Association of Events

A key phrase in Example 31.4 is "the cards are thoroughly shuffled." This has been interpreted to mean that any card is as likely to appear in one position as another, or, in other words, that the cards "are distributed at random." This is the object of shuffling.

There will be many other occasions to use the phrase "at random." A ball drawn from an urn will be said to be drawn "at random" if every ball has the same chance of being selected; a group of n balls will be said to be drawn "at random" if any (every) permutation of n balls is equally likely to be chosen; a ball will be said to be placed in boxes "at random" if it is equally likely to go into any box; or a group of balls will be placed in boxes "at random" if they might with equal likelihood have gone into any permutation of the boxes.

These ideas may be phrased in the following definition:

DEFINITION 33.1. *An event is said to occur "at random" if it is one of the possible results of an experiment, and if all these results are equally likely.*

Example 31.4 is also significant in another important respect. The procedure pairs off the words of the medium against the cards as they are dealt; in mathematical language it puts the words and the cards in 1–1 ("one-to-one") correspondence. This is a common phenomenon. Other examples are: distributing balls in boxes, where n_j, the number of balls in a box, is in 1–1 correspondence with j, the serial number of the box; or placing electrons in atomic orbits; or particles in the energy states of an atom; or alleles in the genes of a chromosome, or many other situations.

Such situations may be referred to in general as putting a set of events in 1–1 correspondence with a set of objects; in the context of Example 31.4 the events would be the words and the objects the cards. The process by which such a correspondence is set up will be said to be random if the events are as likely to be associated with one permutation of objects as with any other. This conforms to the general definition given above.

In discussing Example 31.4 we noted that, so long as the cards were dealt at random, it did not matter whether the choice of words was systematic or not. This is a general proposition:

THEOREM 33.1. *An experiment which associates a set of events with a set of objects in 1–1 correspondence is random if* either *the events* or *the objects occur in random order.*

This theorem is capable of sophisticated proof, but in view of its plausibility this will not be undertaken.

We note one point of warning, however. The fact that two sets of phenomena are quite independent of one another does not necessarily imply randomness. Suppose, for instance, that the "medium" in Example 31.4 had a personal predisposition to call the earlier cards black and the later ones red. Suppose also that, for some unexplained reason, there was a tendency for black cards to appear preferentially in the early part of the deal. The experiment would then not be random, and if it were repeated many times the medium might consistently achieve a better than random score, without possessing any occult powers.

But bias in either half of the experiment would not destroy its random character if the other half were truly random.

34. Conditional Probabilities

Not all questions are as direct as those treated in § 31. Some contain provisos that materially affect the probability desired. For instance, the question, What is the probability that Christmas falls on Monday? has been found to have the answer $\frac{1}{7}$. But the question, What is the probability that Christmas falls on Monday if it does not fall on either Friday or Saturday? is also a proper subject for the theory of probability, and it is immediately obvious that the answer is no longer $\frac{1}{7}$.

The answer to a question of this kind is called a "conditional[2] probability" and will be represented by the symbol $P(B|A)$, which may be read "the probability that B happens if A does."

Problems of this type are sometimes exceedingly difficult to solve, but in many cases they are almost as simple as if the restrictive condtions had not been applied. This is true, for instance, in the case of the question asked above. If Christmas does not fall on either Friday or Saturday it must fall on one of the remaining days of the week, of which there are five. As these are equally likely, the answer to the question is $\frac{1}{5}$. It may be written symbolically as

$$P \text{ (Sunday} \,|\, \text{not Friday or Saturday)} = \tfrac{1}{5}.$$

Note that this argument is possible because the additional information supplied by the proviso has not altered the relative likelihood of the remaining days. It has removed two days of the week from consideration, thus leaving the remaining five as a complete group. But it did not modify our state of ignorance regarding these five in any essential way; they are still equally likely.

The following is another example in which the proviso does not alter the relative probabilities:

EXAMPLE 34.1.—*If an even face falls uppermost in tossing a die, what is the probability that it is greater than 3?*

Here the events 1, 3, 5 have been removed from consideration, but 2, 4, 6 remain equally likely, and the answer is

$$P \,(>3 \,|\, \text{even)} = \tfrac{2}{3}.$$

Not all provisos are of this kind. The following is a case in which the relative probabilities are surely affected:

EXAMPLE 34.2.—*An election involves three candidates, X, Y, and Z, of whom X and Z are campaigning on quite similar platforms, whereas Y's is radically different. Public opinion polls have shown X and Y to have equal probability of election, and Z somewhat less. What is the probability that X will win if Z withdraws?*

---

[2] Sometimes "contingent."

By the statement of the existing situation, X and Y are equally likely candidates. If Z withdraws, the complete group of candidates will have been reduced from three to two. Up to this point the situation is similar to the two illustrations previously considered. But in view of the similarity of platforms, Z's supporters are more likely to transfer to X than to Y. It would therefore violate reason to assert that X still has only an equal chance to win.

In the examples which follow, the information supplied by the proviso does not alter the relative probabilities and answers can be obtained by using the primary definition of probability. Other cases, such as the election example just mentioned, would require a different approach; in that case, perhaps another sampling of public opinion. Consider the following example:

EXAMPLE 34.3.—*If the first four cards of a poker hand have been dealt and all are spades, what is the probability that the remaining card will also be a spade?*

After four spades have been dealt, 48 cards remain, of which 9 are spades. Since the proviso has not destroyed the random character of the remaining deal, the desired probability is

$$P(5\,|\,4) = \tfrac{3}{16}.$$

EXAMPLE 34.4.—*If, in the experiment in psychic research described in Example 31.4, the first card to appear is black but is called red by the medium, what is the chance that at the end of the trial there will be exactly three red cards in the red positions?*

The medium having called the first card red is left with three reds and four blacks. These she will call in some order, which is again our "standard order."

As the first card dealt was black, the only way in which the remainder can match up in exactly three reds is for all of the remaining red positions in the standard order to be matched with red cards. If this is done there are left three blacks and one red with which to fill the four black positions. It is obvious that the red card can be placed in any one of the four positions, after which the placing of the three black cards gives no new arrangement. Thus it is seen that the total number of permutations in the subgroup which satisfies the conditions of the problem is 4. As the complete group consists of $P^{3,4}_{3,4} = 35$, the desired probability is $\tfrac{4}{35}$.

The result of Example 31.4 was $\tfrac{8}{35}$; hence the medium's chance of scoring 75% is reduced by half if her first attempt is wrong.

It is interesting to see how much greater her chances are if she gets the first card right. Therefore the following example may be considered:

begin

EXAMPLE 34.5.—*If, in the experiment in psychic research described in Example 31.4, the medium places the first card correctly, what is her chance of having exactly three correct cards in each position?*

Note that the statement of this example is somewhat different from the statement of the preceding one. The preceding example stated definitely that the first card in the standard order was black but was called red by the medium. As the problem is stated at present the color of the first card is not known. It is only known that the medium called it correctly.

Suppose, to begin with, that the first card is black and is correctly called. There are then left three black cards in the standard order. To satisfy the stated condition one red card must be placed in these positions, which can be done in three ways. After filling the two remaining positions with black cards the one black card which remains can be placed in either of the four red positions. The total number of permutations satisfying the stated condition is thus $3 \cdot 4 = 12$. Since the total number of permutations is again $P_{3,4}^{3,4} = 35$, the probability is $\frac{12}{35}$.

This answer was obtained on the supposition that the first card to fall was black. By reason of symmetry,[3] the same result would be obtained if it was red and was correctly called. Hence the answer is $\frac{12}{35}$ in this case also.

If, therefore, the medium guesses correctly at the first attempt, her chances of scoring exactly 75% are increased by half.

35. Some Instructive Illustrations; A Transition Matrix

The following example is a little different from those in § 34, though only conditional probabilities are concerned:

EXAMPLE 35.1.—*The players agree to risk $1 on the toss of coin but have not examined their pocketbooks. Upon doing so they find they have just $5 between them. What is the probability that player A will have just j dollars after the first throw?*

There is a deficiency in the statement of this example: we are not told how much money player A has in his purse. Since we do not know this, we must content ourselves with the consideration of various alternatives and the conditional probabilities to which they lead.

Suppose, first, that A finds $1 in his purse. Then, if the coin is fair, he is equally likely to have $2 or nothing after the first throw; he cannot have $1, nor more than $2. That is $P(j|1) = \frac{1}{2}$ if j is 0 or 2, and $P(j|1) = 0$ for all other values of j.

Similarly, if we assume he has $2 to begin with, we have $P(j|2) = \frac{1}{2}$ for $j = 1$ or 3, and $P(j|2) = 0$ for other values.

---

[3] § 38 will provide the basis for dealing with the general case.

What if he finds no money in his purse? It is then unreasonable to expect player B to risk loss with no expectation of gain. Hence there will be no change in the financial condition of player A; or, in other words, $P(j|0) = 1$ for $j = 0$, and $P(j|0) = 0$ for any other j.

Proceeding in this way we consider all possible alternatives and set forth the conditional probabilities $P(j|k)$ in Table 35.1.

TABLE 35.1

TABLE OF $P(j|k)$ FOR EXAMPLE 35.1

j	$k = 0$	$k = 1$	$k = 2$	$k = 3$	$k = 4$	$k = 5$
0	1	$\frac{1}{2}$	0	0	0	0
1	0	0	$\frac{1}{2}$	0	0	0
2	0	$\frac{1}{2}$	0	$\frac{1}{2}$	0	0
3	0	0	$\frac{1}{2}$	0	$\frac{1}{2}$	0
4	0	0	0	$\frac{1}{2}$	0	0
5	0	0	0	0	$\frac{1}{2}$	1

Such an array of conditional probabilities is called a *transition matrix*. It contains a column for each condition k that could exist *before* a chance experiment is performed, and a row for each condition j that could exist *after* the experiment; and displays, for each j and k, the conditional probability $P(j|k)$.[4]

Clearly, in this instance, the matrix contains all the information necessary to determine the probability of j, that is, of any possible state of A's purse *after* the experiment, if we knew the probabilities of the k's, that is, of its possible states beforehand.

This is precisely the significance of such matrices in general: they permit us to take the set of probabilities appropriate to our state of ignorance before an experiment, and determine how the experiment will modify—or "transform"—that set. We shall see later (Chapter X) how they are used, and the meaning of the present statements will become clearer then.

Before passing on to the next subject it should be noted that the method of solution used in these problems consists solely of the application of the definition of probability and the second general law of composition of events. Many problems of a much more complicated nature are capable of formal solution by the same means although the actual numerical computation is often much more difficult. Success in treating problems of this kind is contingent on two essentials: a vivid and accurate mental picture of what is desired, and constant

---

[4] Transition matrices are commonly written with $P(j|k)$ in the j'th *column* and k'th *row*. See Footnote 3, § 133, in explanation of the convention here adopted.

caution that the conditions regarding equal likelihood, mutual exclusiveness, and independence are not violated.

Finally, it must not be thought that there is only one way of obtaining the solution of such problems as these. That is rarely true in any mathematical work. In the present instance there are interrelations among some of the examples and some of the problems which follow and, by recognizing these, some answers may be obtained more simply. A little later, when the ideas needed for this purpose have been introduced, we shall show how this can be done.

Problems

1. In Problem 31.5, if the connector has not come to rest within 0.66 sec., what is the chance that it will come to rest within the next 0.33 sec?

2. In Problem 31.5, if the connector has not come to rest within 0.66 sec. after starting, what is the chance that it will come to rest within the following intervals after starting: 1.00–1.50 sec.? 0.66–10.00 sec.? 0.20–0.50 sec.?

3. If zero is not acceptable as a first digit of the numbers in Problem 31.17 what is the probability that even and odd digits alternate?

4. In Problem 31.17, what is the probability that even and odd digits alternate if the first digit is 0? If it is j? Compare with the answer to Problem 31.17.

5. If, in the problem of Example 31.4, the first two cards drawn are black, but the medium calls one black and the other red, what is her chance of having a score of 75%?

6. If, in Example 31.4, there are six red and two black cards, and if the first card to appear is red, but is called black by the medium, what is the chance that the black pile will contain only one red card?

7. Under the circumstances of Problem 6, if the first card to appear is black, but is called red by the medium, what is the chance that she will score 75%? Is the answer the same as in Problem 6? Why?

8. Under the circumstances of Problem 6, if the first card to appear is red and is correctly called, what is the chance of a 75% score?

9. The product of a lamp manufacturer has averaged 5% bad over an entire year. A small retailer gets a shipment of twenty cartons of five. It does not follow, of course, that he has received just five bad lamps, for his "sample" of the gross product may have been better or worse than the average. A customer purchases one carton. How much greater is his chance of having no bad lamps if the shipment was 1% better than the average, than it would have been if the shipment had been 1% worse than the average?

10. Two dice are tossed. One is red and one white. What is the probability of an ace appearing on the red die, if an ace appears on the white one? If 5 appears?

11. An urn contained 7 red and 5 black balls. If four have been drawn from it, what is the probability that the next one drawn will be red?

12. If two dice are tossed, what is the probability that the result is *not* a pair of sixes?

[Compute the complementary probability.]

13. What is the probability of a poker hand containing at least one spade?

14. An urn contains 10 balls, of which 2 are white, 5 are red, and 3 are black. A drawing is made; then all balls of the color drawn are removed from the urn. Construct the transition matrix for the probability of the second ball being white, red, or black.

15. The process described in Problem 14 can be extended to a third drawing. Suppose this is done, and construct a transition matrix for the third drawing.

[Since the conditional probabilities depend only on which pair of colors have already been drawn and not upon the order in which they were drawn, the set of prior conditions can be taken as w,r, w,b, r,b.]

16. Suppose that, in Example 35.1, a first toss has already been made and the loser has paid. The players agree to continue the game under the same conditions. Form the transition matrices for the second and third tosses.

17. The columns in Table 35.1 all add up to 1. Show that this is a necessary consequence of the definition of a transition matrix.

36. Representation of Conditional Probability in the Sample Space

The logical character of conditional probabilities can be illuminated by reference to Fig. 11.1, which is reproduced here for convenience.

The complete sample space of the experiment is represented by the area within the largest curve I; everything which can possibly occur is encompassed by this curve. Similarly the sample points corresponding to the event B are represented by the area within curve B. By definition, then, the unconditional probability that B occurs is the ratio of the weight of the points in B to the weight of all points in I.

But the proviso A is also a chance event —something which may or may not occur —and it also corresponds to some portion of the sample space, such as that within the

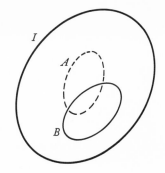

FIG. 11.1

dotted curve. Hence, in saying "if A happens" we rule out of consideration all that portion of the sample space I which lies outside of the dotted curve. In effect, this creates a new sample space within the dotted curve and leaves for the subspace corresponding to the event $B|A$ only the shaded region $A \cap B$ in which the two curves overlap.

If in this process the relative probabilities of the primary events have not been altered, they can easily be adjusted to a scale appropriate to the new sample space by dividing each by the weight of the area A; that is, by $P(A)$.

Thus we have the law

$$P(B|A) = \frac{P(A \cap B)}{P(A)},$$

or, as we shall more often write it,[5]

$$P(B|A) = \frac{P(A, B)}{P(A)}. \tag{36.1}$$

Thus, in Example 34.1, the proviso (event A) is that an even face falls uppermost. The probability of this is $P(A) = \frac{1}{2}$. The event B corresponds to a face greater than 3. The event $A \cap B$ means both even and greater than 3 and therefore includes the primary events 4 and 6. Hence, $P(A,B) = \frac{1}{3}$. Substituting these into equation (36.1), we get $P(B|A) = \frac{1}{3} \div \frac{1}{2} = \frac{2}{3}$, as before.

Similarly, in Example 34.4, the chance that the first card dealt is black (and therefore fails to match the standard order) is $\frac{1}{2}$. This is $P(A)$. To get $P(A,B)$ we note that, of the 70 possible permutations of the red and black cards, only the four described in the discussion of Example 34.4 fail to match at just the first position (which is proviso A) and no other red position (which is event B). Hence $P(A,B) = \frac{4}{70}$. Substituting these into (36.1) leads again to $P(B|A) = \frac{4}{35}$.

The law (36.1) is valid, if correctly interpreted, even when the relative weights of the sample points are altered by the proviso as in Example 34.2, but to demonstrate this by the concept of sample space requires considerable elaboration.[6] We shall therefore accept it on faith until § 65, when a more satisfactory proof can be given.

37. Compound Probabilities

When equation (36.1) is cleared of fractions it leads to the following theorem:

---

[5] $A \cap B$ means "both A and B occur"; for simplicity of notation we shall understand that this is also the meaning of A, B in the symbol $P(A, B)$.

[6] Reasoning otherwise, many mathematicians would say simply that the experiment, and therefore the sample space, was no longer the same, and hence (36.1) no longer has meaning. I prefer not to do this, since the question raised by Example 34.2 is entirely reasonable and it would be a serious limitation on the sample space concept if it could not cover such questions.

See also in this connection the second approach to Example 138.1 in § 138. Questions such as, What is the chance that the third ball drawn will be white if the second is red? cannot be answered by a naïve interpretation of Fig. 11.1, although they obviously have meaning and can be treated in other ways.

THEOREM 37.1: *The probability that event A occurs and is accompanied[7] by event B is the product of the probability that A occurs by the conditional probability that if A occurs B likewise occurs. In symbolic form,*

$$P(A, B) = P(A) P(B|A). \tag{37.1}$$

This theorem is analogous to the second general law of composition of events (§ 17). It will be proved along with (36.1) in § 65. It can be extended to any number of consecutive events. To verify this, consider three events A, B, and C, and call the simultaneous occurrence of A and B "event D." Then by (37.1),

$$P(D, C) = P(D) P(C|D) \tag{37.2}$$

and also

$$P(D) = P(A) P(B|A). \tag{37.3}$$

Substituting (37.3) into (37.2) and exhibiting the fact that $D \equiv A, B$, we get

$$P(A, B, C) = P(A) P(B|A) P(C|A, B).$$

This process can be extended indefinitely and would give

$$P(A_1, A_2, \ldots, A_j) = P(A_1) P(A_2|A_1) \ldots P(A_j|A_1, A_2, \ldots, A_{j-1}).$$

Some examples follow:

EXAMPLE 37.1.—*The letters of the word* **tailor** *are written on cards. The cards being first thoroughly shuffled, four are drawn in order. What is the probability that the result is* **oral**?

Of the six equally likely choices for the first letter only one is an **o**. Hence the chance of getting a group beginning with **o** is $\frac{1}{6}$. After this card has been drawn five remain. Hence, if **o** is first drawn, the chance of drawing **r** next is $\frac{1}{5}$. Hence the chance of drawing **o** followed by **r** is $\frac{1}{30}$. If **o** and **r** are first drawn the chance of next drawing **a** is $\frac{1}{4}$. Therefore the chance of drawing **o r a** is $\frac{1}{120}$. Finally, if these three letters have appeared, the chance that the next trial will produce **l** is $\frac{1}{3}$. Thus the answer to the problem is $\frac{1}{360}$. Naturally this is the same result as was obtained in Example 31.2.

---

[7] If A and B can occur simultaneously the law is true as stated. Sometimes there is a sequence of events as in the statement "a man is shot and dies." In this case "accompanied" must be replaced by "followed," and the number given by this theorem then represents the probability of A happening and being followed by B. The order cannot be reversed.

For instance, there is a certain chance that a man will be shot. *If he is shot* there is a chance that he will die. The product of these is the probability that he will die from a gunshot wound. It is not the same as the chance that he "dies and is then shot"—the latter being a much less common occurrence.

Problem 35.14 also deals with a situation in which the order of events is important.

The solution of the problem as it is here given has required the use of the unconditional probability of drawing an **o**, together with three additional probabilities, each of which stands in the relationship of a conditional probability to all those that precede it.

EXAMPLE 37.2.—*In the psychic research experiment of Example 31.4, what is the chance that the first card drawn is wrongly placed, and that all but two are correctly placed?*

The chance that the first card is wrongly placed is evidently $\frac{1}{2}$. If the first card was wrongly placed, the chance of having only two wrong is, by Example 34.4, $\frac{4}{35}$. Hence the solution of this problem is $\frac{1}{2} \cdot \frac{4}{35} = \frac{2}{35}$.

EXAMPLE 37.3.—*Each of two groups of cards contains four reds and four blacks. One group, which we shall call Group I, is first thoroughly shuffled and laid out face down. Group II is then shuffled and its cards dealt out on top of those of Group I. What is the chance that the first card dealt from each group is black, and that of the remaining pairs just five are matched colors?*

The chance that the first card of Group I is black is $\frac{1}{2}$. If so, the chance that the card placed on it is black is $\frac{1}{2}$. Therefore, the chance that the first card is black and matched by a black is $\frac{1}{4}$. But if the first card is matched, the (conditional) chance of having just two unmatched pairs has been found in Example 34.5 to be $\frac{12}{35}$. Therefore the answer to the problem is $\frac{1}{4} \cdot \frac{12}{35} = \frac{3}{35}$.

Problems

1. In Problem 31.17, what is the probability that the first digit is j, where j is a specified number from 0 to 9, and the digits alternate? What is it in Problem 35.3?

2. Referring to Example 37.1, if each card drawn is replaced and shuffled before another is drawn, what is the probability of **oral**. Has it been increased or decreased by replacing the cards?

3. In Example 37.1 what is the chance of a result **till** if the cards are not replaced? If they are? Has replacing the cards increased or decreased the chances?

4. Confirm the result of Example 31.3 by the method of § 37.

5. Solve Problem 31.15, by the method of § 37.

The next three problems refer to the experiment explained in Example 37.3, except that it is assumed that six red and two black cards are used:

6. What is the probability that the first card of Group I is black, the first from Group II red, and that there are just two unmatched pairs?

7. What is the probability that the first cards are both red and that there are just two unmatched pairs?

8. What is the probability that the first cards are red and black, respectively, and that there are just two unmatched pairs?

9. In the psychic research experiment of Example 31.4, what is the chance that the first card is correctly called, and that only one card of each color is incorrectly placed?
[Use the result of Example 34.5.]

10. Under the conditions of Problem 31.10, what is the chance that the first pair are both red, and two of the remaining pairs unmatched?

11. Under the conditions of Problem 31.10, what is the chance that the first pair are both black, and two of the remaining pairs unmatched?

12. An urn contains 7 red and 5 black balls. Four are drawn in order. What is the probability that they are all black?

13. In tossing a penny, what is the probability that heads will appear on the first j throws?

14. In tossing a penny, what is the probability that there will be a run of just j heads before a tail appears?

15. In tossing a die, what is the probability that the ace will appear *for the first time* on the j'th throw?

38. Alternative Compound Probabilities

Many problems which resemble those of the last section in form, require the use of Convention II in their solution.

EXAMPLE 38.1.—*The numbers* 1, 2, 3, 4, 5 *are written on cards, of which two are drawn without replacement. What is the chance that the combination thus drawn is even?*

Obviously, what the first card is does not matter, and the second is as likely to be one as another; hence the answer must be $\frac{2}{5}$. But suppose the problem is attempted by the argument of § 37. The possible results appear schematically as follows:

1	2	3	4	5
2* 3 4* 5	1 3 4* 5	1 2* 4* 5	1 2* 3 5	1 2* 3 4*

Since *any* number is admissible for the first choice, the unconditional probability of drawing an allowable first number is 1. But what is the conditional probability of a suitable second choice? Every first choice is associated with four possible second choices, of which *sometimes one and sometimes two are suitable*. There is no unambiguous value for the conditional probability. This situation is not covered by equation (37.1).

It is, however, possible to find the probability of "an even number beginning with 1." It is $\frac{1}{5}\cdot\frac{2}{4} = \frac{1}{10}$. The same is true of "an even number beginning with 3," or "with 5"; whereas the probabilities for numbers beginning with 2 and 4 are each $\frac{1}{5}\cdot\frac{1}{4} = \frac{1}{20}$.

These five compound events are mutually exclusive: therefore the chance of one or the other happening is the sum of their separate probabilities, which is $\frac{2}{5}$. As an even number can result in no other way, this must be the desired probability. Naturally, it checks the result obtained directly. In general:

THEOREM 38.1: *If an event can be expressed as the sum of a number of alternative compound events which are mutually exclusive and whose separate probabilities can be found, the probability of the original event can be found by Convention II. It is essential that no manner of occurrence of the original event shall be overlooked.*

As an equation, this statement would become

$$P(B) = \sum_A P(A, B), \tag{38.1}$$

the sum to be taken over every admissible A. Or, using (37.1),

$$P(B) = \sum_A P(A) P(B|A). \tag{38.2}$$

It is particularly evident, in this symbolic form, that the events A, like the differential elements in an integral, are a sort of "catalytic agent," introduced for the purpose of enabling our computation to be carried out, though not themselves a part of the result.

Example 38.1, for instance, is concerned *only* with the second number drawn. That is evident from the way the solution was obtained in the first sentence after the statement of the example. The set of events A (an "even" or an "odd" first digit), in effect, artificially subdivided event B into parts that could be more conveniently dealt with.

It should also be noted that, although all the probabilities $P(B|A)$ on the right-hand side are "conditional," the $P(B)$ to which they give rise is not.[8]

As for the range of summation implied in the Σ, it is always allowable to have it cover the complete group of events A; but if some $P(B|A)$ is zero, the A to which it corresponds may be omitted without error.

---

[8] That is, not conditional in any way upon the set A: the whole process may be predicated upon the desire to obtain a probability which is conditional with respect to some event or events not entering the present discussion.

Thus, if Example 38.1 had asked for the probability of an "even number less than 30," combinations beginning with 3, 4, or 5 could have been omitted; they could also equally well have been included since the accompanying conditional probabilities would have been zero.

Finally, a particular case which is of sufficient importance to merit special mention is that in which the extraneous group consists of an event A and its complement A'. Then the formula reads:

$$P(B) = P(A) P(B|A) + P(A') P(B|A'). \tag{38.3}$$

Thus in Example 38.1 the first number must be either *even* (A) or *not even* (A'), the respective probabilities being

$$P(A) = \tfrac{2}{5},$$
$$P(A') = \tfrac{3}{5}.$$

As the conditional probabilities associated with them have already been said to be

$$P(B|A) = \tfrac{1}{4},$$
$$P(B|A') = \tfrac{2}{4},$$

the solution of the example is

$$P(B) = \tfrac{2}{5} \cdot \tfrac{1}{4} + \tfrac{3}{5} \cdot \tfrac{2}{4} = \tfrac{2}{5},$$

as before.

Example 38.2.—*If the two groups of cards to which reference is made in Example 37.3 contain six red and two black cards each, what is the chance that the first pair is matched and the score is 75%?*

Here the "catalytic events A" may be the pairs composed of the first card in each group. The complete set of these is rr, rb, br, and bb, whose probabilities are $\tfrac{9}{16}$, $\tfrac{3}{16}$, $\tfrac{3}{16}$, and $\tfrac{1}{16}$, respectively. Event B is then "the first pair matched and the score 75%." The conditional probability of this for $A \equiv$ rr (first card in each group red) is $P(B|\text{rr}) = \tfrac{10}{21}$; also $P(B|\text{rb}) = P(B|\text{br}) = 0$, since the first pair does not match; and $P(B|\text{bb}) = \tfrac{6}{7}$. Hence the answer to the problem is $\tfrac{9}{16} \cdot \tfrac{10}{21} + \tfrac{1}{16} \cdot \tfrac{6}{7} = \tfrac{9}{28}$.

Example. 38.3.—*If the two groups of cards to which reference is made in Example 37.3 contain six red and two black cards each, what is the chance that the first pair fails to match and the score is 75%?*

The values of $P(A)$ are the same as before. But now $P(B|\text{rr})$ and $P(B|\text{bb})$ are zero, since these pairs do not fail to match, and we readily find that $P(B|\text{rb}) = P(B|\text{br}) = \frac{2}{7}$.[9] The substitution of these values in (38.2) leads to the results $\frac{3}{16} \cdot \frac{2}{7} + \frac{3}{16} \cdot \frac{2}{7} = \frac{3}{28}$.

39. Some Instructive Illustrations; a Contingency Matrix

The transition matrix in § 35 displayed the complete set of conditional probabilities $P(j|k)$ corresponding to the experiment described in Example 35.1. The probabilities $P(j,k)$ may be similarly displayed. In fact, since $P(j,k) = P(k) P(j|k)$, Table 35.1 may be converted into such a matrix by multiplying every entry in the column for $k = 0$ by $P(0)$, every entry in the column for $k = 1$ by $P(1)$, etc.

To be specific, suppose that A and B started out as in Problem 31.19 and have already completed three throws. Then the probability $P(k)$ that A now has k dollars is set forth in Table 39.1.[10]

TABLE 39.1

Probability that A has k dollars after three rounds of play if his initial capital was \$2.

k	0	1	2	3	4	5
$P(k)$	$\frac{1}{4}$	$\frac{1}{4}$	0	$\frac{3}{8}$	0	$\frac{1}{8}$

If we multiply the columns of Table 35.1 by these factors, we get Table 39.2.

Clearly the numbers in this table give the probability that A had k dollars after the third round *and* j after the fourth; whereas those in the transition matrix were the probability that he had j dollars after the fourth round *if* he had k after the third.

---

[9] This is also the answer to Problem 35.6. There is, however, a psychological difference between the two; for, if I am not mistaken, the medium who was confronted with the necessity of calling "red" six times and "black" but twice would be almost certain to say "red" the first time. Hence in Problem 35.6 only one set of objects (the cards) can be said to fall in random order; the other (the words) cannot; whereas in Example 38.3 both sets of objects are random.

Perhaps this fact may be used to emphasize the point about the axiom of equal likelihood to which we have already referred in § 3. There is a vast difference between the assertions "Two events are equally likely when they differ in no known pertinent attribute" and "Two events are equally likely when we do not know what difference their pertinent attributes make." The first statement leaves us with many situations to which the fundamental method of measuring probability cannot be applied—as in the present instance where, though I feel certain the psychological bias exists, I am wholly unable to state its extent. The second virtually says, "Whenever you cannot measure the probabilities of a group of events, call them equally likely," which is a sheer absurdity.

The reason the two answers are alike is because, by Theorem 33.1, a matching experiment is random if either one of the matched sets falls in random order.

[10] See Problem 31.19.

Such a matrix of all possible values of $P(j,k)$ is called by statisticians a *contingency matrix*.[11] We shall meet such matrices again briefly in Chapter XI.[12]

Contingency matrices have the interesting property that the sum of any column is $P(k)$, and the sum of any row $P(j)$, as indicated by the marginal entries in Table 39.2. This is a consequence of (38.1). The numbers in the

TABLE 39.2

Table of $P(j,k)$ for Example 35.1, if A's initial capital was \$2 and three rounds of play had already been completed.

j	$k = 0$	$k = 1$	$k = 2$	$k = 3$	$k = 4$	$k = 5$	$P(j)$
0	$\frac{1}{4}$	$\frac{1}{8}$	0	0	0	0	$\frac{3}{8}$
1	0	0	0	0	0	0	0
2	0	$\frac{1}{8}$	0	$\frac{3}{16}$	0	0	$\frac{5}{16}$
3	0	0	0	0	0	0	0
4	0	0	0	$\frac{3}{16}$	0	0	$\frac{3}{16}$
5	0	0	0	0	0	$\frac{1}{8}$	$\frac{1}{8}$
$P(k)$	$\frac{1}{4}$	$\frac{1}{4}$	0	$\frac{3}{8}$	0	$\frac{1}{8}$	

bottom row, of course, are just those in Table 39.1. The numbers in marginal column, $P(j)$, give the unconditional probabilities of A having j dollars after the fourth round, and are new.

40. Some Instructive Illustrations; The Psychic Research Problem

Certain interesting relations exist between the probabilities which have been obtained in the case of the psychic research example. In the first place, confining attention to the case of four red and four black cards, there is obviously no pertinent distinction between the four red positions in the standard order which would make a black card more likely to fall in one of them than another. Hence the unconditional probability that the medium is wrong the first time she says "red" must be the same as the unconditional probability that she is wrong the second time she says "red," or the third, or the fourth. Furthermore, since the card that falls in either of these positions is just as likely to be black as red, this unconditional probability is $\frac{1}{2}$. All this is axiomatic.

Likewise there is no distinction between the first occurrence of the word "red" and its subsequent occurrences which would cause the

---

[11] The term is also used (by some writers, exclusively so) for a matrix which displays the *number of individuals in a sample* who have both characteristics j and k, rather than for the underlying *probabilities* $P(j,k)$.

[12] See, especially, § 155 and Problems 164.15, 164.16, 164.24, 164.25.

conditional probability of a 75% score to be different if one were known to have been incorrectly called rather than another. That is, if by accident we happened to observe that the third (or any other) card which the medium called "red" was actually black, but had no significant information regarding the others, the probability of a 75% score would be $\frac{4}{35}$, just as in Example 34.4.

But if a 75% score is to be obtained at all, one or the other of the red positions in the standard order must be filled by black cards. As the four *compound* events ("first red position occupied by a black card and a 75% score," "second red position occupied by a black card and a 75% score," etc.) are mutually exclusive, it follows that the *unconditional* probability of a 75% score is the sum of four compound probabilities, each equal to $\frac{1}{2} \cdot \frac{4}{35}$. This works out to be $\frac{8}{35}$, the result already obtained in Example 31.4.

Another result which can be obtained out of this same argument is the following: To say that the first card is *correctly* called and the score is 75% is equivalent to saying that either the second, the third, or the fourth black card is *incorrectly* called, the rest being correct in each case. The probability of each of these alternatives, however, is $\frac{1}{2} \cdot \frac{4}{35} = \frac{2}{35}$. Hence the probability that the first card is correctly called and the score is 75% works out to be $\frac{2}{35} + \frac{2}{35} + \frac{2}{35} = \frac{6}{35}$; a result which has already been obtained.[13]

Another result may easily be obtained from the use of (37.1), if we regard "event A" as meaning that the first card is correctly called and "event B" that a 75% score is obtained. In this case, (37.1) states that the probability that the first card is called correctly and the score is 75% is the product of the unconditional probability of calling the first card correctly—which is known to be $\frac{1}{2}$—by the conditional probability of obtaining such a score under these circumstances, which we denote merely by $P(B|A)$. Equating $\frac{1}{2}P(B|A)$ to the result obtained in the preceding paragraph, it is found that $P(B|A) = \frac{12}{35}$. This again is identical with the result of Example 34.5.

Many more relationships of this kind can be built up between the numbers already obtained. These are sufficient, however, to illustrate to what extent the theorems developed in the last few sections are capable of simplifying the solution of problems of this type.

41. Some Instructive Illustrations; A Generalization of the Psychic Research Problem

After having used the psychic research experiment explained in Example 31.4 so profusely for illustrative purposes, it would be

---

[13] See Problem 37.9

unnatural to pass it by without obtaining a solution of somewhat greater generality than the special cases already considered. Hence the following general case is given:

EXAMPLE 41.1.—*Each of two sequences contains m events of one kind and n of another. The sequences are placed in one-to-one correspondence by a random process. What is the chance that there are just p pairs which fail to match?*

Phrased in terms of "cards" and "medium" it reads:

EXAMPLE 41.2.—*If, in the psychic research experiment explained in Example 31.4, there are m red and n black cards, what is the chance of just p incorrect cards in each pile?*

The simplest way to solve the problem is by means of the fundamental definition of probability—just as Example 31.4 itself was solved. The order in which the medium calls the cards forms a "standard order," whereas the order in which the cards actually appear may be any one of the $P_{m,n}^{m,n}$ possible permutations of m red and n black things. These represent a complete group of equally likely and mutually exclusive events.

To satisfy the conditions of the problem, those positions which are red in the standard order must be filled by some possible permutation of p blacks and $m - p$ reds, which can be done in $P_{m-p,p}^{m-p,p}$ ways, whereas those which are black in the standard order must be filled by some possible permutation of p reds and $n - p$ blacks, which can be done in $P_{n-p,p}^{n-p,p}$ ways. Each of the possible ways in which the standard red positions can be filled is capable of association with each of the possible ways in which the standard black positions can be filled. Therefore the total number of events in the wanted subgroup is

$$P_{m-p,p}^{m-p,p} \cdot P_{n-p,p}^{n-p,p}.$$

The desired probability is therefore

$$P(p) = \frac{P_{m-p,p}^{m-p,p} \cdot P_{n-p,p}^{n-p,p}}{P_{m,n}^{m,n}}.$$

This can also be written in the form

$$P(p) = \frac{C_p^m \, C_p^n}{C_m^{m+n}},$$

a form which is itself capable of logical interpretation.

42. Some Instructive Illustrations; Independent Trials

A very fundamental class of compound events is that in which the two events are independent. This means that the conditional probability of the second event occurring is the same whether the first event did or did not occur: $P(B|A) = P(B|A')$. If this is substituted in (38.3), it leads to

$$P(B|A) = P(B|A') = P(B),$$

since $P(A) + P(A') = 1$. Under such circumstances (37.1) becomes

$$P(A, B) = P(A) \cdot P(B).$$

THEOREM 42.1. *If the events A and B are independent, the probability that both occur is the product of their unconditional probabilities.*

Dice problems are of interest in the subject of probability largely because they typify this class of events. The following is a simple example:

EXAMPLE 42.1.—*What is the chance of throwing an ace exactly once in six throws of a die?*

This problem can be solved by the use of alternative compound probabilities. The possible cases are

$$+ - - - - -, \quad - + - - - -, \quad - - + - - -,$$
$$- - - + - -, \quad - - - - + -, \quad - - - - - +.$$

Taking the first case, the probability of throwing an ace on the first throw is $\frac{1}{6}$. The probability of not throwing an ace on any of the remaining throws is $(\frac{5}{6})^5$, since the events are all independent. The probability of the first compound event is therefore $\frac{1}{6}(\frac{5}{6})^5$.

The other cases lead to the same factors, although they appear in different orders, which does not affect the result. Since all cases are mutually exclusive the chance that one or the other occurs, which is what the problem asks for, is $6 \cdot \frac{1}{6} \cdot (\frac{5}{6})^5 = (\frac{5}{6})^5$.

Let us see what this problem really teaches. Since the throws are independent the chance of throwing one ace and five "not aces" in some preassigned order is always $\frac{1}{6}(\frac{5}{6})^2$, regardless of the order chosen. Hence it is necessary to add together as many of these equal quantities as there are distinct orders in which the result may appear. The number of distinct orders, however, is just the number of permutations of six things of which five are "not aces" and one is an "ace," that is $P_{5,1}^{5,1}$.

In general, the probability of throwing exactly n aces in m throws *in a preassigned order* is $(\frac{1}{6})^n (\frac{5}{6})^{m-n}$, regardless of the order chosen. The probability of doing so *in some unspecified order* is this quantity multiplied by the number of different orders in which the n aces and $m - n$ not-aces can appear. The second factor is clearly $P_{n,m-n}^{n,m-n} = m!/n!(m - n)!$, and since this is also the value of C_n^m it can be conveniently represented by that symbol. The solution of the general problem therefore is

$$P_m(n) = C_n^m \left(\tfrac{1}{6}\right)^n \left(\tfrac{5}{6}\right)^{m-n}.$$

It is now a simple matter to extend this formula into the following general theorem:

THEOREM 42.2. *If the probability of an event occurring in a single trial is p, the chance that it occurs exactly n times in m INDEPENDENT trials is*

$$P_m(n) = C^m p^n (1 - p)^{m-n}. \tag{42.1}$$

This is one of the most fundamental theorems of the Theory of Probability. It will receive full discussion later. For the present, one additional example will suffice.

EXAMPLE 42.2.—*What is the probability that, in a game of poker, a player will receive in succession three identical hands?*

This is equivalent to the question, What is the chance that both the second and third hands will be identical with the first?

There are $C_5^{52} = 2,598,560$ different hands which might be dealt. The probability of dealing one which is specified in advance—say, a second hand just like the first—is the reciprocal of this, $3.848 \cdot 10^{-7}$. The question then is, What is the chance of doing this twice in two consecutive attempts? Obviously the answer is given by (42.1) with $m = 2$, $n = 2$, and $p = 3.848 \cdot 10^{-7}$. It is $1.481 \cdot 10^{-13}$.

43. Some Instructive Illustrations; A Generalization of the Problem of Independent Trials

We can easily derive as a corollary to this theorem another which is frequently useful. Speaking again in terms of the dice problem which we have considered, but writing n_1 where we previously wrote n, we ask for the conditional probability $P_m(n_2|n_1)$ that there are n_2 deuces among the m trials, *if there are n_1 aces.*

This is easily obtained, for when an ace does not appear, there are five equally likely events, of which one is deuce and four "not deuces." Hence the (conditional) probability of deuce is $\tfrac{1}{5}$. Since there are $m - n_1$ such trials and they are independent, an application of (42.1) gives

$$P_m(n_2|n_1) = C_{n_2}^{m-n_1} \left(\tfrac{1}{5}\right)^{n_2} \left(\tfrac{4}{5}\right)^{m-n_1-n_2}.$$

Of course, by (37.1), the chance of just n_1 aces and n_2 deuces is the product of this expression by the unconditional probability of n_1 aces.

If we go another step we find as the conditional probability of n_3 threes in m trials, *if there are known to be just n_1 aces and n_2 deuces,* is

$$P(n_3|n_1, n_2) = C_{n_3}^{m-n_1-n_2} \left(\tfrac{1}{4}\right)^{n_3} \left(\tfrac{3}{4}\right)^{m-n_1-n_2-n_3};$$

and by multiplying this factor in with the two already found we can obtain the probability of exactly n_1 aces, n_2 deuces and n_3 threes.

Carrying this process on step by step we eventually find the probability of exactly n_1 aces, n_2 deuces, . . . , n_6 sixes. After common factors have been cancelled out the result is

$$P_m(n_1, n_2, \ldots, n_6) = \frac{m!}{n_1!\, n_2! \ldots n_6!} \left(\tfrac{1}{6}\right)^m,$$

it being understood, of course, that $n_1 + n_2 + \ldots + n_6 = m$.

This, too, is easily converted into a general theorem, although the fact that the six faces of the die are equally likely makes it rather difficult to guess what it is to be. For that reason, and also because the alternative form of proof is interesting in itself, we sketch a proof of the general case by a different line of argument.

If we have a complete and mutually exclusive set of events the individual probabilities of which are $p_1, \ldots, p_a$, and if we make m independent trials, the chance that the first event occurs just n_1 times, the second n_2 times, and so on *in a specified order* is just

$$p_1{}^{n_1} p_2{}^{n_2} \ldots p_a{}^{n_a},$$

no matter what order may be specified. Hence to get the chance of the first event occurring n_1 times, the second n_2 times, and so on, *regardless of order*, it is necessary only to multiply this quantity by the number of possible permutations. This gives us immediately

THEOREM 43.1. *If the events denoted by the subscripts* 1, 2, . . . , a *are mutually exclusive and form a complete set, and if their respective probabilities of occurrence are* $p_1, p_2, \ldots, p_a$, *the chance that they will occur with the frequencies* $n_1, n_2, \ldots, n_a$ *in* $m = n_1 + \ldots + n_a$ *independent trials is*

$$P_m(n_1, n_2, \ldots, n_a) = P^{n_1, n_2, \ldots, n_a}_{n_1, n_2, \ldots, n_a}\, p_1{}^{n_1} p_2{}^{n_2} \ldots p_a{}^{n_a}. \tag{43.1}$$

This is known as the multinomial distribution. The name arises from the fact that powers of the multinomial expression $p_1 + p_2 + \ldots + p_a$ can be expanded in terms of the form (43.1) in a way precisely analogous to the "binomial" expansion of $(p_1 + p_2)^m$.[14] If there are just two events, (43.1) reduces to (42.1); whereas if there are six equally likely events it reduces to the result obtained in our consideration of the tossing of a die.

---

[14] See Problem 50.15 at the end of this chapter.

44. Some Instructive Illustrations; A Typical Urn Problem

Consider the following example:

EXAMPLE 44.1.—*An urn contains five red and ten black balls. Eight times in succession a ball is drawn out but it is replaced before the next drawing takes place. What is the probability that the balls drawn were red on two occasions and black on six?*

Since the balls are replaced before the next drawing takes place the condition of the urn is always the same just before every trial, and therefore the chance of drawing a red ball or a black ball is the same for each of the trials. In other words, the trials are completely independent. Theorem 42.2 therefore applies to this case.

The chance of drawing a red ball is $\frac{1}{3}$ and the chance of drawing a black ball $\frac{2}{3}$. Hence the chance of drawing exactly two reds and six blacks in eight trials is

$$C_2^8(\tfrac{1}{3})^2(\tfrac{2}{3})^6 = \tfrac{1792}{6561}.$$

45. Some Instructive Illustrations; Another Typical Urn Problem

In the last example the trials were independent of one another. A different result is obtained if this condition is not satisfied, as may be seen from the following example:

EXAMPLE 45.1.—*An urn contains five red and ten black balls. Eight of these are drawn out and placed in another urn. What is the chance that the latter then contains two red and six black balls?*

This example resembles the former one in that it might be very simply stated as, What is the chance of drawing exactly two red balls in eight trials? It differs in that the trials are not independent; that is, the chance of drawing a red ball on the first attempt is $\frac{5}{15}$, whereas the chance of drawing a red ball on the second attempt is either $\frac{4}{14}$ or $\frac{5}{14}$ according as the first ball was red or black. We shall obtain the solution by two methods.

First, we note that there are $P_{6,2}^{6,2} = C_2^8$ orders in which the two red and six black balls may appear. If each of these orders is separately considered, the probability of drawing the balls in exactly this order may be found. The sum of all these terms will then be the desired answer. This appears to require the computation of $C_2^8 = 28$ terms, which would involve a considerable amount of labor. Fortunately, however, they are all equally likely, as the following (perhaps unnecessary) argument will show:

Three of the possible 28 orders are

r r b b b b b b

b b b b b b r r

b b r b r b b b.

Consider the first of these. The chance of choosing a red ball first is $\frac{5}{15}$. *If this is done,* the chance of choosing a red the next time is $\frac{4}{14}$. *If both these events have taken place,* the chances that the next six balls are each black are $\frac{10}{13}, \frac{9}{12}, \frac{8}{11}, \frac{7}{10}, \frac{6}{9}, \frac{5}{8}$, respectively. Therefore the chance that all of these events take place is

$$\frac{5}{15} \cdot \frac{4}{14} \cdot \frac{10}{13} \cdot \frac{9}{12} \cdot \frac{8}{11} \cdot \frac{7}{10} \cdot \frac{6}{9} \cdot \frac{5}{8}.$$

If the second case is considered the answer takes the form

$$\frac{10}{15} \cdot \frac{9}{14} \cdot \frac{8}{13} \cdot \frac{7}{12} \cdot \frac{6}{11} \cdot \frac{5}{10} \cdot \frac{5}{9} \cdot \frac{4}{8};$$

whereas if the third group is considered the result is

$$\frac{10}{15} \cdot \frac{9}{14} \cdot \frac{5}{13} \cdot \frac{8}{12} \cdot \frac{4}{11} \cdot \frac{7}{10} \cdot \frac{6}{9} \cdot \frac{5}{8}.$$

Now, although the separate fractions differ, the product is the same for every case. As a matter of fact, this property is common to all the terms. Every time a ball is chosen, whether red or black, the number of balls remaining in the urn is reduced by one so that the denominator of the next conditional probability is also reduced by one. This means that no matter what the order of choice may be the array of factors in the denominator will always be the same. Likewise whenever a red ball is chosen the numerator for the next conditional probability of a red ball is reduced by one. But the numerator of the next conditional probability for a black choice remains unchanged. Thus to the red choices correspond fractions the numerators of which are always 5 and 4, while to the black choices correspond numerators 10, 9, 8, 7, 6, and 5. In other words, all orders are equally likely and the answer to the problem is

$$C_2^8 \frac{5! \, 10! \, 7!}{3! \, 4! \, 15!} = \frac{140}{429}.$$

It is considerably larger than that obtained when the balls were replaced. Decimally, the answer to the present problem is 0.326, whereas the answer to the other was 0.273.

This same answer can also be obtained in another way. Suppose the balls are all tagged to establish their identities. There are then P_8^{15} ways in which eight can be drawn out, all of which are equally likely. In order to solve the problem by means of the fundamental definition of probability it is necessary only to determine how many of these ways represent just two red balls and six black balls. This number may be found by observing that there are C_2^5 ways of choosing two red balls for the group and C_6^{10} ways of choosing six black balls. This makes a total of $C_2^5 C_6^{10}$ different *combinations* of tagged balls. Each of these, however, is capable in itself of P_8^8 permutations. Thus, the total number of permutations satisfying the conditions of the problem is found to be $C_2^5 C_6^{10} P_8^8$, and the answer is

$$\frac{C_2^5 C_6^{10} P_8^8}{P_8^{15}}.$$

This is easily reduced to the form already found.

It is possible to generalize this solution and obtain a working theorem. Suppose the problem had read:

EXAMPLE 45.2.—*An urn contains m red and n black balls. If p + q are drawn in order and placed in another urn, what is the chance that the latter contains just p red balls and q black ones?*

If the balls were all tagged there would be P_{p+q}^{m+n} equally likely permutations. Any trial would give some one of these.

There would also be a total of $C_p^m C_q^n$ combinations of p red and q black balls each of which would be capable within itself of P_{p+q}^{p+q} permutations. Therefore the total number of permutations that satisfy the conditions of the problem, and therefore compose the desired subgroup, is $C_p^m C_q^n P_{p+q}^{p+q}$. Dividing the number of elements in the subgroup by the number of elements in the complete group the probability of drawing exactly p reds and q blacks is found to be

$$P_{m,n}(p,q) = \frac{C_p^m C_q^n P_{p+q}^{p+q}}{P_{p+q}^{m+n}} = \frac{C_p^m C_q^n}{C_{p+q}^{m+n}}.$$

In words this theorem reads:

THEOREM 45.1. *If a group of m things of one kind and n things of another exists, and if this group is reduced by eliminating one thing at a time, the thing being chosen quite without respect to those characteristics which differentiate kind from kind, the probability that the first p + q stages will remove p things of the first kind and q of the second is*

$$P_{m,n}(p,q) = \frac{C_p^m C_q^n}{C_{p+q}^{m+n}}. \tag{45.1}$$

This is known as the "hypergeometric distribution."

46. Particle Physics; the Bose–Einstein, Fermi–Dirac, and Maxwell–Boltzmann Statistics

In the part of modern physics that deals with atoms, nuclei, and their radiations, two distinct types of particles are recognized. One is characterized by the fact that no two can be in the same energy state at the same time. Electrons, protons, neutrons, and a number of other elementary particles belong in this class. The other group permits—in fact encourages—multiple occupancy of energy states. Photons, nuclei, and atoms containing an even number of elementary particles belong to this group.

It is shown in treatises on theoretical physics that systems of particles of the first kind demand symmetric solutions of the wave equations, and that systems of the second kind demand antisymmetric solutions. But why a particle is of one type rather than the other—why a photon, for example, is not of the "symmetric" type—has never been adequately explained.

Among the important questions that arise concerning particle systems are those that deal with the group of states which—at a moment of observation—might be found occupied; that is, with the energy state of the system as a whole. These give rise to questions of probability entirely analogous to those encountered in the distribution of balls in boxes by various chance processes. We consider in this section three such processes, which lead to the three types of distribution most commonly met in physical theory.

Suppose, then, that there are a boxes into which n balls are to be placed, and ask for the probability that there will be just j_1 balls in box 1, j_2 in box 2, etc. This is the general question. The three processes will be differentiated by whether a ball about to be placed is attracted to or repelled from boxes which are already occupied, or whether there is no influence of either kind.

First, suppose that a ball is repelled by (cannot enter) a box which is already occupied. Then[15] the boxes occupied will be a group of n selected from the a available boxes. There are C_n^a such groups, and since they are equally likely the probability of each is $1/C_n^a$. That is, in this case,

$$\left.\begin{array}{ll} P(j_1, j_2, \ldots, j_a) = 1/C_n^a, & \text{if } j_i = 0 \text{ or } 1, \quad \sum j_i = n; \\[2mm] P(j_1, j_2, \ldots, j_a) = 0 & \text{otherwise.} \end{array}\right\} \quad (46.1)$$

Next, suppose that a ball is neither repelled by nor attracted to an occupied box; instead the balls are independent and equally likely to enter one cell as another. To deal with this case, first imagine the balls to be numbered and distributed in order. The chance of any one of these falling in a preassigned box is $1/a$, quite independently of the rest; the chance that the first j_1 fall in box 1, the next j_2 in box 2, etc., is therefore $1/a^n$. There are, however, $P_{j_1, j_2, \ldots, j_a}^{j_1, j_2, \ldots, j_a}$ different orders in which the same final distribution could have been produced, so the probability of this distribution is[16]

$$P(j_1, j_2, \ldots, j_a) = \frac{n! \, a^{-n}}{j_1! \, j_2! \cdots j_a!}, \qquad \sum j_i = n. \quad (46.2)$$

The third case is that in which balls are attracted to occupied boxes.

---

[15] See Problem 29.11.

[16] Note that this is a special case of the multinomial distribution (43.1) with all the p_j equal.

This would be trivial, if the attraction were absolute, since only the first ball would be placed by a chance process and the rest would of necessity follow it. It is necessary instead to consider some specific, but less absolute, law of attraction. Suppose, for this purpose, that a ball is $i + 1$ times as likely to enter a cell which is already occupied by i balls as it is to enter an empty cell. This requires that the chance of the $(k + 1)$st ball entering a cell in which there are i balls be $(i + 1)/(a + k)$.[17] Then the chance that the first j_1 balls fall in box 1 is clearly $1 \cdot 2 \ldots j_1/a(a + 1) \ldots (a + j_1 - 1)$. Thereafter, the chance of the next j_2 balls falling in box 2 is $1 \cdot 2 \ldots j_2/(a_1 + j_1)(a_1 + j_1 + 1) \ldots (a_1 + j_1 + j_2 - 1)$. Continuing this process, the probability of all boxes being filled in this order comes out to be

$$\frac{j_1! \, j_2! \ldots j_a!}{a(a + 1) \ldots (a + n - 1)}.$$

It is readily seen that in this situation, as in Example 45.1, this probability remains the same regardless of the order in which the balls enter the boxes: the denominator increases by one as each ball is placed, and that portion of the numerator that corresponds to a particular box increases by one whenever a ball arrives at this box. The desired probability $P(j_1, j_2, \ldots, j_a)$ can therefore be obtained by multiplying the above fraction by the number of possible sequences of arrival, which is $P^{j_1, j_2, \ldots, j_a}_{j_1, j_2, \ldots, j_a}$, thus giving

$$P(j_1, j_2, \ldots, j_a) = \frac{n!(a - 1)!}{(a + n - 1)!} = 1/C_n^{a + n - 1}, \qquad \sum j_i = n. \tag{46.3}$$

The first of these results, (46.1), is the basic formula in what physicists call the *Fermi–Dirac statistics*;[18] as has been said, it applies to systems of electrons, protons, etc. The basic formula in the *Bose–Einstein statistics*, which applies to systems of photons, etc., is (46.3). These are the chance processes involving repulsion and attraction, respectively. Note that both formulas are independent of the j's; that is, $P(j_1, j_2, \ldots, j_a)$ has the same value for every partition of n.

There are no known particles which conform to the neutral process (46.2), but it is an important approximation to the behavior of many complex systems and is known as the *Maxwell–Boltzmann statistics*.[19] It is the only one for which the probability differs for different partitions of n.

---

[17] To see this, let the cells be occupied by $i_1, i_2, \ldots, i_a$ balls, and let α be the chance of entering an empty cell. Then the probability of entering each of the cells, respectively, is $(i_1 + 1)\alpha, (i_2 + 1)\alpha, \ldots$. Since these must sum to 1, and since the i's are a partition of k, we have $\alpha \Sigma i + a\alpha = (k + a)\alpha = 1$, or $(i + 1)\alpha = (i + 1)/(a + k)$.

[18] This use of the word "statistics" is not precise, or at all events does not conform to the distinction which was made in § 13 between probability and statistics. However, it is well-established in "statistical" mechanics and other phases of physical theory. Fortunately, these have so little in common with statistics in the ordinary sense that confusion is not likely to occur.

[19] Note that this is a special case of the multinomial distribution (43.1).

47. Some Instructive Illustrations; A Problem in Matching

A problem of a greater difficulty, which needs repeated use of alternative compound probabilities for its solution, is the following:

EXAMPLE 47.1.   *A deck of cards contains r_1 red and b_1 black cards. It is thoroughly shuffled and m cards are dealt face down in a row. Then from another deck, which contains r_2 red and b_2 black cards, m cards are dealt on top of the first m. In this way m pairs of cards are obtained. The cards in any pair may be either of like or of unlike color. What is the chance that there are exactly n matched pairs?*

This example bears an obvious resemblance to Examples 37.3 and 41.2, but differs from them in a very important respect which makes it much more difficult to solve. In the previous problems the number of red and black cards was both known and known to be equal in both sequences, whereas in the present case the number of reds and blacks dealt from the first pack is neither known nor known to be equal to the number dealt from the second pack.

As the number of reds dealt from the first pack is unknown, the natural thing to do is to assign a letter j to represent it. So far as is known j may have any value between zero and m.

Next we denote by $P(j)$ the chance of the assumed number of reds being the true one, and by $P(n|j)$ the chance of n matched pairs if it is. Then, by (38.2)

$$P(n) = \sum_{j=0}^{m} P(j)\, P(n|j), \qquad (47.1)$$

$P(n)$ being the symbol chosen for the answer to the problem.

Now obviously $P(j)$ is a special case of formula (45.1), the p and q of (45.1) being j and $m - j$, respectively, while m and n are r_1 and b_1. That is

$$P(j) = \frac{C_j^{r_1} C_{m-j}^{b_1}}{C_m^{r_1 + b_1}}. \qquad (47.2)$$

Hence $P(n)$ can be found if $P(n|j)$ can be found, so one of the indefinite features of the problem has been removed. The next step will eliminate another.

If there are exactly n matched pairs, there must be either n pairs of red cards and no black pairs, or $n - 1$ red pairs and one black pair, or some other combination of numbers having the sum n. If, then, $P(k, n - k|i)$ is the probability of just k red and $n - k$ black pairs, when there are j reds in the bottom row,

$$P(n|j) = P(0, n|j) + P(1, n - 1|j) + \dots = \sum_{k=0}^{n} P(k, n - k|j). \qquad (47.3)$$

The final step is to find $P(k, n - k|j)$. This is done by an argument exactly like that of § 38.

The order in which the bottom row of cards appears is unknown; but whatever that order is, it may be called the "standard order." On the other hand, the top row is some possible permutation of m cards chosen from the $r_2 + b_2$ cards of the deck. If the separate identities of all these cards are taken into account, the total number of permutations of this kind is $P_m^{r_2+b_2} = (r_2 + b_2)!/(r_2 + b_2 - m)!$. These permutations are all equally likely, they are mutually exclusive, and they form a complete set. Therefore the desired probability $P(k, n - k|j)$ can be found by finding the subgroup which matches the standard order in exactly k reds and $n - k$ blacks. To find this number, it is easiest to find the number of possible *combinations*, and then the number of permutations of which each combination is capable within itself. The product is the desired number of *permutations*.

The k red cards which match reds in the standard order can be chosen in $C_k^{r_2}$ ways, without taking account of order. With them may be combined any one of $C_{j-k}^{b_2}$ combinations of blacks. Then, from the remaining $b_2 - j + k$ blacks the $n - k$ which match can be chosen in $C_{n-k}^{b_2-j+k}$ ways; whereas the $(m - j) - (n - k)$ reds which fall on blacks can be chosen in $C_{(m-j)-(n-k)}^{r_2-k_1}$ ways from among the $r_2 - k$ reds which remain. The total number of *combinations* of cards which may be dealt in the top row is therefore

$$C_k^{r_2} C_{j-k}^{b_2} \ C_{n-k}^{b_2-j+k} \ C_{(m-j)-(n-k)}^{r_2-k}.$$

Those cards which stand in the red positions of the standard order can be permuted among themselves in every possible way without in any way affecting the number of matches. The same is obviously also true of the cards which stand in the black positions of the standard order. The number of permutations of the first kind is $P_j^j = j!$ and the number of permutations of the second kind is $P_{m-j}^{m-j} = (m - j)!$. When the product of four C's written above is multiplied by these two P's it gives the desired subgroup. Hence:

The probability of matching the standard order in exactly k reds and $n - k$ blacks if the standard order contains exactly j reds and $m - j$ blacks is:[20]

---

[20] This formula has been worked out without the slightest reference to the limits within which the numbers k and $j - k$ must be confined. That there are such limits is obvious. For instance, the number of red pairs cannot be negative, which means that k must be greater than or equal to zero. Similarly, the number of black pairs cannot be negative, which means that $n - k \geq 0$ or $k \leq n$. On the other hand, the number of red pairs cannot exceed the number of red cards in the standard order; that is, $k \leq j$, and the number of black pairs cannot exceed the number of blacks in the standard order, which means that $n - k \leq m - j$. If any one of these four conditions is violated, $P(k, n - k|j)$ must be zero.

We have already noted some cases where formulas of this kind automatically took the correct value zero when the sensible limits upon the variable quantity were transgressed. It is interesting to note that (47.4) actually vanishes when *any* of the above conditions is violated. For instance, for $k < 0$, $C_k^{r_2}$ vanishes. If $k > j$, $C_{j-k}^{b_2}$ vanishes. If $k > n$, $C_{n-k}^{r_2-j+k}$ vanishes. If $(n - k) > (m - j)$, $C_{(n-j)-(n-k)}^{r_2-k}$ vanishes.

There are still other conditions. The number of red cards dealt from the first pack, j, cannot exceed r_1, nor can $m - j$ exceed b_1. In either case a factor of (47.2) vanishes. Similarly the number of red matches, k, must not exceed either r_1 or r_2; if the latter condition were violated the first factor of (47.4) would vanish, whereas if the former were, k would certainly exceed any admissible value of j, and the second factor of (47.4) would vanish. The number of black matches, $n - k$, must not exceed either b_1 or b_2; violating the latter would make the third factor of (47.4) vanish (since $j - k$ is necessarily positive), whereas if $n - k > b_1$, the last factor would vanish (since $m - j \leq b_1$).

In other words, either $P(j)$ or $P(k, n - k|j)$ automatically takes the value 0 whenever *any* one of the limits is transgressed. We can therefore substitute (47.2), (47.3) and (47.4) in (47.1) without worry on this point, provided the limits of summation are kept sufficiently large. This fact simplifies the notation in (47.5) and (47.6).

$$P(k,n - k|j) = \frac{C_{k^2}^{r_2} C_{j-k}^{b_2} \; C_{n-k}^{b_2-j+k} \; C_{(m-j)-(n-k)}^{r_2-k} \; P_j^j P_{m-j}^{m-j}}{P_m^{r_2+b_2}}. \quad (47.4)$$

All that now remains is to collect and simplify the results. First, note that

$$\frac{P_j^j P_{m-j}^{m-j}}{P_m^{r_2+b_2}} = \frac{1}{C_j^m C_m^{r_2+b_2}}.$$

Then substituting this into (47.4), and (47.4) into (47.3), gives

$$P(n|j) = \frac{1}{C_j^m C_m^{r_2+b_2}} \sum_{k=0}^{n} C_k^{r_2} C_{j-k}^{b_2} C_{n-k}^{b_2-j+k} \; C_{m+k-n-j}^{r_2-k}. \quad (47.5)$$

In writing this expression, the denominator, which does not vary with k, has been taken outside the sign of summation.

Finally, substituting (47.5) and (47.2) into (47.1), and factoring out those terms which do not depend upon j, we have

$$P(n) = \frac{1}{C_m^{r_1+b_1} C_m^{r_2+b_2}} \sum_{j=0}^{m} \frac{C_{j_1}^{r_1} C_{m-j}^{b_1}}{C_j^m} \sum_{k=0}^{n} C_k^{r_2} C_{j-k}^{b_2} C_{n-k}^{b_2-j+k} C_{m+k-n-j}^{r_2-k}. \quad (47.6)$$

This is the desired answer.

48. Some Instructive Illustrations; Another Urn Problem

An urn problem somewhat different from the problems that have been previously considered is the following:

EXAMPLE 48.1.—*An urn contains b black and w white balls. These are drawn out one at a time and placed in a separate container. The drawing is continued until all those balls which remain are of the same color. What is the chance that they are all black?*

Suppose the problem is modified by requiring the drawing to continue until only one ball remains. If this is done, any ball is as likely to be left as any other. Hence the answer to the modified problem is $b/(b + w)$.

This is also the answer to the problem as originally stated, a fact which becomes evident upon noting that when the last ball is black, the residual group (when all are of one color) must also be black, and conversely. On the contrary, if the last ball happens to be white, the residual contents of the urn must likewise be white.

49. Some Instructive Illustrations; Another Urn Problem

The solution of the following problem—like that of the last—involves no great difficulty if good judgment is used in the choice of the method of solution, but it might be very hard otherwise.

EXAMPLE 49.1.—*An urn contains w white balls and b black balls, w being greater than b. These are drawn out one at a time and placed in a second container. The drawing is continued until all the balls have been transferred. What is the chance that throughout this process there are always more white than black balls in the second container?*

The simplest way to attack this problem is by means of a geometrical analogy.

Suppose that, as successive balls are drawn, a graph similar to Fig. 49.1 is constructed in which the abscissa is the total number of balls

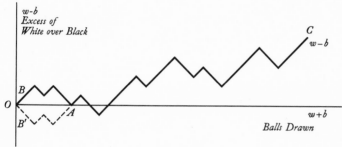

FIG. 49.1

in the second container and the ordinate is the excess of white over black. This curve can be thought of as the chance path traced by a moving point which travels one unit to the right each time a ball is drawn, and either up or down one unit according as that ball is white or black. The final point C obviously has the coordinates $(w + b, w - b)$.

Such a path could be constructed for every possible sequence in which the black and white balls might appear. Clearly these paths will all be different. Conversely, every path which proceeds from O to C and is composed of $\pm 45°$ segments corresponds to a possible sequence. Hence, the total number of such paths, N_{OC}, is $P^{w,b}_{w,b}$. Since this equals C^{w+b}_w, we may write

$$N_{OC} = C^{w+b}_w. \tag{49.1}$$

Suppose now that a path, such as the one shown, touches the axis at some point A. At this stage there are as many black balls as white, which is contrary to the conditions of the problem. Hence, only paths that do not touch or cross the axis correspond to acceptable sequences, and the ratio of their number to the total number of possible paths is the desired probability.

It is simpler to determine the number of paths that cross or touch the axis than the number that do not. We note first that every path must pass through either $(1, 1)$ or $(1, -1)$—that is, B or B'—since the first ball must be either white or black. But *all* paths from B' cross the axis somewhere, and hence are unacceptable. Their number, $N_{B'C}$, is easily found. Since they correspond to the permutations of the w white and $b - 1$ black balls that remain after the first black ball has been drawn, it is $P_{w,b-1}^{w,b-1}$. That is

$$N_{B'C} = C_w^{w+b-1}.$$

Next we shall show that the number of *unacceptable* paths through B equals the *total* number of paths through B'.

If a path P through B is unacceptable, it must touch the axis somewhere, and if it touches more than once there must be a first point, say A. Consider, then, a path P' which is the mirror image of P from O to A, and which follows P identically from A to C. Clearly, for every path P there is just one such a path P'. Conversely, to every path through B' there corresponds just one such unacceptable path through B. This proves the point.

The total number of unacceptable paths, N_{OC}'' is therefore

$$N_{OC}'' = 2C_w^{w+b-1}.$$

Subtracting this from the total of all paths, (49.1), and making some algebraic simplifications, the number of acceptable paths, N_{OC}', is found to be

$$N_{OC}' = \frac{w - b}{w + b} C_w^{w+b}. \tag{49.2}$$

Since all paths (i.e., all permutations of black and white balls) are equally likely, the desired probability is the ratio (49.2) to (49.1), which is

$$\frac{w - b}{w + b}.$$

Note that this ratio is just y/x, where x and y are the coordinates of C. There is, however, a hidden restriction: since w and b are integers, their sum and difference are either both even or both odd. It is not possible to construct any path at all from O to C unless this condition is satisfied.

50. Chance Paths

The last two examples illustrate the extent to which it is sometimes necessary to augment the routine processes of probability theory by common-sense methods in obtaining solutions of comparatively simple problems. The method used in § 49 is especially versatile and is particularly illuminating in discussing repeated trials of the same experiment, a situation to which we shall give special attention in Chapter V. In anticipation of that discussion, a few of the more fundamental properties of such diagrams will be derived here.

Consider, then, a succession of trials such as we have been considering, and let n be the number of successes in m trials. The number of failures is, of course, $m - n$, and the margin of success over failure is $2n - m$. This margin of success, like the plurality of white balls in Example 49.1, changes by $+1$ whenever a trial succeeds, and by -1 when it fails. Hence, if it is plotted against m it generates a chance path similar to Fig. 49.1; but in this case the terminal point of the curve is not fixed in advance as it was in Example 49.1.

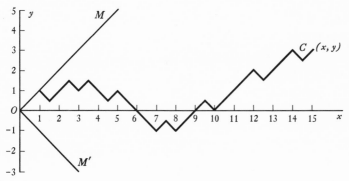

Fig. 50.1 Chance Path Representation of Repeated Trials of an Experiment.
Number of trials: $m = 2x$
Number of successes: $n = x + y$
Margin of success: $2n - m = 2y$

Let Fig. 50.1 be such a diagram. Two general statements can be made at once: (a) It is not possible for the path of an experiment to pass outside the diagonals OM and OM', one of which corresponds to an uninterrupted run of successes, and the other to an uninterrupted run of failures; and (b) the number of trials and the margin of success are either both even, or both odd. This latter point was noted in § 49.

In the interest of simplicity, we shall confine our discussion to even values of m. Equivalent results for the odd values can easily be derived, as certain of the problems which follow will indicate.

For notation, let the number of trials and the margin of success be denoted by

$$m = 2x,$$
$$2n - m = 2y.$$

Then any positive integer x, and any integer y between $-x$ and $+x$, define a point through which the curve may pass. The corresponding n and m are

$$m = 2x,$$

$$n = x + y.$$

We shall be interested, among other things, in the number of times a path crosses or touches the axis; in Fig. 50.1 there are three such "returns to zero" on the path shown. With this in mind, let $v_x(y, r)$ be the number of paths from the origin to the point (x, y) which touch or cross the axis exactly r times. If one of the variables is not specified, its place will be filled by a dot. For example, $v_x(y, \cdot)$ means the total number of paths to C with no restriction on the number of returns to the axis; $v_x(\cdot, r)$ means the number of paths from O which return to the axis just r times, and terminate somewhere on the ordinate through C.[21]

In this notation the three significant results of § 49 may be restated as follows:[22] The total number of paths from O to C is

$$v_x(y, \cdot) = C_{x+y}^{2x}; \tag{50.2}$$

the number of paths that nowhere touch the axis is[23]

$$v_x(y, 0) = \frac{|y|}{x} C_{x+y}^{2x}, \tag{50.3}$$

and the number that touch it at least once is

$$v_x(y, >0) = 2 C_{x+|y|}^{2x-1}. \tag{50.4}$$

The total number of paths from O to an arbitrary point on the ordinate through C can also be set down at once. In our notation it is

---

[21] Such a dot is equivalent to a summation sign; specifically

$$v_x(y, \cdot) = \Sigma_r \, v_x(y, r),$$

$$v_x(\cdot, r) = \Sigma_y \, v_x(y, r). \tag{50.1}$$

[22] To correlate the notation, note that the number of trials is $w + b = 2x$, the number of successes is $w = x + y$, and the margin of success is $w - b = 2y$.

[23] In dealing with Example 49.1, y was tacitly assumed to be positive. However, if a path from O to (x, y) is reflected in the x-axis, it becomes a path from O to $(x, -y)$. Since both of these touch the axis at identical points we have

$$v_x(y, r) = v_x(-y, r). \tag{50.5}$$

Because of this symmetry any formula which holds true for $y \geqq 0$ can be converted into one for $y \leqq 0$ by merely replacing y by $-y$. Or it can be converted into one which is valid for both positive and negative values by substituting the absolute value $|y|$ for y. This has been done when required in (50.3) and (50.4).

$v_x(\,\cdot\,,\,\cdot\,)$ since neither y nor r is specified; and since a path may move either up or down on every trial of the experiment,

$$v_x(\,\cdot\,,\,\cdot\,) = 2^{2x}.$$

The general formula for $v_x(y, r)$ is[24]

$$v_x(y, r) = 2^r \cdot \frac{r + 2|y|}{2x - r}\, C^{2x-r}_{x+|y|}. \qquad (50.6)$$

It is not easily derived by direct logic, but once it has been arrived at by guess or otherwise it can be verified by a process of mathematical induction. This is the approach we shall use. Because of symmetry (see footnote 23), we may confine our attention to positive values of y.

We begin with Fig. 50.2 and note that any path from O to C must, during the last two steps, follow one of the four courses shown. Two of these go through the point $(x - 1, y)$ and one each through $(x - 1, y - 1)$ and $(x - 1, y + 1)$. Furthermore, these final portions can in each case be joined onto any path whatever from O to their starting points. We conclude, therefore, that

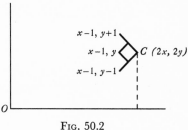

FIG. 50.2

$$v_x(y, r) = v_{x-1}(y - 1, r) + 2v_{x-1}(y, r) + v_{x-1}(y + 1, r), \quad y \geqq 1. \qquad (50.7)$$

The case of $y = 0$ needs to be separately considered. Geometrically the situation is the same as before, but now the terminal point is itself a return to the axis. Therefore, the paths preceding the final portions must have only $r - 1$ returns. In view of this and (50.5), we have

$$v_x(0, r) = 2v_{x-1}(1, r - 1) + 2v_{x-1}(0, r - 1). \qquad (50.8)$$

These equations give the values of v for any integer x provided its values for the next smaller integer are known; they are therefore in precisely the form needed to verify the correctness of (50.6).

The demonstration is quite simple. When (50.6) is substituted into the right-hand side of (50.7), it leads to

$$v_x(y, r) = 2^r \frac{r + 2y}{2x - r - 2} \left(C^{2x-r-2}_{x+y-2} + 2\, C^{2x-r-2}_{x+y-1} + C^{2x-r-2}_{x+y} \right)$$

$$+ \frac{2^{r+1}}{2x - r - 2} \left(C^{2x-r-2}_{x+y} - C^{2x-r-2}_{x+y-2} \right). \qquad (50.9)$$

The quantities in the two parentheses can easily be reduced to C^{2x-r}_{x+y} and $-(2y + r)C^{2x-r}_{x+y}/(2x - r)$, respectively: and when these are substituted for

---

[24] Note that if $y > x$ or $y < -x$, $x + |y| > 2x - r$. Thus the formula (50.6) automatically gives $v = 0$ for any point outside the sector MOM'.

the parentheses, (50.9) collapses into (50.6). The formula is, therefore valid for all values of y different from zero.

To show that it also applies when $y = 0$ we substitute (50.6) into (50.8), which leads to

$$v_x(0, r) = 2^r \frac{r}{2x - r - 1} (C_x^{2x-r-1} + C_{x-1}^{2x-r-1})$$

$$+ \frac{2^r}{2x - r - 1} (C_x^{2x-r-1} - C_{x-1}^{2x-r-1}). \qquad (50.10)$$

Again the first parenthesis becomes C_x^{2x-r}, and the second $-rC_x^{2x-r}/(2x - r)$; and when these are substituted into (50.10), it collapses to

$$v_x(0,r) = 2^r \frac{r}{2x - r} C_x^{2x-r}. \qquad (50.11)$$

This, however, is precisely the value taken by (50.6) for $y = 0$. Hence, if (50.6) holds for any integer x, it must also hold for the next higher integer, and so on for all integers.

To complete the proof, therefore, we need only demonstrate that (50.6) is true for some one value of x.

TABLE 50.1

VALUES OF $v_x(y, r)$

$x = 1$

r \ y	0	± 1
0	0	1
1	2	

$x = 3$

r \ y	0	± 1	± 2	± 3
0	0	5	4	1
1	4	6	2	
2	8	4		
3	8			

$x = 2$

r \ y	0	± 1	± 2
0	0	2	1
1	2	2	
2	4		

$x = 4$

r \ y	0	± 1	± 2	± 3	± 4
0	0	14	14	6	1
1	10	18	10	2	
2	20	16	4		
3	24	8			
4	16				

When x is small, however, it is a simple matter to construct all possible paths from O to any terminal point on the vertical line through $2x$. Then, by counting the number which terminate at y after touching the axis r times, a table of $v_x(y,r)$ can be constructed. This has been done in Table 50.1 for $x = 1, 2, 3, 4$. In the case of $x = 1$, for example, there are only four possible paths. One is a 45° line terminating at $y = 1$; another is its mirror image terminating at $y = -1$; and there are two broken lines ter-minating at $y = 0$, one lying above the axis and the other below. For the latter pair, $r = 1$; for the others, $r = 0$. This leads to the first section of Table 50.1.

The reader may easily confirm the fact that all the numbers in Table 50.1 agree with (50.6), thus completing the proof.[25]

The formulas (50.2) to (50.6) do not, of course, yield probabilities directly. They give the number of paths of the type illustrated in Fig. 50.1 that lead outward from a starting point O, return to the axis (or not) as specified by r, and terminate at C (or elsewhere) as specified by y. But they lead us directly to certain questions of probability which arise in connection with repeated independent trials of an experiment and help to clarify some of the more puzzling answers. The discussion of these will, however, be deferred until §§ 66–69, Chapter V, when it will be more meaningful.

Problems

1. Make use of the results of Problems 37.6, 37.7, and 37.8 to obtain the solution of Example 38.3.

2. Solve Problem 35.3, using the result of Problem 37.1, and the method of alternate compound probabilities.

3. In 100 throws of a penny, what is the chance that there will be more than 5 heads?

[Use Appendix III to compute the complementary probability.]

4. In Problem 37.12, what is the chance of just 1 red ball? Of 2? Of 3? Of 4?

5. If n persons are selected at random from among m_1 men and m_2 women, what is the chance that the first j will be men and the rest women?

6. What is the answer to Problem 5 if the order of choice is immaterial?

7. Derive the answer to Problem 6 directly from Problems 23.8 and 23.9.

8. In the first paragraph of § 40 it is stated that the unconditional probability of any black card being incorrectly called is $\frac{1}{2}$. Since there are four black cards the chance that either the first or the second or the third or the fourth is incorrectly called works out to be $\frac{1}{2} + \frac{1}{2} + \frac{1}{2} + \frac{1}{2} = 2$. What is wrong with this argument?

9. If p +'s and n −'s are distributed at random along a line, what is the chance that no two −'s are adjacent?

10. By the use of (45.1) prove that $\sum\limits_{p=0}^{r} C_p^m C_{r-p}^n = C_r^{m+n}$.

[25] As a matter of fact, with a certain amount of ingenuity, (50.6) may be inferred from an examination of Table 50.1. An algebraic formula for the numbers in the row $r = 0$ is already known from (50.3). Inspection of the table quickly shows that if any element is doubled, and the one below it subtracted, the result is the element to the left of the latter. Starting from these observations, the form of (50.6) reveals itself without too great difficulty.

11. Verify the result of Problem 35.11 by the use of alternative compound probabilities.

[Use Problems 4, above, and 37.12.]

12. If, in Example 47.1, the number of red and black cards was equal and very large, what would be the value of $P(n)$?

13. The number of ballots cast for two candidates A and B in an election was 3278 and 2133, respectively. If the ballots are selected at random when counted, what is the probability that A is constantly ahead?

14. Show that

$$\sum P_{n_1, n_2, \ldots, n_a}^{n_1, n_2, \ldots, n_a} p_1^{n_1} p_2^{n_2} \cdots p_a^{n_a} = 1$$

if the p's correspond to a complete set of events and the sum is extended to all the partitions of m into a parts.

[Use Theorem 43.1.]

15. Using the result of Problem 14, show that, provided $x_1, x_2, \ldots, x_a$ are any positive numbers whatever,

$$\sum P_{n_1, n_2, \ldots, n_a}^{n_1, n_2, \ldots, n_a} x_1^{n_1} x_2^{n_2} \cdots x_a^{n_a} = (x_1 + x_2 + \ldots + x_a)^m.$$

[The numbers $p_i = x_i / \Sigma_i x_i$ are a possible set of probabilities in Theorem 43.1.]

16. Prove that

$$v_x(y, > r) = 2^{r+1} C_{x+y}^{2x-r-1}.$$

[Use (29.8), Problem 29.44.]

17. Prove that

$$v_x(\cdot, r) = 2^r C_x^{2x-r}. \tag{50.12}$$

[Use (29.9), Problem 29.45.]

18. Since $v_x(\cdot, \cdot)$ includes all possible paths with just $2x$ segments, show that

$$\sum_{j=0}^{x} 2^j C_x^{2x-j} = 2^{2x}. \tag{50.13}$$

19. Using (50.12) and (50.13), show that

$$v_x(\cdot, > r) = \sum_{j=r+1}^{x} 2^j C_x^{2x-j} = 2^{2x} - \sum_{j=0}^{r} 2^j C_x^{2x-j}.$$

20. Show that the number of paths from O to $(2x, 2y)$ that touch the axis exactly r times but never cross it is

$$2^{-r} v_x(y, r), \qquad y \neq 0. \tag{50.14}$$

[Consider each point of return in turn, and use the reflection principle. The portion beyond the last return cannot be reflected without leading to $(x, -y)$.]

21. Show that the answer to Problem 20 when $y = 0$ is

$$2^{1-r} \nu_x(0, r). \tag{50.15}$$

22. The number of paths from O to an arbitrary point on the ordinate to $m = 2x$ that touch the axis exactly r times but do not cross it is

$$2 \sum_{y=0}^{x-r} 2^{-r} \nu_x(0, r) = 2 C_{x-1}^{2x-r-1}.$$

[Use (29.9), (50.14) and (50.15).]

23. In Problem 21, how many paths lie above the axis?

24. The number of paths from O to $(2x, 2y)$ that never cross the axis, although they may or may not return to it, is

$$\sum_{r=0}^{x-y} 2^{-r} \nu_x(y, r) = \frac{2y+1}{x+y+1} C_{x-y}^{2x}, \qquad y \neq 0;$$

$$\sum_{r=1}^{x} 2^{1-r} \nu_x(0, r) = \frac{2}{x+1} C_x^{2x}, \qquad y = 0. \tag{50.16}$$

[Use $r + 2y \equiv 2(x + y) - (2x - r)$ and (29.7), Problem 29.43.]

25. The number of paths from O to an arbitrary point on the ordinate to $m = 2x$ which never cross the axis, though they may or may not touch it, is $2C_x^{2x}$.

[This may be obtained by summing (50.16) from $y = -x$ to $y = x$. It can also be obtained by the following geometrical argument: Let the solid portion of Fig. 50.3 represent a solution of the problem. If a new

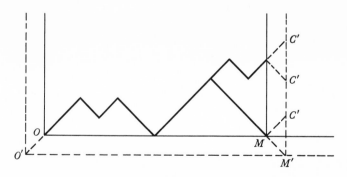

Fig. 50.3

axis is drawn one unit below the true one, this path may be extended by the dotted line OO' and by a unit extension at the other end. Any extended path from O' to an arbitrary point C' which nowhere returns to the new axis, and any extended path from O' to M' which returns only at M', has the desired properties between O and M. There are, however, two such dotted extensions at the right for every admissible path. Hence the answer is

$$\tfrac{1}{2}\nu_{x+1}\left(\cdot,0\right) + \tfrac{1}{2}\nu_{x+1}\left(0,1\right),$$

which, by (50.11) and (50.12), is $2C_x^{2x}.$]

26. Prove that

$$\sum_{j=i}^{x+i-r-y}\frac{i}{j}\,\frac{r+2y-i}{x+y-j}C_{j-1}^{2j-i-1}\,C_{x+y-j-1}^{2x-2j-r+i-1} = \frac{r+2y}{2x-r}\,C_{x+y}^{2x-r}, \quad y>0.$$

[If the path returns to zero r times between O and C, the i'th return must be at some intermediate value of x.]

27. The formulas of § 50 were obtained for even values of $m = 2x$, $n = 2y$. If expressed in terms of m and n, (50.6) in particular becomes

$$\nu_m(r,n) = 2^r\frac{r+n}{m-r}\,C_{(m+n)/2}^{m-r}, \quad n>0.$$

Show that this is also a valid formula when both m and n are odd.

[Any path terminating in (m, n) must have passed through either $(m-1, n-1)$ or $(m-1, n+1)$.]

28. How many paths are there from O to $(2x + 1, 2y + 1)$ that return to the axis at just r points?

[Any such path must pass through either $(2x, 2y)$ or $(2x, 2y + 2)$.]

Answers to Problems at End of § 31

1. $\frac{3}{8}$. 2. (a) $\frac{1}{4}$; (b) $\frac{1}{8}$; (c) $\frac{3}{8}$; (d) $\frac{1}{2}$. 3. (a) $\frac{1}{365}$; (b) $\frac{31}{365}$; (c) $\frac{1}{365}$; (d) $\frac{120}{365}$. 4. $\frac{1}{10}$. 5. 0.06; 0.66; 0. 6. 0.95. 7. $\frac{1}{70}$. 8. $\frac{1}{28}$. 9. $\frac{3}{7}$. 10. $\frac{8}{35}$. 11. $\frac{1}{3}$ if the milkman selects bottles at random; 0 if he disposes of the older milk first; 1 if he disposes of the fresh milk first. 12. $C_5^{800}/C_5^{1000} = 0.32686$; $C_3^{800}\,C_2^{200}/C_5^{1000} = 0.20506$. 13. $\frac{1}{2}$; $\frac{1}{2}$; $\frac{5}{6}$. 14. 1.05/5.95. 15. $\frac{1}{60}$. 16. $\frac{2j-1}{36}$. 17. $(\frac{1}{2})^4$. 18. $\frac{105}{512}$; $\frac{2,401}{4,096}$; $\frac{147}{256}$.

19. If the sequence TT occurs, A will have nothing left regardless of whether the (hypothetical) third toss led to TTT or TTH. Hence:

j	0	1	2	3	4	5
$P(j)$	$\frac{1}{4}$	$\frac{1}{4}$	0	$\frac{3}{8}$	0	$\frac{1}{8}$

20. After the first throw:

j	0	1	2	3	4	5
$P(j)$	0	$\frac{1}{2}$	0	$\frac{1}{2}$	0	0

after the second:

j	0	1	2	3	4	5
$P(j)$	$\frac{1}{4}$	0	$\frac{1}{2}$	0	$\frac{1}{4}$	0

Answers to Problems at End of § 35

1. $\frac{15}{94}$. **2.** $\frac{51}{94}$ if the end-points of the time interval are included, $\frac{18}{47}$ otherwise; 1; 0. **3.** $(\frac{1}{2})^4$. **4.** $(\frac{1}{2})^4$; same. **5.** $\frac{1}{5}$. **6.** $\frac{2}{7}$. **7.** $\frac{2}{7}$. Yes. If the role of cards and medium are interchanged, the two are symmetrical.
8. $\frac{10}{21}$. **9.** 82% vs. 73%. **10.** $\frac{1}{6}$; same; the statements about the white die convey no information pertinent to the question asked. **11.** $\frac{7}{12}$; the fact that four balls have been drawn contributes no pertinent information so long as their color is unknown. **12.** $1 - \frac{1}{36}$. **13.** $1 - (P_5^{39}/P_5^{52}) = \frac{2109}{9520}$.

14.

Color of Second Ball	Color of First Ball		
	w	r	b
w	0	$\frac{2}{5}$	$\frac{2}{7}$
r	$\frac{5}{8}$	0	$\frac{5}{7}$
b	$\frac{3}{8}$	$\frac{3}{5}$	0

15.

Color of Third Ball	Colors of First Two Balls		
	wr	wb	rb
w	0	0	1
r	0	1	0
b	1	0	0

16. Since $p(j|k)$ depends only on how much money A has, and not on how he acquired it, the transition matrix is the same for all tosses.

Answers to Problems at End of § 37

1. $\frac{1}{10}(\frac{1}{2})^4$; $\frac{1}{9}(\frac{1}{2})^4$. **2.** $1/6^4$; decreased. **3.** 0; $1/6^4$; increased. **6.** $\frac{3}{56}$. **7.** $\frac{15}{56}$.
8. $\frac{3}{56}$. **9.** $\frac{6}{35}$. **10.** $\frac{6}{35}$. **11.** 0. **12.** $\frac{1}{99}$. **13.** $1/2^j$. **14.** $1/2^{j+1}$. **15.** $5^{j-1}/6^j$.

Answers to Problems at End of § 50

3. $1 - 2^{-100} \sum\limits_{0}^{5} C_j^{100} = 0.9^{22}37$ (that is, 22 nines followed by 37). **4.** $\frac{14}{99}$, $\frac{14}{33}$, $\frac{35}{99}$, $\frac{7}{99}$. **5.** $m_1! \, m_2! \, (m_1 + m_2 - n)!/(m_1 - j)!(m_2 - n + j)!(m_1 + m_2)!$.
6. $P_{j,n-j}^{j,n-j}$ times the answer to Problem 5, or $C_j^{m_1} C_{n-j}^{m_2}/C_n^{m_1+m_2}$. **8.** Not mutually exclusive. **9.** C_n^{p+1}/C_n^{p+n}. See Problem 29.13. **12.** The chance of a match in any pair would be $\frac{1}{2}$; hence $C_n^m/2^m$. **13.** 1145/5411. **23.** $2^{-r}v_x(0, r)$.

28. $2^r \dfrac{r + 2\,|y| + 1}{2x - r + 1} \, C_{x+|y|+1}^{2x-r+1}$.

Chapter V

Probability and Experiment; Bernoulli's Theorem

51. Introductory Remarks

The reader who has dealt at all with statistics will have noticed that, in defining probability, nothing whatever was said about the frequency with which an event will happen. It has been said that, in tossing a penny, heads is "equally likely to appear as tails," never that "heads will appear as often as tails." The reason is that the latter statement is not true. Try it and see. It is not even true "in the long run," unless that phrase is used in a special sense which comes dangerously near to begging the question.

Neither is it true that "in a large number of independent *runs*, heads will as often exceed tails as tails will exceed heads"; for a *run* is also an *event* and in this respect has the same logical standing as a single trial.

If such statements were true, probability would be an experimental science, which I am quite convinced it is not.

What is true is the fact that the outcome of an experiment may change the measure of a probability—just as any other accretion of pertinent information would do. If a large number of throws showed twice as many heads as tails, and we were carrying the weak end of a bet, we would probably insist on changing the penny. It would be more probable, because of the experiment, that the coin was loaded than it had been before the experiment began.

An experiment may even be undertaken with the view to finding out whether a penny is good or bad, and if bad, how bad. But if so, in a strict logical sense, we will never find out. Not only will we never learn what the probability of tails is (i.e., *how bad* the penny is), we cannot even determine with finality *whether* it is bad; because any result, no matter how one-sided it may be, would not have been impossible with a good penny. We will be led to a *presumption*, perhaps a very strong one, that the penny is bad, or even to a *presumption* as to the approximate measure of the probability, but to nothing more.[1]

Why these things are true—that is, why we cannot with certainty determine the magnitude of a probability, but can nevertheless use experiment as a practical means for its approximate measure—is, broadly speaking, the subject of this chapter. Before the answers can be given, suitable foundations must be laid. So, with the questions in mind, we proceed to the foundation building. For this purpose some rather elementary, but perhaps not very familiar, mathematical ideas must be discussed.

52. Limits and Things which Approach Them

In mathematics the meaning of the phrase "something approaches a limit" is the same as its use in everyday speech.

Consider the very simple function $y = x^2$, or its graph (Fig. 52.1). It is quite clear that y approaches zero as x approaches zero. It is even true that $y = 0$ when $x = 0$. In other words, y not only *approaches*, but *reaches*, its limit.

Next consider Fig. 52.2. It is similar to Fig. 52.1 in a general way; however, y is no longer sharply defined, but instead is only known to

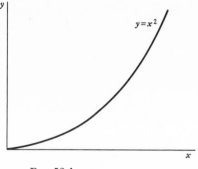

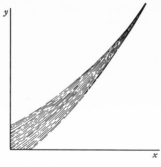

Fig. 52.1   Fig. 52.2

lie somewhere within a certain band of uncertainty represented by the shaded area. In this case, neither mathematics nor common sense would assert that y approaches zero (or any other number) as x approaches zero.

As a third illustration, suppose a man has a thread a foot long. First he cuts off half of it, then half of the remainder, and so on. What he

---

[1] See in this connection § 13.

has left after successive cuts gives the sequence of numbers

$$1, \tfrac{1}{2}, \tfrac{1}{4}, \tfrac{1}{8}, \tfrac{1}{16}, \tfrac{1}{32}, \ldots, \qquad (52.1)$$

which are plotted in Fig. 52.3. Clearly the remnant "approaches zero as time goes on." But it does not approach the limit continuously, as did the variable in Fig. 52.1, but through a discrete set of values instead. Furthermore, it does not reach its limit, since no term of the sequence is zero.

A somewhat similar sequence of numbers is the following:

$$0.100{,}000, \ 0.400{,}00, \ 0.550{,}0, \ 0.625, \ 0.66, \ 0.6, \ 0. \qquad (52.2)$$

If it is understood that these are not exact values, but decimal approximations, and that in each case the digits beyond the last one written are uncertain, the sequence does not clearly define a limit. The situation is, in fact, quite analogous to Fig. 52.2. Of course, if we observe the difference between successive numbers closely, we may infer a law of formation leading to the limiting value 0.7. But this would be a presumptive inference, not a demonstrable fact.

Finally, although it is not germane to the present discussion, we may note that just at the point where we expect an otherwise well-behaved variable to reach its limit, it sometimes misbehaves and takes a quite different value. Figure 52.4, for example, is the graph of a function

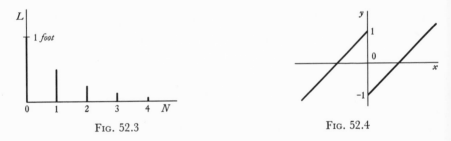

FIG. 52.3   FIG. 52.4

that can be defined by an infinite series of sine functions, a Fourier series. It consists of two straight lines which obviously approach the limit $+1$ as x approaches zero from the left and -1 as it approaches zero from the right. But, when $x = 0$, the value given to y by the defining series is zero—a value which it certainly does not approach from either side.[2]

---

[2] This is a consequence of defining y by means of Fourier series, not an inherent property of two line segments that fail to meet. The point is, not that the function *must* so behave, but that it *may*.

It is important for mathematical purposes to have a definition of "approaching a limit" which agrees with the concept expressed above, is precise enough for logical studies, and can be applied conveniently to test doubtful situations. As we shall be interested primarily in discrete sequences such as (52.1) and (52.2); we phrase the definition in a way most appropriate to that use. It is as follows:

DEFINITION 52.1. *An ordered set of numbers is said to approach a limit if, having chosen in advance a number ϵ, which may be as small as we like but not zero, and having removed a finite part of the set, no two of the numbers which remain differ by as much as ϵ.*

Consider, for example, the sequence (52.1). If a particular value of ϵ is chosen, there is some power of $\frac{1}{2}$ smaller than ϵ. Thus, if ϵ is 0.000,001, $(\frac{1}{2})^{20} < \epsilon$; if it is still smaller, some power N can be found such that $(\frac{1}{2})^N < \epsilon$, this N being a finite number. If the first N terms of the set are removed, no two of the remainder differ by as much as ϵ. Hence the set approaches a limit.

There is a defect to this definition: it does not state what "the limit" is. This defect can be removed in one or the other of two ways:

(*a*) If the set contains a number q which need not be cancelled no matter how small ϵ is made, q is the limit.

(*b*) If a new number q can be added to the set, and need not be cancelled no matter how small ϵ is made, q is the limit.

Obviously, in the first case the set contains its limit, or in technical language "is closed"; whereas in the second case the limit is not contained in the set, or the set "is open."

Our example is a case of an "open set"; for if we try *any* member of the set, say, $(\frac{1}{2})^m$, we can choose ϵ so small that it must be excluded: for example, $\epsilon = (\frac{1}{2})^{m+1}$ would do. But if we arbitrarily include zero in the set, zero need never be cancelled. Hence our set is an "open set" with the "limit zero" which it "does not contain."

53. The Upper Bound of a Set

Among a *finite* set of numbers, one possesses the property of being at least as big as any other. It is the "largest." Sometimes there are several which possess this property. If so there are several "largest" numbers, as in the set 1, 2, 7, 7, 7.

This statement is only safe of finite sets, however. Among an infinity of numbers there need not be any largest number. There are two ways in which this rather unexpected result can come about. They can be very simply illustrated by the following examples:

There is no largest integer among the infinity of positive integers, for no matter what integer may be chosen there is always one larger than this. In this case the numbers in the set do not have any limit as to size; that is, they are not "bounded."

There is no largest number in the set of fractions $\frac{1}{2}, \frac{2}{3}, \frac{3}{4}, \ldots$, all of which are of the form $m/(m + 1)$, for if there were, it could be obtained by giving m some particular value M. Whatever M may be, however, $m = M + 1$ always results in a larger fraction: that is, $(M + 1)/(M + 2)$ is bigger than $M/(M + 1)$. In this case the set of numbers is actually "bounded" (there is no number bigger than 1), and has the limit 1; but it is "open" since 1 is not a member of the set.

Suppose, however, that the set is modified by including the integer 1. It is now a "closed" set and 1 is its largest number. In either case 1 is called the "least upper bound" of the set, the only difference being that the closed set contains its least upper bound (which is also the limit of the sequence); the open set does not.

Among numbers which represent probabilities there can be no unbounded sets, for such numbers are inherently contained between zero and one. But there may be either open or closed sets. In fact, the sequence $\frac{1}{2}, \frac{2}{3}, \frac{3}{4}, \ldots$ is capable of interpretation in terms of probability. If an infinity of urns is provided, each containing one white ball, and if in one of these urns is placed one black ball, in another two black balls, in a third three black balls and so on, the chance that a ball drawn at random from one of the urns is black is either $\frac{1}{2}$ or $\frac{2}{3}$ or $\frac{3}{4}$ or $m/(m + 1)$, according to the urn from which the ball is drawn. Clearly there is no urn for which the probability is as great or greater than that for all remaining urns. The set is "open."

If, however, an additional urn is provided with black balls only, *this* will have the probability 1 which is actually greater than for any other urn. The set is now "closed."

In either of these cases 1 is the least upper bound of the probability. In the second case it is reached (by the urn with only black balls); in the first case it is not.

Now it happens that almost all statistical studies are based upon sets of probabilities that approach a bound as a limit but do not contain it, and a great deal of logical confusion has arisen from loose thinking about them. Hence it is essential to obtain a clear picture of the significance of the upper bound in such cases.

As a step in this direction, take the set of events already mentioned: the drawing of a black ball from the various urns each having just one white ball. Can it be asserted that, by choosing wisely the urn from which we draw, we can be assured of obtaining a black ball? It cannot. So long as the urn contains a white ball—as all the urns do—the outcome is unknown. The most we can say is, that by passing from urn to urn, the importance of our ignorance can be made less and less. The limiting condition is certainty, but that limit cannot be reached.

Choose your urn: make it as far along in the sequence as you like. I'll take the first one. We draw. We want black, but neither is certain to get it. *The only difference lies in the importance of our states of ignorance; yours is of less moment than mine.*

"But," you say, "if we draw repeatedly, my superiority will manifest itself." Weak logic cannot be strengthened by obfuscation; but I'll follow you this once into what, if we kept on, would soon become an infinite regression. Name your number of trials. Make it as big as you like. You cannot be sure you will not draw white *every time*, and I black. But we'll agree it is extremely improbable.

What I am aiming to make clear is that "extremely improbable" is as far as we can go, and that *that* is not arrived at by trial, but by judgment in advance. A trial can only tell us what has happened; our intelligence can go further than that and say whether it was a miracle or not.

54. Regarding Probability as a Limit

Many students of the subject have sought to define the probability of a head appearing when a penny is tossed as the limit of the ratio of the number of heads to the number of throws, as the number of throws is increased indefinitely. Such a definition implies as a fundamental postulate that the ratio obtained in this way *actually approaches a limit.* If this were so, the definition would be logically possible and would be superior to the one which we have set up in one important respect; for as we have already said, there are many situations to which our definition cannot be applied, whereas the limit definition could be applied equally well[3] to almost any case. The trouble is that the fundamental postulate is only tenable provided the trials are *not independent,*[4] whereas the definition implies, even when it does not

---

[3] And also equally badly. In theoretical discussions it would always be applicable, in practice never, for we can never cause our number of trials to "approach infinity" in a practical sense. This difficulty is a superficial one, however. The utility of experiment is exactly the same no matter which point of view we start from.

[4] Unless "approaches a limit" means something logically different from its usual mathematical definition.

explicitly state, that the trials *are independent* and that they are made *under the same essential conditions.*[5]

To see how this inconsistency arises, let us consider the matter of tossing pennies, and let h_n denote the number of heads observed in n tosses. We form, in particular, the sequence of ratios

$$\frac{h_1}{1}, \frac{h_2}{2}, \frac{h_3}{3}, \frac{h_4}{4}, \ldots, \frac{h_n}{n}, \ldots,$$

stretching out toward infinity as throw after throw is made. The definition which we are criticizing affirms that this sequence approaches a limit. But we can only properly make such an affirmation provided, after a finite number of terms have been eliminated, we are assured that no two of the remainder differ by more than some preassigned quantity ϵ. In fact, it must be possible to make this assertion for *any* ϵ, no matter how small; but for our purposes it is quite sufficient to consider only the value $\epsilon = \frac{1}{4}$.

Consider in particular the terms corresponding to $n = N$ and $n = 2N$, and suppose to begin with that h_N/N exceeds $\frac{1}{2}$. If every throw from $N + 1$ to $2N$ should happen to yield a tail, h_{2N} and h_N would be equal and

$$\frac{h_N}{N} - \frac{h_{2N}}{2N} = \frac{1}{2}\frac{h_N}{N} > \frac{1}{4} > \epsilon.$$

Obviously it cannot be asserted that this will not happen unless the result of a particular throw depends on what has gone before.

On the other hand, if h_N/N does not exceed $\frac{1}{2}$, and if the throws

---

[5] That is, that the probability of success does not change from trial to trial.

To see the importance of this, consider the question, What is the probability that a screw chosen at random from the output of a machine will be defective? If we attempt to answer this by getting the ratio of defectives to total output, we need only let the machine run year after year and record the results. Eventually, as the machine wears out, all the screws will be bad, and hence the ratio will, in time, approach the limit 1. This is a genuine limit; but it is quite clearly not responsive to the question asked.

To be responsive to the question we must keep the machine at a constant level of performance. But if we do this, as the body of the text will show, we cannot assert that the success ratio will have a limit.

Note also that "a constant level of performance" means precisely that the chance of a defective unit remains constant; that is, every screw is "equally likely" to be bad. So, to be responsive to the intent of our question, we have again had to introduce the primary concept of equally likely events.

Those readers who are familiar with the concept of a Kollektiv, which had quite a vogue during the second quarter of this century, will recognize that the above example conforms in every respect to that concept. The fact that it gives the wrong answer (or, more properly, answers the wrong question) is the most convincing evidence of the futility of that approach.

from $N + 1$ to $2N$ should all yield heads, h_{2N} would be $h_N + N$, and

$$\frac{h_{2N}}{2N} - \frac{h_N}{N} = \frac{1}{2} - \frac{1}{2}\frac{h_N}{N} \geq \frac{1}{4} \geq \epsilon;$$

and it cannot be asserted that this will not happen, either. It is therefore impossible to say that the sequence has a limit.

The situation is not unlike that of Fig. 52.2. There is an element of uncertainty about h_N/N, similar to the band of uncertainty in y, which is sufficiently serious to invalidate the existence of a limit.

The trouble lies, fundamentally, in the fact that the set of probabilities corresponding to a run of one head, two heads, three heads, and so on, though it has the limit zero, never reaches that limit. If it ever did reach it, say for a value N, runs of more than N heads would be impossible, and the ratio of heads to throws would also have a limit. This would then be a theorem, not a postulate. But so long as the throws are independent, the next throw after a long run of heads may also be a head: no length of run is impossible, and the ratio *need not* (though it very probably will) *approach a limit*.

To look at it from a slightly different point of view, the trouble lies in the fact that the two positive assertions "The trials are independent" and "The sequence approaches a limit" are inconsistent and cannot be made the basis for a definition.

What can be done is this: an *a priori* definition of probability being allowed, it can be *proved* that the PROBABILITY of any two terms differing by more than ϵ can be made as small as desired by taking N large enough. *It is the a priori probability, not the sequence of experimental ratios, which has a limit.* This will become more apparent in the course of the next few sections.

55. Regarding Repeated Independent Trials

Consider an urn in which three balls are placed: one white and two black. Suppose repeated drawings are made from this urn, the ball being returned after each. According to (42.1) the chance of *just n white balls in m trials is*

$$P_m(n) = C_n^m \left(\tfrac{1}{3}\right)^n \left(\tfrac{2}{3}\right)^{m-n}.$$

Suppose now that five trials are made in succession. Any one of six things may happen: None of the trials may give a white ball, or one of them, or two, or three, or four, or five. The probability of each of these six events can be computed, the results being given in Table 55.1.

In this case there are two "most probable" events. One white ball or two white balls are equally likely to appear, and either is more probable than any other possible result.

TABLE 55.1

THE PROBABILITY OF n SUCCESSES IN FIVE TRIALS
IF THE PROBABILITY OF SUCCESS IN A SINGLE TRIAL IS $\frac{1}{3}$

n	Probability	n	Probability	n	Probability
0	0.1317	2	0.3292	4	0.0412
1	0.3292	3	0.1646	5	0.0041

If ten trials are made instead of five there are eleven possible results. The probabilities of these eleven individually are given in Table 55.2. In this case there is one "most probable" number of white balls, three. The least probable number is ten, for which the value given in the table is 0.0000 since it is less than one-half of 0.0001. The exact probability is $1/59,049 = 0.0000169$.

TABLE 55.2

THE PROBABILITY OF n SUCCESSES IN TEN TRIALS
IF THE PROBABILITY OF SUCCESS IN A SINGLE TRIAL IS $\frac{1}{3}$

n	Probability	n	Probability	n	Probability
0	0.0173	4	0.2276	8	0.0030
1	0.0867	5	0.1367	9	0.0003
2	0.1951	6	0.0569	10	0.0000
3	0.2601	7	0.0163		

If fifty trials are made, the results are as shown in Table 55.3. Again there are two equally likely results, 16 and 17, each of which is more probable than any other.

TABLE 55.3

THE PROBABILITY OF n SUCCESSES IN FIFTY TRIALS
IF THE PROBABILITY OF SUCCESS IN A SINGLE TRIAL IS $\frac{1}{3}$

n	Probability	n	Probability	n	Probability
<5	0.0000	13	0.0679	23	0.0202
		14	0.0898	24	0.0113
5	0.0001	15	0.1077	25	0.0059
6	0.0004	16	0.1178	26	0.0028
7	0.0012	17	0.1178	27	0.0012
8	0.0033	18	0.1080	28	0.0005
9	0.0077	19	0.0910	29	0.0002
10	0.0157	20	0.0704	30	0.0001
11	0.0287	21	0.0503		
12	0.0470	22	0.0332	>30	0.0000

The first and last entries mean, not that these cases cannot occur, but that their chances of occurrence are less than one in 20,000. As a matter of fact there is a finite probability for drawing a white ball in every one of the fifty trails, but it is exceedingly small. In fact it is[6]

$$\frac{1}{3^{50}} = \frac{1}{717,897,000,000,000,000,000,000}.$$

56. The Limiting Condition as the Number of Trials Is Greatly Increased

The probabilities in Tables 55.1 to 55.3 are plotted as ordinates in Fig. 56.1.

In this form of graphical presentation several facts stand out at once:

1. There is an orderly progression from one graph to the next.

2. The most probable number of successes increases progressively; that is, the greater the number of trials the greater the most probable number of successes.

3. The probability of this most probable number decreases progressively; that is, the greater the number of trials the less the chance of coming out with the most probable result.

4. An increasing number of different results have probabilities comparable to that of the most probable one. This can be expressed quite simply by saying: the greater the number of trials, the greater the spread of the chart. In other words, the probability of missing the most probable result by more than a stated amount increases constantly as the number of trials is increased.

This last point is worthy of some further discussion.

Consider, for example, the chance of missing the most probable result by more than five units. If only five trials are made, it is impossible to do so and the probability asked for is zero. If ten trials are made, the probability of missing the most probable result by more than five units, though quite small, is a finite value. It is the sum of the last two entries in Table 55.2, which is 0.0003. In the case of fifty trials the chance of missing the most probable result by more than

---

[6] Numbers such as this are inconceivable. I suggest, as an entertaining exercise of the imagination which is worth while just once, the computation of the dimensions of a container which would hold 3^{50} beads. Having done this, if *just one* were black and the rest all white, and if the bunch were thoroughly mixed, the chance of drawing the black one would be the fraction in question. "Too small to matter," you say: yet the chance of getting the one you *did* get was no greater!

five is[7] 0.13. Moreover, this probability can be made as large as we please by taking the number of trials large enough. Thus, for 100 trials it is 0.29, for 1000 trials 0.74, and for 1,000,000 trials about 0.99.

Although these figures are based upon missing the most probable result by *five* units, the same qualitative facts apply to missing it by any preassigned number of units.

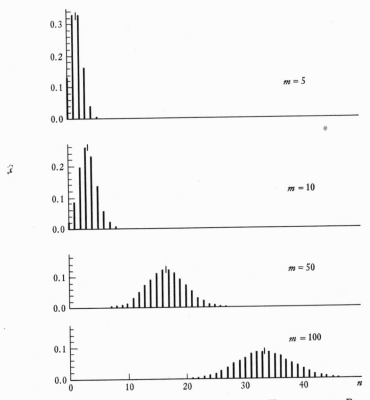

Fig. 56.1   The Probability of n Successes in m Trials if the Probability of Success in a Single Trial is $1/3$.

Theorem 56.1.[8] *In an infinity of trials the probability approaches certainty that the observed result will differ from the most probable result by more than any preassigned number, no matter how large.*

---

[7] This figure is obtained as follows: In Table 55.3 the most probable value of n is 16 or 17. To miss the average of these by more than 5 would require that n be less than 11.5 or more than 21.5. Adding the entries for $n \leq 11$ and $n \geq 22$ gives 0.13.

A method of deriving such figures for large values of m, without separately computing and summing a vast number of terms, will be explained in § 113.

[8] In what follows, this will be referred to as the first half of Bernoulli's Theorem.

It is this spreading out of the diagram which is responsible for the decreasing probability of the most probable result. As the number of ordinates of comparable length increases, the magnitude of each must necessarily be decreased.

Put in still another form this statement becomes: The probability of missing the most probable result by more than five is the sum of all the ordinates which lie *outside* a band width of five on each side of the highest ordinate. Since this sum increases progressively as the number of trials is increased, the sum of all the ordinates *within* the band must correspondingly decrease.

5. The most probable number of successes is always approximately one-third the number of trials.

This is illustrated in the figure by a short vertical line drawn near the top of the curve at that value of n which corresponds to $m/3$. In the case of five trials $m/3$ is $\frac{5}{3}$ and lies between 1 and 2. These are the two most probable results. In the case of ten trials $m/3$ is $\frac{10}{3}$ and lies between 3 and 4. The most probable number of successes is 3. For fifty trials the line comes at $\frac{50}{3}$ and it was found that 16 and 17 were each equally likely. For 100 the line comes at $\frac{100}{3}$ and 33 is the most probable number of successes.

This suggests the rule that, if p is the probability of success in a single trial, the most probable number in m trials is mp if this is an integer, or one of the adjacent integers if it is not. Although it is not always safe to generalize particular cases in this fashion, in the present instance the inference is correct, as will be shown in § 59.

Figure 56.1 is interesting from another point of view. Since the ordinates which represent the probabilities occur at unit intervals while intermediate values of n have no significance, it is possible to erect a rectangle of unit width upon each ordinate, thus producing a set of rectangles the areas of which are equal to the probabilities of the values of n upon which they stand.

When so treated the diagram takes the form shown in Fig. 56.2, in which the graphs corresponding to five trials and ten trials are drawn exactly as explained. The other graphs differ from these only in the fact that the vertical sides of the rectangles, which contribute nothing to the interpretation of the graphs, are omitted, leaving only a broken line. This broken line has two unique properties. One is the property from which it was derived—that the area under each step is the probability of the corresponding value of n. The other property comes from the fact that the set of values of n is complete; it is that the area under the entire broken curve is unity.

A curve constructed in this fashion is called a *distribution curve* for the variable n. Clearly, the area under such a curve and between the vertical lines bounding the interval (n_1, n_2) is the probability that n lies within that interval.[9]

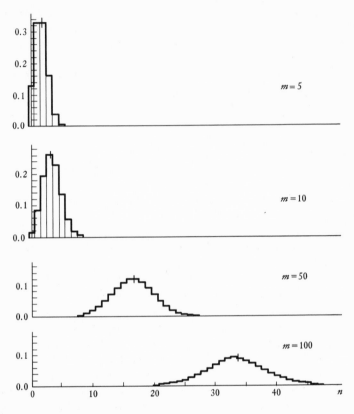

FIG. 56.2　AN ALTERNATIVE FORM OF FIG. 56.1.

57. Bernoulli's Theorem

The fact that the most probable number of successes in Figs. 56.1 and 56.2 is just about ⅓ the number of trials suggests replotting the curves with n/m instead of n as abscissa. This leads to a distribution curve for the proportion of successes, or as we shall more óften call it, a "percentage distribution curve." But in order that the two unique properties of such curves, to which reference was made in § 56, may be conserved, the *areas* of the rectangles must be kept constant no matter

---

[9] For reasons explained in § 10, such curves are also often referred to as *density curves.*

what happens to the *ordinates*. Naturally, since the curve for $m = 100$, say, will be condensed more laterally than the curve for $m = 10$, it must also be stretched more vertically, with the result that the curves will be differently related than before.

The reconstructed family is shown in Fig. 57.1 for $m = 50, 100,$ and 1000.[10] Again there is a marked progressive tendency among the

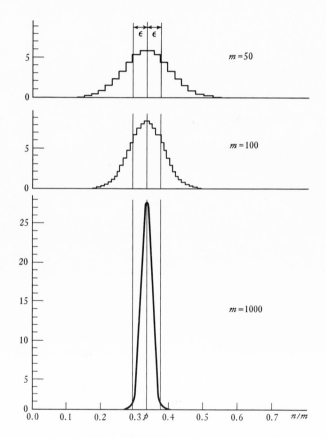

FIG. 57.1   AN ALTERNATIVE FORM OF FIG. 56.1.

curves, but the laws of progression are no longer the same as before. They may now be stated as:

1. The most probable proportion of successes remains approximately the same as m increases.

---

[10] For $m = 1000$ the steps are so small that they cannot be shown.

2. This most probable proportion is always as near to p as it can be, considering the fact that n must always be an integer.

3. The height of the rectangle which represents this most probable proportion *increases* as the number of trials increases.

4. The spread of the percentage distribution curve *decreases* as the number of trials is increased. That is, although the chance of missing the most probable value of n by more than a preassigned *amount* gets greater and greater as the number of trials increases—a fact to which attention was called in the last section—the chance of missing it by a given *percentage* decreases continually.

It is easy to see that the chance of n/m differing from $\frac{1}{3}$ by less than a preassigned amount ϵ is represented in Fig. 57.1 by the area bounded laterally by a pair of vertical lines[11] ϵ units to each side of $\frac{1}{3}$. In the figure ϵ is taken as 0.04. With only 50 trials, more than half the area lies outside these limits. That is, the proportion of successes is more likely to lie outside the limits 0.293 and 0.373 than inside them. In the case of 100 trials, the area outside the boundary is considerably reduced, and the proportion of successes is more likely to lie between the prescribed limits than not. In the case of 1000 trials, almost the entire area lies between these limits: there is very little probability that in so extensive an experiment the proportion of successes would differ from $\frac{1}{3}$ by as much as 0.04. By increasing m still further, a point would eventually be reached where the chance of the proportion of successes lying outside the prescribed range would be smaller than any arbitrarily fixed quantity. In other words, as m approaches infinity the chance of n/m lying outside the limits $p - \epsilon$, $p + \epsilon$ approaches zero, and the chance that it lies within these limits approaches certainty.

This tendency has been illustrated by the use of $\epsilon = 0.04$ and $p = \frac{1}{3}$, but the conclusion would be the same no matter what values were chosen. If, for example, ϵ were taken as 0.000001, the chance of n/m lying within $p - \epsilon$, $p + \epsilon$ would be extremely small for a hundred trials or even a thousand trials; but it would get larger and larger as the number of trials was increased until, with some very large number of trials, say a million million, it would be almost certainty. This fact can be expressed in the form of a theorem as follows:

THEOREM 57.1.   BERNOULLI'S THEOREM.   *If the chance of an event occurring upon a single trial is p, and if a number of independent trials are made, the probability that the ratio of the number of successes to the number*

---

[11] Of course those "steps" which lie partly within this band and partly outside it are either to be entirely included, or else entirely excluded, according as their midpoints lie within or without the band.

of trials differs from p by less than ε, where ε is any preassigned quantity, however small, can be made as near certainty as may be desired by taking the number of trials sufficiently large.

Sometimes the content of a theorem such as this is made clearer by throwing mathematical discretion to the winds and stating it in the form of everyday language. The present appears to be a case of this sort, and therefore we restate the theorem as follows:

If the probability of an event is p, and if an infinity of trials are made, the proportion of successes is sure to be p.

This, of course, is exactly the statement which, in § 54, we said was untrue; yet it is as certainly "true" in one sense as it is *not* "true" in another. It fails to stand the test of mathematical rigor, as the argument of § 54 shows. But our everyday life is not conducted on such rigorous requirements as to "truth." You say, "Are you sure he is coming tomorrow?" and receive the answer, "Yes." Both you and your informant understand what you mean: the event is contingent upon his not dying, for example, and perhaps on many other unforeseen circumstances. It is, in fact, not sure at all; it is merely very probable: so probably that the residual doubt is not worth expression. Our statement is in the same class.

By painstaking experiment with a penny we can learn the extent of the bias in favor of tails, in the sense that the chance of serious error is negligible. Or we can accumulate vital statistics and learn the chance of a man, about whose state of health we have no special information, dying at forty, with quite enough assurance for the purposes of a life insurance company. But we should not be unaware of the logical status of what we are doing. We are putting to practical use an approximate method of measuring probability, to which we have been led by Bernoulli's Theorem. We are not laying the logical foundations for the Theory of Probability.

58. Résumé

It has seemed impossible to discuss Bernoulli's Theorem without travelling rather far afield at times, and as these excursions have removed emphasis somewhat from the facts upon which it should rest, it is probably desirable to put those facts together in a compact form. As they divide into two sets, one concerned with the *number* of times an event occurs, the other with the *proportion* which that number bears to the number of trials, they will be listed in parallel columns.

Facts about the Number of Successes	*Facts about the Proportion of Successes*
(1) In m independent trials under the same essential conditions, the number of times an event occurs, n, may take any value from 0 to m.	(1) In m independent trials under the same essential conditions, the proportion of times an event occurs, n/m, may take any value from 0 to 1.
(2) There is a "most probable" number of successes. (There may be two.)	(2) There is a "most probable" proportion of successes. (There may be two.)
(3) This most probable number is pm when pm is an integer; otherwise it is one (or both) of the adjacent integers.	(3) This most probable proportion is either p, or the integral multiple of $1/m$ next smaller than p, or the one next larger than p, or both.
(4) The chance of the number of successes differing from the most probable number by less than a fixed amount, *no matter how large*, approaches *zero* as the number of trials is indefinitely increased.	(4) The chance of the proportion of successes differing from the most probable proportion by less than a fixed amount, *no matter how small*, approaches *unity* as the number of trials is indefinitely increased.
Loosely: In an infinity of trials the difference between the actual number of successes and the most probable number will be infinite.	Loosely: In an infinity of trials the difference between the actual proportion of successes and the most probable proportion will be zero.

59. Mathematical Justification

So far this discussion has been based on common-sense inferences rather than proofs and has avoided formal mathematics entirely. That defect must now be corrected.

Item (1) of the above list does not require proof. To justify items (2) and (3), note that, by (42.1),

$$P_m(n) = C_n^m p^n (1 - p)^{m-n}.$$

Hence the ratio of two consecutive terms is

$$\frac{P_m(n)}{P_m(n-1)} = \frac{m-n+1}{n}\frac{p}{1-p} = \frac{1 - \dfrac{n}{m} + \dfrac{1}{m}}{\dfrac{n}{m}}\frac{p}{1-p}.$$

Now, reducing the numerator of the last number (by cancelling $1/m$) makes this member too small. Hence

$$\frac{P_m(n)}{P_m(n-1)} > \frac{1 - \dfrac{n}{m}}{1-p} \cdot \frac{p}{\dfrac{n}{m}}. \tag{59.1}$$

Similarly, reducing the denominator by inserting $-1/m$ makes the last member too large. Hence

$$\frac{P_m(n)}{P_m(n-1)} < \frac{1 - \dfrac{n-1}{m}}{1-p} \cdot \frac{p}{\dfrac{n-1}{m}}. \tag{59.2}$$

To establish our theorem we need only notice that, if $n \leqq pm$, both factors on the right of (59.1) are 1 or greater, and therefore $P_m(n) > P_m(n-1)$. In like manner, if $n-1 \geqq pm$, (59.2) gives $P_m(n) < P_m(n-1)$.

These results, interpreted graphically, say that each ordinate of Fig. 56.1 is bigger than the preceding one *up to the stroke at mp* (and including the ordinate at mp if there is one); and similarly that *beyond mp* every ordinate is smaller than the preceding one. Hence the first ordinate past the stroke is bigger than all that follow, and the last one before the stroke is bigger than all that precede. Either one of these is larger than the other, in which case it is a maximum; or else they are equal, in which case they constitute a pair of maxima.

This argument applies to Fig. 57.1 as well as to Fig. 56.1 since they are identical except for scale. Hence the proof covers items (2) and (3) in both columns of the résumé.

60. Stirling's Formula

To justify item (4) it is necessary to estimate the value of $C_n^m P^n (1-p)^{m-n}$ when both m and n are large. Under these circumstances, however, C_n^m contains three factorials of large numbers. An approximation to $n!$ when n is large is therefore required. It is not necessary that the difference between the true and approximate values be small; it is the percentage error which is of consequence. For example, a formula which gave a result 3.0415×10^{64} for $50!$ would be a good approximation, for it differs from $50!$ only in the fifth place. But the actual magnitude of the difference is nevertheless a very large number. It is of the order of magnitude of 10^{60}.

In § 21, $m!$ was defined as

$$m! = \int_0^\infty x^m\, e^{-x}\, dx, \tag{21.2}$$

which, interpreted graphically, means that it is the area between the curve

$$y = x^m\, e^{-x}$$

and the x-axis. The first indication as to how to proceed is supplied by the curves for various values of m. It appears from Fig. 60.1a that when m is large the principal contribution to the integral is made by that part of the curve in the neighborhood of the maximum ordinate. The "tails" in the neighborhood of $x = 0$ and $x = \infty$ dwindle away very rapidly and contribute relatively little to the integral. This suggests that the area will be roughly proportional to the maximum ordinate, at least in the sense that the ratio of the two will not vary with m in such an extreme fashion as does the factorial itself.

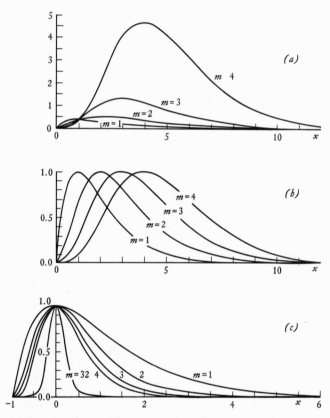

FIG. 60.1   ILLUSTRATING THE CHANGES OF VARIABLE BY MEANS OF WHICH STIRLING'S FORMULA IS OBTAINED.

It is a simple matter to determine this maximum ordinate Y. It turns out to occur at the point $x = m$ and to have the value

$$Y = m^m e^{-m}. \tag{60.1}$$

Dividing (21.2) by Y and denoting the ratio by $f(m)$, we have

$$f(m) = \frac{m!}{Y} = \int_0^\infty (x/m)^m e^{m-x} \, dx. \tag{60.2}$$

This integral can also be interpreted as the area under a curve: the particular curve, of course, being identical with the corresponding one in Fig. 60.1a, except that the vertical scale has been reduced in such a way as to make the maximum ordinate unity. Such a set of curves is shown in Fig. 60.1b.

Next, these curves are shifted so that the maximum ordinate of each lies on the y-axis (which means that x is replaced by a new variable $x' = x - m$), and then contracted in the direction of the x-axis in the ratio 1 to m (by replacing x' by a new variable $x'' = x'/m$). The result of the two substitutions (after dropping the primes, which are of no further service) is

$$f(m) = m \int_{-1}^{\infty} [(x + 1) e^{-x}]^m \, dx. \tag{60.3}$$

The curves corresponding to this integral are shown in Fig. 60.1c.

The next step in our process is an ingenious one, only to be justified by the fact that it works. We replace x by a new variable u, defined by the equation

$$(x + 1) e^{-x} = e^{-u^2}; \tag{60.4}$$

or what amounts to the same thing,

$$x - \log(x + 1) = u^2.$$

Then we have

$$dx = 2u \, du + 2\frac{u}{x} \, du$$

and (60.3) breaks up into the sum of the two terms

$$f(m) = m \int e^{-mu^2} 2u \, du + 2m \int e^{-mu^2} \frac{u}{x} \, du.$$

For the moment we disregard the question of the limits of integration.

The first term in this expression integrates immediately into $-e^{-mu^2}$; that is, into $-[(x + 1)e^{-x}]^m$. As this quantity vanishes for both $x = -1$ and $x = \infty$, the first term is zero. This leaves us finally with the integral

$$f(m) = 2m \int e^{-mu^2} \frac{u}{x} \, du. \tag{60.5}$$

There is now nothing to do but to evaluate this integral directly. But to do this it is necessary to obtain an expression for x in terms of u, and as (60.4) is transcendental the solution can be obtained only as a series. It is found that[12]

$$\frac{u}{x} = \sqrt{2}(\tfrac{1}{2} + \tfrac{1}{12}u^2 + \tfrac{1}{432}u^4 - \tfrac{139}{194400}u^6 + \ldots)$$

$$- (\tfrac{1}{3}u + \tfrac{4}{135}u^3 - \tfrac{4}{2835}u^5 + \ldots). \tag{60.6}$$

---

[12] The region of convergence of this series is $|u| < \sqrt{2\pi}$. We do not here attempt to justify its use with infinite limits.

As for the limits of integration, (60.4) shows that $u^2 = \infty$ both when $x = -1$ and when $x = \infty$. Hence u is $\pm \infty$ at both limits of integration. If the limits were equal the integral would vanish,[13] which is clearly wrong. Hence one limit must be $+\infty$ and the other $-\infty$. Assigning them incorrectly would merely change the sign of the integral; and as the value of the factorial must be positive that error would be detected at once. By trial it is found that $+\infty$ should be the upper limit and $-\infty$ the lower one. Then, substituting (60.6) into (60.5) and integrating term by term, we get

$$f(m) = \sqrt{2\pi m}\left(1 + \frac{1}{12m} + \frac{1}{288m^2} - \frac{139}{51840m^3} + \cdots\right)$$

and therefore, by (60.1) and (60.2),

$$m! = \sqrt{2\pi m}\; m^m\, e^{-m}\left(1 + \frac{1}{12m} + \frac{1}{288m^2} - \frac{139}{51840m^3} + \cdots\right). \qquad (60.7)$$

This is known as Stirling's formula.[14] As an illustration of its use we may compute 100! which turns out to be

$$100! = \sqrt{200\pi}\,100^{100}\,e^{-100}(1 + \tfrac{1}{1200} + \tfrac{1}{2880000} - \cdots)$$

$$= 9.3326215^{157}.$$

This is identical with the result given in Appendix I.

Table 60.1 contains several additional factorials, together with their Stirling Approximations to one and four terms. It will be noticed that for values of m greater than 10 even the simpler formula gives quite acceptable accuracy. For smaller values it would not generally be used because of the ease with which the factorials themselves may be found.

TABLE 60.1

COMPARISON OF THE FACTORIAL WITH ITS STIRLING APPROXIMATIONS

m	True Value	One Term		Four Terms	
	$m!$	$m!$	% Error	$m!$	% Error
1	1	0.922137	8	0.999711	0.03
2	2	1.919005	4	1.999986	0.0007
5	120	118.0192	2	120.0000	
10	3,628,800	3,598,696	0.8	3,628,800	
100	9.3326215^{157}	9.324847^{157}	0.08	9.3326215^{157}	

[13] If u is defined by the principal branch of the logarithm, u^2 is positive for every value of x on the path of x-integration. Therefore, the u does not leave the real axis. As there are no singularities of u/x on the real axis, other than at $u = \pm \infty$, a path from infinity to a finite point and back could only return via the same branch of the function.

[14] The name is usually applied to the first term only:

$$m! = \sqrt{2\pi m}\; m^m\, e^{-m}.$$

61. Another Approximate Formula

We still need an approximation to $(1 + x/m)^m$ when m is very large. Obviously, when m is very large $1 + x/m$ is only slightly different from 1. Hence any *moderate* power would also be but slightly different from 1; but the m'th power is not moderate, so the difference may be considerable.

A very satisfactory approximation can be derived by using the Taylor Series for $\log (1 + x/m)$, which gives

$$\log \left(1 + \frac{x}{m}\right)^m = m \log \left(1 + \frac{x}{m}\right) = x - \frac{x^2}{2m} + \frac{x^3}{3m^2} - \cdots$$

Hence

$$\left(1 + \frac{x}{m}\right)^m = e^{x - (x^2/2m) + (x^3/3m^2) - \cdots}, \tag{61.1}$$

which obviously approaches the limit e^x as m approaches infinity. Unity would therefore have been a very poor approximation. The fact that

$$\lim_{m \doteq \infty} \left(1 + \frac{x}{m}\right)^m = e^x \tag{61.2}$$

is the first important result of this section.

If we like, we may think of e^x as a *first approximation* to the value of $(1 + x/m)^m$, when m is large, and of (61.1) as a higher approximation. For many purposes, however, it is more convenient to segregate the factor $e^{-(x^2/2m) + (x^3/3m^2) - (x^4/4m^3) + \cdots}$ and expand it in a series of decreasing powers of m. This gives

$$\left(1 + \frac{x}{m}\right)^m = e^x \left[1 - \frac{x^2}{2} \frac{1}{m} + \left(\frac{x^4}{4} + \frac{2x^3}{3}\right) \frac{1}{2!m^2}\right.$$

$$- \left(\frac{x^6}{8} + x^5 + \frac{3x^4}{2}\right) \frac{1}{3!m^3}$$

$$\left. + \left(\frac{x^8}{16} + x^7 + \frac{13x^6}{3} + \frac{24x^5}{5}\right) \frac{1}{4!m^4} + \cdots\right]. \tag{61.3}$$

This is the second important result of the section.

62. Justification of the First Half of Bernoulli's Theorem

We are now ready to justify Bernoulli's Theorem by proving two things:

(*a*) *That the maximum ordinate in Fig. 56.1 approaches zero as m becomes infinite.* As there are only a finite number of ordinates between $mp - \epsilon$ and $mp + \epsilon$, and as none exceeds the maximum, the sum of all of them must therefore approach zero, which proves half the theorem.

(b) *That in Fig. 57.1 the ordinates (except those in the immediate vicinity of $n/m = p$) decrease so rapidly as m becomes infinite that the sum of all those which lie outside the band ultimately vanishes.* This will prove the other half. The proof of (a) will be given in this section; the proof of (b) in the next.

We begin with the formula

$$P_m(n) = C_n^m p^n (1 - p)^{m-n}, \tag{42.1}$$

and replace all factorials by their Stirling approximations. The result is

$$P_m(n) = \sqrt{\frac{m}{2\pi n(m-n)}} \left(\frac{m(1-p)}{m-n}\right)^m \left(\frac{(m-n)p}{n(1-p)}\right)^n. \tag{62.1}$$

Now let n, for the present argument, represent the most probable n. Then it does not differ from mp by more than a unit. Hence

$$mp - 1 < n < mp + 1,$$

$$m(1 - p) - 1 < m - n < m(1 - p) + 1.$$

Replacing the denominators by *smaller* numbers, and the numerators by *larger* ones, increases the right-hand side of (62.1), so that

$$P_m(n) < \sqrt{\frac{m}{2\pi(mp - 1)[m(1 - p) - 1]}}$$

$$\times \left(\frac{m(1-p)}{m(1-p)-1}\right)^m \left(\frac{m(1-p)+1}{mp-1}\frac{p}{1-p}\right)^n. \tag{62.2}$$

From this point on we consider the three terms separately.

The first factor approaches zero with increasing m, for m occurs twice in the denominator and only once in the numerator. Hence if the other factors do not become infinite our proposition is proved.

The second factor, however, is of the form

$$\frac{1}{\left(1 - \dfrac{1}{m(1 - p)}\right)^m},$$

which reduces to (61.3) if $-1/(1 - p)$ is called x. Hence this factor approaches $e^{-1/(1-p)}$ and does not become infinite.

The third factor can be rearranged so as to take the form

$$\left(\frac{1 + \dfrac{1}{m(1 - p)}}{1 - \dfrac{1}{mp}}\right)^n.$$

As the quantity within the parentheses is obviously greater than unity, the factor will be increased if n is replaced by something larger than itself, as, for example, by $mp + 1$. Thus the third factor is less than

$$\frac{\left(1 + \dfrac{1}{m(1 - p)}\right)^{mp} \left(1 + \dfrac{1}{m(1 - p)}\right)}{\left(1 - \dfrac{1}{mp}\right)^{mp} \left(1 - \dfrac{1}{mp}\right)}.$$

As m approaches infinity the last part of this product reduces to unity; whereas by identifying mp with the m of (61.3), and $p/(1 - p)$ with x, the numerator of the first part becomes $e^{p/(1-p)}$; and by a similar process the denominator becomes e^{-1}. Combining these limiting values it is found that the product of the last two factors approaches 1, and hence (62.1) must vanish. This proves the theorem.

63. Justification of the Second Half of Bernoulli's Theorem

The second half of Bernoulli's Theorem is easier to justify. Consider an n equal to $m\eta$, where η is not exactly p. Then (62.1) becomes

$$P_m(n) = \sqrt{\frac{1}{2\pi\eta(1 - \eta)m}} z^m,$$

where

$$z = \left(\frac{1 - p}{1 - \eta}\right)^{1 - \eta} \left(\frac{p}{\eta}\right)^{\eta}.$$

Our first step is to show that z is always less than unity. This is best done by finding the maximum value of z: or rather of $\log z$, for that is easier. We have

$$\log z = (1 - \eta)[\log(1 - p) - \log(1 - \eta)] + \eta(\log p - \log \eta),$$

whence

$$\frac{d \log z}{d\eta} = \log\left(\frac{1 - \eta}{1 - p} \cdot \frac{p}{\eta}\right). \tag{63.1}$$

If this is to be zero—as it must be for a maximum value—η must equal p; and when $\eta = p$, $\log z = 0$. Hence the maximum value of z is unity. For any other value of η, $z < 1$.

Finally suppose η is set equal to that one of the quantities $p - \epsilon$, $p + \epsilon$ which happens to give the larger ordinate in Fig. 57.1. Then we know from § 59 that outside the range bounded by these quantities *all* the ordinates are smaller than the one at η: that is, they are all less than $\sqrt{1/2\pi\eta(1-\eta)}mz^m$. As there are less than m of them, their sum cannot exceed $\sqrt{1/2\pi\eta(1-\eta)}\sqrt{m}z^m$. But since $z < 1$, the quantity $\sqrt{m}z^m$ can be made as small as we like by taking m sufficiently large. In other words, the sum of all ordinates outside the range $p + \epsilon > n/m > p - \epsilon$ can be made as small as we wish by taking m large enough.

This proves the second half of our theorem. Later on, in § 112, we shall find that, if we were to draw another set of distribution curves for the variable $n/\sqrt{m}$, the separate curves of this set would be almost indistinguishable for large values of m. This is already suggested by the fact that the first factor of (62.2), which is the one that vanishes with increasing m, does so because of the occurrence of $\sqrt{m}$ in the denominator. Hence the maximum ordinates of the curves of Fig. 56.2 would all be about equal if they were multiplied by the square roots of their respective values of m. But if the areas of the individual rectangles are not to be altered, such a change can be brought about only by condensing the curves laterally in the same ratio, which is equivalent to plotting the distribution functions for $n/\sqrt{m}$.

Although the present is not a suitable place to prove it, this is actually the case: As the number of trials is increased the peaks of Fig. 56.2 become lower and lower in proportion to the reciprocals of the square roots of the number of trials, while the curves spread out laterally to greater and greater extents, in proportion to the square roots of m.

64. Regarding the Experimental Determination of Probability

Bernoulli's Theorem states, in substance, that the chance of an important difference existing between p, the probability of success in a single trial, and n/m, the proportion of successes in m independent trials, may be made as small as we please by making the number of trials sufficiently large. If this is true, it is quite obvious that n/m may be accepted for most practical purposes as an approximation to the probability p; and this affords a new way of measuring probability.

In the case of a perfectly good penny, for instance, we could either form the set of equally likely, mutually exclusive events "heads, tails," and conclude at once that the chance of obtaining a head is $\frac{1}{2}$; or we could toss the penny repeatedly and accept the proportion of successes as the value of the probability. In this specific case, of course, the former method would be by far the better, for it gives an *exact* answer, whereas the latter gives only an approximation at best. But there are many questions to which this exact method cannot be applied because no suitable set of alternative events is known. Take, for example, the chance of a man of twenty dying between the ages of fifty and fifty-five: it is quite out of the question to set up a complete set of equally likely events in this case. But it *is* possible to pick out a large number of men of age twenty, and by waiting thirty-five years determine what proportion actually die between the specified ages. If we are willing to admit that the chance of one of them dying is not influenced by what occurs to any of the others, we may accept this proportion as a satisfactory experimental determination of the desired probability.

Bernoulli's Theorem, therefore, furnishes an acceptable makeshift when the direct a priori determination of probability is not feasible.

But we must observe caution in accepting this argument. Bernoulli's Theorem has been proved by the use of (42.1), and (42.1) was derived by the use of (37.1), which has not so far been satisfactorily proved. Hence either Bernoulli's Theorem itself, or the Multiplication Theorem (37.1), must be independently established. As the generalization of the Multiplication Theorem is not difficult so long as the events A and B are independent [as they are supposed to be in deriving (42.1)], we shall give this generalized proof, thereby justifying Bernoulli's Theorem. Afterward we shall find it possible to make use of Bernoulli's Theorem itself to extend the Multiplication Theorem to cases where the events are not independent and their probabilities are not directly obtainable.

65. The Multiplication Theorem

Consider any two *independent* events A and B, the probabilities of which are p and p', respectively. The probability that both occur is some function of p and p', say

$$P(A, B) = f(p, p'). \qquad (65.1)$$

The problem is, to determine the form of the function f.

If the event A happens to include two mutually exclusive parts A_1 and A_2 (as "getting an even number with a die" includes the mutually exclusive events "getting a two" and "getting an even number greater than two") the compound event A, B will also include two mutually exclusive parts A_1, B and A_2, B. By Convention II, therefore,

$$P(A, B) = P(A_1, B) + P(A_2, B), \qquad (65.2)$$

and

$$p = p_1 + p_2;$$

p_1 and p_2 being, of course, the probabilities of A_1 and A_2, respectively. Since (65.1) is supposed to apply to *any* two independent events, (65.2) becomes

$$f(p_1 + p_2, p') = f(p_1, p') + f(p_2, p').$$

This is a functional equation and can be satisfied only if $f(p, p')$ is of the form $p \cdot F(p')$.[15]

Next we notice that there is no logical distinction between the occurrence of "both A and B" and the occurrence of "both B and A": the two expressions are entirely synonymous so long as the events are independent. Hence

$$f(p, p') = f(p', p),$$

or

$$pF(p') = p'F(p).$$

This requires, however, that

$$\frac{F(p)}{p} = \frac{F(p)'}{p'}.$$

Since the left-hand side of this equation does not contain p', it cannot vary as the value of p' changes. But if the left-hand side does not vary with p', the right-hand side cannot. That is, $F(p')/p'$ must be a constant. Call it C. Then $F(p') = Cp'$, and

$$f(p, p') = pF(p') = Cpp'.$$

Finally, if the event A is certain to happen—that is, if $p = 1$—the occurrence of "both A and B" is synonymous with the occurrence of "B," wherefore $f(1, p') = Cp' = p'$. This establishes the fact that $C = 1$ and completes the proof so far as independent events are concerned.

Having thus justified the Multiplication Theorem for all independent events, we are sure that Bernoulli's Theorem is true in general.

We now turn our attention to a pair of events A and B which are *not* independent, and suppose that we make a large number M of *independent trials* of the compound event A, B. Let there be, among these M trials, N_A in which A occurs and N_{AB} in which both A and B occur. Then the ratio $N_A|M$ is not likely to differ much from $P(A)$. Similarly $N_{AB}|N_A$, which is the "proportion of times both A and B occur if A does," is not likely to differ much from $P(B|A)$. Finally $N_{AB}|M$ is not likely to differ much from $P(A, B)$. In fact, the chance of the difference exceeding any preassigned amount can be made as small as we please in all three cases by taking M large enough.

---

[15] We can readily show this if we assume the possibility of expanding $f(p, p')$ in the Taylor Series. We write

$$f(p, p') = a + bp + cp' + dp^2 + \cdots,$$ (65.3)

whence

$$f(p_1, p') + f(p_2, p') = 2a + bp_1 + bp_2 + 2cp' + dp_1^2 + dp_2^2 + \cdots,$$ (65.4)

and

$$f(p_1 + p_2, p') = a + bp_1 + bp_2 + cp' + dp_1^2 + 2dp_1p_2 + dp_2^2 + \cdots.$$ (65.5)

If we equate coefficients of like powers in these equations we get $a = 0$ from the constant terms, $c = 0$ from the terms in p', $d = 0$ from the terms in p_1p_2, and so on. A little consideration shows, in fact, that every term of (65.3) which contains a power of p higher than the first will give rise in (65.5) to cross-products between p_1 and p_2, whereas in (65.4) no such cross-products can exist. It follows, therefore, that (65.3) must reduce to the form

$$p(b + ep' + gp'^2 + \cdots) = pF(p').$$

Let us denote the differences that actually occur by δ, δ', and δ'', respectively, so that

$$P(A) = \frac{N_A}{M} - \delta,$$

$$P(B|A) = \frac{N_{AB}}{N_A} - \delta',$$

$$P(A, B) = \frac{N_{AB}}{M} - \delta''.$$

Then we find by direct computation that

$$P(A)P(B|A) - P(A, B) = -\delta\frac{N_{AB}}{N_A} - \delta'\frac{N_A}{M} + \delta\delta' + \delta''.$$

Now suppose $P(A)P(B|A) - P(A, B) = d$, where $d \neq 0$. Then one or the other of the δ's must exceed $d/4$, for otherwise the right-hand side could not equal d. There is therefore unit probability that either the one or the other will exceed $d/4$, no matter how large M may be. But this is absurd; for Bernoulli's Theorem tells us that this probability (for each one individually, and therefore also for "one or the other") is zero. Hence we must conclude that

$$P(A)P(B|A) = P(A, B).$$

66. Chance Paths

So far this chapter has dealt with certain limiting characteristics which sequences of repeated trials have in common. Little has been said about the life history of an individual sequence. The methods of § 50 enable us to discuss such life histories in detail. The results are interesting—perhaps in some cases unexpected—and throw further light on the inner meaning of Bernoulli's Theorem. They are the subject of this and the following section.

Consider, then, *any* sequence of repeated independent trials for which the probability of success in a single trial is p. Its life history may be represented by a path such as that of Fig. 50.1, in which each success is signaled by a step upward, and each failure by a downward step. Specifically, such a path portrays the history of $m = 2x$ such trials, of which $n = x + y$ succeeded and $m - n = x - y$ failed; moreover these successes and failures followed one another in precisely the same order as the upward and downward steps of the path. Clearly, the probability that precisely this succession of successes and failures would occur in a sequence of independent trials is $p^n(1 - p)^{m-n}$. Expressed in terms of x and y this is $p^{x+y}(1 - p)^{x-y}$ and depends only on the coordinates of C, not on the path by which it was reached.

Hence,

THEOREM 66.1. *If an experiment consists of a sequence of independent trials under like conditions, and if the successes and failures are plotted as a chance path, as in Fig. 50.1, all paths from* $(0, 0)$ *to* $(2x, 2y)$ *are equally likely, and the probability that an experiment will follow a preassigned one of them is* $p^{x+y}(1 - p)^{x-y}$, *where* p *is the probability of success on a single trial.*

This theorem enables us to translate results about paths, such as those arrived at in § 50, directly into probability statements about repeated independent trials. Thus from (50.2) we get:

EXAMPLE 66.1.—*The probability that a repeated experiment will generate some path from* $(0, 0)$ *to* $(2x, 2y)$ *is*

$$P_x(y, \cdot) = C_{x+y}^{2x} p^{x+y}(1 - p)^{x-y}. \qquad (66.1)$$

To verify this we need only note that there are $\nu_x(y, \cdot)$ distinct paths between these points; the "events" (i.e., sequences of successes and failures) to which they correspond are mutually exclusive and (by Theorem 66.1) equally likely. Hence the probability that some one of these events will occur is

$$P_x(y, \cdot) = \nu_x(y, \cdot) p^{x+y}(1 - p)^{x-y},$$

which, by (50.2), becomes (66.1).

Only the form of this result is new. Indeed, when x and y are replaced by m and n it becomes just the familiar $C_n^m p^n (1 - p)^{m-n}$. This is as it should be, since "generating a path from $(0, 0)$ to $(2x, 2y)$" is synonymous with "having n successes in m trials." The next result is new:

EXAMPLE 66.2.—*The probability that the number of successes will always exceed the number of failures throughout* $m = 2x$ *trials, with the final plurality* $2y$, *is*

$$P_x(y, 0) = \frac{|y|}{x} C_{x+y}^{2x} p^{x+y}(1 - p)^{x-y}. \qquad (66.2)$$

This can be found by using (50.3).

Reasoning in a similar way from (50.6) we conclude that

EXAMPLE 66.3.—*The probability that during* $m = 2x$ *trials there will be exactly* r *occasions when the number of successes equals the number of failures, and that the final plurality will be* $2y$, *is*

$$P_x(y, r) = 2^r \frac{r + 2|y|}{2x - r} C_{x+|y|}^{2x-r} p^{x+y}(1 - p)^{x-y}. \qquad (66.3)$$

In fact, so long as the terminal point C is specified, the general relation

$$P = \nu \cdot p^{x+y}(1 - p)^{x-y} \qquad (66.4)$$

will hold, where ν is the number of paths possessing a specified property and P is the probability of the corresponding experiment. For example, ν might be the number of paths with just three changes of direction and P the probability that there would be just two runs of successes and two runs of failures in the first m trials.

If C is not specified, however, (66.4) no longer holds, since paths going to different terminal points are not equally likely. In such cases it is necessary to make use of (50.1). The following example will illustrate this point.

EXAMPLE 66.4.—*The probability that during $m = 2x$ trials the number of successes will always exceed the number of failures is*

$$P_x(> 0, 0) = \sum_{y=1}^{m} \nu_x(y, 0)p^{x+y}(1 - p)^{x-y} = \sum_{y=1}^{m} \frac{y}{x} C_{x+y}^{2x} p^{x+y}(1 - p)^{x-y}.$$

In this example the final plurality, and therefore the terminal point C, is not specified. It is therefore equivalent to asking for the number of possible paths from 0 which nowhere touch the axis, but without specifying the final value of y. By the principle of alternative compound probabilities, this can be found by summing (66.2) over all admissible values of y; in this case all are positive values since there must be more successes than failures.

In the special case of $p = \frac{1}{2}$, that is, when successes and failures are equally likely, it is not necessary to resort to the principle of alternative compound probabilities; for in this case $p^{x+y}(1 - p)^{x-y}$ reduces to 2^{-2x} and no longer depends on y. Hence *all paths are equally likely regardless of the point in which they terminate*, and (66.4) is valid for any class of paths. In this special case the probability required in Example 66.4 could be found by using (50.12). It is[16]

$$P_x(> 0, 0) = \tfrac{1}{2}\nu_x(\cdot, 0)2^{-2x} = 2^{-2x-1}C_x^{2x}, \qquad p = \tfrac{1}{2}. \qquad (66.5)$$

Such paths, in which forward and backward steps are equally likely, are called "random paths." The next three sections will be devoted to considering some of their special properties. Before leaving the more general topic, however, one further point should be noted.

If the path of Fig. 50.1 were reversed from right to left, it would represent an experiment which began with an accumulated number of successes (we shall call it a "handicap") $2y$. Clearly, the number of reversed paths is equal to the number of forward paths and:

(*a*) Successes and failures are interchanged, so that on the reversed path there are $x - y$ and $x + y$ of these, respectively.

---

[16] In (50.12), $\nu_x(\cdot, 0)$ includes paths both above and below the axis. Only those above the axis represent an excess of successes. Hence the factor $\frac{1}{2}$.

(*b*) The reversed paths touch or intersect the axis at precisely the same intermediate points *and also at the terminal point* 0. Thus for the reverse path *r* is greater by 1 than for the forward path (since a terminal intersection is counted but an initial one is not) *unless y* = 0, and the same as the forward path *when y* = 0.[17]

It follows that

THEOREM 66.2. *The probability that successes and failures are equal after* $m = 2x$ *trials, if there was an initial handicap* $2y$, *is*

$$P_x(0, r|y) = v_x(y, r - 1)p^{x-y}(1 - p)^{x+y}$$

$$= \left(\frac{1 - p}{p}\right)^{2y} P_x(y, r - 1), \quad y \neq 0, \qquad (66.6)$$

and

$$P_x(0, r|0) = P_x(0, r), \qquad (66.7)$$

where the notation $|y$ *means "starting with a handicap* $2y$."

In a sense, all the probabilities discussed in this section have been conditional probabilities—specifically, all except (66.6) have implied that the sequence of trials began without any accumulated history of past successes or failures. Thus the $P_x(y, \cdot)$ in (66.1) could have been written $P_x(y, \cdot|0)$ if we had wished to emphasize the fact that the experiment began without a handicap.

67. Random Paths

The classical example of an experiment where success and failure are equally likely is tossing a coin. We shall adopt this analogy, calling an experiment a game, heads successes and tails failures. If there is already an accumulated score when the game begins, it will be referred to as a handicap. Then, using $p = \frac{1}{2}$ and equations (66.2) and (66.3), Theorem 66.2 becomes

THEOREM 67.1. *If a game starts with a handicap* $2y$ *and successes and failures are equally likely, the chance that it is even for precisely the r'th time after* $2x$ *throws is*

$$P_x(0, r|y) = P_x(y, r - 1) = 2^{r-2x-1} \frac{r + 2|y| - 1}{2x - r + 1} C_{x+|y|}^{2x-r+1},$$

$$y \neq 0, \qquad p = \tfrac{1}{2}, \quad (67.1)$$

---

[17] This exception would be avoided if the notation were changed to include the starting point in counting *r*, but then the number of "returns to zero" would be $r - 1$ instead of r, which seems equally undesirable.

if $y \neq 0$, *and*

$$P_x(0, r|0) \equiv P_x(0, r) = 2^{r-2x}\frac{r}{2x - r}C_x^{2x-r}, \qquad p = \tfrac{1}{2}. \qquad (67.2)$$

We may also show that

EXAMPLE 67.1.—*If a game starts with a handicap 2y and successes and failures are equally likely, the chance that it is even after m = 2x throws (although not necessarily for the first time) is precisely the same as the chance of building up a margin 2y from an even start. It is therefore*

$$P_x(0, \cdot|y) = P_x(y, \cdot) = 2^{-2x}C_{x+y}^{2x}, \qquad p = \tfrac{1}{2}. \qquad (67.3)$$

To verify this, it is only necessary to note the 1–1 correspondence between the set of all paths from $(0, 0)$ to $(2x, 2y)$ and the set from $(0, 2y)$ to $(2x, 0)$.

We now return to the discussion of games that start without a handicap.

An important conclusion can be drawn from (67.2). It is, that no matter how large r may be, the probability that the path will return to the axis r times (i.e., that the players will be even r times) approaches 1 as x becomes large enough. This follows from the fact that $\Sigma_x P_x(0, r) = 1$ for any value of r. The proof is outlined in Problems (69.13), (69.14) and (69.15) and is left as an exercise for the reader.[18]

A graph of $P_x(0, r)$, computed from (67.2), is given in Fig. 67.1 for several values of r. It is interesting to note how the largest r is the least probable at small values of x; but rises, crossing the curves for smaller r, and eventually becomes more probable than any smaller r.[19]

EXAMPLE 67.2.—*The probability that player A, who counts heads, will always be ahead of player B throughout the first 2x throws is $2^{-2x-1}C_x^{2x}$.*

This is just the situation which led to (66.5), which is the answer.

EXAMPLE 67.3.—*The chance that there will be r occasions when A and B are even, regardless of who is finally ahead or by how much, is*

$$P_x(\cdot, r) = 2^{r-2x}C_x^{2x-r}, \qquad p = \tfrac{1}{2}. \qquad (67.4)$$

This is verified by using (50.12).

Suppose, now, that we call the path between two points on the axis in Fig. 50.1 a "loop" if it does not touch the axis in between. The end of the loop which begins at $(0, 0)$ is then the point of first return.

---

[18] See also §§ 105 and 106, Chapter VIII.

[19] In fact, for large values of x, $P_x(0, r) \doteq r/\sqrt{4\pi x^3}$. See Problem 69.17.

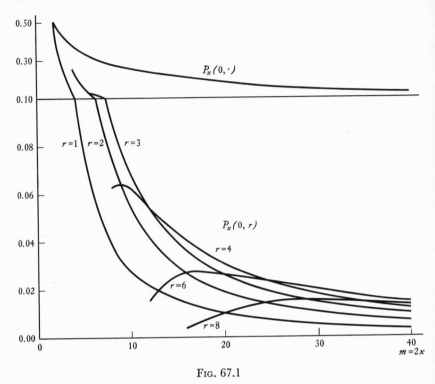

FIG. 67.1

FIG. 67.1

EXAMPLE 67.4.—*The probability that the loop beginning at* $(0, 0)$ *is of length* L (*i.e., that the point of first return is at* $L = 2x$) *is*

$$P(L) = 2^{1-L}\frac{1}{L-1}C_{L/2}^{L-1}, \qquad p = \tfrac{1}{2}. \qquad (67.5)$$

The probability that the path returns for the first time at $L = 2x$ is just $P_x(0, 1)$ and is given by (67.2). When x is replaced by L, this becomes (67.5). Clearly the curve for $P_x(0, 1)$ in Fig. 67.1 is a graphical representation of $P(L)$, since the scale on the horizontal axis is numbered to correspond with $2x = L$.

EXAMPLE 67.5.—*The chance that the players are even on the m'th throw, regardless of how many times they may have been even before is, by* (66.1),

$$P_x(0, \cdot) = 2^{-2x}C_x^{2x}, \qquad p = \tfrac{1}{2}. \qquad (67.6)$$

This result is especially interesting. One might reason carelessly that they are just as likely to be even on one throw as another. However, the plot of (67.6), which is also included in Fig. 67.1, shows that this is certainly not the case. It is not even true in the sense that, as x gets larger, $P_x(0, \cdot)$ settles down to some constant value. For it is easily shown[20] that, for even moderately large values of x,

$$P_x(0, \cdot) \doteq \frac{1}{\sqrt{\pi x}},$$

and hence decreases constantly with increasing x.

The reason can be found from an examination of Fig. 50.1. It arises from the fact that the players were known to be even at the start of the game, and this exerts an influence over the probabilities at any subsequent stage. Specifically, for any x, y must lie between OM and OM'. Thus, as the number of throws increases, y may range over a larger number of values, and the probability of it taking the specific value 0 is reduced. As the game progresses this influence of the starting point varies, but it is never lost.

We must remember, however, that probability measures the importance of our state of ignorance, as we said in Chapter I. Only confusion can result—and all too frequently has resulted—from applying a result that was valid for one situation to another in which the known facts were significantly different. Thus, (67.6) is true only for the person who knows nothing of importance about the progress of the game.[21] For another person, who knows that the players were even on the $2X$'th throw, the correct probability would be $P_{x-X}(0, \cdot)$.[22] For one of the players who knows, for example, that on the $2X$'th throw he is lagging by $2y$ points, it is $P_{x-X}(0, \cdot | y)$, and is given by (67.3).

68. First and Subsequent Passage

An even more illuminating question is the following:

EXAMPLE 68.1.—*What is the chance that the lead changes from one player to the other exactly r times in $m = 2x$ trials?*

The answer is not (67.4) since paths may touch the axis and recede without actually crossing it; such events are included in the count of returns in (67.4) but must be excluded here. Neither is it the same as the probability of $2r$ returns, although this might be suspected from the fact that, whenever a path returns to the axis, it may proceed either by crossing it or by receding from it. Instead, it is

$$P_x(\cdot, r_\downarrow) = 2^{2-2x} C_{x+r_\downarrow}^{2x-1}, \qquad p = \tfrac{1}{2}, \tag{68.1}$$

where, to distinguish between the number of returns, r, and the number of crossings, we use the symbol $r_\downarrow$ for the latter.

---

[20] See Problem 69.12.

[21] Or, if we like, it is true of a game not yet commenced.

[22] That is, in terms of Fig. 50.1, his knowledge would establish a new set of limit lines intersecting at throw X.

The derivation of (68.1), although not especially difficult, is tedious and will not be given here.[23]   Instead we turn our attention to Fig. 68.1, where the distribution (68.1) is plotted for $m = 500$ and $m = 1000$.

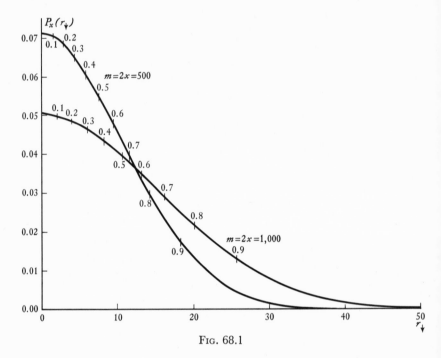

FIG. 68.1

These curves have $r_{\downarrow}$ for abscissa and $P(\cdot, r_{\downarrow})$ as the ordinate. They therefore represent the probability density for $r_{\downarrow}$, and the area under any portion of them is the probability of $r_{\downarrow}$ lying within the corresponding range.[24]   To assist in estimating such areas, vertical markers have been placed on each curve to indicate increments of area equal to 0.1.   Thus, in the case of $m = 1000$ the area to the left of $r_{\downarrow} = 2$ (and hence the probability that the lead will not change more than twice) is 0.1; the area to the right of 25.6 (and hence the chance that it will change at least 26 times) is likewise 0.1.   Both of these statements may be somewhat unexpected.

---

[23] The interested reader will find it outlined in connection with Problem 69.20.

[24] This statement is not precisely true. It would be if the smooth curve were replaced by a set of steps, after the fashion of Fig. 56.2. Also, since fractional values of $r_{\downarrow}$ have no meaning, only full steps should be included in any interval. The reader will readily understand that the smooth curve is a reasonable approximation, and that the markers play the role of scale marks on any measuring instrument. Where fractional values of $r_{\downarrow}$ are mentioned, as in the text, it must also be understood that the probability for one adjacent integer would be somewhat greater and for the other somewhat less.

The fact that the curves peak at $r_1 = 0$ may be even more surprising: no matter how long the game may continue, the most probable number of changes of lead is zero.

But, as is easily seen, the probability of the lead changing more than (say) twenty times is much greater in 1000 trials than in 500, and would be even greater for still longer games. This, at least, should cause no surprise.

69. First Return from a Chance State

We add one further example which may assist in understanding the chance phenomena associated with repeated random trials.

EXAMPLE 69.1.—*Suppose an observer enters a room in which a game is in progress and is told that 2x throws have already occurred, but nothing more. What is the probability that the players will be even for the first time on the 2ξ'th throw thereafter?*

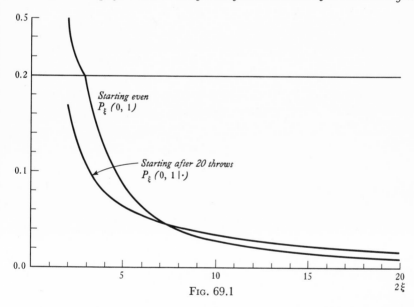

FIG. 69.1

If we knew that the accumulated score at the time of entry was $2y$, the required probability would be $P_\xi(0, 1|y)$ and would be given by Theorem 67.1. Since we do not know y, we must consider all the possibilities and use alternate compound probabilities. Doing so, we arrive at

$$P_\xi(0, 1|\cdot) = \sum_{y=-x}^{x} P_x(y, \cdot) P_\xi(0, 1|y)$$

or the desired probability. When the values of $P_x(y, \cdot)$ and $P_\xi(0, 1|y)$

are taken from (67.1), (67.2), and (67.3), this becomes

$$P_\xi(0, 1|\cdot) = \frac{1}{2^{2x+2\xi-1}\xi}\left[\sum_{y=1}^{x} yC_{x+y}^{2x}C_{\xi-y}^{2\xi} + C_x^{2x}C_{\xi-1}^{2\xi-2}\right]. \quad (69.1)$$

It is not difficult to calculate (69.1). As a numerical example we take $x = 10$; that is, 20 throws have already occurred when the observer enters. The probability that the game first becomes even on the 2ξ'th throw thereafter is plotted in Fig. 69.1. For comparison, $P_\xi(0, 1)$—the chance of the same occurrence if the observer enters at the start of the game—is reproduced from Fig. 67.1.

The curves reveal clearly how the chance of a short wait (six throws or less) is reduced, and the chance of a long one (seven throws or more) increased by the indefinite state of the game after 20 throws, as compared to what they would be from an even start.

Problems

1. The fact that (63.1) is zero at $\eta = p$ has been said to make this the value of η for which z is a maximum. It might just as well be a minimum, however. How do we know which it is?

2. The idea of a distribution curve is obviously a general one. Construct a distribution curve showing the probability of runs of heads of various lengths in tossing a penny.

3. Construct a distribution function for the sums of the numbers appearing when two dice are tossed.

4. Construct a distribution function for the numbers appearing when only one die is tossed.

5. If A and B are tossing a penny, what is the chance that A is never behind B during the first $2x$ throws, although they may or may not be even from time to time? Compute the answer for 20 throws.

6. If A and B are tossing a penny, what is the chance that A is always ahead of B during 20 throws?

7. What is the chance that A is never behind B on $2x$ throws, but on the last throw they are even? Compute for 20 throws.
[See Fig. 50.3.]

8. What is the chance that in $2x$ throws A and B are even exactly r times, including the last throw, but the lead never changes?
[At any point of return the path is equally likely to cross or not. See also Problem 50.21.]

9. Under the conditions of Problem 8, what is the chance that B is never in the lead?

10. Using the results of Problems 7 and 8 show that

$$\sum_{r=0}^{x} rC_x^{2x-r}/(2x - r) = C_x^{2x}/(x + 1).$$

11. Show that the probability that the lead changes *for the first time* on the $2x$'th play is

$$\tfrac{1}{2}P_x(0, 0_{\downarrow}) = 2^{-2x}\frac{1}{x + 1}C_x^{2x}.$$

[One half the paths that touch $(2x, 0)$ will cross. Compare this result with Problem 7.]

12. Using Stirling's formula, show that $C_2^x \doteq 2^{2x}/\sqrt{\pi x}$ when x is large.

13. Using Stirling's Theorem and (67.4), show that, in a sequence of repeated trials with $p = \tfrac{1}{2}$,

$$\lim_{x \to \infty} P_x(\cdot, r) = \frac{1}{\sqrt{\pi x}}. \qquad (69.2)$$

[The fraction $(2x - r)^{2x-r}/x^x(x - r)^{x-r}$ which will appear may be put in the form

$$2^{2x-r}\left(1 - \frac{r}{2x}\right)^x\left(1 + \frac{r}{2(x - r)}\right)^{x-r}.$$

Then use (61.2).]

14. Show that (69.2) implies that

$$\lim_{x \to \infty} P_x(\cdot, \geqq r) = 1. \qquad (69.3)$$

[Find the complementary probability.]

15. Show that (69.3) implies that

$$\sum_{x=r}^{\infty} P_x(0, r) = 1. \qquad (69.4)$$

Method: (69.3) requires that $1 - P_X(\cdot, \geqq r) < \epsilon$, if X is large enough. But if the number of returns at X is r or more, the r'th return must have occurred at some smaller x. Hence

$$1 - \sum_{x=r}^{X} P_x(0, r) < \epsilon.$$

16. Using (69.4), prove that

$$\sum_{j=0}^{\infty} 2^{-2j}C_j^{2j+r}/(2j + r) = 2^r/r.$$

[Direct algebraic verification is also possible but rather complicated.]

17. Using (69.2) and comparing (67.2) with (67.4), show that

$$\lim_{x \to \infty} P_x(0, r) = \frac{1}{\sqrt{4\pi x^3}}.$$

18. A and B will toss a penny $2x$ times. How much is A's chance of being ahead throughout the game increased if he wins the first throw? [See Fig. 50.3. The answer to Problem 11 will be useful.]

19. Show that in $2x$ trials the probability that the game is even r times, the lead changes $r_\downarrow$ of these times, and the final score is $2y$, is

$$P_x(y, r, r_\downarrow) = 2^{-r} C^r_{r_\downarrow} P_x(y, r)$$

$$= 2^{-2x} \frac{r + 2|y|}{2x - r} C^{2|x-r}_{x+|y|} C^r_{r_\downarrow}, \qquad y \neq 0;$$

$$P_x(0, r, r_\downarrow) = 2^{1-r} C^{r-1}_{r_\downarrow} P_x(0, r)$$

$$= 2^{1-2x} \frac{r}{2x - r} C^{2x-r}_x C^{r}_{r_\downarrow}{}^{-1}, \qquad y = 0. \qquad (69.5)$$

20. Derive (68.1).

Outline. Consider a path that returns ρ times, where $\rho \geq r$. At any point of return it is equally likely to cross or not to cross; hence the probability that it crosses at just $r_\downarrow$ points, $P(r_\downarrow|\rho)$, can be found. Next, note that if the final point is on the axis it cannot be a crossing; hence $y = 0$ and $y \neq 0$ must be considered separately. The formal solution is

$$P_x(\cdot, r_\downarrow) = \sum_{\rho=r}^{x} [P_x(0,\rho)P(r_\downarrow|\rho - 1) + P_x(y \neq 0,\rho)P(r_\downarrow|\rho)]$$

with

$$P(r_\downarrow|\rho) = 2^{-\rho} C^\rho_{r_\downarrow}$$

and

$$P_x(y \neq 0,\rho) = P_x(\cdot,\rho) - P_x(0,\rho).$$

To sum the series, use (26.2).

This result may also be obtained by summing $P_x(y, r, r_\downarrow)$, Problem 19, with respect to both y and r.

21. Show that, if $p \neq \frac{1}{2}$, the probability of a loop of length L is

$$P(L) = \frac{2}{L - 1} C^{L-1}_{L/2}[p(1 - p)]^{L/2}. \qquad (69.6)$$

22. Equation (67.5) was derived for $p = \frac{1}{2}$. In that case, either player has the same chance of getting the lead on the first throw *and* of maintaining it for any given length of time. It is not obvious that this is true if $p \neq \frac{1}{2}$. Demonstrate that it is; that is, that $P(A)P(L|A) = P(B)P(L|B) = \frac{1}{2}P(L)$.

[Use the reflection principle and count the forward and backward steps.]

23. Find the chance $P(L|A)$ that the game will be even for the first time at $2x = L$ if A, who holds the advantage with a probability $p > \frac{1}{2}$, gains the first throw. If B gains it.

24. Show that if $p = \frac{1}{2}$,

$$P_x(0, r_\downarrow) = 2^{1-2x} \frac{r_\downarrow + 1}{x} C^{2x}_{x-r_\downarrow-1}.$$

25. What is the equivalent result when $p \neq \frac{1}{2}$?

Answers to Problems

5. $\frac{1}{2}P_x\left(\cdot, 0_\downarrow\right) = 2^{-2x}C_x^{2x}$; 46, 189/262, 144 > $\frac{1}{6}$. **6.** $\frac{1}{2}P_{10}\left(\cdot, 0\right) = 46$, 189/524, 288.

7. $\frac{1}{2}P_x(0, 0_\downarrow) = 2P_{x+1}(0, 1) = 2^{-2x}C_x^{2x}/(x+1)$; 4,199/262,144 $\doteq \frac{1}{60}$.

8. $2^{1-r}P_x(0, r) = 2^{1-2x}{}_rC_x^{2x-r}/(2x-r)$. **9.** $2^{-2x}{}_rC_x^{2x-r}/(2x-r)$.

18. Doubled; from $\frac{1}{2}P_x(\cdot, 0)$ to $P_x(\cdot, 0)$. This can be obtained by noting that all paths from $(1, 1)$ through $(2x - 1, 1)$, except those that terminate at $(2x, 0)$, are admissible if they do not cross the line joining these points. This gives $\frac{1}{2}P_{x-1}(\cdot, 0_\downarrow) - \frac{1}{4}P_{x-1}(0, 0_\downarrow)$, which equals $P_x(\cdot, 0)$. **23.** $P(L|A) = P(L)/2p$; $P(L|B) = P(L)/(2 - 2p)$; where $P(L)$ has the value (69.6.)
25. $2[(r + 1)/x]C_{x}^{2x}{}_{r-1}]p(1 - p)]^x$.

Chapter VI

Probability and Experiment; Bayes' Theorem

70. The "Life on Mars" Paradox

All logical processes are hedged about by a maze of fine distinctions which cannot be included in a formal symbolic expression without making it so complicated as utterly to destroy its usefulness. These distinctions are often important: so important in fact that all sorts of errors may arise through failing to remember them. In particular, in the Theory of Probability there have arisen a host of paradoxes, almost all of which are due to using *formal* logical processes in places where, upon recalling their origin, we should not expect them to apply.

One of these is a very famous one, once used by the adherents of "cogent reason" to confound the "insufficient reasonists." They raise the question, What is the probability of life on Mars? Obviously, they say, we are quite ignorant. Therefore, on the basis of insufficient reason we must admit the answer to be $\frac{1}{2}$.

But the problem can also be attacked this way: What is the probability of no horses on Mars? to which the answer is $\frac{1}{2}$. What is the probability of no cows on Mars? to which the answer is again $\frac{1}{2}$. This process can obviously be extended to every class of animal or vegetable. Say there are n such classes. Then the probability that all these things are true: that is, that there are no horses, no cows, and no other form of life, is $1/2^n$, which is certainly very small. The complementary probability, that there is at least *one* kind of life, is therefore near certainty. Insufficient reason has therefore given two answers, one at least of which must be wrong.

Such is the argument as presented. It has a certain superficial validity, but this rapidly disappears when the underlying assumptions are examined.

The first half implies that we know nothing that is pertinent to

144

answering the question—that is, that our state of knowledge is one of complete equivocation.

The second half, by contrast, implies (*a*) that we know "life" to be a complex of forms, and (*b*) that the occurrence of one of these forms is quite independent of the occurrence of the rest.

These are quite different postulates, and the fact that neither is a realistic approximation to what we know and do not know makes it just a bit harder to think straight about the problem. We cannot object to that: the proposer of the question was entitled to postulate what he would, and we must for the time being divest ourselves of any additional knowledge we possess.

Let us then put ourselves into a very unusual universe, potentially inhabited by many kinds of life, but where, for some obscure reason, they are so entirely independent that the existence (or nonexistence) of one carries no implication as to the likelihood of others existing. What then is the force of the second half of the argument? Merely to demonstrate that this information *is* pertinent. To one who lived in this hypothetical universe where all the untruths upon which the second argument is based were true, the answer *would* be nearly one; just as surely as it is also the answer to the question, What is the chance of at least one head appearing when a handful of pennies is tossed in the air? To a six-weeks old baby, as innocent as the individual to whom the *first* half applies, $\frac{1}{2}$ would be the correct answer. To the Omniscient the answer is either unity or zero. To *us* it is neither—just because we are in neither state of knowledge.

What it *is* to us I cannot say, because I am unable to measure the importance of all the various biological and astronomical facts which are known to bear upon the question; but I am not therefore justified in disregarding *all* I know, as is done in the first half, and calling the probability $\frac{1}{2}$, nor in disregarding *part* of what I know, as is done in the second half, and saying that it is very near certainty.

But if probability measures the importance of our state of ignorance it must change its value whenever we add new knowledge.[1] And so it does. I pick up a coin in the dark, toss it, and ask the probability that heads is uppermost. Without a doubt the answer is $\frac{1}{2}$. This is true even if the coin is biased—even if it is alike on both sides in fact—so long as I have no knowledge which makes tails relatively more (or less) probable than heads.

---

[1] It is sometimes objected that this makes probability a "personal" matter. So it does in a sense, but only in the sense in which it *is* a personal matter—that is, in the sense in which it depends upon individual differences of knowledge. No one would say the probability of heads appearing when a penny is tossed was $\frac{1}{2}$ to one who *knew*. It is only that for all of *us* when none of us knows a thing about it.

But suppose I now take the coin to the light and see that it really has heads on both sides. Immediately the chance of heads being uppermost if I toss it again (or that heads were uppermost when I tossed it before) changes to 1.

This knowledge that the penny is alike on both sides is of such an absolute character that it enables us to state at once the change that it makes in our probability. We might, however, have gotten *inferential* knowledge instead. For example, we might have tossed it a large number of times—100, say—and found that heads appeared every time. Such a thing might happen either with a perfectly good penny or with one that has heads on both sides. It might also happen with a penny which was badly biased. We cannot say with assurance just which situation exists, but certainly the probability that heads will appear upon the next toss is no longer $\frac{1}{2}$. *It has been changed by experiment.*

This then leads us to the question of *how much* it has changed, to which Bayes' Theorem is the clue.

71. Bayes' Theorem

We return to the consideration of the equations (37.1) and (38.2). Obviously, (37.1) can be written either in the form

$$P(A, B) = P(A) P(B|A) \qquad (37.1)$$

or in the form

$$P(A, B) = P(B) P(A|B), \qquad (71.1)$$

provided that, when any questions of order of occurrence are involved, the same order shall apply to both.[2]

---

[2] In the footnote in § 37 we called attention to the fact that the chance that "a man is shot and dies," taken in that temporal, or causative, sequence, is *not* the same as the chance that "he dies and is shot," taken in that order. Suppose we call being shot the "event *A*," and dying "event *B*." Then the *first* order is *A*, *B*, the other *B*, *A*, and their respective probabilities may be denoted by $P(A, B)$ and $P(B, A)$. To the first of these corresponds the pair of equations (37.1) and (71.1); and to the second an exactly similar set which we may write in the form

$$P(B, A) = P(B) P(A|B), \qquad (71.2)$$

$$P(B, A) = P(A) P(B|A). \qquad (71.3)$$

Obviously the right-hand members of these equations are symbolically equivalent to (37.1) and (71.1). But the equivalence stops with the symbolism. For $P(B)$ in (71.1) means "the probability that a man dies," and the $P(A|B)$ means "the probability that a dying man *has been* shot"; while in (71.2), although the $P(B)$ means just what it did before, the $P(A|B)$ means "the probability that, having died, he *will be* shot."

Equations (71.2) and (71.3) would lead to precisely the same equations (71.4) and (71.5); but although formally the same they would refer to the sequence "*B* followed by *A*." Hence they are valid when consistently read in either way; but when the order is of any consequence, as it sometimes is, care must be taken not to mix the two.

We recall that our symbols have the following meanings:

$P(A, B)$.   The probability that A happened[3] and was followed by B.

$P(A)$.   It is not known whether or not B happened. $P(A)$ is the probability that A did.

$P(B)$.   It is not known whether or not A happened. $P(B)$ is the probability that B did.

$P(B|A)$. A is known to have happened. This is the probability that it was followed by B.

$P(A|B)$. B is known to have happened. This is the probability that it was preceded by A.

Since $P(A, B)$ means exactly the same thing in both equations, we may equate their right-hand members and solve for $P(A|B)$. The result is

$$P(A|B) = \frac{P(A)\,P(B|A)}{P(B)}. \qquad (71.4)$$

In other words, given the probability $P(A)$ which would apply if we knew nothing of whether B occurred or not, and the probability $P(B)$ which would apply if we were in total ignorance regarding A, and also the probability of B following A: given these, and knowing that B *did* occur, we can find the probability that it was preceded by A. *Equation* (71.4) *is therefore the clue to interpreting the influence of new knowledge upon probability. It is called Bayes' Theorem.*

Before illustrating its use, we may note that it is usually given in the somewhat different form to which it reduces when (38.2) is substituted for the denominator of (71.4). This form is

$$P(A|B) = \frac{P(A)\,P(B|A)}{\Sigma_A\,P(A)\,P(B|A)}, \qquad (71.5)$$

or, in words:

THEOREM 71.1. BAYES' THEOREM. *If the event B never occurs unless preceded by one or the other of a set of events A, the unconditional probabilities of which are $P(A)$, and if B is known to have happened, the chance that it was preceded by a particular one of the events A is a fraction whose numerator is the product of the unconditional probability of this particular A by the conditional probability of it being followed by B, while the denominator is a sum of exactly similar terms, one for each of the events A.*

---

[3] The use of the past tense is of no significance: present or future would do just exactly as well, except that grammatically the perfect and past are slightly less clumsy than future perfect and future, while the "tenseless present" of logic destroys the sharpness of the distinction between past and present.

72. Some Instructive Illustrations; Bertrand's "Box Paradox"

The following example is an illustration in which there can be no question as to our possession of the information necessary to the use of Bayes' Theorem:

EXAMPLE 72.1.—*Three boxes have in them two coins each. In one box both are gold, in one both are silver, in the other they are mixed. Outside they are of identical appearance. A man chooses a box and takes out a coin, which proves to be gold. What is the chance that the other coin in the box is also gold?*

It is not necessary to use Bayes' Theorem to solve this problem. The solution can be obtained directly as follows: Each of the three gold coins is as likely to be the one chosen as the other. Two are in the box in which "the other is also gold." Hence the answer is $\frac{2}{3}$. It will, however, serve our purpose best to get the answer in two rather roundabout ways corresponding to (71.4) and (71.5), respectively, and for this purpose we choose the following symbolism: A_{gg} for the event "chooses the box with two gold coins," and A_{gs}, A_{ss} for the alternative possibilities; B_g for "picks up a gold coin," and B_s for the opposite.

If we know nothing about what has transpired,[4] the probability of A_{gg} is $P(A_{gg}) = \frac{1}{3}$. Likewise, if we know nothing about what has transpired, one coin is as likely to have been picked up as another. Hence $P(B_g) = \frac{1}{2}$. But *if* the box with two gold coins was chosen, the chance of picking out a gold coin was $P(B_g|A_{gg}) = 1$. Hence after a gold coin has been seen, the probability of the box having two gold coins is given by (71.4) as

$$P(A_{gg}|B_g) = \frac{P(A_{gg})\,P(B_g|A_{gg})}{P(B_g)} = \frac{\frac{1}{3}\cdot 1}{\frac{1}{2}} = \frac{2}{3}.$$

We can phrase the solution another way: $P(A_{ss})$ and $P(A_{gs})$ are also $\frac{1}{3}$, and the conditional probabilities of getting a gold coin *if* the chosen box is *ss* or *gs*, respectively, are $P(B_g|A_{gg}) = \frac{1}{2}$ and $P(B_g|A_{ss}) = 0$. Hence (71.5) becomes:

$$P(A_{gg}|B_g) = \frac{P(A_{gg})\,P(B_g|A_{gg})}{P(A_{gg})\,P(B_g|A_{gg})+P(A_{ss})\,P(B_g|A_{ss})+P(A_{gs})\,P(B_g|A_{gs})}$$

$$= \frac{\frac{1}{3}\cdot 1}{\frac{1}{3}\cdot 1 + \frac{1}{3}\cdot\frac{1}{2} + \frac{1}{3}\cdot 0} = \frac{2}{3}. \tag{72.1}$$

As was to be expected, the answer is the same in all three cases.

---

4 Or, "will transpire."

73. Some Instructive Illustrations; Another Urn Problem

The following is another problem to which Bayes' Theorem affords the solution:

EXAMPLE 73.1.—*A box has had ten balls put in it by the following procedure: An auxiliary container holds equal numbers of black and white balls, thoroughly mixed. A blindfolded man picks one out and places it in the box. He is watched by an assistant who immediately puts another ball* of the same kind *in the auxiliary container and stirs up the contents. Then a second ball is drawn, and so on. After the box has received its ten balls, an experiment is performed by drawing balls repeatedly from it, noting the color, and replacing them. Five such attempts show four black balls and one white. What is the most probable contents of the box?*

Before the experiment, the probability of A white and $10 - A$ black balls was obviously

$$P(A) = C_A^{10}(\tfrac{1}{2})^{10}.$$

If A white balls are there, the chance of drawing one white and four black in five attempts (this is the "event B" which is known to have happened) is

$$P(B|A) = C_1^5 A(10 - A)^4/10^5.$$

Hence Bayes' Theorem gives

$$P(A|B) = \frac{C_A^{10}C_1^5 A(10 - A)^4/10^5 2^{10}}{\sum\limits_{A=0}^{10} C_A^{10}C_1^5 A(10 - A)^4/10^5 2^{10}},$$

or, when the common factors C_1^5, 10^5, and 2^{10} are cancelled,

$$P(A|B) = \frac{C_A^{10}A(10 - A)^4}{\sum\limits_{A=0}^{10} C_A^{10}A(10 - A)^4}. \tag{73.1}$$

Actual computation gives the results shown in Table 73.1. The required probabilities are in the last column. Obviously 4 white and 6 black is the most likely composition.

Before the experiment was performed the most probable composition was half and half. The preponderance of black results has altered the probabilities in the direction which common sense would dictate; but the experimental proportion ($\tfrac{1}{5}$ white) is still only one-third as likely as the most probable proportion ($\tfrac{2}{5}$), and only half as likely as the half-and-half division.

Suppose, instead of five trials, fifty were made, giving 10 white and 40 black. Common sense tells us the experimental evidence must now

TABLE 73.1

A	C_A^{10}	$A(10 - A)^4$	$C_A^{10}A(10 - A)^4$	$P(A|B)$
0	1	0	0	0.00000
1	10	6561	65,610	0.01837
2	45	8192	368,640	0.10323
3	120	7203	864,360	0.24204
4	210	5184	1,088,640	0.30484
5	252	3125	787,500	0.22051
6	210	1536	322,560	0.09032
7	120	567	68,040	0.01905
8	45	128	5,760	0.00161
9	10	9	90	0.00003
10	1	0	0	0.00000

$$\Sigma = 3,571,200$$

be given more weight than before, but common sense does not tell us *how much more*. Bayes' Theorem does. For now we must change the powers of A and $(10 - A)$ in (73.1) to 10 and 40 instead of 1 and 4. This replaces all the numbers in the third column of Table 73.1 by their *tenth* powers, which quite obviously alters the relative values materially.

TABLE 73.2

$$P(A|B)$$

A	After 50 Tests	After 500 Tests
0	0.00000	0.00000
1	0.01334	0.00000
2	0.55276	0.99999
3	0.40714	0.00001
4	0.02657	0.00000
5	0.00020	
6	0.00000	

The new results are shown in the second column of Table 73.2; also, the third column contains the probabilities after 500 tests have given 400 black and 100 white balls. In the last case the experimental evidence completely outweighs any preconceptions arising from our knowledge of how the box was filled. It is 99.999% *sure* that there are just two white balls.

74. Some Instructive Illustrations; The Bad Penny

Let us consider one more example of the use of Bayes' Theorem—again in connection with a problem of no practical consequence, although it may aid us in gaining an accurate picture of what the theorem is good for.

We suppose, to begin with, that a "penny" is given us, and that we are asked to determine whether it is alike on both sides, or normal. Of course the sensible thing to do would be to look and see; but this is not a sensible problem. Instead we propose to find out by tossing it repeatedly and noting what shows up. At the start, before any experiments have been made, there is a certain probability that it is bad (alike on both sides). We cannot say what this is: we may have been told by someone in whom we have considerable confidence that it *is* bad, and in that case the probability is high. Or we may have been told that it is good, and the probability is low. Whatever it is, let it be denoted by $P_0(b)$, and the complementary probability that the penny is good by $P_0(g)$.

Suppose, now, that n throws are made and all of them result in heads. If the penny has heads on both sides, the chance of this is $P(n|b) = 1$; if it is a good penny the chance of a run of n heads is only $P(n|g) = (\frac{1}{2})^n$. Substituting these values in (71.5) we obtain for the probability, *after* the experiment, that the penny is bad,

$$P(b|n) = \frac{P_0(b) \cdot 1}{P_0(b) \cdot 1 + P_0(g) \cdot (\frac{1}{2})^n},$$

or, if we write $P_0(g)/P_0(b) = k$ for simplicity,

$$P(b|n) = \frac{1}{1 + \dfrac{k}{2^n}}.$$

This result depends upon two things, as it should: upon the degree of our assurance before we experiment, which is implied by k, and upon the number of trials carried out. If there is no reason to suspect the penny—for instance, if it is a coin casually picked up on the street—$P_0(g)$ certainly exceeds $P_0(b)$ and k is large; for there is obviously much greater likelihood of this happening on a good coin than a bad one. Suppose we assume that there is only one chance in a million that it is bad, which makes $k = 1,000,000$. Then after ten heads have appeared without interruption the chance of it being bad is[5] $P(b|10) = \frac{1}{1000}$.

---

[5] These are all round numbers based upon the approximation $2^{10} = 1000$, which is plenty near enough for our purpose here. The true value is 1024.

The new probability, though still small, is very much larger than before the experiment was performed. If the run continues and twenty heads appear, the probability becomes $\frac{1}{2}$: twenty heads, in other words, just counterbalance our preconceived notion that the penny was very probably good. Thirty heads, on the other hand, give a probability $P(b|30) = 0.999$. There is now only one chance in a thousand that the penny is not bad.

Of course we would have obtained different figures if we had taken a different value for the *a priori* probability, and we must not lose sight of the fact that we have no way to check this guess. As exact values the answers are worthless, but they illustrate how rapidly an uninterrupted run of luck may wipe out a strong presumption in one direction and replace it by an equally strong presumption in the other. Had we chosen other *a priori* probabilities, the result would have been much the same: if we had guessed the chance of the penny being bad to be the inconceivably small number 0.000,000,000,001, it would still require only fifty heads in succession to replace this probability by 0.999.

Finally, suppose we were mathematically certain that the penny was good—suppose, in other words, that $P_0(b)$ were zero, not approximately, but absolutely. Then k would be infinite, and so also would $k/2^n$ no matter how great n might be. In this case $P(b|n)$ would be zero for every value of n. This, too, is as it should be, for experimental evidence is trivial beside infallible certainty. How we could ever reach such a state of absolute assurance I do not know; but if we could, no amount of experimentation should be allowed to shake our faith.

75. The Uses to which Bayes' Theorem May Be Put

Many important scientific problems are essentially similar to the one we have just been considering. Almost any instance where a scientific generalization is to be made from a limited amount of data could be cited in illustration: for example, the conclusion that all electrons have like charges. One bit of evidence consists of the fact that a certain number have been isolated and their charges measured, and there is a considerable volume of indirect evidence. But how sure are we of the rule? Not absolutely sure, certainly; for though it is pretty generally believed, it has occasionally been contested.

We would be glad, if we could, to get a measure of our certainty in cases such as this; but there is nothing in the Theory of Probability to aid us except Bayes' Theorem, which we can seldom use for the purpose because, as in the problem of the last section, we cannot measure the unconditional probabilities. Any of the answers which we have obtained would be correct IF k had the values assumed; other answers could easily be obtained IF k were something else; but as long as we do not know what k is, we cannot be certain of any of them.

In situations where the *a priori* probabilities cannot reasonably be estimated, and where we therefore cannot obtain a direct answer by Bayes' Theorem, statisticians apply the concept of "confidence limits" which was introduced in § 13 and which will be discussed in greater detail later.

There are, however, three types of service which Bayes' Theorem can render satisfactorily:

First are the cases in which, although the *a priori* probabilities are not known exactly, we have reason to believe we can estimate them to a fair degree of approximation. An example is given in the section immediately following. To such problems I think it is wise to apply the theorem because, although no *exact* information can be expected from this course, *better* information will be obtained than can be gotten in any other way. It will need judicious interpreting, of course, but that is not an uncommon state of affairs when mathematical reasoning is applied to scientific problems.

Second, the theorem is often of service in dealing with problems to which *qualitative* answers are acceptable. Thus in the case of the bad penny of § 74, we might desire to know how many throws would be required to justify the belief that the penny is bad. To this question the answer "not less than twenty nor more than fifty" can safely be given—not very close limits, to be sure, but at least indicating the order of magnitude. A smaller number of throws would give very little information, because of the inherent probability that the penny is good; and a larger number would not increase our certainty to any material extent.[6]

Finally, Bayes' Theorem can often be applied with absolute rigor in the course of a formal mathematical argument. It is unnecessary to introduce artificial illustrations of its use in this direction, however, as sufficient examples will arise naturally in the course of our further studies.[7]

---

[6] This is true, not only because the result given by Bayes' Theorem is already substantially 1, but also because other alternatives, originally neglected because of their inherent absurdity, become of greater and greater consequence as the run proceeds. Suppose, after a run of 100 heads, a tail were to appear. This is impossible with a bad penny, and the chance of it happening with a good penny is so extremely small that hallucination or substitution would merit serious consideration.

[7] Due to numerous inexact statements which have been made of it, Bayes' Theorem has been the subject of much adverse criticism and some authorities have even gone so far as to reject it entirely. This criticism seems to be dying out, the commonly accepted view being much the same as that stated above: that it is just as sound logically as any other part of the Theory of Probability and may be trusted to give reliable results *when we can get a grip on it.* The trouble is that we so seldom can.

76. Some Instructive Illustrations; An Elementary Problem in Sampling

Consider the following problem in the testing of factory output:

EXAMPLE 76.1.—*A factory produces a certain type of screw as a standard product. The screws are collected at the machine in boxes of 1200 each. Long experience has shown that the proportion of these boxes which contain various percentages of bad screws is substantially as follows:*

% of Bad Screws in the Box	Proportion of Boxes Observed to Contain this Percentage of Bad Screws
0	0.78
1	0.17
2	0.034
3	0.009
4	0.005
5	0.002
6	0.000

Two per cent badness has been adopted as a manufacturing standard; that is, any box which contains 2% or less of bad screws is regarded as satisfactory, the aim of the inspection process being to reject those which are poorer. The normal inspection consists in the examination of 50 screws out of each box. A particular box, produced at a time when there was no special reason to suspect that the machines were not operating properly, showed 6 bad screws under normal inspection. What is the probability that the manufacturing standard had not been maintained in the production of this box?

We know from Bernoulli's Theorem that the *proportions* listed in the second column of this table are probably good approximations to the *probabilities* of the various percentages of badness. They may therefore be used as the values of $P(A)$ in (71.5), the "event A" standing successively for the various possible percentages of bad screws in the box. The conditional probabilities then follow from (45.1), p and q being, respectively, 6 and 44, while m and n are $12A$ and $1200 - 12A$. When these are substituted into (71.5), and obvious common factors are cancelled out, they yield the formula

$$P(A|B) = \frac{P(A)\ C_6^{12A}\ \dfrac{(1200 - 12A)!}{(1200 - 12A - 44)!}}{\sum_A P(A)\ C_6^{12A}\ \dfrac{(1200 - 12A)!}{(1200 - 12A - 44)!}}. \tag{76.1}$$

It is a comparatively simple matter to compute the values of this expression. The outline of the computation is shown in Table 76.1. The second column contains the values of $P(A)$ given in the statement of the example; the third column contains the binomial coefficients taken from Appendix III: the fourth column contains the values of $(1200 - 12A)!/(1200 - 12A - 44)!$.

These were found by the use of Appendix II, in which the logarithms of large factorials are given. When these three columns are multiplied together they give the fifth. The entries in this column are the numerators of (76.1), and the sum of the entire column, 3.611^{139}, is the denominator. Hence the desired probabilities are to be found by dividing every entry by 3.611^{139}. The results are shown in the last column.

TABLE 76.1

A	$P(A)$	C_6^{12A}	$\dfrac{(1200 - 12A)!}{(1200 - 12A - 44)!}$		$P(A\|B)$
0	0.78	0.0000	13.721^{134}	0.000^{139}	0.000
1	0.17	9.2400^2	8.746	0.014	0.004
2	0.034	1.3460^5	5.548	0.254	0.070
3	0.009	1.9478^6	3.503	0.614	0.170
4	0.005	1.2272^7	2.201	1.351	0.374
5	0.002	5.0060^7	1.376	1.378	0.382
6	0.000			$\overline{3.611^{139}}$	0.000

The chance that more than 2% are bad is the sum of the last four entries in this column, and is so large as to render it highly probable that trouble exists.

It is unnecessary to say that if the manufacturing situation postulated in the example really existed, this type of computation would be made once for all for such results as were likely to be met. Therefore it would be necessary only to refer to the tabulated probabilities to learn the significance of any set of results: or, more probably, that number of defective screws would be determined for which there was an even chance of trouble existing, and some routine would be established to assure that the trouble was quickly located and corrected. The exact manufacturing conditions would determine what routine was best.

However, the entire problem is, in a way, idealistic. In the first place, we have tacitly assumed in its statement, and in computing our results, that such proportions of product as 1%, 2%, etc., might be bad, but not 1.5% or other fractional percentages. Obviously, this is not the case: for out of the 1200 screws in a box any multiple of $\frac{1}{12}$% is a possibility; and in a more general type of problem the variable might be capable of taking almost any value. We must therefore interpret 0% as including all cases for which the actual percentage is less than $\frac{1}{2}$%; 1% as including all other cases less than 1.5%, and so. It is a matter of experience that such grouping of data frequently causes so little error that the added cost of more complete computation is not warranted. Hence, on the whole, the computation is probably as good as any practical situation of its kind is likely ever to warrant.

Problems

1. The following has been given as an example of the incorrect use of Bayes' Theorem when applied to Example 72.1. (It deals with the chance of getting unlike coins instead of like ones.)
"There is a $\frac{1}{2}$ chance that the coin first seen shall be gold. When gold has been seen, we know that we have chosen one of the first two boxes, but we do not know which. They are equally likely; hence the chance for a gold coin followed by silver is $\frac{1}{4}$. There is an equal chance for a silver coin followed by gold. Hence the total chance is $\frac{1}{2}$."
What is wrong with this argument?

2. The same author gives the following as a correct solution:
"If a gold coin has been seen, the *a priori* chance for the first or second box is $\frac{1}{2}$, but whereas the first has a chance 1 of showing a gold coin the first time, the second has only a chance $\frac{1}{2}$ of doing so. The probability that the gold coin is in the second box is

$$\frac{\frac{1}{2}\cdot\frac{1}{2}}{\frac{1}{2}\cdot 1 + \frac{1}{2}\cdot\frac{1}{2}} = \frac{1}{3}. \tag{76.2}$$

and there is a similar probability for a silver coin."
This argument is also wrong. Explain why.

3. A box has been filled as in Example 73.1. We are told, and have complete faith in the information, that 50 balls have been drawn and have given 10 white and 40 black. We, however, make an independent test by drawing 5 balls, all of which turn out white. What effect has this upon the probabilities of various proportions of the two colors?

4. If the proportions of Example 73.1 turned out to be half and half, how would the probabilities be affected?

5. In the "bad penny" problem of § 74, suppose the first six throws show a run of five heads followed by a tail. What happens to the probabilities?

6. Suppose instead that 600 throws showed a run of 599 heads followed by a tail. Would the situation be any different?
(More than a simple "yes" or "no" is wanted to this problem. Explain as clearly as you can your reactions to it as a problem in logic.)

Answers to Problems

1. Error is in stating "they are equally likely" after gold is seen.

2. *A priori* chance is $\frac{1}{3}$. Compare (76.2) with (72.1).

3. After the preliminary drawing, $P(A|B)$ is (73.1) with $A(10-A)^4$ replaced by $A^{10}(10-A)^{40}$; our additional information changes this to $A^{15}(10-A)^{40}$.

4. In tables such as 73.1 and 73.2, the most probable A would be 5. If the number of trials is large, the probability of any other A is small.

5. The penny is surely good.

6. Examine unlikely possibilities. Maybe the penny was switched?

Chapter VII

Distribution Functions and Continuous Variables

77. Introductory Remarks

The preceding chapters have dealt primarily with discrete sets of events, although the fact that some experimental results may not be limited to a discrete set of values, and that the appropriate sample space would then be continuous, has been mentioned. The present chapter will be devoted to a closer examination of this subject.

We are confronted with two major questions:

First, the primary method of measuring probability has been set up in terms of the total number of different results that an experiment might produce and the proportion of these that have a specified property. When the experimental result can vary continuously, neither the totality of results nor the portion possessing the specified property can be counted. How can the primary method of measurement be extended to such cases?

Second, in the discrete case a change of variable does not alter the associated probability: if we ask for the probability that the number uppermost when a die is cast is x, the answer is $\frac{1}{6}$ for these values of x: 1, 2, 3, 4, 5, 6, and zero for all others; if we ask for the probability that the *square* of the number is x, the admissible values of x have changed to 1^2, 2^2, 3^2, 4^2, 5^2, 6^2, but the probability of each is still $\frac{1}{6}$. In the continuous case the situation is quite different. How can this be dealt with?

These questions will be taken up in turn in the sections that follow.

78. The Random Choice of a Point on a Line Segment

Consider the following simple experiment:

EXAMPLE 78.1.—*The perimeter of a well-balanced wheel is of unit length and carries a uniform scale, such as the scale of a yardstick. A pointer of negligible thickness*

157

is set up opposite this wheel, and the wheel is spun. When it comes to rest the pointer indicates some number on the scale. What is the chance that it lies in the interval between two numbers a and b?[1]

To start with, suppose this interval is 0.7 to 0.8. This is one of ten equally likely and mutually exclusive segments within which the pointer may possibly rest. Hence the definition applies and the probability is $\frac{1}{10}$.

If the interval is 0.70 to 0.71, there are 100 equally likely divisions and the desired probability is $\frac{1}{100}$.

To take a somewhat more general case, let the length of the interval be $b - a = x$, where x is a rational number (i.e., the quotient of two integers n/m). It is then possible to lay off the perimeter of the wheel into m equal divisions, beginning at a. Just n of these lie in the interval from a to b, and hence the probability of the pointer coming to rest within this interval is just $n/m = x$: that is, it is the length of the interval. *Hence, whenever the length of the interval is a rational number, the probability of coming to rest in it is equal to its length.*

But what if the interval is not representable as the quotient of two integers? It is then impossible to find any method of division which divides both the perimeter of the wheel and the segment exactly, and the basic method of measuring probability breaks down.

Since this difficulty arises only when the number x is irrational, it is natural to go for relief to the branch of mathematics that deals with the nature of irrational numbers. When we do this, we find an even more fundamental difficulty: an irrational number cannot be written in our ordinary number system at all and requires a totally different set of ideas for its definition.[2] We get our first insight into the relation which these irrational numbers bear to the rest of our number system—and at the same time an indication of how to overcome our present difficulty—by considering how we deal with them in practical life.

---

[1] It may avoid certain logical difficulties to regard this interval as containing a but not b. That is, if the pointer rested on a, it would be said to be in the interval; but if it rested on b, to be outside it. The only purpose of such a convention is to arrange matters so that the sum of the intervals from a to b and from b to c is just exactly the interval from a to c. If we made any other convention, we would either include one point twice or omit it altogether.

[2] Some rational numbers cannot be written as "decimal fractions" because the base of our number system is 10. The fraction $\frac{1}{3}$ is of this class, for it leads to the "repeating decimal" 0.333 . . . ; but if the base of our number system were a multiple of 3 this difficulty would disappear. Thus, in the duodecimal system $\frac{1}{3}$ would be 0.4, for 0.4 would then mean $\frac{4}{12}$ instead of $\frac{4}{10}$.

The difficulty with irrational numbers is not so superficial. It is fundamental to the logic of number and persists whatever base may be chosen. It can be shown that all rational numbers can be represented by either "repeating" or "terminating decimals." Irrational numbers, on the other hand, cannot be represented either by terminating decimals, by the quotient of two integers, or by repeating decimals.

Suppose we choose $1/\sqrt{2}$ as our illustration. We ordinarily write it as 0.7, or 0.71, or 0.707, understanding in each case that what we have written is the *nearest* tenth, or hundredth, or thousandth. The same idea can be expressed by a sequence of inequalities:

$$0 < \frac{1}{\sqrt{2}} < 1,$$

$$0.7 < \frac{1}{\sqrt{2}} < 0.8,$$

$$0.70 < \frac{1}{\sqrt{2}} < 0.71,$$

$$0.707 < \frac{1}{\sqrt{2}} < 0.708.$$

This sequence could be extended as far as we pleased.

This is not only a *practical* expedient, however. *Logically* it creates one sequence of *rational* numbers, 0, 0.7, 0.70, 0.707, ..., all less than $1\sqrt{2}$, and another *rational* sequence, 1, 0.8, 0.71, 0.708, ..., all greater than $1/\sqrt{2}$, and both of these sequences approach the limit $1/\sqrt{2}$. The same is true of any irrational number: π, for example, is approached by the sequence 3, 3.1, 3.14, 3.141, ..., every term of which is less than π; and also by the sequence 4, 3.2, 3.15, 3.142, ..., every term of which exceeds π. We conclude, therefore, that *every irrational number is the limit of at least two sequences of rational numbers, one approaching it from below, the other from above.*

Let us now return to the discussion of our revolving wheel. If x is irrational, there must be a sequence of rational numbers

$$\frac{n_1}{m_1}, \quad \frac{n_2}{m_2}, \quad \frac{n_3}{m_3}, \dots,$$

all *less* than x, and another

$$\frac{N_1}{M_1}, \quad \frac{N_2}{M_2}, \quad \frac{N_3}{M_3}, \dots,$$

all *greater* than x, both approaching x. Suppose that we locate on the perimeter of the wheel the four points a, $a + n_i/m_i$, $a + x$, $a + N_i/M_i$, the subscript i corresponding to some term in the sequence. (See Fig. 78.1.)

The pointer cannot come to rest in $(a, a + n_i/m_i)$ without being in $(a, a + x)$; hence $P(x) \geqq n_i/m_i$; and by a similar argument

$P(x) \leqq N_i/M_i$. That is

$$\frac{n_i}{m_i} \leqq P(x) \leqq \frac{N_i}{M_i}.$$

This inequality is true for any value of i. But as i increases, n_i/m_i and N_i/M_i converge to the limit x, and as $P(x)$ constantly lies between them, it follows that $P(x) = x$.

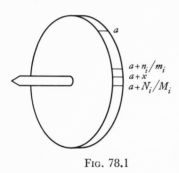

FIG. 78.1

The probability of the pointer lying between a and b is equal to the length of the interval regardless of whether that length is rational or not.

We have required the perimeter of the wheel to be of unit length, but this merely defines the unit in terms of which all lengths are measured. As the *probability* would be the same no matter what unit of length was used,

The probability of lying within an interval of length x upon a wheel, the circumference of which is L, is x/L.

This is, in a sense, an extension upon the definition of "the measure of probability," for that definition cannot be applied to this problem at all. It is made necessary by the fact that "length" is a continuous variable. But the extension is a theorem rather than a new axiom, for it is a logical consequence of the accepted relationship of irrational to rational numbers.

Finally, we note that the revolving wheel of our example serves no other purpose than to assure that the chosen point is equally as likely to lie within one interval as another. The same probability would have been obtained with any other mechanism for which equal intervals were equally likely. We can therefore take as the final form of the theorem at which we have arrived:

THEOREM 78.1 *If a point is placed upon a line segment of length L in such a way that equal intervals are equally likely to contain it, the chance that it lies within an interval of length x is x/L.*

Such a point will be said to be placed "at random" on the line.[3]

---

[3] See § 7.

79. A Paradox Associated with the Random Choice of a Point on a Line Segment

There is a curious paradox associated with this matter of choosing a point on a line segment which is of interest because it throws some light upon—or at least calls attention to—the meaning of zero probability.

It arises in connection with the question, What is the probability that the point chosen is the midpoint of the line L? If an interval of length x is constructed about this midpoint, the chance of the point lying within the interval is x/L, and the chance of lying exactly at the midpoint is less than this. Since this must be true no matter how small the interval becomes, *the probability that a point placed at random upon a line bisects that line is zero.*

This argument could have been carried out equally well for any other point.[4] Hence

THEOREM 79.1 *The probability that a point placed at random upon the line L coincides with any preassigned point is zero.*

However, the random point must have fallen upon some point or other. If, then, zero probability means that the event cannot occur, the random point has done the impossible, for it cannot be where it is and yet it most assuredly is there.

The paradox is only one of many associated with the concept of infinitely large numbers, or of limiting processes in general.

In dealing with a group of m equally likely events, the probability that one of a subgroup n occurs is n/m. So long as m is fixed this ratio cannot vanish unless n is zero; that is, unless none of the possible events has the characteristics specified for the subgroup. In such cases zero probability means impossibility.

But infinity is not a number; it is a characterization of the behavior of a variable which ultimately exceeds any number, and if by some means we keep the number n constant and increase m indefinitely, we face a different situation. If, for example, there are n red balls in a box and $m - n$ white, the probability of drawing a red ball at random is n/m. This can only be zero if $n = 0$; that is, if there is *no* red ball in the box. But if we add more and more white balls—1000, 1,000,000, . . . ,—the probability n/m may be made as small as we please. If we are asked to make it less than ϵ we can add m balls, where $m > 1/\epsilon$. So long as m is finite the resulting probability is also finite and we have no dilemma. But as m becomes infinite the probability in question becomes zero. Logically, therefore, zero probability means impossibility only when the group of events is finite in extent; when the group of events is infinite it means merely that the subgroup of favorable events is but an infinitesimal part of the whole.[5]

---

[4] We are prone to feel—though our better judgment tells us it is not true—that it would be more unusual for the point to bisect the interval than to fall somewhere that "had nothing peculiar about it." Symmetrical effects always impress us unduly. There is a case on record where each of four bridge players drew a complete suit. "Most remarkable," we say: yet actually no less probable than any other set of four hands which might be named. Each had a probability of $4.48 \cdot 10^{-28}$. The remarkable thing about it was its symmetry, not its rarity.

[5] It is unfortunate, in a way, that mathematics has no separate notation for numbers reached through limiting processes. If it had, we could say that zero (the number) as a probability means the thing is impossible; whereas zero (the limit) must be interpreted in terms of the limiting process which gives rise to it.

162 PROBABILITY AND ITS ENGINEERING USES

In a sense, theory and practice diverge at this point, for many things which are logically possible are practical impossibilities. Placing a point upon a line is in this class. We could not bisect a line exactly if we tried our utmost to do it, much less if we cut it at random; and yet the bisecting of the line is not logically impossible. Similarly with an infinity of balls the red ball might *conceivably* be drawn, but the drawing of it would be a miracle rather than a "practical possibility."[6]

80. Extension of the Significance of the Preceding Paragraphs

So far in this chapter we have spoken of "placing a point at random" on a line segment, first by means of a machine of a special type, then somewhat more generally by talking about placing the point, regardless of the mechanism employed. Clearly, however, the talk about "points" and "line segments" has been merely a convenient form of expression; the sense of the argument is more general.

To place a point upon a line which carries a scale is equivalent to choosing a number. Conversely, when a quantity is measured its magnitude can be plotted, thereby determining a point. Hence *locating points on lines* and *measuring quantities* are interchangeable ideas: whatever is true of one of them is true *mutatis mutandis* of the other also. The two fundamental results so far obtained can therefore be framed as follows:

THEOREM 80.1. *If by any process whatever a number is obtained concerning which two things are known:* (1) *that it cannot be less than x_1 nor greater than x_2;* (2) *that it occurs at random between these limits; then the probability that it lies between a and b is $(b - a)/(x_2 - x_1)$, provided, of course, that both a and b lie in the interval in question.*

The probability that the chosen number is equal to any preassigned number x is zero.

In the sections that follow we shall drop our mechanistic ideas as to how the numbers are chosen and shall speak in these more general terms instead.

81. Distribution Functions for Continuous Variables

Most variables which arise in engineering have certain preferred ranges and other ranges that are exceedingly rare. We have mentioned the resistance of a lamp filament as a quantity which cannot be forecast with absolute certainty; yet if the ideal at which production

---

[6] There are propositions which are *logically* as well as *practically* impossible. We usually call them absurdities. For example: "*x* is less than a number which is less than *x*"; or, "He is his mother's father." Bisecting a line is not absurd.

aims is 300 ohms, it is much more likely that a particular lamp will be found to lie within the ten-ohm range between 300 and 310 than in the equal range between 390 and 400.

Such a variable is best thought of in connection with its distribution curve—that is, a curve so constructed that the area under it, between the ordinates at $x = a$ and $x = b$, represents the chance of the variable x lying within these limits. Suppose Fig. 81.1 is such a curve. It follows

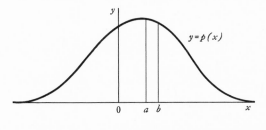

FIG. 81.1

at once that the total area under the curve, from $-\infty$ to $+\infty$, must be unity, for x is certain to have a value between these limits. Suppose we let this curve have the equation $y = p(x)$, and suppose we denote by $p(>a)$ the chance of x exceeding a and by $p(<a)$ the chance of it being less than a. We see immediately that these three functions are related as follows:

$$p(>a) = \int_a^\infty p(x)\,dx,$$

$$p(<a) = \int_{-\infty}^a p(x)\,dx.$$

One gives the area to the right of $x = a$, the other the area to the left. In general, the probability of a value of x between a and b is

$$\int_a^b p(x)\,dx.$$

Suppose, now, that b and a are very nearly equal: say, $b = a + da$. If the curve $y = p(x)$ is continuous in the neighborhood of $x = a$, as it usually is in practice, the figure bounded by the x-axis, the curve, and the two ordinates at a and $a + da$ does not differ much from a rectangle, and hence its area does not differ much from $p(a)\,da$. The difference, in fact, is an infinitesimal of order higher than the first in da, which may usually be ignored. Hence, so long as we deal with very narrow ranges, it is usually quite satisfactory to regard $p(a)$ da as the probability of a value occurring within such a range.[7]

For reasons already explained in § 10, $p(x)$ is often called the *density* of the probability.

As illustrations of distribution functions for variables which are not distributed at random, we give two simple examples. One is a highly artificial case in which the probabilities can be calculated; the other is of the much more common type where they must be inferred as well as may be from the results of a long series of observations, that is, by the use of Bernoulli's Theorem.

82. A Variable which Is Not Distributed at Random

EXAMPLE 82.1.—*Suppose the wheel of Example 78.1 carries on its circumference a logarithmic scale numbered from 1 to 10. What is the probability density for the choice of numbers on this scale?*

Let us denote the *numbers* appearing on the scale by y and their *distances* from the number 1 by x. Then $x = \log y$. This is the definition of a logarithmic scale.

Now choose two *numbers* a and b. The *distance* between them is $\log b - \log a$; and the circumference of the wheel is $\log 10 - \log 1$. Hence the probability of the pointer indicating a number between a and b is $(\log b - \log a)/(\log 10 - \log 1)$.

If we use logarithms to the base 10, this is simply $\log b - \log a$. Our distribution curve, Fig. 82.1, must therefore be of such a nature that for any interval (b, a)

$$\int_a^b p(y)\, dy = \log b - \log a.$$

Differentiating this with respect to b we obtain[8]

$$p(b) = \frac{\log e}{b},$$

---

[7] It is also not unusual to use the phrase "the probability that x takes the value a is $p(a)$," meaning thereby that the chance of x lying between a and $a + da$ differs from $p(a)$ da by an infinitesimal of the second order at least in da; or, in other words, that the ordinate to the distribution curve at a has the length $p(a)$.

[8] Remember that these are logarithms with base 10, and therefore

$$\frac{d}{dx} \log_{10} x = \frac{\log_{10} e}{x}$$

or, if we prefer to write it that way,

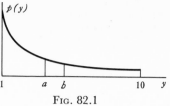

$$p(y) = \frac{\log e}{y}.$$

This is the equation for the distribution
—or density—curve.

FIG. 82.1

This example was solved by direct
application of the definition of probability. Let us now take one
upon which we can get no grip theoretically.

83. Distribution Functions Derived Empirically

EXAMPLE 83.1.—*Construct a distribution curve of length of life: in other words,
a curve the area under any portion of which is a child's chance at birth of dying within
the corresponding range of ages.*

This problem cannot be solved from a purely theoretical standpoint,
since equal age ranges are known not to be equally likely. The best we can
do is to resort to vital statistics and find what proportion of the population
has been observed to die within various age limits. In a sense each life is
an "independent trial," and we can conclude from Bernoulli's Theorem that,
if the cases are numerous enough, the proportion of deaths between any two
age limits is not likely to deviate much from the probability of dying in that
range.

Figure 83.1 was plotted in this
manner from certain German data
given by Czuber in his *Wahrschein-
lichkeitsrechnung*. Its general character
would be much the same for data
taken from almost any civilized
country, although it is obvious that
different conditions of sanitation, and
particularly different customs in the
handling of children, would affect it
somewhat.

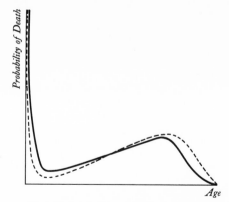

The curve, therefore, gives a child's
chance of dying at a certain age if
he is born at a particular place.
Moreover, the conditions of life are
not static: medical efficiency, for
example, is increasing. Hence the
curve depicts a child's chances of life

FIG. 83.1   A TYPICAL LIFE CURVE.

if born at a given time. In the very nature of things no child can be born
at that time: for the existence of the data implies that the time is past.
Today a child's chances are different, probably in some such way as is
indicated by the dotted line, although such a curve can be based on no
more substantial foundation than the estimation of a "trend"—or rate at
which the probabilities are changing.

The important point, however, is that in this situation the *probabilities* change with time.

When the reverse is true—that is, when the probabilities do not change with time—conditions are said to be in "statistical equilibrium."

Present probability can only be inferred from data already collected when the system under consideration is in statistical equilibrium.

Some conception of the significance of the uncertainties introduced into life insurance by this factor can be obtained by considering the position in which the insurance companies would find themselves if the "trend" were toward shorter rather than longer life. They would then face almost certain loss if they based their rates upon available statistics, and would be forced to estimate as best they could the factor by which present conditions differed from past, with obvious disastrous consequences if they made a wrong guess. As it is they face almost certain gain; which is quite satisfactory to the companies, and not very serious to the policyholder if his company has his interests at heart.

Now, life insurance as such is not a topic of this book. But similar conditions are often met in engineering. Take, for instance, Example 76.1, in which certain empirical data were made the foundation for a solution of a problem in quality control. Perhaps in the case in question such data could be thoroughly relied upon, for screw-making is, I suppose, a rather stable process and not subject to rapid improvement. Suppose, however, that the same sort of argument were attempted in the manufacture of deposited film memories, or solar batteries, or micro-miniature circuitry; by the time enough data were accumulated to define the probability density with reasonable confidence, someone would "improve" the process, and we would be confronted with a set of conditions to which our data no longer applied *exactly*—perhaps not at all.

In other words, manufacturing conditions, like life, are not in statistical equilibrium. Instead, *the probabilities are functions of time*, and those functions are generally unknown.

84. Distribution Functions in Many Variables

The concept of "compound events" in the case of discrete variables has an analog when the variables are continuous. It is "functions of several variables." As an example, suppose we are stamping out metal discs on a punch press, to be used in operating a slot machine. If the slot machine is so constructed as to reject a coin the weight of which deviates too much from standard, we will naturally be interested in the probable variation in weight of our product. The weight, however, depends principally upon two factors: the radius, r, and the thickness, t, of the particular portion of the sheet from which the disc comes. Both of these are subject to variation, and both are obviously continuous variables.

Suppose we represent r and t as Cartesian coordinates, as in Fig. 84.1, and build up a "distribution surface"; that is, a surface such that the volume under any portion of it is equal to the probability of (r, t) lying under that portion. Call the height of such a surface $p(r, t)$. Then the following statements are immediately obvious:

1. The probability of a pair of values within the ranges $(r, r + dr)$, $(t, t + dt)$ is $p(r, t) \, dr \, dt$,[9]

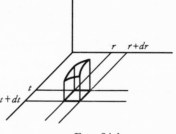

2. The probability that r lies in the range $(r, r + dr)$ is equal to the volume of the vertical slab whose base is bounded by the lines r and $r + dr$; that is,

$$p(r) \, dr = dr \int p(r, t) \, dt. \qquad (84.1)$$

Fig. 84.1

3. The probability that t lies between t and $t + dt$ is represented by a similar slab, and

$$p(t) = \int p(r, t) \, dr. \qquad (84.2)$$

It is understood, of course, that the integrals in (84.1) and (84.2) extend over every possible value of t and r, respectively. They are exact analogs of (38.1).

4. We can, if we wish, think of the occurrence of a radius in the slab between r and $r + dr$ as "event A" and the occurrence of a thickness between t and $t + dt$ as "event B." The argument of § 65 applies as well to these events as to any others, wherefore we have

$$P(A, B) = P(A) \, P(B|A). \qquad (37.1)$$

But, except for infinitesimals of higher order, $P(A,B) = p(r, t) dr \, dt$, $P(A) = p(r)dr$, and (37.1) becomes

$$p(r, t) \, dt \, dt = p(r) \, P(B|A) \, dr$$
$$= p(r) \, p(t|r) \, dr \, dt,$$

if $p(t|r)$ is the limit approached by $p(B|A)/dt$ as dt vanishes. That is,

$$p(r, t) = p(r) \, p(t|r). \qquad (84.3)$$

This is the exact counterpart of (37.1) for the case of continuous variables.

---

[9] "Except for a differential of higher order in dr and dt." The general idea should by now be clear enough to allow the omission of such statements in the future. Differential notation implies a limiting process for complete accuracy.

If we substitute (84.3) into (84.2), we get

$$p(t) = \int p(r)\, p(t|r)\, dr, \qquad (84.4)$$

which is an exact counterpart of (38.2).

5. If we had started from the slab for which t lies between t and $t + dt$, we would have concluded that

$$p(r, t) = p(t)\, p(r|t).$$

Comparing this with (84.3) and making certain obvious transformations, we get

$$p(r|t) = \frac{p(r)\, p(t|r)}{p(t)},$$

or by (84.4),

$$p(r|t) = \frac{p(r)\, p(t|r)}{\int p(r)\, p(t|r)\, dr}.$$

These are the extensions of (71.4) and (71.5). That is, they are Bayes' Theorem for the case of continuous variables.

The above formulas are, of course, not restricted to the particular example from which they were derived. They are, instead, general relations entirely analogous to those already derived for discrete variables. To bring this out more clearly, the corresponding formulas are set opposite one another below. In the continuous case r and t have been replaced by x and y as a further indication of their generality.[10]

---

[10] In treatises on statistics the $p(t)$ and $P(B)$ in (84.2) and (38.1) are often called *marginal probabilities*. The origin of the term is as follows: The contingency matrix for A and B is (see § 39) the rectangular array:

	B_1	B_2		B_b	
A_1	$P(A_1, B_1)$	$P(A_1, B_2)$	—	$P(A_1, B_b)$	$P(A_1)$
A_2	$P(A_2, B_1)$	$P(A_2, B_2)$	—	$P(A_2, B_b)$	$P(A_2)$
A_a	$P(A_a, B_1)$	$P(A_a, B_2)$	—	$P(A_a, B_b)$	$P(A_a)$
	$P(B_1)$	$P(B_2)$	—	$P(B_b)$	

If we sum the columns of this, (38.1) states that we get the various values of $P(B)$; similarly $P(A)$ are the sums of the rows. It is natural to write them in the margins as is done above; hence the word "marginal."

By analogy the term is extended to the case of continuous variables as well.

When used in this context $P(B)$ and $p(x)$ are sometimes written $P(\cdot, B)$ and $p(x, \cdot)$, the dot signifying that the missing variable has been summed (or integrated) out. This is a convenient notation which we have already used from time to time. It should be clearly recognized that $p(x, \cdot)$ means precisely $p(x)$, and $P(\cdot, B)$ precisely $P(B)$; nothing more nor less. The dot exists in recognition of the process by which the probability was determined; it does not characterize or qualify the event.

$$p(x) = \int p(x,y) \, dy \qquad (84.5) \qquad P(B) = \sum_A P(A,B) \qquad (38.1)$$

$$p(x,y) = p(x) \, p(y|x) \qquad (84.6) \qquad P(A, B) = P(A) \, P(B|A) \qquad (37.1)$$

$$p(x) = \int p(x) \, p(y|x) \, dy \quad (84.7) \qquad P(B) = \sum_A P(A) \, P(B|A) \qquad (38.2)$$

$$p(x|y) = p(x) \, p(y|x)/p(y) \quad (84.8) \qquad P(A|B) = P(A) \, P(B|A)/P(B) \quad (71.4)$$

$$p(x|y) = \frac{p(x) \, p(y|x)}{\int p(x) \, p(y|x) \, dy} \qquad (84.9) \qquad P(A|B) = \frac{P(A) \, P(B|A)}{\sum_A P(A) \, P(B|A)} \qquad (71.5)$$

Similar formulas could be written for any number of variables.

As an example, the velocity[11] of a gas molecule can be defined by its components u, v, w in the three coordinate directions x, y, z. The probability that a molecule has a velocity whose components lie within the ranges $(u, u + du)$, $(v, v + dv)$, $(w, w + dw)$ can then be written $p(u, v, w) \, du \, dv \, dw$, $p(u, v, w)$ being the probability density. But to represent this density in a fashion analogous to Fig. 84.1 we would now require three dimensions for u, v, w, and a fourth for p, which is not available. We must, therefore, reason by analogy.

The analogies, however, are fairly obvious. If, for example, $p(u, v, w)$ was given and we wished to limit our consideration to motions normal to the z-axis, we could write as the analog of (84.5).

$$p(u, v) = \int p(u, v, w) \, dw;$$

to consider only the component along the x-axis we would write

$$p(u) = \int \int p(u, v, w) \, dv \, dw;$$

etc. The reader will recognize that both of these, like (84.5) and (38.1), are special cases of the theorem on alternative compound probabilities in § 38, which is itself an application of Convention II.

85. Change of Variable in Distribution Functions; the Jacobian

In studying gas molecules we are not always interested in their velocity. We may want to discuss speed, direction, momentum, energy —any number of things. But as all these are determined by the velocity,[12] we ought to be able to find the probability of any of them in terms of $p(u, v, w)$. This is really the case.

---

[11] We are using the term "velocity" in its vector sense of "speed and direction."

[12] Also the mass, which is generally a constant.

For example, suppose we are required to find the chance that a molecule has a speed between s and $s + ds$.

This would be a simple matter if the probability density were given in terms of speed and two angular coordinates, say $p'(s, \phi, \theta)$; for, by definition, the probability of a velocity within the limits $s, s + ds$;

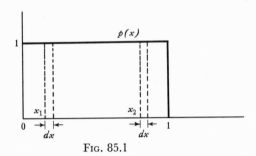

FIG. 85.1

$\phi, \phi + d\phi; \theta, \theta + d\theta$ would then be $p'(s, \phi, \theta)\, ds\, d\phi\, d\theta$; and the theorem on alternative compound probabilities would lead at once to

$$p(s) = \int \int p'(s, \phi, \theta)\, d\phi\, d\theta.$$

But suppose we are given $p(u, v, w)$; how do we find $p'(s, \phi, \theta)$?

The nature of the problem is readily seen from a comparison of Figs. 85.1 and 85.2, which correspond to Examples 78.1 and 82.1.

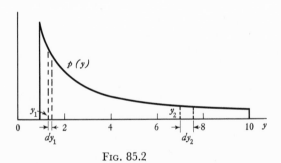

FIG. 85.2

The probability of the pointer resting in the interval $(x_1, x_1 + dx)$ is the same as in the interval $(x_2, x_2 + dx)$. It is therefore equally likely to rest in the intervals bounded by the corresponding values of y. But because of the nature of the transformation $x = \log y$, the corresponding intervals $(y_1, y_1 + dy_1)$ and $(y_2, y_2 + dy_2)$ are not of equal width. Hence, in order that areas may be preserved, the density $p(y)$ must be greater at y_1 than at y_2. A moment's consideration will show that if, at equivalent points on the two curves, dy is greater than dx by a factor k, $p(y)$ must be smaller than $p(x)$ by precisely this factor k. Of course, k is not a constant. By its definition it is dy/dx and varies from point to point. In other words,

$$p(y) = p(x)\frac{dx}{dy}. \tag{85.1}$$

Where more variables are involved the essential problem is the same. Thus, in dealing with the velocity of gas molecules, $p'(s, \phi, \theta)$ cannot be obtained merely by substitution of variables in $p(u, v, w)$. It is also necessary to divide by a factor k, the amount by which the differential element is magnified in passing from $du\ dv\ dw$ to $ds\ d\phi\ d\theta$.

In essence the situation is the same as that met in changing from one coordinate system to another in the integral calculus. But in the calculus it is customary to regard u, v, w and s, ϕ, θ as two ways of defining the location of a point in a single real space; the magnification factor is then included as a part of the "element of volume." In probability theory (and certain other branches of mathematics also) the point of view is different; u, v, w and s, ϕ, θ are thought of as separate sample spaces and the transformation as a means of "mapping" one space on the other. When so regarded the magnification factor must be included as part of the density function to conform to the way in which that function was defined.

This magnification factor is therefore a necessary element in the theory of probability as applied to continuous variables, and a method of computing it is required.

To illustrate how this is done, let us consider first the case of two variables x and y. To represent these requires a plane; any pair of values of x and y determine a point (x, y) somewhere in the plane, and the distribution function $p(x, y)$ is defined as a function which, when integrated over a region dA, gives the probability that the point (x, y) lies within dA. If dA is small enough, $p(x, y)$ is sensibly constant over the entire area and the probability is given by[13] $p(x, y)\ dA$.

Now suppose we have two other variables ξ and η, related to x and y by means of the equations

$$\left.\begin{array}{l} \xi = f(x, y), \\ \eta = \phi(x, y). \end{array}\right\} \tag{85.2}$$

---

[13] In particular, if dA is a rectangle bounded by horizontal and vertical lines, its area may be called $dx\ dy$. The probability in question will then be $p(x, y)\ dx\ dy$. But as it is by no means necessary that the area be of such a shape, we prefer to keep the more general differential dA.

Suppose we choose another plane for the representation of these and seek to determine their distribution function $p(\xi, \eta)$. As the point (x, y) travels around the boundary of dA, the corresponding point (ξ, η) will travel around some curve in its own plane. This curve will bound an area $d\alpha$, which we shall call the "element of area corresponding to dA." Whenever the point (x, y) lies in dA, (ξ, η) lies in $d\alpha$. Therefore

$$p(\xi, \eta) \, d\alpha = p(x, y) \, dA. \tag{85.3}$$

To get $p(\xi, \eta)$, therefore, we must multiply $p(x, y)$ by the quotient $dA/d\alpha$. It is the magnification factor which was called k in earlier paragraphs.

To find this quotient we choose dA as a rectangle bounded by the values x, $x + dx$, y and $y + dy$. (See Fig. 85.3.) As (x, y) travels along

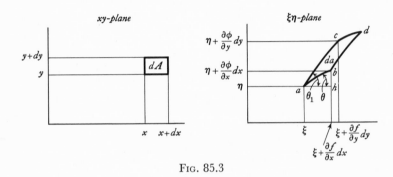

Fig. 85.3

one of the lines which bound this rectangle, (ξ, η) will trace a curve of some form. The element $d\alpha$, therefore, is bounded by four curved elements as shown in the figure. If dx and dy are very small, these elements will be nearly straight and $d\alpha$ will be very nearly a parallelogram. Hence its area is

$$d\alpha = ab \cdot ac \sin (\theta_1 - \theta)$$
$$= (ab \cos \theta) (ac \sin \theta_1) - (ab \sin \theta) (ac \cos \theta_1).$$

However

$$ah = ab \cos \theta = \frac{\partial f}{\partial x} \, dx,[14]$$

$$bh = ab \sin \theta = \frac{\partial \phi}{\partial x} \, dx,$$

---

[14] Partial differential notation is used because y remains constant along this side of our rectangle.

$$ac \cos \theta_1 = \frac{\partial f}{\partial y} \, dy,$$

$$ac \sin \theta_1 = \frac{\partial \phi}{\partial y} \, dy;$$

wherefore

$$d\alpha = \left(\frac{\partial f}{\partial x} \frac{\partial \phi}{\partial y} - \frac{\partial f}{\partial y} \frac{\partial \phi}{\partial x} \right) dA. \tag{85.4}$$

Thus we have found the ratio of $d\alpha$ to dA. It serves our purpose best to write it in the form of a determinant:

$$\frac{\partial(\xi, \eta)}{\partial(x, y)} = \begin{vmatrix} \dfrac{\partial \xi}{\partial x} & \dfrac{\partial \xi}{\partial y} \\[2ex] \dfrac{\partial \eta}{\partial x} & \dfrac{\partial \eta}{\partial y} \end{vmatrix}.$$

Then, by (85.3) and (85.4),

$$p(\xi, \eta) = \frac{p(x, y)}{\dfrac{\partial(\xi, \eta)}{\partial(x, y)}},$$

it being understood, of course, that the x's and y's on the right-hand side are to be expressed in terms of ξ and η by solving (85.2).

In dealing with three or more variables, an exactly similar argument would lead to the ratio of the corresponding volume elements in the form

$$d\alpha = \begin{vmatrix} \dfrac{\partial \xi}{\partial x} & \dfrac{\partial \xi}{\partial y} & \dfrac{\partial \xi}{\partial z} & \cdots & \dfrac{\partial \xi}{\partial w} \\[2ex] \dfrac{\partial \eta}{\partial x} & \dfrac{\partial \eta}{\partial y} & \dfrac{\partial \eta}{\partial z} & \cdots & \dfrac{\partial \eta}{\partial w} \\[2ex] \dfrac{\partial \zeta}{\partial x} & \dfrac{\partial \zeta}{\partial y} & \dfrac{\partial \zeta}{\partial z} & \cdots & \dfrac{\partial \zeta}{\partial w} \\[1ex] \cdots & \cdots & \cdots & & \cdots \\[1ex] \dfrac{\partial \omega}{\partial x} & \dfrac{\partial \omega}{\partial y} & \dfrac{\partial \omega}{\partial z} & \cdots & \dfrac{\partial \omega}{\partial w} \end{vmatrix} dA, \tag{85.5}$$

or, symbolically,

$$d\alpha = \frac{\partial(\xi, \eta, \zeta, \ldots, \omega)}{\partial(x, y, z, \ldots, w)} \, dA.$$

Hence

$$p(\xi, \eta, \zeta, \ldots, \omega) = \frac{p(x, y, z, \ldots, w)}{\dfrac{\partial(\xi, \eta, \zeta, \ldots, \omega)}{\partial(x, y, z, \ldots, w)}}. \tag{85.6}$$

The determinant

$$\frac{\partial(\xi, \eta, \zeta, \ldots, \omega)}{\partial(x, y, z, \ldots, w)},$$

in which the elements are all possible partial derivatives of the new variables with respect to the old, is known as the "Jacobian" of the transformation. Its geometrical significance is contained in the concept which has led us to it: it denotes the degree of local magnification when the old system is mapped on the new. About it we may make three interesting observations:

In the first place, in the one-dimensional case there is only one row and one column in (85.5), which therefore reduces to the derivative of the new variable with respect to the old. This is precisely what we found in discussing Figs. 85.1 and 85.2.

In the second place, there is a perfect reciprocal relationship between our old and new variables. Once $p(\xi, \eta, \zeta, \ldots, \omega)$ is known we could start with it and find $p(x, y, z, \ldots, w)$ by exactly the same argument as was used above. The only essential difference would be that, instead of differentiating the equations $\xi = \xi(x, y, z, \ldots, w)$, $\eta = \eta(x, y, z, \ldots, w), \ldots$ to form the Jacobian, we should want equations defining $x, y, z, \ldots, w$ in terms of $\xi, \eta, \zeta, \ldots, \omega$. Obviously the result of this reciprocal relationship is

$$p(x, y, z, \ldots, w) = \frac{p(\xi, \eta, \zeta, \ldots, \omega)}{\dfrac{\partial(x, y, z, \ldots, w)}{\partial(\xi, \eta, \zeta, \ldots, \omega)}}.$$

But the magnification going from the new coordinates back to the old must be just the reciprocal of the magnification in going from the old to the new. Hence we conclude that

$$\frac{\partial(x, y, z, \ldots, w)}{\partial(\xi, \eta, \zeta, \ldots, \omega)}$$

is the reciprocal of

$$\frac{\partial(\xi, \eta, \zeta, \ldots, \omega)}{\partial(x, y, z, \ldots, w)}.$$

Because of this relation, it is relatively unimportant whether $x, y, \ldots$ are expressed in terms of $\xi, \eta, \ldots$ explicitly, or the converse is true. The Jacobian can be found from either.

Suppose, for instance, that x and y are related to ξ and η by the equations

$$x = \xi \cos \eta,$$
$$y = \xi \sin \eta.$$

Then

$$\frac{\partial(x, y)}{\partial(\xi, \eta)} = \begin{vmatrix} \cos\eta & -\xi\sin\eta \\ \sin\eta & \xi\cos\eta \end{vmatrix} = \xi.$$

But by solving for ξ and η, we find

$$\xi = \sqrt{x^2 + y^2},$$

$$\eta = \tan^{-1}\frac{y}{x};$$

whence

$$\frac{\partial(\xi, \eta)}{\partial(x, y)} = \begin{vmatrix} \dfrac{x}{\sqrt{x^2 + y^2}} & \dfrac{y}{\sqrt{x^2 + y^2}} \\ \dfrac{-y}{x^2 + y^2} & \dfrac{x}{x^2 + y^2} \end{vmatrix} = \frac{1}{\sqrt{x^2 + y^2}} = \frac{1}{\xi} = \frac{1}{\dfrac{\partial(x, y)}{\partial(\xi, \eta)}}.$$

Our third observation is that, since the ratio of two volumes cannot be negative,[15] the determinant which occurs in (85.5) should always be positive. Whether it is or not, however, depends upon the order in which the variables are written down; for interchanging two rows or two columns in a determinant changes its sign. If, for example, the equations of the preceding paragraph had been written in the order

$$y = \xi\sin\eta,$$

$$x = \xi\cos\eta,$$

we would have found that

$$\frac{\partial(y, x)}{\partial(\xi, \eta)} = -\xi.$$

It follows, therefore, that the sign with which our Jacobian appears is largely a matter of accident, and that in every case the positive sign is the correct one.

86. An Example of Change of Variable in Distribution Functions

As an illustration of the use of these ideas, consider again the production of metal discs which was discussed in § 84 and suppose that the probability density $p(r, t)$ is known. In practice this would mean that radius and thickness were measured as part of the inspection routine, and sufficiently extensive data had been accumulated to define

---

[15] In other branches of mathematics the *sign* of the Jacobian has an important significance, but since probabilities are never negative it is unnecessary to discuss the matter.

this function with reasonable assurance. Suppose, further, that $p(w)$, the probability that the weight lies between w and $w + dw$, is wanted.[16] Since[17] $w = tr^2$ this requires that t and r lie in the strip bounded by the curves

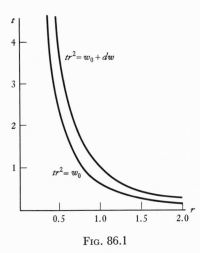

$$tr^2 = w_0,$$

$$tr^2 = w_0 + dw,$$

in Fig. 86.1. That is,

$$p(w)\, dw = \int \int p(r, t)\, dr\, dt,$$

the integral to be taken over the area between the curves.

In this form the integral has rather inconvenient limits, a situation which can be improved by changing to new variables v and w defined by

FIG. 86.1

$$w = tr^2,$$
$$v = r.$$
(86.1)

The Jacobian of this transformation is

$$\frac{\partial(w, v)}{\partial(r, t)} = \begin{vmatrix} 2tr & r^2 \\ 1 & 0 \end{vmatrix} = -r^2.$$

Disregarding the negative sign, this leads to[18]

$$P(w, v) = \frac{p(r, t)}{r^2},$$

where, on the right-hand side, r and t are to be expressed in terms of w and v by solving (86.1). Then, using (84.5),

$$p(w) = \int_0^\infty P(w, v)\, dv.$$
(86.2)

As a numerical example, suppose that $p(r, t)$ is constant over the area $1.10 < t < 1.15$, $1.10 < r < 1.15$, and zero elsewhere. Then, to have total probability 1, $p(r, t) = 400$. (See Fig. 86.2.) In the vw-plane this

---

[16] The reader may wonder why, if w is wanted, it was not measured in the first place. Please be assured that on this point the writer is quite as much in the dark as he.

[17] There is also a density factor. We may suppose the unit of weight to be so chosen that this is unity.

[18] The capital P is used to avoid confusion with the last member of the equation.

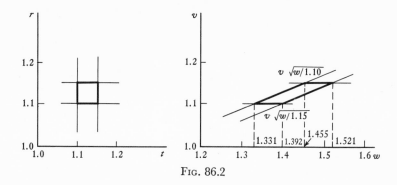

FIG. 86.2

becomes the region bounded by $v = 1.10, v = 1.15,$ $v = \sqrt{w/1.10}$ and $v = \sqrt{w/1.15}.$ But with $p(r, t) = 400,$ (86.2) integrates into

$$p = 400 \left(\frac{1}{1.10} - \sqrt{\frac{1.10}{w}} \right),$$
$$1.331 \leqq w \leqq 1.392,$$

$$p = 400 \left(\sqrt{\frac{1.15}{w}} - \sqrt{\frac{1.10}{w}} \right),$$
$$1.392 \leqq w \leqq 1.455,$$

$$p = 400 \left(\sqrt{\frac{1.15}{w}} - \frac{1}{1.15} \right),$$
$$1.455 \leqq w \leqq 1.521.$$

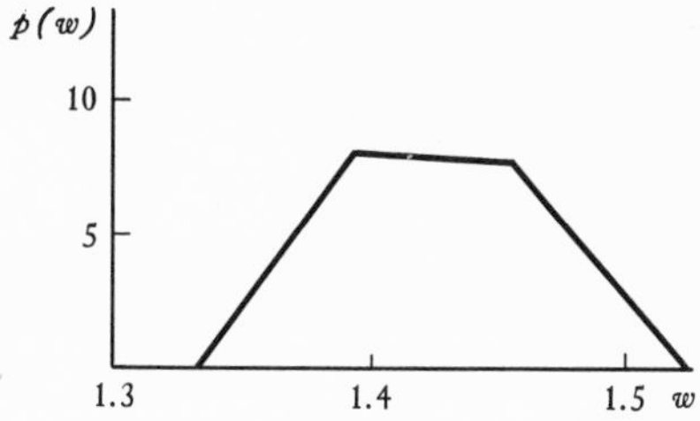

Plotting this we have the distribution curve shown in Fig. 86.3.

FIG. 86.3

87. Derivation of a Distribution Function for the Velocities of Gas Molecules

One of the important problems in physics to which probability theory was first applied, and virtually the only one in which the Normal Law appears as a consequence of a reasonably sound physical argument, is that of the distribution of velocities within a perfect gas. We shall use this as an illustration of the processes which we have been discussing in the present chapter.

Suppose the gas is composed of a large number of particles, similar or dissimilar as the case may be, but all in agitated motion. Assume further that it is contained within a vessel which is not itself in motion. The question before us is, What is the chance of a particular particle having a specified velocity?

To start with, let us make sure we know exactly what the question means. Suppose we phrase it this way: A particular particle is tagged for purposes of identification, and an instant of observation is chosen at random—that is, without any advance information which influences the probability for which we seek. If at that instant we note the velocity of the particle in question, both as to magnitude and direction, what is the chance that its components lie between u and $u + du$, v and $v + dv$, and w and $w + dw$, respectively?

We make these assumptions:

(a) The probability of a given velocity is independent of the part of the vessel in which the particle may be. That is, $p(u, v, w)$ does not depend upon the coordinates x, y, z.

Physically there are two common conditions which violate this assumption: when different parts of the gas are at different temperatures; and when they are at different pressures, as, for example, when the gas is flowing out of an orifice.

(b) All directions of motion are equally likely.

To this we cannot object.

(c) The probability of a component u in the x-direction is independent of any knowledge we may have about the transverse components v and w.

This is the weakest assumption, for it is certainly not obvious, either from a mathematical or a physical point of view, that it should be true. However, we proceed with it.[19]

Let $p(u)$ be the probability of a component u. By assumption (c)

$$p(u, v, w) = p(u) \cdot p(v) \cdot p(w),$$

or

$$\log p(u, v, w) = \log p(u) + \log p(v) + \log p(w).$$

By assumption (b) the function $p(u, v, w)$ must depend on the combination $u^2 + v^2 + w^2$ only; for if we were to replace the three components of velocity by their expressions in terms of speed and direction, the directional variables would all disappear, leaving only the speed. Suppose, then, that we write for the moment

$$\log p(u, v, w) = f(u^2 + v^2 + w^2).$$

We now make our final assumption: that this function f is of such a

---

[19] It is interesting historically to note that Maxwell first derived equation (87.2) by substantially this line of argument. However, he was aware of its weakness and afterwards attempted to improve it by a more sophisticated argument. In Chapter XI of the first edition we gave a derivation quite similar to Maxwell's second approach. It has been omitted in this edition to make space for material of greater present value.

nature that it can be expanded in a series for sufficiently small values of the speed. We then get

$$f(u^2 + v^2 + w^2) = a_0 + a_1(u^2 + v^2 + w^2) + a_2(u^2 + v^2 + w^2)^2 + \ldots$$
$$= \log p(u) + \log p(v) + \log p(w). \tag{87.1}$$

Obviously the third member of this equation is of such a form that no cross-products between u, v, w can be allowed. But such cross-products arise from all the terms of the second member except $a + a_1(u^2 + v^2 + w^2)$: hence the coefficients a_2, a_3, $\ldots$, must be zero. Thus

$$\log p(u, v, w) = a_0 + a_1(u^2 + v^2 + w^2),$$
or
$$p(u, v, w) = A\, e^{a_1(u^2 + v^2 + w^2)}.$$

This equation contains two constants A and a_1, but they are not both arbitrary because of the necessary relation

$$\int_{-\infty}^{\infty} \int_{-\infty}^{\infty} \int_{-\infty}^{\infty} p(u, v, w)\, du\, dv\, dw = 1,$$

which requires that $\pi^3 A^2 = -a_1^3$. If, then, we call $a_1 = -a$, we have as our final law

$$p(u, v, w) = \left(\frac{a}{\pi}\right)^{3/2} e^{-a(u^2 + v^2 + w^2)}. \tag{87.2}$$

This is Maxwell's Equation. It contains only *one* arbitrary constant a, and that can be shown to be completely determined by the temperature of the gas and the mass of the particle under consideration.

88. Some Instructive Illustrations; Change of Variable in Maxwell's Equation

As a second illustration of change of variable, consider the following example:

EXAMPLE 88.1.—*If the probability of a gas molecule having the velocity components u, v, w is given by (73), find the density function in terms of the variables s (speed), θ (longitude), and φ (latitude).*

The relations between the two sets of variables are seen from Fig. 88.1 to be

$$u = s \cos\phi \cos\theta,$$
$$v = s \cos\phi \sin\theta,$$
$$w = s \sin\phi.$$

By differentiation we get

$$\frac{\partial(u, v, w)}{\partial(s, \theta, \phi)} = \begin{vmatrix} \cos\phi\cos\theta & s\cos\phi\sin\theta & -s\sin\phi\cos\theta \\ \cos\phi\sin\theta & s\cos\phi\cos\theta & -s\sin\phi\sin\theta \\ \sin\phi & 0 & s\cos\phi \end{vmatrix}$$

$$= -s^2 \cos\phi,$$

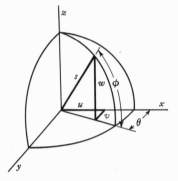

FIG. 88.1 SPHERICAL COORDINATES.

which we know to be the reciprocal of

$$\frac{\partial(s, \theta, \phi)}{\partial(u, v, w)}.$$

Therefore, by (85.6), disregarding the negative sign,

$$p(s, \theta, \phi) = s^2 \cos\phi \, p(u, v, w).$$
$$(88.1)$$

But $u^2 + v^2 + w^2 = s^2$. Substituting this into (87.2), and (87.2) into (88.1), we get finally

$$p(s, \theta, \phi) = (a/\pi)^{3/2} s^2 \cos\phi \, e^{-as^2}.$$
$$(88.2)$$

Equation (88.2) reveals a treacherous point in our argument. By assumption (b), § 87, all directions should be equally likely; without this assumption we could not have asserted that $p(u, v, w)$ was a function of s^2 only. Yet (88.2) contains ϕ as well as s^2, and on first thought would seem to violate one of the assumptions upon which it is based.

The explanation is a simple one. By the brief expression "all directions are equally likely" we really meant this sensible thing: that if a direction were named, the chance of our particle deviating from that direction by an angle less than $d\alpha$, say, would not depend upon the chosen direction. Or, in still other words, if at some instant lines were drawn through the particle in any two directions, and if like cones were instantaneously described about both, the chance of the direction of motion of the particle being within one cone would equal the chance of it being in the other.

Now, if a sphere were described about the common apex of these two cones, they would cut out equal areas on it. Hence assumption (b) requires that the direction of motion be equally likely to intersect this sphere within any two like areas. The element $d\phi \, d\theta$, however, is not of the same area at all places: indeed the element of area is just $r^2 \cos\phi \, d\phi \, d\theta$, if r is the radius; and if we define "element of direction" as the solid angle subtended by this area, the "element of direction" is just $\cos\phi \, d\phi \, d\theta$. Hence the form of (88.2), which may be written

$$p(s, \phi, \theta) \, ds \, d\phi \, d\theta = (a/\pi)^{3/2} s^2 \, e^{-as^2} \, ds \, (\cos\phi \, d\phi \, d\theta),$$

is really in accordance with assumption (b).

89. Information that Can Be Derived from (87.2) and (88.2)

From (88.2) we can easily find the probability that the *speed* of a molecule lies between s and $s + ds$, if we do not care what direction is associated with that speed. We need only integrate $p(s, \theta, \phi)\, ds\, d\theta\, d\phi$ over all possible values of θ and ϕ. However, to include every possible direction we must allow θ to vary from 0 to 2π, and ϕ from $-\pi/2$ to $+\pi/2$. Hence

$$p(s)\, ds = (a/\pi)^{3/2} s^2\, e^{-as^2}\, ds \int_0^{2\pi} d\theta \int_{-\pi/2}^{+\pi/2} \cos\phi\, d\phi,$$

or

$$p(s) = 4\sqrt{a^3/\pi}\, s^2\, e^{-as^2}. \tag{89.1}$$

This, then, is the probability of a molecule having a specified *speed*.

Returning again to (87.2), we ask for the probability that a molecule has u as its component of velocity in the x-direction, regardless of the transverse velocity components with which u may be associated. This is obtained from (87.2) by summing $p(u, v, w)\, du\, dv\, dw$ for every admissible value of v and w, thereby getting

$$p(u) = \int_{-\infty}^{\infty} dv \int_{-\infty}^{\infty} dw\, p(u, v, w)$$

$$= \left(\frac{a}{\pi}\right)^{3/2} e^{-au^2} \int_{-\infty}^{\infty} e^{-av^2}\, dv \int_{-\infty}^{\infty} e^{-aw^2}\, dw. \tag{89.2}$$

Each of the integrals in this expression is $\sqrt{\pi/a}$ and their product is π/a. Hence

$$p(u) = \sqrt{a/\pi}\, e^{-au^2}. \tag{89.3}$$

By symmetry the density functions for v and w are

$$p(v) = \sqrt{a/\pi}\, e^{-av^2},$$

$$p(w) = \sqrt{a/\pi}\, e^{-aw^2}.$$

These equations could have been obtained directly from (87.1), since $\log p(u)$ must clearly be $a_1 u^2$ plus a constant. Since $\log p(v)$ and $\log p(w)$ must contain this same constant, it is $a_0/3$. This leads at once to (89.3). The longer derivation has been given to illustrate the analytical processes by which density functions may be manipulated.

Another type of question which arises frequently in physical problems concerns the type of molecules that pass through a given surface. For instance, we may be thinking of diffusion of a gas through a hole in the wall of the containing vessel, or we may be thinking of the molecules that pass across an imaginary mathematical surface somewhere inside the vessel. The two cases differ principally in the fact that in the former the molecules cross the surface in one direction only, whereas in the latter they cross in both directions. We choose to discuss the latter case.

To be specific in our thinking we phrase the question this way: If a particular molecule has crossed a particular element of surface during a particular short interval of time dt, what is the chance that it had the velocity components u, v, w?

This is obviously a case for the application of Bayes' Theorem; for if we call "having the velocity in question" event A, and "crossing the surface" event B, the question really is, "B having happened, what is the chance that it was accompanied by A?" The answer, we know, is

$$p(u, v, w|B) = \frac{p(u, v, w)\, p(B|u, v, w)}{p(B)}. \tag{89.4}$$

Of the quantities on the right, $p(u, v, w)$ is given by (87.2), and the denominator can be found by summing expressions such as the one in the numerator, provided $p(B|u, v, w)$ can be found. Virtually the entire problem, therefore, lies in finding this last quantity.

Denote the element of area by dA and let the x-axis be normal to it. Then the molecule in question crosses dA during the interval dt provided that, at the beginning of this interval, it was within the slant prism which dA would sweep out if it moved for a time dt with the reversed velocity $-u$, $-v$, $-w$. The volume of this prism is dA times its perpendicular height, or dA times $|u|\, dt$.

The molecule, however, was tagged without reference to its position: it is just as likely to be in one part of the vessel as another. If, then, the total volume is V,

$$p(B|u, v, w) = |u|\, dA\, dt / V. \tag{89.5}$$

This, together with (87.2), gives the numerator of (89.4).

To get $p(B)$, (89.5) must be multiplied by $p(u, v, w)$ and summed over every possible event A with which it may be associated: that is, over every possible set of values of u, v, and w. This gives, when common factors are cancelled,

$$p(u, v, w|B) = \frac{|u|\, e^{-a(u^2 + v^2 + w^2)}}{\displaystyle\int_{-\infty}^{\infty} \int_{-\infty}^{\infty} \int_{-\infty}^{\infty} |u|\, e^{-a(u^2 + v^2 + w^2)}\, du\, dv\, dw}.$$

As in (89.2), the v and w integrals together give a factor π/a. The u integral, which has the *absolute* value of u in its integrand, is by symmetry twice the value obtained between the limits 0 and $+\infty$; that is, $1/a$. Hence the entire denominator becomes π/a^2 and

$$p(u, v, w|B) = \frac{a^2}{\pi} |u| \, e^{-a(u^2 + v^2 + w^2)}.$$

This is the answer required.

We shall not follow the problems of the kinetic theory further.[20]

90. Hyperspherical Coordinates

The system of spherical coordinates is capable of generalization to more than three variables. The nature of the generalization can readily be deduced from Fig. 88.1 by observing that one Cartesian coordinate, z, is given immediately by $r \sin \phi$. The other coordinate axes lie in the plane normal to z, on which the projection of r is $r \cos \theta$. Again, one of the Cartesian coordinates, y, is the product of this projected radius by $\sin \theta$; that is, $r \cos \phi \sin \theta$; the other is the projection on the axis normal both to z and y, that is, $r \cos \phi \cos \theta$. Here the process terminates, since all the dimensions have been exhausted.

At each stage of the process we have projected the radial vector on one axis—thus getting a Cartesian coordinate—and on the space of next lower dimension normal to this axis—thus getting the radial vector for the next stage.

This process, when applied to n coordinates, gives

$$\begin{aligned}
x_1 &= r \sin \theta_1, \\
x_2 &= r \cos \theta_1 \sin \theta_2, \\
x_3 &= r \cos \theta_1 \cos \theta_2 \sin \theta_3, \\
x_{n-1} &= r \cos \theta_1 \cos \theta_2 \ldots \cos \theta_{n-2} \sin \theta_{n-1}, \\
x_n &= r \cos \theta_1 \cos \theta_2 \ldots \cos \theta_{n-2} \cos \theta_{n-1};
\end{aligned} \tag{90.1}$$

in which r is the distance from the point $(x_1, x_2, \ldots, x_n)$ to the origin, and $\theta_1, \theta_2, \ldots, \theta_{n-1}$ are the angles of projection onto spaces of successively lower dimensions.

By straightforward, although somewhat tedious, manipulation, the Jacobian of this transformation is found to be

$$\frac{\partial(x_1, x_2, \ldots, x_n)}{\partial(r, \theta_1, \ldots, \theta_{n-1})} = r^{n-1} \cos^{n-2} \theta_1 \cos^{n-3} \theta_2 \ldots \cos \theta_{n-2}. \tag{90.2}$$

Note that for $n = 2$ this gives the familiar formula for the element of area in circular coordinates,

$$dx_1 \, dx_2 = r \, dr \, d\theta,$$

---

[20] Chapter XI of the first edition contained a more extended discussion.

and for $n = 3$ the element of volume in spherical coordinates,

$$dx_1 \, dx_2 \, dx_3 = r^2 \cos \theta \, dr \, d\theta \, d\phi.$$

Later on the transformation (90.1) and the Jacobian (90.2) will be used in deriving theorems that play a fundamental role in statistical theory.

Problems

1. Find the volume element in cylindrical coordinates.

2. Planck's radiation formula

$$p(\nu) = \frac{a\nu^3}{e^{b\nu} - 1} \tag{90.3}$$

can be interpreted as a "distribution function" in which the variable is the frequency of the light. That is, the probability of unit energy being emitted between frequencies ν and $\nu + d\nu$ is given by (90.3). Find the probability of unit energy being emitted between the wavelengths λ and $\lambda + d\lambda$.

3. What is the probability that the energy of a gas molecule lies between W and $W + dW$?

4. When a gas diffuses outward through an orifice, the equilibrium conditions within the enclosure are destroyed. It is therefore no longer true that the probability of a molecule having specified velocity components is independent of its position. This renders invalid the argument by means of which we determined $p(B|u, v, w)$ in § 89.

Sometimes in physical problems, however, we think of the electrons within a metal as behaving just like the molecules of a gas. If the metal is hot, "thermionic" electrons leak off its surface. They are supposed to get out in such small numbers as not seriously to upset the equilibrium within the metal. Assume this to be true; also assume one is emitted if and only if its x-component of velocity exceeds a positive quantity $\sqrt{E}$.

If the history of an emitted electron is traced back to a moment just before emission, what is the probability that its velocity components were u, v, w?

5. In the case of the thermions mentioned in Problem 4 it is supposed that those which emerge have their v and w unchanged, but that their velocity in the x-direction is changed to a new value u' defined by the law $u^2 - u'^2 = E$.

Assuming this to be true, what is the distribution of velocities after emission?

6. The can containing a gas carries a set of axes x, y, z. It is being translated relatively to a "fixed" set of axes x', y', z' with a velocity U, V, W. By the principle of relativity this is the same thing mechanically as if the x, y, z were "fixed" and the axes x', y', z' were moving with a velocity $-U, -V, -W$ with respect to them. Of course, if the argument of § 87 is true at all, it applies to the can and the axes x, y, z. Find the chance that a particular gas molecule has components of velocity u', v', w' with respect to the axes x', y', z'.

7. Find the volume element in toroidal[20] coordinates; that is, in a system in which any point P which lies in the xz-plane has the coordinates r, θ, 0, whereas if it does not lie in that plane, its first two coordinates are determined in exactly the same manner in the plane which contains both the point and the z-axis, and the third coordinate is the angle between this plane and the xz-plane. The system is illustrated by Fig. 90.1.

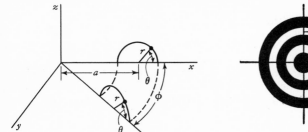

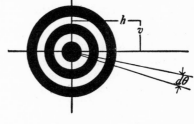

FIG. 90.1 TOROIDAL COORDINATES.   FIG. 90.2

8. In aiming at a target, the bull's-eye will not always be hit. We choose to think of firing over so short a range that there is no appreciable curvature of path and make the following assumptions (see Fig. 90.2).

(*a*) The chance of a horizontal error h in aim is totally independent of any error v vertically.

(*b*) The chance of lying in an angular sector $d\theta$ is the same for any such sector.

Find the chance of a shot having an error between (h, v) and $(h + dh, v + dv)$.

9. In the case of Problem 8, find the chance of the shot hitting between (r, θ) and $(r + dr, \theta + d\theta)$.

10. Suppose the target of Problem 8 to be inclined with respect to the vertical at an angle α. Find the probability of a shot falling between (h', v') and $(h' + dh', v' + dv')$ on this target, the h' and v' being supposed to be measured along its surface.

11. If the target of Problem 10 carries a set of axes x and y which are the 45° diagonals to h' and v', what is $p(x, y)$?

12. In Problem 8, if we choose any direction θ, there is a distance $r(\theta)$ at which the probability of lying within a given element of area dA is exactly p^*. For some other direction the same will be true, although the new

---

[20]The name "toroidal" is due to the fact that any surface defined by the equation $r = $ constant is a "torus" (that is a doughnut). The other coordinate surfaces are: for θ constant, segments of cones having the z-axis as axes; for ϕ constant, planes constaining the z-axis.

distance need not necessarily be the same. The curve

$$r = r(\theta)$$

along all points of which the probability has the same value p^* is called a "curve of equal probability." Find the equation of these curves.

13. Find the curves of equal probability in Problem 10.

14. The evaluation of the Jacobian of (90.1) is an interesting exercise in manipulation. If it is set up in the usual way, the columns will be found to contain common factors which may be divided out. The product of these is the right-hand side of (90.2). To simplify the residual determinant, (a) multiply the first row and divide the second column by $\sin \theta_1$, multiply the second row and divide the third column by $\sin \theta_2$, etc.; (b) then form sums of columns in such a way that all elements below the principal diagonal are zero. The value of the residual determinant will thus be found to be 1.

15. The position of a point in n-dimensional space can be defined by the length of the radial vector to the point, and the angles which it makes with each of the coordinate axes. This gives rise to the following equations:

$$x_1 = \lambda_1\, r,$$

$$x_2 = \lambda_2\, r,$$

$$\cdots$$

$$x_n = \lambda_n\, r,$$

$$\lambda_n^2 = 1 - \lambda_1^2 - \cdots - \lambda_{n-1}^2,$$

in which the λ's are the cosines of the angles of projection. Note that λ_n is not an independent variable. Find the Jacobian of this transformation.

16. When two hard, elastic balls collide with initial velocities u, v, w and u', v', w', their velocities after the collision are

$$\bar{u} = u - \lambda S, \qquad \bar{u}' = u' + \lambda S,$$

$$\bar{v} = v - \mu S, \qquad \bar{v}' = v' + \mu S,$$

$$\bar{w} = w - \nu S, \qquad \bar{w}' = w' + \nu S,$$

where λ, μ, ν are the direction cosines of the line of centers at impact and $S = \lambda(u - u') + \mu(v - v') + \nu(w - w')$. What is the Jacobian of the transformation?

[Reduce the determinant to its principal diagonal by combining columns and then rows.]

17. If the experiment described in Example 78.1 is repeated m times, what is the probability that just n numbers lie in the interval $b - a = x$?

Answers to Problems

1. $r \, dr \, d\theta \, dz$.   **2.** $p(\lambda) = a \, c^4/\lambda^5 (e^{bc/\lambda} - 1)$, if c is the velocity of light.

3. $p(W) = 4 \sqrt{2 a^3 W / m^3 \pi} \; e^{-2aW/m}$.

4. $p(u, v, w|B) = (a^2 u/2\pi) \, e^{-a(u^2 + v^2 + w^2 - E)}$, $u > \sqrt{E}$.

5. $p(u', v, w) = (a^2 u'/2\pi) \, e^{-a(u'^2 + v^2 + w^2)}$, $u' > 0$.

6. $p(u', v', w') = (a/\pi)^{3/2} \, e^{-a[(u'-U)^2 + (v'-V)^2 + (w'-W)^2]}$.

7. $r(a + r \cos \theta) \, dr \, d\theta \, d\phi$.   **8.** $p(h,v) = (a/\pi) \, e^{-a(h^2 + v^2)}$.

9. $p(r, \theta) = (ar/\pi) \, e^{-ar^2}$.   **10.** $p(h', v') = (a/\pi) \cos \alpha \; e^{-a(h'^2 + v'^2 \cos^2 \alpha)}$.

11. $p(x, y) = (a/\pi) \cos \alpha \; e^{-c(x^2 \pm 2bxy + y^2)}$, where $c = a(1 + \cos^2\alpha)/2$ and $b = \sin^2 \alpha/(1 + \cos^2 \alpha)$. The sign of the xy-term depends upon the quadrants in which the positive directions of x and y extend. **12.** $r = c$, where $c^2 = \log (a \, dA/\pi p^*)^{1/a}$.

13. $r' = c'/\sqrt{1 + \tan^2 \alpha \sin^2 \theta'}$, where $c'^2 = \log (a \, dA/\pi p^* \cos \alpha)^{1/a}$.

15. r^{n-1}/λ_n.   **16.** 1.   **17.** $C_n^m x^n (1-x)^{m-n}$.

Chapter VIII

Averages

91. Definition of an Average

DEFINITION 91.1. *The average (or mean) of a set of numbers is such a number that, if every member of the set were replaced by it, their sum would remain unchanged.*

For example, the average weight of a group of men is such that if every man were of the same weight, their aggregate weight would be unaltered. If there were three of them, weighing 140, 160, and 195 pounds, the average would be 165.

Obviously, if the set contains m quantities, of which n_1 have the magnitude x_1, n_2 the magnitude x_2, and so on, this definition is equivalent to the equation

$$m\bar{x} = \sum x_j\, n_j;$$

which leads at once to the formula[1]

$$\mu_1(x) = \bar{x} = \frac{1}{m}\sum x_j\, n_j \tag{91.1}$$

for computing an average.

The following theorem is almost obvious:

THEOREM 91.1. *If $\bar{x}$ is the average of a set of numbers $x_1, x_2, \ldots, x_a$ and y is the average of $y_1, y_2, \ldots, y_a$, the average of the sums $x_1 + y_1$, $x_2 + y_2, \ldots, x_a + y_a$ is $\bar{x} + \bar{y}$.*

92. Mathematical Expectation

Suppose there is a variable x which is capable of taking on any one of the values $x_1, x_2, \ldots, x_a$, and suppose that the chance of it taking these values is $p_1, p_2, \ldots, p_a$. Suppose finally that a total of m independent trials of this quantity is made and that in n_1 of them its value is x_1,

---

[1] $\mu_1(x)$ means "the first moment of x." The reason for this notation will appear in § 93.

in n_2 its value is x_2, and so on. The aggregate value of the quantity x in all the trials is $x_1 n_1 + x_2 n_2 + \ldots + x_a n_a$ and its average per trial is

$$\bar{x} = x_1 \frac{n_1}{m} + x_2 \frac{n_2}{m} + \ldots + x_a \frac{n_a}{m}.$$

We cannot predict in advance what this average $\bar{x}$ is going to be: that is, we cannot predict it with certainty. The only certain way is to try it. But we know from Bernoulli's Theorem that the *chance* of n_1/m differing from p_1 by an important amount becomes smaller and smaller the larger m is made, and a similar argument applies to the other ratios also. Hence, in a large number of trials there is little chance that $\bar{x}$ will differ much from $x_1 p_1 + x_2 p_2 + \ldots + x_a p_a$. We call this quantity the "mathematical expectation" of x.

DEFINITION 92.1. *If x can take only the values $x_1, x_2, \ldots, x_a$ and zero, the probability of each being $p(x_1), p(x_2), \ldots, p(x_a)$ and $p(0)$, the mathematical expectation of x is*[2]

$$\epsilon_1(x) = \sum_{j=0}^{a} x_j p(x_j). \tag{92.1}$$

The following theorem is at once obvious:

THEOREM 92.1. *If a large number of independent trials of the value of x are made, the chance that its average value per trial differs from its mathematical expectation by more than some preassigned quantity is small and may be made as small as we please by sufficiently increasing the number of trials.*

Strictly speaking, this theorem is obvious only when the number of possible values of x is finite; for when there is an infinity of terms, it is not necessarily true that the sum of their limits is equal to the limit approached by their sum. In other words, it is not always proper to take limits of individual terms and add them together unless the number of terms in the sum is finite. This is illustrated, for instance, by the set

$$\frac{\sin x}{1}, \quad \frac{\sin 3x}{3}, \quad \frac{\sin 5x}{5}, \ldots,$$

each term of which approaches the limit zero as x approaches π. The sum of the limits approached by the separate terms is therefore $0 + 0 + \ldots = 0$. But the sum of the terms is a Fourier series which represents the constant $+\pi/2$ for values of x between 0 and π, and the constant $-\pi/2$ for values of x between π and 2π. Therefore it approaches either $+\pi/2$ or $-\pi/2$ as a limit, according to whether we start from values of x smaller than π and ascend toward π or start from values larger than π and descend toward it. In no case can the limit of the sum be made to approach 0.

---

[2] Read "the expectation of x." The reason for the subscript 1 will appear in § 93. When no confusion can arise, $\epsilon_1(x)$ and $\mu_1(x)$ will often be written simply ϵ_1 and μ_1. When no subscript is written, particularly in the expression $\epsilon(x)$, the first expectation is meant.

So it is in the case of our theorem. There are problems in which a very large difference between experimental average and expectation is almost certain, no matter how large the number of trials. One is given in § 103. I know of no case, however, in which such a problem has any practical importance.

Another remark should be made in passing. As we are using the words, an "average" is the result of experiment, whereas a "mathematical expectation" is an advance judgment as to what that average is likely to be. This usage is not universal. Many writers, especially in sciences other than mathematics, use "average" for either idea; others use "expectation" only when a valuable consideration is involved.

We shall attempt to keep the ideas distinct, although we shall usually say "expectation" in preference to the more cumbersome "mathematical expectation."[3]

A simple example will make the general idea of expectation somewhat clearer:

EXAMPLE 92.1.—*Two dice are tossed. If seven appears the player receives a dollar; otherwise nothing. What is his expectation of gain?*

Here the "quantity x" represents money won and can take only two values, one and zero. The probability of the first is the same as the probability of a seven appearing, which is $\frac{1}{6}$; the probability of the other is $\frac{5}{6}$. Hence

$$\epsilon_1(x) = \tfrac{1}{6}\cdot 1 + \tfrac{5}{6}\cdot 0 = \tfrac{1}{6}.$$

The player's expectation of gain is therefore one-sixth of a dollar.

Suppose, now, that the player were required to pay a fixed sum A per throw. After a large number of games he would have received some average amount $\bar{x}$ per game: if $A > x$ he would be the loser, and if $A < \bar{x}$ the winner. We already know, however, that $\bar{x}$ is not likely to deviate appreciably from ϵ_1 if the number of games is great. Hence if $A > \epsilon_1$, that is, if he pays more than $16\frac{2}{3}$ cents per game, he is almost certain to lose in the long run. Conversely, if his payments are less than his expectation, he is almost sure to win. This we know by the second half of Bernoulli's Theorem; for however little his payments may differ from the expectation, the probability that the experimental average will differ by as much as this will approach zero as the number of throws increases.

Clearly, then, the game is not fair in either of these cases; what he could fairly be required to pay per game is a sum equal to his expectation.

---

[3] The adjective "mathematical" pays pentasyllabic deference to another rather mystical concept of "moral expectation," to which we shall refer in passing in § 103. It was introduced when the theory of probability was still very young, to explain something which we now know is better explained without it. Hence the identifying adjective "mathematical" is no longer required.

But suppose he did pay $16\frac{2}{3}$ cents per game; then what? After he has played m games he will have won some number n, and his net winnings will have been $n - \frac{1}{6}m$. By the first half of Bernoulli's Theroem we know that if m is large enough, n will amost certainly differ from $\frac{1}{6}m$ by more than any preassigned quantity, however large. Hence, given games enough, the player is almost sure *either to win or to lose* a very large sum, but which it will be we cannot say. By the *second* half of Bernoulli's Theorem we are equally certain that $(n/m) - \frac{1}{6}$, or in other symbols $\bar{x} - \epsilon_1$, will be negligible: the average net gain *per game* will probably be small.

Now what is true of this example is true in general: *Whenever a gambling game is conducted by repeated independent trials, a player who pays out more per game than his expectation of winning is almost sure in the long run to have an average loss per game substantially equal to the difference; if he pays less than his expectation, he is almost sure in the long run to have an average gain substantially equal to the difference; and if he pays exactly his expectation, his net loss or gain will almost certainly be large, although the average per game will probably be small.*

Let us put this in more vivid terms: If you pay too much you lose a lot; if too little the other fellow does; and if just the right amount, one of you loses, but not very much.

Insurance, viewed from the companies' standpoint, nearly duplicates the conditions of this problem: it would exactly duplicate them if every risk were "equally good,"[4] equal in amount,[5] and paid for in a single premium.[6] Some decades ago many fraternal life companies paid too much per game (that is, the face value of their policies was higher than the premium justified) and they lost money. Conservative companies, on the other hand, pay too little per game (that is, their charges exceed the expectation of their losses), although much of the difference is returned as dividends. They are "gambling on a sure thing." If, instead, they charged the price which is mathematically "fair," they would be about as likely to go bankrupt as not, which would certainly not be a benefit to their policyholders.

EXAMPLE 92.2.—*A penny is tossed repeatedly. If heads appears for the first time on the n'th throw, the player receives n cents and a new game begins. Thus if tails appears twice, followed by heads, the three throws constitute a "game" and the "winnings" are three cents. What is the expectation of gain per game?*

If heads appears for the first time on the first throw, the gain is 1; the probability of this is $p(1) = \frac{1}{2}$. For tails followed by heads the

---

[4] In the case of life insurance, if every man of a given age were equally likely to die at a given time, so far as the company knew when the policy was written. This is not actually true, due to the knowledge they acquire from their physical examinations.

[5] That is, if every life were insured for the same amount.

[6] In practice, the payment of yearly premiums complicates the computation of the company's "expectation of gain." It does not, however, affect what we are about to say.

numbers are 2 and $p(2) = \frac{1}{4}$. In general, the probability of a gain j is $p(j) = 1/2^j$. Hence

$$\epsilon_1(x) = \sum_{j=0}^{\infty} \frac{j}{2^j}.$$

This sum can easily be shown to be 2.[7] To make a fair game, therefore, the player would have to pay the "bank" two cents per game.

93. Derived Averages and Expectations

From any set of numbers $x_1, x_2, \ldots, x_a$ a host of new sets can be obtained by various arithmetical processes. In particular the sets $x_1^2, \ldots, x_a^2$; $x_1^3, \ldots, x_a^3$, and the like, can be built up. Each of these has an average, and these derived averages are just as truly descriptive of the *original* set as $\bar{x}$ was. They are the "mean square" of x, its "mean cube," and so on. We denote them either by $\overline{x^2}, \overline{x^3}, \ldots$ or by $\mu_2(x), \mu_3(x), \ldots$. Thus in general

$$\bar{x^i} = \mu_i(x) = \frac{1}{m} \sum_j x_j^i \, n_j. \tag{93.1}$$

These quantities are called the "moments" of the set of numbers x_j. The reason for this name is as follows:

Suppose the x's were represented on a horizontal axis and that a weight n_j were suspended from each point x_j. The static moment of these weights about the point zero would be exactly μ_1, and their "moment of inertia" or second moment would be μ_2. It is a small generalization to speak of an "i'th moment" as well.

The sum of the i'th powers of $x_1, x_2, \ldots$ would not be changed if each of these *powers* was replaced by $\mu_i(x)$, or if each x was replaced by $\sqrt[i]{\mu_i(x)}$. This is called the *root mean i'th power*. In particular, $\sqrt{\mu_2(x)}$, or $\sqrt{\overline{x^2}}$, is the "root mean square."

To these "average i'th powers" or "i'th moments" correspond "expected i'th powers" or "i'th expectations." By (92.1) they are

$$\epsilon_i(x) = \sum_j x_j^i \, p(x_j).$$

Note that the factor $p(x_j)$ remains unaltered, for the probability that x^i will have the value x_j^i is just the probability that x has the value x_j.

Still more generally, if $f(x)$ is any function of x and x can take only

---

[7] Let $y = x + 2x^2 + 3x^3 + \ldots$. Then $y/x = 1 + 2x + 3x^2 + \ldots$ is the derivative of $1 + x + x^2 + x^3 + \ldots = 1/(1 - x)$. Hence $y/x = 1/(1 - x)^2$, or $y = x/(1 - x)^2$. The series in the text is obtained by putting $x = \frac{1}{2}$. It therefore sums up to the value 2.

the set of discrete values $x_1, x_2, \ldots, x_a$, the expectation of the function is

$$\epsilon(f) = \sum_j f(x_j)\, p(x_j).\tag{93.2}$$

94. Average Values of Continuous Variables

All of the concepts with which the present chapter deals have exact counterparts in the case of continuous variables. The principal formal difference lies in the substitution of integral signs in place of signs of summation.

In the case of averages and moments no problem arises, for the result of m trials is just a set of numbers $x_1, x_2, \ldots, x_m$, whose mean and other moments may be computed directly. In particular, if the sum of these numbers is s, their average is $\bar{x} = s/m$. But the expectation of a continuous variable requires more careful discussion.

To begin with, let us suppose that we are dealing with a variable x, the distribution function for which is known to be $p(x)$. Suppose the total range of variation of this variable to be divided up into elementary intervals of length dx; and suppose that a large number of independent trials of x are made. Within any interval $(x_j, x_j + dx)$ will fall n_j of these values, the sum of which may be denoted by s_j. Then it is obvious that

$$n_j x_j < s_j < n_j(x_j + dx).$$

The sum of *all* the values of x is obviously obtained by adding together the sums for the separate intervals. Let it be denoted by s. Then we have

$$\sum n_j x_j < s < \sum n_j(x_j + dx).$$

The average value of x, which we denote by $\bar{x}$, is obtained by dividing s by the total number of trials made. Hence we have

$$\sum \frac{n_j}{m} x_j < \bar{x} < \sum \frac{n_j}{m} x_j + dx \sum \frac{n_j}{m}.$$

Since $\Sigma\, n_j = m$, x is thus contained between two limits which differ only by dx, a quantity which we may make as small as we like. We conclude, therefore, that

$$\bar{x} = \sum \frac{n_j}{m} x_j + c\, dx\tag{94.1}$$

where $0 < c < 1$.

We also know by Bernoulli's Theorem that if m is large, n_j/m is almost certain to approximate $p(x_j) \, dx$, wherefore $\Sigma \, x_j \, n_j/m$ is almost certain to be close to $\Sigma \, x_j \, p(x_j) \, dx$. If we substitute this in (94.1) and let dx become vanishingly small, we conclude that $\bar{x}$ is not likely to deviate much from

$$\epsilon_1(x) = \int p(x) \, x \, dx. \tag{94.2}$$

This is the "first expectation of x." Obviously the "i'th expectation" is

$$\epsilon_i(x) = \int p(x) \, x^i \, dx.$$

Similarly, if we have any function $f(x)$, its expectation is

$$\epsilon(f) = \int f(x) \, p(x) \, dx. \tag{94.3}$$

Note that this is not only the analog of (93.2); it also follows from (94.2), for by "expectation of f" we clearly mean its first expectation, whence (94.2) gives

$$\epsilon(f) = \int f p(f) \, df. \tag{94.4}$$

Suppose, now, we change variables from f to x; by (85.1),

$$p(f) = p(x) \frac{dx}{df},$$

and when this is substituted in (94.4), it becomes (94.3).

In general, however many variables the quantity f may depend upon, its i'th expectation is given by the law

$$\epsilon_i(f) = \int \int \ldots \int f^i \, p(x_1, x_2, \ldots x_a) \, dx_1 \, dx_2 \ldots dx_a. \tag{94.5}$$

EXAMPLE 94.1.—*What is the expected energy of a molecule in a gas obeying Maxwell's law (87.2)?*

Energy is $W = \frac{1}{2} m s^2$; hence by (94.3) and (89.1)

$$\epsilon(W) = \int \frac{1}{2} m s^2 \, p(s) \, ds$$

$$= 2m \sqrt{\frac{a^3}{\pi}} \int s^4 \, e^{-a s^2} \, ds.$$

If we set $as^2 = z$, this becomes

$$\epsilon(W) = \frac{m}{a\sqrt{\pi}} \int_0^\infty z^{3/2} e^{-z} dz$$

$$= \frac{m}{a\sqrt{\pi}} \left(\frac{3}{2}\right)! = \frac{3}{4}\frac{m}{a}. \tag{94.6}$$

This result could also have been obtained from (87.2) by the use of (94.5), for the energy can also be written $W = m(u^2 + v^2 + w^2)/2$. Hence

$$\epsilon(W) = \int\int\int \frac{m}{2}(u^2 + v^2 + w^2)\, p\,(u,\, v,\, w)\, du\, dv\, dw$$

$$= \frac{m}{2}\left(\frac{a}{\pi}\right)^{3/2}\left\{\int\int\int u^2\, e^{-a(u^2 + v^2 + w^2)}\, du\, dv\, dw\right.$$

$$+ \int\int\int v^2\, e^{-a(u^2 + v^2 + w^2)}\, du\, dv\, dw$$

$$+ \left.\int\int\int w^2\, e^{-a(u^2 + v^2 + w^2)}\, du\, dv\, dw\right\}.$$

The three integrals are equal and each can easily be found to have the value $\pi^{3/2}/2a^{5/2}$, thus leading again to (94.6) for the expected energy.

If the energy of a tagged molecule were noted at a large number of instants far enough apart to constitute "independent" observations, an "average energy" could be obtained. This is nearly certain to be about equal to $\epsilon(W)$. Likewise, if all the molecules in the gas were simultaneously observed, they would constitute a large set of "trials." If those trials were independent— that is, if the chance of one having a specified W were independent of the rest[8]—their average energy would probably not differ greatly from $\epsilon(W)$. For this reason physicists usually speak of $\epsilon(W)$ as the "average energy of the molecules."

95. The Median

DEFINITION 95.1. *The median of a set of numbers is that number which occupies the central position when the sequence is arranged in order of magnitude.*

In other words, there are just as many numbers in the sequence *larger* than the median as there are *smaller* than the median.

Strictly speaking, this definition implies that the number of terms

---

[8] They are not quite independent in fact, for the sum of the energies of all is fixed by the principle of the conservation of energy.

in the sequence is odd. If the number of terms is even, either of the two adjacent numbers, or, better still, their average, can be taken as the median. Due to their arrangement in order of magnitude, it will generally make little difference which of these conventions is adopted.

As an example, the median of the set of numbers

$$-28, \quad -8, \quad -8, \quad -1, \quad -1, \quad +28, \quad +56, \quad +56, \quad +68$$

is -1, since there are just four numbers greater and four numbers less than (or equal to) -1. The average of the sequence, on the other hand, is one-ninth of the sum of the terms, which turns out to be 18.

To the "median" corresponds an "expected median." For example, suppose the chance of x taking the value x_j is $p(x_j)$. A long series of trials will result in n_1 x_1's, n_2 x_2's, and so on. Let these be arranged in order and call the middle one x_i. Then, obviously

$$n_1 + n_2 + \ldots + n_{i-1} < \frac{m}{2},$$

$$n_1 + n_2 + \ldots + n_i > \frac{m}{2}.$$

But in the long run n_j/m is not likely to differ much from $p(x_j)$; so if we divide these inequalities by m throughout they immediately suggest the relations

$$p(x_1) + p(x_2) + \ldots + p(x_{i-1}) < \tfrac{1}{2},$$

$$p(x_1) + p(x_2) + \ldots + p(x_i) > \tfrac{1}{2}.$$

This defines the expected median.

Hence:

DEFINITION 95.2. *The expected median x_i is such a number that there is less than an even chance of either x or x_i being greater than the other.*

For example, in tossing two dice the chances of various sums are as follows:

Sum	2	3	4	5	6	7	8	9	10	11	12
Probability	$\frac{1}{36}$	$\frac{2}{36}$	$\frac{3}{36}$	$\frac{4}{36}$	$\frac{5}{36}$	$\frac{6}{36}$	$\frac{5}{36}$	$\frac{4}{36}$	$\frac{3}{36}$	$\frac{2}{36}$	$\frac{1}{36}$

The expected median is therefore 7, for the chance of the sum exceeding 7 is $\frac{15}{36}$ and the chance of 7 exceeding the sum is also $\frac{15}{36}$.

The general idea is that of a number which we can expect to be exceeded as often as not; but its own chance of repeated occurrence spoils so simple a definition when the variable is capable of only a discrete set of values. On the other hand, if the variable is capable of continuous variation this definition is valid, for in that case the chance of the variable taking *exactly* its median value is zero. By a line of argument exactly similar to that used in § 94 we can show that the expected median of x is that value x_m for which

$$\int_{x_m}^{\infty} p(x) \, dx = \tfrac{1}{2}.$$

Of course the integral of $p(x)$ between the limits $-\infty$ and x_m is also $\tfrac{1}{2}$.

96. The Deviation, Variance and Standard Deviation

So far we have introduced three fundamental probability concepts: that of the "most probable" result, of the "expected" result, and of the "expected median"; and have intimated that a host of derived, or secondary, concepts are possible, of which "expected i'th powers" have been specifically mentioned. In practice these derived concepts are not often applied directly to the numbers of the set, but more usually to their "deviations from the mean" or, more simply, their "deviations."

Thus, to the set of numbers $x_1, x_2, \ldots, x_a$ repeated $n_1, n_2, \ldots, n_a$ times, respectively, there corresponds a mean $\bar{x}$ and a set of deviations from that mean

$$d_1 = x_1 - \bar{x},$$
$$d_2 = x_2 - \bar{x},$$
$$\cdots$$
$$d_a = x_a - \bar{x}, \qquad (96.1)$$

each of which recurs as often as the corresponding x. Obviously the set of d's has its own average, median, and the like.

Of these, two are especially important:

THEOREM 96.1. *The average of a set of d's is zero.*

By definition $\bar{d}$, or $\mu_1(d)$, is

$$\mu_1(d) = \frac{1}{m} \sum d_j \, n_j.$$

But from (96.1),

$$\sum d_j \, n_j = \sum x_j \, n_j - \bar{x} \sum n_j.$$

However $\Sigma \, n_j = m$ and, by (91.1), $\Sigma \, x_j \, n_j = m\bar{x}$. Hence

$$\bar{d} = \mu_1(d) = 0.$$

THEOREM 96.2. *The mean square deviation of a set of numbers is equal to the mean square of the set diminished by the square of their average.*

For

$$\mu_2(d) = \frac{1}{m} \sum n_j (x_j - \bar{x})^2$$

$$= \frac{1}{m} \sum n_j x_j{}^2 - \frac{2\bar{x}}{m} \sum n_j x_j + \bar{x}^2.$$

But by the use of (91.1) and (93.1) this reduces immediately to

$$\mu_2(d) = \overline{x^2} - \bar{x}^2. \tag{96.2}$$

In statistical works the quantity μ_2 is generally called the "sample variance" and is denoted by s^2. Its square root, s, is known as the *sample standard* deviation.[9] Thus, all of the following equations are equivalent to (96.2)

$$s^2 = \overline{d^2} = \mu_2(d) = \overline{x^2} - \bar{x}^2 = \mu_2(x) - [\mu_1(x)]^2.$$

Finally, if a set of numbers $x_1, x_2, \ldots, x_a$ have an expectation ϵ, the quantities

$$\delta_1 = x_1 - \epsilon,$$
$$\delta_2 = x_2 - \epsilon,$$
$$\cdots$$
$$\delta_a = x_a - \epsilon$$

are their deviations from expectation. However, when x has the value x_j, δ has the value δ_j. The probability of either is therefore $p(x_j)$ and

$$\epsilon_1(\delta) = \sum p(x_j) (x_j - \epsilon)$$
$$= \sum x_j p(x_j) - \epsilon \sum p(x_j).$$

Since all possible values of x_j are included in the summation, $\sum x_j p(x_j) = \epsilon_1(x) = \epsilon$ by definition and $\sum p(x_j) = 1$. Hence

$$\epsilon_1(\delta) = 0.$$

THEOREM 96.3. *The first expectation of the deviation is zero.*

Similarly, the second expectation of δ, which is called the variance of x and written var(x), is

$$\epsilon_2(\delta) = \sum p(x_j) (x_j - \epsilon)^2$$
$$= \sum x_j{}^2 p(x_j) - 2\epsilon \sum x_j p(x_j) + \epsilon^2 \sum p(x_j)$$
$$= \epsilon_2(x) - [\epsilon_1(x)]^2.$$

---

[9] This terminology is not universally adopted. Sometimes, for a reason which will appear in § 141, Chapter XI, the sample variance is defined as $n \mu_2/(n - 1)$ instead, and the sample standard deviation as the square root of this quantity.

THEOREM 96.4. *The variance of x is its second expectation reduced by the square of its first expectation.*

The square root of the variance is known as the standard deviation and generally denoted by σ. Thus

$$\sigma^2 = \mathrm{var}(x) = \epsilon_2(x) - [\epsilon_1(x)]^2. \qquad (96.3)$$

All the formulas of this section apply to continuous variables as well as to those which are capable of taking only discrete values.

97. Standard Form of Distribution Functions

A visual impression of the meaning of the expectation and the standard deviation can be obtained by referring back to Figs 56.1 and 56.2. The stroke near the top of each diagram is, in fact, located at the first expectation of n. From the discussion in the preceding section it is clear that it locates the center of gravity of the area under the distribution curve.

Also, in the figures the successive curves spread out more and more widely. The standard deviation is a measure of this spread, or, if we wish to speak of the opposite characteristic, of the compactness of the distribution. If the reader will refer ahead to Fig. 112.1, he will find the same distributions plotted to scales proportional to their standard deviations; they are now equally "compact."

It is often desirable, particularly in statistical studies, to place the origin of coordinates at the expectation of the distribution function and to adopt the standard deviation σ as the unit of measure. This is accomplished by the transformation

$$y = \frac{x - \epsilon_1(x)}{\sigma},$$

whence

$$p'(y) = \sigma p(\sigma y + \epsilon_1),$$

where $p(x)$ is the original distribution function and $p'(y)$ is the same distribution in the new variable. When transformed in this way, the distribution is said to be *in standard form*.[10] That is,

DEFINITION 97.1. *A distribution is in standard form when the scales are so chosen that $\epsilon_1 = 0$ and $\sigma = 1$.*

---

[10] Such functions are customarily said to be "normalized." The word leads to awkward phrases, such as "normalized normal distributions," and occasionally to ambiguities. We therefore adopt the less common, but more convenient, term.

98. Expectation and Variance of a Sum; Covariance

Just as the discussion of § 96 could equally well have been framed in terms of continuous variables by using integrals instead of summations, so the formulas which follow could be derived for discrete variables. We shift to the continuous concept, with its associated integral notation, only to acquaint the reader equally with both.

Suppose, then, that an experiment leads to two numbers, as, for example when two dice are tossed simultaneously, or when the radius and thickness of the discs of § 84 are measured. Call these numbers x and y and let f be any function of them. Then, by (94.5),

$$\epsilon_1(f) = \int \int f p(x,y) \, dx \, dy. \tag{98.1}$$

First, suppose that $f = x + y$. Then

$$\epsilon_1(x + y) = \int \int x \, p(x,y) \, dx \, dy + \int \int y \, p(x,y) \, dx \, dy,$$

or, since the integrals are obviously $\epsilon_1(x)$ and $\epsilon_1(y)$,

$$\epsilon_1(x + y) = \epsilon_1(x) + \epsilon_1(y). \tag{98.2}$$

THEOREM 98.1. *The expectation of the sum of two (or any number) of variables is the sum of their expectations.*

It readily follows that

THEOREM 98.2. *The expectation of the average $\bar{x}$ of the variables $x_1, x_2, \ldots, x_a$ is the average of their expectations. In particular, if all these variables have the same expectation ϵ,*

$$\epsilon_1(\bar{x}) = \epsilon. \tag{98.3}$$

Next, let $f = (x + y)^2 = x^2 + 2xy + y^2$. Then (98.1) breaks into three parts which are easily identified as $\epsilon_2(x)$, $2\epsilon_1(xy)$ and $\epsilon_2(y)$, and we have

$$\epsilon_2(x + y) = \epsilon_2(x) + \epsilon_2(y) + 2\epsilon_1(xy). \tag{98.4}$$

If we now square both sides of (98.2) and subtract them term by term from (98.4), and if we make use of the relation (96.3), we arrive at

$$\text{var}(x + y) = \text{var}(x) + \text{var}(y) + 2[\epsilon_1(xy) - \epsilon_1(x)\,\epsilon_1(y)]. \tag{98.5}$$

The term in brackets is called the *covariance* of the distribution (or the covariance of x and y) and is denoted by covar(xy). We shall discuss its significance in a moment. First, however, recalling that the variance is the square of the standard deviation, we rewrite (98.5) in the form in which it is most commonly met in statistical theory:

$$\sigma^2(x + y) = \sigma^2(x) + \sigma^2(y) + 2 \operatorname{covar}(xy),$$

where

$$\operatorname{covar}(xy) = \epsilon_1(xy) - \epsilon_1(x)\,\epsilon_1(y). \tag{98.6}$$

THEOREM 98.3. *The variance of a sum of two variables is equal to the sum of their variances plus twice their covariance.*

If we had dealt with a larger number of variables $x_1, x_2, \ldots, x_a$ and substituted $f^2 = (x_1 + x_2 + \ldots + x_a)^2$ in (94.5), we would have arrived at the general relation

$$\sigma^2(x_1 + x_2 + \ldots + x_a) = \sum_i \sigma^2(x_i) + 2 \sum{}^*\operatorname{covar}(x_i x_j), \tag{98.7}$$

where the notation Σ^* is used to indicate that the last sum is to be taken for every pair i, j for which $j > i$.

To get an insight into the significance of the covariance term, consider the case of two *independent* variables. Then $p(x,y) = p(x)\,p(y)$ and

$$\epsilon_1(xy) = \int\!\!\int xy\,p(x)\,p(y)\,dx\,dy = \left[\int x\,p(x)\,dx\right]\left[\int y\,p(y)\,dy\right] = \epsilon_1(x)\,\epsilon_1(y).$$

When this is substituted into (98.6) it gives $\operatorname{covar}(xy) = 0$.

THEOREM 98.4. *When two variables are independent, their covariance is zero.*

Covariance, then, is in some sense a criterion of dependence; we can at least say that when it is *not* zero the variables are *not* independent. But the converse of this statement is not true, as will be seen in Problems 110.23 and 110.24. Hence the criterion is not a very reliable one. In particular, if the covariance of the numbers yielded by an experiment is less than that of the numbers yielded by a control experiment, we cannot assert that the former pair are more nearly independent.

The following example may illuminate the subject further.

EXAMPLE 98.1.—*Find the covariance of the distributions $p(h', v')$, Problem 90.10, and $p(x, y)$, Problem 90.11.*

The first of these is easy, for, according to the answers,

$$p(h', v') = (a/\pi) \cos \alpha \left[e^{-ah'^2}\right]\left[e^{-av'^2 \cos \alpha}\right].$$

Since this is in the form $p(h')\,p(v')$, the variables are independent and hence

$$\operatorname{covar}(h'v') = 0.$$

For the second we have

$$p(x, y) = \frac{a}{\pi} \cos \alpha \; e^{-c(x^2 + 2bxy + y^2)}$$

with

$$c = \frac{a}{2}(1 + \cos^2 \alpha), \qquad b = \frac{\sin^2 \alpha}{1 + \cos^2 \alpha}.$$

To evaluate the covariance we introduce two new variables

$$\xi = \sqrt{c}(x + by), \qquad \eta = \sqrt{c(1 - b^2)}\, y.$$

With these, the exponent in $p(x, y)$ reduces to $-(\xi^2 + \eta^2)$, the Jacobian of the transformation is $1/a \cos \alpha$, and

$$xy = \frac{\xi \eta}{a \cos \alpha} - \frac{\eta^2}{2a} \tan^2 \alpha.$$

Hence the integral

$$\epsilon_1(xy) = \int_{-\infty}^{\infty} \int_{-\infty}^{\infty} xy\, p(x, y)\, dx\, dy$$

can be evaluated without difficulty and becomes

$$\epsilon_1(xy) = -\frac{1}{a} \tan^2 \alpha.$$

Similarly, we find that $\epsilon_1(x) = \epsilon_1(y) = 0$; and therefore by (98.6),

$$\mathrm{covar}(xy) = -\frac{1}{a} \tan^2 \alpha.$$

Now let us recall the nature of the problems. Both relate to firing at the same target under identical conditions. The real distribution of hits on the target is clearly the same for both. The only difference is that in one case the positions of these hits are measured relative to one set of axes, and in the other case to a different set. It is this change in the frame of reference, not something inherent in the experiment, that has destroyed the "independence."

To look at the matter from the reverse point of view, a situation in which the variables x and y have non-zero covariance and therefore are clearly *not* independent has been replaced by one in which the variables *are* independent, merely by rotation of the axes.[11]

---

[11] See also §§ 158 to 160, Chapter XI.

99. Résumé

Most of the concepts in this chapter relate to sets of numbers. This is, in a way, a limitation of the general idea of an "event" and its probability, for not every aspect of an "event" is numerically measureable. However, recognizing this limitation, what we have so far learned takes the following form:

Concepts Associated with the Results of Experiment	*Concepts Associated with Advance Judgement*
(1) Of a finite set of numbers, the one that occurs most frequently is called the *mode*.[12]	(1) Of a finite set of numbers, one is the *most probable*. (It is also called the *mode* by some writers.)
(2) If the numbers are arranged in order of magnitude, the one that occupies the middle position is the *median*.	(2) There is a value which the variable has at most an even chance of exceeding, and at least an even chance of either equalling or exceeding. It is the *expected median*.
(3) That number by which every number of the set could be replaced without changing their sum is the *average* or *mean* of the set.	(3) There is an average per trial which a number is most likely to show after *m* independent trials have been made. This average approaches a limiting value as *m* is indefinitely increased. This limiting value is the *expectation* of the number.
(4) If each number is reduced by an amount equal to the average of the set, the resultant numbers are the *deviation from the average*.	(4) If every possible value is reduced by an amount equal to the expectation of the set, the results are the *deviations from expectation*.
(5) The *mean deviation* is zero.	(5) The *expected deviation* is zero.
(6) If each deviation of the set is raised to the *i*'th power, the average of the result is called *the i'th moment* of the deviations. The second moment is known as the *sample variance* (or *mean square deviation*). Its square root is the *sample standard deviation* (or *root mean square deviation*).	(6) If every possible deviation from expectation is raised to the *i*'th power, the resultant set of numbers possesses its own expectation. This is called the *i'th expectation* of the deviations. The second expectation of the deviation is known as the *variance* and its square root is the *standard deviation*.
(6a) The *sample variance* of a set of numbers is equal to the average of their squares, diminished by the square of their average.	(6a) The *variance* of a distribution is equal to its second expectation, diminished by the square of its first expectation.

[12] This statement is not made in the text.

(7) If $x_1, x_2, \ldots, x_a$ and $y_1, y_2, \ldots, y_b$ are two sets of numbers with averages $\bar{x}$ and $\bar{y}$, the average of the x's plus the y's is

$$(a\bar{x} + b\bar{y})/(a + b).$$

If they are equally numerous, and are added in pairs,

$$\overline{x + y} = \bar{x} + \bar{y}$$

and

$$d_i(x + y) = d_i(x) + d_i(y).^{12}$$

(7) If $\epsilon_1(x)$ and $\epsilon_1(y)$ are the expectations of two variables, the expectation of their sum is

$$\epsilon_1(x + y) = \epsilon_1(x) + \epsilon_1(y)$$

and the deviations of the sum are

$$\delta_i(x + y) = \delta_i(x) + \delta_i(y).$$

(8) The *sample covariance* of the number pairs (x_1, y_1), (x_2, y_2), $\ldots$, (x_a, y_a) is the average of the products $x_i y_i$, diminished by the product of the averages $\bar{x}$ and $\bar{y}$.

(8) If an experiment provides two numbers x and y with probability $p(x, y)$, the *covariance* of x and y is the expectation of their product, diminished by the product of their expectations. If the variables are independent, their covariance is zero.

(9) The sample variance of the sums $(x_i + y_i)$ of a set of number pairs (x_i, y_i) is the sum of the sample variance of x, the sample variance of y, and twice their sample covariance.

(9) The variance of $x + y$ is the sum of the variance of x, the variance of y, and twice their covariance.

100. Some Instructive Illustrations; The General Case of Independent Trials

EXAMPLE 100.1.—*Find the expected number of successes in m independent trials of an event with probability of success p.*

The probability of n successes in m trials is

$$p(n) = C_n^m\, p^n\, (1 - p)^{m-n}.$$

The expectation of n is, by (92.1),

$$\epsilon_1(n) = \sum_{n=0}^{m} n\, p(n)$$

$$= \sum_{n=0}^{m} n\, C_n^m\, p^n\, (1 - p)^{m-n}.$$

But

$$n\, C_n^m = m\, C_{n-1}^{m-1}.$$

Hence

$$\epsilon_1(n) = mp \sum_{n=0}^{m} C_{n-1}^{m-1}\, p^{n-1}\, (1 - p)^{(m-1)-(n-1)}.$$

This is of the form[13] (25.2), except that m is replaced by $m - 1$ and n by $n - 1$. Hence the sum of all the terms is $[p + (1 - p)]^{m-1} = 1$, and

$$\epsilon_1(n) = mp.$$

In this case the expected number of successes and the most probable number come out to be equal, except that the expected number may be fractional whereas the most probable number is necessarily an integer (see § 56). The variance and standard deviation are (see Problem 110.2)

$$\epsilon_2(\delta) = mp(1 - p),$$

$$\sigma = \sqrt{mp(1 - p)}.$$

101. Some Instructive Illustrations; The Expectation of the Hypergeometric Distribution

EXAMPLE 101.1.—*Example 45.2 dealt with the probability of drawing just p red and q black balls from an urn which, at the start, held m red and n black. What is the expected number of red balls, if a total of r are drawn?*

If $p + q = r$, the probability of drawing p red balls is, by (45.1),

$$P_{m,n}(p, q) = \frac{C_p^m \, C_{r-p}^n}{C_r^{m+n}}. \tag{101.1}$$

The expected number of red balls—that is, the first expectation of p— is thus

$$\epsilon_1(p) = \sum_{p=0}^{r} p \, \frac{C_p^m \, C_{r-p}^n}{C_r^{m+n}}.$$

Noting that C_r^{m+n} does not vary from term to term and replacing $p \, C_p^m$ by $m \, C_{p-1}^{m-1}$, this becomes

$$\epsilon_1(p) = \frac{m}{C_r^{m+n}} \sum_{p=0}^{r} C_{p-1}^{m-1} \, C_{r-p}^n. \tag{101.2}$$

But if C_{r-p}^n is written $C_{(r-1)-(p-1)}^n$, the sum in (101.2) can be identified with (23.2). Hence

$$\epsilon_1(p) = m \, \frac{C_{r-1}^{m+n-1}}{C_r^{m+n}} = \frac{mr}{m + n}.$$

As in the last example, when this result is integral it is also the most

---

[13] There is one term too many, but this term turns out to be zero because of the factor C_{-1}^{m-1}, which vanishes.

probable number of red balls, and when it is fractional the most probable number of red balls is one of the adjacent integers.

102. Some Instructive Illustrations; A Dice Problem

In the illustrations considered in the last two sections the "expectation" was either equal to or adjacent to the "most probable" result, according to whether both results were integral or not. The following example shows that this is not always so.

EXAMPLE 102.1.—*A die is tossed until an ace appears. What is the most probable number of throws and what is the expected number of throws?*

The chance that the ace appears on the first throw is $p_1 = \frac{1}{6}$. The chance that it does not appear on the first throw but appears on the second is $p_2 = \frac{5}{6} \cdot \frac{1}{6}$. The chance that it does not appear on either of these throws but appears on the third is $p_3 = (\frac{5}{6})^2 \cdot \frac{1}{6}$, and, in general, the chance that it appears for the first time on the j'th throw is $p_j = (\frac{5}{6})^{j-1} \cdot \frac{1}{6}$. It is obvious that the most probable number of throws is 1.

The expected number of throws, on the other hand, is

$$\epsilon_1(j) = \sum_{j=1}^{\infty} j\, p_j = \frac{1}{6}[1 \cdot 1 + 2 \cdot \frac{5}{6} + 3 \cdot (\frac{5}{6})^2 + 4 \cdot (\frac{5}{6})^3 + \ldots].$$

But from Footnote 7, § 92.

$$\frac{1}{(1-x)^2} = 1 + 2x + 3x^2 + \ldots.$$

Comparing this with $\epsilon_1(j)$, we get

$$\epsilon_1(j) = 6.$$

In other words, the expected number of throws is six, although the most probable number is one.

103. Some Instructive Illustrations; The St. Petersburg Paradox

As a final illustration of this kind of computation we take the following very famous problem, the apparently absurd solution of which puzzled men for generations:

EXAMPLE 103.1.—*A penny is tossed until heads appears. If heads appears for the first time on the j'th throw, the player receives 2^{j-1} dollars (i.e., 1, 2, 4, 8, . . . dollars on the first, second, etc., throws). What should the player pay the bank for the privilege of playing a sequence of this sort in order that the game may be equitable?*

If heads appears for the first time on the j'th throw, the player receives $x_j = 2^{j-1}$ dollars. The probability of this happening is $p(x_j) = (\frac{1}{2})^j$. Substituting these into (92.1), it becomes

$$\epsilon_1(x) = \sum x_j p(x_j) = \tfrac{1}{2} + \tfrac{1}{2} + \tfrac{1}{2} + \ldots.$$

There is, however, no logical limit to the number of consecutive tails which may turn up before the first head appears. Hence the series contains infinitely many terms and $\epsilon_1(x) = \infty$. In other words, in order to play a sequence of this sort fairly to the bank, the player must first deposit with the bank an infinite amount of money.

From a common-sense standpoint this is absurd. No sane man would consider paying the bank one hundred dollars for such a chance, much less an infinite amount. And yet the mathematics itself is straightforward and no more questionable than the processes used elsewhere in this book. If the result is incorrect, it throws suspicion upon the entire structure of Probability Theory. It is therefore important to know why the result does not agree with common sense.

A number of answers have been given to this question. Probably the first historically is that given by Daniel Bernoulli, who distinguished between what he termed "mathematical" and "moral" expectation. The former he defined exactly as we have done; the latter he explained as follows:

A dollar is worth more to a beggar than it is to a millionaire. In fact, says Bernoulli, the satisfaction which one gets out of any acquired sum of money is less and less the greater the amount of money which one then has. When, therefore, the player pays out from his moderate fortune a certain sum of money, he pays out something the *moral* value of which is comparatively large. He has a chance—though a very small chance—of winning an enormous amount of money; but if he does, he is then a very wealthy man and his winnings acquire a *moral* value based upon his new, rather than upon his old, economic standing. In other words, his losses, being based upon a comparatively low economic standing, loom larger in his estimation than do his winnings.

By introducing the hypothesis that the relationship between the moral and mathematical expectations is of a logarithmic nature, the computation of the amount which he should pay can be carried out and gives a result which is somewhere within the bounds of reason. It leads to another absurdity, however, since the amount which the player should pay to the bank is different *for different men*, according to their varying degrees of wealth, even though they play against the *same bank*. What the banker would say to such an arrangement is quite obvious. As this is certainly not the true way out of the dilemma it is not necessary to go into the mathematics of it.

Another explanation which has been favored by many statisticians is based upon the fact that, if the amount paid is $x_j = k^{j-1}$ instead of 2^{j-1}, where $k < 2$, the required payment is no longer infinite. In this case, (92.1) becomes

$$\epsilon_1(x) = \frac{1}{2} + \frac{k}{4} + \frac{k^2}{8} + \ldots = \frac{1}{2-k}. \tag{103.1}$$

For instance, if k is 1.5, the player should pay the bank $2.00 for the privilege of playing a sequence, which seems reasonable.

The second explanation of the paradox makes use of these facts, and then concludes that we have no intuitive sense of the immensity of the difference between the situation when $k = 2$ and when $k < 2$, and therefore are unwilling to pay the amount of money which is logically called for. This explanation, too, is open to objection, however; for as k approaches the value 2 the sum (103.1) gets larger and larger, and likewise becomes absurd. Thus, if k were 1.99 instead of 2 (so that instead of paying $2.00 if heads appears on the second throw the bank would pay only $1.99), the player should still pay the bank $100, which no sensible man could be induced to do. Hence, if the trouble is with our intuition, that intuition must go wrong even when dealing with numbers that deviate from $2.00 by amounts which our merchants have done their utmost to make familiar.

I believe the true resolution of the paradox is quite different, and rests upon the fact that in our everyday experience we deal only with individuals who have finite fortunes and who would therefore be incapable of paying back the sums which are required in those very rare cases where there is an extremely long run of tails. To see the effect upon the mathematical expectation if the bank has limited wealth, consider the following alternative form of the problem:

EXAMPLE 103.2.—*What is the equitable payment for playing in the game described in Example 103.1 if the bank's wealth is limited to $1,000,000?*

The probability of heads appearing first on the j'th throw is $(\frac{1}{2})^j$, as before. If so, the bank pays 2^{j-1} if this is less than $1,000,000; otherwise it pays $1,000,000. In other words,

$$p_j = (\tfrac{1}{2})^j, \qquad x_j = 2^{j-1}, \qquad \text{if} \quad 2^{j-1} < 1,000,000;$$
$$\text{i.e.,} \quad \text{if} \quad j \leq 20;$$

$$p_j = (\tfrac{1}{2})^j, \qquad x_j = 1,000,000, \qquad \text{if} \quad 2^{j-1} > 1,000,000;$$
$$\text{i.e.,} \quad \text{if} \quad j > 20.$$

Thus (92.1) becomes:

$$\epsilon_1(x) = \sum_{j=1}^{20} (\tfrac{1}{2})^j \cdot 2^{j-1} + \sum_{j=21}^{\infty} (\tfrac{1}{2})^j \cdot 1,000,000.$$

The first sum obviously is 10. The second is a geometric series the sum of which is

$$\frac{1,000,000}{2^{20}} = 0.9536.$$

In order for play to be equitable against a million-dollar bank, therefore, the player should pay $10.95—a reasonable amount.[14]

If the bank had a billion dollars, the payment would be less than $16; whereas if it had $1,000,000,000,000 the payment would be less than $21.

Taking the other extreme, if the bank had only $100 capital,[15] the payment would be $4.26. If it had $10, it would be $2.63, whereas if it had only $1 (in which case the payment would be $1, no matter how many tails appeared before the first head), the payment would be $1, as it should.

I believe this to be the best resolution of the paradox.[16] If the bank were infinitely wealthy, the expectation would be infinite. Therefore the mathematics is correct. But we are accustomed to deal only with "limited wealth" and cannot conceive of "unlimited amounts of money."

In other words, our intuition is in error, rather than the theory; but only because the theory deals with material for which we have no opportunity to build up intuitive judgments.

104. The Expectation of a Probability

Equations (93.2) and (94.3) give the expectation of any function of x whatever, where the number x is determined by experiment and $p(x)$ is its probability. But $p(x)$ is itself a function of x and therefore also has an expected value $\epsilon(p)$.

Thus, if we toss two dice and add the numbers appearing, we get a sum from 2 to 12. Each of these has a well-defined probability of appearing, which was derived in Problem 69.3. The exact relation is

Sum	2	3	4	5	6	7	8	9	10	11	12
Probability	$\frac{1}{36}$	$\frac{2}{36}$	$\frac{3}{36}$	$\frac{4}{36}$	$\frac{5}{36}$	$\frac{6}{36}$	$\frac{5}{36}$	$\frac{4}{36}$	$\frac{3}{36}$	$\frac{2}{36}$	$\frac{1}{36}$

An experiment which gave the sum $x = 4$ could equally well be said to have determined $p(x) = \frac{3}{36}$. The probability of either result is $p(x) = \frac{3}{36}$.

---

[14] Note that only $0.95 of this arises from the expectation of receiving a million dollars!

[15] All these numbers are based upon the bank's wealth after receiving the payment, not before. In the case of the million-dollar bank the difference is negligible; in some of the figures which follow, however, it is not.

[16] But see also Problem 110.18.

Thus, if we identify $p(x)$ with the $f(x)$ of (93.2), we get

$$\epsilon(p) = \sum [p(x_j)]^2, \tag{104.1}$$

which, in the case of the numbers above, is

$$\left(\tfrac{1}{36}\right)^2 + \left(\tfrac{2}{36}\right)^2 + \left(\tfrac{3}{63}\right)^2 + \cdots + \left(\tfrac{2}{36}\right)^2 + \left(\tfrac{1}{36}\right)^2 = 0.1126.$$

In other words, we may expect the experiment to give a result of which the probability is little greater than $\tfrac{1}{9}$.

As a second example, consider all the various poker hands which can be dealt. There are C_5^{52} of these and each has the same probability $1/C_5^{52}$. In this case (104.1) includes C_5^{52} terms, each equal to $1/(C_5^{52})^2$, and $\epsilon(p) = 1/C_5^{52}$—not a remarkable answer, because when every experiment leads to an equally likely result, we surely expect a result of this degree of probability.

These are simple illustrations of the inner meaning of the expectation of a probability.

The probability of a particular poker hand is less than 0.000,000,4—very much smaller than that of any of the sums that can be obtained from two dice. A particular poker hand will appear much less frequently than a particular sum. But it is not on that account "unusual" or "remarkable"; any other hand would have the same probability; we expect an event of precisely that probability.

In tossing two dice, by contrast, we can expect a probability of about $\tfrac{4}{36}$; 5 or 9 have just about this expected probability and hence, in this sense, are not unusual; 2, 3, 4, 10, 11, and 12 are "unusual" in the sense that they can be expected to occur less often than 5 or 9, and 6, 7, 8 in the sense that they can be expected to occur more often.

Thus, by comparing the probability of an experimental result with its expected probability, we get an indication of the extent to which its frequency of occurrence can be expected to depart from the average, or typical, frequency.

We shall now prove that

THEOREM 104.1. *The expectation of the probability of a complete set of events is least when the events are equally likely.*

Suppose the events are a in number, and that their respective probabilities are $p_1, p_2, \ldots, p_a$. Then the expectation of their probability is

$$\epsilon(p) = p_1{}^2 + p_2{}^2 + \cdots + p_a{}^2,$$

where the p's must satisfy the condition

$$p_1 + p_2 + \cdots + p_a = 1,$$

since the set is complete. Solving the latter of these equations for p_a and substituting in the other, we get

$$\epsilon(p) = p_1{}^2 + p_2{}^2 + \cdots + p_{a-1}{}^2 + (1 - p_1 - p_2 - \cdots - p_{a-1})^2.$$

The variables now are independent and the minimum may be found in the usual way. Differentiating with respect to each variable in turn we get expressions of the form

$$\frac{\partial \epsilon}{\partial p_i} = 2p_i - 2(1 - p_1 - p_2 - \ldots - p_{a-1}) = 2(p_i - p_a).$$

In order that all these equations may be zero every p_i must be equal p_a. This proves the theorem.

As an illustration, the eleven sums that may be obtained in tossing two dice are not equally likely. We have seen that the expectation of their probability is 0.1126. If they were equally likely, however, the probability of each would be $\frac{1}{11}$; and since p could take no other value, its expectation would also be $\frac{1}{11}$. This is indeed less than 0.1126.

A similar theorem can be proved for the case of continuously distributed variables. It reads:

THEOREM 104.2. *The expectation of* $p(x)$ *is least if* x *is distributed at random.*

We shall not stop to prove it.

105. Generating Functions

Consider an experiment which can result in only a discrete set of numbers $x_1, x_2, \ldots, x_a$ and let the probabilities of these be $p(x_j) = p_j$. Then the polynomial (or series, if the number of possible results is unlimited)

$$g(u) = p_1 u + p_2 u^2 + p_3 u^3 + \ldots \qquad (105.1)$$

has the interesting property that its derivatives, at the origin, are

$$\frac{d^i g(0)}{du^i} = i! \, p(x_i). \qquad (105.2)$$

That is, the probability of any one of the events x_i can be obtained by differentiating $g(u)$ i times and setting $u = 0$.

Similarly, the derivatives of the associated function

$$G(u) = p_1 e^{x_1 u} + p_2 e^{x_2 u} + p_3 e^{x_3 u} + \ldots \qquad (105.3)$$

are, at $u = 0$,

$$\frac{d^i G(0)}{du^i} = x_1{}^i p_1 + x_2{}^i p_2 + x_3{}^i p_3 + \ldots.$$

That is,

THEOREM 105.1. *If the set of values* $x_1, x_2, \ldots$ *is complete, the* i*'th derivative of* $g(u)$ *at* $u = 0$ *is* $i! \, p(x_i)$, *and the* i*'th derivative of* $G(u)$ *at* $u = 0$ *is* $\epsilon_i(x)$.

The functions g(u) and G(u) are called generating functions. They are, respectively, the generating functions for the probability of the chance variable x, and for its expectations.[17]

Note that, although $g(u)$ defines the probabilities of the x's, these x's do not appear explicitly in (105.1). Instead, both (105.1) and (105.2) contain a variable u which has no significance whatever; only the analytic behavior of $g(u)$ and $G(u)$ at the origin is of importance.

Note also that, so long as the set of events $x_1, x_2, \ldots$ is complete as required by the theorem,

$$G(0) = g(1) = \sum p_j = 1. \tag{105.4}$$

Consider a simple example. When a die is cast, one of six numbers may appear, and the probability of each is $\frac{1}{6}$. In this case, then, $a = 6$, $x_j = j$, and (105.1) and (105.3) become

$$g(u) = \tfrac{1}{6}(u + u^2 + u^3 + u^4 + u^5 + u^6) = \frac{u}{6}\frac{1 - u^6}{1 - u}, \tag{105.5}$$

$$G(u) = \tfrac{1}{6}(e^u + e^{2u} + e^{3u} + e^{4u} + e^{5u} + e^{6u}) = \frac{e^u - e^{7u}}{6(1 - e^u)}. \tag{105.6}$$

By using the second members of these equations, it is readily seen that $p(3)$, the chance of throwing a 3, is

$$p(3) = \frac{1}{3!}\frac{d^3 g(u)}{du^3}\bigg|_{u=0} = \frac{1}{6 \cdot 3!}(6 + 24u + 60u^2 + 120u^3)_{u=0} = \tfrac{1}{6},$$

as it should be; and that $\epsilon_1(x)$ is

$$\epsilon_1(x) = \frac{dG(u)}{du}\bigg|_{u=0} = \tfrac{1}{6}(1 + 2 + 3 + 4 + 5 + 6) = 3.5,$$

again as it should be. Also, $G(0) = g(1) = 1$, as it should be.

The same results can be obtained, although with somewhat greater difficulty, from the last members of (105.5) and (105.6).

If $G(0)$ and $g(1)$ are not 1, this is evidence that the set of events is not complete. In any such case, as we shall shortly prove, $g(u)/g(1)$ generates *conditional* probabilities: specifically, it generates conditional probabilities on the assumption that those events which were omitted from the set do not occur.

---

[17] $G(u)$ is called the "moment generating function." In a strict sense this is improper, since moments are derived from the numerical results of an experiment, not from its probabilities; but it sounds better than "expectation generating function," and is not likely to be misunderstood.

For example, suppose the even terms are omitted from (105.5) and (105.6), thus leaving

$$g(u) = \tfrac{1}{6}(u + u^3 + u^5),$$
$$G(u) = \tfrac{1}{6}(e^u + e^{3u} + e^{5u}).$$

Here $g(1) = G(0) = \tfrac{1}{2}$; and we find, for example, that

$$\frac{1}{3!}\frac{d^3}{du^3}\frac{g(u)}{g(1)}\bigg|_{u=0} = \tfrac{1}{3},$$

which is clearly the conditional probability of throwing a 3 *if an even face does not appear.* Also

$$\frac{d}{du}\frac{G(u)}{G(0)}\bigg|_{u=0} = 3,$$

which is easily seen to be the expected value of x under the same conditions.

In general, we have

THEOREM 105.2. *If the set of values* $x_1, x_2, \ldots$ *is not complete, the i'th derivative of* $g(u)/g(1)$ *at* $u = 0$ *is* $i!\, p(x_i|*)$, *and the i'th derivative of* $G(u)/G(0)$ *at* $u = 0$ *is* $\epsilon_i(x|*)$, *where* $p(x_i|*)$ *is the conditional probability of* x *taking the value* x_i *if those events which were omitted from the set do not occur, and* $\epsilon_1(x|*)$ *is the expectation of* x *subject to the same condition.*

To prove this theorem, let the occurrence of x_j, one of the values included in the set, be called event A. Then, since the j'th derivative of $g(u)$ at $u = 0$ is still $j!\, p_j$,

$$P(A) = \frac{1}{j!}\frac{d^j g(u)}{du^j}\bigg|_{u=0}.$$

Next, let event B mean that no excluded value of x has occurred. Then $P(B)$ is the sum of the probabilities of all those events which were *not* omitted; that is,

$$P(B) = g(1).$$

Finally, when A occurs, B also automatically occurs; $A, B \equiv A$, and

$$P(A, B) = P(A).$$

Using these values in Bayes' Theorem we get

$$p(x_j|*) = P(A|B) = \frac{P(A, B)}{P(B)} = \frac{P(A)}{P(B)} = \frac{1}{j!g(1)}\frac{d^j g(u)}{du^j}\bigg|_{u=0}. \tag{105.7}$$

This proves half of Theorem 105.2.

To prove the other half, it is necessary only to multiply (105.7) by $x_j{}^i$, and sum over all the values which have been included in the set. This gives

$$\epsilon_i(x|*) = \sum_j x_j{}^i \, p(x_j|*) = \frac{1}{g(1)} \sum_j x_j{}^i \, p_j = \frac{1}{G(0)} \frac{d^i G(u)}{du^i} \bigg|_{u=0},$$

and completes the proof.

106. Some Instructive Illustrations; First Return to Zero Score in a Coin Tossing Game

At this point it may appear that nothing of importance has been accomplished; for to write the series (105.1) at all we must know the values of the probabilities, and if they are known the series for the expectations can be written out directly. But this is not quite true. Sometimes, as will be seen in Example 107.1, generating functions are of assistance in deriving the values of the p_j themselves. Sometimes, also, the series can be summed in a closed form with interesting results. The following example is a case of this sort. It is analogous to Example 67.4, but in the present case successes and failures need not be equally likely.

EXAMPLE 106.1.—*In an experiment with probability of success p, find the generating function for the number of throws that elapse before successes and failures are equal for the first time.*

In the discussion of Example 67.4 (which was phrased in terms of the chance path generated by the experiment), the first return to the axis was denoted by L. We shall retain this notation, L_j thus taking the role of x_j above. Then, since the distance to the first return must be even, $L_j = 2j$.[18]

The applicable formula for the probability is given in Problem 69.21. It is

$$p(L_j) = \frac{2}{2j-1} \, C_j^{2j-1} [p(1-p)]^j. \tag{106.1}$$

Substituting this into (105.1) gives

$$g_L(u) = \sum_{j=1}^{\infty} \frac{2}{2j-1} \, C_j^{2j-1} [p(1-p)u]^j. \tag{106.2}$$

---

[18] We might, alternatively, let $L_j = j$, and assert that $p(L_j) = 0$ when L_j is odd. If this choice were made, u would be replaced by u^2 in (106.2) and (106.3). Then all odd order derivatives of the modified $g(u)$ would vanish, thus indicating (correctly) that the players cannot be even on an odd number of throws. This would be a virtue of the choice $L_j = j$; the principal advantage of using $L_j = 2j$, as we have done, is that (106.3) is much easier to differentiate.

Since $L_j = 2j$ plays the role of x_j in (105.3), it is clear that $G_L(u)$ can be obtained from $g_L(u)$ at any time by substituting e^{2u} for u. Hence it is unnecessary to derive it separately.

The series (106.2) can be summed in finite form by writing $C_j^{2j-1} = (2j-1)C_{j-1}^{2j-2}/j$ and using the result of Problem 29.52. This gives

$$g_L(u) = 1 - \sqrt{1 - 4p(1-p)u}. \tag{106.3}$$

Immediately something important appears, for $g_L(1) < 1$ unless $p = \frac{1}{2}$. Something is therefore missing from the set of events covered by $g_L(u)$. It is this: We have set down the probabilities $p_1, p_2, \ldots, p_j, \ldots$ that the score is even on the second, fourth, $\ldots$, $2j$'th, $\ldots$ trial, but have omitted the possibility that it may *never* be even. To complete the set it would be necessary to include this additional event, with the probability

$$p' = 1 - g_L(1) = \sqrt{1 - 4p(1-p)}.$$

There is, however, no value of L (i.e., j) corresponding to this event. Hence it does not fit comfortably into (105.1) and cannot be included in (105.3) at all.[19]

This situation is in sharp contrast to the earlier discussion of a die with even results excluded. There both conditional and unconditional expectations were available, and we were free to discuss either. Here the concept of an expectation, as applied to the complete set, breaks down entirely[20] and we have no option except to deal with the conditional expectations.

Let us, then, seek the expected number of throws before the two players are equal for the first time, provided they ever are. For this, by Theorem 105.2, we need $G_L(u)/G_L(0)$.

Replacing u by e^{2u} in (106.3) gives

$$G_L(u) = 1 - \sqrt{1 - 4p(1-p)e^{2u}}.$$

Thus

$$p(*) = G_L(0) = 1 \pm (1 - 2p) = 2p, \qquad 0 \leqq p \leqq \tfrac{1}{2},$$
$$= 2 - 2p, \qquad \tfrac{1}{2} \leqq p \leqq 1, \tag{106.4}$$

---

[19] If p' is called p_0, it can be inserted as the first term of (105.1). In this way the deficiency in $g(1)$ is removed; furthermore (105.2) will yield p' as its derivative of zero order. But $G(u)$ would require a corresponding term of the form $e^{x_0 u}$, and it is impossible to find a logical value for x_0. Zero will not do—it implies that a path which never returns to the axis returns instantly! The formal symbol $x_0 = \infty$ will not do—it destroys the function entirely. Any number in between is as obviously wrong.

[20] It would not be without meaning to assert that when a path never returns to the axis, the distance to the point of return is infinite. But I know of no analytical approach that leads to such an assertion through a limiting process, without which the statement is mathematically meaningless.

the sign of the radical being chosen so that $G_L(0)$, which is a probability, lies between 0 and 1. Also,

$$\frac{dG_L(u)}{du}\bigg|_{u=0} = \frac{4p(1-p)}{|1-2p|},$$

whence

$$\epsilon_1(L|*) = \frac{2(1-p)}{1-2p}, \qquad 0 \leq p \leq \tfrac{1}{2},$$

$$= \frac{2p}{2p-1}, \qquad \tfrac{1}{2} \leq p \leq 1. \qquad (106.5)$$

The equations (106.4) and (106.5) are plotted in Fig. 106.1. As is to be expected, they have like ordinates for p and $1 - p$; interchanging "success" and "failure" does not affect the probable number of trials before an equal score results.

When p (or $1 - p$) is very small, $p(*)$ is small; if the probability of success (or failure) is very small, it is quite unlikely that the number of successes will ever equal the number of failures. If they do, it will almost certainly be on the second trial, for thereafter the handicap is too great; in the figure this is portrayed by the fact that $\epsilon(L|*) \doteq 2$ for small values of p (or $1 - p$).

As p (or $1 - p$) increases, there is increasingly greater chance that an even score will occur, and if it does, it may be after a long succession of trials. Hence, both $p(*)$ and $\epsilon(L|*)$ increase steadily with increasing p. As $p \to \tfrac{1}{2}$ there is greater and greater chance that

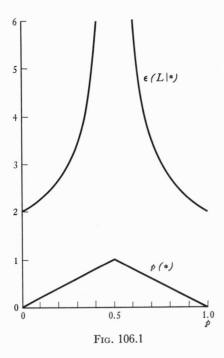

FIG. 106.1

a large accumulation of successes may be wiped out by a subsequent large accumulation of failures; it becomes virtually certain that the score will sometime be equal; but only after so many trials that, as $p \to \tfrac{1}{2}$, it increases beyond all bounds.

107. Some Instructive Illustrations; The Poisson Distribution

Example 106.1 was an illustration of the usefulness of generating functions in studying a situation for which the probabilities are already known. The example which follows illustrates how they can be used in deriving the probabilities when they are unknown.

EXAMPLE 107.1.[21]—*There is a complete set of events* $x_0, x_1, \ldots, x_j, \ldots$ *with probabilities* $p_0, p_1, \ldots, p_j, \ldots$ *which vary with time. These are related by the differential equation*

$$\frac{dp_j}{dt} = k(p_{j-1} - p_j). \tag{107.1}$$

Find the values of p_j.

Let

$$g(u) = \sum_{j=0}^{\infty} p_j u^j$$

be the generating function for the distribution. Then, multiplying (107.1) by u^j and summing for all values of j with the understanding that $p_j = 0$ for negative values of j, we get

$$\frac{d}{dt} g(u) = k(u - 1)g(u).$$

The solution of this is

$$g(u) = ce^{(u-1)kt}.$$

Since it is known that the set of events is complete, $g(1) = 1$ and hence the constant of integration $c = 1$. Thus, finally

$$g(u) = e^{(u-1)kt}.$$

The j'th derivative of this is $(kt)^j e^{(u-1)kt}$, or, when $u = 0$, $(kt)^j e^{-kt}$. Hence by (105.2),

$$p_j = \frac{(kt)^j e^{-kt}}{j!}. \tag{107.2}$$

It is easily verified that (107.2) does in fact satisfy the differential equation (107.1).

---

[21] A physical interpretation of this example will be found in §§ 116–118. The result (107.2) is known as the Poisson distribution function. It is one of great importance in the applications of the Theory of Probability, especially to traffic problems and related fields. It will be discussed in detail in Chapter IX.

108. The Sums of Chance Integers

The set of numbers $x_1, x_2, \ldots$ with which § 105 dealt was entirely general. They could be either positive or negative and either integers or not. Theorems 105.1 and 105.2 applied in any case.

The present section will deal with the important situation where they are positive integers. In such situations there is no need to differentiate between j and x_j for, although the admissible set of integers may not be consecutive, they can be included in a larger consecutive set by assigning probability zero to the excess. Furthermore, as can be seen by comparing (105.1) and (105.3), when $x_j = j$,

$$G(u) = g(e^u). \tag{108.1}$$

Consider, then, an experiment which can result in only the integers $0, 1, 2, \ldots, a$ and let p_i be the probability that the result is i.[22] We ask for the probability, if this experiment is performed twice, that the sum of the resulting numbers will be j. For this to occur, the pair of results must be either 0 and j, or 1 and $j - 1$, etc. Hence the desired probability is

$$p_2(j) = p_0 p_j + p_1 p_{j-1} + p_2 p_{j-2} + \ldots + p_j p_0. \tag{108.2}$$

More generally, consider two independent experiments one of which can give the integer i with probability p_i' and the other with probability p_i''. Then the probability that the sum of a number supplied by the first experiment and a number supplied by the second is j, is

$$p_2(j) = p_0' p_j'' + p_1' p_{j-1}'' + p_2' p_{j-2}'' + \ldots + p_j' p_0''. \tag{108.3}$$

Next, let $g'(u)$ and $g''(u)$ be the generating functions for the two experiments and call the generating function for the sum $g_2(u)$. By definition these three are

$$g'(u) = p_0' + p_1' u + p_2' u^2 + \ldots, \tag{108.4}$$

$$g''(u) = p_0'' + p_1'' u + p_2'' u^2 + \ldots, \tag{108.5}$$

$$g_2(u) = p_2(0) + p_2(1)u + p_2(2)u^2 + \ldots,$$

the last of which, by (108.3), is

$$g_2(u) = p_0' p_0'' + [p_0' p_1'' + p_1' p_0'']u$$
$$+ [p_0' p_2'' + p_1' p_1'' + p_2' p_0'']u^2 + \ldots. \tag{108.6}$$

But if the right-hand members of (108.4) and (108.5) are multiplied together and terms in like powers of u are collected, the product is found to be just (108.6). That is, $g_2(u) = g'(u) \, g''(u)$.

---

[22] For brevity we shall call the results of such an experiment "chance integers."

If the process leading to (108.6) is now regarded as a single experiment, and the numbers resulting from it and from a third independent experiment are added, the generating function for the new sum will obviously be $g'(u) \, g''(u) \, g'''(u)$. Hence, in general,

THEOREM 108.1. *The generating function for the sum of any number of independent chance integers is the product of their separate generating functions.*

An important special case of this theorem is:

THEOREM 108.2. *If $g(u)$ is the generating function for the chance integer resulting from an experiment, and if this experiment is repeated n times, the generating function for the sum of the numbers thus obtained is $[g(u)]^n$.*

EXAMPLE 108.1.—*In a coin tossing experiment the appearance of heads is counted as 1 and the appearance of tails as 0. What is the probability that after n trials the accumulated score will be j?*

The only two possible values for a single trial are 0 and 1, and the probability of each is $\frac{1}{2}$. Hence the generating function for a single trial is

$$g(u) = \tfrac{1}{2} + \tfrac{1}{2}u.$$

The generating function for the score after n trials (which is, of course, the sum of the scores of the separate trials) is therefore

$$g_n(u) = (\tfrac{1}{2} + \tfrac{1}{2}u)^n.$$

This is easy to differentiate and gives

$$j! \, p(j) = \left. \frac{d^j g_n(u)}{du^j} \right|_0 = 2^{-n} \frac{n!}{(n-j)!} (1 + u)^{n-j} \Big|_0 = 2^{-n} \frac{n!}{(n-j)!},$$

or

$$p(j) = 2^{-n} \, C_j^n. \tag{108.7}$$

Clearly a score j means just j successes and $n - j$ failures in n independent trials. The probability of this, however, was already known from (42.1), and agrees with (108.7). The mechanism of generating functions has led to it by another path.

EXAMPLE 108.2.—*A penny and a die are tossed simultaneously. Heads are scored 0 and tails 2 and the faces of the die according to their numbers. What is the chance that the sum of the score from the die and the penny is j?*

For the penny the generating function is

$$g'(u) = \tfrac{1}{2}(1 + u^2),$$

and for the die

$$g''(u) = \tfrac{1}{6}(u + u^2 + u^3 + u^4 + u^5 + u^6). \tag{108.8}$$

Hence, for the sum of the two the generating function is

$$g_2(u) = \tfrac{1}{12}(u + u^2 + 2u^3 + 2u^4 + 2u^5 + 2u^6 + u^7 + u^8).$$
(108.9)

The probabilities p_j are the coefficients of u^j in this polynomial. By summing (108.8), (108.9) can be put in the form

$$g_2(u) = \frac{u}{12} \frac{(1 + u^2)(1 - u^6)}{1 - u},$$

the derivatives of which could also be used to evaluate the probabilities; but the process would be more difficult because of the greater complexity of the algebraic forms. It is therefore simpler in this instance to use the expanded form (108.9).

109. Convolutions

Mathematicians call the sums[23] (108.2) and (108.3) *convolutions*. That is,

DEFINITION 109.1. *A convolution is the sum of all the partial products which can be formed by taking a number from each of two sequences, the choices being taken in such a way that the sum of the subscripts is the same for all pairs.*

There is an analog in the case of continuous variables. If $p'(x)$ and $p''(x)$ are the distribution functions for two independent experiments,

$$p(x) = \int p'(\xi)\, p''(x - \xi)\, d\xi$$
(109.1)

is the distribution function for the sum. This also is called a *convolution*.

EXAMPLE 109.1.—*In the example of the spinning wheel with a uniform scale, § 78, the probability of the pointer coming to rest on the number x was $1/L$ for $0 < x < L$, and 0 elsewhere. If such a wheel is spun repeatedly, what is the probability that, after n trials, the sum of the readings is x?*

After the second trial, (109.1) gives

$$p_2(x) = \int p'(\xi)\, p'(x - \xi)\, d\xi.$$

Since p' is a constant, the essential point in the problem is the determination of the limits of integration. These are set by the fact that neither ξ nor $x - \xi$ can be negative, nor greater than L. Thus

$$p_2(x) = \frac{1}{L^2} \int_0^x d\xi = \frac{x}{L^2}, \qquad 0 < x < L;$$

$$p_2(x) = \frac{1}{L^2} \int_x^{2L} d\xi = \frac{2L - x}{L^2}, \qquad L < x < 2L.$$
(109.2)

---

[23] Sometimes the term is applied to the set of such sums $\{p_2(0), p_2(1), p_2(2), \ldots\}$, rather than to an individual member of the set.

The graph of this density function therefore consists of two straight lines joining the points $(0, 0)$, $(L, 1/L)$ and $(2L, 0)$.
After three trials, the sum would be

$$p_3(x) = \int p_2(\xi)\, p'(x - \xi)\, d\xi,$$

and, as is easily seen from the fact that $p_2(x)$ is a linear function, would consist of three segments, each of the second degree in x, covering the range from 0 to $3L$.

By continuing this process it would be found that $p_n(x)$ extends from 0 to nL and consists of n segments of degree $n - 1$ in x. The precise determination of these is a straightforward problem in integration, though obviously tedious.[24]

EXAMPLE 109.2.—*The result of an experiment is a chance variable x with the distribution function*[25]

$$p'(x) = 1/\pi(1 + x^2).$$

What is the distribution function for the sum of the results from n such experiments?

The sum of two trials has the density function

$$p_2(x) = \frac{1}{\pi^2} \int_{-\infty}^{\infty} \frac{1}{1 + \xi^2} \frac{1}{1 + (x - \xi)^2}\, d\xi. \qquad (109.3)$$

Making use of the formula[26]

$$\frac{a}{\pi} \int_{-\infty}^{\infty} \frac{1}{1 + \xi^2} \frac{1}{a^2 + (x - \xi)^2}\, d\xi = \frac{a + 1}{(a + 1)^2 + x^2}, \qquad (109.4)$$

with $a = 1$, (109.3) becomes

$$p_2(x) = 2/\pi\,(4 + x^2).$$

By repeating this process we find that

$$p_n(x) = n/\pi\,(n^2 + x^2). \qquad (109.5)$$

110. Generating Functions for Continuous Variables

It will be noted that the concept of a generating function has played no part in the discussion of Examples 109.1 and 109.2. Only the convolution integral (109.1), which is the analog of (108.2), was used. There are,

---

[24] See also § 127, Chapter IX, where a similar problem is considered.
[25] This is known as the Cauchy distribution. It has a number of interesting properties which will appear in the problems and in later chapters.
[26] Readers who are familiar with analytic function theory can readily derive (109.4) by the theory of residues. The integrand has poles at $\pm i$ and $x \pm ai$ and vanishes to the fourth order at infinity. Hence the path of integration may be closed by a semicircle in the upper half-plane, thus enclosing i and $x + ai$. The sum of the residues at these points is the right-hand member of (109.4).

however, direct analogs of (105.1) and (105.3) in the case of continuous variables. For a chance variable x with the probability distribution $p(x)$ they are

$$g(u) = \int_{-\infty}^{\infty} p(\xi) u^{\xi} d\xi \tag{110.1}$$

and

$$G(u) = \int_{-\infty}^{\infty} p(\xi) e^{\xi u} d\xi, \tag{110.2}$$

respectively.

We shall not discuss them at length, since to do so would carry us into the subject of Laplacian Transforms, which is beyond the scope of the present volume. We may, however, note in passing that Theorems 108.1 and 108.2 apply equally to the case of continuous chance variables.

Problems

1. In § 100, $\epsilon_1(n)$ was found for the case of *independent* trials. By transformations which are exactly similar to those used there, the summations defining $\epsilon_2(n), \epsilon_3(n), \ldots$ can be reduced to one or more terms of the form (25.2). Find $\epsilon_2(n)$ and $\epsilon_3(n)$.

2. Show that the variance and standard deviation are $mp(1 - p)$ and $\sqrt{mp(1 - p)}$, as stated in § 100. What are the values of $\epsilon_3(\delta)$ and $\epsilon_4(\delta)$?

3. Find the variance of (101.1).

4. On a single try with a perfect penny, what are the first expectation and standard deviation of the number of heads?

5. Toss a penny ten times and record the number of heads appearing. Call it n. Repeat the experiment until you have 50 values of n. With these *experimental* results find their average, the set of deviations d, and the three moments $\mu_1(d), \mu_2(d), \mu_3(d)$.

[It will save time to take ten coins and toss them fifty times. The number of heads can then be counted after each throw.]

6. Find the expectation of n and the first three expectations of δ for the experiment of Problem 5. The results of Problem 2 will aid you.

7. Suppose the game described in Example 103.1 is altered so that if heads do not appear before ten throws the bank captures the stakes and a new game begins. What is the player's expectation of gain?

8. Equation (89.3) is the normal probability law. Find the most probable velocity in the x-direction. The first expectation.

9. Find σ, the standard deviation of u.

10. Suppose σ were adopted as the unit of velocity and denote velocities measured in this new system by u'. Find $p(u')$. We refer, of course, to the velocities in the x-direction only.

11. Find the first three expectations of δ under the conditions of Problem 10. You should not need to compute the first two.

12. In Example 103.1 the bank has \$1,000,000; but instead of paying 2^{j-1} dollars if heads appears first on the j'th throw, it pays $(1.99)^{j-1}$. What is a fair price per game? What is the fair price if the bank pays $(1.5)^{j-1}$ dollars? Compare these values with the results obtained in § 103 upon the assumption that the bank's wealth was infinite.

13. Ten dice are tossed together, the experiment being repeated fifty times. What is the expectation of the number of times three aces appear?

14. If an experiment produces two numbers a and b, and if the value of a which appears is independent of the value of b, show that the expectation of their product is the product of their expectations.

15. The face cards are discarded from two packs and thereafter one card is dealt from each. What is the expectation of the product of the numbers appearing on them?

16. The face cards are discarded from a single pack and then two cards are drawn. What is the expectation of the sum of the numbers appearing on them?

17. Show that the expectation of the probability of a continuous variable is least when the variable is distributed at random.

18. In Example 103.1, suppose the bank's wealth is infinite but the player's time (lifetime?) is limited. What is the equitable payment? Evaluate the special case of one throw per second, 40 hours per week, 50 weeks per year, for ten years.

19. What is the expectation of the length of a continuous run of heads in tossing a penny? The second expectation?
[See Problem 37.14.]

20. What is the expectation of the throw on which ace will first appear in tossing a die?
[See Problem 37.15.]

21. What is the generating function for the lengths of continuous runs of heads in tossing a penny?
[See Problem 37.14.]

22. In tossing dice, what is the generating function for the probability that ace will first appear on the j'th throw?

23. Let $p(x,y)$ be constant over the region bounded by $x = \pm\pi/2$ and $y = \cos x \pm \epsilon$. Find covar (x,y). What is its limiting value as $\epsilon \to 0$; i.e., as the chance relation between x and y approaches the determinate functional relation $y = \cos x$?

24. From the result of Problem 23 infer a property of $y = f(x)$ which will always assure that covar$(xy) = 0$.

25. Reduce to standard form the distribution function for the number x which appears when a die is tossed.

26. Reduce to standard form the distribution $p(x) = \frac{1}{6}$, $0.5 < x < 6.5$; $p(x) = 0$ elsewhere.

27. If the distribution $p(x)$ in Problem 25 is represented by rectangular areas as in Fig. 56.2 instead of by isolated ordinates as in Fig. 56.1, it becomes identical with the distribution described in Problem 26. Why does the probability remain $\frac{1}{6}$ in the one case and not in the other?

28. Find the generating function and the moment generating function for the binomial distribution (42.1).

29. Use the result of Problem 28 to find the first, second, and third expectations of n. Compare with the results of Problem 1.

30. Find the moment generating function for the Poisson distribution (107.2).

31. Find the first, second, and third expectations of j in the Poisson distribution.

32. Reduce the function $p(j) = x^j e^{-x}/j!$ to standard form.

33. If an experiment gives numbers j distributed according to the Poisson distribution, and if the experiment is repeated a times, what is the distribution of the sum J? Of the average $\bar{j}$?

34. If an experiment gives positive numbers x distributed continuously according to the law $x^j e^{-x}/j!$, j being for this purpose a constant, what are the first and second expectations of x?

35. If an experiment gives numbers distributed according to the Cauchy Law $p(x) = 1/\pi(1 + x^2)$, what is the distribution function for the average $\bar{x}$ of the results of a trials?
[Use (109.5).]

36. What are the first and second expectations of the Cauchy distribution?

37. Using the results of Problem 69.23 and Example 106.1, write the generating functions for $P(L|A)$ and $P(L|B)$.
[The important point is the sign of the radical in (106.3). Player A is supposed to have the advantage.]

38. If A, who holds the advantage in the game to which Problem 37 refers, wins the first round, what is the probability $P(*|A)$ that the game will never be even? What is it if B wins the first trial?

39. If, in Problem 37, B wins the first round, what is the expectation of L, the number of throws before they are even for the first time?

40. If $p'(x)$ and $p''(x)$ are two distribution functions in standard form and $p(x)$ is the distribution for the sum of two numbers, one from each, show that the standard form of $p(x)$ is $f(y)$, where $y = x/\sqrt{2}$ and

$$f(y) = \sqrt{2}\, p(\sqrt{2}\, y).$$

[Multiply (109.1) by $x^2 \equiv [\xi + (x - \xi)]^2$ and integrate with respect to x.

It will be necessary to rearrange the order of integrals and use the substitution $\eta = x - \xi$.]

41. Let an experiment have a standardized distribution function $p_1(x)$. Let it be performed repeatedly and let the standardized distribution of the sum after n trials be $p_n(x)$. Show that

$$\frac{1}{\sqrt{2}} p_{2n}(x/\sqrt{2}) = \int_{-\infty}^{\infty} p_n(\xi) \, p_n(x - \xi) \, d\xi. \qquad (110.3)$$

42. If $y = b_1 x_1 + b_2 x_2 + \ldots + b_a x_a$ and $z = c_1 x_1 + c_2 x_2 + \ldots + c_a x_a$, show that

$$\text{covar}(yz) = \sum_i b_i c_i \sigma_i{}^2 + \sum{}^*(b_i c_j + c_i b_j) \, \text{covar}(x_i x_j)$$

where the last sum is taken over every pair i, j for which $j > i$.

43. Find the generating function $g'(u)$ corresponding to a single trial of Example 109.1.

44. What is the generating function for the sum of two trials of Example 109.1? Of n trials?

45. What is the generating function corresponding to the distribution (109.2)? Compare with Problems 43 and 44.

46. Using Theorem 108.1 and equations (105.4) and (108.1), give an independent proof of (98.7).

Answers to Problems

1. $mp[(m - 1)p + 1]$; $mp[(m - 1)(m - 2)p^2 + 3(m - 1)p + 1]$.
2. $\epsilon_3(\delta) = mp(1 - p)(1 - 2p)$; $\epsilon_4(\delta) = mp(1 - p) + 3m(m - 2)p^2(1 - p)^2$.
3. $\sigma^2 = mnr(m + n - r)/(m + n)^2(m + n - 1)$.   4. $\epsilon_1(h) = \frac{1}{2}$, $\sigma^2 = \frac{1}{4}$.
6. $\epsilon_1(n) = 5$; $\epsilon_1(\delta) = 0$; $\epsilon_2(\delta) = 2.5$; $\epsilon_3(\delta) = 0$. 7. $\frac{9}{2} - (A/512)$ if A is the player's stake. Hence for a fair game $A = \$4.49+$. 8. 0; 0. 9. $1/\sqrt{2a}$.
10. $p(u') = e^{-u'^2/2}/\sqrt{2\pi}$. 11. 0; 1; 0. 12. \$10.48; \$2.00. 13. 7.75. 15. $(\frac{11}{2})^2$.
16. 11.
18. $N/(2 + 2^{1-N})$, where N is the number of throws that can be made in the allotted time. With one throw per second and ten years of 40 hour weeks, 50 weeks per year, this would be \$36,000,000 for the first game. It would decrease thereafter as the allowable span of time was used up.
19. 1; 3. 20. 6. 21. $g(u) = 1/(2 - u)$. 22. $g(u) = u/(6 - 5u)$.
23. covar $(xy) = 0$; same. 24. $f(x)$ an even function of x.
25. $\epsilon = 3.5$, $\sigma = \sqrt{35/12}$. Hence the six allowable values of the standardized variable are $y = \pm \sqrt{15/7}$, $\pm \sqrt{27/35}$, $\pm \sqrt{3/35}$. Each has probability $\frac{1}{6}$.
26. $\epsilon = 3.5$, $\sigma = \sqrt{3}$. Hence the range of $y = (x - 3.5)/\sqrt{3}$ is from $-\sqrt{3}$ to $+\sqrt{3}$, and $p(y) = 1/2\sqrt{3}$ between these values and zero elsewhere.
27. Because the area representing a probability must be kept invariant.
28. $g(u) = (1 - p + pu)^n$; $G(u) = (1 - p + pe^u)^m$. 30. $G(u) = e^{(e^u - 1)kt}$.
31. $\epsilon_1(j) = kt$; $\epsilon_2(j) = k^2t^2 + kt$; $\epsilon_3(j) = k^3t^3 + 3k^2t^2 + kt$.

32. $\epsilon = x$, $\sigma^2 = x$, $y_j = (j - x)/x$, $p(y_j) = x^j e^{-x}/j!$.

33.
$$p_a(J) = \frac{(ax)^J e^{-ax}}{J!}; \qquad p_a(\bar{j}) = \frac{(ax)^{a\bar{j}} e^{-ax}}{(a\bar{j})!}.$$

Since $a\bar{j} = J$, an integer, $\bar{j}$ must be a multiple of $1/a$.

34. $j + 1$; $j^2 + 3j + 2$. **35.** $p(\bar{x}) = 1/\pi(1 + \bar{x}^2)$.

36. The second expectation is infinite; the integral defining the first expectation does not converge, though by symmetry we would be justified in assigning the value 0. [This is sometimes known as the "principal value" of the divergent integral.]

37.
$$g\,(u \mid A) = \frac{1 - |\sqrt{1 - 4p(1 - p)u}|}{2p}.$$

$$g_L(u \mid B) = \frac{1 - |\sqrt{1 - 4p(1 - p)u}|}{2 - 2p}.$$

38. $P(* \mid A) = (2p - 1)/p$; $P(* \mid B) = 0$.

39. $\epsilon(L \mid B) = \epsilon(2j \mid B) = \left. \dfrac{dG(u \mid B)}{du} \right|_{u = 0} = 2p/(2p - 1)$.

43. $g'(u) = (u^L - 1)/L \log u$. **44.** $[g'(u)]^2$; $[g'(u)]^n$. **45.** $(u^L - 1)^2/(L \log u)^2$.

Chapter IX

The Distribution Functions Most Frequently Used in Engineering

111. Introductory Remarks

If there is any one distribution function which more than another deserves the adjective "ubiquitous," it is the normal distribution

$$\phi(y) = \frac{1}{\sqrt{2\pi}} e^{-y^2/2}. \tag{111.1}$$

It appears and reappears in mathematical theory with amazing frequency; it appears as a basic law in such physical theories as gaseous dynamics; and like the rafters and studding which, though concealed by plaster and paint, are yet the strength of a house, it is the frequently hidden and sometimes forgotten framework that supports the structures of practical statistics.

Yet I cannot set down, in language that would assist the reader in bridging the gap between detached mathematical logic and practical application, any criteria for judging what experiments will produce results distributed in the normal way, and what will not.

We have seen that the binomial distribution (§ 42) is appropriate to repeated independent trials under like conditions; that both the Bose–Einstein and Fermi–Dirac distributions (§ 46) imply strong dependence of the result of one trial on those which preceded it, the former inciting recurrence of a result previously obtained and the latter forbidding it entirely; later we shall find that the Poisson distribution (§ 116) is appropriate to experiments whose results are distributed at random in time or space. The Normal Law cannot be characterized

227

in any such manner.[1] Even in the Dynamical Theory of Gases, where the validity of the law is most thoroughly established, no completely convincing derivation exists.[2]

Viewed from another angle, there are certain *necessary* (though by no means sufficient) conditions which the results of an experiment must possess if they are to be distributed in this way:

1. There must be just one most probable result.
2. This must be identical with the first expectation of the variable (Problem 110.8).
3. Any deviation, no matter how large, must be possible.
4. Positive and negative deviations from expectation must be equally likely.

All these follow clearly from the character of the graph of (111.1). It requires only a moment's thought to see that situations which satisfy all four of these conditions are by no means common.

Take for example the distribution of the height of men. It is absurd to speak of a man of negative height: such a thing is not merely very infrequent; it simply cannot occur. Yet if height were distributed normally, the third requirement would assign a finite probability to this absurdity.

As a further example, think of the lengths of telephone conversations. Here again negative values are meaningless; but more than that, actual experience has shown that the conversation of most frequent occurrence is very short indeed, certainly much shorter than the average. The distribution function which these call-lengths obey therefore possesses none of the last three properties.

Wherein, then, does the value of the normal distribution lie? We have said that as an exact law its demonstrations have been of a sadly impractical character, and that as an empirical law its own peculiarities are so special that it is seldom obeyed; and it might appear that this left no field of usefulness for it whatever. But this conclusion would be grossly in error, for there are powerful reasons for the popularity of the normal distribution.

Its ubiquity, and therefore its importance, resides in the fact that *almost all other distributions approach it as a limit under suitable circumstances.*

---

[1] Among many attempts, the one most often quoted is the following: If the result of an experiment is caused to deviate from the true (or expected) value because of a very large number of contributory causes, no one of which is comparable in magnitude to the combined effect of the rest, and if in the aggregate these are as likely to produce positive as negative deviations—all this would justify the use of the normal law. But it is generally hopeless to appraise a practical situation against such criteria, especially when (as in the case of a precise determination of the velocity of light or of the molecular weight of oxygen) every precaution has been taken to eliminate controllable causes.

[2] This was touched on in § 87 and was discussed at greater length in Chapter XI of the first edition.

Although it portrays no experimental syndrome exactly, it affords a more or less close resemblance to many. It is like a composite portrait which, although not like any man, somewhat resembles all.[3]

A primary purpose of this chapter is to bring out these relations clearly. And since the careful user of approximations needs to form some judgment of the error which he incurs, much emphasis is placed on means of estimating and improving this.

112. Distribution Functions for Discrete Variables; The Binomial Distribution and Various Approximations to It

The first function of any general consequence which we met in the course of our studies was

$$P_m(n) = C_n^m p^n (1 - p)^{m-n}. \tag{42.1}$$

As we know, it represents the probability of n successes in m *independent* trials, if the chance of success in a single trial is p.

The law is exact, and the conditions underlying it are such that we can be reasonably confident when to use it. Of course, there are comparatively few practical situations in which the same essential conditions can be maintained for a great length of time; but there are many which approximate stability to such an extent that we feel no hesitancy in dealing with them on this basis. For example, take the production of stamped parts made on a punch press. The die in use is certain to wear and thus produce a progressive tendency of some sort; but the trend will usually be slow enough that, if wear is not allowed to progress too far, this trend may be ignored. So, too, with many other features of the process: sheets differ somewhat in thickness, temperatures change, and so on to a great number of factors. Yet if we sort the product into two kinds, "bad" and "good," the various pieces have something like the same chance of being good.

The binomial law, therefore, is one of very broad utility. Its chief objectionable feature is the difficulty of computing it, particularly when m is large and the answer desired is the probability of *exceeding* n instead of *equaling* it. Then a very large number of terms might have to be calculated and added together. There are, however, fairly accurate approximations which can be used in such cases. The foundations for deriving these have been laid in §§ 60 and 61. We shall now complete the proof.

---

[3] We noted in § 46 a similar situation with regard to the Maxwell–Boltzmann distribution which no elementary particle obeys, but which is approximately valid for many complex systems. The generic reason is surely the same. As we shall see in § 122, the normal distribution is a limiting form of the multinomial (alias, Maxwell–Boltzmann) and therefore also of all those for which the latter is an acceptable approximation.

We saw (Fig. 56.2) that as the number of trials is increased, the distribution function becomes flatter and flatter and spreads out more and more widely along the n-axis, but that when plotted against n/m (Fig. 57.1), it becomes higher and spreads less widely as m increases. If instead it is put in standard form—that is, if we plot it against δ/σ— the successive curves appear as in Fig. 112.1 and are so similar that it is

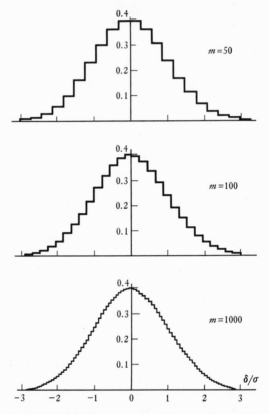

Fig. 112.1   An Alternative Form of Fig. 56.1.

reasonable to assume they approach a definite limit as m becomes infinite. It should be possible, then, to find a smooth curve which is a good approximation, at least when m is very large. We shall seek this approximation in terms of the standardized variable[4]

$$y = \frac{\delta}{\sigma} = \frac{n - mp}{\sqrt{mp\,(1 - p)}}.$$

(112.1)

[4] See §§ 97 and 100.

We begin by replacing all the factorials in (42.1) by their Stirling approximations. If we write $f(m, n)$ for the combination of three series (like the one in parentheses in (60.7)) which arise in doing this, the result is

$$P_m(n) = \frac{1}{\sqrt{2\pi mp(1-p)}} \left(\frac{mp}{n}\right)^{n+\frac{1}{2}} \left(\frac{m-mp}{m-n}\right)^{m-n+\frac{1}{2}} f(m, n). \quad (112.2)$$

With the accuracy we shall require, $f(m, n)$ is

$$f(m, n) = 1 - \frac{1}{12} \frac{m^2 - mn + n^2}{mn(m-n)} + \dots \quad (112.3)$$

Next, since the standard deviation of the binomial distribution is $\sigma = \sqrt{mp(1-p)}$,

$$m = \sigma^2/p(1-p) \quad (112.4)$$

and (112.1) becomes

$$n = \sigma y + \frac{\sigma^2}{1-p}. \quad (112.5)$$

Substituting these into (112.2) gives

$$P_m(n) = \frac{f(m, n)}{\sqrt{2\pi}\,\sigma}\left(1 + \frac{(1-p)y}{\sigma}\right)^{-\sigma^2/(1-p)-\sigma y-\frac{1}{2}} \left(1 - \frac{py}{\sigma}\right)^{-\sigma^2/p+\sigma y-\frac{1}{2}} \quad (112.6)$$

We now take the two brackets in (112.6) and treat them by the same process as was used in § 61. If we call their product Z, we obtain $\log Z = -\frac{1}{2}y^2$

$$+ \frac{1}{\sigma}\left(\frac{(p-1)^2 - p^2}{2.3}y^3 + \frac{(p-1) + p}{2.1}y\right)$$

$$+ \frac{1}{\sigma^2}\left(\frac{(p-1)^3 - p^3}{3.4}y^4 + \frac{(p-1)^2 + p^2}{2.2}y^2\right) + \dots,$$

whence Z itself is equal to e raised to this power. From this exponential we sort out the term $e^{-y^2/2}$, which is independent of σ, and then expand the remainder in a series. The complicated expression which results from this process need not be written here in detail; if it is represented by the symbol Y, we have

$$Z = e^{-y^2/2}\,Y. \quad (112.7)$$

Next, the n and m in (112.3) are replaced by (112.4) and (112.5), giving

$$f(m, n) = 1 - \frac{1 - p + p^2}{12\sigma^2} + \frac{1 - 2p}{12\sigma^3}y + \dots. \quad (112.8)$$

When the series Y in (112.7) and the series (112.8) are multiplied together and the whole is substituted in (112.2), there results

$$
\begin{aligned}
P_m(n) = \frac{1}{\sqrt{2\pi}\,\sigma} e^{-y^2/2} \Bigg[& 1 + \frac{1}{\sigma}(2p-1)\left(\frac{y}{2} - \frac{y^3}{6}\right) \\
& - \frac{1}{\sigma^2}\left(\frac{1-p+p^2}{12} - \frac{3-8p+8p^2}{8}y^2 + \frac{2-7p+7p^2}{12}y^4\right. \\
& \left. - \frac{(2p-1)^2}{72}y^6\right) + \frac{1}{\sigma^3}(2p-1)\left(\frac{-3+p-p^2}{24}y\right. \\
& + \frac{47-74p+74p^2}{144}y^3 - \frac{37-94p+94p^2}{240}y^5 \\
& + \frac{3-10p+10p^2}{144}y^7 - \frac{(2p-1)^2}{1296}y^9\Big) - \cdots\Bigg].
\end{aligned}
$$
(112.9)

This is a series in descending powers of σ, of which the first four terms are given. Clearly, since σ is proportional to $\sqrt{m}$, the accuracy of the approximation improves as the number of trials increases. It will be observed that (except for the σ in the denominator, the presence of which will be explained shortly) the first term of this is just the normal distribution (111.1).

To what end has all this tedious algebra led?

So long as y^3/σ is small,[5] (112.9) gives a good approximation to the binomial distribution. Indeed, if y^3 is small enough—which means we confine attention to the portion of the curve near the peak—the first term of (112.9) is good enough for many purposes. Moreover, when dealing with the special case $p = \frac{1}{2}$, the odd terms in (112.9) vanish because of the presence of the factor $(2p-1)$. Hence:

The normal distribution (111.1) is a fair approximation to the binomial distribution so long as y^3/σ is not too large. In this special case of $p = \frac{1}{2}$ it is somewhat better than otherwise. In the vicinity of the "tails"—that is, when the deviations are large—it is never satisfactory.

It is important that this statement be kept in mind, particularly in making or interpreting statistical tests of significance. And since a statement of this kind is likely to be vague unless sharpened by numerical examples, we present Fig. 112.2, which corresponds to $m = 36$ and $p = \frac{1}{2}$, and Fig. 112.3, which corresponds to the same m but to $p = \frac{1}{10}$. In each case the circles represent exact values of the binomial distribution; they occur, of course, only at integral values of n. The

---

[5] Since $y = \delta/\sigma$, this is equivalent to saying δ^3/σ^4 is small.

curves represent approximations to these values. For reference, each
diagram carries a scale of n along the lower margin and a scale of y
above.

Dealing first with the symmetrical case of Fig. 112.2, we note that the
circles and curve coincide absolutely, so far as is possible to judge from

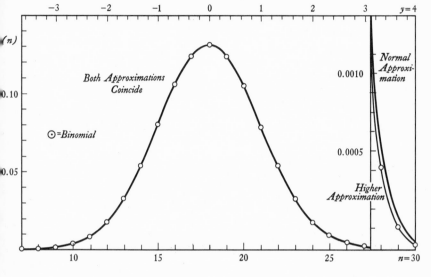

FIG. 112.2 APPROXIMATIONS TO THE BINOMIAL DISTRIBUTION.

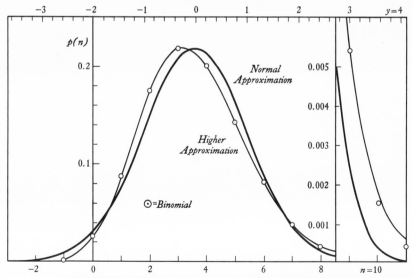

FIG. 112.3 APPROXIMATIONS TO THE BINOMIAL DISTRIBUTION.

the main portion of the drawing. What is more, the first term of (112.9) and the sum of four terms are so nearly coincident that it is impossible to distinguish between them. This continues to be so out to $n = 36$ if the same scale is used. But if the ends of the curves are magnified, as has been done at the right-hand margin of the drawing, they do indeed separate, and the higher approximation represents the true values better than the normal distribution. For example, at $n = 30$ (the extreme edge of the drawing) the normal distribution is in error by more than 50%, whereas the higher approximation is still indistinguishable from the true value on the scale of the drawing.

Next, turning to Fig. 112.3, we find that the first term nowhere represents the binomial with any great degree of exactness, whereas the higher approximation again coincides very well, although there is a perceptible deviation in the expanded portion on the right.

113. Some Instructive Illustrations; Computation of Binomial Sums

Consider the following example:

EXAMPLE 113.1.—*A penny has been tossed 1000 times and heads has appeared 545 times. If the penny is true, what is the chance of deviating this much or more in such an experiment?*

The answer, of course, is $\Sigma_j\, C_j^{1000}/2^{1000}$ summed for all values of $j \geq 545$. This is not easy to compute. We may, however, note that this sum is just the area under part of the binomial distribution curve; and since the normal curve approximates the binomial, the area under the corresponding portions of the two should be about equal. The area under the normal curve can be found by integration, and since tables of the integral exist this is the simpler computation.

Before we can proceed, however, we must note that (112.9) still gives the ordinates of the curve $P_m(n)$. To preserve areas when the variable is changed to y, a factor must be introduced to compensate for the change of scale[6] as explained in § 85. This can be found from the requirement that

$$\int_{-\infty}^{\infty} P_m(y)\, dy = 1;$$

its effect is just to cancel the σ which appears outside the bracket of

---

[6] If the situation involved nothing more than a change of variable, this would be done by introducing the Jacobian, as explained in § 85 and § 90. As a matter of fact, it could also be done here. But this is largely an accident, for the binomial which is being approximated has meaning for us only at *discrete* values of n, and we are replacing it by a continuous function. It is more appropriate, therefore, to make sure that the area under the approximating curve is unity.

(112.9). The first term then becomes precisely the normal distribution function (111.1).

That is,

$$P_m(y) \doteq \phi(y) = \frac{1}{\sqrt{2\pi}} \, e^{-y^2/2}, \tag{113.1}$$

or, if a better approximation is required, $P_m(y)$ is $\phi(y)$ multiplied by the bracketed expression (112.9).

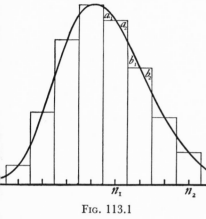

FIG. 113.1

We must also determine the limits of integration. If we refer to Fig. 113.1, which reproduces part of Fig. 112.3, we observe that the sum of the ordinates from n_1 to n_2 is represented by the rectangles above them, which extend from $n_1 - \frac{1}{2}$ to $n_2 + \frac{1}{2}$. It is obvious, therefore, that the area under the smooth curve between n_1 and n_2 is smaller than the area of the corresponding set of rectangles, but the area between the limits $n_1 - \frac{1}{2}$ and $n_2 + \frac{1}{2}$ is a better approximation, since the little triangular areas $a_1, a_2; b_1, b_2; \ldots$ very nearly compensate for one another.

We can, therefore, find a reasonably good approximation to the probability of n lying between two values n_1 and n_2 by using as limits of integration, not the values y_1 and y_2 that correspond to n_1 and n_2, but others which correspond to $n_1 - \frac{1}{2}$ and $n_2 + \frac{1}{2}$ instead. From the general relation (112.5) which exists between y and n we easily find these limits, and write down the formula

$$\sum_{n=n_1}^{n_2} P_m(n) \doteq \int_{y_1 - 1/2\sigma}^{y_2 + 1/2\sigma} P_m(y) \, dy. \tag{113.2}$$

If we substitute (113.1) in this integral and express it in terms of the function

$$\phi_{-1}(y) = \frac{1}{\sqrt{2\pi}} \int_{-\infty}^{y} e^{-y^2/2} \, dy,$$

we are led to the final conclusion that

The sum

$$\sum_{j=n_1}^{n_2} C_j^m \, p^j (1-p)^{m-j}$$

is approximately equal to the integral

$$\frac{1}{\sqrt{2\pi}} \int_{y_1 - 1/2\sigma}^{y_2 + 1/2\sigma} e^{-y^2/2} \, dy = \phi_{-1}(y_2 + 1/2\sigma) - \phi_{-1}(y_1 - 1/2\sigma),$$ (113.3)

where $y = (n - mp)/\sigma$ *and* $\sigma = \sqrt{mp(1 - p)}$.

For Example (113.1) we have

$$\epsilon = mp = 500,$$

$$\sigma = \sqrt{mp(1 - p)} = \sqrt{250},$$

and hence for the lower limit of integration

$$y_1 - \frac{1}{2\sigma} = \frac{44.5}{\sqrt{250}} = 2.814.$$

The upper limit is ∞. Then from Appendix V we find

$$\sum_{n=545}^{1000} C_j^{1000}/2^{1000} \doteq \frac{1}{\sqrt{2\pi}} \int_{2.814}^{\infty} e^{-y^2/2} \, dy = 1 - 0.99754 = 0.00246.$$

By laborious computation the exact value of the sum is found to be 0.00243. Since in this case m is large, the distribution is symmetrical, and y is not too large, the approximation is a good one, as we would expect.

To see what happens when the distribution is not symmetrical, consider the following:

EXAMPLE 113.2.—*A die is cast 1000 times and the ace appears 195 times. What is the chance of a deviation as large or larger than this?*

Here $\epsilon = 166.7$, $\sigma = \sqrt{5000/36} = 11.785$ and hence $y_1 - 1/2\sigma = 2.359$. From Appendix V we find that $1 - \phi_{-1}(2.359) = 0.00923$.

The exact value, obtained by summing the binomial distribution, is 0.01012.

114. Distribution Functions for Discrete Variables; The Poisson Distribution as a Limiting Case of the Binomial

The second important distribution function for discrete variables is the Poisson distribution. It is usually regarded as an approximate form of the binomial when the number of trials m is very large and the probability p very small; and as its derivation from this point of view is the simplest, we shall begin our discussion with it, although we shall shortly see there is another point of view which is of greater practical importance.

We have found in § 100 that the expectation of n in the case of the binomial distribution is $\epsilon = mp$. Suppose, then, that we replace the p in (42.1) by ϵ/m, thus causing the formula to take the form

$$P_m(n) = C_n^m \left(\frac{\epsilon}{m}\right)^n \left(1 - \frac{\epsilon}{m}\right)^{m-n}.$$

By writing out the binomial coefficient and rearranging the factors slightly, this expression can be put into the alternative form

$$P_m(n) = \left[\left(1 - \frac{1}{m}\right)\left(1 - \frac{2}{m}\right) \cdots \left(1 - \frac{n-1}{m}\right)\right]$$

$$\times \left[\left(1 - \frac{\epsilon}{m}\right)^{-n}\right]\left[\left(1 - \frac{\epsilon}{m}\right)^{m}\right] \frac{\epsilon^n}{n!}.$$

Now, remembering that we are dealing with a case in which p is supposed to be very small, it is obvious that only those values of n are of consequence which are very small compared to m. Hence every one of the group of terms enclosed in the first set of brackets is of just about unit magnitude. The same is true also of the quantity $1 - \epsilon/m$ which occurs in the second and third brackets, for ϵ/m, or p, is very small. Hence it follows, since there are comparatively few of these terms in the first two brackets, that their product is also not greatly different from unity.

In the case of the third bracket, however, this argument cannot be applied; for the power to which the quantity $1 - \epsilon/m$ is raised is not moderate, but very large. By (61.2), this bracket is approximately equal to $e^{-\epsilon}$ and hence

$$P_m(n) \doteq \frac{e^{-\epsilon}\epsilon^n}{n!}. \tag{114.1}$$

Just how good this approximation is depends upon the values of m, n and ϵ; of course whatever it is, we could readily improve it to any degree we might desire by the use of processes similar to those in § 112. The result, however, appears to be of little value and probably does not warrant its presentation.

The consequential thing is that, *if p is small enough and m large enough*, the binomial distribution reduces approximately to the form (114.1), which is exactly the Poisson. These conditions are sometimes satisfied sufficiently well to warrant use of the simpler law, as may be shown by the following example, which, because of its unusual subject matter, has become classical.

Certain army records, extending over a period of years, give among other things the number of soldiers killed by the kick of horses. The classified results are shown in Table 114.1. The numbers in the first column are the number of soldiers killed in this way in one corps during one year, and the second column tells how often this record was repeated during the period covered by the data.

Now there are a large number of days in a year, and the chance of a fatality occurring during any one of these days is rather small. What is more, each day is a sort of independent "trial"; so there is some

TABLE 114.1

RECORDS OF SOLDIERS DYING FROM THE
KICK OF HORSES

Number of Deaths	Frequency Observed	Frequency Expected
0........109		108.7
1.........65		66.3
2.........22		20.2
3..........3		4.1
4..........1		0.6
5..........0		0.1
6..........0		0.0

reason for expecting the data of Table (114.1) to follow (114.1) rather closely. To check this supposition there are given, in the third column of the table, the number of times the various records would be expected to have occurred if the distribution accurately obeyed the Poisson distribution with an expectation of $\epsilon = 0.61$. We have at present no better means of checking the agreement of the second and third columns than the mere observation that there does not appear to be any serious disagreement between them. Later on,[7] when we have developed a scientific method of measuring this agreement, we shall find that it is very good indeed.

115. Definitions of the Phrases "Individually at Random" and "Collectively at Random"

We can make better use of this illustration, however, than that of merely showing that data sometimes conform to the Poisson distribution. They can guide us to the conditions under which that distribution is *exactly*, rather than *approximately*, applicable.

We note, to begin with, that these deaths were probably quite *independent* of one another. They occurred infrequently and at widely scattered locations, and there is no reason to suppose that one was

---

[7] See Problem 164.13.

either provoked or deterred by another. If we think of them as determining points on a time axis, we would be inclined to believe that the
location of one such point is influenced little, if at all, by any other.
It seems reasonable also to suppose that they occurred *at random*;
that is, that a man was as likely to have such an accident in one month
or on one day as another.[8]

Moreover, if we turn our attention away from the individual event
and consider instead various periods of time, there seems little reason
to suppose that what happened in one period was much influenced
by what occurred in another. If a statistician kept records of these
deaths and observed an excess during the first half year, he could not
deduce from that fact that there would probably be either an excess or
a deficit in the next half. "It is still a matter of chance."[9] In this respect
the situation differs radically from "putting 100 points at random on
a line of length 10," where, if only 75 points fall in the first eight units,
the (conditional) probability of, say, 14 points in the ninth unit is
greater than it would be if there had been 85.

This is a new concept, and we need a new term and a precise definition for it. We shall say the deaths were "collectively at random."

DEFINITION 115.1. *A set of points is said to be distributed "collectively at
random" along a line segment if the conditional probability of n points falling
in an interval dx is independent of the number of points in any interval outside
dx.*

We shall also say that

DEFINITION 115.2. *A set of points is said to be distributed "individually
at random" along a line segment if each point of the set is placed at random,
independently of any other.*

Note that a set of events (or points) may be collectively random even
if the events are not independent. For example, Easter strollers might

---

[8] We must, of course, not be hypercritical about this statement. Certain points on the
time axis correspond to periods when the men were asleep, and it is quite unlikely that a
death would occur at such an instant. There probably were also different routines established
for week days and Sundays, and these might affect the likelihood of the point lying at one
place rather than another. Perhaps, however, the fact that what we say about this illustration is *not* true when viewed in too great detail may serve the more clearly to point out the
idea we are aiming to convey.

[9] This statement is also probably not true. An excess observed by a statistician at the
middle of the year would probably lead—if it were serious enough—to some sort of "safety
campaign" intended to reduce the number of such accidents. Or, viewed from a somewhat
closer angle, if the men themselves had immediate knowledge of the occurrence of such
deaths, they would probably be led to exert greater care the day following an accident than
at other times, and the probability of a death in an interval of a day just following the occurrence of such an accident would be less than normal.

be dispersed in such a way that the conditional probability of just n of them passing a given point in a minute's time would be independent of the number who had gone before. But Easter strollers generally travel in couples and the time of arrival of one member of the pair is not independent of the other.

A set of points may also be collectively at random even though they are not at random individually. Consider, for instance, the points of impact of cosmic rays upon a strip of photographic film. If, before reaching the film, they must pass through a wedge of lead, more will reach the film through the thin end than through the thick one. The individual points will therefore clearly not be distributed at random along the strip; but the probability of just n points in a given element of length—although it will be a function of position—will not be changed by a knowledge of the number somewhere else. Hence the set is collectively at random.

116. Second Demonstration of the Poisson Distribution

We shall now prove the following theorem:

THEOREM 116.1. *If points are placed upon a line segment at random and independently of one another, and in such a way that the set is collectively at random, the probability of n points lying within any interval of length x is*

$$P(n, x) = \frac{(kx)^n}{n!} e^{-kx}, \tag{116.1}$$

where kx is the expected number of points within the interval.

As notation we shall use $P(n, x)$ for the chance of just n, and $P(> n, x)$ for the chance of more than n, points in the interval x. In outline the proof will run as follows:

(*a*) We shall show that, because the points are placed individually and collectively at random, the probability of one or more points in an interval dx approaches $k\, dx$ as $dx \to 0$;

(*b*) Since they are independent, $P(> 1, dx)$ vanishes to the order $(dx)^2$ as $dx \to 0$;

(*c*) Using this fact, we shall deduce a differential equation for $P(n, x)$ whose solution is (116.1).

(*a*) We focus our attention upon an interval of length x, which we suppose to be subdivided into a large number of equal subintervals $dx_1, dx_2, \ldots, dx_a$. This implies, of course, that $a\, dx = x$.

Then, since the points are placed at random individually, the unconditional probability of just n falling in such a subinterval must be the same for each subinterval. We shall be especially concerned with empty subintervals and for simplicity will write

$$P(0, dx) = 1 - \epsilon, \qquad (116.2)$$

so that ϵ stands for $P(> 0, dx)$. Similarly, we shall set

$$P(0, x) = 1 - \alpha,$$

where $\alpha = P(> 0, x)$.

Also, since the points are distributed collectively at random, the conditional probability of just n points in the subinterval dx_1 must be the same regardless of the number of points in the other intervals. In other words, it is the same as the unconditional probability; in the case of $n = 0$ it is (116.2).

However, the interval x can be empty only if all of the subintervals are empty, and hence we have

$$1 - \alpha = (1 - \epsilon)^a.$$

Taking logarithms and recalling that $a = x/dx$, we find that

$$\frac{\log (1 - \alpha)}{x} = \frac{\log (1 - \epsilon)}{dx}. \qquad (116.3)$$

Note, now, that the left-hand member of this equation depends only on x and upon $1 - \alpha$, the probability that there are no points in x. It does not depend on how this interval is subdivided and remains unchanged as dx varies. Therefore, the right-hand member also remains unchanged as dx varies, and we write

$$\frac{\log (1 - \epsilon)}{dx} = -k$$

or

$$1 - \epsilon = e^{-k\,dx}.$$

For vanishing dx, this becomes

$$\epsilon \equiv P(> 0, dx) \to k\,dx, \qquad dx \to 0, \qquad (116.4)$$

which is what we set out to prove.

So far, however, we have shown only that k is independent of dx, not that it is also independent of x. However, the right-hand side of (116.3) depends only on the probability that there are no points in an interval of size dx, and it remains unaltered if x is either lengthened or shortened by multiples of dx. This can be true only if k is also independent of x. Hence it is a constant.

(b) The phrase, "points are placed independently," is best interpreted by example.

Suppose the points are the instants at which telephone subscribers originate calls. Then each point represents the act of a particular subscriber. To say it was placed at random means that the subscriber was as likely to call within one brief interval dt as another. By Theorem 78.1, we know that the chance of his doing so is then proportional to dt; we may call it $\gamma \, dt$.

To say there is just one point in an interval dt means that one or another of these subscribers, but not more than one, originated a call during that interval. This can be computed from their individual chances of doing so, and, if the interval is short enough, differs little from the sum of their individual chances. Therefore

$$P(1, dt) \rightarrow N\gamma \, dt, \qquad dt \rightarrow 0,$$

if the number of subscribers is N.

Suppose now that we ask for $P(> 1, dt)$, the chance of two or more calls in dt. To bring this about, some group of two or more subscribers would have to originate calls in this time. For any particular pair—say subscribers A and B—the probability of this would be $\gamma^2(dt)^2$ *because they act independently.* For a larger group it would be a higher power of $\gamma \, dt$. The chance that *specified* subscribers $A, B, C, \ldots,$ will do this *if they act independently* is $(\gamma \, dt)^s$, where s is the size of the group. To get $P(> 1, dt)$ we must therefore add together terms of this kind for all possible groups that could be formed. Since s is never less than 2, $(dt)^2$ is a factor in all such terms and we may write

$$P(> 1, dt) \rightarrow k'(dt)^2, \qquad dt \rightarrow 0.$$

Clearly, since $P(> 2, dt)$, $P(> 3, dt), \ldots$ are less than $P(> 1, dt)$, they must also vanish at least as rapidly.

But this would not be true if the subscribers did not act independently. If, for some mysterious reason, subscribers A and B always called simultaneously and the others were associated in similar pairs, $P(> 1, dt)$ would be proportional to dt, not $(dt)^2$. And if, for some reason, all calls were separated by at least a minimum interval, $P(> 1, dt)$ would be zero for sufficiently small dt.

In the general case which we have been discussing, for the same reasons as above,

$$P(> 1, dx) \rightarrow k'(dx)^2, \qquad dx \rightarrow 0, \qquad (116.5)$$

if the points are independenly placed. Furthermore, $P(> 2, dx)$, $P(> 3, dx), \ldots$ must vanish at least as rapidly. This is what we set out to prove in part (b).

(c) Now consider two adjacent intervals of length x and dx. Together they are an interval of length $x + dx$. This combined interval cannot have more than n points in it unless there are more than n in x, or else there are n in x and one or more in dx, or else $n - 1$ in x and two or more in dx, etc. As an equation this statement becomes

$$P(> n, x + dx) = P(> n, x) + P(n, x)\, P(> 0, dx)$$
$$+ P(n - 1, x)\, P(> 1, dx) + \ldots .$$

Then, using (116.4) and (116.5) and letting $dx \to 0$, this reduces to

$$\frac{d P(> n, x)}{dx} = k\, P(n, x). \tag{116.6}$$

But $P(n, x) = P(> n - 1, x) - P(> n, x)$. Differentiating this and using (116.6), we get, finally,[10]

$$\frac{d P(n, x)}{dx} = k[P(n - 1, x) - P(n, x)]. \tag{116.7}$$

This is the set of differential equations which was discussed in § 107, and, as we know, the solution is (116.1).[11]

The fact that kx is the expectation of the number of points in length x has already been verified in Problem 110.31.

117. Discussion of the Poisson Distribution; Problems to which It Is an Appropriate Solution

We have now derived Poisson's distribution in two ways. According to the first, it was an approximation to the binomial, valid when m is large compared to ϵ. The second obtains it as an *exact solution, not an approximation*. It lays down general assumptions as to the nature of our knowledge—or rather, lack of knowledge—concerning the manner in which points follow one after another, asserting: (1) that the probability of one or more points within a specified interval is not influenced by any knowledge we may have concerning the states of other intervals; and (2) that each point lies at random, independently of all the rest.

There are many situations that can best be judged by the second set of criteria. One is the incidence of telephone calls in a telephone exchange. These certainly do not fall collectively at random for any great length of time; for the probability of a large number of calls within a minute at three o'clock in the morning is much smaller than

---

[10] In the equation for $n = 0$ the term $P(-1, x)$ must be given the value zero since the number of points in an interval obviously cannot be negative.

[11] In § 107 the notation was simplified by writing p_n for $P(n, x)$.

in a similar interval at three o'clock in the afternoon. If each call were plotted upon a time axis covering an entire day, some periods would be very dense and others sparse. If, however, we choose a quarter of an hour, say, from that part of the day when the traffic appears to be heaviest, or from any other portion except those in which the traffic density is changing rapidly, it will be approximately true that any small subinterval is as likely to contain n points as any other. Furthermore, there is very slight dependence among the individual calls. Throughout this quarter of an hour, therefore, the distribution of calls is approximately random, both individually and collectively. We conclude that, with x meaning time, (116.1) applies *to any time interval whatsoever lying wholly within the quarter of an hour* or even to the quarter of an hour itself.

This we can infer from our second method of proof. From the first method, on the other hand, we could only infer that the Poisson distribution is obeyed approximately in an interval of sufficiently short duration compared with the quarter of an hour,[12] and we would have no criterion for determining what the words "sufficiently short" mean.

There are many problems of this general type. The emission of β-rays from a radio-active substance is probably the best example in physics, because of the apparently complete independence of the emissions one from another.[13] But there are many others to which the formula applies in much the same general sense as to the problem of telephone calls. We name only a few typical ones:

The electrons emitted from a hot metal (thermions) or from a photosensitive substance under the influence of light (photoelectrons) probably emerge with sufficient independence to meet the criteria for use of the Poisson distribution. The number of line surges in a power transmission system because of the throwing of switches undoubtedly falls into the same class, and the number of bursts of static in radio reception probably does. Demands for service in general, whether upon the cashier of a department store, the stock clerk of a warehouse, or any similar functionary, fall into this pattern unless regularity is artificially injected into the system.

[12] If there were known to be exactly m points in the quarter of an hour, and if they were distributed individually at random, the chance of any one of them lying in an interval of length x would be $p = x/15$, if we measure time in minutes. The chance of just n in this interval would then be given exactly by the binomial distribution, to which the Poisson is known to be an approximation *only when p is small*. Hence x must be much smaller than 15.

[13] If we chose a given sample of our substance and watched *it*, the atoms of which it is composed would gradually transmute themselves into something else. Hence as time went on the number under observation would decrease. We shall find this worth thinking about a little later. For the moment we may suppose that a new atom is somehow fed into the group under observation whenever one leaves it by transmutation.

Hence it comes about that problems which demand to know the number of persons or the quantity of apparatus which will be needed to perform a given service often require the use of the Poisson distribution. The number of operators in a telephone exchange or the number of turnstiles in a subway station are excellent illustrations. We have not yet arrived at a point where it seems wise to undertake the exact discussion of such problems,[14] but we can with profit consider a very simple one which, in spite of its simplicity, is so similar to many more practical ones as to aid in orienting ourselves.

EXAMPLE 117.1.—*In a neighborhood store which has limited storage facilities the average demand for dog-biscuits is 10 boxes per week. The usual practice is to stock up Monday morning. How many packages should be adopted as the standard Monday morning stock in order not to lose more than one sale out of a hundred?*

The chance of a demand for j packages is

$$P(j) = \frac{10^j e^{-10}}{j!},$$

for this is exactly the chance of j points (buyers) in unit time (a week) when the expectation for that period is 10.

If the week begins with n packages in stock, the expected number of lost sales will be

$$\epsilon(L) = \sum_{j=n}^{\infty} (j - n) P(j).$$

If, then, we were to keep records for a large number of weeks, the number of packages which could have been sold if the stock had been unlimited would not differ much from $10m$ nor the number of lost sales from ϵm. It follows that in the long run the proportion of lost sales would be very close to[15]

---

[14] They will be the subject of Chapter XII.

[15] This step in our solution presents an excellent chance for error; for there is a treacherous difference between the "expectation of the proportion of sales lost in the long run" and the "expectation of the proportion of sales lost per week." The difficulty lies, not in computing the correct answer, for either computation is very simple, but in knowing exactly what it is that we are trying to compute.

In the present problem "losing one sale out of a hundred" means that, if we were to keep records over a very long time, the number of lost sales should be about 1% of the number of possible sales.

For the other, we would keep records of the proportion of sales lost each week, and average these. If just j customers appeared, the proportion of lost sales would be $(j - n)/j$. The chance of this occurring is $P(j)$. Hence the expectation would be

$$\epsilon'(L) = \sum_{j=n+1}^{\infty} \frac{j - n}{j} P(j). \tag{117.1}$$

$$\frac{\epsilon(L)}{10} = \frac{1}{10} \sum_{j=n}^{\infty} (j - n) P(j). \qquad (117.2)$$

To answer the question proposed in Example 117.1 it is necessary to find the smallest value of n for which this expression is less than 0.01. This requires a process of straightforward computation, but is much simplified by the use of Appendix VII, which is a table of

$$^{\infty}\Pi'_{\nu} = \sum_{j=\nu}^{\infty} \frac{\epsilon^j e^{-\epsilon}}{j!}.$$

By writing out the value of $P(j)$ and considering separately the parts involving j (Pj) and $n P(j)$, (117.2) is easily reduced to the form

$$\frac{\epsilon(L)}{10} = \sum_{j=n-1}^{\infty} \frac{10^j e^{-10}}{j!} - \frac{n}{10} \sum_{j=n}^{\infty} \frac{10^j e^{-10}}{j!} = {}^{\infty}\Pi'_{n-1} - \frac{n}{10} {}^{\infty}\Pi'_n.$$

TABLE 117.1

n	$^{\infty}\Pi'_{n-1}$	$n\,^{\infty}\Pi_n/10$	$\epsilon(L)/10$
10	0.66718	0.54207	0.12511
11	0.54207	0.45865	0.08342
12	0.41696	0.36386	0.05310
13	0.30322	0.27097	0.03225
14	0.20844	0.18976	0.01868
15	0.13554	0.12519	0.01035
16	0.08346	0.07798	0.00548
17	0.04874	0.04597	0.00277
18	0.02704	0.02570	0.00134
19	0.01428	0.01365	0.00063
20	0.00719	0.00691	0.00028

Table 117.1 shows the details of the computation. The second column contains the values of $^{\infty}\Pi'_{n-1}$ taken from the column headed 10 in Appendix VII. The third column contains $n\,^{\infty}\Pi'_n/10$, and the fourth column, which is the difference of these two, is $\epsilon(L)/10$.

Under the conditions of the problem, the least safe stock is 16.

118. Discussion of the Poisson Distribution; Variable Traffic Density in a Telephone Exchange

Both the Poisson distribution and the mathematical argument by means of which we derived it in § 116 can be applied to traffic in which there is a very definite trend (i.e., to a distribution of points which tend to pack more densely about certain parts of the line than others) provided we know enough about the nature of the trend. We may illustrate this by means of a problem which is not entirely impractical: the incidence of calls in a telephone exchange when the traffic is varying rapidly.

To illustrate exactly what we have in mind, consider the highly idealized case of an exchange in which there is no traffic whatever before nine o'clock in the morning, and in which the traffic density then begins to build up so as to reach a maximum at noon. Suppose this is not due to a tendency of individual subscribers to place their calls late in the morning, but to the fact that no subscriber arrives at his place of business before nine o'clock, and many not until considerably later. Suppose, finally, that we have reason to believe that the subscribers arrive at a uniform rate, so that the number at work is a linear function of the time. Under all these highly artificial conditions, the chance of a call being made during the short interval of time between t and $t + dt$ would be proportional to the number of subscribers then at work, and therefore also to t if nine o'clock is taken as the origin of time.[16]

More generally, assume that the chance of a call arriving in the interval between t and $t + dt$ is some known function[17] $k(t) \, dt$ of the time of day t, and also that the chance of two or more calls in such an interval is an infinitesimal of higher order than $k(t) \, dt$.

Denoting by[18] $p(n, \tau, t)$ the probability that n calls arrive within an interval of length τ beginning at the instant t and focusing attention on two adjacent intervals τ and $d\tau$, we have

$$p(n, \tau + d\tau, t) = p(n, \tau, t) \, p(0, d\tau, t + \tau)$$

$$+ \, p(n - 1, \tau, t) \, p(1, d\tau, t + \tau)$$

$$+ \, p(n - 2, \tau, t) \, p(2, d\tau, t + \tau)$$

$$+ \, \ldots$$

Furthermore,

$$p(0, d\tau, t + \tau) = 1 - p(1, d\tau, t + \tau) - p(2, d\tau, t + \tau) - \ldots$$

Substituting this in the preceding equation and recalling the assumption that $p(2, d\tau, t + \tau)$, $p(3, d\tau, t + \tau), \ldots$ vanish to a higher order than $d\tau$, we obtain

$$\frac{d}{d\tau} p(n, \tau, t) = [p(n - 1, \tau, t) - p(n, \tau, t)] \, k(t + \tau). \qquad (118.1)$$

---

[16] We are here describing a situation in which the calls are not at random individually, but they are independent and collectively at random.

[17] This $k(t) \, dt$ will play the same part in our present discussion that the $k \, dx$ played in § 116. There k was the expected number of points per unit length (calls per unit time, or "calling rate"); here $k(t)$ is the "instantaneous calling rate."

[18] This should be read "probability of n [calls] within [an interval of length] τ beginning at [the instant] t."

Now let $g(u)$ be the generating function for $p(n, \tau, t)$; that is,

$$g(u) = \sum_{n=0}^{\infty} p(n, \tau, t) \, u^n.$$

Multiplying (118.1) by u^n and summing for all values of n, we get[19]

$$\frac{dg(u)}{d\tau} = (u - 1) \, k(t + \tau) \, g(u),$$

or

$$\frac{dg(u)}{g(u)} = (u - 1) \, k(t + \tau) \, d\tau.$$

Hence

$$g(u) = c e^{(u-1) \, K(t,\tau)}, \tag{118.2}$$

where

$$K(t, \tau) = \int_{0}^{\tau} k(t + \tau) \, d\tau$$

and c is the constant of integration. Since $g(1)$ must be 1, $c = 1$. Differentiating (118.2) gives

$$\frac{d^n g(u)}{du^n} = [K(t, \tau)]^n \, e^{(u-1) \, K(t, \tau)},$$

and hence by (105.2)

$$p(n, \tau, t) = \frac{K^n \, e^{-K}}{n!}.$$

This is again the Poisson distribution, with the integral K playing the role of the kx in (116.1). There kx meant the "expected number of points in distance x" or, in the terms of our present example, the "expected number of calls in time x." Here also K is the "expected number of calls in the interval τ," for it is easy to show that

$$\sum n \, p(n, \tau, t) = K.$$

It is obvious, then, that the usefulness of the Poisson distribution is much wider than would be inferred from the discussion of § 116. We must be careful not to swing to the opposite extreme, however, and conclude that it is *universally* applicable to everything which, in the loose sense in which the phrase is applied in everyday speech, occurs "at random."

To illustrate the type of situation to which it does *not* apply we consider still another example.

---

[19] As always, u is supposed to be a variable quite independent of any others in the equation. Specifically, it is not a function of τ, so that $u^n \, dp/d\tau = d(u^n \, p)/d\tau$.

119. Discussion of the Poisson Distribution; The General Problem of β-Ray Emission

In Footnote 13, § 117, we called attention to the fact that as a substance emits β-rays it transmutes itself into a new substance, and thus reduces the amount of the old substance in the sample under observation. This is usually expressed in physics by the assertion that the substance "decays." We now solve the following example:

EXAMPLE 119.1.—*If, at time $t = 0$, there are N atoms of an element in a sample, and if the chance of any one atom decaying in an interval dt is $k\,dt$, what is the chance of exactly j decaying between t and $t + \tau$?*

This problem, like the one in § 118, deals with a set of events which show a definite trend, but there is this vital difference between them: the chance of an event taking place during the interval between t and $t + dt$ was determined solely by t in the preceding case and was independent of the past history of the system, whereas in the present case it is determined solely by the past history of the system and is a function of t only because the past history is. For, in the present instance the chance of an emission in the interval in question is proportional to the amount of sample left and is determined by the number of emissions which have already taken place.[20] The problem is no harder to solve, however, than was Example 117.1.

We start by investigating the chance of *just n β-rays between $t = 0$ and $t = t$*. We can do this most easily, because we know the number of atoms available for transmutation is N at $t = 0$ and (if n have been emitted) $N - n$ at $t = t$.

Using the same notation as in § 118[21] and proceeding with an exactly similar argument, we find that

$$p(n, t + dt, 0) = p(n, t, 0)[1 - (N - n)k\,dt]$$
$$+ p(n - 1, t, 0)(N - n + 1)k\,dt. \qquad (119.1)$$

The remaining terms of the convolution are negligible since the chance of more than one atom decaying during dt is an infinitesimal of higher order. From (119.1) we obtain

$$\frac{d}{dt} p(n, t, 0) + (N - n)k\,p(n, t, 0) = (N - n + 1)k\,p(n - 1, t, 0).$$
$$(119.2)$$

In the case of $n = 0$ the right-hand member is zero, since it is clearly impossible for a negative number of atoms to decay. Thus

$$\frac{d}{dt} p(0, t, 0) + Nk\,p(0, t, 0) = 0$$

---

[20] In mathematical terms, the points (emissions) are independent and individually at random, but they are not collectively at random.

[21] That is, $p(n, t, 0)$ means the chance of n emissions during a time t beginning at $t = 0$. Later $p(n, \tau, t)$ will mean the chance of n emissions during a time τ beginning at $t = t$, as in § 118.

or[22]

$$p(0, t, 0) = e^{-Nkt}.$$ (119.3)

By using this on the right of (119.2) for $n = 1$, $p(1, t, 0)$ can be obtained; and thus in succession $p(2, t, 0), \ldots .$[23] We thus obtain

$$p(n, t, 0) = C_n^N (1 - e^{-kt})^n e^{-(N-n)kt}$$ (119.4)

or, if we write $x = 1 - e^{-kt}$,

$$p(n, t, 0) = C_n^N x^n (1 - x)^{N-n}.$$ (119.5)

This, then, is a general formula for an interval beginning at an instant when the number of molecules is known to be N.

What about the interval from t to $t + \tau$ about which Example 119.1 asked? Now that (119.4) is available, $p(n, \tau, t)$ can easily be found by the use of alternative compound probabilities. If there were n emissions in the time t, the chance that in the next interval τ exactly n' out of the $N - n$ which remain will decay is obviously, by (119.5),

$$p(n', \tau, t | n) = C_{n'}^{N, -n} y^{n'} (1 - y)^{N-n-n'},$$

where

$$y = 1 - e^{-k\tau}.$$

Hence

$$p(n', \tau, t) = \sum_{n=0}^{N-n'} [C_n^N x^n (1 - x)^{N-n}] [C_{n'}^{N, -n} y^{n'} (1 - y)^{N-n-n'}].$$

By noting that $C_n^N C_{n'}^{N,-n} = C_{n'}^N C_n^{N-n'}$ and making certain other rearrangements, this becomes

$$p(n', \tau, t) = C_{n'}^N [(1 - x)y]^{n'} \sum_{n=0}^{N-n'} C_n^{N-n'} x^n [(1 - x)(1 - y)]^{N-n'-n}$$

$$= C_{n'}^N z^{n'} (1 - z)^{N-n'}$$

if

$$z = (1 - x)y = e^{-kt}(1 - e^{-k\tau}).$$

This is the general solution of the problem. *Like* (119.5) *it is a binomial distribution, not a Poisson.* Only when N is very large and k very small (so

---

[22] The constants of integration are determined so that, as the time t drops to zero, the probability of one or more emissions vanishes and the probability of none becomes 1.

[23] Equation (116.7) could also have been solved step by step in this fashion, and very easily. The generating function was introduced as a further illustration of its use, not because it greatly simplified the problem. Its use in (119.2) would give rise to substantial complications, due to the appearance of terms of the form $n p(n, t, 0)$. The reader will recall that such terms arise in $dg(u)/du$; for this reason (119.2) would lead to a differential equation involving both $\partial g/\partial t$ and $\partial g/\partial u$. To obtain (119.4) by this process would be somewhat involved.

that Nk is of moderate size) does it become approximately a Poisson distribution. Under these circumstances the number left after any physically consequential time t is not very greatly different from N, so that the chance of an emission between t and $t + dt$ is virtually independent of t.

120. An Approximation to the Poisson Distribution

Under certain circumstances the normal distribution is an acceptable approximation to the Poisson distribution. We begin with (116.1) and, as usual, denote the deviation from expectation by δ and the standard deviation by σ. A simple algebraic computation then shows that $\epsilon = \sigma^2 = kx$.

From this point on, the procedure is exactly parallel to that carried out in § 112. We first replace n by a new variable $y = \delta/\sigma = (n - \sigma^2)/\sigma$, which measures the deviation in terms of the standard deviation as a unit. We thus get

$$P(n) = \frac{\sigma^{2\sigma^2+2\sigma y}}{(\sigma^2 + \sigma y)!}\, e^{-\sigma^2}.$$

We next replace the factorial by its Stirling approximation and expand the various terms in series. The final result, after much tedious algebra, and after making the change of scale which is required in passing from n to y, is

$$
\begin{aligned}
P(y) = \frac{e^{-y^2/2}}{\sqrt{2\pi}} \Bigg[&1 - \frac{1}{\sigma}\left(\frac{y}{2} - \frac{y^3}{6}\right) - \frac{1}{\sigma^2}\left(\frac{1}{12} - \frac{3y^2}{8} + \frac{y^4}{6} - \frac{y^6}{72}\right) \\
&+ \frac{1}{\sigma^3}\left(\frac{y}{8} - \frac{47y^3}{144} + \frac{37y^5}{240} - \frac{y^7}{48} + \frac{y^9}{1296}\right) \\
&+ \frac{1}{\sigma^4}\left(\frac{1}{288} - \frac{5y^2}{32} + \frac{347y^4}{1152} - \frac{617y^6}{4320} + \frac{23y^8}{960} - \frac{y^{10}}{648} + \frac{y^{12}}{31104}\right) \\
&+ \dots \Bigg].
\end{aligned}
\tag{120.1}
$$

The first term of this series is exactly the same as (111.1). That is,

The normal distribution (111.1) is a satisfactory approximation to the Poisson when y^3/σ is not too large.

To see just how satisfactory the approximation is, we refer to Figs. 120.1 and 120.2, in which the values of the Poisson distribution are represented by circles, whereas the normal and the more complete approximation (120.1) are shown as continuous curves. In Fig. 120.1 the value of ϵ is 10 and in Fig. 120.2 it is 100. The discrepancies between the true values and those given by the normal approximation are considerable in every case, although much more noticeably so for the smaller value of ϵ than for the larger one; but near the center of the range, where the probabilities are high, the percentage error would not be of serious consequence for many purposes. Near the tails,

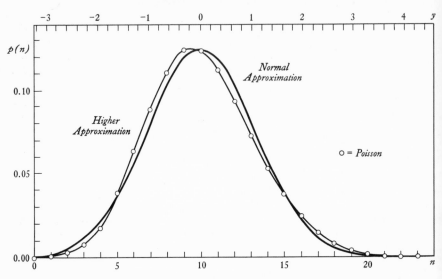

FIG. 120.1 APPROXIMATIONS TO THE POISSON DISTRIBUTION.

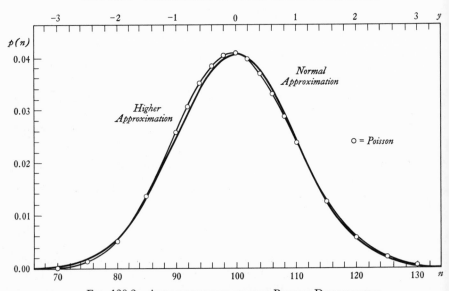

FIG. 120.2 APPROXIMATIONS TO THE POISSON DISTRIBUTION.

however, the percentage error is very large. Therefore this approximation should never be used in those regions. The complete approximation (120.1), on the other hand, agrees very well with the true values throughout the entire range, even in the case of the smaller value of ϵ.

121. Other Distribution Functions

So far this chapter has dealt exclusively with three distribution functions—the binomial, normal, and Poisson. They are three of the most important, but it is well to call attention in passing at this time to the wide variety of others which either have been, or will be, discussed in the course of this book. A number of these are listed under the general heading "Distribution functions" in the index.

122. The Normal Approximation to the Multinomial Distribution

In § 43 it was pointed out that, just as an experiment which can have only two mutually exclusive results, say success and failure, will, when repeated, generate data distributed according to the binomial function, so an experiment which can have several different results will generate data distributed according to the multinomial distribution

$$P_m(n_1, n_2, \ldots, n_a) = \frac{m!}{n_1! \, n_2! \, \ldots \, n_a!} p_1{}^{n_1} p_2{}^{n_2} \ldots p_a{}^{n_a}, \quad (122.1)$$

where a is the number of different results, m is the number of trials, and

$$n_1 + n_2 + \ldots + n_a = m. \quad (122.2)$$

We seek an approximation to (122.1) when the number of trials is large. The argument parallels exactly the one which was used in § 112.

If m is large enough that every n_j can without serious error be replaced by its Stirling approximation, (122.1) can be put in the form

$$P = \frac{1}{(\sqrt{2\pi m})^{a-1} \sqrt{p_1 p_2 \ldots p_a}} \left(\frac{mp_1}{n_1}\right)^{n_1 + \frac{1}{2}} \left(\frac{mp_2}{n_2}\right)^{n_2 + \frac{1}{2}} \ldots \left(\frac{mp_a}{n_a}\right)^{n_a + \frac{1}{2}}. \quad (122.3)$$

Next, as in (112.1), each n_j is replaced by a new variable

$$y_j = \frac{\delta_j}{\sigma_j} = \frac{n_j - mp_j}{\sigma_j},$$

where $\sigma_j = \sqrt{mp_j(1 - p_j)}$. Each factor of (122.3) then becomes

$$\left(1 + \frac{\sigma_j y_j}{mp_j}\right)^{-mp_j - \sigma_j y_j - \frac{1}{2}}. \quad (122.4)$$

Writing these in (122.3), taking the logarithm of both sides, and then expanding the logarithm of each of the factors (122.4) in a series give

$$\log \left[(\sqrt{2\pi m})^{a-1} \sqrt{p_1 p_2 \ldots p_a P} \right]$$

$$= - \sum \left(\sigma_j y_j + \frac{\sigma_j^2 y_j^2}{2 m p_j} + \text{terms of lower order} \right). \quad (122.5)$$

Next we go back to (122.2) and replace all the n's by their corresponding y's. The result is

$$\sum \sigma_j y_j + m \sum p_j = m;$$

whence, since $\sum p_j = 1$, it follows that $\sum \sigma_j y_j = 0$. Therefore, when we remember the value of σ_j^2, (122.5) becomes

$$P(n_1, n_2, \ldots, n_a) = \frac{1}{(\sqrt{2\pi m})^{a-1} \sqrt{p_1 p_2 \ldots p_a}} \, e^{- \frac{1}{2} \Sigma y_j^2 (1 - p_j)}. \quad (122.6)$$

The form of the exponent to which we are thus led suggests the substitution of a new variable $x_j = y_j \sqrt{1 - p_j}$ in place of y_j. A little later we shall discuss what this new variable signifies. For the moment we had best keep our attention focused upon the purely mathematical ideas. Let us, then, change to x_j in place of y_j, thus obtaining

$$P(n_1, n_2, \ldots, n_a) = \frac{1}{(\sqrt{2\pi m})^{a-1} \sqrt{p_1 p_2 \ldots p_a}} \, e^{- \frac{1}{2} \Sigma x_j^2}, \quad (122.7)$$

where

$$x_1 = \frac{n_1 - m p_1}{\sqrt{m p_1}}, \, x_2 = \frac{n_2 - m p_2}{\sqrt{m p_2}}, \ldots, x_a = \frac{n_a - m p_a}{\sqrt{m p_a}}. \quad (122.8)$$

This is the desired approximation to (122.1). It is analogous to the normal approximation to the binomial. We saw in § 113 that the practical value of the latter lies principally in the aid which it gives in estimating the sums of large numbers of ordinates to the distribution curve, not in the computation of a specific ordinate, and this led to integrations with respect to y. So also in the present case we seldom have reason to evaluate $P(n_1, n_2, \ldots, n_a)$ for a particular set of n's, but have frequent reason to be interested in their sum over various ranges. Furthermore, as will appear in the next chapter, these ranges are frequently best expressed in hyperspherical coordinates. We shall, therefore, do two things simultaneously: we shall introduce the change of scale which is necessary in passing from the n's to the x's and shall change the coordinates to hyperspherical form.

Let us, then, call the analogue of (122.6)

$$P(x_1, x_2, \ldots, x_a) = Ke^{-\frac{1}{2}\Sigma x_j^2},\qquad\qquad (122.9)$$

where K is a constant to be determined, and introduce the transformation (90.1) and its Jacobian (90.2). The result is

$$P(r, \theta_1, \ldots, \theta_{a-1}) = Ke^{-\frac{1}{2}r^2} r^{a-1} \cos^{a-2}\theta_1 \cos^{a-3}\theta_2 \ldots \cos\theta_{a-2}.$$
$$(122.10)$$

The constant K can now easily be determined by integrating over all values of r and the angles. Clearly, this requires r to range from 0 to ∞. Also, θ_1 must range from $-\pi/2$ to $+\pi/2$; otherwise x_1 would not take both positive and negative values. A similar argument applies to $\theta_2, \ldots, \theta_{a-2}$. In the case of θ_{a-1}, however, this range is insufficient, since it would not provide for change of sign of x_a. (See equation (90.1).) This one angle must therefore vary from $-\pi$ to $+\pi$.

When (122.10) is integrated between these limits and the result is set equal to 1,[24] it is found that

$$K = (2\pi)^{-a/2}.$$

This value can be inserted in either (122.9) or (122.10). However, when using either formula as an approximation to the multinomial distribution, the fact that the n's must satisfy the equation (122.2) must be kept in mind. This means that the x's in (122.9) are subject to the restriction

$$\sum \sqrt{mp_j}\, x_j = 0,$$

which is a hyperplane through the origin.

How this affects the problem of computation will become clear in §§ 149–151.

Problems

1. Suppose that telephone calls, each of length T, occur individually and collectively at random, the calling rate being n per unit time. What is the probability that, at the instant t, there are *exactly j* in progress?

2. What is the probability that *more than j* are in progress?

3. What is the chance of *two or more* calls in an interval of length dt? If every call is followed by a "danger interval"—that is, an interval of length dt within which another call, if it arrives, will interfere with the first—what is the probability that a call will be interfered with during its danger interval? Why are these answers not equal?

---

[24] See Footnote 6, § 113.

4. At the time 0 an observer begins to note the arrival of calls. What is the probability that the *first* call arrives between t and $t + dt$?

5. What is the probability that the interval between a call and its next succeeding call lies between t and $t + dt$?

6. What is the expected time of waiting in Problem 4? The expected time interval in Problem 5?

7. With respect to Problem 6 the following argument can be made: The time $t = 0$ at which the observer enters must lie in an interval between calls. It is just as likely to lie near the beginning as the end of the interval. That is, its average position is the middle of the interval. Hence the average waiting time of the observer will be half the average interval between calls.
    The correct answers to Problem 6 do not satisfy this condition. Explain the paradox.

8. Suppose an exchange is suddenly "cut into service" at the height of busy hour traffic. Call the instant $t = 0$. For negative values of t the calling rate is zero. Hence there are no calls in any interval. For $t > 0$ the calling rate is n per unit time: hence the Poisson distribution applies to any interval lying wholly in this time. But if an interval begins at a time $t < 0$ and ends at $t + \tau > 0$, the calling rate is not constant. What is the probability of just j calls in such an interval?

9. In Problem 8, assume $n = 3$, $\tau = 1$, and draw curves for $P_j(\tau, t)$ covering values of t from -2 to $+1$, for each of the following values of j: 0, 1, 2, 3. Discuss the characteristic features—particularly maxima—of these curves.

10. In Problem 5, what is the most probable length of interval? The standard deviation of the length? The expected length?

11. In Example 119.1, what amount of substance can be expected to remain after a time t?

12. What *proportion* of the amount present at time t can be expected to decay during the next second? Note that t does not appear in your answer.

13. What is the expected time of emission of the first β-particle?
    [Use (119.3).]

14. Footnote 15 in § 117 refers to a different expectation than that computed in Table 117.1. Taking values of $P(j)$ from Appendix VI, find the value of n for which the expected proportion of losses per week would be less than 0.01.
    [Write (117.2) in the form
$$\epsilon'(L) = {}^\infty\Pi_{n+1} - n \sum_{j=n+1}^{\infty} P(j)/j.]$$

15. In a town of 5000 people, what is the probability that 20 or more were born on Christmas?
    [Use the Poisson approximation and Appendix VII.]

16. A penny is tossed 1000 times. What, approximately, is the probability of just h heads?

123. Further Remarks About the Normal Distribution

It is interesting to note that the normal distribution $\phi(y)$ has so far appeared only as an approximation to the binomial, Poisson, and multinomial distributions, all of which are discrete distributions. However, the normal function is also important in relation to continuous distributions.

In the first place, any such distribution can be represented by a series whose terms are $\phi(y)$ and its successive derivatives.[25] These series, which are similar in many ways to the familiar Fourier Series, are the subject of §§ 124 and 125.

In the second place, it can be shown that the results of any experiment, no matter how they are distributed, possess this remarkable property: that if it is repeated time after time and the observed results are averaged, the distribution function for the average will approach $\phi(y)$ as the number of trials increases.[26] This is the subject of §§ 127 and 128.

124. Hermite Polynomials; The Gram–Charlier Series

The successive derivatives of the normal function

$$\phi(y) = \frac{1}{\sqrt{2\pi}} e^{-y^2/2} \qquad (111.1)$$

are

$$\phi'(y) = \frac{-1}{\sqrt{2\pi}} e^{-y^2/2}\, y,$$

$$\phi''(y) = \frac{1}{\sqrt{2\pi}} e^{-y^2/2} \left(y^2 - 1\right),$$

$$\phi'''(y) = \frac{-1}{\sqrt{2\pi}} e^{-y^2/2} \left(y^3 - 3y\right),$$

---

[25] As a mathematical theorem, this statement would require some qualification and would read that "the series converges almost everywhere provided certain integrals exist." In practice, however, the conditions are always satisfied, principally because the results of an experiment are always confined to a finite range.

[26] As a mathematical theorem this statement also requires qualification, and in § 128 we present a distribution for which it is not true. But again the statement is always true in practice for the reason stated in footnote 25.

or in general,

$$\phi^i(y) = \frac{(-1)^i}{\sqrt{2\pi}} e^{-y^2/2} H_i(y), \qquad (124.1)$$

where $H_i(y)$ is written briefly for the "Hermite Polynomial"[27]

$$H_i(y) = y^i - 1 \, C_2^i y^{i-2} + 1 \cdot 3 \, C_4^i y^{i-4} - 1 \cdot 3 \cdot 5 \, C_6^i y^{i-6} + \cdots$$

$$= \sum_j (-\tfrac{1}{2})^j y^{i-2j} \frac{i!}{j! (i - 2j)!}. \qquad (124.2)$$

The sum is to run from $j = 0$ to the largest value for which $i - 2j \geq 0$. These H's and ϕ's possess the remarkable property that the integral of the product $H_i(y) \, \phi^i(y)$ taken from $-\infty$ to $+\infty$ is zero, no matter what the values of i and j may be, so long as they are not equal. This property, which is known in mathematics as "biorthogonality," is always a very valuable one; for it permits us to make use of a very simple

---

[27] The first thirteen of the polynomials are:

$H_0 = 1,$
$H_1 = y,$
$H_2 = y^2 - 1,$
$H_3 = y^3 - 3y,$
$H_4 = y^4 - 6y^2 + 3,$
$H_5 = y^5 - 10y^3 + 15y,$
$H_6 = y^6 - 15y^4 + 45y^2 - 15,$
$H_7 = y^7 - 21y^5 + 105y^3 - 105y,$
$H_8 = y^8 - 28y^6 + 210y^4 - 420y^2 + 105,$
$H_9 = y^9 - 36y^7 + 378y^5 - 1260y^3 + 945y,$
$H_{10} = y^{10} - 45y^8 + 630y^6 - 3150y^4 + 4725y^2 - 945,$
$H_{11} = y^{11} - 55y^9 + 990y^7 - 6930y^5 + 17325y^3 - 10395y,$
$H_{12} = y^{12} - 66y^{10} + 1485y^8 - 13860y^6 + 51975y^4 - 62370y^2 + 10395.$

There are many interesting relations between these polynomials. A few of the more useful ones follow:

$$y^n = \sum_{j=0}^{[n/2]} C_{2j}^n \frac{(2j)!}{2^j j!} H_{n-2j}(y), \qquad (124.3)$$

where $[n/2]$ means the integral part of $n/2$; i.e., $n/2$ or $(n - 1)/2$ according as n is even or odd.

$$H_i(y + z) = \sum_{j=0}^{i} C_j^i y^j H_{i-j}(z). \qquad (124.4)$$

$$H_i\left(\frac{y + z}{\sqrt{2}}\right) = 2^{-i/2} \sum_{j=0}^{i} C_j^i H_j(y) H_{i-j}(z). \qquad (124.5)$$

method of expanding an arbitrary function, $f(y)$, into a series of the form

$$f(y) = c_0 \phi(y) + c_1 \phi'(y) + c_2 \phi''(y) + \dots . \qquad (124.6)$$

To show this, suppose we multiply both sides of this equation by $H_i(y)$ and then integrate the result term by term between the limits $-\infty$ and $+\infty$. Because of the fact that the functions are biorthogonal, every term on the right-hand side of the equation will vanish except the term for which the two indices are equal, thus giving us the relation

$$\int_{-\infty}^{\infty} H_i(y) f(y) \, dy = c_i \int_{-\infty}^{\infty} H_i(y) \, \phi^i(y) \, dy,$$

or

$$c_i = \frac{\displaystyle\int_{-\infty}^{\infty} H_i(y) f(y) \, dy}{\displaystyle\int_{-\infty}^{\infty} H_i(y) \, \phi^i(y) \, dy}.$$

Now, by straightforward integration we find that the denominator of this expression is equal to $(-1)^i \, i!$; wherefore

$$c_i = \frac{(-1)^i}{i!} \int_{-\infty}^{\infty} H_i(y) f(y) \, dy. \qquad (124.7)$$

In words, *the coefficients in the series which represents $f(y)$ are simply the product of known numerical factors by the integrals from minus infinity to plus infinity of the products of the Hermite polynomials into the function which is to be expanded.*

Of course all this is true only when the integrals (124.7) exist and the series (124.6) converges. There is never any question about either when $f(y)$ is a distribution function arising from a practical experiment, principally because such functions are always zero for values of y outside some finite range. In principle, then, we have in (124.6) a means of representing the distribution of any statistical data as accurately as may be desired.

However, certain practical difficulties remain. To evaluate (124.7) we need to know what the function $f(y)$ is, *and in the case of statistical studies we almost never do.* What we usually know is that certain observations have given us certain results. They admittedly do not represent the function exactly; but they are the best we have, and the problem before us is that of making the very best possible use of them. In the attempt to do this, we shall be much better pleased with a result that does not obviously disagree with the data than we will with another result that still is grossly in error even after we have done our best with it, no matter how sound the latter may be theoretically.

We can perhaps illustrate this idea a bit better by reference to a more familiar type of expansion. It is well known that the function e^{-x^2} can be represented for every value of x by means of a Taylor Series. If, however, we possessed data which obeyed this law, though we did not know it did, and if our data were only extensive enough to permit the determination of three coefficients in our Taylor Series, we would be hard put to find a series which possessed even the major characteristics of the function in question. Certainly no three-term polynomial would do. But we might get something of practical utility from the use of the function $a \cot^{-1}(b + c x^2)$ which, theoretically, is not the right thing to begin with at all.

The same general situation exists with reference to the Gram–Charlier Series. So far as their application to statistical data is concerned, fine-spun theories regarding convergence and the like are likely to be a work of supererogation; for it is usually possible to determine no more than three or four coefficients at the most, and the practical question is simply how far the simple expressions thus derived are capable of representing our data.[28]

Nevertheless, the series and the mathematical theory behind them have very substantial merits. For one thing, once the coefficients have been determined they are easy to compute because extensive tables of the functions $\phi^i(y)$ are available to assist us.[29] They therefore provide more convenient approximations to the binomial, Poisson, and other distributions than the power series which were obtained earlier. This will be shown in §§ 125 and 126. They will also enable us to demonstrate, in § 127, one of the most remarkable theorems in the Theory of Probability—a theorem which is also one of the foundations of Statistics.

---

[28] A means of testing "goodness of fit" will be derived in § 149, Chapter XI.
[29] Appendix V is a table of $\phi(y)$, its first six derivatives, and its integral

$$\phi_{-1}(y) = \int_{-\infty}^{y} \phi(y)\, dy.$$

Larger tables of $\phi^i(y)$ for values of i up to 20, are given in *Tables of the error function and of its first twenty derivatives*, The Annals of the Computation Laboratory of Harvard University, 1952. Harvard University Press, Cambridge, Mass.; Oxford University Press, London, England.

Appendix IV contains a related function

$$\Phi(y) = 1 - \int_{-y}^{+y} \phi(y)\, dy.$$

125. Gram–Charlier Approximation to the Binomial Distribution

In § 112, in seeking a way to approximate the binomial distribution, we arrived at the formidable series (112.9). Computation of this in any individual case is likely to be tedious. But by comparing the terms of this series with the known expressions for Hermite polynomials it is a simple matter to throw it into the form

$$
P_m(y) = \phi + \frac{2p-1}{6\sigma}\phi''' + \frac{1}{\sigma^2}\left(\frac{6p^2-6p+1}{24}\phi^{iv} + \frac{4p^2-4p+1}{72}\phi^{vi}\right)
$$

$$
+ \frac{2p-1}{\sigma^3}\left(\frac{12p^2-12p+1}{120}\phi^v + \frac{6p^2-6p+1}{144}\phi^{vii}\right)
$$

$$
+ \frac{4p^2-4p+1}{1296}\phi^{ix}\Bigg) + \dots \tag{125.1}
$$

This series, which is of the Gram–Charlier type, is much easier to evaluate than (112.9) because of the aid that may be obtained from tables such as the one in Appendix V. This is particularly obvious if, as in Examples 113.1 and 113.2, we wish to sum a large number of values of $P_m(n)$ by means of the integral (113.2). If this were done by integrating (112.9), it would lead to another series likewise containing various powers of y, and we should have to compute these powers for both limits of integration and form the appropriate sums. On the other hand, if (125.1) is substituted into (113.2), the integral of $\phi'''(y)$ is $\phi''(y)$, the integral of $\phi^{iv}(y)$ is $\phi'''(y)$, and in general the integral of $\phi^i(y)$ is $\phi^{i-1}(y)$. All these quantities may be taken directly from the table in Appendix V, even the integral of $\phi(y)$ being given under the heading $\phi_{-1}(y)$. It therefore becomes an exceedingly simple matter to carry out the computation of (113.2)

EXAMPLE 125.1.—*Find the chance of n successes in 100 trials of an event the probability of which is 0.1.*

This example does not demand a sum and therefore no integration is involved. The problem is the direct computation of (125.1).

We have $p = 0.1$, $m = 100$ and therefore $\sigma = 3$, whence (125.1) becomes

$$
P_{100}(y) = \phi - \frac{2}{45}\phi''' + \left(\frac{23}{10,800}\phi^{iv} + \frac{2}{2,025}\phi^{vi}\right)
$$

$$
+ \left(\frac{1}{50,625}\phi^v - \frac{23}{243,000}\phi^{vii} - \frac{4}{273,375}\phi^{ix}\right) + \dots, \tag{125.2}
$$

the argument of the ϕ's being $y = (n-10)/3$.

Table 125.1 illustrates the degree of accuracy which may be expected of this formula; but the form of the table requires some explanation.

In the first place, (125.2) gives the values of $P_{100}(y)$, not $P_{100}(n)$. To get the latter it is necessary to introduce the proper change of scale, which from § 113[30] we know to be $1/\sigma = \frac{1}{3}$. Hence the values from which the table is derived are not the numbers given by (125.2) but one-third of them instead.

In the second place, although we have given in the second column the true values of the binomial distribution, the Gram–Charlier approximations to it are indicated, not by their actual values, but by their errors; for it is the errors in which we are principally interested.

In the third place, the four columns of deviations correspond: (1) to the Normal Law, which is represented by the first term of (125.1); (2) to the second approximation obtained by including the term which has the first power of σ in its denominator; (3) the approximation obtained by including the second power of σ also, and (4) the complete expression, so far as we have written it. That the convergence of the series is a fairly rapid one is obvious from the rapid vanishing of the Δ's.[31]

EXAMPLE 125.2.—*Find the chance of n or more successes in 100 trials of an event the probability of which is 0.1.*

---

[30] In § 113 the factor σ was introduced on the ground that it was required to make the area under the curve 1. But only the first term of (112.9) was considered in determining this area. We can now establish the fact that the area remains unity no matter how many terms are included. For $\int \phi^i(y)dy = \phi^{i-1}(y)$ and for $i \geq 1$, $\phi^{i-1}(y)$ is zero at both limits of integration. Hence, the terms beyond the first in (125.1)—or in (112.9) or (124.6)—change the shape of the distribution curve but do not alter the area under it.

[31] To these remarks we may also add the following observations, which will probably be of less interest to the elementary student than to those already familiar with the subject.

In the first place, various writers, of whom Edgeworth is perhaps the best known, have pointed out that to get the "best" results from a Gram–Charlier Series the terms should be associated in an order different from the "natural" one. Specifically, the term of zero order must either be used alone, or else in some one of the combinations

$$0, 3;$$
$$0, 3, 4, 6;$$
$$0, 3, 4, 6, 5, 7, 9.$$

Now this is just exactly the way the terms have grouped themselves in (125.1) and (125.2); and we see at once that the rule may be said to be a natural consequence (in the case of Binomial expansions at least) of the attempt to arrange the terms in descending powers of σ.

In the second place, there is a common rule to the effect that the coefficient of the term of order 6 is approximately equal to half the square of the coefficient of order 3. In the case of (125.1) and (125.2) this is identically true, if by the "term of order 6" we mean that one which occurs in combination with ϕ^{iv}. This, however, is not the entire term of order 6: the first *unwritten* term of (125.1) would also contain ϕ^{vi}, but as it has a higher power of σ in its denominator it can be expected to be of little importance by comparison with the part accounted for by the common rule.

It would appear, therefore, that to obtain the best results from the use of the Gram–Charlier Series, *some* other order than the natural one is required. Whether that suggested by Edgeworth is the "best in the long run" will depend largely upon what we mean by that phrase. Certainly it is not to be expected that any order of summation can be devised which will not, in an exceptional case, be less exact than some other order which happened to be peculiarly appropriate to that exceptional case.

[In the first edition of this book, this footnote was extended to include some comments on the literature of the day. They are not repeated here since their interest is now largely historical.]

Here $P_m(y)$ is again (125.2), but it must be integrated between the limits $y = (n - 10.5)/3$ and ∞. As stated above, this requires only that ϕ be replaced by ϕ_{-1} and the other ϕ^i's by ϕ^{i-1}. Table 125.2 contains the results. The approximation is not quite so good as in Table 125.1 but it would still be quite sufficient for most purposes.

TABLE 125.1

THE BINOMIAL DISTRIBUTION $C^{100} (0.1)^n (0.9)^{100-n}$ AND SEVERAL GRAM–CHARLIER APPROXIMATIONS TO IT

n	True Value	Δ_0	Δ_1	Δ_2	Δ_3
0	0.00003	+0.00048	−0.00013	−0.00006	−0.00002
1	0.00030	+ 118	− 0	− 5	− 2
2	0.00162	+ 218	+ 32	+ 6	+ 1
3	0.00589	+ 285	+ 64	+ 18	+ 5
4	0.01587	+ 212	+ 52	+ 14	+ 3
5	0.03387	− 71	− 16	− 7	− 3
6	0.05958	− 491	− 95	− 22	− 5
7	0.08890	− 824	− 107	− 14	− 1
8	0.11482	− 834	− 31	+ 4	− 1
9	0.13042	− 462	+ 76	+ 12	+ 1
10	0.13187	+ 111	+ 111	− 1	− 1
11	0.11988	+ 592	+ 53	− 14	+ 1
12	0.09879	+ 770	− 33	− 2	+ 2
13	0.07430	+ 635	− 82	+ 12	− 1
14	0.05130	+ 370	− 59	+ 14	− 3
15	0.03268	+ 48	− 7	+ 2	− 1
16	0.01929	− 130	+ 30	− 8	+ 2
17	0.01059	− 185	+ 37	− 9	+ 3
18	0.00543	− 163	+ 22	− 4	+ 1
19	0.00260	− 113	+ 6	+ 1	− 1
20	0.00117	− 66	− 4	+ 3	− 1
21	0.00050	− 34	− 6	+ 2	− 0
22	0.00020	−0.00015	−0.00005	+0.00001	+0.00000

126. Gram–Charlier Approximation to the Poisson Distribution

We can carry out a similar line of argument with respect to the series (120.1) which was obtained as an approximation to the Poisson distribution.

It is found to reduce easily to the Gram–Charlier form

$$P(y) = \phi - \frac{1}{\sigma}\frac{\phi'''}{6} + \frac{1}{\sigma^2}\left(\frac{\phi^{iv}}{24} + \frac{\phi^{vi}}{72}\right) - \frac{1}{\sigma^3}\left(\frac{\phi^{v}}{120} + \frac{\phi^{vii}}{144} + \frac{\phi^{ix}}{1{,}296}\right)$$
$$+ \frac{1}{\sigma^4}\left(\frac{\phi^{vi}}{720} + \frac{13\phi^{viii}}{5{,}760} + \frac{\phi^{x}}{1{,}728} + \frac{\phi^{xii}}{31{,}104}\right) + \cdots,$$

from which either the probability of n taking a particular value or the chance of it lying within a specified range could be computed. The Poisson distribution is of sufficient importance, however, that extensive tables have been

TABLE 125.2

CERTAIN GRAM–CHARLIER APPROXIMATIONS TO THE SUM OF A BINOMIAL SERIES

n_1	True Value	Δ_0	Δ_1	Δ_2	Δ_3
0	1.00000	−0.00023	+0.00020	+0.00002	−0.00001
5	0.97629	− 967	− 187	− 99	− 81
10	0.54871	+ 1747	+ 47	− 7	− 6
15	0.07257	− 576	+ 143	+ 65	+ 80
20	0.00198	−0.00121	−0.00015	+0.00011	+0.00009

prepared, not only of $P(n) = \epsilon^n e^{-\epsilon}/n!$ itself, but also of the function

$$\Pi(n) = \sum_{n}^{\infty} P(n)$$

which represents the probability that n is not less than a specified value. Appendices VI and VII are skeleton tables of this sort.[32] Obviously, with such tables available, we have very little use for a series expansion.

127. The Central Limit Theorem

The central limit theorem may be stated as follows:

THEOREM 127.1. *If an experiment leads to a number x with the distribution $p(x)$, and if the integrals*

$$\int_{-\infty}^{\infty} x^i\, p(x)\, dx$$

exist for all values of i, the sum of the results of n independent trials of this experiment has a distribution which, in standard form, approaches the normal distribution (111.1) *for large values of n.*

---

[32] More extensive tables are found in *Poisson's Exponential Binomial Limit*, by E. C. Molina, D. Van Nostrand Co., Inc., Princeton, N.J.

This theorem has been demonstrated in many ways. The proof which we shall give not only establishes the fact that the process approaches the stated limit; it also provides a method of computing the successive approximations, and it gives an indication of the manner and the rate of the approach to the limit. For simplicity of presentation we shall not prove the theorem exactly as stated, but instead shall prove that those distribution functions for which $n = 2, 2^2, \ldots, 2^a$ approach the stated limit. The same argument can be applied to the complete series, but the added complexity (which is principally a matter of notation) is not warranted here.

Assume, then, that the standard form of $p(x)$ is $p_0(x)$ and that it has a Gram–Charlier expansion

$$p_0(x) = \sum_j \alpha_{0,j} \phi^j(x);$$

and let the distributions for the sums of $2^1, 2^2, \ldots, 2^a$ trials, *also in standard form*, be, respectively,

$$p_1(x) = \sum_j \alpha_{1,j} \phi^j(x),$$
$$p_2(x) = \sum_j \alpha_{2,j} \phi^j(x), \qquad (127.1)$$
$$\cdots$$
$$p_a(x) = \sum_j \alpha_{a,j} \phi^j(x).$$

Now consider the sum of 2^{a+1} trials. This can be regarded as the sum of its two halves, which are themselves sums of 2^a trials.[33] Hence, by (110.3),

$$\frac{1}{\sqrt{2}} p_{a+1}(x/\sqrt{2}) = \int_{-\infty}^{\infty} p_a(\xi) p_a(x - \xi) \, d\xi. \qquad (127.2)$$

If each of the p's in this equation is replaced by its Gram–Charlier series and the equation is multiplied throughout by $H_s(x/\sqrt{2})$ and then integrated, we get, by virtue of (124.7),

$$(-1)^s s! \, \alpha_{a+1,\, s} = \sum_i \sum_j \alpha_{a,i} \alpha_{a,j} \int_{-\infty}^{\infty} dx \int_{-\infty}^{\infty} d\xi \, H_s(x/\sqrt{2}) \, \phi^i(\xi)\phi^j(x-\xi).$$

Next, let $x = \xi + \eta$, and replace H_s by (124.5). This gives

$$(-1)^s s! \, \alpha_{a+1,s} = \sum_i \sum_j \sum_{k=0}^{s} \frac{\alpha_{a,i} \alpha_{a,j}}{2^{s/2}} C_k^s$$

$$\times \int_{-\infty}^{\infty} d\xi \int_{-\infty}^{\infty} d\eta \, H_k(\xi) \, H_{s-k}(\eta) \, \phi^i(\xi) \, \phi^j(\eta).$$

---

[33] It is this fact that allows the notation to be simplified when only the chosen subsequence is used.

This equation looks very complicated; but, because the H's and ϕ's are orthogonal, the ξ integral vanishes for every i except $i = k$, and the η integral vanishes for every j except $j = s - k$. Hence the complication evaporates, and we are left with the simple convolution

$$\alpha_{a+1,s} = \sum_{k=0}^{s} \frac{\alpha_{a,k}\,\alpha_{a,s-k}}{2^{s/2}}. \tag{127.3}$$

Thus, *in the series for the sum of 2^{a+1} trials the coefficient $\alpha_{a+1,s}$ is the convolution of the first $s + 1$ coefficients of the series for 2^a trials divided by $2^{s/2}$.* As we shall see, it is this factor $2^{s/2}$ that causes convergence to the normal distribution. There is, however, some further simplification to be introduced.

Since all the distributions are standardized we have

$$\int_{-\infty}^{\infty} p_a(x)\, dx = 1, \qquad \int_{-\infty}^{\infty} x\, p_a(x)\, dx = 0, \qquad \int_{-\infty}^{\infty} x^2\, p_a(x)\, dx = 1.$$

If we replace $p_a(x)$ in these integrals by (127.1) and note that $1 = H_0(x)$, $x = H_1(x)$ and $x^2 = H_2(x) + H_0(x)$, we find from the orthogonality property that

$$\alpha_{a,0} = 1, \qquad \alpha_{a,1} = 0, \qquad \alpha_{a,2} = 0.$$

Hence, for every a, the second and third terms of the Gram–Charlier series are missing, and in the convolution (127.3) several terms drop out.

Taking advantage of these simplifications, we find that (127.3) becomes for $s = 3$ simply $\alpha_{a+1,3} = \alpha_{a,3}/\sqrt{2}$; and since this is valid for any value of a it can be used repeatedly to get

$$\alpha_{a,3} = \frac{\alpha_{a-1,3}}{\sqrt{2}} = \frac{\alpha_{a-2,3}}{2} = \dots = \frac{\alpha_{0,3}}{2^{a/2}}. \tag{127.4}$$

By a similar process we also find

$$\alpha_{a,4} = \frac{\alpha_{0,4}}{2^a},$$

$$\alpha_{a,5} = \frac{\alpha_{0,5}}{2^{3a/2}},$$

$$\alpha_{a,6} = \frac{\alpha_{0,6}}{2^{2a}} + \frac{\alpha_{0,3}^{\,2}}{2^{a+2}},$$

$$\alpha_{a,7} = \frac{\alpha_{0,7}}{2^{5a/2}} + \frac{\alpha_{0,3}\,\alpha_{0,4}}{2^{(3a+2)/2}},$$

$$\alpha_{a.8} = \frac{\alpha_{0,8}}{2^{3a}} + \frac{\alpha_{0,3}\,\alpha_{0,5}}{2^{2a+1}} + \frac{\alpha_{0,4}^{\,2}}{2^{2a+2}},$$

$$\tag{127.5}$$

and so on. Now all of these approach zero as the number of trials $n = 2^a$ becomes infinite; only the first coefficient $\alpha_{a,0}$ remains constantly equal to 1. *This proves the theorem.*

What is more, we observe that the higher order terms vanish more rapidly than the lower ones; the exact relation is somewhat complicated, but the progressive relation can be clearly established. Hence it comes about that, even with a relatively unfavorable starting distribution, the distribution for the sum of only a modest number of trials can be approximated quite well by a few Gram–Charlier terms.

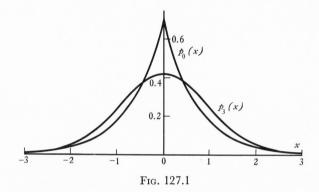

FIG. 127.1

As an example consider the case of the starting function shown in Fig. 127.1. To the right of the axis it is the exponential $e^{-\sqrt{2x}}/\sqrt{2}$; to the left, the mirror image of that exponential.[34]

The exact distributions for the sums of 2, 4, and 8 numbers taken from this starting function can be computed directly by the use of (127.2), and when put in standard form are, for $x \geqq 0$,

$$p_1(x) = e^{-2x}(x + \tfrac{1}{2}),$$

$$p_2(x) = e^{-2\sqrt{2x}}(\tfrac{2}{3} x^3 + \sqrt{2}\, x^2 + \tfrac{5}{4} x + \tfrac{5}{16}\sqrt{2}),$$

$$p_3(x) = e^{-4x}\Big(\tfrac{16}{315} x^7 + \tfrac{16}{45} x^6 + \tfrac{6}{5} x^5 + \tfrac{5}{2} x^4$$

$$+ \tfrac{55}{16} x^3 + \tfrac{99}{32} x^2 + \tfrac{429}{256} x + \tfrac{429}{1024}\Big).$$

---

[34] This is a severe example, for though there is no formal difficulty in deriving the coefficients, the Gram–Charlier series is, in fact, divergent. However, it belongs to the class of series which often give a reasonable approximation if they are terminated in the neighborhood of their smallest term.

In this severe example, the series for the starting function is of no use whatever; but nevertheless when the coefficients of the series for $p_2(x)$, $p_3(x)$, ... are derived by (127.5), these functions are approximated quite well with only a few terms.

The last of these is also plotted in Fig. 127.1. It is, of course, symmetrical about $x = 0$.

The coefficients of the Gram–Charlier series for $e^{-\sqrt{2}x}/\sqrt{2}$ can also be obtained without difficulty and are[35]

$$\alpha_{0,0} = 1.00000, \qquad \alpha_{0,6} = 0.04167,$$

$$\alpha_{0,4} = 0.12500, \qquad \alpha_{0,8} = 0.02344.$$

From these the coefficients of the series for $p_3(x)$ are easily found by (127.5). They are

$$\alpha_{3,0} = 1.00000, \qquad \alpha_{3,6} = 0.00065,$$

$$\alpha_{3,4} = 0.01562, \qquad \alpha_{3,8} = 0.00015.$$

Note that, as was to be anticipated, these decrease much more rapidly than those of the starting function.

When this series is computed it gives values which, to the scale of the drawing in Fig. 127.1, are indistinguishable from $p_3(x)$. Furthermore, both sets of values are so close to the normal curve as to be just barely distinguishable to that scale.

As a second example, consider the starting function shown in Fig. 127.2.[36] It is defined by

$$p_0(x) = \frac{1}{2\sqrt{3}}, \qquad -\sqrt{3} < x < \sqrt{3},$$

$$p_0(x) = 0, \qquad |x| > \sqrt{3}. \tag{127.6}$$

The successive convolutions of this can, in principle, be calculated, but the labor of doing so becomes rapidly prohibitive.

It is not difficult, however, to evaluate the integrals (124.7) and thus determine the coefficients of a Gram–Charlier series for (127.6). They are

$\alpha_{0,0} =$	$1.0000,$	$\alpha_{0,8} =$	$-8.9286^{-4},$	$\alpha_{0,16} =$	$2.2623^{-8},$
$\alpha_{0,2} =$	$0.0000,$	$\alpha_{0,10} =$	$4.3170^{-5},$	$\alpha_{0,18} =$	$-1.4561^{-9},$
$\alpha_{0,4} =$	$-5.0000^{-1},$	$\alpha_{0,12} =$	$1.7338^{-7},$	$\alpha_{0,20} =$	$7.0978^{-11}.$
$\alpha_{0,6} =$	$9.5238^{-3},$	$\alpha_{0,14} =$	$-2.2596^{-7},$		

[35] Since the function is symmetrical, the odd terms drop out.

[36] This also is a severe example, but for a different reason. There is here no question of convergence. But a very large number of terms would be required before the series for $p_0(x)$ could reproduce the sharp discontinuities. In fact, the series converges so slowly that the sum of the terms to and including $\phi^{(20)}(x)$ gives the curve shown in the figure, which is still far short of reproducing the discontinuities. But in the series for $a = 3$ the higher order terms are so greatly attenuated that only those up to $\phi^{(8)}(x)$ are needed to define $p_3(x)$ accurately. The coefficients for both series are given in the text. Because some are very small, the decimal position of the first non-zero digit is indicated by an exponent. Thus $7.0978^{-11} \equiv 7.0978 \cdot 10^{-11}$.

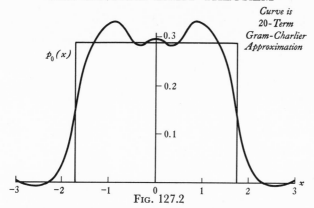

FIG. 127.2

Using these, the coefficients for $a = 3$ can readily be found to be

$$\alpha_{3,0} = \quad 1.0000, \qquad \alpha_{3,6} = 1.4884^{-4},$$
$$\alpha_{3,2} = \quad 0.0000, \qquad \alpha_{3,8} = 8.0218^{-6},$$
$$\alpha_{3,4} = -6.2500^{-3},$$

and these lead to the circled points in Fig. 127.3. The contribution of terms of higher order would not be detectable on the scale of the drawing. For comparison the solid curve is the normal distribution.

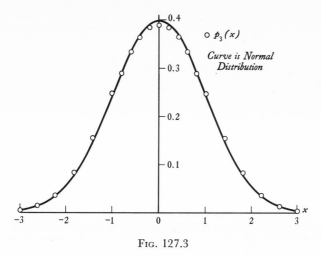

FIG. 127.3

One cautionary remark should, however, be made regarding these examples. They have been chosen to illustrate how rapidly the convolutions destroy features of the starting distribution which, from a purely mathematical point of view, are rather extreme. But both are symmetrical so that the coefficients of all terms of odd order are zero.

Now asymmetry is not mathematically remarkable, but it disappears less rapidly under the convolutions than the apparently radical features of Figs. 127.1 and 127.2. This can be seen from the fact that the denominator of α_3 in (127.4) is $2^{a/2}$, whereas all other α's have at least 2^a in their denominator. That is, the value of a required to reduce the asymmetrical term $\phi'''(x)$ by a given percentage is about twice as large as for any term of higher order. This means that approximately the square of the number of convolutions is required.

It is dangerous to put numbers in such a statement, but if flatness, corners, etc., are almost obliterated in samples of 8, as our examples suggest, we might expect asymmetry to disappear in samples of 64.

Figure 127.4 illustrates this point. The starting distribution, $p_0(x)$, is asymmetrical, although not more so than is true of many met in practice.[37]

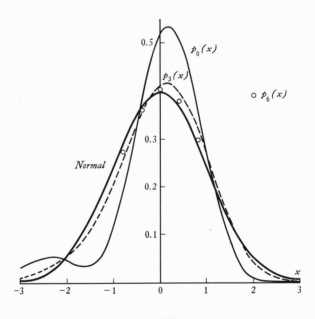

FIG. 127.4

The distribution of the averages of samples of 8 is $p_3(x)$; it is still noticeably skew and departs significantly from the normal distribution. Even $p_6(x)$, which relates to samples of 64, for which a few points are shown, departs perceptibly from the normal.

---

[37] The equation for $p_0(x)$ is

$$p_0(x) = \phi(x) + \tfrac{1}{6}\phi'''(x) + \tfrac{1}{10}\phi^{iv}(x).$$

The maximum departure of $p_6(x)$ from the normal is 0.01, just about the same as the maximum departure of the third convolution in the symmetrical case of Fig. 127.2.

128. Comments on the Central Limit Theorem

To recapitulate the preceding section: We have demonstrated the central limit theorem for all starting functions which can be represented by Gram–Charlier series and have shown that the approach to the normal distribution is surprisingly rapid even when the starting functions have rather discouraging characteristics.

There are distributions, however, which do not obey the theorem. The most important, theoretically, is the Cauchy distribution

$$p(x) = \frac{1}{\pi(1 + x^2)}. \tag{128.1}$$

This has a bell-shaped graph similar in general appearance to the normal curve; but the similarity is deceiving. In fact, the variance of (128.1) is infinite (see Problem 110.36); hence it cannot be put in standard form. It cannot be represented, even formally, by a Gram–Charlier series since the integrals (124.7) which would determine the coefficients are infinite. Furthermore, as we have seen in Example 109.2, if numbers are determined by an experiment which obeys it, their sum obeys a law of similar form and hence certainly does not approach the normal distribution $\phi(y)$.

The central limit theorem is of great importance to Statistics, and in preparation for our discussion of that subject in the next chapter we make two further observations here.

First: We have required the distribution functions $p_1(x)$, $p_2(x)$, $\ldots$ to be put in standard form at every stage, but we have not kept track of the changes of scale which this implied. We now rectify this deficiency. In doing this it will be convenient to use, for the moment, a notation slightly different from that in § 127.

Let the chance variable given by the experiment be x and its distribution $p(x)$, as in the statement of the theorem. To put this in standard form, it is necessary to introduce the new variable

$$z = (x - \epsilon)/\sigma,$$

where ϵ and σ are the expectation and standard deviation of $p(x)$.

If n independent trials are made, and if the sum of the z's is denoted by Z, we know by Theorems 98.1 and 98.3 that the expectation and variance of this sum are $\epsilon_n = 0$ and $\sigma_n^2 = n$. Hence, in the standard form of the sum,

$$y = \frac{Z - \epsilon_n}{\sigma_n} = Z/\sqrt{n}.$$

It is this standardized variable y to which the theorem refers, and whose distribution is therefore approximately

$$\phi(y) = \frac{1}{\sqrt{2\pi}} e^{-y^2/2}.$$

By change of variable this can be written explicitly in terms of either X, the sum of the original numbers, or $\bar{x}$, their average; for clearly $Z = n\bar{z} = n(\bar{x} - \epsilon)/\sigma$, whence

$$y = \sqrt{n}(\bar{x} - \epsilon)/\sigma. \tag{128.2}$$

Hence

$$p_n(\bar{x}) = \frac{\sqrt{n}}{\sqrt{2\pi}\,\sigma} e^{-n(\bar{x}-\epsilon)^2/2\sigma^2}. \tag{128.3}$$

Also, since $X = n\bar{x}$,

$$p_n(X) = \frac{1}{\sqrt{2\pi n}\,\sigma} e^{-(x - n\epsilon)^2/2n\sigma^2}.$$

Second, we may note that the central limit theorem applies not only to x, but to functions of x as well; for if $p(x)$ is the distribution of x and f is a function of x, the distribution of f may be found by change of variable, and, so long as $p(f)$ does not violate the conditions imposed by the central limit theorem, the theorem also applies to the sum of values selected from this f-distribution. This observation is especially important when applied to powers of x, for it enables us to state the following theorem:

THEOREM 128.1. *If an experiment leads to a number x with a suitable distribution*[38] *$p(x)$, and if n values of x are obtained by independent trials of this experiment and m_i is the i'th moment of these values, the distribution of m_i (in standard form) is approximately normal for large values of n.*

A particularly important case is the second moment, $i = 2$. If we write $w = x^2$, it is clear that $\epsilon_1(w) = \epsilon_1(x^2) \equiv \epsilon_2(x)$, $\epsilon_2(w) = \epsilon_4(x)$ and $\sigma^2(w) = \epsilon_2(w) - [\epsilon_1(w)]^2 = \epsilon_4(x) - [\epsilon_2(x)]^2$. Hence to put w in standard units we would have to write

$$z = \frac{w - \epsilon(w)}{\sigma(w)} = \frac{x^2 - \epsilon_2(x)}{\sqrt{\epsilon_4(x) - [\epsilon_2(x)]^2}}.$$

Now suppose a sample of n x's is obtained and z_i is computed for each of the x_i's. Since z is expressed in standard units, the distribution

---

[38] We do not state the conditions which $p(x)$ must theoretically satisfy, but note only that these are always met if $p(x) = 0$ for x larger than some number X. Since x is always limited in any practical experiment, the theorem is in effect universally true.

of the sum has an expectation 0 and variance n. Hence to put the sum in standard units we would write, in the notation of § 97,

$$y = \frac{\Sigma z_i}{\sqrt{n}} = \sqrt{n}\bar{z} = \frac{\mu_2(x) - \epsilon_2(x)}{\sigma^*}$$ (128.4)

where

$$n\,\sigma^{*2} = \epsilon_4(x) - [\epsilon_2(x)]^2.$$ (128.5)

By the theorem, this variable y is normally distributed.

129. Empirical Families of Curves; Transformation of Variable

Let us think for the moment of any two distribution curves, such as those shown in Fig. 129.1. They are decidedly dissimilar, but being distribution functions they necessarily enclose equal areas. Suppose, now, that we start

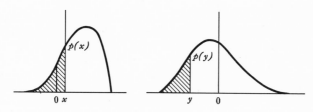

FIG. 129.1

from the left and lay off on each an equal area A, as, for example, the shaded areas in the figures. Finally, suppose we call the y and x which bound these areas "corresponding" values. Such a process could obviously be carried out for any area A (or for any x), thus relating a y to every x. Let us imagine the corresponding pairs to be plotted as in Fig. 129.2. By this means we have found a function of x the distribution of which is exactly in accordance with the right-hand curve of Fig. 129.1.

In other words, *no matter what the distribution of x may be, there is some function y(x) of such a nature that the distribution of y will conform to any law we may desire.* For example, we might cause it to be represented by a straight line, so that equal ranges of y were equally probable.

Little has ever been done in the matter of finding to what extent this form of transformation might be utilized in deriving distribution laws

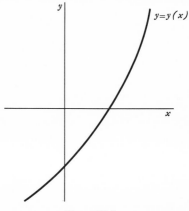

FIG. 129.2

for empirical data,[39] but it has been used now and then to throw unusual types of distribution curves into forms that conformed better to established types, especially to the normal curve.

Problems

1. Using (128.4) and (128.5), write the explicit equations for the approximate distributions of $p(\mu_2)$ and $p(\Sigma x_i^2)$.

2. When a penny is tossed, the distribution for the number of heads has only two points, 0 and 1, with probabilities $1 - p$ and p. Using the results of Problem 110.4, and the central limit theorem, find the probability of h heads in 1000 trials. Compare with Problem 122.16.

3. An "experiment" consists in tossing a penny ten times and noting the number of heads. Consequently the expectation and standard deviation are 5 and $\sqrt{5/2}$, respectively. If this experiment is repeated 100 times, write an approximate formula for the distribution of the sum of the results.

4. In Problem 3, the deviations $\delta_j = h_j - 2.5$ have the following expectations: $\epsilon_1 = 0$, $\epsilon_2 = 5/2$, $\epsilon_3 = 0$, $\epsilon_4 = 35/2$. (See Problem 110.2.) Write, in standard units, the approximate distribution for $\mu_2(\delta) = \Sigma \delta_j^2/100$.

5. If an approximate solution of Problem 122.15 is obtained by using the normal function (111.1) or the Gram–Charlier series (125.1), what is the result? Compare with the answer to Problem 122.15.

6. If an experiment yields numbers distributed according to the normal law $\phi(x) = e^{-x^2/2}/\sqrt{2\pi}$, write an approximate equation for the distribution of the sum of the squares of n experimental results.

7. If in Problem 6 there are 50 trials, what is the probability of a sum $\Sigma x_i^2 = \chi^2 \geq 50$? Of $\chi^2 \leq 50$? Of $\chi^2 = 50$?

[In case of difficulty, reread § 113.]

8. In Problem 7, what is the chance of $25 \leq \chi^2 \leq 75$?

9. If an experiment yields numbers lying between 6 and 7, with uniform probability in this interval and zero probability elsewhere, write an approximate formula for the distribution of the sum of 50 trials.

10. In Problem 9, what is the approximate distribution of $\chi^2 = \Sigma x_i^2$?

11. In Problem 9, what is the probability that the sum $X \geq 331$? That $320 \leq X \leq 327$?

12. In Problem 10, what is the probability that $\chi^2 < 2050$?

---

[39] It would seem that there might be some point to the attempt to treat statistical data by finding what transformation would result in a completely random distribution: that is, in equal probabilities for all intervals within a certain range.

Answers to Problems at End of § 122

1. $P(j, T) = \dfrac{(nT)^j}{j!} e^{-nT}.$

2. $^\infty\Pi'_{j+1} = \displaystyle\sum_{i=j+1}^{\infty} \dfrac{(nT)^i}{i!} e^{-nT}.$

3. $P(> 1, dt) = 1 - (1 + ndt) e^{-ndt}; 1 - e^{-ndt} \doteq ndt;$ the first is the *unconditional* probability that two or more calls might fall in a preassigned interval chosen independently of the process by which calls originate; the second is the *conditional* probability of a second call, in an interval immediately following the first.

4. $ne^{-nt} dt.$ **5.** $ne^{-nt} dt.$ **6.** $1/n$; same.

7. The observer, in effect, marks a new point on the time axis, independently of those made by the arrival of calls. It is proportionally more likely to fall in a long interval than a short one.

8. $P(j, \tau + t) = \dfrac{[n(\tau + t)]^j}{j!} e^{-n(\tau+t)}.$ **10.** $0, \sqrt{2}/n, \quad 1/n.$

11. $\epsilon(N - n) = N - \epsilon(n) = Ne^{-kt}.$ **12.** $e^{-k}.$ **13.** $1/Nk.$ **14.** $n = 15.$

15. $\epsilon = 13.70;$ $^\infty\Pi'_{20} = 0.066.$

16. $P_{1000}(h) = (1/\sqrt{500\,\pi})\, e^{-(h-500)^2/500}.$

Answers to Problems at End of § 129

1. $p(\mu_2) = \dfrac{1}{\sqrt{2\pi}\,\sigma^*} e^{-[\mu_2 - \epsilon_2(x)]^2/2\sigma*^2};$

$p(\textstyle\sum x_i^2) = \dfrac{1}{\sqrt{2\pi}\,n\,\sigma^*} e^{-[\Sigma x_i^2 - n\,\epsilon_2(x)]^2/2n^2\,\sigma*^2}.$

2. $p(h) = (1/\sqrt{500\,n})\, e^{-(h - 500)^2/500}.$

3. Same as Problem 2.

4. $\phi(y) = e^{-y^2/2}/\sqrt{2\pi},$ with $y = 2\sqrt{5}(2\mu_2 - 5)/3.$ **5.** $0.059; 0.066.$

6. $P(\chi^2) = (1/\sqrt{4\pi\,n})\, e^{-(\chi^2 - n)^2/4n},$ where $\chi^2 = \sum x_i^2.$

7. $1 - \phi_{-1}(- 0.05) = 0.52;$ $0.52;$ $0.04.$ **8.** $0.99.$

9. $\epsilon = 13/2;$ $\sigma^2 = 1/12;$ $p_{50}(X) = \sqrt{3/25\pi}\, e^{-3(X - 325)^2/25}.$

10. $\epsilon_2 = 127/3,$ $\epsilon_4 = 9031/5,$

$p_{50}(\chi^2) = \sqrt{9/12680\,\pi}\; e^{-9(\chi^2 - 6350/3)^2/12680},$ with $\chi^2 = \sum x_i^2.$

11. With $y_0 = 5.5\,\sqrt{6/25},$ $y_1 = -5.5\,\sqrt{6/25},$ and $y_2 = 2.5\,\sqrt{6/25},$ the answers are, respectively: $1 - \phi_{-1}(y_0) = 0.004;$ $\phi_{-1}(y_2) - \phi_{-1}(y_1) = 0.89.$

12. With $y = -66.67\,\sqrt{9/6340},$ $\phi_{-1}(y) = 0.006.$

Chapter X

Matrix Methods and Markov Processes

130. Introductory Remarks; Processes

When we began our discussion of Bernoulli's Theorem we presented, in Fig. 56.1, the probability distributions for the number of successes in 5, 10, 50, and 100 independent trials of an experiment. Similar graphs could also be presented for 1, 2, 3, . . . trials; the ones in Fig. 56.1 were a selection from this infinite family, or sequence, of distributions. If we think of these curves as being generated one by one as time goes on, it is not unnatural to say that each trial changes the distribution from what it was immediately beforehand to what it became immediately after.

Of course, if we were to perform such an experiment repeatedly, it would either succeed or fail on each trial and the result of n trials would be a specific history, not a distribution. A gambler risking money on the toss of a die does not receive in return a probability distribution; he experiences a clear-cut succession of gains and losses. So, in the derivation of Bernoulli's Theorem, and even more in our discussion of chance paths, we thought and spoke of such specific, if hypothetical, histories.

However, there are many situations in which it is not only more natural, but mathematically better to consider the distribution (or population) as the entity under discussion. If, for example, two related varieties of corn are cross-fertilized, and subsequent generations are then produced by some process of selection, our primary interest centers in the composition of successive generations. Or if a nuclear chain reaction is set up in a particular way, we are not so much concerned with individual nuclear behavior as with whether the process will in time grow into an explosion, or stabilize into a power reactor. In such situations we are, in effect, not conducting a single sequential experiment; instead we are simultaneously generating a large number of such simple histories—so many, in fact, that the proportionate composition of the entire system at any time is about equal to the corresponding distribution of probabilities.

This will be the nature of the emphasis in the present chapter. Also, in keeping with general usage, we shall often speak of the experimental procedure as a "process," thus emphasizing its continuing, or sequential, aspect.

We have already met "processes" on several occasions. Repeated independent trials of a dichotomy such as were studied in Chapter V constitute a process which is often referred to as "the Bernoulli process." The telephone calls in § 116 were originated by a process which placed them individually and collectively at random; it is known as the Poisson process. The decaying radioactive material in § 119 produces particles by a different process. The control of quality in manufacturing, the spread of epidemic diseases, and the diffusion of gases are all processes which can often be most conveniently studied from the point of view now under discussion.

The subject is a broad one, and we shall not go into it deeply. We shall, however, present some of the simpler and more basic ideas. As illustrations we shall use principally the simple coin-tossing game referred to in Example 35.1, and the contrasting urn scheme of Problems 35.14 and 35.15.

We shall also use some elementary notions regarding matrices, which will be introduced in the two sections which follow.

131. Matrices

Any rectangular array of numbers is a matrix. It may, or may not, be square. Such arrays are frequently set off by brackets as an indication that the concepts of matric algebra are being invoked. Thus:

$$A = \begin{bmatrix} 1 & 3 & 2 & 5 \\ 0 & 2 & 0 & 4 \\ 3 & 0 & 0 & 1 \end{bmatrix}, \qquad B = \begin{bmatrix} 2 & \frac{1}{2} \\ \frac{1}{4} & 1 \\ 0 & 0 \\ 1 & 0 \end{bmatrix}, \qquad (131.1)$$

$$T = \begin{bmatrix} 1 & \frac{1}{2} & 0 & 0 & 0 & 0 \\ 0 & 0 & \frac{1}{2} & 0 & 0 & 0 \\ 0 & \frac{1}{2} & 0 & \frac{1}{2} & 0 & 0 \\ 0 & 0 & \frac{1}{2} & 0 & \frac{1}{2} & 0 \\ 0 & 0 & 0 & \frac{1}{2} & 0 & 0 \\ 0 & 0 & 0 & 0 & \frac{1}{2} & 1 \end{bmatrix}, \qquad D = \begin{bmatrix} \frac{1}{4} \\ 0 \\ \frac{1}{2} \\ 0 \\ \frac{1}{4} \\ 0 \end{bmatrix} \qquad (131.2)$$

are matrices of three rows and four columns, four rows and two columns, six rows and six columns, and six rows and one column, respectively.

It is important to have a compact and convenient notation, since otherwise a great deal of space would be required in writing out arrays. We shall therefore write $A = [a_{j,k}]$ for the matrix

$$A = \begin{bmatrix} a_{0,0} & a_{0,1} & \cdots & a_{0,n} \\ a_{1,0} & a_{1,1} & \cdots & a_{1,n} \\ \cdots & \cdots & & \cdots \\ a_{m,0} & a_{m,1} & \cdots & a_{m,n} \end{bmatrix}$$

when the numerical values of the elements need not be displayed. Note, particularly, that the first subscript indexes the *rows*, and the second index the *columns*, of the matrix.

A matrix with but a single row or single column, such as the matrix D in (131.2), is often called a "vector" because of its interpretation in mechanics and geometry. Such matrices require only one index, but to distinguish between horizontal and vertical arrays it is desirable to replace the missing index by a dot and write $[a_{.,k}]$ and $[a_{j,.}]$, respectively.

Finally, when a single column matrix stands alone and its individual elements must be displayed, it also is very wasteful of space. To avoid this we shall sometimes display the elements horizontally between arrows. Thus $\downarrow \frac{1}{4}, 0, \frac{1}{2}, 0, \frac{1}{4}, 0 \downarrow$ would be identical with the matrix D in (131.2) above.

Two matrices are especially important in probability theory. One is a single column matrix which displays a complete set of probabilities. It thus affords yet another method of representing a distribution function, for which reason we shall call it a *distribution matrix*. D, above, is, in fact, such a matrix. It relates to the coin tossing game described in Problem 31.19. Reading down the column it gives the probabilities that A, who had \$2 to begin with, will have just \$0, \$1, . . . , \$5 after the first two throws. (See Problem 31.20.)

The other matrix which is especially important in the Theory of Probability is the *transition matrix*, which we have already met in § 35. This is a matrix whose columns correspond to a set of events identified by the index number k, whose rows likewise correspond to a set of events identified by j, and whose elements are the conditional probabilities $P(j|k)$.[1] *It is important that both sets of events be complete.* T, above, is such a matrix; specifically, it is the transition matrix derived in § 35 and relates to the same coin-tossing game as D.

---

[1] These conditional probabilities are often called *transition probabilities* when they occur in a transition matrix or are otherwise met in discussing the sequence of distributions generated by a process.

132. Multiplication of Matrices

There is an extensive algebra of matrices, but the only operation which we shall use is multiplication.[2]

The product AB of two matrices $A \equiv [a_{j,k}]$ and $B \equiv [b_{j,k}]$ is a matrix C which has, in row j and column k, the element

$$c_{j,k} = \sum_i a_{j,i} b_{i,k}. \tag{132.1}$$

That is, $c_{j,k}$ is obtained by multiplying the elements in the j'th *row* of A by the elements in the k'th *column* of B, and adding.

For example, if A and B are the matrices (131.1), the element in the second row and first column of their product would be computed by multiplying 0, 2, 0, 4, in order, by 2, $\frac{1}{4}$, 0, 1, thus getting

$$(0 \times 2) + (2 \times \tfrac{1}{4}) + (0 \times 0) + (4 \times 1) = 4\tfrac{1}{2}.$$

Proceeding in this way for the other elements we would obtain

$$C = AB = \begin{bmatrix} 7\frac{3}{4} & 3\frac{1}{2} \\ 4\frac{1}{2} & 2 \\ 7 & \frac{3}{2} \end{bmatrix}.$$

Note that this process can be carried out only when the number of *columns* in A and the number of *rows* in B are equal, and that the product always has the same number of rows as A, and the same number of columns as B. In particular, if a distribution matrix $D \equiv [d_{j,\cdot}]$ is multiplied by a transition matrix $T \equiv [t_{j,k}]$, the result is a single column matrix $D' = TD$ of which the elements are, by (132.1)

$$d'_{j,\cdot} = \sum_i t_{j,i} d_{i,\cdot}. \tag{132.2}$$

The reader can readily prove the important theorem (see Problem 138.15) that in forming the product ABC it does not matter which pair of factors is multiplied first; that is, that

$$(AB)C = A(BC). \tag{132.3}$$

Note, however, that the product BA is not in general equal to AB. Indeed, with the A and B defined in (131.1), the product BA does not even exist, since there are only two numbers in a row of B—not enough to pair up with the three numbers in a column of A. But even if this were not true, the products would only in exceptional cases be equal.

---

[2] Other parts of the algebra of matrices would be very helpful in a more recondite discussion of processes.

The reader can readily verify this in the case of the square matrices

$$A = \begin{bmatrix} 3 & 6 \\ 4 & 0 \end{bmatrix}, \qquad B = \begin{bmatrix} 2 & 7 \\ 1 & 4 \end{bmatrix},$$

for which the two products are

$$AB = \begin{bmatrix} 12 & 45 \\ 8 & 28 \end{bmatrix}, \qquad BA = \begin{bmatrix} 34 & 12 \\ 19 & 6 \end{bmatrix}.$$

133. The Transition Matrix as an Operator

Let us now recall that the elements of a distribution matrix are the probabilities of a complete set of mutually exclusive events. If these events are called A_j and their probabilities $P(A_j)$, the factors $d_{i,.}$ in (132.2) become

$$d_{i,.} = P(A_i).$$

Also, the elements of the transition matrix are the conditional probabilities $P(B_k|A_j)$, where the B_k are another complete set of mutually exclusive events. Hence, in (132.2)

$$t_{j,i} = P(B_j|A_i).$$

If we substitute these into (132.2), it becomes

$$d'_{j,.} = \sum_i P(B_j|A_i)P(A_i);$$

and when we compare this with (38.2), we see at once that

$$d'_{j,.} = P(B_j).$$

In other words, the matrix $D' \equiv [d'_{j,.}]$ is precisely the distribution matrix for the set of events B. Thus we have the fundamental theorem:

THEOREM 133.1. *If D and D' are the distribution matrices for two complete sets of mutually exclusive events A_j and B_k, and if T is the transition matrix from A to B [i.e., $t_{j,k} = P(B_k|A_j)$], then*

$$D' = TD. \tag{133.1}$$

This theorem is valid in any situation in which (38.2) is, and (38.2) depends only on (37.1) and the fundamental Conventions I and II.

It is therefore of very great generality since, as we have seen in § 65, (37.1) is valid wherever the symbols have meaning. Its principal interest, however, is in connection with sequential processes and we therefore restate it in language more appropriate to that application.

THEOREM 133.2. *If D_{n-1} is the matrix of the probability distribution just prior to the n'th trial of a sequential process and T_n is the transition matrix for that trial, the matrix for the probability after the n'th trial is*

$$D_n = T_n D_{n-1}. \qquad (133.2)$$

In particular, if the transition matrix is the same for all trials,

$$D_n = T D_{n-1}, \qquad (133.3)$$

where T is the constant transition matrix.

In the language of operators we would express this by saying that T_n (or T) is an operator which transforms the matrix D_{n-1} into the matrix D_n.[3] It is therefore, in a very real sense, the mathematical equivalent of the experiment so far as the theory of probability is concerned.

134. Some Instructive Illustrations; Reconsideration of Example 35.1

Let us now consider again Example 35.1, which we restate in slightly different language:

EXAMPLE 134.1.—*Two players, who have just $5 between them, agree to risk $1 on the toss of a coin. If, at some time, A's chance of having j of the 5 dollars is given by the distribution $P(j)$, how is this distribution modified by the next throw?*

The statement of this example indicates that the distribution matrix

---

[3] It is appropriate at this point to mention that many, if not most, writers place the conditional probability $P(j|k)$ in the j'th *column* and k'th *row* of the transition matrix; in other words, they write T with the rows and columns interchanged. The distribution matrix is then written as a single *row* (which is an advantage), and the order of the factors in (133.2) is interchanged so that it becomes

$$D_n = D_{n-1} T_n.$$

But in dealing with operators, the operator T is universally written to the left of the operand D, and conformity with this convention has seemed to me sufficiently desirable to justify a departure in the convention for T.

There is, of course, another way out of the difficulty by adopting column to row multiplication, but this would undoubtedly be more confusing than the one I have chosen.

just before the coin is tossed is $D_{n-1} = \downarrow P(0), P(1), \ldots, P(5) \downarrow$, and we have seen in § 35 that the process has the transition matrix T in (131.2). Hence, by (133.3), D_n is the product of the two.

Let us try some numerical examples:

When this example first appeared (in Problem 31.19) it was stated that A had just \$2. With this explicit knowledge,

$$P_0(j) = 1, \qquad j = 2,$$
$$P_0(j) = 0, \qquad j \neq 2,$$

and the matrix D_0 is $\downarrow 0, 0, 1, 0, 0, 0 \downarrow$. Hence

$$D_1 = TD_0 = \begin{bmatrix} 1 & \frac{1}{2} & 0 & 0 & 0 & 0 \\ 0 & 0 & \frac{1}{2} & 0 & 0 & 0 \\ 0 & \frac{1}{2} & 0 & \frac{1}{2} & 0 & 0 \\ 0 & 0 & \frac{1}{2} & 0 & \frac{1}{2} & 0 \\ 0 & 0 & 0 & \frac{1}{2} & 0 & 0 \\ 0 & 0 & 0 & 0 & \frac{1}{2} & 1 \end{bmatrix} \cdot \begin{bmatrix} 0 \\ 0 \\ 1 \\ 0 \\ 0 \\ 0 \end{bmatrix} = \begin{bmatrix} 0 \\ \frac{1}{2} \\ 0 \\ \frac{1}{2} \\ 0 \\ 0 \end{bmatrix}.$$

This will be found to be the same as the answer to the first part of Problem 31.20. If we wish to answer to the second part, we need only form the product TD_1 which easily works out to be

$$D_2 = \downarrow \tfrac{1}{4}, 0, \tfrac{1}{2}, 0, \tfrac{1}{4}, 0 \downarrow.$$

Repeating this procedure once again we obtain

$$D_3 = TD_2 = \downarrow \tfrac{1}{4}, \tfrac{1}{4}, 0, \tfrac{3}{8}, 0, \tfrac{1}{8} \downarrow$$

for the distribution after the third throw, a result already obtained by other means in Problem 31.19. Obviously, the procedure can be extended as often as we like.

Since $D_1 = TD_0$ and $D_2 = TD_1$ we have, by substitution, $D_2 = T(TD_0)$. But by (132.3) this is the same as $D_2 = (TT)D_0$. That is, D_2 can also be found by first multiplying the transformation matrix by itself, and then multiplying the distribution D by this new transformation matrix. Similarly, $D_3 = TD_2 = T^3D_0$; or, in general, after n repetitions of the process, D_n will be T^nD_0 where the operator T^n is the n-fold product of T by itself.

More labor is involved in multiplying T by itself than in forming single-column products such as TD_0 and TD_1. Hence, if the only object is to obtain D_1 or D_2 the latter would be the preferred method. But when large values of n are involved the reverse is usually true, since T^4 may be obtained as $T^2 \cdot T^2$; T^8 as $T^4 \cdot T^4$, and so on. In this way even the 64th power requires only six multiplications.

In the present instance, the successive distribution functions rapidly converge to a limiting form, as can be seen by forming the powers of T up to T^{64}. With an accuracy of five decimal places the last of these is[4]

$$T^\infty = T^{64} = \begin{bmatrix} 1 & 0.8 & 0.6 & 0.4 & 0.2 & 0 \\ 0 & 0.0 & 0 & 0.0 & 0 & 0 \\ 0 & 0 & 0.0 & 0 & 0.0 & 0 \\ 0 & 0.0 & 0 & 0.0 & 0 & 0 \\ 0 & 0 & 0.0 & 0 & 0.0 & 0 \\ 0 & 0.2 & 0.4 & 0.6 & 0.8 & 1 \end{bmatrix}.$$

The reader will have no difficulty in verifying that the product TT^{64} is the same as T^{64}; and of course the same is true of all higher powers as the symbol T^∞ indicates. We may therefore conclude that the process with which we are dealing is of such a character that, no matter what distribution function D_0 we may have initially, repeated applications of the process (i.e., repeated rounds of the game) will eventually lead to the limiting distribution $T^\infty D_0$. Furthermore, this distribution is such that A either has all or none of the money; and the chance that he has all is precisely equal to the proportion of the joint capital with which he started.

135. Some Instructive Illustrations; A Problem in Bose–Einstein Statistics

As a second example we return to the process described in § 46, which was phrased in terms of placing balls in boxes, and consider the following:

EXAMPLE 135.1.—*There is a set of "a" empty boxes into which balls are placed one after another. These are attracted toward boxes already occupied to such an extent that a ball is $i + 1$ times as likely to enter a cell which already has i balls in it as to enter an empty cell. After n balls have been placed, what is the probability that there are just j balls in the first box?*

The transformation matrix for the ν'th step in the process is easily constructed, for if there are already k balls in the first box after $\nu - 1$ balls have been placed, there will either be the same number or one

---

[4] The terms written 0 are absolutely zero; those written 0.0 are smaller than 0.000005.

more afterward. In symbols this becomes

$$P_\nu(j \mid j - 1) = \frac{j}{a + \nu - 1},$$

$$P_\nu(j \mid j) = \frac{a + \nu - j - 1}{a + \nu - 1}, \tag{135.1}$$

$$P_\nu(j \mid k) = 0, \text{ otherwise.}$$

But, unlike Example 134.1 in which the transformation matrix was the same at each step of the process, here the conditional probabilities $P(j \mid k)$ and hence the matrix formed from them is different for different values of ν.

Let us write down a few of these matrices. To start with, all cells are empty, and hence k can have only one value, 0. The transformation matrix for the first step of the process can have only one column and is easily seen to be

$$T_1 = \begin{bmatrix} \dfrac{a - 1}{a} \\[2ex] \dfrac{1}{a} \end{bmatrix}.$$

For the second step (i.e., the placing of the second ball), $\nu = 2$ and we have

$$T_2 = \begin{bmatrix} \dfrac{a}{a + 1} & 0 \\[2ex] \dfrac{1}{a + 1} & \dfrac{a - 1}{a + 1} \\[2ex] 0 & \dfrac{2}{a + 1} \end{bmatrix}.$$

Similarly,

$$T_3 = \begin{bmatrix} \dfrac{a + 1}{a + 2} & 0 & 0 \\[2ex] \dfrac{1}{a + 2} & \dfrac{a}{a + 2} & 0 \\[2ex] 0 & \dfrac{2}{a + 2} & \dfrac{a - 1}{a + 2} \\[2ex] 0 & 0 & \dfrac{3}{a + 2} \end{bmatrix},$$

$$T_4 = \begin{bmatrix} \dfrac{a + 2}{a + 3} & 0 & 0 & 0 \\[2ex] \dfrac{1}{a + 3} & \dfrac{a + 1}{a + 3} & 0 & 0 \\[2ex] 0 & \dfrac{2}{a + 3} & \dfrac{a}{a + 3} & 0 \\[2ex] 0 & 0 & \dfrac{3}{a + 3} & \dfrac{a - 1}{a + 3} \\[2ex] 0 & 0 & 0 & \dfrac{4}{a + 3} \end{bmatrix}.$$

Others could be written without difficulty, but we turn our attention instead to the matrix of the initial distribution D.

Since we know that the box was initially empty, this consists only of $P_0 = 1$; hence we may write

$$D_0 = [1],$$

a matrix of just one row and one column. The first step of the process (i.e., placing the first ball) transforms this into $D_1 = T_1 D_0$, which, as the reader can readily verify, is identical with T_1. For the second step we have

$$D_2 = T_2 D_1 \equiv T_2 T_1,$$

for the third

$$D_3 = T_3 D_2 = T_3 T_2 T_1,$$

and so on. Carrying out the indicated operations, we have:

$$D = [1], \quad D_1 = \begin{bmatrix} \dfrac{a-1}{a} \\[2ex] \dfrac{a-1}{a(a-1)} \end{bmatrix}, \quad D_2 = \begin{bmatrix} \dfrac{a-1}{a+1} \\[2ex] \dfrac{2(a-1)}{(a+1)a} \\[2ex] \dfrac{2(a-1)}{(a+1)a(a-1)} \end{bmatrix},$$

$$D_3 = \begin{bmatrix} \dfrac{a-1}{a+2} \\[2ex] \dfrac{3(a-1)}{(a+2)(a+1)} \\[2ex] \dfrac{6(a-1)}{(a+2)(a+1)a} \\[2ex] \dfrac{6(a-1)}{(a+2)(a+1)a(a-1)} \end{bmatrix}.$$

The law of formation of these terms is now quite obvious. The denominators are $(a + n - 1)!/(a + n - j - 2)!$ and the numerators $n!(a - 1)/(n - j)!$. Hence we infer that the answer to the question in Example 135.1 is

$$P_n(j) = \frac{n!(a + n - j - 2)!(a - 1)}{(a + n - 1)!(n - j)!} = \frac{a - 1}{a + n - 1}\frac{C_j^n}{C^{a+n-2}}. \quad (135.2)$$

The validity of this inference is easily established by induction. It would have been difficult to obtain the result by the methods of § 46.

136. Some Instructive Illustrations; A Waiting-Line Problem

As a further example, we take a familiar kind of problem.

EXAMPLE 136.1.—*A barber shop has only one barber, who takes exactly 15 minutes to serve each customer. The times at which customers arrive are individually and collectively random and the expectation of the number arriving during a 15-minute interval is* ϵ. *What is the probability that there are just j customers in the shop one-half hour after the shop opens for business? It will be assumed that customers who arrive before opening time leave at once, so that there is not a waiting line at the start of business.*

We can readily set up the transformation matrix corresponding to this process.

If, at any instant, there are k customers in the shop, one will have been served and will have left within 15 minutes (which we will call a "unit of time"). The conditional probability $P(j|k)$ of j customers in the shop at the end of the interval, therefore, is just the chance that $j - k + 1$ arrived during it. We know from the discussion of § 116, however, that the probability of this is

$$P(j|k) = \frac{\epsilon^{j-k+1}}{(j-k+1)!}\, e^{-\epsilon}, \qquad k > 0. \tag{136.1}$$

This argument applies only when there is at least one customer in the shop to begin with. If, instead, it is empty at the start of the interval, all who arrive during the unit interval will still be there at its end. Thus, for $k = 0$,

$$P(j|0) = \frac{\epsilon^j}{j!}\, e^{-\epsilon}. \tag{136.2}$$

Using these values we may now write the transformation matrix

$$T = \begin{bmatrix} e^{-\epsilon} & e^{-\epsilon} & 0 & 0 & \cdots \\[2mm] \epsilon\, e^{-\epsilon} & \epsilon\, e^{-\epsilon} & e^{-\epsilon} & 0 & \cdots \\[2mm] \dfrac{\epsilon^2}{2!} e^{-\epsilon} & \dfrac{\epsilon^2}{2!} e^{-\epsilon} & \epsilon\, e^{-\epsilon} & e^{-\epsilon} & \cdots \\[2mm] \dfrac{\epsilon^3}{3!} e^{-\epsilon} & \dfrac{\epsilon^3}{3!} e^{-\epsilon} & \dfrac{\epsilon^2}{2!} e^{-\epsilon} & \epsilon\, e^{-\epsilon} & \cdots \\[2mm] \cdots & \cdots & \cdots & \cdots & \cdots \end{bmatrix}.$$

This matrix is infinite, for there is no limit to the number of customers who may arrive in a unit of time if the traffic is in fact random.

We know the shop was empty to begin with; hence the initial distribution D_0 was $\downarrow 1, 0, 0, \ldots \downarrow$; that is, the probability of any number of customers greater than 0 is 0. If we form the product $D_1 = TD_0$ we get, for the distribution function at the end of the first period,

$$D_1 = \quad \downarrow e^{-\epsilon}, \quad \epsilon e^{-\epsilon}, \quad \frac{\epsilon^2}{2} e^{-\epsilon}, \quad \dots \downarrow \;,$$

which is precisely the Poisson distribution, as would be expected.

At the end of the second period it would be $D_2 = TD_1$, which can readily be shown to be

$$D_2 = \quad \downarrow (1 + \epsilon)e^{-2\epsilon}, \quad \frac{\epsilon}{2!}(2 + 3\epsilon)e^{-2\epsilon}, \quad \frac{\epsilon^2}{3!}(3 + 7\epsilon)e^{-2\epsilon},$$

$$\frac{\epsilon^3}{4!}(4 + 15\epsilon)e^{-2\epsilon}, \quad \dots \downarrow \;,$$

the general term being

$$P_2(j, \cdot) = \frac{\epsilon^j}{(j + 1)!}[j + 1 + (2^{j+1} - 1)\epsilon]e^{-2\epsilon}.$$

This is the answer required.

It is a simple matter in principle to carry this process forward step by step for as many periods as may be desired, although the algebraic complexity of the expressions would increase quite rapidly. In doing so we would determine how the load builds up after the establishment opens for business—or, more precisely, how the distribution matrix D changes during this transient period. As a matter of experience, however, we are aware that as time goes on, the knowledge that the shop was empty when the doors first opened will be less and less important, and the situation will settle down to what, in some sense of the term, is a steady state. It will be more profitable to explore this avenue than to follow the step-by-step development of the distribution matrix further. We therefore consider the following question:

EXAMPLE 136.2.—*What is the probability that there are just j customers in the barber shop of Example 136.1 after the effects of the opening have worn off and a state of equilibrium has been established?*

The word "equilibrium" has come into this question quite smoothly —it is a word we would be likely to use in everyday speech. Just what do we mean by it? Certainly not that the number of customers will remain fixed. The barber will still be idle at times, and at other times several customers will be waiting. What we mean, quite clearly, is that the *probabilities* of these conditions will no longer be changing— that instead the distribution matrix will no longer vary with time.

This state is called *statistical equilibrium*, a term of sufficient importance to warrant a formal definition.

DEFINITION 136.1. *A system is said to be in statistical equilibrium when the probability of finding it in any specified condition is independent of the time at which it is examined.*

But to say that the distribution matrix does not change with time is equivalent to saying that the same D appears on both sides of the matrix equation

$$D = TD;$$

that is:

$$
\begin{bmatrix} P(0) \\ P(1) \\ P(2) \\ P(3) \\ \cdots \end{bmatrix}
=
\begin{bmatrix}
e^{-\epsilon} & e^{-\epsilon} & 0 & 0 & \cdots \\
\epsilon\, e^{-\epsilon} & \epsilon\, e^{-\epsilon} & e^{-\epsilon} & 0 & \cdots \\
\dfrac{\epsilon^2}{2!} e^{-\epsilon} & \dfrac{\epsilon^2}{2!} e^{-\epsilon} & \epsilon\, e^{-\epsilon} & e^{-\epsilon} & \cdots \\
\dfrac{\epsilon^3}{3!} e^{-\epsilon} & \dfrac{\epsilon^3}{3!} e^{-\epsilon} & \dfrac{\epsilon^2}{2!} e^{-\epsilon} & \epsilon\, e^{-\epsilon} & \cdots \\
\cdots & \cdots & \cdots & \cdots & \cdots
\end{bmatrix}
\cdot
\begin{bmatrix} P(0) \\ P(1) \\ P(2) \\ P(3) \\ \cdots \end{bmatrix}.
$$

If we perform the multiplications, we get

$$P(0) = e^{-\epsilon}[P(0) + P(1)],$$
$$P(1) = \epsilon\, e^{-\epsilon}[P(0) + P(1)] + e^{-\epsilon} P(2),$$
$$P(2) = \frac{\epsilon^2}{2!} e^{-\epsilon}[P(0) + P(1)] + \epsilon\, e^{-\epsilon} P(2) + e^{-\epsilon} P(3),$$

and so on.

To solve these equations, let us call the combination $P(0) + P(1)$ which reappears in each of them q. Then, by the first equation,

$$P(0) = e^{-\epsilon} q,$$

and

$$P(1) = q - P(0) = (1 - e^{-\epsilon})q.$$

Then, by the second equation,

$$P(2) = e^{\epsilon} P(1) - \epsilon q = (e^{\epsilon} - 1 - \epsilon)q.$$

Continuing this process, each of the P's can be expressed in turn in terms of q, and finally q can be determined from the requirement that $\Sigma_j P(j) = 1$. The complete solution will be found in § 188. For the present we note that q turns out to be $(1 - \epsilon)e^\epsilon$, and hence

$$P(0) = 1 - \epsilon,$$
$$P(1) = (1 - \epsilon)(e^\epsilon - 1),$$
$$P(2) = (1 - \epsilon)[e^{2\epsilon} - e^\epsilon(1 + \epsilon)],$$

and so on.

As a numerical example, suppose $\epsilon = \frac{1}{2}$. This means that only 1 customer is expected to arrive during twice the time it takes the barber to serve him. It is therefore not surprising that $P(0)$, the chance that the barber is idle, is $\frac{1}{2}$. The other probabilities are:

$$P(1) = 0.3244, \qquad P(3) = 0.0378,$$
$$P(2) = 0.1226, \qquad P(4) = 0.0109.$$

137. Markov Processes

The examples in the preceding sections belong to the class known as Markov processes. What this means is that at any stage of the process the conditional probabilities are independent of the course of events by which the system arrived at the state in which it then is. More exactly:

DEFINITION 137.1. *A process is a Markov process if the transition matrix T_n at the n'th stage remains the same no matter what information may or may not be supplied regarding preceding stages.*

The significance of this may be sharpened somewhat by an example of a repeated experiment which is *not* Markovian. Problems 35.14 and 35.15 describe such a process. We shall discuss it in considerable detail in § 138. Here we need only note that the conditional probability of drawing a white ball on the second trial is *not* independent of information regarding the first. On the contrary, it is 0 if the first ball is known to have been white, and $\frac{2}{5}$ or $\frac{2}{7}$, respectively, if it is known to have been red or black; if the color of the first ball is not known this conditional probability has still another value.

By contrast, in Example 136.1 the equations (136.1) and (136.2) still give $P(j|k)$ correctly even if we are told that at some prior time (say one hour ago) there were three people waiting. The transition from k to j can come about *only* through the arrival of $j - k + 1$ new customers within the interval under consideration; it is not affected by the congestion at other times. It is true, of course, that if there were (say) five customers waiting an hour ago, the shop could not be empty now, since only four would have been served. But this inference relates to the present state of the shop—or, if we like, to the present distribution matrix D—not to the conditional probabilities in T. It is still true that *if the shop had been empty* at the start of the present interval, the chance of j persons in it at the end would be (136.2), and *if it had had k persons* at the start, the chance of j at the end would be (136.1).

The situation in Example 134.1 is essentially the same. In Example 135.1 it is slightly different; for whereas in Examples 134.1 and 136.1 the transition matrix is the same at all stages, in Example 135.1 it varies from stage to stage. But the reader will readily confirm that here also the conditional probabilities are unaltered by additional information regarding earlier stages. It makes no difference if there were 1, 2, or 8 balls in the first box three stages back, the conditional probabilities (135.1) remain the same.

Therefore all three processes are Markovian. The difference between them is expressed by saying that when the matrix T is the same at all stages the process is *stationary*, whereas when T depends on v, as in Example 135.1, it is *nonstationary*.

Markov processes are met in such widely diverse fields of science as genetics, nuclear physics, epidemiology, and telephone engineering. They have been the subject of a vast amount of mathematical study extending over the last quarter century. What has evolved is an extensive and important general theory, an adequate discussion of which would carry us beyond the proper bounds of this volume. We shall therefore not pursue it further here.

We shall, however, give a number of examples of its use. In fact, most of Chapter XII, which deals with the general subject of traffic problems, is concerned in one way or another with the limits approached by the distributions which Markov processes generate.

Returning to Examples 134.1, 135.1 and 136.1: These have also differed in the character of their objectives. In 134.1 and 135.1 we were primarily interested in following the distribution from stage to stage of the process. In other words, our attention was focused on how this distribution changed with time. In 136.2, by contrast (and to some extent in 134.1 also), we investigated the limiting condition which the distribution approached as time went on. These "conditions of statistical equilibrium" are also a matter of great concern; not only *what* they are, but also, in some situations, *whether* they exist at all. The difference between a nuclear reactor and a nuclear bomb, for example, lies precisely in the fact that the chance process in the former *does* approach a condition of statistical equilibrium and in the latter *does not*. This difference must somehow be implicit in the transformation matrices for the two processes; how it may be inferred from them is also a part of the broad theory of Markov processes.

138. Some Instructive Illustrations; A Non-Markovian Process

The validity of matrix methods is not limited to Markov processes. In fact, as we remarked in connection with Theorem 133.1, the fundamental relation (133.1) is valid wherever its symbols have meaning. To emphasize this point, and also to present an example of a process which is not Markovian, we take up again the scheme described in Problems 35.14 and 35.15 and propose the following question:

EXAMPLE 138.1.—*An urn contains 10 balls, of which 2 are white, 5 red, and 3 black. A drawing is made and its color noted. Then, before a second drawing occurs, all balls of this color are removed. What is the probability that the ball selected on the second drawing is white, red, or black?*

It is clear that the chance of drawing white, red, or black on the first drawing is $\frac{1}{5}$, $\frac{1}{2}$, or $\frac{3}{10}$, respectively. Hence the probability distribution after the first step in the process is represented by the matrix

$$D_1 = \downarrow \tfrac{1}{5} \quad \tfrac{1}{2} \quad \tfrac{3}{10} \downarrow . \tag{138.1}$$

The transformation matrix T_2 for the second step has been found in Problem 35.14. Using these we find that D_2, the distribution after the second step, is[5]

$$D_2 = T_2 D_1 = \begin{array}{c} w \\ r \\ b \end{array} \begin{bmatrix} 0 & \frac{2}{5} & \frac{2}{7} \\ \frac{5}{8} & 0 & \frac{5}{7} \\ \frac{3}{8} & \frac{3}{5} & 0 \end{bmatrix} . \begin{bmatrix} \frac{1}{5} \\ \frac{1}{2} \\ \frac{3}{10} \end{bmatrix} = \begin{array}{c} w \\ r \\ b \end{array} \begin{bmatrix} \frac{2}{7} \\ \frac{19}{56} \\ \frac{3}{8} \end{bmatrix} . \tag{138.2}$$

where the $w \; r \; b$ labels head the columns of the transformation matrix.

That is, the chance that the second ball is white (or red or black, respectively) is $\frac{2}{7}$ (or $\frac{19}{56}$ or $\frac{3}{8}$).

So far the argument has been quite straightforward. But if we now ask for the probability of the various colors on the third drawing—that is, for D_3—a new difficulty arises. What occurs on the third drawing depends not only on the outcome of the second trial, but on the previous history also. This does not mean that a transformation matrix T_3 cannot be found, but it certainly creates a more complex situation. We shall approach it in two ways.

For the first approach we may suppose that when a ball is drawn it is placed in an auxiliary container, and we regard the contents of this container after each drawing as the object of our study. Then it is clear that D_1, (138.1), is the distribution matrix for the result of the first drawing. After the second drawing, however, the contents of the auxiliary container will be either w,r, w,b or r,b, and the transition matrix to this set of possibilities will be composed of conditional probabilities such as $P(w,r|w)$, $P(w,r|r)$, and so on. These are easily evaluated and lead to

$$T_2' = \begin{array}{c} w,r \\ w,b \\ r,b \end{array} \begin{bmatrix} \frac{5}{8} & \frac{2}{5} & 0 \\ \frac{3}{8} & 0 & \frac{2}{7} \\ 0 & \frac{3}{5} & \frac{5}{7} \end{bmatrix} .$$

---

[5] For clarity, especially in subsequent matrices, the rows and columns are indexed with initials of the corresponding colors.

The first row of this, for example, states that the probability $P(w,r|w)$ of drawing a white and a red on the first two trials, if the first trial gives white, is $\frac{5}{8}$, whereas $P(w,r|r) = \frac{2}{5}$ and $P(w,r|b) = 0$. Then, operating on D_1 with this transition matrix, we obtain

$$D_2' = T_2' D_1 = \downarrow \begin{array}{ccc} w,r & w,b & r,b \\ \frac{13}{40} & \frac{9}{56} & \frac{18}{35} \end{array} \downarrow. \tag{138.3}$$

The validity of this result is readily checked by first principles.

If we now ask for the probability that the third ball will be white, red, or black, we need only operate on (138.3) with the transition matrix derived in Problem 35.15, thus getting

$$D_3 = \downarrow \begin{array}{ccc} w & r & b \\ \frac{18}{35}, & \frac{9}{56}, & \frac{13}{40} \end{array} \downarrow. \tag{138.4}$$

But we could also ask a different question, namely, What is the probability of each combination of colors which may be in the auxiliary container after the third trial? Since there is just one possibility w,r,b its probability must be 1, and the corresponding distribution matrix degenerates into the single term $D' = [1]$. This is obvious from first principles. But it is likewise obvious from first principles that the conditional probabilities $P(w,r,b|w,r)$, $P(w,r,b|w,b)$, $P(w,r,b|r,b)$ are all unity. From these we may form the single-rowed transformation matrix

$$T_3' = w,r,b \begin{array}{ccc} w,r & w,b & r,b \\ [\ 1 & 1 & 1 \ ]; \end{array} \tag{138.3}$$

and if we operate on (138.3) with this we get

$$D_3' = \begin{array}{c} w,r,b \\ [\ 1 \ ], \end{array}$$

which is again true, even if trivial.

For the second approach we consider, not the contents of the auxiliary container, but simply the color of the ball drawn on a particular trial. In such a context, questions such as, What is the chance of drawing red on the third attempt if the second trial gave white? are not without meaning, even though the result of the first trial is not specified. We should therefore be able to form a matrix T_3'', composed of such conditional probabilities, which when operating on D_2 would lead to D_3. The only problem is to compute the conditional probabilities. This may be done as follows:

Taking first the conditional probability of red on the third trial if the second was white, we note that

$$P(\cdot, \ w,r) \equiv P(b,w,r) = \frac{3}{35}$$

since neither the sequence w,w,r nor r,w,r is possible. Also, considering only the first two trials,

$$P(\cdot, w) = P(r,w) + P(b,w) = \frac{2}{7}$$

since the sequence ww is not possible. But by (37.1),

$$P(\cdot, w,r) = P(\cdot, w) \, P(r|\cdot,w),$$

and upon substitution of the known numerical values

$$P(r|\cdot, w) = \tfrac{3}{10}.$$

This is the desired conditional probability.
Computing the other elements of T_3'' in a similar way, we obtain

$$T_3'' = \begin{matrix} & \cdot,w & \cdot,r & \cdot,b \\ w \\ r \\ b \end{matrix} \begin{bmatrix} 0 & \frac{12}{19} & \frac{4}{5} \\ \frac{3}{10} & 0 & \frac{1}{5} \\ \frac{7}{10} & \frac{7}{19} & 0 \end{bmatrix}.$$

The reader will have no difficulty in demonstrating that when D_2, (138.2), is multiplied by this matrix the result is (138.4).
Thus Theorems 133.1 and 133.2 have confirmed their validity throughout several alternative interpretations of their symbols.

Problems

1. An urn contains three balls, one white and two black. Repeated drawings are made from this in the fashion of § 55. If $D_m = [P_m(n)]$ is the distribution for n, the number of white balls drawn in the first m trials, what is T_m, the transition matrix for the m'th trial?
[This is sometimes referred to as the Bernoulli process.]

2. If the process of Problem 1 is modified by keeping score on a binary counter which cannot carry over beyond two digits (in other words, it can count 0, 1, 2, 3 but then returns to zero), what is the transition matrix for the m'th trial?

3. If there is no accumulated score on the counter of Problem 2 when the process begins, what is the distribution of probabilities after the second trial? After the eighth?

4. If the counter showed an accumulated score of 3 when the trial began, what would the distribution be after the eighth trial?

5. What is D_∞, the limit approached by D_m as $m \to \infty$? Does this depend on the initial registration of the counter?

6. Is Problem 2 a Markov process? Is it stationary?

7. Is Problem 1 a Markov process? It is stationary?

8. Suppose the barber shop of Example 136.1 has only two chairs for waiting customers, and that anyone who arrives when these are occupied goes away at once and does not return. What is the transition matrix?

9. What is the distribution when statistical equilibrium has been established? Evaluate this for $\epsilon = \tfrac{1}{2}$.

10. What percentage of the potential traffic does the barber lose for lack of adequate seating?
[Compare the results of Problem 9 with those of Example 136.1.]

11. There are many people in a room. They are approached one at a time and asked in what month they were born. Consider a particular month—say January—and after n trials let the probability that just j of the birthdays fall in this month be $P(j)$. Then

$$D_n = \,\downarrow P(0), P(1), \ldots, P(n) \downarrow$$

is the corresponding distribution matrix. Find the transformation matrix for the n'th interrogation.

12. Before the count begins in Problem 11, no birthdays have been determined to be in January. Hence the initial distribution is $D_0 = [1]$. Find successively $D_1 = T_1 D_0$, $D_2 = T_2 D_1$, $D_3 = T_3 D_2$. Compare with (42.1).

13. Balls are placed one by one at random in a set of five boxes. Let $P(j)$ be the probability that just j of these boxes are occupied after n balls have been placed, and let D_n be the distribution matrix for these probabilities. Construct the transition matrix appropriate to the placing of the n'th ball.

14. Using the result of Problem 13, find the distribution of probabilities after 4 balls have been placed, and after a condition of statistical equilibrium is established.

15. Prove (132.3) by induction.

[Call $B' = BC = [b'_{jk}]$ and $A' = AB = [a'_{jk}]$; then by repeated use of (132.1) write expressions for the elements of $(AB)C$ and $A(BC)$.]

16. Establish the validity of (135.2) by induction.

[Use (135.1) to derive the relation

$$(a + \nu - 1)\, P_\nu(j) = (a + \nu - j - 2)\, P_{\nu-1}(j) + j\, P_{\nu-1}(j - 1).$$

Then show that this is satisfied by (135.2) for all ν.]

17. Only one element of T''_3, § 138, was computed in the text. Derive the remaining terms of the matrix.

Answers to Problems

1. Two answers are possible: (a) Taking account of the fact that n cannot exceed m, we can write the matrix of $m - 1$ rows and m columns

$$T_m = \begin{bmatrix} \frac{2}{3} & 0 & 0 & \cdots & 0 \\ \frac{1}{3} & \frac{2}{3} & 0 & \cdots & 0 \\ 0 & \frac{1}{3} & \frac{2}{3} & \cdots & 0 \\ \cdots & \cdots & \cdots & \cdots & \cdots \\ 0 & 0 & 0 & \cdots & \frac{2}{3} \\ 0 & 0 & 0 & \cdots & \frac{1}{3} \end{bmatrix},$$

or (b) we can extend this to an infinite matrix with all elements of the principal diagonal $\frac{2}{3}$, and all elements of the adjacent diagonal $\frac{1}{3}$. It is then necessary to regard D_m also as an infinite matrix with all elements zero beyond $n = m$.

2.
$$T_m = \begin{bmatrix} \frac{2}{3} & 0 & 0 & \frac{1}{3} \\ \frac{1}{3} & \frac{2}{3} & 0 & 0 \\ 0 & \frac{1}{3} & \frac{2}{3} & 0 \\ 0 & 0 & \frac{1}{3} & \frac{2}{3} \end{bmatrix}.$$

3. $D_0 = \;\downarrow 1, 0, 0, 0 \downarrow,$

$$T^8 = \begin{bmatrix} \frac{1377}{6561} & \frac{1808}{6561} & \frac{1904}{6561} & \frac{1472}{6561} \\ \frac{1472}{6561} & \frac{1377}{6561} & \frac{1808}{6561} & \frac{1904}{6561} \\ \frac{1904}{6561} & \frac{1472}{6561} & \frac{1377}{6561} & \frac{1808}{6561} \\ \frac{1808}{6561} & \frac{1904}{6561} & \frac{1472}{6561} & \frac{1377}{6561} \end{bmatrix};$$

D_8 is identical with the first column of T^8.

4. $D_0 = \;\downarrow 0, 0, 1, 0 \downarrow$; hence D_8 is identical with the third column of T^8.

5. $\downarrow \frac{1}{4}, \frac{1}{4}, \frac{1}{4}, \frac{1}{4} \downarrow$; no, since all columns of T^∞ are alike. This can be inferred from inspection of T^8 and proved by induction. It is in contrast to Example 134.1 where the columns of T^∞ were different, and the ultimate condition of statistical equilibrium depended upon the initial distribution.

6. Yes; yes.

7. Yes; yes, if T_m is written as an infinite matrix. Strictly speaking, if T_m is written in finite form it varies with m; but since the option of an invariant infinite matrix exists the process would usually be called stationary.

8.
$$T = \begin{bmatrix} e^{-\epsilon} & e^{-\epsilon} & 0 & 0 \\ \epsilon e^{-\epsilon} & \epsilon e^{-\epsilon} & e^{-\epsilon} & 0 \\ \frac{1}{2}\epsilon^2 e^{-\epsilon} & \frac{1}{2}\epsilon^2 e^{-\epsilon} & \epsilon e^{-\epsilon} & e^{-\epsilon} \\ 1 - (1 + \epsilon + \frac{1}{2}\epsilon^2)e^{-\epsilon} & 1 - (1 + \epsilon + \frac{1}{2}\epsilon^2)e^{-\epsilon} & 1 - (1 + \epsilon)e^{-\epsilon} & 1 - e^{-\epsilon} \end{bmatrix}$$

9. $P(0) = e^{-\epsilon}/D, P(1) = (1 - e^{-\epsilon})/D, P(2) = (e^\epsilon - 1 - \epsilon)/D,$

$P(3) = [e^{2\epsilon} - (1 + 2\epsilon)e^\epsilon + (\epsilon + \frac{1}{2}\epsilon^2)]/D$ where

$D = e^{2\epsilon} - 2\epsilon e^\epsilon + \frac{1}{2}\epsilon^2;$

$P(0) = 0.5077, P(1) = 0.3294, P(2) = 0.1245, P(3) = 0.0384.$

10. With plenty of chairs the barber is idle $\frac{1}{2}$ of the time; with only 2, 0.5077. He loses $0.0077/0.5000 = 1.5\%$ of the potential traffic.

11.
$$T_n = \begin{bmatrix} \frac{11}{12} & 0 & 0 & \cdots & 0 & 0 \\ \frac{1}{12} & \frac{11}{12} & 0 & \cdots & 0 & 0 \\ 0 & \frac{1}{12} & \frac{11}{12} & \cdots & 0 & 0 \\ \cdots & \cdots & \cdots & \cdots & \cdots & \cdots \\ 0 & 0 & 0 & \cdots & \frac{1}{12} & \frac{11}{12} \\ 0 & 0 & 0 & \cdots & 0 & \frac{1}{12} \end{bmatrix}.$$

This is a matrix of n rows and $n - 1$ columns. It can be replaced by an infinite matrix. See answer to Problem 1.

12. $D_1 = \downarrow \frac{11}{12}, \frac{1}{12} \downarrow, D_2 = \downarrow (\frac{11}{12})^2, 2\cdot\frac{11}{12}\cdot\frac{1}{12}, (\frac{1}{12})^2 \downarrow,$

$D_3 = \downarrow (\frac{11}{12})^3, 3(\frac{11}{12})^2 \frac{1}{12}, 3\cdot\frac{11}{12}(\frac{1}{12})^2, (\frac{1}{12})^3 \downarrow.$

These are the values taken by (42.1) with $p = \frac{1}{12}$ and $m = 1, 2, 3,$ respectively.

13.

$$T = \begin{bmatrix} 0 & 0 & 0 & 0 & 0 & 0 \\ 1 & \frac{1}{5} & 0 & 0 & 0 & 0 \\ 0 & \frac{4}{5} & \frac{2}{5} & 0 & 0 & 0 \\ 0 & 0 & \frac{3}{5} & \frac{3}{5} & 0 & 0 \\ 0 & 0 & 0 & \frac{2}{5} & \frac{4}{5} & 0 \\ 0 & 0 & 0 & 0 & \frac{1}{5} & 1 \end{bmatrix}.$$

14. $D_4 = \downarrow 0, \frac{1}{125}, \frac{28}{125}, \frac{72}{125}, \frac{24}{125}, 0 \downarrow,$

$D_\infty = \downarrow 0, 0, 0, 0, 0, 1 \downarrow.$

Chapter XI

The Foundations of Statistics

139. Introductory Remarks

We have already remarked in § 13 that Probability Theory and Statistical Theory deal with diametrically opposed aspects of the same broad subject. The former is concerned with inferences which can be made regarding the outcome of an experiment when the controlling circumstances (the probabilities) are specified; the latter asks what inferences can be drawn regarding the probabilities from the known results of an experiment.

This book is devoted to the former subject, and it is not the purpose of this chapter—as it has not been the purpose elsewhere—to give the reader a working knowledge, or even a connected account, of the other. But the foundations of Statistical Theory rest on the Theory of Probability, and a clear understanding of the nature of these foundations is an important adjunct of both disciplines. It is the purpose of this chapter to discuss this subject.

The discussion will be concerned with four typical questions with which statisticians have to deal:

1. The best estimate of the true magnitude of a quantity which can be made from several more or less inexact measurements. This is the subject of §§ 140 to 144.

2. The best answer which can be given to the question: "Are the results of an experiment consistent with the belief (hypothesis) that they are distributed in a prescribed way?" This is discussed in §§ 145 to 153.

3. Are two sequences of experimental results dependent or independent? This is discussed in §§ 154 to 160.

4. When a random sample is taken (i.e., independent trials of an experiment are made), what is the distribution function for the average, variance. or other statistics of the sample? This is discussed in §§ 161 to 164.

140. Precision of Measurement

Suppose a quantity is in some manner to be measured; that is, determined by means of an experiment. In general, the result of a single experiment is not precise, and it is a matter of common experience that the precision can be improved by repeating the measurement a number of times and taking the average of the results. But when this is done we still have only an estimate, not the true value, and the essential question of the trustworthiness of the estimate still remains.

If the separate measurements differ only slightly from one another, as for example in the group 16.15, 16.17, 16.13, 16.15, 16.15, we would normally assume that the true value was very close to their average 16.15. If, on the other hand, they scattered widely, as in the group 13.27, 17.94, 11.51, 20.16, 17.87, which also has the average 16.15, the uncertainty would certainly be greater. Can we, from the data themselves, derive limits within which we may reasonably assume that the true value lies?

Such questions arise in many human activities. Perhaps they reach their greatest urgency in the precise determination of fundamental constants of science, such as the velocity of light, the energy equivalent of heat, Planck's constant, or the diameter of the earth's orbit. We shall consider an example of this general type.

EXAMPLE 140.1.—*Table 140.1 contains measurements of the diameter of Saturn's ring which were made by Bessel in the years 1829–1831. What is the best estimate possible as to the true diameter?*

In such a situation we would like to use Bayes' Theorem, since it would give the most informative answer. But to do so we would need: first the *a priori* probability $p(X)$ that the true value is X, which we do not have; second, the conditional probability $p(x_j|X)$ of making a reading x_j if the true value is X, which we also do not know. So this direct avenue of attack is closed to us.

TABLE 140.1

BESSEL'S MEASURES OF SATURN'S RING

38.91	39.35	39.41	39.02	39.32	39.25	39.40	39.01
38.93	39.14	39.36	38.86	39.31	39.47	39.20	39.51
39.17	39.29	39.42	39.21	39.04	39.32	39.30	39.17
39.57	39.40	39.41	39.60	39.46	39.33	39.43	39.54
39.30	39.28	39.43	39.45	39.03	39.62	39.36	39.72

$n = 40$; $\bar{x} = 39.3075$; $\Sigma d_j^2 = 1.58815$; $s^2 = 0.0397$; $s = 0.1992$.

From the start, however, we must keep in mind this fact: It is a *merit* of Bayes' Theorem, not a *weakness*, that it takes account of the inherent likelihood of an event. It would be well to read again § 74 and note that the information sought does not depend solely on the experimental evidence, but on all the other bits of knowledge which go into the making up of our advance judgment as to the goodness of our coin.

It is a matter of cold fact that the reliance which we dare place in the result of an experiment depends upon the inherent plausibility of the result as well as upon the accuracy with which it has been attained. Any substitute for Bayes' Theorem which does not require the knowledge of the a priori *probabilities must therefore be incapable of giving the* a posteriori *probabilities.*

Being, therefore, unable to get a mathematical measure of the assurance with which we may accept our estimate because we do not first possess a mathematical measure of its inherent plausibility, we turn to the task of finding the best possible makeshift. Fortunately the makeshift is not a very unsatisfactory one when its meaning is clearly understood, but we must repeat that it *does not tell us how probable our estimate is. Nothing can tell us that which does not require the* a priori *probabilities.*

We reason as follows:
There is some probability distribution $p_0(x)$ which corresponds to the experimental conditions. It is unknown to us, but may be represented schematically by Fig. 140.1. It has a first expectation and standard deviation which we will denote by ϵ and σ.

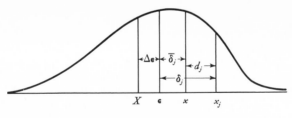

FIG. 140.1

We note, to begin with, that ϵ is not necessarily identical with the true value X, since either the observer or the measuring instrument may be biased in such a way as to introduce a systematic error. Presumably Bessel made the measurements by moving a cross-wire first to one side of the ring and then the other. If the pitch of the screw which moved the cross-wire was slightly in error, all the readings would tend to be too large or too small. Moreover, it is known that different observers make systematically different judgments when they attempt to locate a cross-wire at the exact edge of an object in their field of view. Because of this the curve $p_0(x)$—and hence its expectation ϵ—might be somewhat different for different observers. Hence we must assume a systematic error $\Delta\epsilon$ between ϵ and X, as the figure shows.

The average of the 40 readings in Example 140.1 is still another number x. This also is indicated in the figure, and its displacement from ϵ is represented by $\bar{x} - \epsilon = \delta$.

We cannot expect to learn from the table of data how large the bias $\Delta\epsilon$ is, or even if it exists. Only some independent information as to the approximate magnitude of X, or regarding the peculiarities of the observer or his instrument, could assist in estimating bias. $\Delta\epsilon$ must therefore remain unresolved.

But thanks to the central limit theorem we *can* get some insight into the probable discrepancy, δ, between $\bar{x}$ and ϵ. We have 40 trials of an experiment, which are presumed to be independent and to have the distribution $p_0(x)$. By (128.2) their average should (approximately) obey the normal law with

$$y = \sqrt{n}\,(\bar{x} - \epsilon)/\sigma = \sqrt{n}\,\delta/\sigma. \qquad (140.1)$$

That is, for reasonably large n, the distribution of the average δ should be

$$p(\delta) \doteq \frac{\sqrt{n}}{\sqrt{2\pi}\sigma}\, e^{-n\bar{\delta}^2/2\,\sigma^2}. \qquad (140.2)$$

This we know without more specific information about the nature of the experiment and the consequent distribution $p_0(x)$ than is provided by the constants ϵ and σ.[1]

But what is δ? It is the difference between $\bar{x}$ and ϵ; in other words, the error that we would commit if we accepted $\bar{x}$ as an estimate of ϵ. We can say either that, if ϵ were known (it is not), the distribution of x would be given by (140.2), or with equal accuracy that, if $\bar{x}$ is known (as it is), the distribution of ϵ is given by (140.2). Thus we have the

THEOREM 140.1. *If $\bar{x}$ is the average of n independent measurements made under constant experimental conditions, the probability that the correct value X lies between $\epsilon_1 + \Delta\epsilon$ and $\epsilon_2 + \Delta\epsilon$ is approximately*

$$\phi_{-1}(y_2) - \phi_{-1}(y_1),$$

where y_1 and y_2 are obtained by substituting ϵ_1 and ϵ_2 in (140.1). In this

---

[1] The theoretical requirements for the validity of the central limit theorem are always satisfied in practice, as was noted in footnotes 25 and 26, § 123.

expression $\Delta\epsilon$ *is the personal or instrumental bias of the measurement and* σ *is its standard deviation.*[2]

We still do not know the value of σ. The standard deviation of the sample, $s = 0.1992$, has been computed in Table 140.1, but this differs from σ for two reasons: first, because of accidental peculiarities in the composition of the sample; second, because the sample deviations $d_j = x_j - \bar{x}$ are measured from the average $\bar{x}$, not from the (unknown) expectation ϵ as would be required in computing σ.

There are, at this point, two courses of action open to us. One is, to retain the assumption with which we began, that the distribution function $p_0(x)$ can be of any form, and ask how best to estimate the ϵ and σ in (140.1). This will be done in the next section.

If, on the other hand, we abandon the generality of $p_0(x)$ and assume instead that it is the *normal* distribution, it is possible to obtain limiting values for x *without knowing its* σ. This will be done in § 163.

141. Estimation of Parameters

It will be simpler, for the moment, to think of the n trials as constituting a single experiment by means of which a set of numbers $(x_1, x_2, \ldots, x_n)$ are determined with probability $p(x_1, x_2, \ldots, x_n)$. Since the trials are independent, we obviously have

$$p(x_1, x_2 \ldots, x_n) = p_0(x_1)\, p_0(x_2) \ldots p_0(x_n). \qquad (141.1)$$

We ask for the best estimates which can be made from the data at hand of the expectation ϵ and variance σ^2 of $p_0(x)$. As is customary in statistical theory, we shall differentiate between the true value and an estimate by a circumflex accent; thus $\hat{\epsilon}$ and $\hat{\sigma}^2$ will represent our estimates of ϵ and σ^2.

What shall we mean by a "best estimate"? We are dealing with data from which certain statistics—in our case $\bar{x}$ and s—have been computed. In theory the expectations of these, $\epsilon_1(\bar{x})$ and $\epsilon_1(s)$, can be

---

[2] If the reader feels that this statement has somehow circumvented the requirements of Bayes' Theorem, he should note that the distribution in Fig. 140.1 is, in reality, the $p(x_j|X)$ of Bayes' Theorem. Our argument has told us only that, if the ϵ_X and σ_X of this are known, the limiting form of $p_n(\bar{\delta}_j|X)$ is also known.

If we assume in addition that (*a*) Fig. 140.1 is the same for every X, (in which case ϵ_X, σ_X and $p_n(\bar{\delta}|X)$ are independent of X), and (*b*) the *a priori* probability $p(X)$ is constant for all possible values and zero elsewhere, Bayes' Theorem will yield the stated Theorem. In other words, these two assumptions are implicit in our argument.

Similar remarks would also be in order at many other points throughout this chapter, and in fact throughout most of Statistical Theory. It is equally unwise to be unaware, as I fear many statisticians are, of the logical insufficiency of their practices, or to be unnecessarily disturbed about it. Until we have something better, which in this case is unlikely, we had best use what we have thoughtfully—and thankfully.

computed from (141.1); but since $p_0(x)$ depends on ϵ and σ this can in practice be done only by assigning them specific values $\hat{\epsilon}$ and $\hat{\sigma}$. For one such choice, $\bar{x}$ may be very close to $\epsilon(\bar{x})$, and s to $\epsilon(s)$, and for another far apart. It seems sensible to say that a good estimate, in the light of the data at hand, is one that makes the difference small; and that the "best estimate" is the one which makes the difference as small as possible.

This is the sense in which the phrase is used in statistical theory. It is important enough to restate more concisely.

CRITERION: *If an experiment has produced a sample of data from which certain statistics k_1, k_2, ... have been computed, and if this experiment is presumed to be characterized by a probability distribution containing certain parameters γ_1, γ_2 ... the values of which are as yet unknown, the "best estimates" of these parameters are defined to be those values $\hat{\gamma}_1$, $\hat{\gamma}_2$, ... for which* $[k_1 - \epsilon_1(k_1)]^2$, $[k_2 - \epsilon_1(k_2)]^2$, ... *are as small as possible.*

These conditions are clearly satisfied if it is possible to make each statistic k_j *equal* to its expectation—in our case $\bar{x} = \epsilon_1(\bar{x})$ and $s^2 = \epsilon_1(s^2)$.

We already know from (98.3) that

$$\epsilon_1(\bar{x}) = \epsilon,$$

and hence the "best" estimate of ϵ (i.e., the one which makes $\epsilon_1(\bar{x}) = \bar{x}$), is $\hat{\epsilon} = \bar{x}$.

The sample variance s^2 requires special consideration. By definition it is

$$s^2 = \frac{x_1^2 + x_2^2 + \ldots + x_n^2}{n} - \bar{x}^2$$

$$= \frac{x_1^2 + x_2^2 + \ldots + x_n^2}{n} - \left(\frac{x_1 + x_2 + \ldots + x_n}{n}\right)^2$$

$$= \frac{n-1}{n^2}(x_1^2 + x_2^2 + \ldots + x_n^2) - \frac{2}{n^2}\sum{}^* x_i x_j, \qquad (141.2)$$

where the sum Σ^* is to be taken over all pairs i, j for which $j > i$. Thus $\epsilon_1(s^2)$ is the sum of the expectations of all the terms on the right of (141.2).

Consider first a term of the form x_i^2. By (141.1) its expectation is

$$\epsilon_1(x_i^2) = \int \int \ldots \int x_i^2 \, p_0(x_1) \ldots p_0(x_i) \ldots p_0(x_n) \, dx_1 \ldots dx_i \ldots dx_n,$$

which breaks up into n separate integrals

$$\int p_0(x_1) \, dx_1 \ldots \int x_i^2 \, p_0(x_i) \, dx_i \ldots \int p_0(x_n) \, dx_n.$$

All factors in this are 1 except $\int x_i{}^2 \, p_0(x_i) dx_i$; and since $p_0(x_i)$ is the same for all the x_i's, this latter factor is, by (96.3)

$$\epsilon_1(x_i{}^2) = \epsilon_2(x_i) = \sigma^2 + \epsilon^2. \tag{141.3}$$

When terms of form $x_i x_j$ are similarly considered, we find by (98.6) that

$$\epsilon_1(x_i x_j) = \epsilon^2, \tag{141.4}$$

since the variables are independent. Thus $\epsilon_1(s^2)$ consists of n identical terms of the form (141.3) and $n(n-1)/2$ identical terms of the form (141.4); and taking account of the coefficients by which they are multiplied in (141.2) they add up to

$$\epsilon_1(s^2) = \frac{n-1}{n} \sigma^2.$$

To make $\epsilon_1(s^2) = s^2$, therefore, we must set

$$\hat{\sigma}^2 = \frac{n}{n-1} s^2.$$

If we had approached the matter less thoughtfully, we would probably have chosen $\hat{\epsilon} = \bar{x}$ and $\hat{\sigma} = s$ as our estimates of the parameters. The first of these would have been the "best estimate" in the sense of the accepted criterion, but the other would not. The fundamental reason, as is clear from (141.2), is that the squares of the x's enter s^2 not only directly, but also through the term in $\bar{x}^2$.

DEFINITION 141.1. *A statistic which is itself the "best estimate" of a parameter is called by statisticians an "efficient statistic."*

The reader will note that the argument of this section did not depend upon the nature of the particular example we have been discussing, but in the case of $\hat{\epsilon}$ only upon (98.2), which is perfectly general, and in the case of $\hat{\sigma}$ upon the independence of the variables $x_1, x_2, \ldots, x_n$. Hence we may state the following

THEOREM 141.1. *If n independent trials are made of an experiment characterized by the distribution function $p_0(x)$, the efficient statistics for estimating ϵ and σ are $\bar{x}$ and $\sqrt{n/(n-1)} \, s$, respectively. That is*

$$\hat{\epsilon} = \bar{x},$$

$$\hat{\sigma}^2 = \frac{n}{n-1} s^2.$$

142. Precision of Measurement; Numerical Examples

Returning now to Example 140.1, we quickly get the estimates

$$\hat{\epsilon} = \bar{x} = 39.3075,$$

$$\hat{\sigma} = \sqrt{40/39}\, s = 0.2018,$$

$$y = \sqrt{40}\, \delta/\hat{\sigma} = 31.34\, \delta.$$

It is now a simple matter to estimate the probability that ϵ lies within any desired interval around $\bar{x}$. For example, if ϵ is not to differ from $\bar{x}$ by more than 0.05, δ must be between ± 0.05, and y between ± 1.567. The probability of this is[3] $\phi_{-1}(1.567) - \phi_{-1}(-1.567)$. It may be found from Appendix V. However, since the limiting values of y are equal and opposite in sign, it can be found more easily from the function $\Phi(y)$, in Appendix IV, which gives the *complement* of $\phi_{-1}(y) - \phi_{-1}(-y)$ directly. That is, $\Phi(y)$ represents the area of *both* tails beyond the limits $\pm y$. With $y = 1.567$, we find that the area of the tails is 0.117; hence the probability that ϵ differs from $\bar{x}$ by less than 0.05, is 0.883.

Alternatively, we can ask for the limits within which it is 99% certain that ϵ lies. The area of tails is then 0.01; from Appendix IV, $y = 2.576$; hence $\delta = 0.0822$ and $\epsilon = 39.3075 \pm 0.0822$.

Clearly, the uncertainty concerning ϵ is quite small.[4] It is true that in making these computations we have assumed that σ is in fact $\hat{\sigma}$. If this estimate were considerably in error the limiting values of y would be affected proportionally, as can be seen from (140.1). But the variability of the separate measurements is so slight that no large error in estimating σ is to be anticipated.[5]

A more serious reservation concerns the possibility of systematic bias in the measurements; that is, the $\Delta\epsilon$ of Fig. 140.1. This cannot be judged from the data alone. It can only be inferred or rejected on the basis of other evidence regarding the experimental conditions. Therefore it is sometimes passed over in silence in textbooks on the practice of statistics, although it is in fact one of the major possibilities for which the careful investigator should be alert.

A second numerical example of a radically different sort is afforded by the set of measurements mentioned in the opening paragraphs of § 140. They are reproduced in Table 142.1.

---

[3] See § 113.

[4] Note that only 5 of the 40 separate measurements fall within these limits; yet our argument gives us good reason to assume that ϵ does.

[5] See also § 163.

EXAMPLE 142.1.—*A quantity has been measured five times with the results 13.27, 17.94, 11.51, 20.16, 17.87. What is the best estimate possible as to its true value, and within what limits can it be said to lie with probability 0.99?*

Here $\hat{\epsilon} = \bar{x} = 16.15$ and $\hat{\sigma} = \sqrt{5/4}\, s = 3.608$.

Assuming no systematic bias, the best estimate of the true value is $\hat{X} = 16.15$.

To answer the second question, we find from Appendix IV that there is 0.01 probability that ϵ lies outside $y = \pm 2.576$. But by (140.1),

$$\delta = \hat{\sigma} y / \sqrt{n} = 1.614 y,$$

and hence the limiting values of δ are ± 4.16. We thus conclude that $X = \epsilon = 16.15 \pm 4.16$ with probability 0.99.

TABLE 142.1

x	d	d^2
13.27	− 2.88	8.29
17.94	+ 1.79	3.20
11.51	− 4.64	21.53
20.16	+ 4.01	16.08
17.87	+ 1.72	2.96
80.75	0.00	52.06

$= 5;$ $\bar{x} = 16.15;$ $s^2 = 10.41;$ $s = 3.226.$

Here, even if there is no systematic bias and $\hat{\sigma}$ is not greatly in error, the uncertainty as to the true value of the measured quantity is very wide.[6] It is, in fact, $\pm 25\%$.

143. Levels of Confidence; Confidence Intervals

In both these examples we would have obtained other values for δ if we had used another probability value. Thus in the last example, with probability 0.95, $y = \pm 1.960$ and $\delta = \pm 3.16$. Hence, statements such as $X = 16.15 \pm 4.16$ and $X = 16.15 \pm 3.16$ are not fully informative unless there is an indication of the assumed probability. They are therefore usually accompanied by the phrase "at the

---

[6] In this case, at the 1% level, the range of uncertainty is almost as wide as the spread between the largest and smallest measurements.

306   PROBABILITY AND ITS ENGINEERING USES

99% level" or "at the 95% level," indicating that the chance of X falling *outside* the indicated interval is 0.01 or 0.05, respectively.[7] These intervals are known as *confidence intervals*, and the probabilities with which they are associated as *levels of confidence*.

144. Distribution of Variance; First Approximation

We have noted that these limits are only as accurate as the estimate $\hat{\sigma}$ upon which they are based. We can, if we like, use Theorem 128.1, and in particular the equation for σ^*, to obtain an estimate of the uncertainty in $\hat{\sigma}$. To do this, we identify δ in Fig. 140.1 with the x of the theorem and δ^2 with w. Then the theorem, together with (128.4) and (128.5), states that the average of n δ^2's is normally distributed and has standard deviation σ^*. We do not know σ^*, but just as in the examples already dealt with, the best estimate of it is

$$\hat{\sigma}^{*2} = \frac{n}{n-1} \, s^{*2} = \frac{1}{n-1} \{\mu_4(d) - [\mu_2(d)]^2\} \, .$$

From Table 140.1 we can compute $\mu_4(d) = 0.004262$ and $\mu_2(d) = 0.03970$. Hence $\hat{\sigma}^{*2} = 0.00006887$, $\hat{\sigma}^* = 0.008299$.

But in (128.4) $\epsilon_2(x) \equiv \epsilon_2(\delta) \equiv \sigma^2$ and $\mu_2(x) - \epsilon_2(x) = \Delta\sigma^2$. Hence, with 0.01 probability $(y = 2.576)$, $\Delta\sigma^2 = \pm\, 2.576\, \hat{\sigma}^* = 0.0214$; whence $\sigma^2 = 0.0407 \pm 0.0214$. Thus, finally, there is 0.99 probability that σ lies in the interval $(0.139, 0.249)$.

In the case of the second example, the size of the sample is so small that we cannot expect the central limit theorem to yield more than a crude approximation. If we nevertheless carry through the same process we get $\mu_4(d) = 161.8$, $\mu_2(d) = 10.41$, $s^{*2} = 10.71$, $\hat{\sigma}^{*2} = 13.37$, $\hat{\sigma}^* = 3.66$. Hence, with 0.99 probability, $\Delta\sigma^2 = 9.42$ and $\sigma^2 = 13.02 \pm 9.42$; finally $\sigma = (1.90, 4.74)$.

The process which is carried out arithmetically in the two preceding paragraphs can also be treated algebraically and leads to the result that the standard deviation of the distribution of $\hat{\sigma}$ is approximately[8]

$$\sigma(\hat{\sigma}) = \sqrt{\frac{\mu_4(d) - [\mu_2(d)]^2}{4n\mu_2(d)}} \, .$$

---

[7] The variability of a measurement is often shown by writing the limits which correspond to $y = 1$. The probability of lying within the stated limits is then 0.3173, and the level of confidence 32%.

With this convention, the diameter of Saturn's ring would be stated as

$$39.3075 \pm 0.0319.$$

To find the limits corresponding to any other level of confidence it is necessary only to multiply the second figure by the appropriate y; e.g., by 2.576 for the 99% level.

[8] This formula is not as soundly based as the one for $\hat{\sigma}^*$. For one thing, it involves approximating a term of the form $\sqrt{a^2 + b^2}$ by $a + b^2/2a$ under circumstances where b may be comparable in magnitude to a. For another, Theorem 128.1 applies to $\hat{\sigma}^2$, but does not apply to $\hat{\sigma}$ since the latter is neither the sum nor the average of powers of δ, but the *square root* of such a sum. Hence we cannot say without further justification that $\hat{\sigma}$ is normally distributed.

In practice, however, the general level of uncertainty is often high enough that a little more may be inconsequential. This is certainly true in our second example, and probably in our first one also.

If this approximation were used, it would give for the intervals above (0.151, 0.253) and (2.30, 4.91).

The reader will observe how great the uncertainty in $\hat{\sigma}$ is. Even in the first example, where there is a large amount of good data, the first digit of σ is somewhat uncertain. Hence, although the method of improving the precision of measurement by averaging is a valid and valuable one, the limits of uncertainty assigned by the central limit theorem to the best estimate are often only rough approximations and should be so regarded. We shall see in § 163 how better limits can sometimes be obtained, especially when n is small.

145. The Accepted Criterion as to Goodness of Fit

We turn our attention now to a related, but somewhat more general subject—the testing of hypotheses. As in § 140, let us begin with a specific example.

EXAMPLE 145.1.—*There is a case on record where a die was thrown 315,672 times, with the result that either 5 or 6 appeared 106,602 times. Was the die true, and, if not, what was the probability of the appearance of 5 or 6?*

We have again a situation to which Bayes' Theorem cannot be applied, since we do not know the *a priori* probabilities. It is, of course, less extreme than that of Example 140.1; for in the present instance we can at least say that, *if p has the value $\hat{p}$, the conditional probability of* the observed result is $C_{106,602}^{315,672}\ \hat{p}^{106,602}\ (1-\hat{p})^{209,070}$ whereas in Example 140.1 neither the *a priori* nor the conditional probabilities were known. But in essence the situation is unchanged, and our first necessity is to agree on some criterion against which to evaluate the question presented to us.

A simple illustration will help in getting our ideas fixed. Suppose we were attempting to measure the probability of a certain event occurring and conducted an experiment which gave 20 successes in 50 trials. Suppose, moreover, that because of certain collateral evidence, which we need not discuss, we reached the conclusion that a fair estimate of the probability was $\frac{1}{2}$. From Table 55.3 we find that *if this estimate is correct* the chance of getting 20 successes in 50 trials is only 0.0704. The particular result in question was therefore not very likely. But by glancing over the table we quickly observe that no other result was much more likely to occur, and many of them were even less likely. Obviously under these circumstances it is unfair to conclude that our estimate is an unreasonable one. The question that really presents itself is, How likely would we be to get a result the probability of which is no greater than 0.0704? We can easily answer this question by adding together the probabilities of all possible results except those from 14 to 19, thus getting the answer 0.368. Obviously, then, the chance of getting a result that was at least as unusual as 20 successes is big enough that we need not discard our assumed probability as an untenable one.

To take another simple example, suppose we have dealt a pack of cards and have observed the order in which they fell. Suppose by *a priori* reasoning we have formed the hypothesis that all orders are equally likely. On the basis of this estimate we compute the chance of getting the observed result and find it to be 1/52!, which is inconceivably small. Are we therefore justified in discarding our hypothesis? Certainly not, for any order at all would be just as improbable. The thing that counts is; on the basis of our hypothesis we were *sure* to get a result as unlikely as this.

What we have done in both these illustrations is:

(*a*) By some means we formed a more or less plausible estimate of the probabilities which the experiment was designed to measure; and

(*b*) We computed the chance that another experiment, so conducted that its probabilities were really equal to these estimates, would lead to a result at least as improbable as the one under discussion.

We may express the matter in terms more commonly used by statisticians as follows:

(*a*) We consider the results of our experiment and from them estimate the proportions in which the different kinds of individuals are contained in the population; and

(*b*) We compute the chance that another sample, taken from this assumed population, would be at least as unusual as the sample under discussion.

The accepted criterion for assessing the acceptability of a hypothesis is precisely the same. It may be phrased concretely as follows:

CRITERION. *The accepted criterion for testing a hypothesis is, not how likely it is that the hypothesis is correct, nor how likely our experimental result was if the hypothesis was correct, but instead the chance of getting a result at least as unusual as the one observed, if the hypothesis was correct.*

The first step in our process—that of forming a hypothesis—is likely to present itself in a wide variety of forms. Sometimes it requires the estimation of only one probability, as in the first example above; sometimes it requires the estimation of many, as in the card illustration where we really estimated 52! probabilities at once, making them all equal; sometimes the number may be infinite, as in finding the chance of a metal stamping differing from standard by a specified amount. The last case, indeed, requires that we give the equation of a distribution curve, rather than the values of certain discrete numbers.

Naturally, the methods of forming our estimates of these probabilities are going to vary widely, not only with the number of variables with which we must deal, but also with the amount of collateral information which we may possess and which influences our choice. For this part of our work the various distribution functions discussed in Chapter IX will be our principal stock of tools.

Once our estimate has been formed, however, the other half of the process follows the same set of ideas quite consistently, no matter whether we may be dealing with a single probability or with an entire distribution curve. In what follows it will be our purpose, so far as possible, to cause this underlying unity to show through the confusion of algebraic detail which we cannot entirely avoid.

146. Some Instructive Illustrations; The Biased Die

We return to the consideration of Example 145.1.

If the die was a true die, the expectation was just one-third the number of throws, or 105,224. The difference is not very great—about $1\frac{1}{3}\%$—certainly not great enough to convince us offhand that the die was bad. We therefore begin with the assumption that it was *good* and attempt to find out whether that assumption is plausible. To this end we apply our criterion of goodness of fit, and compute the probability that an experiment *conducted with a true die* would give a result that is at least as unlikely as 106,602 5's or 6's.

This is not very difficult. In fact, the case is one to which the binomial distribution applies directly,[9] the number of trials being 315,672 and the (assumed) probability $\frac{1}{3}$. We know that with so large a number of trials the binomial distribution is very accurately approximated by the normal law, provided we choose our unit of measure properly.

On the basis of our hypothesis the deviation of our result from expectation is 1,378 and the standard deviation is $\sqrt{mp(1 - p)} = 264.9$. Measured in terms of this unit the deviation from expectation is $y = 5.20$. Obviously, larger deviations than this are less probable and smaller ones more probable; so our problem becomes that of finding the chance of a deviation at least as big as 5.20.

---

[9] The binomial distribution assumes independent trials *under the same essential conditions.* To avoid monotony, we frequently omit this phrase, but it must be remembered as a basic assumption in many of our discussions. The present is a case at point.

If, as Weldon's experiments proceeded, the corners wore off, or other changes occurred, a systematic drift of the results would probably occur. Such a drift could be detected, if complete data were available, by comparing the last half of the series with the first.

The discussion in the text assumes throughout that conditions were constant throughout the test.

It is clear, in the problem at hand, that any result greater than 106,602 would have been at least as remarkable as that specific one; so, however, would have been results that were equally far removed from expectation on the smaller side. Hence, in our computation we must include both tails of the distribution curve, which can be done by the use of the $\Phi(y)$ in Appendix IV. Entering this with $y = 5.20$ we find, from the last entries in the table, that $\Phi(y) < 0.000,001$. From a larger table its value could be found to be 0.000,000,2. Hence *the chance of a true die giving as improbable a result as did our experiment is only about one in five million.* It is therefore quite likely that the die is asymmetrical *unless there is a very powerful* a priori *reason for thinking otherwise.* As we have no such powerful prejudice, we reject our first estimate of p and seek a better one.

Suppose we adopt, as our second estimate of the probability, the proportion of times a 5 or 6 was actually observed; for we know from Bernoulli's Theorem that this is not likely to differ much from the true value of p. This gives us $\hat{p} = 0.337,699$. But upon this assumption we find that $y = 0$. Naturally any experiment which we might perform would show a deviation as large as this; or, in other words, $\Phi(y)$ is, for this case, unity. But surely this does not mean that our new estimate is absolutely accurate. Instead it merely reflects the fact that we have artificially forced an agreement between the estimate and the experiment by computing the one from the other.

Later on, in dealing with more complicated examples, we shall find that we must always compensate for any such forcing and it will be well for the student to keep in mind until then the present illustration, in which the absurdity of accepting the uncompensated $\Phi(y)$ is quite apparent. The very simplicity of our example, however, makes the present an unsuitable time to discuss the matter. Instead we shall circumvent the difficulty by another method of approach.

We wish to know how far we can trust this experimental approximation to the probability. Surely we can place no confidence in the last 9 of the 0.337,699, for if we had tossed the die just once more we would of necessity have had a frequency ratio of either 0.337,696 or 0.337,702. On the other hand, to write merely 0.33 would be unduly conservative, for we have seen that the departure from 0.333,333 is almost certainly significant, and that departure occurs only in the third place.

Suppose we regard the data as the result of a grand experiment, designed to *measure* the probability p of an imperfect die by repeated independent trials. The precision of such a measure, like any other, may be discussed by the methods of § 141. Here p plays the role of x in that discussion, and the experiment has given us a "best estimate"

$\hat{p} = 0.337,699$. We ask for the interval within which this may be said to lie at, say, the 99% level of confidence. The only significant difference is that, in our present problem, we know the form of the distribution function and can therefore compute $\hat{\sigma}$ from $\hat{p}$ by means of the formula,[10] $\hat{\sigma} = \sqrt{m\hat{p}(1 - \hat{p})} = 265.7$, whereas in §§ 140 to 142 we had to estimate $\hat{\sigma}$ independently from the experimental data. Hence, at the 99% level, the limiting expectations are $m\hat{p} = 106,602 \pm 684$, and therefore the limiting values of p are[11] 0.3377 ± 0.0022.

If, then, p is less than 0.3355 or greater than 0.3399, there is less chance than one in a hundred that an attempt to repeat the experiment would give a result that differed from expectation by as much as did the one under discussion.

We could also have approached the question by assuming various probabilities to be the true one—just as we have already assumed first $\frac{1}{3}$ and then 0.337,699 to be the true one—and finding whether the experiment deviated significantly from them. We list the computations involved in Table 146.1.

TABLE 146.1

Assumed p	Expected Number of 5's or 6's	Deviation	Standard Deviation	y	$\Phi(y)$
0.333	105,119	+1483	264.9	+5.699	0.0000
0.335	105,750	+ 852	265.2	+3.213	0.0013
0.337	106,382	+ 220	265.6	+0.828	0.4076
0.339	107,013	− 411	266.0	−1.545	0.1224
0.341	107,645	−1043	266.4	−3.915	0.0001

It is obvious that the experimental result was not unusual if then probability is 0.337 or 0.339, but would have been quite unusual for $p = 0.335$, and exceedingly so for the other values. Hence, unless there is a powerful reason for doubting it, we are forced to conclude that p is probably between 0.335 and 0.340.

---

[10] This is the standard deviation for the expected number of successes. We could equally well have written the standard deviation for the average number of successes (which is also our best estimate of p). This is $\sigma(\hat{p}) = \sqrt{\hat{p}(1 - \hat{p})/m}$ and would have given directly, at the 99% level, $\Delta p = \pm 0.0022$.

[11] Alternatively, we could write $p = 0.3377 \pm 0.00084$ without mention of a level of significance. It would then be understood that 0.00084 is $\hat{\sigma}_p$ and is to be multiplied by the appropriate y for any desired level.

This is quite consistent with the confidence limits obtained above.[12]

147. Discussion of Example 145.1

There are several things that should be said about the arguments which have been used in the last section.

To begin with, it should be noted that we have done two things that are, in a sense at least, quite distinct. First, we attempted to answer the questions, "Is $\frac{1}{3}$ a sensible value of p?" and "Is 0.337,699 a sensible value for p?" Then we attempted to answer the question, "Within what limits have we succeeded, by our experiment, in confining p?" The first question asks about the legitimacy of our guesses, the second asks about the precision of our experiment.

To deal with these questions we adopted a criterion by means of which to judge whether the *results* of an experiment were compatible with a *hypothesis* regarding it. When applied to the hypothesis $\hat{p} = \frac{1}{3}$, this criterion gave an unambiguous answer: the hypothesis was not consistent with the data. When applied to the hypothesis $\hat{p} = 0.337,699$, it again gave an unambiguous answer: the hypothesis was most certainly consistent with the data. But, as we saw, the consistency in question had been artificially produced. The only one disposable parameter in the assumed binomial distribution was p, and we had so chosen it as to make agreement inevitable.

But while in this latter case compatibility was no longer a useful criterion, we were still able to obtain a meaningful answer to the second question by the theory set forth in §§ 140 and 141. This, it will be recalled, was derived from the Central Limit Theorem.

The breakdown in the test of compatibility (or "goodness of fit," as it is more commonly known) in testing our second hypothesis is especially worthy of note. It is indicative of something that always occurs when parameters of an assumed distribution are artificially forced to agree with experimental data. In the example above the breakdown was complete, and therefore so obvious as to be harmless. But the effect of such artificial forcing seldom reveals itself in such a cooperative manner. We shall have more to say on this matter in § 149.

148. Some Instructive Illustrations; Weldon's Dice Data

The figures which we gave in Example 145.1 were totals obtained from an experiment made by the English biologist, Weldon, who

---

[12] This example emphasizes the caution which should be exercised in accepting a statistical ratio as the measure of a probability. Even after 315,672 trials, even the third digit is in doubt at the 99% level.

performed it under circumstances somewhat different from those stated in the example. Instead of using one die he used twelve, throwing all twelve at once and recording the number of 5's and 6's that appeared. Table 148.1 contains a summary of his results. We shall

TABLE 148.1

WELDON'S DICE DATA

Number of 5's or 6's	Observed Frequency	Frequency Ratio
0	185	0.007033
1	1,149	0.043678
2	3,265	0.124116
3	5,475	0.208127
4	6,114	0.232418
5	5,194	0.197445
6	3,067	0.116589
7	1,331	0.050597
8	403	0.015320
9	105	0.003991
10	14	0.000532
11	4	0.000152
12	0	0.000000

Total 26,306

now turn our attention to the data in this form, considering in particular the two questions which follow:

EXAMPLE 148.1.—*Are the data in Table 148.1 consistent with the assumption that the twelve dice were unbiased?*

EXAMPLE 148.2.—*Are the data in Table 148.1 consistent with the assumption that the probability of 5 or 6 had the same value 0.3377 for each of the twelve dice?*[13]

[13] If we admit that the dice are very probably all different, and denote the probabilities of showing 5 or 6 by p', p'', ..., p^{xii}, we can so determine these p's that all of Weldon's observed values agree with their expectations. This is exactly analogous to what we did in the latter half of § 146. Before we could place much reliance in our results, however, we should be forced to find within what limits each of these values would have to be confined if the actual observations were not to be too improbable. That is, we should have to determine the precision of this experimental determination of the various p's.

This procedure is probably a more logical one to follow than either of those outlined in the examples, but unfortunately it requires a great deal of computation in finding the first estimates of the p's, and requires a more complicated form of statement regarding the limits to which they must be confined. In fact, it is not a practical method at all unless the problem justifies considerable labor.

The questions which we have formulated are, on the other hand, not at all difficult to deal with from a computational standpoint.

We shall find that it is best to carry these two examples through simultaneously, as most of our remarks about one of them will be equally true of the other also.

Our argument will be very similar to that in § 146. We shall sum up the probabilities of all events which, by our hypothesis, are less likely than the one that occurred; and to do this we shall replace the sum by an integral. But we shall have to deal with a larger number of variables.

The first step is to determine how much the data of Table 148.1 deviate from what we would have expected from our two hypotheses.

When twelve dice are thrown, the chance that just j show 5's or 6's is, in either case, given by the binomial distribution[14]

$$p_j = C_j^{12} p^j (1 - p)^{12-j};$$

the only difference being that the p is $\frac{1}{3}$ in one case and 0.3377 in the

TABLE 148.2

DISCUSSION OF WELDON'S DICE DATA IF DICE WERE TRUE

Number of 5's and 6's	Probability	Observed Frequency	Expected Frequency	Deviation from Expectation	Divergence
j	p_j	n_j	$\epsilon(n_j)$	δ_j	$\dfrac{\delta_j^2}{\epsilon(n_j)}$
0	0.007707	185	202.75	− 17.75	1.554
1	0.046244	1,149	1,216.50	− 67.50	3.745
2	0.127171	3,265	3,345.37	− 80.37	1.931
3	0.211952	5,475	5,575.61	−100.61	1.815
4	0.238446	6,114	6,272.56	−158.56	4.008
5	0.190757	5,194	5,018.05	+175.95	6.169
6	0.111275	3,067	2,927.20	+139.80	6.677
7	0.047689	1,331	1,254.51	+ 76.49	4.664
8	0.014903	403	392.04	+ 10.96	0.306
9	0.003312	105	87.12	+ 17.88	3.670
10	0.000497	14⎫			
11	0.000045	4⎬ 14.31		+ 3.69	0.952
12	0.000002	0⎭			
			26,306.02		$\chi^2 = 35.491$

---

[14] We would ordinarily write $P(j)$ instead of p_j, but the uses which we are to make of the symbol in the present case are such that it is desirable to use the simpler symbol.

other. The second columns of Tables 148.2 and 148.3 are obtained by direct computation from this formula.

The third column contains the observed frequences taken from Table 148.1. The fourth column gives the expected value of each n_j; since each of Weldon's 26,306 throws constituted an independent trial this is just $26,306p_j$. The fifth column shows the deviations from expectation.

We must next attempt to find out how compatible these deviations are with the hypotheses set forth in the examples.

Viewed broadly, the j's constitute a complete set of mutually exclusive events, for on a single throw of the twelve dice there must be either no successes, or one, or two, or some other number not exceeding twelve. Moreover, Weldon's 26,306 throws constitute repeated independent trials of exactly the kind contemplated in § 43, and if we desired, we could compute from equation (43.1) the chance that another 26,306 throws conducted under the conditions laid down in

TABLE 148.3

DISCUSSION OF WELDON'S DICE DATA IF DICE WERE EQUALLY BIASED

Number of 5's and 6's	Probability	Observed Frequency	Expected Frequency	Deviation from Expectation	Divergence
j	p_j	n_j	$\epsilon(n_j)$	δ_j	$\dfrac{\delta_j^2}{\epsilon(n_j)}$
0	0.007123	185	187.38	− 2.38	0.030
1	0.043584	1,149	1,146.51	+ 2.49	0.005
2	0.122225	3,265	3,215.24	+ 49.76	0.770
3	0.207736	5,475	5,464.70	+ 10.30	0.019
4	0.238324	6,114	6,269.35	− 155.35	3.849
5	0.194429	5,194	5,144.65	+ 79.35	1.231
6	0.115660	3,067	3,042.54	+ 24.46	0.197
7	0.050549	1,331	1,329.73	+ 1.27	0.001
8	0.016109	403	423.76	− 20.76	1.017
9	0.003650	105	96.03	+ 8.97	0.838
10	0.000558	14 ⎫			
11	0.000052	4 ⎬	16.11	+ 1.89	0.222
12	0.000002	0 ⎭			
			26,306.00		$\chi^2 = 8.179$

Example 148.1 would exactly reproduce Weldon's results. That, however, is not quite what we need. Instead the criterion laid down in § 145 requires the probability that such a test would give a result that is *no more likely* than Weldon's, which would seem to require the addition of a prodigious number of terms of the form (43.1).

In § 122, however, we learned that the multinomial distribution can be approximately represented by the normal law (122.7) in which, as we see from (122.8), each x_j^2 is, in the notation of Tables 148.2 and 148.3,

$$x_j^2 = \frac{(n_j - mp_j)^2}{mp_j} = \frac{\delta_j^2}{\epsilon(n_j)}. \tag{148.1}$$

These values of x_j^2 are set forth in the last columns of the tables. The sum χ^2 at the foot of each of these columns therefore corresponds to the Σx_j^2 which occurs in the exponent of (122.7). It is, in other words, equivalent to the r^2 in the hyperspherical coordinates of (122.10).

This approximation permits us to simplify the use of our criterion in much the same way that, in the case of the binomial distribution, we calculated sums by integrating the normal function.

149. The Measure of the Goodness of Fit, $P(>\chi^2)$

In Tables 148.2 and 148.3 we have 13 different variables, but it will be wise for us to think for a moment in terms of only three so that we may visualize certain geometrical ideas. Suppose, then, that we had only the three variables n_1, n_2, n_3, so that (122.7) reduced simply to

$$P(n_1, n_2, n_3) = K\, e^{-\frac{1}{2}(x_1^2 + x_2^2 + x_3^2)} = K\, e^{-\frac{1}{2}r^2}.$$

Clearly, $P(n_1, n_2, n_3)$ has the same value at all points of the sphere

$$x_1^2 + x_2^2 + x_3^2 = r^2. \tag{149.1}$$

Clearly, also, the larger r is, the smaller the probability. Hence the combinations of n's which are less likely than the one observed are precisely those for which $r^2 > \chi^2$.

When written explicitly in terms of the n's (149.1) becomes the ellipsoid

$$\frac{(n_1 - mp_1)^2}{mp_1} + \frac{(n_2 - mp_2)^2}{mp_2} + \frac{(n_3 - mp_3)^2}{mp_3} = r^2. \tag{149.2}$$

In a space of a dimensions the situation is the same. To any value of r there corresponds an ellipsoid in the space of $(n_1, n_2, \ldots, n_a)$. Different values of r define a set of such ellipsoids, all having the same center $(mp_1, mp_2, \ldots, mp_a)$, and no two intersecting. They form a sort of nest, one within another, of such a nature that the probability P decreases progressively as we go outward from their common center.

This nest of ellipsoids is a representation of the probabilities assigned by our working hypothesis ($p = \frac{1}{3}$ or $\hat{p} = 0.3377$) to the sets of n's which lie on them. The shell for which $r^2 = \chi^2$ is the one upon which the experimental data lie. Hence, to find the sum of the probabilities of all less likely events we need only integrate over all the volume *outside* the χ^2-ellipsoid.

The ellipsoid (149.2) in n-space becomes the sphere (149.1) in x-space, with its center at the origin and its radius equal to r. This, indeed, is the significance of the x's; they are deviations measured in such units that equal "vector deviations" are equally likely, no matter what their "directions." Our integration, therefore, extends over all those admissible values that lie outside a sphere of radius χ.

In a moment we shall discuss this word "admissible," for some sets of values of $\{n_j\}$ are not. Leaving this out of account for the moment, however, we note that if we use hyperspherical coordinates, (122.10) gives at once

$$P_{a'}(r) = K' e^{-r^2/2} r^{a'-1}, \tag{149.3}$$

where K' includes the constant obtained by integrating over all values of the θ's, and a' is the number of dimensions in the space over which we integrate. Outside a three-dimensional sphere, for example, the integrand would be $e^{-r^2/2} r^2 \, dr$.

The total probability outside the χ^2-sphere is (writing $r^2 = 2u$)

$$P(> \chi^2) = K'' \int_{\chi^2/2}^{\infty} e^{-u} u^{\frac{1}{2}a'-1} \, du. \tag{149.4}$$

Why are not all sets of n_j's admissible? For one thing, they must satisfy the equation

$$n_1 + n_2 + \ldots n_a = m, \tag{122.2}$$

or, in terms of the x's,

$$\sqrt{p_1}\, x_1 + \sqrt{p_2}\, x_2 + \ldots + \sqrt{p_a}\, x_a = 0. \tag{149.5}$$

This is required by both Example 148.1 and Example 148.2. It is therefore not fair to use, as a criterion for the plausibility of our assumed conditions, the unconditional probability of getting a result that is as unusual as Weldon's. Instead we must get the *conditional* probability that a test, conducted with the probabilities listed in Table 148.3, *but required to satisfy the auxiliary condition (149.5)*, would give a more unusual result than Weldon's.

In addition, Example 148.2 differs from Example 148.1 in precisely the same way that the second discussion of Example 145.1 differed from the first: an unnatural degree of agreement has been forced upon the data by the act of computing $\hat{p} = 0.3377$ from it. To be exact, this requires that

$$\sum jn_j = m\sum j\hat{p}_j,$$ (149.6)

or

$$\sum j\sqrt{\hat{p}_j}\, x_j = 0.$$ (149.7)

So, in dealing with this example we shall have to get the conditional probability of a less likely set of n's, *if both (149.5) and (149.7) are* satisfied.

Thinking again in terms of three dimensions, we note that both (149.5) and (149.7) are of the form

$$b_1 x_1 + b_2 x_2 + b_3 x_3 = 0$$

and define planes which pass through the origin. With one such condition, the admissible points are those lying in this plane; and the admissible region of integration is the exterior of the circle in which it is intersected by the χ^2-sphere. With two conditions, the admissible region is reduced to the line in which the two planes meet.

The same situation exists in general. A single linear[15] condition upon our variables (there is never less than one, because the condition (122.2) must always be satisfied) reduces us from a space of a dimensions to one of $a - 1$ dimensions and requires that we integrate (149.3) over all those portions of this space which are further from the origin than a certain predetermined amount χ. And q conditions reduce us to a space of $a - q$ dimensions, again requiring an integration over all that region that lies outside a hypersphere of radius χ. So far as computation is concerned, therefore, we are interested only in the integral of $K\, e^{-r^2/2}$ in a space of $a' = a - q$ dimensions. This explains the use of a' instead of a in (149.4).

All that remains is to determine the constant K'', which is easily done by observing that the integral of the probability density over the entire space must be unity. This leads to

$$P_{a'}(> \chi^2) = \frac{1}{(\tfrac{1}{2}a' - 1)!} \int_{\chi^2/2}^{\infty} e^{-u}\, u^{\frac{1}{2}a' - 1}\, du.$$ (149.8)

---

[15] Such conditions usually arise from using the moments of the data to determine parameters of the distribution. This (fortunately) leads to *linear* "equations of constraint," so that other possibilities need not be discussed.

This formula, like many others of frequent use, has been reduced to the form of tables, one of which is given in Appendix VIII. The values of P are given on the headings of the columns, and the values of χ^2 in the body of the table. In order to find the probability of any estimate, therefore, it is necessary only to determine a', locate χ^2 in the body of the table, and read the corresponding value of P from the column heading.

150. The Solution of Examples 148.1 and 148.2

We are now prepared to renew our discussion of Weldon's data, with the direct purpose of determining whether the fact that his results were classified as indicated in Table 148.1 affects our conclusion that the dice were probably biased.

There were originally 13 possible events corresponding to $j = 0$, 1, ..., 12, but in Tables 148.2 and 148.3 the last three were combined and regarded as a single event "more than 9 fives or sixes." The reason for this is to be found in the first steps of the derivation of (122.7), where every $n_j!$ was replaced by its Stirling approximation. This is inaccurate when n_j is too small. But how we divide the data up is entirely a matter for our own judgment—we can always combine several events into a more inclusive event if we wish, and thus assure that a fair number of observations fall in each.

Due to this grouping there are just $a = 11$ classes in Table 148.2; and since (122.2) must also be satisfied, $a' = 10$. Thus we enter Appendix VIII with $a' = 10$ and find that $\chi^2 = 35.49$ is well off the right-hand side of the table; hence the probability of such an occurrence with true dice is very much less than 0.01. From a more extensive table it would be found to be about 0.0001. Looked at as a whole, as we did in § 148, Weldon's result appeared to be even less likely, but from either standpoint it appears highly probable that the dice were inaccurate.

Passing now to Example 148.2, we have made use of *two* linear relations among the n_j's: (122.2) and (149.6). Hence we must enter Appendix VIII with $a' = 9$ and $\chi^2 = 8.179$. We find $P = 0.52$. That is, if all dice were identically biased so that the probability of throwing a 5 or 6 was 0.3377, a divergence as great as that observed could be expected at least as often as not.

I must emphasize again that these figures, taken only by themselves, *decidedly do not say that the dice were biased.* They only force one of two conclusions upon us:

(1) *Either* the dice are biased,
(2) *Or* a very unexpected thing has happened.

It is only because we feel that conclusion (1) is a plausible one—as of course we do in this case—that we choose it in preference to the less plausible (2).

151. Résumé of the Test of Goodness of Fit

We have arrived at the chi-squared test through the consideration of an experiment for which the multinomial distribution was clearly appropriate. But the test itself is not limited to such a narrow use. On the contrary, it is one of the most versatile tests in Statistical Theory, and applies to substantially any situation where it is desired to test whether data are or are not consistent with a postulated distribution, whatever its form. In the case of data which can reasonably be assumed to be drawn from a normal population its use is even more general.

It is beyond the scope of this book to follow these ramifications, but a few remarks are possible.

Suppose, then, that we are concerned with an experiment which has led to certain data, and with a hypothesis that a certain probability distribution is appropriate to the experiment. We wish to test the plausibility of this hypothesis by means of the criterion set forth in § 145.

The experiment may be such that only a discrete set of events may occur—as was the case with the dice problem which we have been considering—or it may concern itself with such a variable as the diameter of Saturn's ring, which can take any value in a continuous interval. In either case we may divide the entire range of variation into intervals (or classes) such as those shown in Fig. 151.1. If the variable can take only a discrete set of values, it may often be natural to make each of these values a distinct class; we did this in the case of the dice experiment, except that the infrequent values 10, 11, and 12 were classed together. But this is not necessary. We can classify our data largely as we see fit. The classes need not even contain equal ranges of the variable, as an indication of which we have made them obviously unequal in the figure.

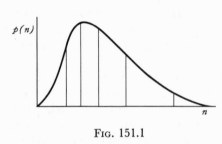

$p(n)$

n

FIG. 151.1

To each of these classes corresponds a definite probability, represented in Fig. 151.1 by the area under the corresponding segment of the curve. Hence we can compute the probability of m events partitioning themselves among the classes in such a way that these are exactly n_j in the j'th class. When we do so we obtain the multinomial distribution (122.1). This is too complicated for purposes of computation but is quite accurately represented by the generalized normal distribution

$$P(n_1, n_2, \ldots, n_a) = K\, e^{-\frac{1}{2}\Sigma_j x_j^2} = K\, e^{-\frac{1}{2}r^2},$$

provided none of the numbers n_j is too small. This generalized normal distribution has as its single variable the quantity r^2 formed from the sum of the "divergences" (148.1) of the individual classes, the term "divergence" meaning the square of the deviation of n_j from its expectation, divided by the expectation.

To test the plausibility of our hypothesis we find the sum of the divergences of the experimental data, which we call χ^2, and then ask for the chance of an experiment giving a less likely (i.e., a larger) value of r^2 than this. The answer is the integral of (149.3) over all values of r which exceed χ. It is given by (149.8), or for practical purposes by the table in Appendix VIII. If the $P(> \chi^2)$ thus obtained is not too small, we conclude that our assumed distribution is a plausible one *in the sense that the observations would not be miraculous if it were the correct one*; if the probability is very small, we conclude that the experiment was probably conducted under conditions which differed materially from those assumed.

The assurance we feel in these conclusions must be tempered by our judgment as to their inherent plausibility. We must not, for instance, accept a preposterous assumption merely because we get a high value of P; or reject one which is almost certain to be true as being disproved by a low value of P: for a low value of P merely says that the result is unusual, not that it could not occur.

When we compute P we find that it has different values according to the number of classes into which we have divided our range of possibilities. Hence the table of P's is a double-entry table, arranged according to values of χ^2 and the "class-number" a'. Moreover, we find that this class-number is not the total number of classes a, but the number that, under the conditions of the problem, may be assigned values arbitrarily—that is, the number of *independent* classes. Since the sum of all the n_j's must equal the total number of events, no more than $a - 1$ of them can ever be assigned arbitrarily; and if in addition we make use of our data to compute constants of our assumed formula, as in the case of Table 148.3 we used the data to find the appropriate value of p, we must reduce the class-number by one for each such condition. This is the only difficulty in the *application* of the test for goodness of fit; its *justification*, as we have seen, is another matter.

152. Null Hypothesis; Errors of Types I and II

The concepts so far presented in this chapter are often stated by statisticians in an equivalent, but slightly different form.

To every hypothesis there is a complementary, or counter hypothesis. Thus, in Example 145.1, when we ask, Was the die true? we are seeking to choose between two alternative hypotheses

A. The die is true;
B. The die is biased.

One of these may be called the *null hypothesis* and the other the *test hypothesis*. Which is which? Since the two are assumed to be complementary, it would appear to be immaterial which choice is made, but there is a pragmatic consideration which usually is observed and which can be illustrated as follows:

To *prove* hypothesis A (or to disprove B) would be most difficult, for no matter how great the accumulation of favorable evidence, there would always be a residual chance that the die was at least slightly biased. But to *disprove* it and therefore accept B is less difficult.

It is customary in statistical practice to call that one of a pair of alternative hypotheses which can most readily be proved false the null hypothesis.[16]

Thus, in the case of Example 145.1, we would call A above the "null hypothesis." In § 146 we found convincing evidence that it was false. We therefore *rejected* the null hypothesis and *accepted* the test hypothesis instead.

We could also frame for Example 145.1 the pair of hypotheses

A. Null hypothesis: The probability p lies outside the limits 0.3377 $\pm$ 0.0030.

B. Test hypothesis: The probability p lies inside the limits 0.3377 $\pm$ 0.0030.

Here again it would be virtually impossible to prove B false, but the phrasing of the hypotheses implies our intention not to *accept* it unless we have adequate reason to *reject* the other. As a matter of fact, we do have such reason: we found in § 146 that the 99% confidence interval was only ± 0.0022, so that the chance that the null hypothesis is true is very remote.

When we state the problem this way, we may also agree on the weight of evidence (i.e., a probability p_1) on which we will *reject* A, and the probability p_2 on which we will *accept* B. These need not be the same. In the second treatment of Example 145.1, for instance, we might take $p_1 = 0.80$ and $p_2 = 0.99$. Then, since we found in § 146 that the confidence interval is narrower than $\pm$ 0.0030 at the 99% level, we would *both* reject A and accept B. But if we had found that the interval was $\pm$ 0.0030 at a 90% level of confidence,

---

[16] Some statisticians restrict the term "null hypothesis" to statements of precisely the form "A parameter of the population has a stated value." In the above example, "$p = \frac{1}{3}$." The above definition is broader, and I believe more in keeping with general usage. It includes, for example, statements such as "In America, the distribution of income is independent of the distribution of intelligence quotient."

Note in this connection the discussion of Example 145.1 which follows immediately above, and also Example 155.1.

we would do neither—we would say simply that both hypotheses remained undecided.[17]

Now clearly, since statistical evidence is seldom absolute, any of the following situations may exist:

The null hypothesis may be	and from the data we may infer it is
True	True
	False: Type I error
False	True: Type II error
	False

In the second and third of these eventualities our conclusion would be wrong. They are often referred to as errors of Type I and II, as indicated.

Thus, in Example 145.1, the null hypothesis was "The die is true." We rejected it on the basis of the evidence. But the data could have been obtained with a true die; the chance of this is fantastically small, but not zero. If this very unlikely event occurred, we made an error of Type I.

It could also happen (although in the example it did not) that a biased coin by accident gave heads and tails in almost identical numbers. In such a case we would erroneously accept the null hypothesis. This would be an error of Type II.

The example which follows is a further illustration of the use of the χ^2-test. Our discussion of it is phrased in the jargon of the present section, so that the reader may become somewhat more familiar with its use.

153. Some Instructive Illustrations; Some Telephone Data

EXAMPLE 153.1.—*In Chapter XII we shall find that there is reason to believe that the probability of just n pieces of telephone apparatus being in use at a given instant is often given by the Poisson formula. One case, in particular, to which we should expect this formula to apply reasonably well is the type of automatic equipment known as the "sender." Table 153.1 records 3754 observations upon the number of senders busy in a panel type machine switching exchange. Are these observations consistent with the Poisson distribution?*

Here a suitable null hypothesis and test hypothesis are, respectively:

The data are compatible with the Poisson distribution; and
They are not.

The Poisson Law is determined solely by its expectation ϵ. In the case of our data the average number of busy senders is 10.44, and if we use this value as our estimate of $\hat{\epsilon}$, the Poisson formula gives the values shown in the third

---

[17] Note that $p_1 > p_2$ would be absurd.

TABLE 153.1

NUMBER OF BUSY SENDERS IN A TELEPHONE EXCHANGE

Number Busy	Observed Frequency	Expected Frequency	Deviation, δ	Divergence, x^2
0	0 ⎤			
1	5 ⎬	7.24	+ 11.76	19.10
2	14 ⎦			
3	24	20.83	+ 3.17	0.48
4	57	54.36	+ 2.64	0.13
5	111	113.50	− 2.50	0.06
6	197	197.49	− .49	0.00
7	278	294.53	− 16.53	0.93
8	378	384.38	− 6.38	0.11
9	418	445.89	− 27.89	1.74
10	461	465.51	− 4.51	0.04
11	433	441.82	− 8.82	0.18
12	413	384.38	+ 28.62	2.14
13	358	308.69	+ 49.31	7.88
14	219	230.20	− 11.20	0.54
15	145	160.22	− 15.22	1.45
16	109	104.54	+ 4.46	0.19
17	57	64.20	− 7.20	0.81
18	43	37.24	+ 5.76	0.89
19	16	20.46	− 4.46	0.97
20	7	10.68	− 3.68	1.27
21	8	5.31	+ 2.69	1.36
22	3	2.52	+ 0.48	0.09
		3753.99	+ 0.01	$\chi^2 = 40.36$

column under the heading "Expected Frequency."[18] The deviations from expectation are listed in the fourth column, the divergences in the fifth, and their total, which is χ^2, at the bottom. The quantities are all large enough that there is no occasion to combine the classes, except the top three. Hence there are in all 21 classes. However, since we have made use of $\Sigma n_j = 3754$ and determined $\hat{\epsilon}$ from the data, only 19 of these classes are independent. We therefore look up the entry 40.36 in the row of Appendix VIII which

[18] These values can be found approximately by interpolation between columns 10 and 11 of Appendix VI. However, linear interpolation in this table is not very accurate, and the expected frequencies in Table 153.1 were taken from a larger table of $^\infty P_j{}'$.

corresponds to the class number 19, and find that it is beyond the right-hand margin of the table—apparently at about $P = 0.005$.

The fit is none too good, and if we consider only the statistical data, we would reject this distribution as unsuitable. But because of the theoretical basis which underlies the choice of the Poisson distribution, the *a priori* probability of its validity is strong, and the weight of statistical evidence required to avoid the hazard of a Type I error is correspondingly great.

Perhaps, under the circumstances, the prudent course would be to re-examine the experiment closely for anything that could cause the traffic *not* to be individually and collectively random, as required by the Poisson distribution.[19]

It would then be up to the investigator to decide whether to reject the null hypothesis, with some chance of an error of Type I, or accept it, with an obvious danger of an error of the other kind.

154. Dependence and Independence; Introductory Remarks

We come now to the third topic of this chapter: the determination of whether two chance variables are or are not independent, and in this connection it is important to understand just what independence— or rather, the lack of it—implies.

Consider, first, the case of a hermetically sealed and rigid container filled with air. We know that the pressure of the gas will change as the air temperature changes. Air temperature and air pressure, therefore, are clearly not independent.

Next, suppose this sealed container and an open bucket of water are standing side by side, and suppose we keep a record of the pressure in the container and the rate at which water evaporates. Again, the two will rise and fall together.

Finally, suppose that a careful record was made of the skin pigment and annual income of all residents of a community. Again, there would be a tendency for the two to be related.

But there is an obvious progression in these three examples. In the first, if our measurements were precise, they could be repeated exactly as often as we wish: in fact, if the temperature range was not too great, the two would be linearly related. There is, in this case, a direct functional relationship.

The second case is less absolute. Even with precise measurement the data would be different on different days, because the rate of evaporation would vary with wind and humidity as well as temperature.

If the data for the three examples were plotted, the results would resemble those in Fig. 154.1. In the first case, there would be a single, well-defined pressure for each temperature, and hence just one point on each ordinate. In the second, several different rates of evaporation

---

[19] In particular, why were 2, 3, and 4 senders found busy more often than anticipated?

would have been observed for each specific pressure in the container, but the points would nevertheless be relatively compact. In the third case, a very wide scattering can be expected; for both among light-skinned and dark-skinned persons, some will be much more prosperous than others.

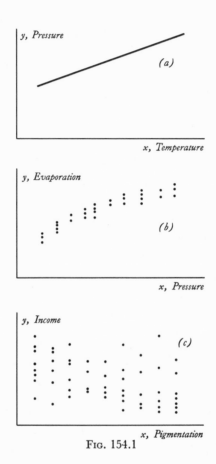

FIG. 154.1

We express this difference by saying that in the second and third cases the variables are *correlated*, whereas in the first they are *functionally related*.

We can also say, from our general knowledge of sociological factors, that there will be systematic differences between charts of the third kind made in different communities. In Mobile or Johannesburg, for example, we would expect a stronger correlation than in San Francisco or Tel Aviv, and it is just possible that in New Delhi there may be none at all. These are important and interesting inferences: too important in fact to be left solely to the vague, and by no means identical, impressions which various persons would receive from looking at the charts themselves. We need a rational method of deciding whether two chance variables are in fact correlated; and also a quantitative index for the nature and extent of the dependence, if one exists.

For the first of these we already have the necessary equipment, as the example which follows will show.

155. Some Instructive Illustrations; A Test of Independence

EXAMPLE 155.1.—*An experiment which gives a pair of numbers x and y was repeated 100 times with the results set forth in the main body of Table 155.1. It is desired to know whether the chance variables x and y are independent.*

If the variables are independent, the distribution $p(x,y)$ must be of the form $p(x)\,p(y)$. Of course, we do not know either $p(x,y)$, $p(x)$, or $p(y)$, but we may estimate $p(x)$ and $p(y)$ from the data, and then use the

TABLE 155.1

y	$x=1$	$x=2$	$x=3$	$x=4$	$x=5$	$x=6$	$x=7$	$x=8$	$n(y)$
$+2$		1		1		1			3
$+1$	1		3			1			5
0		4		2		2			8
-1	4		10		1		1		16
-2		7		13		6		1	27
-3			12		12		1		25
-4				5		4		3	12
-5					3		1		4
$n(x)$	5	12	25	21	16	13	4	4	100

χ^2-test to determine whether the hypothesis of independence (our null-hypothesis) must be rejected. To simplify the computation we classify the numbers in pairs, thus producing Table 155.2.

In this table, the sum of a row is the total number of y's in the class; when divided by 100 it is the *proportion* of y's in the class, which we take as our estimate $\hat{p}(y)$. Similarly from the columns we get $\hat{p}(x)$; and for our estimate of the joint distribution we take $\hat{p}(x,y) = \hat{p}(x)\,\hat{p}(y)$. The expected number in any class (x,y) is just 100 times this product, and is recorded in the table in parentheses.

Squaring the difference of the numbers in each box, dividing by the expectation, and adding we get $\chi^2 = 20.40$. Three of the $\hat{p}(y)$'s and three of the $\hat{p}(x)$'s have, however, been computed from the data (the fourth is fixed by the requirement that $\Sigma p = 1$), and we have also made the sum of the expectations equal to the number of trials.[20] This is a total of 7 conditions. Hence $a' = 16 - 7 = 9$; and with this we find $P(> \chi^2) = 0.016$. There is, then, only one chance in 60 that the data are independent.

TABLE 155.2

y	$x = 1,2$	$x = 3,4$	$x = 5,6$	$x = 7,8$	$\hat{p}(y)$
+2, +1	2 (1.36)	4 (3.68)	1 (2.32)	1 (0.64)	0.08
0, −1	8 (4.08)	12 (11.04)	3 (6.96)	1 (1.92)	0.24
−2, −3	7 (8.84)	25 (23.92)	18 (15.08)	2 (4.16)	0.52
−4, −5	0 (2.72)	5 (7.36)	7 (4.64)	4 (1.28)	0.16
$\hat{p}(x)$	0.17	0.46	0.29	0.08	1.00

$$\chi^2 = 20.40; \quad a' = 16 - 7 = 9; \quad P = 0.016.$$

156. Regression

To study the second question raised in § 154—the nature and extent of the dependence of correlated chance variables—we need to study a diagram such as part (c) of Fig. 154.1 in detail.

Consider, then, a single ordinate on this chart (i.e., the class of persons of a particular complexion), and let Fig. 156.1 represent the

[20] Contingency tables, such as Table 155.1, are not necessarily square. Note, however, that if all but one of the $\hat{p}$'s on each margin are determined from the data, the number of conditions is precisely the number of classes along the bottom and one side of the table, leaving for a' the number of classes in a table with one less column and one less row; in our case 3 × 3.

distribution of income in this particular class. In this figure, then, the abscissa represents annual income and the ordinate the proportion of the class which has that income. Also, let ϵ be the expectation and σ the standard deviation of this distribution. Then, as we know, ϵ has the very important property that, if the income of the entire population was shared equally, the income of each would be ϵ. It is, therefore, the one single parameter that best describes the prosperity of this group.

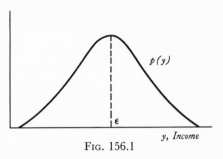

Fig. 156.1

But ϵ also has another interesting property: if differences in income are measured from some arbitrary value η', and a person selected at random has income y, the expected value of the square of the difference $(y - \eta')^2$ is least when $\eta' = \epsilon$. This merely says in words that $\epsilon_2(y)$ is a minimum when the origin is so chosen that $\epsilon_1(y) = 0^{21}$, which by (96.3) is clearly true. The point on $p(y)$ which possesses these properties is called the "point of regression."

DEFINITION 156.1. *In the distribution $p(y)$ for a single chance variable, the point of regression is the point at which y has its expected value $\epsilon_1(y)$.*

Suppose, now, we return to part (c) of Fig. 154.1. There is on every ordinate, a point of regression, and taken together these define a curve, the *curve of regression*. Hence

DEFINITION 156.2. *In the distribution $p(x,y)$ for two chance variables x and y, the curve of regression of y on x is the locus of the conditional expectations $\epsilon_1(y|x)$. That is, it is defined by the equation*

$$y = \epsilon_1(y|x).$$

We have said that the point of regression on a single ordinate is the point which best described the prosperity of that particular class in the population. In the same sense the curve of regression is the curve which best describes the way prosperity varies from class to class.

---

[21] Written as an equation, this statement is that

$$I(x) = \int (y - \eta')^2 p(y|x) \, dy \tag{156.1}$$

is a minimum when $y = \eta'$. The notation $I(x)$ and $p(y|x)$ expresses the fact that this statement is true for every x.

All that has been said so far refers to the idealized population of statistical theory, which, like the sample space and distribution function of probability theory, is an abstract concept. Any specific body of data, even if it includes every person in the real community, must be thought of as a sample drawn from this idealized population. We ask, therefore, what we may learn regarding the ideal population from the data at hand.

Here the result of § 141 comes at once to our service; the best estimate we can make of the point of regression on any one ordinate is clearly $\hat{e} = \bar{y}$, both symbols referring, as did Fig. 156.1, to that segment of the population characterized by a particular x. Hence, taking account of the practical necessity of dividing x into finite segments (classes):

THEOREM 156.1. *The best estimate of the curve of regression of y on x that can be formed from a sample of data is a curve passing through the means of the classes into which the variable x is partitioned.*

In principle this is very nice. But we have seen that in practice the precision of such estimates is low—that is, the confidence interval is likely to be quite wide—because the quantity of data is limited. There

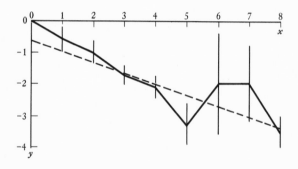

FIG. 156.2

are exceptions. The number of people in the United States is so large that, even if classified by year of birth, there will be more than 1,000,000 in all classes except the very aged. Hence the average income for each class, if complete and accurate data were available, should not differ widely from the theoretical expectation; in other words, these averages should define the curve of regression of income on age quite precisely.

Where data are less plentiful—and this is the more usual case—the situation is likely to resemble Fig. 156.2. This represents the two chance variables x and y (which, except for the fact that y is negative, might be age and income in a limited sample of a community);[22] it is presumed classified in intervals with midpoints at $x = 1, 2, 3, \ldots$; and in each group the best estimate of the point of regression and its interval of uncertainty (confidence interval) are indicated. Clearly in this case the jaggedness of the curve is a statistical artifact and conveys no reliable information. Still, there is an indication of a general downward slope, as shown by the dotted line.

In such a situation, where the *curve* of regression cannot reliably be established, the *line* that "best" represents the data may still be useful. It is called *the line of regression of y on x*. Even when the curve of regression could be derived, the line of regression is not without significance, for it portrays the average rate of increase of [the expectation of] y throughout the range of x under investigation.

157. Correlation

How can such a "best" line be determined?

To discuss this question we leave the sample for the moment and turn our attention to the ideal population.

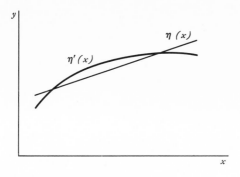

Fig. 157.1

Suppose, then, that we have two chance variables x and y with a distribution function $p(x, y)$, and let the curve of regression of y on x be represented in Fig. 157.1 by

$$\eta'(x) = \epsilon_1(y|x). \tag{157.1}$$

---

[22] It is, in fact, derived from the data of Example 155.1, which will be discussed in greater detail later.

This can be defined in either of two ways: (a) As the curve which, at every value of x, passes through the conditional expectation of y for that x. This is the definition given in § 156. (b) As that curve, among all the curves which can be drawn in the xy-plane, for which the expectation of $(y - \eta')^2$ is least; that is, the curve for which

$$I = \int \int (y - \eta')^2 p(x,y) \, dx \, dy \qquad (157.2)$$

is a minimum.[23]

This suggests two possible criteria for the "best" line $\eta(x)$. It might be that line which most nearly approximates the curve of regression (in the sense that the expectation of $(\eta - \eta')^2$ is a minimum). Or it might be the line for which, among all lines in the xy-plane,

$$I = \int \int (y - \eta)^2 p(x, y) \, dx \, dy \qquad (157.3)$$

is least. It can be shown that these definitions lead to the same line[24]

$$y - \epsilon_1 (y) = \frac{\text{covar}(x, y)}{\sigma_x^2} [x - \epsilon_1(x)]. \qquad (157.4)$$

---

[23] To show that these statements are equivalent, substitute (156.1) and $p(x,y) = p(x) \, p(y|x)$ in (157.2), which gives

$$I = \int I(x) \, p(x) \, dx.$$

Suppose, now, that $\eta'(x) + \delta\eta(x)$ represents any other curve than (157.1), and let the $I(x)$ and I derived from it be $I(x) + \delta I(x)$ and $I + \delta I$. Then, by footnote 21, § 156, $\delta I(x) \geqslant 0$ for every x. Hence, since $p(x)$ is also positive, $\delta I = \int p(x) \, \delta I(x) \, dx \geqslant 0$. That is, any departure from (157.1) increases the value of I.

[24] The demonstrations proceed as follows: To minimize (157.3) with $\eta(x) = \alpha x + \beta$ we have

$$\partial I / \partial \alpha = -2 \int \int (y - \alpha x - \beta) x \, p(x,y) \, dx \, dy = -2[\epsilon_1(xy) - \alpha \epsilon_2(x) - \beta \epsilon_1(x)],$$

$$\partial I / \partial \beta = -2[\epsilon_1(y) - \alpha \epsilon_1(x) - \beta].$$

Setting both of these zero and solving for α and β, we get an equation $y = \eta(x)$ which can easily be put in the form (157.4).

For the other definition we must minimize the integral $I' = \int (\eta' - \eta)^2 p(x) \, dx$ with $\eta' = \epsilon(y|x) = [1/p(x)] \int y \, p(x,y) \, dy$ and $\eta = \alpha x + \beta$. This requires that both $\partial I'/\partial \alpha$ and $\partial I'/\partial \beta$ vanish. But

$$\partial I' / \partial \alpha = -2 \int (\eta' - \eta) x \, p(x) \, dx = -2 \int \int xy \, p(x,y) \, dx \, dy + 2 \int x(\alpha x + \beta) \, p(x) \, dx$$

which, when expressed as expectations is precisely the first of the pair derived above. Similarly $\partial I'/\partial \beta$ gives the second of the pair.

Hence

THEOREM 157.1. *The line of regression of y on x passes through the center of gravity* $[\epsilon_1(x), \epsilon_1(y)]$ *of* $p(x,y)$ *and has a slope* $\mathrm{covar}(x,y)/\sigma_x^2$.

Finally, if the distribution function is put in standard form by writing

$$\eta = \frac{y - \epsilon_1(y)}{\sigma_y}, \qquad \xi = \frac{x - \epsilon_1(x)}{\sigma_x},$$

(157.4) becomes

$$\eta = \frac{\mathrm{covar}(x,y)}{\sigma_x \sigma_y} \xi. \tag{157.5}$$

The reader can readily verify that the coefficient in this equation is equivalent to either $\mathrm{covar}(\xi, \eta)$ or $\epsilon_1(\xi\eta)$.

DEFINITION 157.1. *The quantity*

$$\epsilon_1(\xi\eta) = \mathrm{covar}(x,y)/\sigma_x\sigma_y$$

is called the "correlation coefficient" of the chance variables x and y. It is usually denoted by the symbol r_{xy}. *In this notation* (157.5) *becomes* $\eta = r_{xy}\xi$.

THEOREM 157.2. *The slope of the line of regression of y on x is equal to the correlation coefficient* r_{xy} *when the distribution is in standard form. When not standardized, the slope is* $r_{xy}\sigma_y/\sigma_x$.

158. Discussion of Regression and Correlation

Let us now interpret the results of §§ 156 and 157 in terms of Fig. 154.1.

We set out to find a means of setting forth quantitatively the nature of the dependence of y on x. We found a single well-defined curve, the curve of regression, which accomplishes this end in the sense that the ordinate to this curve, for any x, is the single number which best describes the affluence of that segment of the population. We also found that the variance of the vertical deviations $[y - \epsilon_1(y|x)]^2$ is smaller for that curve than for any other. We found, moreover, that the best estimate of this curve which can be formed from a sample of data is just the curve drawn through the average ordinate of each of the classes (intervals) into which we may elect to subdivide the abscissa.

Unless the sample of data is very large, these averages do not represent $\epsilon_1(y)$ very precisely, and so the result of this construction is likely to be a jagged line whose wiggles convey no significant information.

In such cases it is customary to construct—not the curve which best fits the data—but the *line* which fits best. This is called the *line of regression*. If the distribution is not in standard form, it passes through the point $[\epsilon_1(x), \epsilon_1(y)]$ and has the slope $r_{xy}\sigma_y/\sigma_x$, where r_{xy} is the correlation coefficient. In standard coordinates it passes through the origin and has slope r_{xy}.

It can be shown (see problems 164.34 and 164.35) that the absolute value of r never exceeds 1. It is ± 1 when, and only when, there is a linear functional relation between the variables; that is, when the graph is clear-cut, as in part (*a*) of Fig. 154.1, and is a straight line. A smaller value of r may imply *either* an experiment in which the results scatter, as in parts (*b*) and (*c*), *or* that a functional relation exists but is non-linear. In particular, $r = 0$ means that the line of regression which best fits the experiment is horizontal; this can imply *either* that the chance variables are independent, *or* that the curve of regression is symmetrical,[25] as in Fig. 158.1.

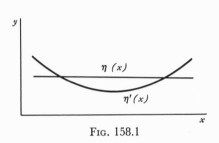

FIG. 158.1

Thus, *whereas r = 1 or any value closely approximating it is clear-cut evidence of a strong dependence of the variables upon one another, r = 0 or values closely approximating it do not, without supporting evidence, imply independence*. (We have already seen, in § 155) how a less ambiguous test can be applied.)

On the other hand, the slope of the line of regression, which is $r_{xy}\sigma_y/\sigma_x$, has an unambiguous meaning. It is the average rate at which y increases with x; or, more precisely, the average change from class to class of the expectation of y in each class.

Finally, in any of the figures 154.1 to 158.1, the horizontal and vertical axes could have been interchanged, and all our arguments would have applied equally well. Thus we would have been led to the notions of a curve of regression and a line of regression *of x on y*. These also afford a best fit to the experiment, but in the sense of minimum variance in the *horizontal* direction as our figures are drawn. To obtain its equation we need only interchange x and y throughout in (157.4) or (157.5). Since $r = \operatorname{covar}(x,y)/\sigma_x\sigma_y$ is symmetrical in x and y and therefore insensitive to interchange of axes, the line of regression of x on y must be

$$\xi = r\,\eta, \text{ or } \eta = \frac{1}{r}\xi.$$

---

[25] More precisely, that the "weighted curve" $y = p(x)\,\eta'(x)$ is symmetrical.

THEOREM 158.1. *When $p(x,y)$ is put in standard form, the lines of regression of y on x and of x on y make equal and opposite angles with the 45° diagonal. Otherwise, the equation of the line of regression of x on y is (157.4) with x and y interchanged.*

159. Some Instructive Illustrations; An Example of Correlated Chance Variables

EXAMPLE 159.1.—*It has been shown in § 155 that the variables x and y of Table 155.1 are not independent.*[26] *Study the nature of the dependence and derive the correlation coefficient and line of regression.*

Along the right-hand margin of Table 155.1 are the values of $n(y) = \Sigma_x n(x,y)$, from which we easily compute

$$\bar{y} = \frac{1}{100} \sum y\, n(y) = -2.02,$$

$$\overline{y^2} = \frac{1}{100} \sum y^2\, n(y) = 6.58,$$

and hence

$$s_y^2 = 2.50.$$

Similarly from the marginal numbers at the bottom we get

$$\bar{x} = 4.06, \qquad \overline{x^2} = 19.34, \qquad s_x^2 = 2.86.$$

Finally, by multiplying each entry in the table by the corresponding xy and adding, we get

$$\mu_1(xy) = \frac{1}{100}\sum_x \sum_y x\, y\, n(x,y) = -9.16.$$

The sample covariance is therefore

$$\text{covar}(x,y) = -9.16 + 2.02 \cdot 4.06 = -0.96,$$

whence

$$r_{xy} = -0.96/\sqrt{2.86 \cdot 2.50} = 0.36.$$

Finally, by (157.4), based on these estimates the line of regression is

$$y + 2.02 = -0.34(x - 4.06). \tag{159.1}$$

Figures 156.2 and 159.1 give a graphical representation of these results. In Fig. 159.1 the groups of dots (which should, in fact, be concentrated at the center of each group) represent the data of Table 155.1. A line drawn through the average of the y's at each value of x

---

[26] More precisely, the hypthesis that they are independent was rejected.

results in the jagged line of Fig. 156.2. As we have said, it is the "best estimate" of the curve of regression; but as can be seen from the vertical strokes, which are the 68% confidence limits, it is not very precise. The straight line is the line of regression (159.1) as determined by the data. It indicates a well-defined tendency for y, on the average, to be larger when x is large than when x is small.

The data of this example were derived from an experiment of the coin-tossing type whose theoretical distribution is known. (See § 160.) It is therefore possible to compute both the theoretical curve of regression and the theoretical regression line. These also are shown in Fig. 159.1, the curve being drawn in, and the linear approximation indicated by dotted line segments near the borders of the diagram.

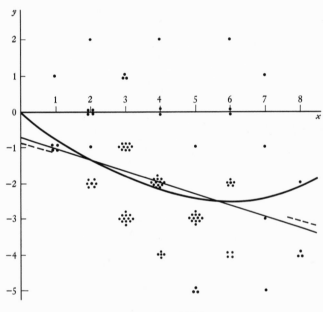

FIG. 159.1

The sample regression line lies quite close to the theoretical one. More significantly, however, both are quite close to the theoretical regression *curve* in the interval from $x = 2$ to $x = 6$, where more than 85% of the results are concentrated.

This example also illustrates another point to which reference was made in § 158. Theoretically x can take values from 0 to 12, although in the experiment neither $x = 0$ nor $x > 8$ occurred. Over the complete range the curve of regression is a parabola symmetrical about the midpoint $x = 6$. Hence, as was said in Footnote 25, § 158, the correlation coefficient would be zero and the line of regression horizontal if the distribution of x were also symmetrical about $x = 6$. Neither would then have given an indication of the true nature of the dependence of y on x, which would have been a rising one over part of the range, and a falling one over an *equally important* part. In our example, both the correlation coefficient and the line of regression reflect the heavy concentration of probability density in the interval $x = 2$, $x = 6$, and report that over this important region y tends to increase numerically as x increases.

160. Rotation of Axes; Correlation Vectors

Let x and y be a pair of chance variables with the distribution $p(x, y)$, and let us introduce new variables u and v by the transformation

$$u = x \cos \alpha + y \sin \alpha,$$
$$v = -x \sin \alpha + y \cos \alpha. \qquad (160.1)$$

This corresponds to a counterclockwise rotation of the axes through the angle α, as indicated in Fig. 160.1.

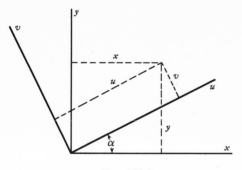

Fig. 160.1

We wish to determine how the correlation coefficient r_{uv} is related to r_{xy}. This requires some rather tedious algebra, but is not otherwise difficult.

From (160.1) we get at once

$$\epsilon_1(u) = \epsilon_1(x) \cos \alpha + \epsilon_1(y) \sin \alpha,$$

$$\epsilon_1(v) = -\epsilon_1(x) \sin \alpha + \epsilon_1(y) \cos \alpha,$$

$$\epsilon_1(uv) = [\epsilon_2(y) - \epsilon_2(x)] \cos \alpha \sin \alpha + \epsilon_1(xy) (\cos^2 \alpha - \sin^2 \alpha).$$

If we now multiply the first two of these and subtract from the second, we obtain, after some simple modifications

$$2 \operatorname{covar}(u,v) = -(\sigma_x^2 - \sigma_y^2) \sin 2\alpha + 2r_{xy} \sigma_x \sigma_y \cos 2\alpha.$$

Note, now, that covar(u, v), and therefore r_{uv} also, will vanish if α is so chosen that the second member of this equation is zero; that is, if $\alpha = \alpha_0$, where

$$\tan 2\,\alpha_0 = \frac{2\,r_{xy}\sigma_x\sigma_y}{\sigma_x{}^2 - \sigma_y{}^2}. \tag{160.2}$$

THEOREM 160.1 *If x and y are correlated chance variables, the linear combinations u and v (160.1), have zero correlation if the angle* α *has the value* α_0 *defined by (160.2).*

It can also be shown (see Problems 164.39, 164.40, and 164.41) that

THEOREM 160.2 *If x and y are correlated chance variables, the linear combinations u and v (160.1), have maximum correlation when* $\alpha = \alpha_0 \pm \pi/4$.

Thus, in Example 155.1, $\tan 2\hat{\alpha}_0 = 5.33$, or $\hat{\alpha}_0 = -39°\,42'$. We conclude that the chance variables

$$u = 0.769x - 0.639y,$$
$$v = 0.639x + 0.769y, \tag{160.3}$$

should be independent.

As a matter of fact, the data of Table 155.1 were obtained as follows:

A penny and a die were tossed six times and the number of heads recorded as u and the number of aces as v. This was repeated 100 times with the results shown in Table 160.1. Obviously, from the nature of the experiment, these variables u and v should be independent.

TABLE 160.1

v	$u = 0$	$u = 1$	$u = 2$	$u = 3$	$u = 4$	$u = 5$	$u = 6$
0		4	7	12	5	3	
1	1	4	10	13	12	4	1
2	1	3	2	1	6	1	3
3		1		2	1	1	
4			1	1			

Then the sum and difference of each pair was computed and called

$$x = v + u,$$
$$y = v - u. \tag{160.4}$$

These pairs x and y constitute the data for Table 155.1. As we have seen they have a correlation coefficient $r_{xy} = -0.34$. But, of course, the linear combinations

$$u = \tfrac{1}{2}(x - y),$$

$$v = \tfrac{1}{2}(x + y),$$

$$(160.5)$$

being independent, should have $r_{uv} = 0$.

Now, comparing (160.5) with (160.3) we see two differences: the four coefficients in (160.3) are not identical, and they are not $\tfrac{1}{2}$. The first of these differences is explained by the fact that the true angle between the x, y and u, v axes should be 45°, as is evident from (160.5); the estimate supplied by our data has missed this by a little over 5°. The second difference is explained by the fact that the transformation (160.4) does not preserve areas (its Jacobian is 2), whereas a rotation does. If (160.4) were adjusted to preserve areas, all coefficients in both (160.4) and (160.5) would be 0.707; and if $\hat{\alpha}_0$ had been 45°, the coefficients in (160.3) would have been the same.

Hence, within the accuracy permitted by our data, the experiment has led us to that pair of chance variables which, under the conditions of the experiment, were independent.

161. The Distribution of Statistics

In several of the examples with which we have dealt so far we have seen the necessity of estimating the parameters of a distribution function from whatever sample of data is at hand. This estimate is usually obtained from the corresponding statistic of the sample. Thus, in Example 140.1 the expectation and standard deviation were estimated from the sample average and standard deviation; in Example 148.2 the bias of the dice (expectation) was estimated from the sample mean; and in computing the line of regression in Example 159.1 we made use of two averages, two standard deviations, and a covariance, all derived from the sample of data.

Clearly, it is important to know how trustworthy these estimates are.

In §§ 140 and 144 we saw how such information can be obtained from the Central Limit Theorem when the sample is large enough. That derivation, as was emphasized at the time, applies equally well regardless of the distribution function which characterizes the experiment. We now approach the problem from a different point of view which is less restrictive regarding the size of the sample, but which places more severe restrictions upon the nature of the experiment. Specifically, *we shall assume that the numbers supplied by the experiment are normally distributed.*

162. The Distribution of the Mean; The Distribution of Variance, Second Approximation

Let an experiment yield a chance variable x with the distribution

$$p(x) = \frac{1}{\sqrt{2\pi}\,\sigma}\, e^{-(x-\varepsilon)^2/2\sigma^2},$$

and let $x_1, x_2, \ldots, x_n$ be the results of n independent trials of this experiment. This can also be written (see Fig. 140.1)

$$p(\delta) = \frac{1}{\sqrt{2\pi}\,\sigma}\, e^{-\delta^2/2\sigma^2},$$

and we may speak of the experiment as having given a set of values $\delta_j = x_j - \varepsilon$ instead of x_j. Then

$$p(\delta_1, \delta_2, \ldots, \delta_n) = \frac{1}{(2\pi)^{n/2}\sigma^n}\, e^{-\Sigma \delta_i^2/2\sigma^2}. \tag{162.1}$$

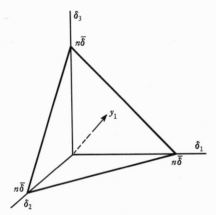

FIG. 162.1

We wish to determine the mean

$$\delta = \frac{\delta_1 + \delta_2 + \cdots + \delta_n}{n} \tag{162.2}$$

and sample variance[27]

$$s^2 = \frac{\delta_1^2 + \delta_2^2 + \cdots + \delta_n^2}{n} - \delta^2. \tag{162.3}$$

We first note that like values of δ lie upon a hyperplane with the equation (162.2). This plane has equal intercepts $n\delta$ on all coordinate axes, as indicated for three dimensions in Fig. 162.1. For different values of δ these planes are parallel; and since the perpendicular to the origin is of length $\sqrt{n}\,\delta$ they are at unit distance apart for unit change in

$$y_n = \sqrt{n}\,\delta. \tag{162.4}$$

Suppose, then, we rotate our coordinate axes so that one, which we call y_n, falls along this normal to the δ-planes, and the others, y_1,

---

[27] Note that all δ's in (162.3), but not in (162.2), could be replaced by d's. That is, the sample variance is the same whether the deviations are measured from ε or from x.

$y_2, \ldots, y_{n-1}$, fall where they may. Clearly, since all scale factors are preserved, the Jacobian is 1, and the distance to a point is given by

$$\sum y_i^2 = \sum \delta_i^2. \tag{162.5}$$

Then (162.1) becomes

$$p(y_1, y_2, \ldots, y_n) = \frac{1}{(2\pi)^{n/2}\,\sigma^n}\,e^{-\sum y_i^2/2\sigma^2}. \tag{162.6}$$

However, by (162.3) and (162.5),

$$\sum y_i^2 = n(\bar\delta^2 + s^2) \tag{162.7}$$

or

$$p(y_1, y_2, \ldots, y_n) = \frac{1}{(2\pi)^{n/2}\,\sigma^n}\,e^{-n\bar\delta^2/2\sigma^2}\,e^{-ns^2/2\sigma^2}. \tag{162.8}$$

This gives at once the

THEOREM 162.1. *If $x_1, x_2, \ldots, x_n$ are the results of n independent trials of an experiment for which*

$$p(x) = \frac{1}{\sqrt{2\pi}\,\sigma}\,e^{-(x-\varepsilon)^2/2\sigma^2},$$

the mean and variance of the sample are independently distributed.

If we integrate out all the y's of (162.6) except y_n,[28] the second exponent in (162.8) disappears leaving

$$p(y_n) = \frac{1}{\sqrt{2\pi}\,\sigma}\,e^{-n\bar\delta^2/2\sigma^2},$$

or, introducing the Jacobian of (162.4),

$$p(\delta) = \frac{\sqrt{n}}{\sqrt{2\pi}\,\sigma}\,e^{-n\bar\delta^2/2\sigma^2}, \tag{162.9}$$

which is precisely what we found in (128.3)

If, on the other hand, we integrate out y_n, we are left with an expression precisely similar in form to (162.6), but with n replaced by $n-1$. Let us, then, introduce polar coordinates exactly as in § 149, with

$$r^2 = y_1^2 + y_2^2 + \ldots + y_{n-1}^2 = ns^2, \tag{162.10}$$

---

[28] Note that, by (162.4) and (162.7), $n\bar\delta^2 = y_n^2$ and $ns^2 = y_1^2 + y_2^2 + \ldots + y_{n-1}^2$.

and integrate out the angular coordinates. The result for $P(r)$ is just (149.3) with $a' = n - 1$, and with r replaced by r/σ.

To obtain the distribution of s we must introduce the Jacobian which, by (162.10), is $\sqrt{n}$ and hence can be absorbed in the general constant K. When this is done and the constant is determined in the usual way we get

$$p(s) = \frac{2\,(n/2)^{(n-1)/2}}{\sigma^{n-1}[\frac{1}{2}(n-3)]!}\,s^{n-2}\,e^{-ns^2/2\sigma^2} \qquad (162.11)$$

and

$$p(> s^2) = \frac{1}{[\frac{1}{2}(n-3)]!}\int_{ns^2/2\sigma^2}^{\infty} e^{-\gamma}\,\gamma^{(n-3)/2}\,d\gamma$$

$$= P_{n-1}(> n\,s^2/\sigma^2),$$

where P_{n-1} is the χ^2 - distribution defined by (149.8). Hence

THEOREM 162.2. *If $x_1, x_2, \ldots, x_n$ are the results of independent trials of an experiment for which*

$$p(x) = \frac{1}{\sqrt{2\pi}\,\sigma}\,e^{-(x-\varepsilon)^2/2\sigma^3},$$

the mean of the sample has the normal distribution (162.9) with standard deviation $\sigma/\sqrt{n}$, and the variance has the χ^2-distribution with $n-1$ degrees of freedom and with $\chi^2 = n\,s^2/\sigma^2$.

As illustrations we may use Examples 140.1 and 142.1 for which we have already found 99% confidence limits for s in § 144.

For the first we have $n = 40$. This is beyond the limits of Appendix VIII, but by using the method explained in the footnote to that table we find, for $P = 0.99$ and 0.1, $\chi^2 = 20.80$ and 61.62, respectively. From Table 140.1 we have $s^2 = 0.0397$.

Then, from Theorem 162.2 we find that if $n\,s^2/\sigma^2 = 1.588/\sigma^2$ is outside the limits stated—that is, if $\sigma^2 > 0.0763$ or $\sigma^2 < 0.0258$—there is less than one chance in 100 of getting the observed s^2. Hence we conclude that—at the 99% level—the confidence limits on σ are 0.161 and 0.276. This compares favorably with the limits (0.139, 0.249) obtained in § 144, as it should, since the size of the sample is fairly large.

For Example 142.1 we have $n = 5$, so that from Appendix VIII the limiting values of χ^2 are found to be 0.297 and 13.277. From Table 142.1 we find $s^2 = 10.41$; whence $\sigma^2 = n\,s^2/\chi^2 = (3.920, 175.2)$ and $\sigma = (1.98, 13.24)$. In this case the sample is so small that we would not expect the central limit theorem to give a very accurate approximation, and as we see from the earlier limits (1.90, 4.74), it did not. Note particularly that the confidence interval given by the more accurate χ^2 approximation is *fully twice* as wide as the earlier approximation.

163. The Distribution of $\bar{\delta}/s$; the *t*-Distribution

We remarked in § 140 that it is possible to establish confidence limits for the expectation ϵ *without a knowledge of the standard deviation*, provided we know (or assume) that the distribution is normal. This may be done by the argument which follows.

Since δ and s are known to be independently distributed, $p(\delta, s)$ is the product of their separate distribution functions (162.9) and (162.11). Suppose, then, that we introduce two new variables

$$\alpha = \delta/s,$$
$$\gamma = n s^2/2\sigma^2$$

into this product, and multiply by the Jacobian of the transformation, which is

$$\frac{\partial(\delta, s)}{\partial(\alpha, \gamma)} = \frac{\sigma^2}{n}.$$

The result is

$$p(\alpha, \gamma) = \frac{1}{\sqrt{\pi}[\frac{1}{2}(n - 3)]!}\gamma^{(n - 2)/2} e^{-(1+\alpha^2)\gamma}. \tag{163.1}$$

To find the distribution of the ratio $\delta/s = \alpha$ which we seek, it is only necessary to integrate (163.1) with respect to γ. This gives

$$p(\alpha) = \frac{(\frac{1}{2}n - 1)!}{\sqrt{\pi}[\frac{1}{2}(n - 3)]!(1 + \alpha^2)^{n/2}}. \tag{163.2}$$

Note that σ does not occur in either the definition of α or this equation. Hence we have the

THEOREM 163.1. *The distribution of $\alpha = \delta/s$ in random samples of size n taken from a normal population is* (163.2). *Both α and $p(\alpha)$ are independent of the standard deviation of the population.*

In statistical practice it is more common to use the ratio

$$t = \sqrt{n}\,\delta/\hat{\sigma} \tag{163.3}$$

instead of α. Since $\hat{\sigma} = \sqrt{n/(n - 1)}\, s$, this is equivalent to

$$t = \sqrt{n - 1}\,\alpha,$$

344 PROBABILITY AND ITS ENGINEERING USES

and, if we write $n' = n - 1$, (163.2) becomes

$$p(t) = \frac{[\tfrac{1}{2}(n' - 1)]!}{\sqrt{n'\pi}\,[\tfrac{1}{2}(n' - 2)]!\,\left(1 + \dfrac{t^2}{n'}\right)^{(n'+1)/2}}.$$

As in the case of the normal and χ^2 distributions, what is usually wanted is not the density $p(t)$, but instead $p(>|t|)$, the probability of the observed magnitude t being exceeded. Appendix IX is a table of such probabilities. It is organized in the same way as Appendix VIII. That is, each row corresponds to a particular value of n' (which is one less than the sample size), and each column to a particular value of the probability $2p(>|t|)$. The corresponding number in the body of the table is the value of $|t|$ beyond which the area under *both* tails of the curve is equal to the stated probability.[29]

As numerical illustrations let us take again Examples 140.1 and 142.1.

For the former we have, from Table 140.1, $n = 40$, $\hat{\sigma} = 0.2017$; and from Appendix IX we find that $t = \pm 2.708$ is the value for which the area of *both* tails is 0.01. Substituting in (163.3) gives $\delta = \pm 0.0864$; whence $\epsilon = 39.3075 \pm 0.0864$. As would be expected, since the sample is fairly large, this is quite close to the 99% confidence interval 39.3075 ± 0.0822 obtained in § 142.

By contrast, for the small sample of Example 142.1 we find from Table 142.1 that $n = 5$, $\hat{\sigma} = 3.608$, and from Appendix IX that $t = 4.604$ at the 99% level. Hence the 99% confidence limits for ϵ are 16.15 ± 7.43—much wider than the limits 16.15 ± 4.16 obtained in § 142.[30]

164. The Distribution of the Ratio of Two Variances

Another statistic that plays an important role in modern statistical theory is the ratio of the variances of two samples. The problem arises as follows:

Suppose the numbers x supplied by an experiment have the normal

---

[29] Two sets of tables exist, one for $p(> t)$, the other for $2p(> t)$—that is, for the area of one tail and both tails—and the distinction is not always clearly indicated. The reader is cautioned to be on his guard concerning this. As stated in the text, Appendix IX gives the area of both tails.

[30] The reason these limits are wider than those given in § 142 can be visualized as follows: Those in § 142 were computed for $\sigma = \hat{\sigma}$. But, due to sampling variations, the true value of σ may be either larger or smaller, and what is needed is a sort of weighted average of the values of δ corresponding to all these possibilities. If the distribution of s were symmetrical, this weighted average would be just the δ found in § 142. But the distribution is not symmetrical, as is easily seen from (162.11), and the large positive values of $\Delta\sigma$ contribute disproportionately to δ.

distribution function

$$p(\delta) = \frac{1}{\sqrt{2\pi}\,\sigma_x}\,e^{-\delta^2/2\sigma^2},$$

and that a sample of m values $\delta_1, \delta_2, \ldots, \delta_a$ has been obtained from it. We know that the s_x of these has the distribution (162.11) with n replaced by m and s by s_x.

Suppose also that an independent experiment which, *as a hypothesis to be tested*, we assume to have the same distribution function, has yielded n values of y. Under the test hypothesis the distribution of s_y is also given by (162.11). Hence

$$p(s_x, s_y) = k\,s_x^{\,m-2}\,s_y^{\,n-2}\,e^{-(ms_x{}^2 + ns_y{}^2)/2\sigma^2}. \qquad (164.1)$$

We now ask for the probability of the ratio s_x^2/s_y^2 taking the value β. If we use the transformation

$$\beta = s_x^2/s_y^2,$$
$$\gamma = n\,s_y^2/2\sigma^2$$

whose Jacobian is $4\sigma^4\gamma/n^2$, and absorb all constant multipliers into the symbol k', (164.1), becomes

$$p(\beta, \gamma) = k'\,\beta^{(m-3)/2}\,\gamma^{(m+n-4)/2}\,e^{-(1+m\beta/n)\gamma}.$$

To get $p(\beta)$ we need only integrate with respect to γ. This gives

$$p(\beta) = \frac{k''\,\beta^{(m-3)/2}}{(m\beta + n)^{(m+n-2)/2}}. \qquad (164.2)$$

This is the desired distribution.

However, in this instance as in the preceding section, it is customary to use

$$F = \hat{\sigma}_x^2/\hat{\sigma}_y^2, \qquad m' = m - 1, \qquad n' = n - 1$$

instead of β, m, and n. With these substitutions (164.2) becomes

$$p_{m', n'}(F) = k'''\,\frac{F^{\frac{1}{2}m'-1}}{\left(1 + \dfrac{m'}{n'}F\right)^{(m'+n')/2}},$$

in which, to make $\int p(F)\,dF = 1$, k''' must have the value

$$k''' = \tfrac{1}{2}\,\frac{m'\,n'}{m'+n'}\,C_{m'/2}^{(m'+n')/2}\left(\frac{m'}{n'}\right)^{m'/2}.$$

Extensive tables of this function, or rather of

$$P(< F) = \int_0^F P_{m',n'} (F) \, dF,$$

exist and are used in modern statistical practice in a variety of ways. It would carry us much beyond the scope of the present book to explain them in detail. We shall therefore content ourselves with a single, very simple, illustration.

EXAMPLE 164.1.—*In connection with Example 140.1, was there a change in the diameter of the ring or in the precision of the observations between the first and last halves of the series?*

By considering separately the first 20 observations we find that

$$n_1 = 20, \qquad \bar{x}_1 = 39.2755, \qquad s_1^2 = 0.04286.$$

Similarly, for the remaining observations

$$n_2 = 20, \qquad \bar{x}_2 = 39.3395, \qquad s_2^2 = 0.03450.$$

It is readily established that each of the means, $\bar{x}_1$ and $\bar{x}_2$, lies within the confidence limits of the other. (see Problem 164.23). Hence the data give no indication of a change in the diameter.[31]

There is, however, a substantial difference in the dispersion of the measurements as indicated by s_1^2 and s_2^2, and we may raise the question whether this is greater than would be expected between random samples. To answer this, we could look up the ratio[32] $F = s_1^2/s_2^2$ in a suitable table and would find that $P(< F) = 0.68$. There is, therefore, about one chance in three that an independent experiment conducted under identical conditions would show a larger disparity in variance than was observed. Clearly, we have no basis for rejecting the idea (the null hypothesis) that the quality of the observations was maintained.

Problems

1. A "direct advertising" sales campaign is under consideration, and a trial batch of 1000 circulars is sent out. It results in 19 favorable replies. Assuming that the binomial distribution sufficiently well represents the situation, state an upper and lower limit to the number of replies that may be expected from 100,000 circulars, it being understood that the limiting expectations are to be such that, beyond them, the chance of the trial batch showing 19 returns is less than 0.01.

2. How large a test batch must be used in Problem 1 in order that the

---

[31] Also, assuming the diameter fixed, there is no evidence of a change in the systematic error $\Delta \epsilon$, Fig. 140.1, if there was one.

[32] Since the groups are equally numerous, $\hat{\sigma}_1^2/\hat{\sigma}_2^2 = s_1^2/s_2^2$. In entering the table we use $m' = n' = 19$.

upper and lower limits expected from a subsequent batch of 100,000 shall not differ by more than 100?

3. What is the least number of favorable replies in Problem 1 to assure a lower limit of expectation of 2%?

4. Plans are being laid for a direct advertising campaign, which will not be profitable unless at least 2% of those circularized return favorable replies. A trial run of 1000 circulars will be made to test whether the campaign will be a success. Formulate a recommendation for the interpretation of the results of the trial run: (a) What shall be the "acceptance number" (i.e., the number of favorable replies that shall be accepted as conclusive)? (b) What shall be the "rejection number"? (c) What procedure do you recommend in doubtful cases?

5. The results of 27 independent repetitions of Problem 110.5 are recorded in Table 164.1. Are the results contained in the column headed "Totals" consistent with the assumption that the pennies were unbiased?

TABLE 164.1

Number of Heads	Frequency of Occurrence (Individual Results)									
0	0	0	0	1	0	0	0	0	0	0
1	0	0	1	0	0	1	0	0	0	0
2	1	2	2	0	1	2	0	2	0	1
3	5	6	8	6	4	4	7	7	4	4
4	13	10	6	10	14	10	9	9	13	9
5	11	11	8	6	10	13	10	13	15	10
6	13	12	14	11	12	12	9	12	10	16
7	4	7	7	11	7	7	8	4	5	7
8	2	1	2	5	2	1	6	3	2	3
9	1	1	2	0	0	0	1	0	1	0
10	0	0	0	0	0	0	0	0	0	0
Average	5.10	5.10	5.20	5.42	5.14	5.02	5.48	5.00	5.18	5.38

Number of Heads	Frequency of Occurrence (Individual Results)									
0	0	0	0	0	0	0	0	0	0	0
1	2	1	0	1	1	0	0	1	0	0
2	1	3	2	3	4	2	3	1	3	3
3	7	12	3	11	3	8	9	7	6	4
4	16	7	9	7	8	8	7	7	7	7
5	10	6	20	10	11	12	8	13	14	15
6	7	11	7	8	11	11	12	9	12	11
7	4	6	7	5	8	8	5	8	4	6
8	2	4	2	5	4	1	5	3	1	4
9	1	0	0	0	0	0	1	1	3	0
10	0	0	0	0	0	0	0	0	0	0
Average	4.68	4.82	5.12	4.82	5.18	5.00	5.14	5.20	5.14	5.22

TABLE 164.1 *Continued*

Number of Heads	Frequency of Occurrence (Individual Results)							Totals	Total for First 24	Total for Last 3
0	0	0	0	0	0	0	0	1	1	0
1	1	0	2	0	0	1	0	12	11	1
2	2	1	1	1	2	2	1	46	41	5
3	4	6	4	5	10	6	5	165	144	21
4	11	13	16	10	12	12	7	267	236	31
5	9	8	10	14	12	12	15	306	267	39
6	14	14	7	12	7	11	8	293	267	26
7	7	5	7	7	5	5	11	175	154	21
8	2	2	3	1	2	1	1	70	66	4
9	0	1	0	0	0	0	2	15	13	2
10	0	0	0	0	0	0	0	0	0	0
Average	5.10	5.12	4.90	5.12	4.70	4.80	5.42	5.0926	5.1075	4.8733

6. Each individual column in Table 164.1 may be regarded as an independent experiment to determine the average number of heads. The individual averages are all shown at the bottom of the columns. Using classes bounded by $- \infty$, 4.89, 4.99, . . . , 5.39, $+ \infty$ determine whether these averages are consistent with the theoretical distribution.

7. Consider the following null hypothesis: The last three columns came from the same population as the first 24. Should it be rejected?

8. Consider the following null hypothesis: The penny was biased and favored heads in the ratio indicated by the grand average 5.0926. Should it be rejected on the evidence of the Totals column?

9. Using the same classes as in Problem 6, determine whether the averages are consistent with $p = 0.50926$.

10. If the averages in Problem 5 are considered as a sample of data without regard for their origin, and $\hat{\epsilon}$ and $\hat{\sigma}$ determined from them, should the hypothesis that they are consistent with a normal distribution be rejected?

11. Assuming the penny is unbiased, what are the 95% confidence limits for the average of the Totals column?

12. Considering the results of Problems 5–11 as a whole, what is your conclusion regarding the penny used in the experiments?

13. Test the goodness of fit of the Poisson Law in the case of Table 114.1.

14. Using the known distribution of s^2, write the distribution function for s in random samples of n.

15. Test the hypothesis that u and v of Table 160.1 are independent. [Assume the origin of the data is unknown and make $u > 4$ and $v > 2$ single classes.]

16. From § 160 it would be expected that the data of Table 160.1 would fit the distribution $p(u, v) = (\frac{5}{12})^6 C_u^6 C_v^6 \, 5^{-v}$. Test this hypothesis. Compare with Problem 15.

17. An experiment is being tested to judge whether it conforms to a given distribution function. Two experimental values fall in a class for which the expectation is zero. What conclusion can be drawn?

18. The first two columns of Table 164.2 are the record of 1000 numbers obtained by a sampling process. Find the best estimate of the expectation and standard deviation of the distribution from which they were derived. (Ignore the third column.)

19. In Problem 18, what is the confidence interval for ϵ at the 90% level?

20. Are the results recorded in Table 164.2 compatible with the normal distribution at the 90% level of confidence? (Ignore the third column.)

TABLE 164.2

Marking	Number Observed	Theoretical Probability
−3.0	5	0.0030
−2.5	9	0.0092
−2.0	36	0.0278
−1.5	55	0.0656
−1.0	123	0.1210
−0.5	165	0.1747
0.0	203	0.1974
+0.5	172	0.1747
+1.0	123	0.1210
+1.5	68	0.0656
+2.0	31	0.0278
+2.5	8	0.0092
+3.0	2	0.0030
	1000	1.0000

21. Table 164.2 was, in fact, constructed as follows: The probability that a chance variable which obeys the normal law will lie in the intervals $(-\infty, -2.75)$, $(-2.75, -2.25)$, $(-2.25, -1.75)$, ..., was recorded in Column 3. Then 1000 chips were marked. Three had the marking -3, nine -2.5, twenty-eight -2.0, and so on; the number with each marking being $1000p_j$, where p_j is the number in the third column. These chips were then placed in a box, thoroughly mixed, and one drawn out. After its marking had been noted it was replaced, the contents of the box again

mixed, and another drawing made. The results of 1000 such drawings were distributed as shown in the second column of Table 164.2.

In the light of this knowledge as to the origin of the data, what is the probability that another similar experiment would deviate from expectation at least as much as this one did?

22. If Weldon's results were recorded by a careless amanuensis who had a tendency to omit some aces and threes, how would the appraisal of the results be affected?

23. Using the data of Example 164.1, find the 90% confidence limits for ϵ as determined by the first and second halves of the observations. [Use the t-test.]

24. A penny and a die were thrown six times and u, the number of heads, and v, the number of aces, recorded. This experiment was repeated 100 times with the results shown in Table 164.3. Test this for independence of u and v.

TABLE 164.3

v	$u = 0$	$u = 1$	$u = 2$	$u = 3$	$u = 4$	$u = 5$	$u = 6$	$n(v)$
0		3	9	9	4	3		28
1	3	4	12	9	13	5		46
2	1	1	3	9	3	1	1	19
3			2	2	2			6
4								0
5				1				1
$n(u)$	4	8	26	30	22	9	1	100

25. Test Table 164.3 for goodness of fit to the theoretical distribution $p(u, v) = (\frac{5}{12})^6 C_u^6 C_v^6 5^{-v}$.

26. In Table 164.3, find $\hat{\epsilon}_u$ and $\hat{\epsilon}_v$ and the confidence interval for each at the 90% level.

[Use the t-test. It is fully justified in this case since both u and v have binomial distributions with n large.]

27. Find $\hat{\sigma}_u^2$ and $\hat{\sigma}_v^2$ from Table 164.3 and the 90% confidence limits of each.

28. Table 164.4 bears the same relation to Table 164.3 as Table 155.1 to Table 160.1. Test the two for compatibility, using the following classes: $x = (1, 2, 3), (4, 5), (6, 7, 8)$; $y = (0, 1, 2), (-1, -2), (-3, -4, -5)$.

29. In Table 164.4, find the angle of rotation and the linear combinations of x and y which lead to uncorrelated variables u and v.

30. In Table 164.4, what is the line of regression of y on x?

TABLE 164.4

y	$x = 1$	$x = 2$	$x = 3$	$x = 4$	$x = 5$	$x = 6$	$x = 7$	$x = 8$	$n(y)$
$+2$		1					1		2
$+1$	3		1		2				6
0		4		3		2			9
-1	3		12		9		2		26
-2		9		9		3			21
-3			9		13			1	23
-4				4		5		1	10
-5					3				3
$n(x)$	6	14	22	16	27	10	3	2	100

31. Prove the following theorem: If an experiment yields a chance variable x which is normally distributed, and if x_1, x_2, $\ldots$, x_n are the results of n independent trials of this experiment, then the linear functions

$$y_i = \sum_j c_{ij} x_j$$

are independent and normally distributed provided the coefficients c_{ij} define a rotation of axes about the point $[\epsilon_1(x), \epsilon_1(x), \ldots, \epsilon_1(x)]$.

[Translate origin to the center of gravity, use (162.5), and translate back.]

32. Show that the theorem of Problem 31 is also valid if the results of the experiments obey the distribution $p(x_i) = e^{-k_i x_i}/k_i$ where the k_i need not be equal.

33. If x and y are *independent* chance variables, what is the curve of regression of y on x?

34. Prove that r_{xy} is never greater than 1 in absolute value.
[Use the definition $r_{xy} = \epsilon_1(\xi\eta)$ and the inequality $(|\xi| - |\eta|)^2 \geqq 0$.]

35. Prove that $r_{xy} = \pm 1$ when *and only when* x and y are linearly related.
[Consider the case $(|\xi| - |\eta|)^2 = 0$ in Problem 34.]

36. If $r_{xy} = \pm 1$, and u,v correspond to a rotation of axes, what is the value of r_{uv}?
[Use the result of Problem 35.]

37. If x_1 and x_2 are independent chance variables with the distributions

$$e^{-x_1^2/2\sigma_1^2}/\sqrt{2\pi}\,\sigma_1 \text{ and } e^{-x_2^2/2\sigma_2^2}/\sqrt{2\pi}\,\sigma_2,$$

find the distribution of $t = x_1/x_2$.

38. If two large random samples of size n and m are taken from a population with standard deviation σ, what is the distribution of the ratio $t = \bar{\delta}_u/\bar{\delta}_m$?
[Use (128.3) and the result of Problem 37.]

39. If axes are rotated, as in § 160, show that

$$\sigma_u^2 = \sigma_x^2 \cos^2 \alpha + 2r_{xy}\, \sigma_x\, \sigma_y \cos \alpha \sin \alpha + \sigma_y^2 \sin^2 \alpha,$$

$$\sigma_v^2 = \sigma_x^2 \sin^2 \alpha - 2r_{xy}\, \sigma_x\, \sigma_y \cos \alpha \sin \alpha + \sigma_y^2 \cos^2 \alpha.$$

40. Using the α_0 defined by (160.2) and the results of Problem 39, show that

$$r_{uv} = \frac{\sin 2\,(\alpha_0 - \alpha)}{\sqrt{\sin^2 2(\alpha_0 - \alpha) + \left(\dfrac{1}{r_{xy}^2} - 1\right)\sin^2 2\alpha_0}}.$$

41. Hence, show that r_{uv} takes its maximum value at $\alpha = \alpha_0 \pm \pi/4$.

Answers to Problems

1. This can be solved in several ways. (a) As the problem is stated, if the expectation is 100,000ϵ, the chance of 19 or more from a sample of 1000 is $1 - \phi_{-1}(y) = 0.01$ for the lower limit, and the chance of 19 or less is $\phi_{-1}(y) = 0.01$ for the upper limit, where $y = (19 - 1000\epsilon)/\sqrt{1000\epsilon(1 - \epsilon)}$. This gives a quadratic in ϵ which can be solved directly. The result is 100,000ϵ = (1125, 3193). (b) More simply, the 0.01 confidence limits of $\hat{p}$ from a sample of 1000 are $\Delta p = \pm\, 0.0111$, whence 100,000p = (890, 3010).

2. 449,000. **3.** By method (a), 33; by method (b), 29.

5. Yes. Combining 0, 1 and 9, 10: $a' = 8$, $\chi^2 = 10.52$, $P(> \chi^2) = 0.23$. **6.** No. $a' = 6$, $\chi^2 = 20.49$, $P(> \chi^2) = 0.002$.

7. No. Combining 0, 1 and 9, 10: $a' = 8$, $\chi^2 = 5.60$, $P(> \chi^2) = 0.69$.

8. No. Combining 0, 1 and 9, 10: $a' = 7$, $\chi^2 = 5.92$, $P(> \chi^2) = 0.55$.

9. Probably not. $a' = 5$, $\chi^2 = 11.07$, $P(> \chi^2) = 0.05$. **10.** Probably. $\hat{\epsilon} = 5.107$, $\hat{\sigma} = 0.2084$, $a' = 4$, $\chi^2 = 10.32$, $P(> \chi^2) = 0.04$.

11. (4936, 5084).

12. The totals are entirely consistent with either the hypothesis of a true penny or of one biased to $p = 0.5107$. The averages are quite unusual on either hypothesis and also do not conform well to a normal distribution. The difficulty is the high concentration of averages in the class (5.09, 5.19). Taken as a whole, $p = 0.5107$ is only moderately better than $p = 0.5$. It is not possible on the evidence to reach a firm conclusion.

The study (which deals with data from an actual experiment, unmodified in any way) illustrates the importance of considering data from several angles before drawing firm inferences. If Problem 5 only had been used, the penny would appear true; if Problem 6 only, this hypothesis would certainly have been rejected.

13. Combining $n > 3$ into one class, $a' = 3$, $\chi^2 = 0.610$, $P(> \chi^2) = 89\%$.

14.
$$\frac{2(n/2)^{(n-1)/2}}{\left(\dfrac{n-3}{2}\right)! \, \sigma^{n-1}} s^{n-2} e^{-ns^2/2\sigma^2}.$$

15. $a' = 15$, $\chi^2 = 12.36$, $P(> \chi^2) = 0.65$. There is no reason to reject the hypothesis.

16. $a' = 23$, $\chi^2 = 14.72$, $P(> \chi^2) = 0.90$.

17. The experiment does not obey the given distribution. Zero expectation implies either that negative and positive values are equally likely, or that the event cannot occur. Since events do not occur a negative number of times, the second meaning applies.

18. $\hat{\epsilon} = 0.0015$, $\hat{\sigma}^2 = 1.0342$. **19.** 0.0015 ± 0.0528. **20.** With $\hat{\epsilon} = 0.0015$, $\hat{\sigma}^2 = 1.0342$ we find $\chi^2 = 7.19$, $a' = 10$, and $P(> \chi^2) = 0.71$. Since this exceeds 0.10 the answer is "yes." **21.** $a' = 12$, $\chi^2 = 7.21$, $P(> \chi^2) = 0.84$.

23. 39.2755 ± 0.0821; 39.3395 ± 0.0737. **24.** Combining $u = 0$, 1 and 5, 6, and $v = 3$, 4, 5 into single classes: $\chi^2 = 8.960$, $a' = 12$, $P(> \chi^2) = 0.71$. **25.** $a' = 19$, $\chi^2 = 12.014$, $P(> \chi^2) = 0.88$.

26. $n = 100$, $t = 1.662$, $s_u = 1.263$, $s_v = 0.930$, $\hat{\epsilon}_u = 2.89$, $\hat{\epsilon}_v = 1.07$; hence $\epsilon_u = 2.89 \pm 0.21$, $\epsilon_v = 1.07 \pm 0.15$. Note that the theoretical values $\epsilon_u = 3$, $\epsilon_v = 1$ are within these intervals.

27. $\hat{\sigma}_u^2 = 1.614$, $\hat{\sigma}_v^2 = 0.874$. By the method of § 144 the confidence limits are $(1.103, 2.093)$ and $(0.461, 1.269)$, respectively; by the method of § 162 they are $(1.106, 2.161)$ and $(0.599, 1.170)$.

28. There are two null hypotheses: (a) Table 164.4 was drawn from the population of Table 155.1; $a' = 8$, $\chi^2 = 5.46$, $P(> \chi^2) = 0.71$. (b) Table 155.1 was drawn from the population of Table 164.4; $a' = 8$, $\chi^2 = 5.77$, $P(> \chi^2) = 0.67$.

29. $\tan 2\alpha_0 = -6.350$, $\alpha_0 = -40° 32'$, $u = 0.760\,x - 0.650\,y$, $v = 0.650\,x + 0.760\,y$.

30. $y + 1.82 = -0.284\,(x - 3.96)$. **33.** $y = \epsilon_1(y)$, a constant. **36.** Since u and v are also linearly related, $r_{uv} = \pm 1$.

37. $p(t) = \sigma_1\sigma_2/\pi\,(\sigma_2^2\,t^2 + \sigma_1^2)$. **38.** $p(t) = \sqrt{mn}/\pi\,(nt^2 + m)$.

Chapter XII

The Theory of Probability as Applied to Problems of Congestion*

165. Introductory Remarks

"Problems of Congestion" arise in any phase of industrial life in which demands for service arise from a multiplicity of sources acting more or less independently of one another. For example, the turnstiles through which passengers pass into a subway platform are used by numerous individuals who act independently of one another to a large degree, though perhaps influenced by common working hours to travel for the most part at certain peak hours. The demands made upon a cash-carrier system in a large store are "independent" in the same broad sense, though obviously they are influenced by peak shopping hours.

We have already had an example of one closely related problem. In § 117 we investigated the stock of dog-biscuit which should be carried by a grocery store under certain specified conditions. This, which we may for brevity refer to as the "warehouse problem," is in fact the simplest of all congestion problems. In it, the only question asked is: "How many demands will be made within a given time?" Obviously this question is also *part* of the problem raised by the turnstile or the cash-carrier, but not the whole problem; for the passenger who uses the turnstile does not remove it permanently from service, as the purchaser of dog-biscuit removes it permanently from stock. Instead, the turnstile is "returned to service" after the passenger is

---

* Except for necessary changes in reference numbers and a few minor corrections, this chapter is identical with Chapter X of the first edition.

through with it: that is, *after a certain period called the holding-time.* This holding-time is a new element in the situation.

The fundamental turnstile problem[1] therefore formulates itself as follows: "Knowing the expected number of demands per unit time and the expected holding-time, how many paths (turnstiles, say) must be provided in order that the proportion of persons inconvenienced shall not exceed a preassigned amount?"

This question is, however, still quite indefinite, for "inconvenienced" may mean a number of different things under different circumstances. In the case of the turnstile or cash-carrier it almost certainly means "delayed," for the user does not disappear if no apparatus is available. If, however, we spoke of the number of chairs in a barber shop, a period of congestion would probably result in a loss of trade—and would therefore be to a certain degree its own cure, for the periods of congestion would obviously be shorter than if all the customers waited until served. This is probably no comfort to the barber, but we—and he—must face the facts nevertheless.

I doubt if my readers are likely to become barber-shop engineers; but there are other places where problems of an exactly analogous kind are faced in engineering experience. In telephone engineering, for instance, a certain number of trunk lines are provided between two exchanges, and when they are all busy the subscriber is given a "busy signal" which causes him to hang up his receiver and repeat his call later on. This is not quite a case of "lost traffic," for he very probably does repeat; but unless he repeats very soon—before the congestion is quite thoroughly cleared out—the length of such periods will be much the same as if he were to go away entirely.

We have, therefore, two quite fundamental divisions in this problem of congestion: a "delayed traffic" division and a "lost traffic" division. It is our purpose in the present chapter to indicate how the Theory of Probability can be applied to these two problems, and to two others which we shall explain as they arise.

As the methods of solution are the same no matter what the particular engineering application may be, it makes little difference in what language we phrase our study. As telephone practice offers examples of widely diverse conditions, we shall choose it; and to make the study more understandable we give the following general explanation of the terms which we are to use:[2]

When a subscriber makes a call, it is designed for some particular person and must therefore be steered toward that person, either by

---

[1] Such problems are now commonly called "queueing problems."
[2] It need hardly be said that it is not intended as a description of a telephone exchange.

human intervention—as in manual practice—or by mechanical intervention—as in machine-switching (automatic) systems. Whatever performs this steering function we call a "switch."

Obviously a switch must pass a call on to something else. We call that something a "channel." Such a channel will ordinarily be one of a "group" performing identical functions—that is, any one of the group could accommodate our call. There may be other channels to which our call might have been assigned if it were going somewhere else—to a different office, say; these however are not part of our "group." There may also be other channels leading to the place we wish our call sent, and which are available to *other* subscribers though not to *us*. These also are not part of our "group." When we speak of a "group of channels" we shall mean a group each member of which is capable of performing identical functions for identically the same calls as any other.

Usually these calls can come from a number of sources. For example, if the group serves calling subscribers directly, there will usually be a number of subscribers capable of using any channel of the group in exactly the same way.[3] This is the "group of sources" corresponding to the "group of channels." In such cases, there must be something to locate a suitable channel and associate the calling source with it. Whatever performs this function, whether human or mechanical, we shall term a "switch."

We need no further knowledge of telephony for the purposes of our discussion.

166. Notation

The principal symbols used are the following:

n—the calling rate, that is, the expected number of calls *per source per hour*.

T—the expected duration of a call, measured in *hours* unless otherwise noted.

λ—the number of sources in our group.

ν—the number of channels in our group.

p—the probability that a given source (sometimes a given channel) is busy at a random instant of observation.

$P(j)$—the probability that if a particular group is examined at a random instant it will be found to contain exactly j busy members.

Π—the probability of a call being lost by reason of insufficient equipment.

ϵ—the expected traffic density of our group; that is, the expected number of busy sources (or channels).

---

[3] But the source need not be a subscriber. It may be a switch to which he has already entrusted his call.

To any of these symbols will be affixed such subscripts and super-scripts as are necessary to characterize the particular conditions to which they are applied.

167. General Assumptions

We make the following assumptions as to the nature of our problem:

Assumption 1—The system is in statistical equilibrium; in other words, the probability of finding it in any specified condition is independent of the time at which it is examined.

It is quite true that no telephone exchange ever actually reaches a con-dition of statistical equilibrium. Its traffic varies from a light load at night to a peak sometime during the day, and then falls off again. During the time when the traffic is increasing, the probability of a large number of busy switches is also increasing and therefore varying with the time. On the other hand, when the traffic is decreasing, the probability of lost calls is also decreasing. It is not hard to see that the probability of losing calls always lags somewhat behind the traffic, reaching its peak shortly after the peak load is reached, and its minimum shortly after the minimum load occurs. This was illustrated in a simple way by the results of Problems 122.8 and 122.9. But when the periodic fluctuation of the traffic is sufficiently slow, the peak value of the probability is substantially the same as the probability of loss figured on the basis of statistical equilibrium with the traffic density at its peak value; and in such cases it is safe to make the assumption stated above, designing the exchange entirely for the conditions of busy hour traffic.

Assumption 2—Connection of sources to channels and their disconnection therefrom is effected instantaneously.

This assumption is entirely tenable as long as the time consumed in the operations of connecting and disconnecting is small compared to the duration of the average conversation. In other cases an independent investigation is necessary; but to take into account such minor complica-tions would only serve to obscure the main purpose of the present discussion.

Assumption 3—The expected traffic density is the same for every source.

This assumption is justified only by the fact that it is difficult to make any other which more nearly agrees with practical conditions. It does not mean that each subscriber originates the same number of calls. It means that the number of seconds in the busy hour during which a source is expected to be busy is the same for all sources.

The assumption is evidently not satisfied in practice and some notion of the nature of the errors to which it leads is desirable. In an article on "The Theory of Telephone Probabilities Applied to Trunking Problems" in the *Bell System Technical Journal* for November, 1922, E. C. Molina has shown that it is on the side of safety, at least when the probability of congestion is small, as it usually is under operating conditions.

Assumption 4—Busy sources make no calls.

If this assumption is ignored, formulas will be obtained which give the same probability of loss for the same amount of traffic, regardless of whether the number of sources is less than or greater than the number of available channels. As an extreme example, consider the case of 20 sources, each originating five calls per hour, and the alternative case of five sources, each originating 20 calls per hour, the average duration of the calls being two minutes in each case. If each of these groups is assigned ten channels, such a formula would say that the proportion of lost calls is the same in both cases. However, it is obvious from a common-sense standpoint that if there are only five sources they cannot make use of more than five channels. Hence in the second illustration no calls can possibly be lost, whereas it is possible for the twenty sources of the first illustration to want more than ten channels at once.

Assumption 5—Either every channel which can serve a source S_1 can also serve S_2, or else no channel can serve them both.

We have really inferred this in the explanation given in § 165. There are cases in telephone practice (the "graded multiple" is a good example) which violate it.

Assumption 6—The number of busy channels in a group is equal to the number of busy members in its group of sources, except that in case lost calls are not instantly wiped out, the number of busy sources may exceed the total number of channels. When this latter situation arises, all channels are busy.

This assumption is violated whenever the group of channels goes in only one of a number of different directions to which the sources have access; for obviously a source may be sending a call in one of these other directions. It is less often false in other engineering fields than in telephony.

168. Some Problems of Lost Traffic

In order to illustrate the general principles involved we shall develop six formulas for the probability of a call being lost. They illustrate well the extent to which shades of meaning must be carefully considered in dealing with such problems, arising as they do, on the one hand, from three slightly different assumptions as to how the traffic originates, and on the other hand from two as to what happens when a call is lost. The three which deal with the origination of calls are:

Assumption 7—The probability that a particular source will originate a call during a given time interval is the same for every interval at the beginning of which it is idle. It is not in any way influenced by the condition of its group of channels. (Alternative to Assumptions 8 and 9.)

Assumption 8—The calls which are assigned to the group of channels are distributed individually and collectively at random. That is, the chance of the group being assigned a call during a test interval is independent of the state of either group. (Alternative to Assumptions 7 and 9.)

The difference between these assumptions may be illustrated as follows: If a group of ten channels is accessible to fifteen subscribers and to them only, it seems scarcely reasonable to assert that the chance of a call being originated within a second is the same if all trunks are busy at the beginning of the second as it is if all trunks are idle; for when all trunks are idle there are three times as many possible sources as when all are busy. To make such an assertion implies that individual subscribers are more likely to call when the group is busy than when it is idle: and this in turn implies foreknowledge on their part. However, it is this assertion that is contained in Assumption 8. Unreasonable as it appears from this extreme illustration it will be found that it is often very near the fact when the sources of calls are not the subscribers themselves, but interoffice trunks and the like.[4]

A more reasonable assertion in case the subscriber is the source would be that the chance of a call originating during a short test interval is proportional to the number of idle subscribers; that is, in the case of the above illustration, that it is three times as great when all channels are idle as when all are busy. This is the condition implied by Assumption 7. It also is sometimes very near the truth, even when the sources are not subscribers' lines.

Assumption 9—The probability of a call being assigned to the group of channels by some one of its sources is independent of the condition of either group, unless all sources are busy, in which case it is zero. In other words: calls are distributed individually and collectively at random, except that none is made when all channels are busy. (Alternative to Assumptions 7 and 8.)

The discrepancies between the results given by 7 and 8 are frequently large enough for practical traffic densities that the use of the wrong formula would result either in inadequate or in extravagant installation. The results of 8 and 9 are generally so nearly alike as to be interchangeable in practice. The principal difference is that, although the use of 8 may, in extreme cases, require more channels than sources, 9 does not fall into this difficulty. Such a result is so absurd, however, that no one would put faith in it; so that the advantage which 9 appears to have in this respect is of doubtful value.

The assumptions dealing with what happens to lost traffic are:

Assumption 10—If a call is lost because no channel is available, the source which made it nevertheless continues to demand service. If during this time a channel becomes available it will be siezed and rendered unavailable for others

---

[4] It should also be noted that Assumption 8 implies, either that the chance of all sources being simultaneously busy is zero, or that Assumption 4 is violated. Any procedure which violates the latter assumption will be carefully avoided.

for the entire period that would have been required for the call if it had been successful, though the call will still be regarded as lost. (Alternative to Assumption 11).

Assumption 11—If a call is lost by virtue of insufficient equipment its holding-time is zero. (Alternative to Assumption 10.)

Assumption 10, of couse, does not correspond to what actually takes place in telephone practice. If a call is unsuccessful, especially if the subscriber is informed of this fact, he is more likely to hang up his receiver quickly than otherwise. But there are problems to which Assumption 10 appears rigorously applicable. I believe certain types of fire-alarm apparatus are so designed that the sending mechanism continues to attempt to send an alarm for a fixed time, whether or not the alarm circuit is already in use.

In order to avoid a considerable amount of circumlocution these two conditions will be spoken of briefly as "lost calls held" and "lost calls cleared," and each will be considered under a separate topical heading.[5]

169. The Elementary Probabilities; Lost Calls Held

The two events of prime importance in a telephone system are the inception of a call and its termination. If the probability of the occurrence of each of these events is known under all circumstances, it should be possible to determine exactly how much equipment is needed. Hence the attack will be begun by evaluating them in accordance with the assumptions given above, using, to begin with, 7 and 10 as the particular pair of alternatives.

Suppose a source is tested at a certain instant and observed for a short time, dt, thereafter. At the moment when it is first tested it must be either idle or busy. The probability that it is busy has already been denoted by p; the probability that it is idle must therefore be $1 - p$. If the source is busy at the beginning of this interval, the only way in which it can originate a call is for the subscriber to close the call in progress and start another one during the interval. The chance of this happening can be made negligibly small by choosing a sufficiently short time interval dt. Then it will be true that if the source is busy at the beginning of dt, it cannot possibly originate a call before dt ends.

The chance that a source, idle at the beginning of dt, becomes busy before its end is denoted by $p(b|i)$, and the chance of the source originating a call during the time interval dt, assuming that nothing

---

[5] "Lost calls held" must not be confused with "delayed calls"; for the latter stand by until served *and then consume a time equal to their holding time*—as would be the case if the fire-alarm mechanism were restrained from starting until its circuit was free.

is known about its condition at the beginning of that interval, by $p(b)$. Then by the rule for alternative compound probabilities the relationship

$$p(b) = (1 - p) \cdot p(b|i) + p \cdot p(b|b) \qquad (169.1)$$

may be written down at once. In words this relation expresses the logical proposition: the chance of a source becoming busy during a random time interval must be equal to the chance that it is idle and being idle becomes busy, plus the chance that it is busy and being busy becomes busy again. The latter of these has already been said to be negligible, and in accordance with the results of § 116 the random chance of a source originating a call is obviously $p(b) = n\,dt$, to the same degree of approximation. Hence, inserting this value into equation (169.1), the chance of an idle line becoming busy is found to be

$$p(b|i) = \frac{n\,dt}{1 - p}. \qquad (169.2)$$

This is one of the elementary probabilities.

If the chance of a source becoming *idle* during dt is considered, the logical proposition

$$p(i) = (1 - p) \cdot p(i|i) + p \cdot p(i|b) \qquad (169.3)$$

is obtained, which expresses the fact that if a source becomes idle, it must either be idle and become idle again (the chance of which is negligibly small) or else it must be busy and become idle. However, the source obviously becomes idle just as often as it becomes busy, and if nothing whatever is known about the condition of the line at the beginning of the time interval dt, the chance of it becoming idle during that interval must be the same as the chance of it becoming busy. In other words, $p(i) = p(b) = n\,dt$. Inserting this value into (169.3) it is found that

$$p(i|b) = \frac{n\,dt}{p}. \qquad (169.4)$$

If, instead of one source only, the entire group of λ sources are examined and j of them are found busy at the beginning of the interval, the chance that some of these j busy sources will become idle during dt is just j times as great as the chance for one individual source. Also, if Assumption 7 is adopted, the chance that one of the $\lambda - j$ idle sources will become *busy* is just $\lambda - j$ times as great as the chance for one individual source. These latter probabilities are therefore[6]

$$\frac{j\,n\,dt}{p} \tag{169.5}$$

and

$$\frac{(\lambda - j)\,n\,dt}{1 - p}, \tag{169.6}$$

respectively. In both these formulas p represents the chance that an instant observation, chosen at random, finds the line busy. It is obviously equal to the proportion of the hour during which the line may be expected to be busy; that is, to nT. (See §§ 78–80.)

170. Introduction of the Assumption of Statistical Equilibrium; Lost Calls Held

It is now possible to introduce the condition stated in Assumption 1; that is, to assert that the *probability* of the system being in any specified condition is the same at the end of the time interval dt as at its beginning.

Consider first a time at which all sources are idle. The chance of this condition existing is very small if the group has anything like the total amount of traffic which it can safely handle. Nevertheless, the condition *might* occur and therefore has some finite probability. This may be denoted by $^{\lambda}P'(0)$, the prime signifying the condition of lost calls held and the λ and 0 referring to the total number of sources in the group and to the number which are busy. Since there are λ idle sources the chance of *some one* of them becoming busy during a time dt is $\lambda n\,dt/(1 - p)$, and the probability that *none* will become busy during this length of time is

$$1 - \frac{\lambda\,n\,dt}{1 - p}.$$

---

[6] There are two statements of a negative context which it is worth while making with respect to these elementary probabilities. In the first place, passing from (169.2) to (169.6) *does not imply that the calling rate n is the same for all sources.* It is quite true that if the *j* sources which are busy happen to be those which call with the least frequency, the chance of a call originating during the time *dt* is greater than that given by (169.6); whereas if they happen to be those which call with the greatest frequency the reverse is the case. To mention special cases such as these, however, implies special knowledge regarding the particular sources which are busy, and this, of course, is not allowable. If the properly weighted average of these probabilities is formed it is found to be identical with (169.6) above.

In the second place *it is nowhere assumed that all calls are of the same length.* What *is* assumed is what is stated in Assumption 3—that *p* is the same for every source. Although the method of derivation which has been used is entirely free from the implication of equal holding times, the assumption of equality has been so frequently employed by other writers, even when their results could just as well have been obtained without it, that it seems well to point out that it is not here involved.

Hence the chance that all the sources are idle both at the beginning and at the end of the interval is

$$\left(1 - \frac{\lambda\, n\, dt}{1 - p}\right) {}^{\lambda}P'(0).$$

This is not, however, the total probability that none of the sources is busy at the end of this interval, for it *might* happen that at the beginning of the interval one source was busy, and that during the interval this source became idle. Denoting the probability that exactly one source is busy by ${}^{\lambda}P'(1)$, and noting that the probability of this source becoming idle is, by formula (169.5), dt/T, it is easily seen that the probability of it being busy at the beginning of the interval and idle at the end is

$$\frac{dt}{T}\cdot {}^{\lambda}P'(1).$$

There are other things that might conceivably happen during dt which would leave the entire group of sources idle when this interval closes. For example, two sources might be busy and both of them become idle. But if the chance of a particular source becoming idle is dt/T, the chance that both of two busy sources will become idle is the square of this, and is therefore of the second order in the very small quantity dt. In fact, a little consideration serves to show that the probability of any one change taking place in the condition of the set of sources is of the first order in dt; the probability of any two changes is of the second order; and so on. Since quantities of the second or higher orders in dt are so small as to be negligible, it follows that there is no need of considering the possibility of more than one such change taking place. Hence, to the first order of small quantities, the probability of all the sources of the system being idle at the end of the interval dt is the sum of the probability that all were idle at its beginning and remained so, and of the probability that one only was busy at the start and that this one became idle. These quantities having already been found, the probability of all sources being idle at the end of dt is easily seen to be

$$\left(1 - \frac{\lambda\, n\, dt}{1 - p}\right) {}^{\lambda}P'(0) + \frac{dt}{T} {}^{\lambda}P'(1).$$

To accord with the assumption of statistical equilibrium this must be the same as ${}^{\lambda}P'(0)$. Forming the equation to which this fact leads and making a few obvious cancellations, it is found that

$$\frac{\lambda\, n}{1 - p} {}^{\lambda}P'(0) = \frac{1}{T} {}^{\lambda}P'(1). \qquad (170.1)$$

A similar argument may be applied to the case where every source is busy. The probability that some one of the sources will become idle being $\lambda \, dt/T$, it follows that the probability of none of them becoming idle is $1 - \lambda \, dt/T$. If, therefore, the probability that λ sources are busy at the beginning of the interval is denoted by $^\lambda P'(\lambda)$, the chance that they will be busy both at the beginning and at the end of the interval is

$$\left(1 - \frac{\lambda \, dt}{T}\right) {}^\lambda P'(\lambda). \tag{170.2}$$

There is only one other way in which λ sources of the system may be busy at the end of the interval without more than one event taking place in the meantime. This occurs in case $\lambda - 1$ sources are busy at the start and the remaining one becomes busy before the interval ends. The probability of this is the product of the probability $^\lambda P'(\lambda - 1)$ that exactly $\lambda - 1$ sources are busy at the beginning of the interval, and the probability $n \, dt/(1 - p)$ that the remaining one becomes busy before it ends. Adding this product to (170.2), and remembering that the result must be $^\lambda P'(\lambda)$, we obtain the equation

$$\frac{n}{1 - p} {}^\lambda P'(\lambda - 1) = \frac{\lambda}{T} {}^\lambda P'(\lambda). \tag{170.3}$$

In general, the condition of j and only j sources busy at the end of the interval may occur in either of three ways:

(a) By exactly j being busy at the beginning of the interval and no calls being originated or discontinued during it, the probability of which is

$$\left(1 - \frac{\lambda - j}{1 - p} n \, dt - \frac{j}{T} dt\right) {}^\lambda P'(j).$$

(b) By exactly $j - 1$ being busy at the beginning of the interval and one new call originating, the probability of which is

$$\frac{\lambda - j + 1}{1 - p} n \, dt \, {}^\lambda P'(j - 1).$$

(c) By exactly $j + 1$ being in progress at the beginning of the interval and one being completed, the probability of which is

$$\frac{j + 1}{T} dt \, {}^\lambda P'(j + 1).$$

by summing these three terms to get the complete probability of exactly j busy sources at the end of the interval, and setting this probability equal to $^\lambda P'(j)$, an equation is obtained which may easily be reduced to the form

$$\left(\frac{\lambda - j + 1}{1 - p} n\right) {}^\lambda P'(j - 1) - \left(\frac{\lambda - j}{1 - p} n + \frac{j}{T}\right) {}^\lambda P'(j)$$

$$+ \left(\frac{j + 1}{T}\right) {}^\lambda P'(j + 1) = 0. \qquad (170.4)$$

171. The Probability Formulas Corresponding to Assumptions 7 and 10

If the equations (170.1), (170.3), and (170.4) were linearly independent they would be sufficient to determine the value of the probabilities $^\lambda P'(j)$ for each j from 0 to λ; for there are exactly $\lambda + 1$ of these probabilities and there are exactly $\lambda + 1$ equations corresponding to them. It so happens, however, that they are not linearly independent and an additional equation is necessary to solve the problem. This is readily obtained by remembering that

$$\sum_{j=0}^{\lambda} {}^\lambda P'(j) = 1. \qquad (171.1)$$

Solving these equations, which may be done by the theory of determinants,[7] it is found that

$$^\lambda P'(j) = C_j^\lambda p^j (1 - p)^{\lambda - j}. \qquad (171.2)$$

This equation gives with absolute accuracy the probability of exactly j busy sources out of a total of λ at an arbitrary instant when a test is made, provided Assumptions 7 and 10 are satisfied. It is, therefore, the probability that exactly j subscribers will wish to use the group of channels simultaneously.

The formula itself is the usual binomial distribution for the probability of an event happening j times in λ independent trials, if the probability of success in a single trial is p. The problem could have been so phrased that the answer would have been apparent at once: the longer method was adopted because it emphasizes the underlying hypotheses, and leaves no doubt as to the exact meaning of the answer when obtained.

To find the probability of a call being lost we make use of the following argument: If we choose an interval at random, and observe the system during this interval, a call may or may not occur. If it does,

---

[7] An alternative method of solution is: to find $^\lambda P'(1)$ in terms of $^\lambda P'(0)$ from (170.1); then by writing $j = 1$ in (170.4) to find $^\lambda P'(2)$ in terms of $^\lambda P'(0)$; next by writing $j = 2$ in (170.4) to find $^\lambda P'(3)$ in terms of $^\lambda P'(0)$; and so on. After every $^\lambda P'(j)$ has been so expressed, $^\lambda P'(0)$ may be found from (171.1).

it may or may not be lost; but since the interval has been chosen at random, without regard for the state of the system, "the probability that it is lost if it occurs" is just exactly the thing that we mean by the words "the probability of loss."

In the form in which we have stated it, however, this is a conditional probability, and to it the formula (37.1) may be applied at once if we let the symbol A, B mean "a call occurs and is lost," the symbol A, "a call occurs," and the symbol B, "it is lost."

As for the chance of a call occurring and being lost—that is, $P(A, B)$ —that is just

$$\sum_{j=v}^{\lambda} {}^{\lambda}P'(j) \frac{(\lambda - j)\, n\, dt}{1 - p} = \lambda n\, dt \sum_{j=v}^{\lambda-1} C_j^{\lambda-1} p^j (1 - p)^{\lambda - j - 1}$$

for if more than v sources are busy during our interval dt and a call occurs it will of necessity be lost. And as for the chance of a call occurring,—that is, $P(A)$—that is just $\lambda n\, dt$. So substituting these values in (37.1) and making certain simple rearrangements, we get for $P(B)$, or ${}^{\lambda}\Pi_v'$, the form

$$^{\lambda}\Pi_v' = \left(\frac{\lambda - \epsilon}{\lambda}\right)^{\lambda-1} \sum_{j=v}^{\lambda-1} C_j^{\lambda-1} \left(\frac{\epsilon}{\lambda - \epsilon}\right)^j \qquad (171.3)$$

where ϵ, or λp, is the expected traffic density in the group.

172. The Probability Formulas Corresponding to Assumptions 8 and 10

Formulas (171.2) and (171.3) are more complicated than is necessary for many purposes, for it frequently happens that the traffic arises from a very large number of sources, each one of which is busy but a small fraction of the time. In such cases the number of idle sources— and therefore the chance of a new call—is substantially the same at every instant, and we should expect to be able to find a suitable formula in a simpler form. Indeed we find, by allowing the number of sources λ to increase indefinitely without changing either ϵ or v, that (171.3) approaches the simpler expression

$$^{\infty}\Pi_v' = e^{-\epsilon} \sum_{j=v}^{\infty} \frac{\epsilon^j}{j!}. \qquad (172.1)$$

This formula is much used in computing trunk groups.

The corresponding formula for the probability of exactly j busy sources is obtained by taking the limit of (171.2), the result being, as we have seen in § 114,

$$\infty P'(j) = \frac{\epsilon^j \, e^{-\epsilon}}{j!}.$$ (172.2)

which is just the familiar Poisson Formula.

The manner in which (172.1) has been derived suggests that it is only accurate when the number of sources greatly exceeds the number of channels to which they have access. As a matter of fact, this is true if each source is independent of the rest as required by Assumption 7. However, the usefulness of (172.1) is actually much broader than this statement would imply, as can be shown by placing it upon a slightly different foundation, as follows:

Since $\epsilon = \lambda n T = \lambda p$, it follows that as λ is increased indefinitely, nT and p must each decrease according to the law $nT = p = \epsilon/\lambda$. Inserting this in (169.6) we find that the chance of a call being originated when j sources are busy is

$$\left(1 - \frac{j}{\lambda}\right) \frac{\epsilon}{1 - \frac{\epsilon}{\lambda}} \frac{dt}{T},$$

a quantity which approaches the limit $\epsilon \, dt/T$ as λ increases indefinitely. Since this limit is independent of j it follows that *formula (172.1) corresponds to Assumption 8, that is, to the case where the calls are distributed individually and collectively at random.*

From a practical standpoint Assumption 8 is inconsistent with a limited number of sources, for in practice it must always be true that the chance of a new call being originated when all the sources are busy is zero; and it is therefore dependent on the number of busy sources to just that extent.

This practical difficulty is reflected in the theory in the sense that the combination of Assumptions 8 and 10 is inconsistent with Assumption 4 unless the number of sources is infinite. For the purpose of this paragraph, therefore, Assumption 4 may be regarded as ignored. The same difficulty will not arise when Assumption 8 is combined with Assumption 11 unless the number of channels is at least as great as the number of sources.

Practically speaking, these difficulties in harmonizing our assumptions are unimportant unless the chance of all sources being busy simultaneously is quite large. Moreover, it is actually true that (172.1) and (172.2) are extremely valuable in many cases where the number of sources exceeds the number of channels by a sufficiently wide margin.

173. The Probability Formulas Corresponding to Assumptions 9 and 10

The practical analogue of Assumption 8 in the case of a limited number of sources is Assumption 9, which states that so long as any sources are idle the chance of a new call being originated is independent of their number, but that as soon as all sources become busy the chance of a new call being originated drops to zero. If the method of computation which has been used in obtaining formula (171.3) is applied to this set of assumptions the results

$$P'(j) = \frac{\dfrac{\epsilon^j}{j!}}{\sum_{j=0}^{\lambda} \dfrac{\epsilon^j}{j!}} \tag{173.1}$$

and

$$\Pi'_{\nu} = \frac{\sum_{j=\nu}^{\lambda-1} \dfrac{\epsilon^j}{j!}}{\sum_{j=0}^{\lambda} \dfrac{\epsilon^j}{j!}} \tag{173.2}$$

are obtained.

It can be shown that in most instances these formulas give approximately the same values as those obtained from (172.1) and (172.2). Practical conditions usually require that the probability of loss shall be small. This means, of course, that the terms in the numerator of (173.2) must be small, and it is easy to see that if this is true the difference between the denominator and a similar expression summed from zero to infinity is negligibly small. The latter expression, however, is the series expansion for e^{ϵ}. If this approximation is substituted for the denominator, (173.1) immediately becomes identical with (172.2).

Likewise if it is true that λ is much larger than ν the difference between the numerator of (173.2) and a similar expression summed from ν to infinity will be negligible and (173.2) will reduce to (172.1). In other words, (173.1) is always sensibly equal to (172.2) under practical conditions, and (173.2) is approximately equal to (172.1) except when the number of sources is very nearly the same as the number of channels. These qualitative assertions will be given quantitative illustration in §§ 179 and 180.

The one vital difference between (173.2) and (172.1) is that (172.1) does not depend upon λ at all and therefore gives a finite probability of loss even when the number of channels exceeds the number of sources—an absurd result to which (173.2) does not lead.

This absurdity is merely the practical manifestation of the remark made in § 172: that Assumption 8 is not strictly tenable in any case where the number of sources is limited.

The present section and the two which precede it contain formulas corresponding to the conditions of lost calls held, both when the sources of calls are assumed to be independent and when they are assumed to be dependent upon one another in such a way that the chance of a call originating is not influenced by the number of busy sources. It is necessary next to obtain analogous results for the condition of lost calls cleared.

174. The Elementary Probabilities; Lost Calls Cleared

A careful consideration of the derivation of (169.2) shows that the form of this equation is not affected by shifting to the assumption of lost calls cleared. The value of p, however, is somewhat altered, due to the fact that unsuccessful calls contribute nothing to the busy time of the sources. Hence instead of $p = nT$ we now have $p = (1 - \Pi)nT$.

In the development of the second elementary probability, the term $p(i/i)$, which occurs in (169.3) is no longer zero, since it can no longer be asserted that the probability of an idle source becoming busy and idle again during the interval dt is negligible; for if such an idle source were to originate a call at a time when there was no available channel to receive it, it would instantly become idle again. Thus, in effect, an idle source becomes idle, and $p(i|i)$ is not zero. Instead, $p(i|i)$ is now equal to the probability that all channels are occupied during dt, and that our source, which is idle, originates a call. We find at once

$$p\,(i|i) \,=\, \Pi\,\frac{n\,dt}{1 - p}.$$

Inserting this into (169.3), we get

$$p(i|b) \,=\, \frac{(1 \,-\, \Pi)n\,dt}{p};$$

and then remembering that p is now $(1 - \Pi)\,nT$, we are again led to the same formula dt/T as before.

It is obvious from a common-sense standpoint that the progress of a successful call, after its connection is established, should be in no way influenced by unsuccessful calls. In particular, the probability of termination and the holding time should be unaltered, whatever becomes of the unsuccessful calls. It would seem apparent, therefore, that if the chance of a busy line becoming idle is expressed in terms of dt and T only, the formula which results must be valid either for lost calls held or for lost calls cleared. This would establish the validity of (169.4) even if the method by which it was originally derived had introduced Assumption 9.

175. The Probability Formulas Corresponding to Assumptions 7 and 11

Having seen that both elementary probabilities are expressible in the same form as in the preceding case, it may be inferred at once that the form of equations (170.1) and (170.4) remains unchanged. This inference is borne out by an independent investigation. There is this difference in the circumstances, however: that, whereas in the preceding case the maximum number of sources which might be simultaneously busy was λ, in the present instance the number is ν. Equations (170.3) and (171.1) must therefore be reconsidered.

Suppose the probability of exactly ν channels being simultaneously busy is $\lambda P''(\nu)$, the λ and ν having the same significance as before and the double prime relating to the condition of lost calls cleared. If the system is to be in this condition at the end of a short interval dt, it may either have been so at the beginning of the interval and remained unchanged, or else it may have had just one idle channel at the beginning of the interval, this one becoming busy meanwhile. Taking both of these possibilities into account and introducing the principle of statistical equilibrium in exactly the same fashion as has been done above, it may be easily seen that (170.3) must be replaced by

$$\frac{\nu}{T}\,{}^{\lambda}P''(\nu) = \frac{\lambda - \nu + 1}{1 - p}\, n\,{}^{\lambda}P''(\nu - 1).$$

Similarly the sum of the probabilities of each number of busy sources from 0 to ν must be equal to unity, since it is impossible for this number to exceed λ. This gives

$$\sum_{j=0}^{\nu} {}^{\lambda}P''(j) = 1,$$

which takes the place of (171.1).

Having thus obtained the necessary independent equations, we can carry out their solution very easily by the use of determinants. The result is

$$ {}^{\lambda}P''(j) = \frac{C_j^{\lambda}\left(\dfrac{nT}{1 - p}\right)^{j}}{\displaystyle\sum_{j=0}^{\nu} C^{\lambda}\left(\dfrac{nT}{1 - p}\right)^{j}}. \tag{175.1}$$

It is desirable to express this formula in terms of the traffic density of the group. This traffic density is, as before, $\epsilon = \lambda\,nT$; whence

$$p = \frac{(1 - \Pi)\,\epsilon}{\lambda}.$$

Hence in terms of ϵ, (175.1) becomes

$$^{\lambda}P''(j) = \frac{C^{\lambda}\left(\dfrac{\epsilon}{\lambda - (1 - \Pi)\,\epsilon}\right)^{j}}{\displaystyle\sum_{j=0}^{\nu} C^{\lambda}\left(\dfrac{\epsilon}{\lambda - (1 - \Pi)\,\epsilon}\right)^{j}}. \qquad (175.2)$$

The probability of loss is obtained by the same argument as in § 171. The chance of a call being originated during a short interval of observation is $\lambda\, n\, dt$ as before. The chance of a call being lost, however, is much simpler, since it is now impossible for more than ν sources to be busy simultaneously. It is

$$^{\lambda}P''(\nu)\,\frac{\lambda - \nu}{1 - p}\, n\, dt.$$

The ratio of these two quantities is the probability of loss. It is easily seen to be

$$^{\lambda}\Pi''_{\nu} = \left(\frac{\lambda - \nu}{\lambda}\right)\frac{^{\lambda}P''(\nu)}{1 - p} = \frac{1}{1 - p}\,\frac{C_{\nu}^{\lambda-1}\left(\dfrac{nT}{1 - p}\right)^{\nu}}{\displaystyle\sum_{j=0}^{\nu} C_{j}^{\lambda}\left(\dfrac{nT}{1 - p}\right)^{j}}.$$

A less obvious form, but one which is more convenient for computation is

$$^{\lambda}\Pi''_{\nu} = \frac{C_{\nu}^{\lambda-1}\left(\dfrac{\epsilon}{\lambda - (1 - \Pi)\,\epsilon}\right)^{\nu}}{\displaystyle\sum_{j=0}^{\nu} C_{j}^{\lambda-1}\left(\dfrac{\epsilon}{\lambda - (1 - \Pi)\,\epsilon}\right)^{j}}. \qquad (175.3)$$

176. The Probability Formulas Corresponding to Assumptions 8 and 11

Formulas (175.2) and (175.3) are analogous to (171.2) and (171.3). From them others may be derived which are appropriate when the sources are independent and their number greatly exceeds the number of channels, or when the sources, though not very numerous, are so related that as more and more of them become busy the individual calling rates of those which remain idle increase at a rate which just neutralizes their decrease in number. This is done by taking the limits of (175.2) and (175.3) as λ becomes infinite, just as was done in § 172. In this way formulas analogous to (172.1) and (172.2) are obtained. They are

$$^\infty P''(j) = \frac{\dfrac{\epsilon^j}{j!}}{\displaystyle\sum_{j=0}^{\nu}\frac{\epsilon^j}{j!}} \tag{176.1}$$

and

$$^\infty \Pi_\nu'' = \frac{\dfrac{\epsilon^\nu}{\nu!}}{\displaystyle\sum_{j=0}^{\nu}\frac{\epsilon^j}{j!}}. \tag{176.2}$$

As has been said in connection with formulas (172.1) and (172.2), Assumption 8 is not tenable if it is possible for all sources to be busy simultaneously, for in this case there are no idle sources left to originate calls. This manifests itself in the fact that (176.2), like (172.1), gives a finite probability of loss, even when $\lambda < \nu$. For this reason, Assumption 4 must be ignored in developing (176.2) if, $\lambda \leqq \nu$.

177. The Probability Formulas Corresponding to Assumptions 9 and 11

No change is made in either (176.1) or (176.2) when Assumption 8 is replaced by Assumption 9, unless $\lambda \leqq \nu$. However, if $\lambda < \nu$ they become, respectively,

$$P''(j) = \frac{\dfrac{\epsilon^j}{j!}}{\displaystyle\sum_{j=0}^{\lambda}\frac{\epsilon^j}{j!}} \tag{177.1}$$

and

$$\Pi_\nu'' = 0. \tag{177.2}$$

These formulas are identical with (173.1) and (173.2).[8] That this is to be expected is obvious since, when no calls are lost, what happens to lost calls is immaterial.

---

[8] When $\lambda \leqq \nu$ the upper index of summation in the numerator of (173.2) is less than the lower index, so that the formula is meaningless as written in § 173. Its true value, however, is zero, as listed in Table 178.2.

178. Recapitulation of Formulas

Formulas have now been obtained corresponding to each of the six alternative pairs of assumptions, and it is desirable to collect them together for purposes of reference. This is done in Tables 178.1 to 178.3.

Table 178.1 represents schematically the relationship of the various

TABLE 178.1

Schematic Representation of Notation

Assumptions as to Origination of Calls	Assumptions as to Treatment of Lost Calls	
	Lost Calls Cleared (Assumption 11)	*Lost Calls Held* (Assumption 10)
Sources Independent (Assumption 7)	I $^{\lambda}P''(j)$ $^{\lambda}\Pi_{\nu}''$	II $^{\lambda}P'(j)$ $^{\lambda}\Pi_{\nu}'$
Calls occur individually and collectively at random (Assumption 8)	III $^{\infty}P''(j)$ $^{\infty}\Pi_{\nu}''$	IV $^{\infty}P'(j)$ $^{\infty}\Pi_{\nu}'$
Calls occur individually and collectively at random, unless all sources are busy; then none occur (Assumption 9)	V $P''(j)$ Π_{ν}''	VI $P'(j)$ Π_{ν}'

Note.—The Roman numerals are for the purpose of identification in connection with the curves which follow.

Formulas I, II, III, and IV are known, respectively, by the names Engset, binomial, Erlang, and Poisson.

formulas to the sets of assumptions upon which they are based; whereas Tables 178.2 and 178.3 give the formulas themselves.

In developing these probabilities in the preceding pages there has been no need to write down the circumstances under which they take the value zero. This was evident from the context. In the tables, however, these limiting conditions are given in order that no ambiguity may be involved.

TABLE 178.2

PROBABILITY OF LOSS

Assumptions[a]	Formulas		Reference Number
7 and 11	$\lambda\Pi_\nu'' = 0$ $\lambda\Pi_\nu'' = \dfrac{C_j^{\lambda-1}\left(\dfrac{\epsilon}{\lambda-(1-\Pi)\epsilon}\right)^\nu}{\displaystyle\sum_{j=0}^{\nu} C_j^{\lambda-1}\left(\dfrac{\epsilon}{\lambda-(1-\Pi)\epsilon}\right)^j}$	$\lambda \leqq \nu$ $\lambda > \nu$	(175.3)
7 and 10	$\lambda\Pi_\nu' = 0$ $\lambda\Pi_\nu' = \left(\dfrac{\lambda-\epsilon}{\lambda}\right)^{\lambda-1}\displaystyle\sum_{j=\nu}^{\lambda-1} C_j^{\lambda-1}\left(\dfrac{\epsilon}{\lambda-\epsilon}\right)^j$	$\lambda \leqq \nu$ $\lambda > \nu$	(171.3)
8 and 11 (4 ignored if $\lambda \leqq \nu$)	$\infty\Pi_\nu'' = \dfrac{\dfrac{\epsilon^\nu}{\nu!}}{\displaystyle\sum_{j=0}^{\nu}\dfrac{\epsilon^j}{j!}}$	$\lambda \geqq 0$	(176.2)
8 and 10 (4 ignored if λ is finite)	$\infty\Pi_\nu' = e^{-\epsilon}\displaystyle\sum_{j=\nu}^{\infty}\dfrac{\epsilon^j}{j!}$	$\lambda \geqq 0$	(172.1)
9 and 11	$\Pi_\nu'' = 0$ $\Pi_\nu'' = {}^\infty\Pi_\nu''$	$\lambda \leqq \nu$ $\lambda > \nu$	(177.2)
9 and 10	$\Pi_\nu' = 0$ $\Pi_\nu' = \dfrac{\displaystyle\sum_{j=\nu}^{\lambda-1}\dfrac{\epsilon^j}{j!}}{\displaystyle\sum_{j=0}^{\lambda}\dfrac{\epsilon^j}{j!}}$	$\lambda \leqq \nu$ $\lambda > \nu$	(173.2)

[a] Unless explicitly stated all assumptions from 1 to 6 are used.

TABLE 178.3

PROBABILITY OF CONGESTION j

Assumptions[a]	Formulas	Reference Number
7 and 11	$$\lambda P''(j) = \frac{C_j^\lambda \left(\dfrac{\epsilon}{\lambda - (1 - \Pi)\epsilon}\right)^j}{\sum\limits_{j=0}^{\nu} C_j^\lambda \left(\dfrac{\epsilon}{\lambda - (1 - \Pi)\epsilon}\right)^j} \qquad j \leqq \nu$$ $$\lambda P''(j) = 0 \qquad\qquad\qquad\qquad\qquad j > \nu$$	(175.2)
7 and 10	$$\lambda P'(j) = \left(\frac{\lambda - \epsilon}{\lambda}\right)^\lambda C_j^\lambda \left(\frac{\epsilon}{\lambda - \epsilon}\right)^j \qquad j \geqq 0$$	(171.2)
8 and 11 (4 ignored if $\lambda < \nu$)	$$\infty P''(j) = \frac{\dfrac{\epsilon^j}{j!}}{\sum\limits_{j=0}^{\nu} \dfrac{\epsilon^j}{j!}} \qquad j \leqq \nu$$ $$\infty P''(j) = 0 \qquad\qquad j > \nu$$	(176.1)
8 and 10 (4 ignored if λ is finite)	$$\infty P'(j) = e^{-\epsilon} \frac{\epsilon^j}{j!} \qquad j \geqq 0$$	(172.2)
9 and 11	$$P''(j) = P'(j) \qquad \lambda \leqq \nu$$ $$P''(j) = \infty P''(j) \qquad \lambda \geqq \nu$$	(177.1)
9 and 10	$$P'(j) = \frac{\dfrac{\epsilon^j}{j!}}{\sum\limits_{j=0}^{\lambda} \dfrac{\epsilon^j}{j!}} \qquad j \leqq \lambda$$ $$P'(j) = 0 \qquad\qquad j > \lambda$$	(173.1)

[a] Unless explicitly stated all assumptions from 1 to 6 are used.

179. Numerical Comparison of Formulas; The Dependence of the Probability of Loss upon the Number of Sources when the Traffic Density of the Group Is Held Constant

In order to gain some conception of the magnitude of the differences between these various formulas, it is desirable to present a few numerical examples that illustrate the essential points of their behavior.

In the first place, the extent to which they depend upon the number of sources may be considered. To illustrate this point a group of ten channels[9] is chosen and it is assumed that this group receives its traffic, sometimes from a few busy sources, sometimes from many relatively idle ones, but always in such a way that the traffic density is 4. The

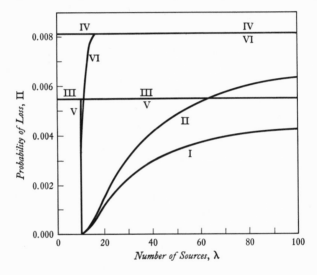

FIG. 179.1   COMPARISON OF VARIOUS FORMULAS FOR PROBABILITY OF LOSS WHEN THE TRAFFIC DENSITY IS HELD CONSTANT.

results plotted against λ, the number of sources, are shown in Fig. 179.1, each curve corresponding to one of the formulas of Table 178.2.

The two formulas corresponding to the assumption of independent sources (the top row in the scheme of Table 178.1) give the Curves

---

[9] Attention should be called to the fact that in this and the following sections the particular numerical values chosen are such as to give quite appreciable differences between the various formulas. It would be a mistake to infer that the differences are always of this order of magnitude. As a matter of fact they may be either larger or smaller. It may be stated as a rough general rule—although this rule like most others has its exceptions—that where the groups of channels are large, the differences will be smaller than those here obtained, and vice versa.

I and II. These coincide with the λ-axis so long as $\lambda \leqq \nu$, and rise gradually as λ increases beyond this value.

The formulas corresponding to Assumption 8 give horizontal lines, as is to be expected from the fact that the assumption implies independence of λ. They are designated III and IV. That they are asymptotic to the Curves I and II is evident from the fact that (176.2) and (172.1) were obtained as limiting cases of (175.3) and (171.3). They do not approach the λ-axis even when $\lambda < \nu$, a fact which is merely the graphical equivalent of the statement already made—that they give a finite probability of loss even when the number of channels exceeds the number of sources.

Curves V and VI, which correspond to the third row in Table 178.1, occupy an intermediate position. They coincide with the λ-axis for $\lambda < \nu$ and thus avoid the absurd results to which formulas (176.2) and (172.1) give rise. Indeed, the purpose of the modification of Assumption 8 contained in Assumption 9 was exactly to avoid this absurdity.

For all values of λ which exceed ν, Curve V coincides with Curve III. That this is as it should be is seen from the fact that when λ exceeds ν it is not possible for all the sources to be simultaneously busy, and hence the modification of Assumption 8 plays no part whatever. Curve VI, on the other hand, while it rises more steeply than II, does not jump abruptly from zero to its maximum value but approaches the latter asymptotically. The reason for this lies in the fact that if lost calls are held, there can be more than ν in progress at one time. In this case, more than one must clear before a successful call can be made. Thus, those calls which fail still produce a "hang-over" effect, which interferes with the chance of success of other calls. This "hang-over" becomes greater and greater as the number of sources is increased. Indeed, it is this effect which is responsible for the fact that all of the curves corresponding to the first column of Table 178.1 show smaller probabilities of loss than do the analogous curves of the second column.

It may seem surprising at first thought that the "hang-over" effect should ever produce an increase in the number of lost calls as great as that which is necessary to account for the difference between Curves III and IV. In fact, Curve III says that, if lost calls are cleared, only about 0.5% of the calls are lost, and Curve IV says that this small proportion, if held instead of cleared, is capable of increasing the proportion of loss by about 50%. It should be remembered in this connection, however, that the very fact that calls are lost implies that they are originated at a time when the system is already congested. Therefore, unless they are quickly disposed of, a very few of them may lengthen the period of congestion to a considerable extent and increase the proportion of loss correspondingly.

That there is no "hang-over" effect when λ exceeds ν by 1 is evident from a common-sense point of view. Hence the modified Assumption 8 should give exactly the same results regardless of whether lost calls are held or cleared. In other words, Curves III, V, and VI should all cross at the value $\lambda = 11$. That they do so is evident from the figure, as well as from the fact that in this case (176.2), (177.2) and (173.2) are all identical.

180. Numerical Comparison of Formulas; The Dependence of the Allowable Traffic Density upon the Number of Sources, when the Proportion of Loss Is Fixed

The curves of Fig. 179.1 show very satisfactorily the essential differences between the results to which our various combinations of assumptions lead. They are open to the objection, however, that they give an exaggerated idea of the practical importance of these differences. Ordinarily probability formulas are not used, as is done here, to compute the proportion of loss which corresponds to a preassigned amount of traffic, but for the converse purpose of computing the maximum allowable traffic density when the allowable proportion of loss is known. Since small changes in the traffic density produce large changes in the proportion of loss, formulas that give widely different results when used in the former way may agree surprisingly well when used in the latter.

In order that no such erroneous impressions may be produced, curves showing the traffic density corresponding to a loss of one call in one hundred are shown in Fig. 180.1. As before, a group of ten channels is considered and the number of sources is varied through the range from 0 to 100. The different curves correspond to the six alternative formulas of Table 178.2.

Formulas (176.2) and (172.1) again lead to the straight lines III and IV, which extend unbroken even when $\lambda < 10$. Formula (177.2) leads to Curve V which coincides with III when $\lambda > 10$. Similarly, (173.2) leads to a curve which crosses III and V at $\lambda = 11$, and for all subsequent values practically coincides with IV. From a practical standpoint these four curves are sufficiently alike that any one of them might be used in place of any other.

Curves I and II, however, which are obtained from formulas (175.3) and (171.3) and therefore correspond to the first row of Table 178.1, differ from the others by amounts which are of engineering importance. For instance, when the number of sources is 15 they allow these sources to originate about 20% more traffic than is allowable when the other formulas are adopted.

In other words, little change of practical consequence is introduced in our results by shifting from the assumption of lost calls held to the assumption of lost calls cleared; or by shifting from Assumption 8 to its modified form 9. *The only difference which is of serious consequence comes from using, on the one hand, the assumption of independent sources (Assumption 7) and on the other the assumption that the chance of a new call being made during short period of observation is not affected by the state of the system when that period of observation begins (Assumption 8 or 9).*

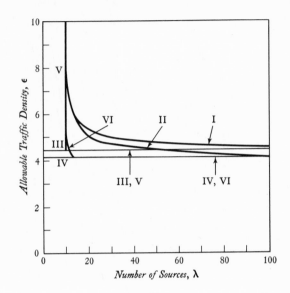

FIG. 180.1   COMPARISON OF VARIOUS FORMULAS FOR THE ALLOWABLE TRAFFIC
DENSITY WHEN THE PROBABILITY OF LOSS IS HELD CONSTANT

181. Charts for Purposes of Computation

Since all of the formulas of Table 178.2 group themselves into two similar classes in such a way that members of the *same* class give very similar results, whereas members *of different* classes do not agree so well, it will be sufficient for the further purposes of this study, as well as for most practical needs, to confine attention to a typical pair. For this purpose that pair is chosen which corresponds to the extreme conditions represented by Curves I and IV in Figs 179.1 and 180.1. All the other formulas give results which lie intermediate to these two but agree with the one or the other of them sufficiently well that no account need generally be taken of the differences.

Figure 181.1 is a working chart computed in accordance with equation (175.3). The entire figure corresponds to a loss of one call per thousand. Each curve corresponds to a group of channels, the size of which is indicated by the attached number. The numbers

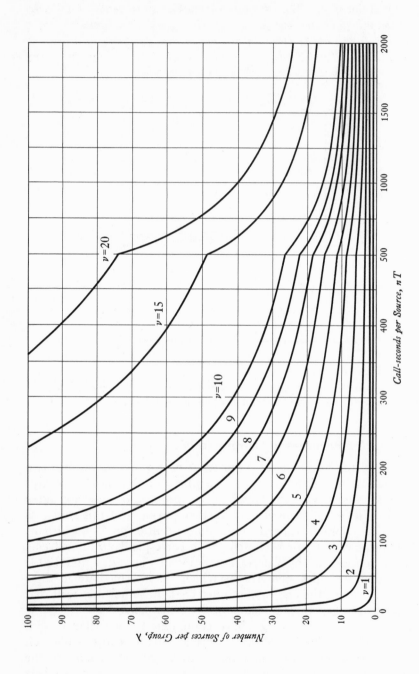

Fig. 181.1 Working Chart for the Engset Formula. Probability of
Loss = 0.001

along the left-hand margin represent the number of sources, and the numbers at the bottom give values of 3600ϵ (i.e., n, the number of calls *per hour*, multiplied by T, the holding time *in seconds*).[10]

As an illustration of the use of this chart, suppose it is desired to assign to a group of ten channels a group of sources, each of which originates on the average three calls of 100 seconds duration per hour. Then $nT = 300$ call seconds. Entering the chart, it is found from the curve for $\nu = 10$ that the ordinate corresponding to this value is $\lambda = 41$. Hence 41 sources may be assigned to the group of ten channels.

As another illustration, suppose 200 sources are to be accommodated by switches capable of reaching ten trunks each. Suppose on the average these sources originate during the busy hour two calls of an average duration of 140 seconds, and that it is required to find how they shall be grouped. Multiplying the calling rate by the holding time gives 280 call seconds. Entering the chart with this value it is found that each group of trunks is capable of accommodating 43 sources. Therefore 4 full groups of trunks are required. There then remain 28 sources to be accommodated by the odd group. The point upon the chart which corresponds to $\lambda = 28$ and $3600\epsilon = 280$ lies between the curves marked 7 and 8. Hence the odd group will require 8 channels to carry its traffic. The grouping of the sources will therefore be 4 groups of 43 and 1 group of 28, and the channels required will be 4 groups of 10 and 1 group of 8, or a total of 48.

Figure 181.2 is a similar chart except that it corresponds to a probability of loss of one call per hundred. Its use is identical with that of Fig. 181.1.

In Fig. 181.3 are given working curves corresponding to the formula (172.1). Their use is slightly different from that of the curves in Figs 181.1 and 181.2. The size of the group of channels is now represented by the numbers along the horizontal axis instead of by those on the curves, while the curves themselves correspond to a particular value of the probability of loss. Curves are given for $\Pi = 0.01$ and $\Pi = 0.001$. The vertical axis now represents the maximum allowable traffic density, from which the number of sources must be determined since the values of λ do not explicitly occur.

The use of this chart may be illustrated by solving exactly the same problems as before. In the first case a group of 10 channels is available. Entering the chart, the allowable traffic density for such a group (for a loss of one call in a thousand) is found to be $\epsilon = 2.96$. The number of sources that can be accommodated is the largest number the traffic from which does not exceed this density. The traffic density for a single source is $nT = 0.0833$. Hence the number of sources that can safely be accommodated is $2.96/0.0833 = 35$. This number corresponds to the 41 obtained from the use of Fig. 181.1.

In the second illustration, where it is necessary to accommodate 200 sources originating on the average two calls of 140 seconds holding time

---

[10] In the telephone industry, calling rate and holding time are usually stated in this way.

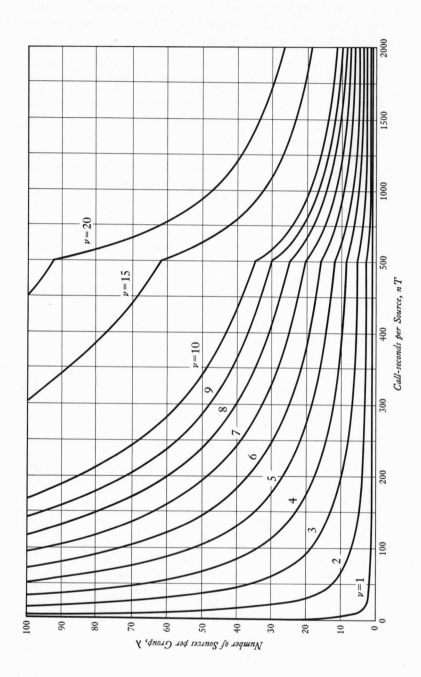

Fig. 181.2 Working Chart for the Engset Formula. Probability of Loss = 0.01.

apiece, the average traffic density of a source is $nT = 0.0778$. Since the traffic density of a group may be 2.96 we find that the number of sources that can be accommodated is $2.96/0.0778 = 38$. There are therefore required 5 full groups of 10 trunks each, together with an odd group sufficiently large to handle the traffic from the remaining 10 sources. These 10 sources give rise to a traffic density amounting to $0.0778 \times 10 = 0.778$.

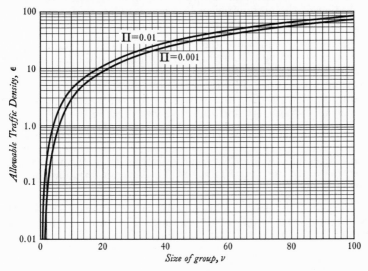

FIG. 181.3   WORKING CHART FOR THE POISSON FORMULA.

Entering the chart with this value it is found that the number of trunks required for this odd group is 5. The total number of trunks is therefore 55. The difference between this result and that obtained from Fig. 181.1 is about 14%.

By means of charts such as these, computations can be carried out without the expenditure of an undue amount of time. That is, the complicated formulas listed in Table 178.2 can actually be reduced to a form in which their use for practical purposes is feasible. Figures 181.1, 181.2, and 181.3 do not cover a sufficient range of values to make them satisfactory for such purposes; and, indeed, it would be difficult to print, in pages such as these, charts on a scale large enough to be of much practical value. It is evident, however, that constructing such charts is possible; and since they need be made but once, the fact that the computations involved in producing them are tedious is a matter of minor importance.

Problems

1. In a certain bootblack "parlor" of a railroad terminal, the expectation of the number of customers during the peak period is 75 per hour. On the

average a shine requires 4 minutes. Assume that a prospective customer, if the chairs are all full, merely looks in the door and walks away. Assume also that the customers arrive individually and collectively at random. What probability formula would you use to find the number of chairs required in order that the proportion of lost trade should not exceed 0.01?

2. Use the Poisson Formula as a means of obtaining a first approximation to the number of chairs required in Problem 1. Then find, by computation for neighboring values of v, the correct number.

3. It is desired to measure the number of bursts of static per second by means of a recording chronograph. Assuming that the expected number per second is $n = 1.7$, and that the expected duration of each is $T = 0.3$ second, what proportion will not give distinct signals?

[Assume that overlapping bursts will be recorded as one; also that the bursts occur individually and collectively at random.]

4. The chronograph record consists of a number of separate entries of measurable duration. It is possible to read directly, therefore, the number of separate entries n^* and their average duration T^*. Due to overlapping, however, these are not equal to n and T. Develop formulas for n and T in terms of n^* and T^*.

5. During an hour, such a chronograph record showed 18,241 separate entries, the aggregate length of which was 2977 seconds. What figures do you deduce for the frequency and duration of the static pulses?

182. Some Hunting Problems

We now turn to a different class of problems: those which concern the amount of traveling which the "switch" must do in steering a call along its way. Such problems are of importance for two reasons: first, because the amount of wear to which a switch is subject ordinarily decreases with decreasing travel; second, because in many cases the time consumed in the hunting operation increases the period required to complete the connection by just that much. We choose again a number of problems which typify, in the main, the methods of solution, without requiring an explanation of any of the technical details of telephony.

In the first place, we must notice that the "switches" themselves may be of either of two types. Each switch may be permanently connected to a "source", its function being to select a channel for that source to use when the source needs it. Such switches are technically known as "selectors." Or it may be permanently connected to the channel and, when a channel is needed by one of its group of sources, it may go in search of the "calling" source. Such switches are technically known as "finders." In either case, of course, the "group of switches" is synonymous with one of the groups about which we have been speaking—that is, it is immaterial whether we speak of a "group of sources" or of the "group of selector switches" to which those sources are connected; and the same is true of channels and finder switches. In our present study it will be simpler to think in terms of the switches in each case.

The second point which we must notice especially is that, although the switches are assumed to be identical and to reach the same group, they may not reach the various members of that group in the same order. To be explicit about this, we may think of a group of six selectors, represented schematically by the arrows of Fig. 182.1; and

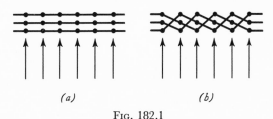

(a) *(b)*

Fig. 182.1

we may suppose that they reach a group of three channels represented by the horizontal lines. So far our description applies equally well to either part (*a*) or part (*b*) of the figure. But all six switches in the arrangement (*a*) reach channel 1 first, channel 2 next, and channel 3 last; in arrangement (*b*) each channel appears in the lowest ("preferential") position before two switches, in the second-choice position before two others, and finally as last-choice positions for the remaining two. Condition (*a*) is known technically as a "straight multiple" and condition (*b*) as a "slipped multiple."[11]

The third point which we must notice concerns the behavior of the switch when it is released from service. Customarily it does one of two things: (1) returns to a "rest position," so that all idle switches are lined up in a neat schematic row as shown in Fig. 182.1; or (2) stays where it is, so that idle switches may be most anywhere, as shown in Fig. 182.2.

Fig. 182.2

Finally, in the fourth place, the switches may hunt singly or in groups. When they hunt as a group, the switch which first succeeds in its search takes charge of the call and the rest stop hunting.

---

[11] Not all "slipped multiples" are arranged exactly as in (*b*), but we shall use the term for this simplest arrangement only.

Naturally, a difference in any of these three essentials may very profoundly affect the length of hunt; so separate consideration must, in general, be given to each possibility. We shall take up a number of cases in order.

183. Individual Hunting from a Normal Position

ONE FINDER STARTS FROM NORMAL REST POSITION. STRAIGHT MULTIPLE.

The simplest of all possible problems is that of a single finder hunting over a straight multiple. Obviously, how far it must go is determined solely by the position of the source which wants it. If there are ν sources and all have the same calling rate, the expected number of terminals tested will be

$$\epsilon(k) = \frac{\nu + 1}{2};$$ (183.1)

and the probability of testing more than a specified number k will be

$$p(> k) = 1 - \frac{k}{\nu}.$$ (183.2)

ONE FINDER STARTS FROM NORMAL REST POSITION. SLIPPED MULTIPLE.

If the multiple, instead of being "straight," is "slipped," the formulas (183.1) and (183.2) are still unchanged. The principal difference between this case and the former one lies in the fact that in this case all sources get equivalent grades of service, since all appear equally often in the favorable position, whereas in the former case those which appear nearest the rest position get a better grade of service than the others. The grade of service, averaged over all lines, is the same in both cases, however.

For our second problem we may state the conditions as follows:

ONE SELECTOR STARTS FROM NORMAL REST POSITION. STRAIGHT MULTIPLE.

Each channel appears in the same position before every switch; all switches start from rest; if every channel is busy the switches do not repeat the test, but return to normal and discard the call. Under these circumstances it is evident that the channels are not equally used. The first to be tested will be in use most of the time, whereas the last in the group will seldom be busy. It is not true, however, as might be supposed at first thought, that when six channels are busy it is always the lowest six, for the following reason: if, when the last call preceding the one under consideration was made, the first six channels were busy, this last preceding call was assigned to the seventh channel; but between that time and the present, one of the six calls which were originally in progress may have been discontinued. This would leave exactly six busy channels, but they would not be the lowest six and a hunt of seven terminals would not be required. For example, if the call which occupied the lowest channel in the group has been discontinued, the switch which handles our present call need only test this lowest channel in order to find accommodation; so instead of hunting seven terminals it need hunt only one.

What we must find is the probability that *the first k channels are busy and the next is idle.* This we may easily do by noting what would happen if, for some reason, all those calls which did not find service among these k channels were instantly cleared. Obviously this would have no effect whatever upon the service rendered by these k channels. *Hence the chance of the first k channels being simultaneously busy is equal to the probability of all k busy on the basis of formula*[12] (176.1).

Hence we have[13]:

$$_{[k]}P = {}^{\infty}\Pi_k'' = \frac{\dfrac{\epsilon^k}{k!}}{1 + \epsilon + \dfrac{\epsilon^2}{2!} + \ldots + \dfrac{\epsilon^k}{k!}}.$$

The probability which we desire—that is, $_{[k]}P_{k+1}$—may be obtained by subtracting from all the cases in which the first k channels are busy those cases in which the $(k + 1)$'st channel is also busy. The latter cases, however, are represented by the probability $_{[k+1]}P$, which is given by the same law as $_{[k]}P$. We therefore have for the probability of hunting exactly $k + 1$ terminals

$$p(k + 1) = {}_{[k]}P - {}_{[k+1]}P.$$

Similarly the probability of hunting exactly k terminals is

$$p(k) = {}_{[k-1]}P - {}_{[k]}P = {}^{\infty}\Pi_{k-1}'' - {}^{\infty}\Pi_k''.$$

---

[12] We shall assume that calls are distributed individually and collectively at random. Other assumptions could easily be used, but this will be quite sufficient for our present purposes.

[13] The notation has this significance: $_1P$ means "the first trunk busy"; $_{1,3}P_2$ "the first and third busy and the second idle"; $_{[4]}P_5$ means "the first four busy and the fifth idle"; $_6P_{[5]}$ means "the first five idle and the sixth busy." The scheme, I think, is obvious.

The expected hunt under these circumstances is[14]

$$\epsilon(k) = \sum_{k=1}^{\nu} k\,p(k).$$

This can be thrown into the form

$$\epsilon(k) = \sum_{k=0}^{\nu-1} {}_{[k]}P,$$

which is more suitable for numerical calculation.

ONE TRUNK SELECTOR STARTS FROM NORMAL REST POSITION. SLIPPED MULTIPLE.

If the multiple is so arranged that each channel appears as often in one position as in any other the situation is quite different. In this case busy channels will be distributed in haphazard fashion over the entire bank instead of being concentrated near the bottom, and the chance of an idle channel being near the bottom of the group will be materially greater than in the preceding example. The solution of the problem is obtained by the following argument:

The probability of exactly j busy channels is denoted by[15] $P(j)$. If these j busy channels are distributed at random over the entire group, the chance that the first k tested by the switch are all busy is

$$_{[k]}P = \frac{C_k^j}{C_k^\nu}.$$

The probability of testing more than k terminals is found by summing the product of these two expressions for every possible value of j. Formally it is given by the formula

$$p(> k) = \sum_{j=k}^{\nu} {}_{[k]}P \cdot P(j).$$

Using formula (176.1) for $P(j)$, we find that

$$p(> k) = \frac{(\nu-k)!}{\nu!} \frac{\displaystyle\sum_{j=k}^{\nu} \frac{\epsilon^j}{(j-k)!}}{\displaystyle\sum_{i=0}^{\nu} \frac{\epsilon^i}{i!}}.$$

---

[14] Note how the assumption of "lost calls cleared" is justified by the fact that, when all ν channels are busy, the switches discard the call. Hence the chance of hunting just ν terminals is just $_{[\nu-1]}P$, and $p(>\nu) = 0$.

[15] We shall use for it the formula $\infty P''(j)$, to conform to the conditions as we have laid them down. In other circumstances some other formula might be needed.

If, now, we call $j - k$ by a new symbol (which may as well be i as anything, since the two summations are entirely independent) this becomes[16]

$$p(> k) = \epsilon^k \frac{(\nu - k)!}{\nu!} \frac{\displaystyle\sum_{i=0}^{\nu-k} \frac{\epsilon^i}{i!}}{\displaystyle\sum_{i=0}^{\nu} \frac{\epsilon^i}{i!}} = \frac{{}^{\infty}\Pi_{\nu}''}{{}^{\infty}\Pi_{\nu-k}''}. \tag{183.3}$$

As before,

$$p(k) = p(> k - 1) - p(> k). \tag{183.4}$$

We may also find the expected hunt, which is

$$\epsilon(k) = \sum_{k=0}^{\nu} k\, p(k).$$

This, however, can be further reduced to a form which is more suitable for purposes of computation by noting that when written out in full it is:

$$\epsilon(k) = p(> 0) - p(> 1)$$
$$+ 2p(> 1) - 2p(> 2)$$
$$+ 3p(> 2) - \ldots$$
$$\ldots - (\nu - 1)p(> \nu - 1)$$
$$+ \nu p(> \nu - 1),$$

which is obviously equal to

$$\epsilon(k) = \sum_{k=0}^{\nu-1} p(> k).$$

As an illustration of the extent to which the average hunt is reduced by slipping the multiple, the results of a numerical example computed in accordance with each of these formulas may be presented. The case chosen is one in which the total number of channels is $n = 100$ and the expected number busy is $\epsilon = 34.49$. If each channel appears in the same position before all the switches, the average number of terminals tested is found to be 19.6; whereas if the multiple is slipped, the average number of tests is only 1.53.

---

[16] Except for $k = \nu$. It is obvious, from a common-sense standpoint, that the switch cannot hunt more than ν terminals. Hence $p(> \nu) = 0$. The formula fails to give this because the switch might (logically) fail in its ν'th trial if all channels were busy, and in that case additional trials *would be needed* for success.

184. Individual Hunting with Stay-Put Switches

In studying the problem of individual hunting with stay-put switches we shall assume that the switch is capable of hunting over the entire group of channels no matter from what position it may start, but that if no idle trunk is then found it will not repeat the test. Otherwise when all trunks are busy the number of terminals tested before an idle trunk is found would depend upon the length of time which elapses before a trunk becomes idle and the speed with which the test is made, both of which questions we wish to avoid.

ONE STAY-PUT SELECTOR HUNTING OVER A STRAIGHT MULTIPLE.

We consider only the case of selector switches, as the other case is trivial. It is obvious that after the system has been in operation for a certain length of time, the switches will be distributed at random over the terminal bank. Since the busy channels are likewise distributed at random over the bank they are also at random with respect to any switch. Hence in this case the hunting probabilities follow exactly the same law as if the switches started from a normal position and hunted over a slipped bank. The formulas to be applied are therefore (183.3) and (183.4).

ONE STAY-PUT SELECTOR HUNTING OVER A SLIPPED MULTIPLE.

Since the positions of the busy channels are distributed at random with respect to any one switch, even when the multiple is straight, it follows that no change is introduced if a slipped multiple is used, and formulas (183.3) and (183.4) again apply.

185. Group Hunting with Stay-Put Switches

Under this heading we shall consider two distinct cases distinguished in the following manner: When a group of switches of the stay-put variety are all started at once it may happen that the first to reach the desired terminal[17] may be, not a single switch, but two or more that are accidentally moving together. The problem then arises as to what disposition is to be made of them, for it is obviously not desirable to allow them all to connect with it. There are two alternatives: one is to allow some one of the group to seize the terminal; the other is to pass them all by and wait until it is tested by a switch which is traveling alone.

---

[17] "Terminal" is here used as a general term meaning "source or channel."

GROUP OF STAY-PUT FINDER SWITCHES HUNTING OVER A STRAIGHT MULTIPLE. IF TWO ARRIVE AT ONCE, ONE TAKES CHARGE OF THE CALL.

In the first case, if λ switches are searching over a straight multiple, the solution is easily obtained by this line of thought: Any individual switch is just as likely to be on one terminal as another, quite independently of where the other switches may be. Then let the heavy line of Fig. 185.1 be the calling source, there being in all ν sources and λ switches. The chance that a particular switch is on some one of the k bracketed sources to begin with is k/ν; and the chance that it is *not* there is $1 - k/\nu$. As the positions of the switches are quite independent, the chance that no one of the λ switches is on any of the bracketed sources is $(1 - k/\nu)^\lambda$. But this is just the condition under which the switches would have to make *more than* k tests in order to reach the calling source. Hence we have:

FIG. 185.1

$$p(> k) = \left(1 - \frac{k}{\nu}\right)^\lambda. \tag{185.1}$$

As before

$$p(k) = p(> k - 1) - p(> k) = \left(1 - \frac{k - 1}{\nu}\right)^\lambda - \left(1 - \frac{k}{\nu}\right)^\lambda. \tag{185.2}$$

The expectation of k—that is, the number of tests we may expect the switches to make before giving service—is

$$\epsilon_1(k) = \sum k\,p(k) = \frac{1^\lambda + 2^\lambda + 3^\lambda + \ldots + \nu^\lambda}{\nu^\lambda}.$$

GROUP OF STAY-PUT FINDER SWITCHES HUNTING OVER A STRAIGHT MULTIPLE. IF TWO OR MORE ARRIVE AT ONCE NEITHER TAKES CHARGE OF THE CALL.

In the second case which we have mentioned the formula is decidedly more complicated and requires the use of the principle of alternative compound probabilities for its evaluation. We begin as follows:

If there are just i' switches resting on the k bracketed sources of Fig. 185.1, the chance that there are exactly i on the source next below them is given by the formula

$$_k p(i|i') = C_i^{\lambda - i'} \left(\frac{1}{\nu - k}\right)^i \left(1 - \frac{1}{\nu - k}\right)^{\lambda - i' - i}.$$

Evidently if the i' switches which rest on the k sources are so arranged that no source has exactly one switch, the test must exceed k terminals. That is, it will be more than $k + 1$ if $i \neq 1$, and if $i = 1$ it will be exactly $k + 1$. Hence if we knew the probability of there being i' switches on the bracketed sources so arranged that no source has on it exactly one switch, we would be able to compute the probability of a hunt of any desired magnitude by merely building up the proper form of alternative compound probability. For the moment we may content ourselves with writing a symbol for it, in the hope that later on we may be able to find a formula for it. Let us choose for this purpose the notation $_kP(i')$, the prefixed subscript being added in this case, as in the case of $_kp(i|i')$, to call attention to the fact that the probability depends upon the particular value of k which we choose to consider. Then we have at once, as a formal expression for our solution,

$$p(k + 1) = \sum_{i' = 0}^{\lambda - 1} {_kP(i')} \, {_kp(i|i')}. \tag{185.3}$$

As for the determination of an expression for $_kP(i')$, we notice that if there are exactly i' switches on $k + 1$ sources, and if these switches are arranged in the fashion described, it must be true, either that all are on the first k and none on the $(k + 1)$'st, or that all but *two* are on the first k and those two are on the $(k + 1)$'st, or that all but three are on the first k and those three on the $(k + 1)$'st, or some similar arrangement. The only cases which are excluded are those which would require only one on the first k or only one on the $(k + 1)$'st, since either of these cases would require a *single* switch on some source. Hence we have the recursion formula

$$_{k+1}P(i') = {_kP(i')} \, {_kp(0|i')} + {_kP(i' - 2)} \, {_kp(2|i' - 2)}$$

$$+ {_kP(i' - 3)} \, {_kp(3|i' - 3)} + \cdots$$

$$= \sum_{i = 0}^{i'} {_kP(i' - i)} \, {_kp(i|i' - i)},$$

it being understood that the values $i = 1$ and $i = i' - 1$ are not to be included in the summation. From this recursion formula it is possible to obtain $_{k+1}P(i')$ if $_kP(i')$ is known. Hence if the values of this function are known for any one value of k they may be found for all others. But it is obvious at once that

$$_1P(i') = C_i^\lambda \frac{(\nu - 1)^{\lambda - i'}}{\nu^\lambda}.$$

With this as a start, it requires only routine algebra to show that[18]

$$_2P(i') = C_{i'}^\lambda \frac{(\nu - 2)^{\lambda - i'}}{\nu^\lambda} (2^{i'} - 2i' + i' \, C_{i'-2}^0),$$

$$_3P(i') = C_{i'}^\lambda \frac{(\nu - 3)^{\lambda - i'}}{\nu^\lambda} [3^{i'} - 3i' \, 2^{i'-1} + 3i'(i' - 1) - i'(i' - 1) \, C_{i'-3}^0],$$

and in general

$$_kP(i') = C_{i'}^\lambda \frac{(\nu - k)^{\lambda - i'}}{\nu^\lambda} \left(\sum_{h=0}^{k-1} (- 1)^h \, C_h^k \frac{i'!}{(i' - h)!} (k - h)^{i' - h} \right.$$

$$\left. + (- 1)^k \frac{i'!}{(i' - k + 1)!} \, C_{i'-k}^0 \right).$$

We now have formulas for both $_kP(i')$ and $_kp(i|i')$, and can therefore substitute them in (185.3). Some more routine algebra then shows that

$$p(k + 1) = \sum_{h=0}^{k} (- 1)^h \frac{\lambda!}{(\lambda - h - 1)!} \, C_h^k \frac{(\nu - h - 1)^{\lambda - h - 1}}{\nu^\lambda} \quad (185.4)$$

when $k + 1 < \nu$, and

$$p(\nu) = \sum_{h=0}^{\nu-1} (- 1)^h \frac{\lambda!}{(\lambda - h)!} \, C_h^{\nu-1} \frac{(\nu - h)^{\lambda - h}}{\nu^\lambda}. \quad (185.4)$$

For completeness we quote also the expected number of tests:

$$\epsilon_1(k) = \frac{\lambda!}{\nu^\lambda} \sum_{h=0}^{\nu-1} (- 1)^h \, C_{h+1}^\nu \frac{(\nu - h)^{\lambda - h}}{(\lambda - h)!}. \quad (185.5)$$

These formulas probably serve no other useful purpose, so far as this text is concerned, than that of showing how complicated problems of this general type can become.

GROUP OF STAY-PUT FINDER SWITCHES HUNTING OVER A SLIPPED MULTIPLE. IF TWO OR MORE ARRIVE AT ONCE, ONE TAKES CHARGE OF THE CALL.

GROUP OF STAY-PUT FINDERS HUNTING OVER A SLIPPED MULTIPLE. IF TWO OR MORE ARRIVE AT ONCE, NEITHER TAKES CHARGE OF THE CALL.

The method by means of which (185.1) and (185.2) are derived can be applied without change to the case of a slipped multiple. Hence these formulas are equally valid in this case. The same is true of (185.4) and (185.5). In both cases the mental picture upon which the

---

[18] These expressions have different values according as i' is, or is not, equal to k. This has been taken account of by the terms having the factors $C_{i'-k}^0$ which vanish for all values of i' except $i' = k$.

argument is based requires some modification; but the steps to be followed and the results themselves are identical throughout.

GROUP OF STAY-PUT SELECTORS HUNTING OVER A STRAIGHT MULTIPLE. IF TWO OR MORE ARRIVE AT ONCE, ONE TAKES CHARGE OF THE CALL.

If instead of finders, however, we are dealing with selectors, the hunts are in all cases likely to be shorter. If two or more can arrive at once and still take charge of the call, the formula by means of which the results are expressed is not very difficult to obtain. We fall back upon the similar case with only one selector, for which the solution is given by (183.3) and (183.4). It is obvious that any member of the group at present under consideration might be the *one selector* previously considered. Hence each of the group must obey the laws obeyed by that one. This being understood, the chance that some i switches would need to hunt exactly k terminals while the rest hunt more than k is

$$C_i^\lambda \, [p_1(k)]^i \, [p_1(> k)]^{\lambda - i},$$

the $p_1(k)$ being given by (183.4) and $p_1(> k)$ by (183.3). Hence the chance of a hunt of just k terminals is[19]

$$
\begin{aligned}
p_\lambda(k) &= \sum_{i=1}^{\lambda} C^\lambda \, [p_1(k)]^i \, [p_1(> k)]^{\lambda - i} \\
&= [p_1(k) + p_1(> k)]^\lambda - [p(> k)]^\lambda \\
&= [p_1(> k - 1)]^\lambda - [p_1(> k)]^\lambda \\
&= \left(\frac{{}_\infty \Pi''_\nu}{{}_\infty \Pi''_{\nu - k + 1}} \right)^\lambda - \left(\frac{{}_\infty \Pi''_\nu}{{}_\infty \Pi''_{\nu - k}} \right)^\lambda .
\end{aligned}
$$

The chance of a hunt of more than k terminals is

$$p_\lambda(> k) = [p_1(> k)]^\lambda = \left(\frac{{}_\infty \Pi''_\nu}{{}_\infty \Pi''_{\nu - k}} \right)^\lambda ,$$

and the expected hunt is

$$\epsilon_1(k) = \sum_{k=0}^{\nu - 1} \left(\frac{{}_\infty \Pi''_\nu}{{}_\infty \Pi''_{\nu - k}} \right)^\lambda .$$

As an illustration of the extent to which group hunting may reduce the average hunt we may consider the same illustration as before.

We found that with a straight multiple and a switch which starts from normal, the average number of terminals tested was 19.6. With stay-put switches, only one being assigned, or with a random slip in the

---

[19] Except for $k = \nu$. The formula in this case lacks the negative term.

multiple, this was reduced to 1.53. If the switches stay put and are started in groups of two, three, four, or five, the answers are, respectively, 1.14, 1.04, 1.014, and 1.005. Remembering that the minimum is a test of one terminal, the extent to which the test is reduced by starting a group is evident.

186. The Problem of Double Connections

One type of problem which frequently presents itself in connection with the use of apparatus by a considerable number of different people is that of preventing one person from seizing what is already in use and thus causing inconvenience to somebody else. This is frequently accomplished by operating a relay, or some similar device, which cuts off access to the particular channel which has been assigned. Obviously, such a blocking device will ordinarily require time for its operation, and during at least a portion of this time it will be possible for another source to seize the already busy channel, thus creating what is technically termed a "double connection." We are interested in determining what proportion of calls can be expected to suffer inconvenience from this source.

Problems of this type ordinarily arise in checking up whether a proposed system does or does not meet certain specified standards, and since we can tolerate much larger errors in studying such problems than in studying losses, we need not be so careful of the exactness of our assumptions. In particular, we may assume that the calls occur individually and collectively at random, and that, in assigning channels to calling sources, it is a matter of pure chance which of the idle channels is chosen. As always, we denote the number of channels by ν, the calling rate by n, and the expected holding time by T.

Let us suppose that we observe the group for a short time dt, at the beginning of which exactly j channels are busy. The chance that a call is made during this interval is obviously $n\lambda\,dt$; and if so, the chance that it is assigned to some *particular* channel which we have set out to watch is $n\lambda\,dt/(\nu - j)$.

Next we write down, by the use of alternative compound probabilities, the chance $p(b)$ that this particular channel is seized during dt, if we do not know how many channels are already in use. Denoting by $P(j)$ the probability that exactly j channels are busy at the beginning of this interval, it is:

$$p(b) = \sum_{j=0}^{\nu-1} P(j)\frac{n\lambda dt}{\nu - j} = n\lambda dt \sum_{j=0}^{\nu-1} \frac{P(j)}{\nu - j}. \qquad (186.1)$$

If we assume that lost calls are instantly cleared, $P(j)$ must be given the form (176.1); whence (186.1) becomes

$$\frac{dt}{T} \frac{\sum_{j=0}^{\nu-1} \dfrac{\epsilon^{j+1}}{(\nu-j)\,j!}}{\sum_{j=0}^{\nu} \dfrac{\epsilon^{j}}{j!}}, \tag{186.2}$$

which we shall denote simply as $f(\epsilon)\,dt/T$, $f(\epsilon)$ meaning, of course, the fraction in (186.2).

It remains to determine the relation of this result to the probability of double connections. From the fashion in which we have derived it we are assured that it represents the probability of a call being made upon a particular idle channel during a particular short interval of observation. One way of making this observation, however, would be to introduce a call and see if it is interfered with. Hence it is obvious that what we have obtained is the probability that our call will be followed by another within so short a time as to result in a double connection. In other words $f(\epsilon)\,dt/T$ is the probability that a call will be involved in a double connection by virtue of the fact that another call *originating later than itself* obtains access to the same trunk. It is just as likely, however, to interfere with someone else who arrived earlier, as to be interfered with by someone who arrives later. Hence $f(\epsilon)\,dt/T$ is only half of the total probability that a call will be involved in a double connection. This leads us at once to

$$p(dc) = 2p(b) = \frac{2\,dt}{T}f(\epsilon).$$

In order to facilitate computations, a chart of the function $f(\epsilon)$ has been prepared for a considerable number of values of ν between 1 and 100. This chart, with the abscissas measured in terms of ϵ/ν instead of ϵ for the sake of compactness, is presented as Fig. 186.1. Its use may be illustrated by a simple example:

Suppose there are 20 trunks handling 288 calls per hour, each with an average holding time of 100 seconds. Then $T = 1/36$, $n\lambda = 288$, $\epsilon = n\lambda T = 8$ and $\nu = 20$; so that $\epsilon/\nu = 0.04$. Referring to Fig. 186.1, we find that for this case $f(\epsilon) = 0.720$.[20] Suppose that the unguarded interval is 0.05 second, then the probability of a double connection is:

$$p(dc) = \frac{2 \times 0.05}{100}0.720 = 0.00072.$$

---

[20] These values are given with greater accuracy than is obtainable from the sketchy diagram of Fig. 186.1.

This means that under these circumstances, 72 calls out of every 100,000 would be involved in double connections, due account being taken of the fact that every double connection involves two calls.

Other problems involving double connections can be worked equally well provided the value of $f(\epsilon)$ is taken from the proper one of the curves of Fig. 186.1.

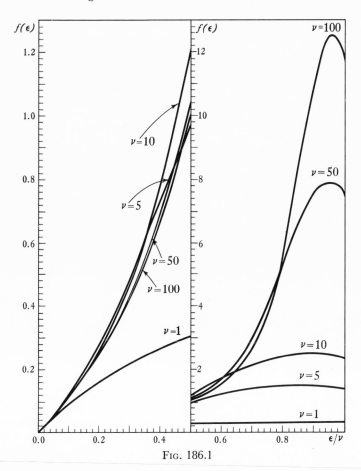

FIG. 186.1

187. Delays in Awaiting Service

The problems presented by systems which operate upon a delay basis instead of a loss basis—that is, in which a call is not discarded when there is no apparatus to handle it, but is merely held over until something becomes free—are much the most complicated with which the traffic statistician must deal. There are several reasons for this:

In the first place, we have seen in our study of the probability of loss that our results are quite independent of the lengths of individual calls. They are the same in any two systems which possess the same traffic density, whether that traffic density be made up of many short calls or a few long ones, and whether the calls are all of the same length or of different lengths. When we come to the study of delay problems, however, this is no longer true. It can be seen at a glance, for example, that if the calls are all of like length, the delays will be greater the greater the length may be. Thus, a system which had an expectation of three twenty-minute calls per hour, and one which had an expectation of sixty one-minute calls, should be identical so far as probability of loss is concerned; but it is obvious from a common-sense standpoint that the person who sought service and found no available apparatus in the first case would face the prospect of a longer wait before some became idle than in the second. It is perhaps not so easy to see from an intuitive standpoint that the distribution of call lengths—whether they are all of like length or not, and if not, how they differ—also affects the problem; but once we come to formulating our results we find that this is true.

In the second place, when we were dealing with loss problems, we were able to affirm that the end-points of calls, like their points of origin, were distributed at random. But this is no longer true in the case of systems with waiting arrangements. Thus, if calls are all of unit length, and if there are just five trunks, there can be only five calls in progress at any time, and hence no more than five can terminate within the same unit of time. They may still originate at random, but the delays to which some of them are subjected smooth out the distribution of their end-points. It is to this fact, indeed, that most of the mathematical difficulties are due.

In the third place, in a system which operates upon a loss basis, every subscriber who is inconvenienced at all is inconvenienced in just the same way as every other: his call is discarded. But in a delay system some suffer delays of negligible length, others long delays. It is no longer sufficient to specify the standard of service by a mere statement that such and such a proportion of calls is delayed: it becomes necessary to say instead what proportion is delayed *more than a specified time*. This adds one more complication to the problem.

As a result of these various complexities there are only two delay problems which have sufficiently simple solutions to justify their presentation in a text such as this. Indeed, the rest have in many instances been dealt with in an approximate fashion only, and can be said to have been "solved" only in the sense that engineering design can be carried out with reasonable assurance that a sufficient factor of safety exists, but not in the sense that the factor of safety is known. We present these two solutions only, as illustrations of the simpler methods of attack.

In the first place, if all the calls must be accommodated by a single channel instead of by a group of channels, and if they are also all of the same length, a rigorous solution can be found. We speak of this as the case of "noncooperative channels."

In the second place, if call lengths are governed by an exponential distribution function (which has the effect of rendering their end-points "random" in spite of the attempts of the system to smooth them out) a general solution can be obtained even if there is a group of channels instead of a single one.

188. Calls of Equal Length at Noncooperative Channels; The Probability of Congestion j[21]

We shall assume that calls originate individually and collectively at random, and that if at any time the congestion is so great that more than one is awaiting service, they will be served in the order in which they originated. As in the case of the problem of loss, we denote by $P(j)$ the chance that there are just j sources either seeking service or being served at the same time—that is, that the congestion is j. We also assume, as always, that the system is in statistical equilibrium, so that these probabilities are independent of time.

Let n be the calling rate and T the holding time. Then, since it is impossible for calls to overlap, the proportion of time during which our channel can be expected to be busy is nT, and its expected idle time is $1 - nT$. This latter, however, is obviously $P(0)$. Hence, using the notation $nT = \epsilon$ as before, we have

$$P(0) = 1 - \epsilon.$$

Next we consider an interval of length exactly equal to the holding time, and ask, What is the probability that the congestion is exactly j at the end of this interval? Obviously, there will be j calls in progress at the end of the interval provided there was none in progress when it began and just j came in meanwhile, or provided there was a congestion of 1 when the interval started and j came in meanwhile (for the one which was in progress will have discontinued before the interval ends), or provided there were 2 in progress at the beginning of the interval and $j - 1$ came in, and so on. As the system is in statistical equilibrium, the probability of any one of these states at the beginning

---

[21] Compare this section with § 136.

of the interval is equal to the probability of the same state at its end hence we arrive at the law

$$P(j) = [P(0) + P(1)]\frac{\epsilon^j e^{-\epsilon}}{j!} + P(2)\frac{\epsilon^{j-1} e^{-\epsilon}}{(j-1)!} + P(3)\frac{\epsilon^{j-2} e^{-\epsilon}}{(j-2)!}$$
$$+ \ldots + P(j+1) e^{-\epsilon}. \tag{188.1}$$

Suppose, now, that we write down the first few of these equations. They are:

$$P(0) = [P(0) + P(1)] e^{-\epsilon},$$
$$P(1) = [P(0) + P(1)] \epsilon e^{-\epsilon} + P(2) e^{-\epsilon},$$
$$P(2) = [P(0) + P(1)]\frac{\epsilon^2}{2!} e^{-\epsilon} + P(2) \epsilon e^{-\epsilon} + P(3) e^{-\epsilon}.$$

These equations can easily be solved in order and give (when we remember that $P(0) = 1 - \epsilon$)

$$P(1) = (1 - \epsilon)(e^\epsilon - 1),$$
$$P(2) = (1 - \epsilon)[e^{2\epsilon} - e^\epsilon(1 + \epsilon)],$$
$$P(3) = (1 - \epsilon)\left[e^{3\epsilon} - e^{2\epsilon}(1 + 2\epsilon) + e^\epsilon\left(\epsilon + \frac{\epsilon^2}{2}\right)\right],$$

the general rule being, as can be shown by more elaborate methods, that $P(j)$ is always the product of two factors, of which the first is $(1 - \epsilon)$, and the second is composed of a series of exponential terms with suitable coefficients. These coefficients are, in every instance after the first, the sum of two terms taken from the power series expansion of the exponential which they multiply: and specifically they are the first and second, the second and third, the third and fourth, and so on, respectively. The general formula therefore is

$$P(j) = (1 - \epsilon) \sum_{k=1}^{j} (-1)^{j-k} e^{k\epsilon}\left(\frac{(k\epsilon)^{j-k}}{(j-k)!} + \frac{(k\epsilon)^{j-k-1}}{(j-k-1)!}\right).$$

189. Calls of Equal Length at Noncooperative Channels; The Expected Delay

Our next objective is the determination of the expected delay $\epsilon(\tau)$. It is at once obvious that the sum $0 \cdot P(0) + 1 \cdot P(1) + 2 \cdot P(2) + \ldots$ represents the aggregate expected lengh of all calls in a typical unit of time. This means, not the aggregate of the times during which they are obtaining service, but the sum obtained by adding to those "intervals of use," the delays as well. However, the aggregate of all the intervals of use is ϵ. Similarly, the aggregate of all the delays is obtained by multiplying the expected number of calls by the expected delay $\epsilon(\tau)$. Thus we arrive at the relation

$$\epsilon + n\epsilon(\tau) = \sum_{j=0}^{\infty} j\, P(j). \qquad (189.1)$$

From this equation the expected delay $\epsilon(\tau)$ may be obtained, provided we can evaluate the summation which occurs in the right-hand member. To do this we return to the equation (188.1), which for our present purpose may be written in the form

$$P(j) = \sum_{k=0}^{j} P(j+1-k)\frac{\epsilon^k\, e^{-\epsilon}}{k!} + P(0)\frac{\epsilon^j\, e^{-\epsilon}}{j!}.$$

It is impossible to substitute this formula in (189.1) and thereby evaluate $\epsilon(\tau)$, for the attempt to do so leads us to a worthless identity. However, we can accomplish our purpose by a somewhat indirect artifice.

If we form, not the sum $\Sigma\, j\, P(j)$, but the sum $\Sigma\, j^2\, P(j)$ instead, and if we then interchange the order of the k and j summations in the usual manner, we arrive at the equation

$$\sum_{j=0}^{\infty} j^2\, P(j) = \sum_{k=0}^{\infty}\sum_{j=k}^{\infty} j^2\, P(j+1-k)\frac{\epsilon^k\, e^{-\epsilon}}{k!} + P(0)\sum_{j=0}^{\infty} j^2\frac{\epsilon^j\, e^{-\epsilon}}{j!}. \qquad (189.2)$$

Direct evaluation gives us the result

$$\sum_{j=0}^{\infty} j^2\frac{\epsilon^j\, e^{-\epsilon}}{j!} = \epsilon(\epsilon+1). \qquad (189.3)$$

This takes care of the last term of (189.2).

As for the double summation, it can be simplified by replacing the element of summation j by a new element $h = j - k + 1$. Since $j^2 = h^2 + 2h(k-1) + (k-1)^2$, the double summation splits up into three terms:

$$\sum_{k=0}^{\infty} \frac{\epsilon^k\, e^{-\epsilon}}{k!} \sum_{h=1}^{\infty} h^2\, P(h),$$

$$2 \cdot \sum_{k=0}^{\infty} (k-1)\frac{\epsilon^k\, e^{-\epsilon}}{k!} \sum_{h=1}^{\infty} h\, P(h),$$

$$\sum_{k=0}^{\infty} (k-1)^2\frac{\epsilon^k\, e^{-\epsilon}}{k!} \sum_{h=1}^{\infty} P(h).$$

In the form in which the terms now appear the h- and k- summations are independent of one another and their values can readily be found. Actual evaluation gives for the k-summations the results 1, $\epsilon - 1$, and $\epsilon^2 - \epsilon + 1$, respectively; whereas the first h-summation is identical with the left-hand side of (189.2),[22] and the last h-summation is $1 - P(0)$. Hence, when we substitute all these relations, together with (189.3), into (189.2), we obtain

$$\sum_{k=0}^{\infty} k\, P(k) = \frac{\epsilon^2 - 2\epsilon}{2(\epsilon - 1)}. \tag{189.4}$$

We now return to (189.1) and note that, since $nT = \epsilon$, the left-hand member can be written

$$\left(1 + \frac{\epsilon(\tau)}{T}\right)\epsilon.$$

Combining (189.1) and (189.4) and making use of this relationship, we arrive finally at a formula for the expected delay

$$\frac{\epsilon(\tau)}{T} = \frac{1}{2} \cdot \frac{\epsilon}{1 - \epsilon}. \tag{189.5}$$

190. Exponential Distribution of Holding Times; Delays at Co-operative Groups of Channels

We found in our discussion of probability of loss—and the same applies equally here—that the entire problem could be expressed in terms of two "elementary probabilities": the probability that a new call arrives during a test interval dt at the beginning of which the congestion is j, and the probability of one ending during such an interval. As we are assuming that the sources which originate calls have no knowledge of the state of the system, and therefore cannot be influenced by it until they have actually placed a call, the first of these elementary probabilities is here just what it was in the problem of loss. Every difference that exists between the two types of service must therefore be attributable to some difference in the second elementary probability. Let us, then, think for a moment about the chance of a call, known to be in progress at the time $t = 0$ at which we begin to observe it, ending before $t = dt$.

Our problem contemplates no change in the nature of the call *after service is given*. Hence the fact that we observe a call to be in progress means merely that it must end within a time equal to its own holding time, and the probability that it will end during the time

---

[22] The difference in the lower limit of summation is unimportant, since the term corresponding to $j = 0$ is itself zero.

dt is therefore $dt/\bar{T}$, just as before, *unless we are given information which leads us to infer something about the time at which it began.* But when the degree of congestion is known, this probability is altered—for otherwise, as we have already said, both elementary probabilities, and therefore $P(j)$ itself, would be the same as in the loss problem. Hence *a knowledge of the degree of congestion must, by inference at least, convey information regarding the times at which calls were given service.*[23]

Now it is a peculiar property of the exponential distribution of holding times that even *absolute* knowledge of the time at which a call was given service does not affect its chance of ending during dt; and obviously if *absolute* knowledge does not, *inferential* knowledge cannot. This is why the delay problem can be easily solved when such a distribution of call lengths is postulated.

To show that the length of time a call has been in progress does not affect the probability of its termination, when the call lengths are distributed in accordance with the law[24]

$$p(T) = \frac{1}{\bar{T}} e^{-T/\bar{T}}, \tag{190.1}$$

is a very simple mathematical problem. Suppose the call is known to have been in progress just t seconds. It must then be at least t seconds long, the probability of which is

$$p(> t) = \int_t^\infty p(T)\, dT = e^{-t/\bar{T}}.$$

If it ends during dt it must have had a length lying between t and $t + dt$, the probability of which is

$$p(t)\, dt = \frac{dt}{\bar{T}} e^{-t/\bar{T}}.$$

The quotient of these[25] is the chance that the call ends during dt

---

[23] This statement is undoubtedly true, as the above argument shows, and that without regard to how the lengths of the calls may be distributed. I have frequently attempted to formulate a direct argument to replace the *reductio ad absurdum* here given. Such an argument should give a value for the elementary probability of termination under congestion j, and it would be a very easy matter to formulate a complete solution if this were known. The direct relationship, however, still remains as baffling as ever.

[24] For the time being we write $\bar{T}$ and $\bar{\tau}$, instead of $\epsilon(T)$ and $\epsilon(\tau)$, in order to simplify the appearance of our equations.

[25] Obviously $p(t)\, dt$ (the chance of a call ending during dt) is the chance of it lasting until $t = 0$ [which is $p(> t)$] multiplied by the conditional chance that it does not last beyond $t + dt$ [which we may write $p(< t + dt| > t)$]. The first two have been computed, and the third is exactly the probability for which we are seeking.

and turns out to be $dt/\bar{T}$. As this is independent of t, the statement is proved.

191. Exponential Distribution of Holding Times; The Probability of Congestion j

Suppose there are ν channels serving λ sources, each of which latter originates an average of n calls per unit time. Suppose, further, that the call lengths are distributed according to the exponential law (190.1). Then the principle of statistical equilibrium leads to the set of equations

$$\left.\begin{aligned}
&(1 - \lambda \alpha \, dt) \, P(0) + \frac{dt}{\bar{T}} P(1) = P(0), \\[1em]
&(\lambda \alpha \, dt) \, P(0) + \left[1 - (\lambda - 1) \alpha \, dt - \frac{dt}{\bar{T}}\right] P(1) \\[0.5em]
&\qquad + \frac{2 \, dt}{\bar{T}} P(2) = P(1), \\[1em]
&\qquad \cdots \qquad\qquad \cdots \qquad\qquad \cdots \\[1em]
&(\lambda - \nu + 1) \alpha \, dt \, P(\nu - 1) + \left[1 - (\lambda - \nu) \alpha \, dt - \frac{\nu \, dt}{\bar{T}}\right] P(\nu) \\[0.5em]
&\qquad + \frac{\nu \, dt}{\bar{T}} P(\nu + 1) = P(\nu), \\[1em]
&(\lambda - \nu) \alpha \, dt \, P(\nu) + \left[1 - (\lambda - \nu - 1) \alpha \, dt - \frac{\nu \, dt}{\bar{T}}\right] P(\nu + 1) \\[0.5em]
&\qquad + \frac{\nu \, dt}{\bar{T}} P(\nu + 2) = P(\nu + 1), \\[1em]
&\qquad \cdots \qquad\qquad \cdots \qquad\qquad \cdots \\[1em]
&\alpha \, dt \, P(\lambda - 1) + \left[1 - \frac{\nu \, dt}{\bar{T}}\right] P(\lambda) = P(\lambda),
\end{aligned}\right\} \tag{191.1}$$

where

$$\alpha = \frac{n}{1 - n\bar{T} - n\bar{\tau}}.$$

These equations differ from those obtained in § 169 in just two respects: The first is that sources are effectively busy, so far as the origination of calls is concerned, whether they are actually being served or are only awaiting service. Hence p, in (169.2), takes the form $n(\bar{T} + \bar{\tau})$, and gives for $n/(1 - p)$ the quantity which we have called α. But in the second elementary probability (169.4) p means, as before, $n\bar{T}$; for it is only when we find the source actually being served that there is a chance of that service coming to an end during dt.

In the second place, when the congestion exceeds the number of available channels, the number of calls in progress is equal to ν, not to j. Hence in place of (169.5) we must now write $j\,dt/\bar{T}$, provided $j \leq \nu$, but $\nu\,dt/\bar{T}$ for all larger values of j.

From the first of the equations (191.1), $P(1)$ may be found in terms of $P(0)$. Then from the second $P(2)$ can be found in terms of $P(0)$, and so on.[26] As we should expect, the result takes different forms according as j is less than or greater than ν. It is

$$P(j) = C_j^\lambda \beta^j P(0), \qquad\qquad j \leq \nu$$

$$P(j) = \frac{j!}{\nu!}\nu^{\nu-j} C_j^\lambda \beta^j P(0), \qquad j \geq \nu$$

where β has been written for the quantity

$$\beta = \frac{n\bar{T}}{1 - n\bar{T} - n\bar{\tau}}. \qquad (191.2)$$

So far the constant $P(0)$ in these equations is arbitrary, but it may be determined by means of the condition

$$\sum_0^\lambda P(j) = 1.$$

It is found to be given by the equation

$$\frac{1}{P(0)} = (1 + \beta)^\lambda + \sum_{j=\nu+1}^\lambda C_j^\lambda \beta^j \left(\frac{j!}{\nu!}\nu^{\nu-j} - 1\right).$$

These formulas apply in case the number of sources is limited and the sources are independent. If, on the other hand, the calls occur individually and collectively at random, the solutions take somewhat simpler forms that may be obtained by setting λ infinite in the above expressions. They are

$$P(j) = \frac{\epsilon^j}{j!} P(0), \qquad\qquad j \leq \nu$$

$$P(j) = \frac{\epsilon^j}{\nu!}\nu^{\nu-j} P(0), \qquad j \geq \nu$$

---

[26] The labor of solving (191.1) is much less if determinants are used than by the scheme suggested; but adeptness as well as knowledge is required.

where ϵ is the expected traffic density, computed quite without regard to delays, and where $P(0)$ is found to be

$$\frac{1}{P(0)} = e^\epsilon + \frac{1}{(\nu - \epsilon)} \frac{\epsilon^\nu}{(\nu - 1)!} - \sum_{j=\nu}^{\infty} \frac{\epsilon^j}{j!}.$$

192. Exponential Distribution of Holding Times; The Expected Delay

The probability $P(j)$ represents the proportion of time during which j calls are being served or are awaiting service. If j is not greater than ν, these calls are all being served, whereas if j exceeds ν, ν of them are obtaining service and the remaining $j - \nu$ are standing by waiting for an idle trunk. It follows, therefore, that the aggregate length of all calls served per unit time must be given by

$$\sum_{j=0}^{\nu} j\, P(j) + \sum_{j=\nu+1}^{\lambda} \nu\, P(j),$$

and the aggregate length of all the delays which occur per unit time must be

$$\sum_{j=\nu+1}^{\lambda} (j - \nu)\, P(j).$$

If the latter of these is divided by the expected number of calls per unit time, the expected delay, $\bar{\tau}$, is obtained. However, the average number of calls is $\lambda n = \epsilon/\bar{T}$. Hence we have the formula

$$\frac{\bar{\tau}}{\bar{T}} = \frac{1}{\epsilon} \sum_{j=\nu+1}^{\lambda} (j - \nu)\, P(j).$$

This can also be thrown into the form[27]

$$\frac{\bar{\tau}}{\bar{T}} = \frac{1}{\epsilon} \frac{\nu^\nu}{\nu!} \frac{P(0)}{{}^\infty P'(\lambda)^*} \left[\left(\lambda - \nu - \frac{\nu}{\beta} \right)(1 - {}^\infty\Pi'^*_{\lambda-\nu}) + \frac{\nu}{\beta} {}^\infty P'(\lambda - \nu + 1)^* \right],$$

$$(192.1)$$

where the asterisk following a P or Π indicates that this symbol is to be evaluated as if the expected traffic density were ν/β.

From this equation it is quite possible to find $\bar{\tau}$, although it occurs implicitly on the right-hand side due to the relation (191.2). The

---

[27] In this case (as in several others which follow) we do not attempt to explain the method by means of which one form of equation follows from another. In each such case, however, the only processes required are those of routine algebra. They contain nothing of interest from a probability standpoint.

process of computation consists in assigning to β such values as may be desired, computing the corresponding $\bar{\tau}$'s from (192.1), and then finding n from (191.2). In this way a table of corresponding values of n and $\bar{\tau}$ is obtained, from which the delay corresponding to any calling rate may be found by interpolation.

The computations are not at all simple; but they can be performed when it is necessary to answer questions of sufficient importance to justify the expense. In many cases it is satisfactory to assume that the calls originate individually and collectively at random, in which case the formula is much simpler. It is derived by exactly the same line of argument and is found to be

$$\frac{\bar{\tau}}{\bar{T}} = \frac{1}{(\nu - \epsilon)^2} \frac{\epsilon^\nu}{(\nu - 1)!} P(0).$$

193. Exponential Distribution of Holding Times; The Probability of a Delay Exceeding the Length τ If Calls Are Served in the Order in which They Originate

If a test call finds exactly j calls ahead of it, the delay to which it will be subjected will exceed the length τ if, and only if, $j - \nu$ or less calls end during the time τ. In case j is known, therefore, the probability of a delay as great as τ can be found by determining the probability that a preassigned number of calls end during a given time τ. This is our next objective.

If we consider any time interval dt, at the beginning of which all trunks are busy, we know from § 191 that the probability that a call ends during this interval is $\nu \, dt / \bar{T}$. We also know from § 190 that the chance of a call ending during any such interval is altogether independent of what may have happened in any other. Hence these end-points are distributed individually and collectively at random with an expectation of $\nu / \bar{T}$ per unit length, and the chance that exactly i end during the time τ is

$$\left(\frac{\nu\tau}{\bar{T}}\right)^i \frac{e^{-\nu\tau/\bar{T}}}{i!},$$

which we shall denote simply by $^\infty P'(i)^{**}$, the two asterisks indicating that the probability is to be computed as if the expected traffic density were $\nu\tau/\bar{T}$. The chance of $j - \nu$ or less terminating during this time (or, what amounts to the same thing, the probability of a delay exceeding τ) is

$$p(> \tau | j) = \sum_{i=0}^{j-\nu} {}^\infty P'(i)^{**} = 1 - {}^\infty \Pi'^{**}_{j-\nu+1}.$$

All this is true only provided we know that exactly j calls are either in progress or awaiting service when our test call occurs. However, during the proportion $P(j)$ of the time, j calls *are* in progress; and the calling rate during such intervals is $(\lambda - j)\alpha$ calls per unit time. It therefore follows that the number of calls originated per unit time which find just j calls preceding them and are delayed more than τ seconds is

$$(\lambda - j)\,\alpha\,P(j)\,p(> \tau|j).$$

This formula obviously applies for any value of j; and since any call which is delayed a longer time than τ must have been preceded by *some* number of calls, it follows that the number per unit time which may be expected to be delayed more than τ may be obtained by summing this expression for such values of j as are capable of causing delays. The result is

$$\sum_{j=v}^{\lambda} (\lambda - j)\,\alpha\,P(j)\,p(> \tau|j).$$

When this result is divided by λn (i.e., by the total number of calls which are expected to originate per unit time) it gives us the probability of a test call experiencing a delay greater than τ.

This formula can also be put in a somewhat more convenient form for purposes of computation. It is, in fact, equal to

$$P(> \tau) = \frac{v^v}{\epsilon(v - 1)!} \frac{P(0)}{^\infty P'(\lambda)^*} \sum_{j=v}^{\lambda-1} {}^\infty P'(\lambda - j - 1)^*(1 - {}^\infty\Pi'^{**}_{j-v+1}). \quad (193.1)$$

As in every other case, it becomes much simpler if we assume that the calls originate individually and collectively at random. The result is then

$$P(> \tau) = P(0)\frac{\epsilon^v}{(v - \epsilon)(v - 1)!}e^{(\epsilon - v)\tau/\bar{T}}. \quad (193.2)$$

It must be borne in mind that these results are valid only if calls are served in the order in which they originate. If apparatus is assigned in some other fashion a different distribution of delays will occur. The results of §§ 192, 194, and 195, however, do not depend upon this assumption.

194. Exponential Distribution of Holding Times; The Proportion of Delayed Calls

By setting τ equal to 0 in $P(> \tau)$ we obtain the proportion of delayed calls. From (193.1) we get

$$P(> 0) = \frac{v^v}{\epsilon(v - 1)!}P(0)\frac{1 - {}^\infty\Pi'^*_{\lambda-v}}{^\infty P'(\lambda)^*};$$

the asterisk having the same meaning as always. From (193.2) we get the even simpler formula

$$P(> 0) = P(0) \frac{\epsilon^\nu}{(\nu - \epsilon)(\nu - 1)!}.$$

195. Exponential Distribution of Holding Times; The Expected Delay of Delayed Calls

The expected delay, $\bar{\tau}$, obtained in § 192 is analogous to the result which would be obtained by placing a large number of test calls, noting the delay to which each was subjected, adding all these delays together, and dividing by the number of calls. Many of the calls, however, would be subject to no delay, and the average thus derived would apportion the total delay among these as well as among the delayed calls.

If we desire to know, not this expected delay $\bar{\tau}$ but the delay $\bar{\tau}_\delta$ which a call may be expected to have *if it is delayed at all*, we need only divide $\bar{\tau}$ by the proportion of delayed calls, $p(> 0)$. The result is

$$\frac{\bar{\tau}_\delta}{\bar{T}} = \frac{1}{\nu} \frac{\left(\lambda - \nu - \dfrac{\nu}{\beta}\right)(1 - {}^\infty\Pi'^*_{\lambda-\nu}) + \dfrac{\nu}{\beta} {}^\infty P'(\lambda - \nu + 1)^*}{1 - {}^\infty\Pi'^*_{\lambda-\nu}};$$

or, if calls occur individually and collectively at random,

$$\frac{\bar{\tau}_\delta}{\bar{T}} = \frac{1}{\nu - \epsilon}.$$

These results may complete our discussion. It is obvious that we might, by introducing various shades of meaning into our assumptions, prolong the study indefinitely, and that quite without the necessity of ever passing far from conditions for which we might easily find analogues in practice. What we have done, however, has probably shown the two things for which it was devised: the highly complex nature of the problems to which "traffic" in its most general sense leads us, and something—though by no means all—of the methods which in part at least meet the needs of such problems. If at the same time we have painted a rather wearisome picture, no great harm will have been done; for after all it was only the old masters to whom the gods granted a virgin field in which to grow those things which were easiest, and to them no tools were given. We, who have inherited the implements of their fashioning, cannot well complain if the fields require more labor.

Problems

1. Prove (183.1) and (183.2).

2. What is the probability of hunting more than k terminals with a single selector starting from rest, and a straight multiple? What is the probability of hunting more than ν?

3. Prove that the exponential law (190.1) is the only distribution of holding times which possesses the property discussed in § 190.

[Let $p(T)$ be the distribution for call lengths T. Let event A mean "the call has been in progress for a length of time t," which is synonymous with $T > t$. Let B mean "the call will continue at least an additional time τ," which is synonymous with $T > t + \tau$. Then write

$$P(A, B) = P(A) \, P(B|A),$$

observing that $P(A, B) \equiv P(B)$. It is then easily established that $P(B|A)$ can only be independent of t when $p(T)$ has the form (190.1.)]

4. Find the probability that a call is delayed, no matter how much, at a noncooperative channel.

5. The $\epsilon(\tau)$ given by (189.5) is the "unconditional" expectation of delay. It is the analogue of an "average delay" formed from a number of calls, some of which suffered no delay at all. We could, however, eliminate from this group all those that suffered no delay, leaving only the "delayed calls"; and we could then make use of this residual group to find the "average delay of delayed calls." To such an average corresponds a "conditional expectation," namely, "the expectation of delay if the call is delayed," or in symbolical form $\epsilon_\delta(\tau)$. Find $\epsilon_\delta(\tau)$ at a noncooperative channel.

Answers to Problems at End of § 181

1. $^\infty\Pi_\nu''$, (176.2).   2. First approximation, 12; corrected value, 11.
3. $\epsilon = 0.51, \nu = 1$. Hence, using $^\infty\Pi_\nu'$, 40% will not be distinct. 4. We have: $n^*T^* = \Pi$, $n(1 - \Pi) = n^*$, from which $n = n^*/(1 - n^*T^*)$. But also $\Pi = 1 - e^{-\epsilon} = 1 - e^{-nT}$, whence $nT = -\log(1 - n^*T^*)/\log e$. Thus, finally, $T = -(1 - n^*T^*)\log(1 - n^*T^*)/n^*\log e$. 5. $T = 0.06$ second; frequency 105,400 per hour.

Answers to Problems at End of § 195

2. $^\infty\Pi_k''$; 0.   4. ϵ.   5. $\epsilon_\delta(\tau) = T/2(1 - \epsilon)$.

APPENDICES

n	$n!$	n	$n!$	n	$n!$
1	1	36	$3.719\ 9333\ ^{41}$	71	$8.504\ 7859\ ^{101}$
2	2	37	$1.376\ 3753\ ^{43}$	72	$6.123\ 4458\ ^{103}$
3	6	38	$5.230\ 2262\ ^{44}$	73	$4.470\ 1155\ ^{105}$
4	$2.4\ ^{1}$	39	$2.039\ 7882\ ^{46}$	74	$3.307\ 8854\ ^{107}$
5	$1.20\ ^{2}$	40	$8.159\ 1528\ ^{47}$	75	$2.480\ 9141\ ^{109}$
6	$7.20\ ^{2}$	41	$3.345\ 2527\ ^{49}$	76	$1.885\ 4947\ ^{111}$
7	$5.040\ ^{3}$	42	$1.405\ 0061\ ^{51}$	77	$1.451\ 8309\ ^{113}$
8	$4.032\ 0\ ^{4}$	43	$6.041\ 5263\ ^{52}$	78	$1.132\ 4281\ ^{115}$
9	$3.628\ 80\ ^{5}$	44	$2.658\ 2716\ ^{54}$	79	$8.946\ 1821\ ^{116}$
10	$3.628\ 800\ ^{6}$	45	$1.196\ 2222\ ^{56}$	80	$7.156\ 9457\ ^{118}$
11	$3.991\ 6800\ ^{7}$	46	$5.502\ 6222\ ^{57}$	81	$5.797\ 1260\ ^{120}$
12	$4.790\ 0160\ ^{8}$	47	$2.586\ 2324\ ^{59}$	82	$4.753\ 6433\ ^{122}$
13	$6.227\ 0208\ ^{9}$	48	$1.241\ 3916\ ^{61}$	83	$3.945\ 5240\ ^{124}$
14	$8.717\ 8291\ ^{10}$	49	$6.082\ 8186\ ^{62}$	84	$3.314\ 2401\ ^{126}$
15	$1.307\ 6744\ ^{12}$	50	$3.041\ 4093\ ^{64}$	85	$2.817\ 1041\ ^{128}$
16	$2.092\ 2790\ ^{13}$	51	$1.551\ 1188\ ^{66}$	86	$2.422\ 7095\ ^{130}$
17	$3.556\ 8743\ ^{14}$	52	$8.065\ 8175\ ^{67}$	87	$2.107\ 7573\ ^{132}$
18	$6.402\ 3737\ ^{15}$	53	$4.274\ 8833\ ^{69}$	88	$1.854\ 8264\ ^{134}$
19	$1.216\ 4510\ ^{17}$	54	$2.308\ 4370\ ^{71}$	89	$1.650\ 7955\ ^{136}$
20	$2.432\ 9020\ ^{18}$	55	$1.269\ 6403\ ^{73}$	90	$1.485\ 7160\ ^{138}$
21	$5.109\ 0942\ ^{19}$	56	$7.109\ 9859\ ^{74}$	91	$1.352\ 0015\ ^{140}$
22	$1.124\ 0007\ ^{21}$	57	$4.052\ 6920\ ^{76}$	92	$1.243\ 8414\ ^{142}$
23	$2.585\ 2017\ ^{22}$	58	$2.350\ 5613\ ^{78}$	93	$1.156\ 7725\ ^{144}$
24	$6.204\ 4840\ ^{23}$	59	$1.386\ 8312\ ^{80}$	94	$1.087\ 3662\ ^{146}$
25	$1.551\ 1210\ ^{25}$	60	$8.320\ 9871\ ^{81}$	95	$1.032\ 9978\ ^{148}$
26	$4.032\ 9146\ ^{26}$	61	$5.075\ 8021\ ^{83}$	96	$9.916\ 7793\ ^{149}$
27	$1.088\ 8869\ ^{28}$	62	$3.146\ 9973\ ^{85}$	97	$9.619\ 2760\ ^{151}$
28	$3.048\ 8834\ ^{29}$	63	$1.982\ 6083\ ^{87}$	98	$9.426\ 8904\ ^{153}$
29	$8.841\ 7620\ ^{30}$	64	$1.268\ 8693\ ^{89}$	99	$9.332\ 6215\ ^{155}$
30	$2.652\ 5286\ ^{32}$	65	$8.247\ 6506\ ^{90}$	100	$9.332\ 6215\ ^{157}$
31	$8.222\ 8387\ ^{33}$	66	$5.443\ 4494\ ^{92}$	101	$9.425\ 9478\ ^{159}$
32	$2.631\ 3084\ ^{35}$	67	$3.647\ 1111\ ^{94}$	102	$9.614\ 4667\ ^{161}$
33	$8.683\ 3176\ ^{36}$	68	$2.480\ 0355\ ^{96}$	103	$9.902\ 9007\ ^{163}$
34	$2.952\ 3280\ ^{38}$	69	$1.711\ 2245\ ^{98}$	104	$1.029\ 9017\ ^{166}$
35	$1.033\ 3148\ ^{40}$	70	$1.197\ 8572\ ^{100}$	105	$1.081\ 3968\ ^{168}$

n	$n!$	n	$n!$	n	$n!$
106	$1.146\ 2806^{170}$	141	$1.898\ 1438^{243}$	176	$1.979\ 0311^{320}$
107	$1.226\ 5202^{172}$	142	$2.695\ 3641^{245}$	177	$3.502\ 8851^{322}$
108	$1.324\ 6418^{174}$	143	$3.854\ 3707^{247}$	178	$6.235\ 1354^{324}$
109	$1.443\ 8596^{176}$	144	$5.550\ 2938^{249}$	179	$1.116\ 0892^{327}$
110	$1.588\ 2455^{178}$	145	$8.047\ 9261^{251}$	180	$2.008\ 9606^{329}$
111	$1.762\ 9526^{180}$	146	$1.174\ 9972^{254}$	181	$3.636\ 2187^{331}$
112	$1.974\ 5069^{182}$	147	$1.727\ 2459^{256}$	182	$6.617\ 9181^{333}$
113	$2.231\ 1927^{184}$	148	$2.556\ 3239^{258}$	183	$1.211\ 0790^{336}$
114	$2.543\ 5597^{186}$	149	$3.808\ 9226^{260}$	184	$2.228\ 3854^{338}$
115	$2.925\ 0937^{188}$	150	$5.713\ 3840^{262}$	185	$4.122\ 5130^{340}$
116	$3.393\ 1087^{190}$	151	$8.627\ 2098^{264}$	186	$7.667\ 8741^{342}$
117	$3.969\ 9372^{192}$	152	$1.311\ 3359^{267}$	187	$1.433\ 8925^{345}$
118	$4.684\ 5258^{194}$	153	$2.006\ 3439^{269}$	188	$2.695\ 7178^{347}$
119	$5.574\ 5858^{196}$	154	$3.089\ 7696^{271}$	189	$5.094\ 9067^{349}$
120	$6.689\ 5029^{198}$	155	$4.789\ 1429^{273}$	190	$9.680\ 3227^{351}$
121	$8.094\ 2985^{200}$	156	$7.471\ 0629^{275}$	191	$1.848\ 9416^{354}$
122	$9.875\ 0442^{202}$	157	$1.172\ 9569^{278}$	192	$3.549\ 9679^{356}$
123	$1.214\ 6304^{205}$	158	$1.853\ 2719^{280}$	193	$6.851\ 4381^{358}$
124	$1.506\ 1417^{207}$	159	$2.946\ 7023^{282}$	194	$1.329\ 1790^{361}$
125	$1.882\ 6772^{209}$	160	$4.714\ 7236^{284}$	195	$2.591\ 8990^{363}$
126	$2.372\ 1732^{211}$	161	$7.590\ 7051^{286}$	196	$5.080\ 1221^{365}$
127	$3.012\ 6600^{213}$	162	$1.229\ 6942^{289}$	197	$1.000\ 7841^{368}$
128	$3.856\ 2048^{215}$	163	$2.004\ 4016^{291}$	198	$1.981\ 5524^{370}$
129	$4.974\ 5042^{217}$	164	$3.287\ 2186^{293}$	199	$3.943\ 2893^{372}$
130	$6.466\ 8555^{219}$	165	$5.423\ 9107^{295}$	200	$7.886\ 5787^{374}$
131	$8.471\ 5807^{221}$	166	$9.003\ 6917^{297}$		
132	$1.118\ 2487^{224}$	167	$1.503\ 6165^{300}$		
133	$1.487\ 2707^{226}$	168	$2.526\ 0757^{302}$		
134	$1.992\ 9427^{228}$	169	$4.269\ 0680^{304}$		
135	$2.690\ 4727^{230}$	170	$7.257\ 4156^{306}$		
136	$3.659\ 0429^{232}$	171	$1.241\ 0181^{309}$		
137	$5.012\ 8887^{234}$	172	$2.134\ 5511^{311}$		
138	$6.917\ 7865^{236}$	173	$3.692\ 7734^{313}$		
139	$9.615\ 7232^{238}$	174	$6.425\ 4257^{315}$		
140	$1.346\ 2012^{241}$	175	$1.124\ 4495^{318}$		

$$\tfrac{1}{2}! = \tfrac{1}{2}\sqrt{\pi}; \quad (-\tfrac{1}{2})! = \sqrt{\pi}; \quad (n + \tfrac{1}{2})! = (n + \tfrac{1}{2})(n - \tfrac{1}{2})(n - \tfrac{3}{2}) \ldots \tfrac{3}{2} \cdot \tfrac{1}{2}\sqrt{\pi}.$$

n	$\log n!$	n	$\log n!$	n	$\log n!$
1	0.000 000 0000	41	49.524 428 9249	81	120.763 212 7414
2	0.301 029 9957	42	51.147 678 2153	82	122.677 026 5938
3	0.778 151 2504	43	52.781 146 6709	83	124.596 104 6861
4	1.380 211 2417	44	54.424 599 3473	84	126.520 383 9722
5	2.079 181 2460	45	56.077 811 8611	85	128.449 802 8979
6	2.857 332 4964	46	57.740 569 6928	86	130.384 301 3492
7	3.702 430 5364	47	59.412 667 5507	87	132.323 820 6018
8	4.605 520 5234	48	61.093 908 7881	88	134.268 303 2739
9	5.559 763 0329	49	62.784 104 8681	89	136.217 693 2806
10	6.559 763 0329	50	64.483 074 8725	90	138.171 935 7900
11	7.601 155 7180	51	66.190 645 0486	91	140.130 977 1823
12	8.680 336 9641	52	67.906 648 3922	92	142.094 765 0097
13	9.794 280 3164	53	69.630 924 2618	93	144.063 247 9582
14	10.940 408 3521	54	71.363 318 0216	94	146.036 375 8118
15	12.116 499 6111	55	73.103 680 7111	95	148.014 099 4171
16	13.320 619 5938	56	74.851 868 7381	96	149.996 370 6502
17	14.551 068 5152.	57	76.607 743 5938	97	151.983 142 3844
18	15.806 341 0203	58	78.371 171 5874	98	153.974 368 4601
19	17.085 094 6212	59	80.142 023 5990	99	155.970 003 6547
20	18.386 124 6169	60	81.920 174 8494	100	157.970 003 6547
21	19.708 343 9116	61	83.705 504 6844	101	159.974 325 0285
22	21.050 766 5924	62	85.497 896 3739	102	161.982 925 2003
23	22.412 494 4285	63	87.297 236 9234	103	163.995 762 4250
24	23.792 705 6702	64	89.103 416 8973	104	166.012 795 7643
25	25.190 645 6788	65	90.916 330 2540	105	168.033 985 0633
26	26.605 619 0268	66	92.735 874 1895	106	170.059 290 9286
27	28.036 982 7910	67	94.561 948 9922	107	172.088 674 7063
28	29.484 140 8223	68	96.394 457 9049	108	174.122 098 4618
29	30.946 538 8202	69	98.233 306 9957	109	176.159 524 9597
30	32.423 660 0749	70	100.078 405 0357	110	178.200 917 6449
31	33.915 021 7688	71	101.929 663 3844	111	180.246 240 6237
32	35.420 171 7471	72	103.786 995 8808	112	182.295 458 6463
33	36.938 685 6870	73	105.650 318 7410	113	184.348 537 0898
34	38.470 164 6040	74	107.519 550 4607	114	186.405 441 9411
35	40.014 232 6484	75	109.394 611 7241	115	188.466 139 7815
36	41.570 535 1491	76	111.275 425 3164	116	190.530 597 7707
37	43.138 736 8732	77	113.161 916 0415	117	192.598 783 6325
38	44.718 520 4698	78	115.054 010 6442	118	194.670 665 6398
39	46.309 585 0768	79	116.951 637 7355	119	196.746 212 6012
40	47.911 645 0682	80	118.854 727 7225	120	198.825 393 8472

Taken from the 18-place table of C. F. Degen, Havniae, 1824,

n	log n!	n	log n!	n	log n!
121	200.908 179 2175	161	286.880 282 1167	201	377.200 084 6975
122	202.994 539 0482	162	289.089 797 1313	202	379.505 436 0669
123	205.084 444 1597	163	291.301 984 7357	203	381.812 932 1048
124	207.177 865 8448	164	293.516 828 5837	204	384.122 562 2722
125	209.274 775 8578	165	295.734 312 5279	205	386.434 316 1333
126	211.375 146 4029	166	297.954 420 6160	206	388.748 183 3537
127	213.478 950 1239	167	300.177 137 0871	207	391.064 153 6991
128	215.586 160 0935	168	302.402 446 3688	208	393.382 217 0341
129	217.696 749 8038	169	304.630 333 0735	209	395.702 363 3202
130	219.810 693 1561	170	306.860 781 9948	210	398.024 582 6149
131	221.927 964 4518	171	309.093 778 1052	211	400.348 865 0702
132	224.048 538 3830	172	311.329 306 5521	212	402.675 200 9312
133	226.172 390 0240	173	313.567 352 6553	213	405.003 580 5346
134	228.299 494 8223	174	315.807 901 9035	214	407.333 994 3080
135	230.429 828 5908	175	318.050 939 9522	215	409.666 432 7679
136	232.563 367 4992	176	320.296 452 6200	216	412.000 886 5190
137	234.700 088 0664	177	322.544 425 8864	217	414.337 346 2529
138	236.839 967 1528	178	324.794 845 8887	218	416.675 802 7465
139	238.982 981 9530	179	327.047 698 9197	219	419.016 246 8613
140	241.129 109 9887	180	329.302 971 4248	220	421.358 669 5421
141	243.278 329 1014	181	331.560 649 9997	221	423.703 061 8158
142	245.430 617 4457	182	333.820 721 3876	222	426.049 414 7903
143	247.585 953 4832	183	336.083 172 4774	223	428.397 719 6533
144	249.744 315 9753	184	338.347 990 3004	224	430.747 967 6717
145	251.905 683 9775	185	340.615 162 0288	225	433.100 150 1898
146	254.070 036 8333	186	342.884 674 9730	226	435.454 258 6289
147	256.237 354 1681	187	345.156 516 5795	227	437.810 284 4861
148	258.407 615 8835	188	347.430 674 4288	228	440.168 219 3331
149	260.580 802 1519	189	349.707 136 2330	229	442.528 054 8154
150	262.756 893 4109	190	351.985 889 8339	230	444.889 782 6515
151	264.935 870 3582	191	354.266 923 2012	231	447.253 394 6314
152	267.117 713 9462	192	356.550 224 4299	232	449.618 882 6162
153	269.302 405 3770	193	358.835 781 7389	233	451.986 238 5373
154	271.489 926 0978	194	361.123 583 4688	234	454.355 454 3947
155	273.680 257 7960	195	363.413 618 0802	235	456.726 522 2570
156	275.873 382 3943	196	365.705 874 1515	236	459.099 434 2599
157	278.069 282 0468	197	368.000 340 3777	237	461.474 182 6059
158	280.267 939 1337	198	370.297 005 5680	238	463.850 759 5630
159	282.469 336 2580	199	372.595 858 6444	239	466.229 157 4639
160	284.673 456 2407	200	374.896 888 6400	240	468.609 368 7056

n	$\log n!$	n	$\log n!$	n	$\log n!$
241	470.991 385 7482	281	567.673 298 3669	321	666.832 041 9066
242	473.375 201 1142	282	570.123 547 4752	322	669.339 897 7783
243	475.760 807 3878	283	572.575 333 9108	323	671.849 100 3006
244	478.148 197 2141	284	575.028 652 2508	324	674.359 645 3108
245	480.537 363 2985	285	577.483 497 1108	325	676.871 528 6718
246	482.928 298 4056	286	579.939 863 1439	326	679.384 746 2718
247	485.320 995 3589	287	582.397 745 0407	327	681.899 294 0245
248	487.715 447 0397	288	584.857 137 5284	328	684.415 167 8682
249	490.111 646 3868	289	587.318 035 3712	329	686.932 363 7662
250	492.509 586 3955	290	589.780 433 3691	330	689.450 877 7060
251	494.909 260 1169	291	592.244 326 3581	331	691.970 705 6998
252	497.310 660 6577	292	594.709 709 2095	332	694.491 843 7835
253	499.713 781 1789	293	597.176 576 8299	333	697.014 288 0170
254	502.118 614 8955	294	599.644 924 1603	334	699.538 034 4838
255	504.525 155 0760	295	602.114 746 1763	355	702.063 079 2909
256	506.933 395 0413	296	604.586 037 8873	336	704.589 418 5683
257	509.343 328 1646	297	607.058 794 3367	337	707.117 048 4691
258	511.754 947 8706	298	609.533 010 6007	338	709.645 965 1694
259	514.168 247 6346	299	612.008 681 7891	339	712.176 164 8676
260	516.583 220 9826	300	614.485 803 0438	340	714.707 643 7847
261	518.999 861 4900	301	616.964 369 5394	341	717.240 398 1636
262	521.418 162 7813	302	619.444 376 4823	342	719.774 424 2697
263	523.838 118 5298	303	621.925 819 1108	343	722.309 718 3897
264	526.259 722 4566	304	624.408 692 6944	344	724.846 276 8323
265	528.682 968 3306	305	626.892 992 5338	345	727.384 095 9274
266	531.107 849 9672	306	629.378 713 9603	346	729.923 172 0262
267	533.534 361 2286	307	631.865 852 3357	347	732.463 501 5010
268	535.962 496 0226	308	634.354 403 0522	348	735.005 080 7449
269	538.392 248 3026	309	636.844 361 5317	349	737.547 906 1719
270	540.823 612 0668	310	639.335 723 2255	350	740.091 974 2162
271	543.256 581 3576	311	641.828 483 6145	351	742.637 281 3327
272	545.691 150 2617	312	644.322 638 2085	352	745.183 823 9962
273	548.127 312 9087	313	646.818 182 5461	353	747.731 598 7016
274	550.565 063 4715	314	649.315 112 1942	354	750.280 601 9636
275	553.004 396 1654	315	651.813 422 7480	355	752.830 830 3166
276	555.445 305 2474	316	654.313 109 8306	356	755.382 280 3146
277	557.887 785 0165	317	656.814 169 0928	357	757.934 948 5307
278	560.331 829 8124	318	659.316 596 2128	358	760.488 831 5574
279	562.777 434 0157	319	661.820 386 8958	359	763.043 926 0060
280	565.224 592 0470	320	664.325 536 8742	360	765.600 228 5067

n	log n!	n	log n!	n	log n!
361	768.157 735 7086	401	871.409 558 5503	441	976.394 942 7311
362	770.716 444 2792	402	874.013 784 6034	442	979.040 365 0005
363	773.276 350 9042	403	876.619 089 6496	443	981.686 768 7267
364	775.837 452 2878	404	879.225 471 0147	444	984.334 151 6968
365	778.399 745 1523	405	881.832 926 0379	445	986.982 511 7078
366	780.963 226 2377	406	884.441 452 0715	446	989.631 846 5665
367	783.527 892 3019	407	887.051 046 4807	447	992.282 154 0896
368	786.093 740 1206	408	889.661 706 6438	448	994.933 432 1036
369	788.660 766 4868	409	892.273 429 9518	449	997.585 678 4446
370	791.228 968 2108	410	894.886 213 8085	450	1000.238 890 9584
371	793.798 342 1205	411	897.500 055 6304	451	1002.893 067 5003
372	796.368 885 0603	412	900.114 952 8464	452	1005.548 205 9351
373	798.940 593 8922	413	902.730 902 8981	453	1008.204 304 1371
374	801.513 465 4944	414	905.347 903 2392	454	1010.861 359 9900
375	804.087 496 7621	415	907.965 951 3359	455	1013.519 371 3866
376	806.662 684 6070	416	910.585 044 6665	456	1016.178 336 2293
377	809.239 025 9572	417	913.205 180 7215	457	1018.838 252 4293
378	811.816 517 7571	418	915.826 357 0033	458	1021.499 117 9074
379	814.395 156 9670	419	918.448 571 0263	459	1024.160 930 5929
380	816.974 940 5636	420	921.071 820 3167	460	1026.823 688 4246
381	819.555 865 5393	421	923.696 102 4125	461	1029.487 389 3500
382	822.137 928 9022	422	926.321 414 8635	462	1032.152 031 3255
383	824.721 127 6762	423	928.947 755 2308	463	1034.817 612 3165
384	827.305 458 9006	424	931.575 121 0874	464	1037.484 130 2971
385	829.890 919 6301	425	934.203 510 0175	465	1040.151 583 2500
386	832.477 506 9347	426	936.832 919 6166	466	1042.819 969 1667
387	835.065 217 8998	427	939.463 347 4916	467	1045.489 286 0472
388	837.654 049 6254	428	942.094 791 2606	468	1048.159 531 9003
389	840.243 999 2267	429	944.727 248 5528	469	1050.830 704 7430
390	842.835 063 8337	430	947.360 717 0084	470	1053.502 802 6010
391	845.427 240 5911	431	949.995 194 2785	471	1056.175 823 5081
392	848.020 526 6581	432	952.630 678 0254	472	1058.849 765 5067
393	850.614 919 2085	433	955.267 165 9217	473	1061.524 626 6475
394	853.210 415 4303	434	957.904 655 6512	474	1064.200 404 9891
395	855.807 012 5259	435	960.543 144 9082	475	1066.877 098 5988
396	858.404 707 7119	436	963.182 631 3974	476	1069.554 705 5515
397	861.003 498 2186	437	965.823 112 8344	477	1072.233 223 9305
398	863.603 381 2907	438	968.464 586 9449	478	1074.912 651 8271
399	866.204 354 1864	439	971.107 051 4652	479	1077.592 987 3405
400	868.806 414 1777	440	973.750 504 1416	480	1080.274 228 5779

n	log n!	n	log n!	n	log n!
481	1082.956 373 6543	521	1190.962 607 0282	561	1300.302 596 6937
482	1085.639 420 6925	522	1193.680 277 5312	562	1303.052 333 0093
483	1088.323 367 8233	523	1196.398 779 2200	563	1305.802 841 4042
484	1091.008 213 1849	524	1199.118 110 5070	564	1308.554 120 5081
485	1093.693 954 9235	525	1201.838 269 8104	565	1311.306 168 9560
486	1096.380 591 1928	526	1204.559 255 5546	566	1314.058 985 3871
487	1099.068 120 1540	527	1207.281 066 1698	567	1316.812 568 4460
488	1101.756 539 9760	528	1210.003 700 0923	568	1319.566 916 7818
489	1104.445 848 8351	529	1212.727 155 7644	569	1322.322 029 0481
490	1107.136 044 9152	530	1215.451 431 6340	570	1325.077 903 9038
491	1109.827 126 4073	531	1218.176 526 1550	571	1327.834 540 0121
492	1112.519 091 5101	532	1220.902 437 7873	572	1330.591 936 0409
493	1115.211 938 4293	533	1223.629 164 9964	573	1333.350 090 6628
494	1117.905 665 3783	534	1226.356 706 2534	574	1336.109 002 5552
495	1120.600 270 5772	535	1229.085 060 0354	575	1338.868 670 3999
496	1123.295 752 2537	536	1231.814 224 8251	576	1341.629 092 8833
497	1125.992 108 6424	537	1234.544 199 1108	577	1344.390 268 6965
498	1128.689 337 9852	538	1237.274 981 3865	578	1347.152 196 5349
499	1131.387 438 5308	539	1240.006 570 1517	579	1349.914 875 0986
500	1134.086 408 5351	540	1242.738 963 9115	580	1352.678 303 0922
501	1136.786 246 2610	541	1245.472 161 1766	581	1355.442 479 2246
502	1139.486 949 9781	542	1248.206 160 4631	582	1358.207 402 2092
503	1142.188 517 9632	543	1250.940 960 2927	583	1360.973 070 7640
504	1144.890 948 4996	544	1253.676 559 1924	584	1363.739 483 6111
505	1147.594 239 8778	545	1256.412 955 6947	585	1366.506 639 4772
506	1150.298 390 3946	546	1259.150 148 3374	586	1369.274 537 0932
507	1153.003 398 3539	547	1261.888 135 6637	587	1372.043 175 1945
508	1155.709 262 0662	548	1264.626 916 2222	588	1374.812 552 5205
509	1158.415 979 8486	549	1267.366 488 5667	589	1377.582 667 8153
510	1161.123 550 0247	550	1270.106 851 2562	590	1380.353 519 8270
511	1163.831 970 9248	551	1272.848 002 8550	591	1383.125 107 3079
512	1166.541 240 8858	552	1275.589 941 9327	592	1385.897 429 0146
513	1169.251 358 2509	553	1278.332 667 0640	593	1388.670 483 7079
514	1171.962 321 3699	554	1281.076 176 8288	594	1391.444 270 1529
515	1174.674 128 5989	555	1283.820 469 8119	595	1394.218 787 1186
516	1177.386 778 3005	556	1286.565 544 6035	596	1396.994 033 3784
517	1180.100 268 8436	557	1289.311 399 7987	597	1399.770 007 7095
518	1182.814 598 6034	558	1292.058 033 9976	598	1402.546 708 8935
519	1185.529 765 9612	559	1294.805 445 8055	599	1405.324 135 7159
520	1188.245 769 3049	560	1297.553 633 8325	600	1408.102 286 9663

n	log n!	n	log n!	n	log n!
601	1410.881 161 4383	641	1522.615 809 4311	681	1635.434 357 6708
602	1413.660 757 9295	642	1525.423 344 4591	682	1638.268 142 0455
603	1416.441 075 2417	643	1528.231 555 4320	683	1641.102 562 7492
604	1419.222 112 1803	644	1531.040 441 2994	684	1643.937 618 8509
605	1422.003 867 5550	645	1533.850 001 0140	685	1646.773 309 4224
606	1424.786 340 1791	646	1536.660 233 5320	686	1649.609 633 5381
607	1427.569 528 8702	647	1539.471 137 8127	687	1652.446 590 2752
608	1430.353 432 4495	648	1542.282 712 8186	688	1655.284 178 7134
609	1433.138 049 7421	649	1545.094 957 5154	689	1658.122 397 9353
610	1435.923 379 5771	650	1547.907 870 8720	690	1660.961 247 0260
611	1438.709 420 7874	651	1550.721 451 8606	691	1663.800 725 0734
612	1441.496 172 2095	652	1553.535 699 4563	692	1666.640 831 1679
613	1444.283 632 6840	653	1556.350 612 6376	693	1669.481 564 4025
614	1447.071 801 0552	654	1559.166 190 3859	694	1672.322 923 8729
615	1449.860 676 1709	655	1561.982 431 6859	695	1675.164 908 6775
616	1452.650 256 8831	656	1564.799 335 5253	696	1678.007 517 9171
617	1455.440 542 0471	657	1567.616 900 8948	697	1680.850 750 6952
618	1458.231 530 5222	658	1570.435 126 7885	698	1683.694 606 1179
619	1461.023 221 1712	659	1573.254 012 2031	699	1686.539 083 2936
620	1463.815 612 8607	660	1576.073 556 1386	700	1689.384 181 3336
621	1466.608 704 4609	661	1578.893 757 5081	701	1692.229 899 3516
622	1469.402 494 8456	662	1581.714 615 5875	702	1695.076 236 4637
623	1472.196 982 8923	663	1584.536 129 1159	703	1697.923 191 7887
624	1474.992 167 4819	664	1587.358 297 1953	704	1700.770 764 4479
625	1477.788 047 4993	665	1590.181 118 8406	705	1703.618 953 5649
626	1480.584 621 8325	666	1593.004 593 0698	706	1706.467 758 2659
627	1483.381 889 3733	667	1595.828 718 9037	707	1709.317 177 6797
628	1486.179 849 0171	668	1598.653 495 3662	708	1712.167 210 9374
629	1488.978 499 6625	669	1601.478 921 4839	709	1715.017 857 1726
630	1491.777 840 2120	670	1604.304 996 2866	710	1717.869 115 5213
631	1494.577 869 5712	671	1607.131 718 8068	711	1720.720 985 1220
632	1497.378 586 6495	672	1609.959 088 0798	712	1723.573 465 1157
633	1500.179 990 3595	673	1612.787 103 1441	713	1726.426 554 6455
634	1502.982 079 6174	674	1615.615 763 0406	714	1729.280 252 8573
635	1505.784 853 3427	675	1618.445 066 8134	715	1732.134 558 8991
636	1508.588 310 4583	676	1621.275 013 5094	716	1734.989 471 9214
637	1511.392 449 8907	677	1624.105 602 1781	717	1737.844 991 0771
638	1514.197 270 5694	678	1626.936 831 8719	718	1740.701 115 5213
639	1517.002 771 4275	679	1629.768 701 6462	719	1743.557 844 4117
640	1519.808 951 4015	680	1632.601 210 5589	720	1746.415 176 9081

n	log n!	n	log n!	n	log n!
721	1749.273 112 1728	761	1864.075 452 8940	801	1979.790 716 7537
722	1752.131 649 3704	762	1866.957 407 8654	802	1982.694 891 1220
723	1754.990 787 6677	763	1869.839 932 4033	803	1985.599 606 6673
724	1757.850 526 2339	764	1872.723 025 7619	804	1988.504 862 7160
725	1760.710 864 2405	765	1875.606 687 1971	805	1991.410 658 5964
726	1763.571 800 8612	766	1878.490 915 9667	806	1994.316 993 6382
727	1766.433 335 2720	767	1881.375 711 3306	807	1997.223 867 1729
728	1769.295 466 6514	768	1884.261 072 5507	808	2000.131 278 5337
729	1772.158 194 1797	769	1887.146 998 8905	809	2003.039 227 0553
730	1775.021 517 0398	770	1890.033 489 6156	810	2005.947 712 0742
731	1777.885 434 4167	771	1892.920 543 9937	811	2008.856 732 9284
732	1780.749 945 4978	772	1895.808 161 2940	812	2011.766 288 9576
733	1783.615 049 4724	773	1898.696 340 7879	813	2014.676 379 5032
734	1786.480 745 5324	774	1901.585 081 7486	814	2017.587 003 9081
735	1789.347 032 8714	775	1904.474 383 4511	815	2020.498 161 5169
736	1792.213 910 6858	776	1907.364 245 1724	816	2023.409 851 6756
737	1795.081 378 1736	777	1910.254 666 1912	817	2026.322 073 7322
738	1797.949 434 5355	778	1913.145 645 7882	818	2029.234 827 0358
739	1800.818 078 9739	779	1916.037 183 2459	819	2032.148 110 9376
740	1803.687 310 6936	780	1918.929 277 8485	820	2035.061 924 7900
741	1806.557 128 9016	781	1921.821 928 8824	821	2037.976 267 9471
742	1809.427 532 8069	782	1924.715 135 6355	822	2040.891 139 7646
743	1812.298 521 6206	783	1927.608 897 3975	823	2043.806 539 5998
744	1815.170 094 5562	784	1930.503 213 4602	824	2046.722 466 8115
745	1818.042 250 8289	785	1933.398 083 1170	825	2049.638 920 7601
746	1820.914 989 6564	786	1936.293 505 6630	826	2052.555 900 8074
747	1823.788 310 2582	787	1939.189 480 3954	827	2055.473 406 3170
748	1826.662 211 8561	788	1942.086 006 6129	828	2058.391 436 6537
749	1829.536 693 6738	789	1944.983 083 6161	829	2061.309 991 1843
750	1832.411 754 9372	790	1947.880 710 7074	830	2064.229 069 2767
751	1835.287 394 8742	791	1950.778 887 1909	831	2067.148 670 3005
752	1838.163 612 7147	792	1953.677 612 3724	832	2070.068 793 6267
753	1841.040 407 6909	793	1956.576 885 5598	833	2072.989 438 6282
754	1843.917 779 0368	794	1959.476 706 0622	834	2075.910 604 6788
755	1846.795 725 9884	795	1962.377 073 1908	835	2078.832 291 1543
756	1849.674 247 7839	796	1965.277 986 2586	836	2081.754 497 4317
757	1852.553 343 6634	797	1968.179 444 5800	837	2084.677 222 8897
758	1855.433 012 8691	798	1971.081 447 4713	838	2087.600 466 9083
759	1858.313 254 6450	799	1973.983 994 2506	839	2090.524 228 8692
760	1861.194 068 2373	800	1976.887 084 2376	840	2093.448 508 1552

n	$\log n!$	n	$\log n!$	n	$\log n!$
841	2096.373 304 1510	881	2213.781 955 7223	921	2331.979 160 6232
842	2099.298 616 2425	882	2216.727 424 3075	922	2334.943 891 5443
843	2102.224 443 8171	883	2219.673 385 0110	923	2337.909 093 2453
844	2105.150 786 2638	884	2222.619 837 2760	924	2340.874 765 2165
845	2108.077 642 9727	885	2225.566 780 5467	925	2343.840 906 9493
846	2111.005 013 3358	886	2228.514 214 2686	926	2346.807 517 9360
847	2113.932 896 7461	887	2231.462 137 8885	927	2349.774 597 6701
848	2116.861 292 5984	888	2234.410 550 8542	928	2352.742 145 6463
849	2119.790 200 2886	889	2237.359 452 6152	929	2355.710 161 3603
850	2122.719 619 2143	890	2240.308 842 6219	930	2358.678 644 3089
851	2125.649 548 7744	891	2243.258 720 3259	931	2361.647 593 9898
852	2128.579 988 3692	892	2246.209 085 1803	932	2364.617 009 9022
853	2131.510 937 4003	893	2249.159 936 6392	933	2367.586 891 5459
854	2134.442 395 2710	894	2252.111 274 1580	934	2370.557 238 4222
855	2137.374 361 3857	895	2255.063 097 1933	935	2373.528 050 0331
856	2140.306 835 1504	896	2258.015 405 2029	936	2376.499 325 8818
857	2143.239 815 9723	897	2260.968 197 6460	937	2379.471 065 4727
858	2146.173 303 2602	898	2263.921 473 9826	938	2382.443 268 3111
859	2149.107 296 4240	899	2266.875 233 6744	939	2385.415 933 9033
860	2152.041 794 8753	900	2269.829 476 1838	940	2388.389 061 7569
861	2154.976 798 0267	901	2272.784 200 9748	941	2391.362 651 3803
862	2157.912 305 2925	902	2275.739 407 5123	942	2394.336 702 2831
863	2160.848 316 0883	903	2278.695 095 2626	943	2397.311 213 9759
864	2163.784 829 8307	904	2281.651 263 6931	944	2400.286 185 9702
865	2166.721 845 9382	905	2284.607 912 2723	945	2403.261 617 7787
866	2169.659 363 8302	906	2287.565 040 4700	946	2406.237 508 9151
867	2172.597 382 9277	907	2290.522 647 7571	947	2409.213 858 8941
868	2175.535 902 6529	908	2293.480 733 6056	948	2412.190 667 2314
869	2178.474 922 4293	909	2296.439 297 4888	949	2415.167 933 4439
870	2181.414 441 6819	910	2299.398 338 8811	950	2418.145 657 0491
871	2184.354 459 8370	911	2302.357 857 2581	951	2421.123 837 5661
872	2187.294 976 3219	912	2305.317 852 0964	952	2424.102 474 5145
873	2190.235 990 5656	913	2308.278 322 8740	953	2427.081 567 4151
874	2193.177 501 9982	914	2311.239 269 0697	954	2430.061 115 7898
875	2196.119 510 0512	915	2314.200 690 1638	955	2433.041 119 1614
876	2199.062 014 1574	916	2317.162 585 6374	956	2436.021 577 0537
877	2202.005 013 7508	917	2320.124 954 9731	957	2439.002 488 9914
878	2204.948 508 2667	918	2323.087 797 6543	958	2441.983 854 5005
879	2207.892 497 1418	919	2326.051 113 1657	959	2444.965 673 1077
880	2210.836 979 8139	920	2329.014 900 9930	960	2447.947 944 3407

n	$\log n!$	n	$\log n!$	n	$\log n!$
961	2450.930 667 7284	1001	2570.605 078 2996	1041	2690.973 503 8239
962	2453.913 842 8004	1002	2573.605 946 0211	1042	2693.991 371 5429
963	2456.897 469 0876	1003	2576.607 246 9542	1043	2697.009 655 8513
964	2459.881 546 1215	1004	2579.608 980 6670	1044	2700.028 356 3500
965	2462.866 073 4348	1005	2582.611 146 7287	1045	2703.047 472 6404
966	2465.851 050 5612	1006	2585.613 744 7094	1046	2706.067 004 3250
967	2468.836 477 0353	1007	2588.616 774 1800	1047	2709.086 951 0066
968	2471.822 352 3926	1008	2591.620 234 7121	1048	2712.107 312 2893
969	2474.808 676 1697	1009	2594.624 125 8783	1049	2715.128 087 7775
970	2477.795 447 9039	1010	2597.628 447 2521	1050	2718.149 277 0765
971	2480.782 667 1338	1011	2600.633 198 4077	1051	2721.170 879 7926
972	2483.770 333 3988	1012	2603.638 378 9202	1052	2724.192 895 5324
973	2486.758 446 2390	1013	2606.643 988 3656	1053	2727.215 323 9036
974	2489.747 005 1959	1014	2609.650 026 3206	1054	2730.238 164 5145
975	2492.736 009 8116	1015	2612.656 492 3628	1055	2733.261 416 9741
976	2495.725 459 6293	1016	2615.663 386 0708	1056	2736.285 080 8923
977	2498.715 354 1930	1017	2618.670 707 0237	1057	2739.309 155 8796
978	2501.705 693 0478	1018	2621.678 454 8017	1058	2742.333 641 5473
979	2504.696 475 7396	1019	2624.686 628 9857	1059	2745.358 537 5074
980	2507.687 701 8153	1020	2627.695 229 1575	1060	2748.383 843 3727
981	2510.679 370 8227	1021	2630.704 254 8996	1061	2751.409 558 7566
982	2513.671 482 3105	1022	2633.713 705 7954	1062	2754.435 683 2733
983	2516.664 035 8283	1023	2636.723 581 4291	1063	2757.462 216 5378
984	2519.657 030 9267	1024	2639.733 881 3857	1064	2760.489 158 1658
985	2522.650 467 1572	1025	2642.744 605 2511	1065	2763.516 507 7736
986	2525.644 344 0722	1026	2645.755 752 6119	1066	2766.544 264 9783
987	2528.638 661 2248	1027	2648.767 323 0555	1067	2769.572 429 3977
988	2531.633 418 1694	1028	2651.779 316 1701	1068	2772.601 000 6504
989	2534.628 614 4610	1029	2654.791 731 5449	1069	2775.629 978 3556
990	2537.624 249 6556	1030	2657.804 568 7696	1070	2778.659 362 1333
991	2540.620 323 3101	1031	2660.817 827 4349	1071	2781.689 151 6041
992	2543.616 834 9822	1032	2663.831 507 1322	1072	2784.719 346 3895
993	2546.613 784 2307	1033	2666.845 607 4537	1073	2787.749 946 1114
994	2549.611 170 6151	1034	2669.860 127 9925	1074	2790.780 950 3928
995	2552.608 993 6959	1035	2672.875 068 3422	1075	2793.812 358 8570
996	2555.607 253 0343	1036	2675.890 428 0977	1076	2796.844 171 1284
997	2558.605 948 1926	1037	2678.906 206 8540	1077	2799.876 386 8317
998	2561.605 078 7339	1038	2681.922 404 2076	1078	2802.909 005 5925
999	2564.604 644 2221	1039	2684.939 019 7551	1079	2805.942 027 0372
1000	2567.604 644 2221	1040	2687.956 053 0944	1080	2808.975 450 7927

n	log n!	n	log n!	n	log n!
1081	2812.009 276 4866	1121	2933.687 702 5306	1161	3055.985 850 8433
1082	2815.043 503 7474	1122	2936.737 695 3876	1162	3059.051 056 9714
1083	2818.078 132 2040	1123	2939.788 075 1438	1163	3062.116 636 6861
1084	2821.113 161 4862	1124	2942.838 841 4551	1164	3065.182 589 6664
1085	2824.148 591 2244	1125	2945.889 993 9775	1165	3068.248 915 5918
1086	2827.184 421 0497	1126	2948.941 532 3680	1166	3071.315 614 1422
1087	2830.220 650 5938	1127	2951.993 456 2841	1167	3074.382 684 9982
1088	2833.257 279 4891	1128	2955.045 765 3837	1168	3077.450 127 8410
1089	2836.294 307 3689	1129	2958.098 459 3256	1169	3080.517 942 3522
1090	2839.331 733 8668	1130	2961.151 537 7691	1170	3083.586 128 2139
1091	2842.369 558 6174	1131	2964.205 000 3741	1171	3086.654 685 1090
1092	2845.407 781 2558	1132	2967.258 846 8009	1172	3089.723 612 7207
1093	2848.446 401 4177	1133	2970.313 076 7108	1173	3092.792 910 7328
1094	2851.485 418 7397	1134	2973.367 689 7653	1174	3095.862 578 8297
1095	2854.524 832 8589	1135	2976.422 685 6269	1175	3098.932 616 6963
1096	2857.564 643 4131	1136	2979.478 063 9582	1176	3102.003 024 0180
1097	2860.604 850 0406	1137	2982.533 824 4229	1177	3105.073 800 4809
1098	2863.645 452 3807	1138	2985.589 966 6850	1178	3108.144 945 7713
1099	2866.686 450 0732	1139	2988.646 490 4091	1179	3111.216 459 5764
1100	2869.727 842 7583	1140	2991.703 395 2604	1180	3114.288 341 5837
1101	2872.769 630 0773	1141	2994.760 680 9048	1181	3117.360 591 4813
1102	2875.811 811 6718	1142	2997.818 347 0087	1182	3120.433 208 9579
1103	2878.854 387 1843	1143	3000.876 393 2391	1183	3123.506 193 7025
1104	2881.897 356 2576	1144	3003.934 819 2636	1184	3126.579 545 4049
1105	2884.940 718 5357	1145	3006.993 624 7502	1185	3129.653 263 7553
1106	2887.984 473 6626	1146	3010.052 809 3679	1186	3132.727 348 4443
1107	2891.028 621 2835	1147	3013.112 372 7858	1187	3135.801 799 1632
1108	2894.073 161 0439	1148	3016.172 314 6738	1188	3138.876 615 6039
1109	2897.118 092 5901	1149	3019.232 634 7025	1189	3141.951 797 4585
1110	2900.163 415 5688	1150	3022.293 332 5429	1190	3145.027 344 4199
1111	2903.209 129 6278	1151	3025.354 407 8665	1191	3148.103 256 1814
1112	2906.255 234 4150	1152	3028.415 860 3456	1192	3151.179 532 4368
1113	2909.301 729 5794	1153	3031.477 689 6529	1193	3154.256 172 8805
1114	2912.348 614 7702	1154	3034.539 895 4617	1194	3157.333 177 2072
1115	2915.395 889 6376	1155	3037.602 477 4459	1195	3160.410 545 1125
1116	2918.443 553 8322	1156	3040.665 435 2800	1196	3163.488 276 2922
1117	2921.491 607 0053	1157	3043.728 768 6390	1197	3166.566 370 4426
1118	2924.540 048 8089	1158	3046.792 477 1984	1198	3169.644 827 2606
1119	2927.588 878 8954	1159	3049.856 560 6343	1199	3172.723 646 4437
1120	2930.638 096 9181	1160	3052.921 018 6236	1200	3175.802 827 6898

n	$m=0$	$m=1$	$m=2$	$m=3$	$m=4$	$m=5$	$m=6$	$m=7$	$m=8$	$m=9$	$m=10$
0	1	1	1	1	1	1	1	1	1	1	1
1		1	2	3	4	5	6	7	8	9	10
2			1	3	6	10	15	21	28	36	45
3				1	4	10	20	35	56	84	120
4					1	5	15	35	70	126	210
5						1	6	21	56	126	252
6							1	7	28	84	210
7								1	8	36	120
8									1	9	45
9										1	10
10											1

n	$m=11$	$m=12$	$m=13$	$m=14$	$m=15$	$m=16$	$m=17$	$m=18$	$m=19$
0	1	1	1	1	1	1	1	1	1
1	11	12	13	14	15	16	17	18	19
2	55	66	78	91	105	120	136	153	171
3	165	220	286	364	455	560	680	816	969
4	330	495	715	1001	1365	1820	2380	3060	3876
5	462	792	1287	2002	3003	4368	6188	8568	11628
6	462	924	1716	3003	5005	8008	12376	18564	27132
7			1716	3432	6435	11440	19448	31824	50388
8					6435	12870	24310	43758	75582
9							24310	48620	92378
10									92378

n	$m = 20$	$m = 21$	$m = 22$	$m = 23$	$m = 24$	$m = 25$
1	2.0^{1}	2.1^{1}	2.2^{1}	2.3^{1}	2.4^{1}	2.5^{1}
2	1.90^{2}	2.10^{2}	2.31^{2}	2.53^{2}	2.76^{2}	3.00^{2}
3	1.140^{3}	1.330^{3}	1.540^{3}	1.771^{3}	2.024^{3}	2.300^{3}
4	4.845	5.985	7.315	8.855	1.0626^{4}	1.2650^{4}
5	1.5504^{4}	2.0349^{4}	2.6334^{4}	3.3649^{4}	4.2504	5.3130

Since C_0^m is equal to unity for every value of m it is not tabulated beyond $m = 20$.

n	$m = 20$	$m = 21$	$m = 22$	$m = 23$	$m = 24$	$m = 25$
6	3.876 0 ^{4}	5.426 4 ^{4}	7.461 3 ^{4}	1.009 47 ^{5}	1.345 96 ^{5}	1.771 00 ^{5}
7	7.752 0	1.162 80 ^{5}	1.705 44 ^{5}	2.451 57	3.461 04	4.807·00
8	1.259 70 ^{5}	2.034 90	3.197 70	4.903 14	7.354 71	1.081 575 ^{6}
9	1.679 60	2.939 30	4.974 20	8.171 90	1.307 504 ^{6}	2.042 975
10	1.847 56	3.527 16	6.466 46	1.144 066 ^{6}	1.961 256	3.268 760
11		3.527 16	7.054 32	1.352 078	2.496 144	4.457 400
12				1.352 078	2.704 156	5.200 300
13						5.200 300

n	$m = 26$	$m = 27$	$m = 28$	$m = 29$	$m = 30$
1	2.6 ^{1}	2.7 ^{1}	2.8 ^{1}	2.9 ^{1}	3.0 ^{1}
2	3.25 ^{2}	3.51 ^{2}	3.78 ^{2}	4.06 ^{2}	4.35 ^{2}
3	2.600 ^{3}	2.925 ^{3}	3.276 ^{3}	3.654 ^{3}	4.060 ^{3}
4	1.495 0 ^{4}	1.755 0 ^{4}	2.047 5 ^{4}	2.375 1 ^{4}	2.740 5 ^{4}
5	6.578 0	8.073 0	9.828 0	1.187 55 ^{5}	1.425 06 ^{5}
6	2.302 30 ^{5}	2.960 10 ^{5}	3.767 40 ^{5}	4.750 20	5.937 75
7	6.578 00	8.880 30	1.184 040 ^{6}	1.560 780 ^{6}	2.035 800 ^{6}
8	1.562 275 ^{6}	2.220 075 ^{6}	3.108 105	4.292 145	5.852 925
9	3.124 550	4.686 825	6.906 900	1.001 5005 ^{7}	1.430 7150 ^{7}
10	5.311 735	8.436 285	1.312 3110 ^{7}	2.003 0010	3.004 5015
11	7.726 160	1.303 7895 ^{7}	2.147 4180	3.459 7290	5.462 7300
12	9.657 700	1.738 3860	3.042 1755	5.189 5935	8.649 3225
13	1.040 0600 ^{7}	2.005 8300	3.744 2160	6.786 3915	1.197 5985 ^{8}
14		2.005 8300	4.011 6600	7.755 8760	1.454 2268
15				7.755 8760	1.551 1752

n	$m = 31$	$m = 32$	$m = 33$	$m = 34$	$m = 35$
1	3.1 ^{1}	3.2 ^{1}	3.3 ^{1}	3.4 ^{1}	3.5 ^{1}
2	4.65 ^{2}	4.96 ^{2}	5.28 ^{2}	5.61 ^{2}	5.95 ^{2}
3	4.495 ^{3}	4.960 ^{3}	5.456 ^{3}	5.984 ^{3}	6.545 ^{3}
4	3.146 5 ^{4}	3.596 0 ^{4}	4.092 0 ^{4}	4.637 6 ^{4}	5.236 0 ^{4}
5	1.699 11 ^{5}	2.013 76 ^{5}	2.373 36 ^{5}	2.782 56 ^{5}	3.246 32 ^{5}
6	7.362 81	9.061 92	1.107 568 ^{6}	1.344 904 ^{6}	1.623 160 ^{6}
7	2.629 575 ^{6}	3.365 856 ^{6}	4.272 048	5.379 616	6.724 520
8	7.888 725	1.051 8300 ^{7}	1.388 4156 ^{7}	1.815 6204 ^{7}	2.353 5820 ^{7}
9	2.016 0075 ^{7}	2.804 8800	3.856 7100	5.245 1256	7.060 7460
10	4.435 2165	6.451 2240	9.256 1040	1.311 2814 ^{8}	1.835 7940 ^{8}

n	$m = 31$	$m = 32$	$m = 33$	$m = 34$	$m = 35$
11	$8.467\ 2315^{7}$	$1.290\ 2448^{8}$	$1.935\ 3672^{8}$	$2.860\ 9776^{8}$	$4.172\ 2590^{8}$
12	$1.411\ 2052^{8}$	$2.257\ 9284$	$3.548\ 1732$	$5.483\ 5404$	$8.344\ 5180$
13	$2.062\ 5308$	$3.473\ 7360$	$5.731\ 6644$	$9.279\ 8376$	$1.476\ 3378^{9}$
14	$2.651\ 8252$	$4.714\ 3560$	$8.188\ 0920$	$1.391\ 9756^{9}$	$2.319\ 9594$
15	$3.005\ 4020$	$5.657\ 2272$	$1.037\ 1583^{9}$	$1.855\ 9675$	$3.247\ 9432$
16	$3.005\ 4020$	$6.010\ 8039$	$1.166\ 8031$	$2.203\ 9614$	$4.059\ 9290$
			$1.166\ 8031$	$2.333\ 6062$	$4.537\ 5676$
					$4.537\ 5676$

n	$m = 36$	$m = 37$	$m = 38$	$m = 39$	$m = 40$
1	3.6^{1}	3.7^{1}	3.8^{1}	3.9^{1}	4.0^{1}
2	6.30^{2}	6.66^{2}	7.03^{2}	7.41^{2}	7.80^{2}
3	7.140^{3}	7.770^{3}	8.436^{3}	9.139^{3}	9.880^{3}
4	$5.890\ 5^{4}$	$6.604\ 5^{4}$	$7.381\ 5^{4}$	$8.225\ 1^{4}$	$9.139\ 0^{4}$
5	$3.769\ 92^{5}$	$4.358\ 97^{5}$	$5.019\ 42^{5}$	$5.757\ 57^{5}$	$6.580\ 08^{5}$
6	$1.947\ 792^{6}$	$2.324\ 784^{6}$	$2.760\ 681^{6}$	$3.262\ 623^{6}$	$3.838\ 380^{6}$
7	$8.347\ 680$	$1.029\ 5472^{7}$	$1.262\ 0256^{7}$	$1.538\ 0937^{7}$	$1.864\ 3560^{7}$
8	$3.026\ 0340^{7}$	$3.860\ 8020$	$4.890\ 3492$	$6.152\ 3748$	$7.690\ 4685$
9	$9.414\ 3280$	$1.244\ 0362^{8}$	$1.630\ 1164^{8}$	$2.119\ 1513^{8}$	$2.734\ 3888^{8}$
10	$2.541\ 8686^{8}$	$3.483\ 3014$	$4.727\ 3376$	$6.357\ 4540$	$8.476\ 6053$
11	$6.008\ 0530$	$8.549\ 9215$	$1.203\ 3223^{9}$	$1.676\ 0560^{9}$	$2.311\ 8014^{9}$
12	$1.251\ 6777^{9}$	$1.852\ 4830^{9}$	$2.707\ 4751$	$3.910\ 7974$	$5.586\ 8535$
13	$2.310\ 7896$	$3.562\ 4673$	$5.414\ 9503$	$8.122\ 4254$	$1.203\ 3223^{10}$
14	$3.796\ 2972$	$6.107\ 0868$	$9.669\ 5541$	$1.508\ 4504^{10}$	$2.320\ 6930$
15	$5.567\ 9026$	$9.364\ 1998$	$1.547\ 1287^{10}$	$2.514\ 0841$	$4.022\ 5345$
16	$7.307\ 8721$	$1.287\ 5775^{10}$	$2.223\ 9974$	$3.771\ 1261$	$6.285\ 2102$
17	$8.597\ 4966$	$1.590\ 5369$	$2.878\ 1143$	$5.102\ 1118$	$8.873\ 2379$
18	$9.075\ 1353$	$1.767\ 2632$	$3.357\ 8001$	$6.235\ 9144$	$1.133\ 8026^{11}$
19		$1.767\ 2632$	$3.534\ 5264$	$6.892\ 3264$	$1.312\ 8241$
20				$6.892\ 3264$	$1.378\ 4653$

n	$m = 41$	$m = 42$	$m = 43$	$m = 44$	$m = 45$
1	4.1^{1}	4.2^{1}	4.3^{1}	4.4^{1}	4.5^{1}
2	8.20^{2}	8.61^{2}	9.03^{2}	9.46^{2}	9.90^{2}
3	$1.066\ 0^{4}$	$1.148\ 0^{4}$	$1.234\ 1^{4}$	$1.324\ 4^{4}$	$1.419\ 0^{4}$
4	$1.012\ 70^{5}$	$1.119\ 30^{5}$	$1.234\ 10^{5}$	$1.357\ 51^{5}$	$1.489\ 95^{5}$
5	$7.493\ 98$	$8.506\ 68$	$9.625\ 98$	$1.086\ 008^{6}$	$1.221\ 759^{6}$
6	$4.496\ 388^{6}$	$5.245\ 786^{6}$	$6.096\ 454^{6}$	$7.059\ 052$	$8.145\ 060$
7	$2.248\ 1940^{7}$	$2.697\ 8328^{7}$	$3.222\ 4114^{7}$	$3.832\ 0568^{7}$	$4.537\ 9620^{7}$
8	$9.554\ 8245$	$1.180\ 3018^{8}$	$1.450\ 0851^{8}$	$1.772\ 3263^{8}$	$2.155\ 5320^{8}$
9	$3.503\ 4356^{8}$	$4.458\ 9181$	$5.639\ 2200$	$7.089\ 3051$	$8.861\ 6314$
10	$1.121\ 0994^{9}$	$1.471\ 4430^{9}$	$1.917\ 3348^{9}$	$2.481\ 2568^{9}$	$3.190\ 1873^{9}$

n	$m = 41$	$m = 42$	$m = 43$	$m = 44$	$m = 45$
11	$3.159\ 4620^{9}$	$4.280\ 5614^{9}$	$5.752\ 0043^{9}$	$7.669\ 3391^{9}$	$1.015\ 0596^{10}$
12	$7.898\ 6549$	$1.105\ 8117^{10}$	$1.533\ 8678^{10}$	$2.109\ 0683^{10}$	$2.876\ 0022$
13	$1.762\ 0076^{10}$	$2.551\ 8731$	$3.657\ 6848$	$5.191\ 5526$	$7.300\ 6209$
14	$3.524\ 0153$	$5.286\ 0229$	$7.837\ 8960$	$1.149\ 5581^{11}$	$1.668\ 7133^{11}$
15	$6.343\ 2275$	$9.867\ 2428$	$1.515\ 3266^{11}$	$2.299\ 1162$	$3.448\ 6743$
16	$1.030\ 7745^{11}$	$1.665\ 0972^{11}$	$2.651\ 8215$	$4.167\ 1481$	$6.466\ 2642$
17	$1.515\ 8448$	$2.546\ 6193$	$4.211\ 7165$	$6.863\ 5380$	$1.103\ 0686^{12}$
18	$2.021\ 1264$	$3.536\ 9712$	$6.083\ 5905$	$1.029\ 5307^{12}$	$1.715\ 8845$
19	$2.446\ 6267$	$4.467\ 7531$	$8.004\ 7243$	$1.408\ 8315$	$2.438\ 3622$
20	$2.691\ 2894$	$5.137\ 9161$	$9.605\ 6692$	$1.761\ 0394$	$3.169\ 8708$
21	$2.691\ 2894$	$5.382\ 5787$	$1.052\ 0495^{12}$	$2.012\ 6164$	$3.773\ 6558$
22			$1.052\ 0495$	$2.104\ 0990$	$4.116\ 7154$
23					$4.116\ 7154$

n	$m = 46$	$m = 47$	$m = 48$	$m = 49$	$m = 50$
1	4.6^{1}	4.7^{1}	4.8^{1}	4.9^{1}	5.0^{1}
2	1.035^{3}	1.081^{3}	1.128^{3}	1.176^{3}	1.225^{3}
3	$1.518\ 0^{4}$	$1.621\ 5^{4}$	$1.729\ 6^{4}$	$1.842\ 4^{4}$	$1.960\ 0^{4}$
4	$1.631\ 85^{5}$	$1.783\ 65^{5}$	$1.945\ 80^{5}$	$2.118\ 76^{5}$	$2.303\ 00^{5}$
5	$1.370\ 754^{6}$	$1.533\ 939^{6}$	$1.712\ 304^{6}$	$1.906\ 884^{6}$	$2.118\ 760^{6}$
6	$9.366\ 819$	$1.073\ 7573^{7}$	$1.227\ 1512^{7}$	$1.398\ 3816^{7}$	$1.589\ 0700^{7}$
7	$5.352\ 4680^{7}$	$6.289\ 1499$	$7.362\ 9072$	$8.590\ 0584$	$9.988\ 4400$
8	$2.609\ 3282^{8}$	$3.144\ 5750^{8}$	$3.773\ 4899^{8}$	$4.509\ 7807^{8}$	$5.368\ 7865^{8}$
9	$1.101\ 7163^{9}$	$1.362\ 6491^{9}$	$1.677\ 1066^{9}$	$2.054\ 4556^{9}$	$2.505\ 4337^{9}$
10	$4.076\ 3504$	$5.178\ 0668$	$6.540\ 7159$	$8.217\ 8225$	$1.027\ 2278^{10}$
11	$1.334\ 0783^{10}$	$1.741\ 7134^{10}$	$2.259\ 5200^{10}$	$2.913\ 5916^{10}$	$3.735\ 3739$
12	$3.891\ 0618$	$5.225\ 1401$	$6.966\ 8534$	$9.226\ 3735$	$1.213\ 9965^{11}$
13	$1.017\ 6623^{11}$	$1.406\ 7685^{11}$	$1.929\ 2825^{11}$	$2.625\ 9678^{11}$	$3.548\ 6052$
14	$2.398\ 7754$	$3.416\ 4377$	$4.823\ 2062$	$6.752\ 4887$	$9.378\ 4566$
15	$5.117\ 3876$	$7.516\ 1630$	$1.093\ 2601^{12}$	$1.575\ 5807^{12}$	$2.250\ 8296^{12}$
16	$9.914\ 9385$	$1.503\ 2326^{12}$	$2.254\ 8489$	$3.348\ 1090$	$4.923\ 6897$
17	$1.749\ 6950^{12}$	$2.741\ 1889$	$4.244\ 4215$	$6.499\ 2704$	$9.847\ 3794$
18	$2.818\ 9531$	$4.568\ 6481$	$7.309\ 8370$	$1.155\ 4258^{13}$	$1.805\ 3529^{13}$
19	$4.154\ 2467$	$6.973\ 1998$	$1.154\ 1848^{13}$	$1.885\ 1685$	$3.040\ 5943$
20	$5.608\ 2330$	$9.762\ 4797$	$1.673\ 5679$	$2.827\ 7527$	$4.712\ 9212$
21	$6.943\ 5266$	$1.255\ 1760^{13}$	$2.231\ 4239$	$3.904\ 9919$	$6.732\ 7446$
22	$7.890\ 3711$	$1.483\ 3898$	$2.738\ 5657$	$4.969\ 9897$	$8.874\ 9815$
23	$8.233\ 4307$	$1.612\ 3802$	$3.095\ 7700$	$5.834\ 3357$	$1.080\ 4325^{14}$
24		$1.612\ 3802$	$3.224\ 7604$	$6.320\ 5303$	$1.215\ 4866$
25				$6.320\ 5303$	$1.264\ 1061$

n	$m = 51$	$m = 52$	$m = 53$	$m = 54$	$m = 55$
1	5.1^{1}	5.2^{1}	5.3^{1}	5.4^{1}	5.5^{1}
2	1.275^{3}	1.326^{3}	1.378^{3}	1.431^{3}	1.485^{3}
3	$2.082\ 5^{4}$	$2.210\ 0^{4}$	$2.342\ 6^{4}$	$2.480\ 4^{4}$	$2.623\ 5^{4}$
4	$2.499\ 00^{5}$	$2.707\ 25^{5}$	$2.928\ 25^{5}$	$3.162\ 51^{5}$	$3.410\ 55^{5}$
5	$2.349\ 060^{6}$	$2.598\ 960^{6}$	$2.869\ 685^{6}$	$3.162\ 510^{6}$	$3.478\ 761^{6}$
6	$1.800\ 9460^{7}$	$2.035\ 8520^{7}$	$2.295\ 7480^{7}$	$2.582\ 7165^{7}$	$2.898\ 9675^{7}$
7	$1.157\ 7510^{8}$	$1.337\ 8456^{8}$	$1.541\ 4308^{8}$	$1.771\ 0056^{8}$	$2.029\ 2772^{8}$
8	$6.367\ 6305$	$7.525\ 3815$	$8.863\ 2271$	$1.040\ 4658^{9}$	$1.217\ 5664^{9}$
9	$3.042\ 3124^{9}$	$3.679\ 0754^{9}$	$4.431\ 6136^{9}$	$5.317\ 9363$	$6.358\ 4020$
10	$1.277\ 7712^{10}$	$1.582\ 0024^{10}$	$1.949\ 9100^{10}$	$2.393\ 0713^{10}$	$2.924\ 8649^{10}$
11	$4.762\ 6017$	$6.040\ 3729$	$7.622\ 3753$	$9.572\ 2853$	$1.196\ 5357^{11}$
12	$1.587\ 5339^{11}$	$2.063\ 7941^{11}$	$2.667\ 8314^{11}$	$3.430\ 0689^{11}$	$4.387\ 2974$
13	$4.762\ 6017$	$6.350\ 1356$	$8.413\ 9297$	$1.108\ 1761^{12}$	$1.451\ 1830^{12}$
14	$1.292\ 7062^{12}$	$1.768\ 9663^{12}$	$2.403\ 9799^{12}$	$3.245\ 3729$	$4.353\ 5490$
15	$3.188\ 6752$	$4.481\ 3814$	$6.250\ 3478$	$8.654\ 3277$	$1.189\ 9701^{13}$
16	$7.174\ 5193$	$1.036\ 3195^{13}$	$1.484\ 4576^{13}$	$2.109\ 4924^{13}$	$2.974\ 9251$
17	$1.477\ 1069^{13}$	$2.194\ 5588$	$3.230\ 8783$	$4.715\ 3359$	$6.824\ 8282$
18	$2.790\ 0908$	$4.267\ 1977$	$6.461\ 7566$	$9.692\ 6349$	$1.440\ 7971^{14}$
19	$4.845\ 9472$	$7.636\ 0381$	$1.190\ 3236^{14}$	$1.836\ 4992^{14}$	$2.805\ 7627$
20	$7.753\ 5156$	$1.259\ 9463^{14}$	$2.023\ 5501$	$3.213\ 8737$	$5.050\ 3729$
21	$1.144\ 5666^{14}$	$1.919\ 9181$	$3.179\ 8644$	$5.203\ 4145$	$8.417\ 2882$
22	$1.560\ 7726$	$2.705\ 3392$	$4.625\ 2573$	$7.805\ 1218$	$1.300\ 8536^{15}$
23	$1.967\ 9307$	$3.528\ 7033$	$6.234\ 0425$	$1.085\ 9300^{15}$	$1.866\ 4422$
24	$2.295\ 9191$	$4.263\ 8498$	$7.792\ 5531$	$1.402\ 6596$	$2.488\ 5895$
25	$2.479\ 5927$	$4.775\ 5118$	$9.039\ 3616$	$1.683\ 1915$	$3.085\ 8510$
26	$2.479\ 5927$	$4.959\ 1853$	$9.734\ 6971$	$1.877\ 4059$	$3.560\ 5973$
27			$9.734\ 6971$	$1.946\ 9394$	$3.824\ 3453$
28					$3.824\ 3453$

n	$m = 56$	$m = 57$	$m = 58$	$m = 59$	$m = 60$
1	5.6^{1}	5.7^{1}	5.8^{1}	5.9^{1}	6.0^{1}
2	1.540^{3}	1.596^{3}	1.653^{3}	1.711^{3}	1.770^{3}
3	$2.772\ 0^{4}$	$2.926\ 0^{4}$	$3.085\ 6^{4}$	$3.250\ 9^{4}$	$3.422\ 0^{4}$
4	$3.672\ 90^{5}$	$3.950\ 10^{5}$	$4.242\ 70^{5}$	$4.551\ 26^{5}$	$4.876\ 35^{5}$
5	$3.819\ 816^{6}$	$4.187\ 106^{6}$	$4.582\ 116^{6}$	$5.006\ 386^{6}$	$5.461\ 512^{6}$
6	$3.246\ 8436^{7}$	$3.628\ 8252^{7}$	$4.047\ 5358^{7}$	$4.505\ 7474^{7}$	$5.006\ 3860^{7}$
7	$2.319\ 1740^{8}$	$2.643\ 8584^{8}$	$3.006\ 7409^{8}$	$3.411\ 4945^{8}$	$3.862\ 0692^{8}$
8	$1.420\ 4941^{9}$	$1.652\ 4115^{9}$	$1.916\ 7973^{9}$	$2.217\ 4714^{9}$	$2.558\ 6208^{9}$
9	$7.575\ 9684$	$8.996\ 4625$	$1.064\ 8874^{10}$	$1.256\ 5671^{10}$	$1.478\ 3143^{10}$
10	$3.560\ 7051^{10}$	$4.318\ 3020^{10}$	$5.217\ 9482$	$6.282\ 8356$	$7.539\ 4028$

n	$m = 56$	$m = 57$	$m = 58$	$m = 59$	$m = 60$
11	$1.489\ 0222^{11}$	$1.845\ 0927^{11}$	$2.276\ 9229^{11}$	$2.798\ 7177^{11}$	$3.427\ 0013^{11}$
12	$5.583\ 8331$	$7.072\ 8552$	$8.917\ 9479$	$1.119\ 4871^{12}$	$1.399\ 3588^{12}$
13	$1.889\ 9127^{12}$	$2.448\ 2960^{12}$	$3.155\ 5816^{12}$	$4.047\ 3764$	$5.166\ 8634$
14	$5.804\ 7320$	$7.694\ 6447$	$1.014\ 2941^{13}$	$1.329\ 8522^{13}$	$1.734\ 5899^{13}$
15	$1.625\ 3249^{13}$	$2.205\ 7981^{13}$	$2.975\ 2626$	$3.989\ 5567$	$5.319\ 4089$
16	$4.164\ 8952$	$5.790\ 2201$	$7.996\ 0183$	$1.097\ 1281^{14}$	$1.496\ 0838^{14}$
17	$9.799\ 7534$	$1.396\ 4649^{14}$	$1.975\ 4869^{14}$	$2.775\ 0887$	$3.872\ 2168$
18	$2.123\ 2799^{14}$	$3.103\ 2552$	$4.499\ 7201$	$6.475\ 2070$	$9.250\ 2957$
19	$4.246\ 5598$	$6.369\ 8397$	$9.473\ 0949$	$1.397\ 2815^{15}$	$2.044\ 8022^{15}$
20	$7.856\ 1356$	$1.210\ 2695^{15}$	$1.847\ 2535^{15}$	$2.794\ 5630$	$4.191\ 8445$
21	$1.346\ 7661^{15}$	$2.132\ 3797$	$3.342\ 6492$	$5.189\ 9027$	$7.984\ 4657$
22	$2.142\ 5824$	$3.489\ 3485$	$5.621\ 7282$	$8.964\ 3774$	$1.415\ 4280^{16}$
23	$3.167\ 2958$	$5.309\ 8782$	$8.799\ 2268$	$1.442\ 0955^{16}$	$2.338\ 5332$
24	$4.355\ 0317$	$7.522\ 3275$	$1.283\ 2206^{16}$	$2.163\ 1432$	$3.605\ 2387$
25	$5.574\ 4406$	$9.929\ 4723$	$1.745\ 1800$	$3.028\ 4005$	$5.191\ 5438$
26	$6.646\ 4484$	$1.222\ 0889^{16}$	$2.215\ 0361$	$3.960\ 2161$	$6.988\ 6167$
27	$7.384\ 9426$	$1.403\ 1391$	$2.625\ 2280$	$4.840\ 2641$	$8.800\ 4802$
28	$7.648\ 6906$	$1.503\ 3633$	$2.906\ 5024$	$5.531\ 7304$	$1.037\ 1995^{17}$
29		$1.503\ 3633$	$3.006\ 7266$	$5.913\ 2291$	$1.144\ 4960$
30				$5.913\ 2291$	$1.182\ 6458$

n	$m = 61$	$m = 62$	$m = 63$	$m = 64$	$m = 65$
1	6.1^{1}	6.2^{1}	6.3^{1}	6.4^{1}	6.5^{1}
2	1.830^{3}	1.891^{3}	1.953^{3}	2.016^{3}	2.080^{3}
3	$3.599\ 0^{4}$	$3.782\ 0^{4}$	$3.971\ 1^{4}$	$4.166\ 4^{4}$	$4.368\ 0^{4}$
4	$5.218\ 55^{5}$	$5.578\ 45^{5}$	$5.956\ 65^{5}$	$6.353\ 76^{5}$	$6.770\ 40^{5}$
5	$5.949\ 147^{6}$	$6.471\ 002^{6}$	$7.028\ 847^{6}$	$7.624\ 512^{6}$	$8.259\ 888^{6}$
6	$5.552\ 5372^{7}$	$6.147\ 4519^{7}$	$6.794\ 5521^{7}$	$7.497\ 4368^{7}$	$8.259\ 8880^{7}$
7	$4.362\ 7078^{8}$	$4.917\ 9615^{8}$	$5.532\ 7067^{8}$	$6.212\ 1619^{8}$	$6.961\ 9056^{8}$
8	$2.944\ 8278^{9}$	$3.381\ 0985^{9}$	$3.872\ 8947^{9}$	$4.426\ 1654^{9}$	$5.047\ 3816^{9}$
9	$1.734\ 1764^{10}$	$2.028\ 6591^{10}$	$2.366\ 7690^{10}$	$2.754\ 0585^{10}$	$3.196\ 6750^{10}$
10	$9.017\ 7170$	$1.075\ 1893^{11}$	$1.278\ 0553^{11}$	$1.514\ 7321^{11}$	$1.790\ 1380^{11}$
11	$4.180\ 9415^{11}$	$5.082\ 7132$	$6.157\ 9026$	$7.435\ 9578$	$8.950\ 6900$
12	$1.742\ 0590^{12}$	$2.160\ 1531^{12}$	$2.668\ 4244^{12}$	$3.284\ 2147^{12}$	$4.027\ 8105^{12}$
13	$6.566\ 2223$	$8.308\ 2812$	$1.046\ 8434^{13}$	$1.313\ 6859^{13}$	$1.642\ 1074^{13}$
14	$2.251\ 2762^{13}$	$2.907\ 8984^{13}$	$3.738\ 7266$	$4.785\ 5700$	$6.099\ 2559$
15	$7.053\ 9988$	$9.305\ 2750$	$1.221\ 3173^{14}$	$1.595\ 1900^{14}$	$2.073\ 7470^{14}$
16	$2.028\ 0247^{14}$	$2.733\ 4245^{14}$	$3.663\ 9520$	$4.885\ 2694$	$6.480\ 4594$
17	$5.368\ 3005$	$7.396\ 3252$	$1.012\ 9750^{15}$	$1.379\ 3702^{15}$	$1.867\ 8971^{15}$
18	$1.312\ 2512^{15}$	$1.849\ 0813^{15}$	$2.588\ 7138$	$3.601\ 6888$	$4.981\ 0590$
19	$2.969\ 8318$	$4.282\ 0830$	$6.131\ 1643$	$8.719\ 8781$	$1.232\ 1567^{16}$
20	$6.236\ 6467$	$9.206\ 4785$	$1.348\ 8561^{16}$	$1.961\ 9726^{16}$	$2.833\ 9604$

n	$m = 61$	$m = 62$	$m = 63$	$m = 64$	$m = 65$
21	$1.217\ 6310^{16}$	$1.841\ 2957^{16}$	$2.761\ 9435^{16}$	$4.110\ 7997^{16}$	$6.072\ 7723^{16}$
22	$2.213\ 8746$	$3.431\ 5056$	$5.272\ 8013$	$8.034\ 7448$	$1.214\ 5545^{17}$
23	$3.753\ 9613$	$5.967\ 8358$	$9.399\ 3415$	$1.467\ 2143^{17}$	$2.270\ 6888$
24	$5.943\ 7720$	$9.697\ 7332$	$1.566\ 5569^{17}$	$2.506\ 4911$	$3.973\ 7053$
25	$8.796\ 7825$	$1.474\ 0555^{17}$	$2.443\ 8288$	$4.010\ 3857$	$6.516\ 8767$
26	$1.218\ 0160^{17}$	$2.097\ 6943$	$3.571\ 7498$	$6.015\ 5785$	$1.002\ 5964^{18}$
27	$1.578\ 9097$	$2.796\ 9257$	$4.894\ 6200$	$8.466\ 3698$	$1.448\ 1948$
28	$1.917\ 2475$	$3.496\ 1572$	$6.293\ 0829$	$1.118\ 7703^{18}$	$1.965\ 4073$
29	$2.181\ 6954$	$4.098\ 9429$	$7.595\ 1000$	$1.388\ 8183$	$2.507\ 5886$
30	$2.327\ 1418$	$4.508\ 8372$	$8.607\ 7801$	$1.620\ 2880$	$3.009\ 1063$
31	$2.327\ 1418$	$4.654\ 2835$	$9.163\ 1207$	$1.777\ 0901$	$3.397\ 3781$
32			$9.163\ 1207$	$1.832\ 6241$	$3.609\ 7142$
33					$3.609\ 7142$

n	$m = 66$	$m = 67$	$m = 68$	$m = 69$	$m = 70$
1	6.6^{1}	6.7^{1}	6.8^{1}	6.9^{1}	7.0^{1}
2	2.145^{3}	2.211^{3}	2.278^{3}	2.346^{3}	2.415^{3}
3	$4.576\ 0^{4}$	$4.790\ 5^{4}$	$5.011\ 6^{4}$	$5.239\ 4^{4}$	$5.474\ 0^{4}$
4	$7.207\ 20^{5}$	$7.664\ 80^{5}$	$8.143\ 85^{5}$	$8.645\ 01^{5}$	$9.168\ 95^{5}$
5	$8.936\ 928^{6}$	$9.657\ 648^{6}$	$1.042\ 4128^{7}$	$1.123\ 8513^{7}$	$1.210\ 3014^{7}$
6	$9.085\ 8768^{7}$	$9.979\ 5696^{7}$	$1.094\ 5334^{8}$	$1.198\ 7747^{8}$	$1.311\ 1598^{8}$
7	$7.787\ 8944^{8}$	$8.696\ 4821^{8}$	$9.694\ 4390$	$1.078\ 8972^{9}$	$1.198\ 7747^{9}$
8	$5.743\ 5721^{9}$	$6.522\ 3616^{9}$	$7.392\ 0098^{9}$	$8.361\ 4537$	$9.440\ 3509$
9	$3.701\ 4131^{10}$	$4.275\ 7704^{10}$	$4.928\ 0065^{10}$	$5.667\ 2075^{10}$	$6.503\ 3529^{10}$
10	$2.109\ 8055^{11}$	$2.479\ 9468^{11}$	$2.907\ 5238^{11}$	$3.400\ 3245^{11}$	$3.967\ 0452^{11}$
11	$1.074\ 0828^{12}$	$1.285\ 0633^{12}$	$1.533\ 0580^{12}$	$1.823\ 8104^{12}$	$2.163\ 8429^{12}$
12	$4.922\ 8795$	$5.996\ 9623$	$7.282\ 0256$	$8.815\ 0836$	$1.063\ 8894^{13}$
13	$2.044\ 8884^{13}$	$2.537\ 1763^{13}$	$3.136\ 8726^{13}$	$3.865\ 0751^{13}$	$4.746\ 5835$
14	$7.741\ 3632$	$9.786\ 2516$	$1.232\ 3428^{14}$	$1.546\ 0301^{14}$	$1.932\ 5376^{14}$
15	$2.683\ 6726^{14}$	$3.457\ 8089^{14}$	$4.436\ 4341$	$5.668\ 7769$	$7.214\ 8069$
16	$8.554\ 2064$	$1.123\ 7879^{15}$	$1.469\ 5688^{15}$	$1.913\ 2122^{15}$	$2.480\ 0899^{15}$
17	$2.515\ 9430^{15}$	$3.371\ 3637$	$4.495\ 1516$	$5.964\ 7204$	$7.877\ 9326$
18	$6.848\ 9561$	$9.364\ 8991$	$1.273\ 6263^{16}$	$1.723\ 1414^{16}$	$2.319\ 6135^{16}$
19	$1.730\ 2626^{16}$	$2.415\ 1582^{16}$	$3.351\ 6481$	$4.625\ 2744$	$6.348\ 4158$
20	$4.066\ 1171$	$5.796\ 3797$	$8.211\ 5379$	$1.156\ 3186^{17}$	$1.618\ 8460^{17}$
21	$8.906\ 7327$	$1.297\ 2850^{17}$	$1.876\ 9229^{17}$	$2.698\ 0767$	$3.854\ 3953$
22	$1.821\ 8317^{17}$	$2.712\ 5049$	$4.009\ 7899$	$5.886\ 7129$	$8.584\ 7896$
23	$3.485\ 2432$	$5.307\ 0749$	$8.019\ 5798$	$1.202\ 9370^{18}$	$1.791\ 6083^{18}$
24	$6.244\ 3941$	$9.729\ 6373$	$1.503\ 6712^{18}$	$2.305\ 6292$	$3.508\ 5662$
25	$1.049\ 0582^{18}$	$1.673\ 4976^{18}$	$2.646\ 4613$	$4.150\ 1326$	$6.455\ 7618$

n	$m = 66$	$m = 67$	$m = 68$	$m = 69$	$m = 70$
26	1.654 2841 ^{18}	2.703 3423 ^{18}	4.376 8399 ^{18}	7.023 3013 ^{18}	1.117 3434 ^{19}
27	2.450 7913	4.105 0753	6.808 4177	1.118 5258 ^{19}	1.820 8559
28	3.413 6021	5.864 3934	9.969 4687	1.677 7886	2.796 3144
29	4.472 9959	7.886 5980	1.375 0991 ^{19}	2.372 0460	4.049 8346
30	5.516 6949	9.989 6908	1.787 6289	3.162 7280	5.534 7740
31	6.406 4844	1.192 3179 ^{19}	2.191 2870	3.978 9159	7.141 6439
32	7.007 0923	1.341 3577	2.533 6756	4.724 9626	8.703 8785
33	7.219 4284	1.422 6521	2.764 0097	5.297 6853	1.002 2648 ^{20}
34		1.422 6521	2.845 3041	5.609 3139	1.040 6999
35				5.609 3139	1.121 8628

n	$m = 71$	$m = 72$	$m = 73$	$m = 74$	$m = 75$
1	7.1 ^{1}	7.2 ^{1}	7.3 ^{1}	7.4 ^{1}	7.5 ^{1}
2	2.485 ^{3}	2.556 ^{3}	2.628 ^{3}	2.701 ^{3}	2.775 ^{3}
3	5.715 5 ^{4}	5.964 0 ^{4}	6.219 6 ^{4}	6.482 4 ^{4}	6.752 5 ^{4}
4	9.716 35 ^{5}	1.028 790 ^{6}	1.088 430 ^{6}	1.150 626 ^{6}	1.215 450 ^{6}
5	1.301 9909 ^{7}	1.399 1544 ^{7}	1.502 0334 ^{7}	1.610 8764 ^{7}	1.725 9390 ^{7}
6	1.432 1900 ^{8}	1.562 3891 ^{8}	1.702 3045 ^{8}	1.852 5079 ^{8}	2.013 5955 ^{8}
7	1.329 8907 ^{9}	1.473 1097 ^{9}	1.629 3486 ^{9}	1.799 5791 ^{9}	1.984 8298 ^{9}
8	1.063 9126 ^{10}	1.196 9016 ^{10}	1.344 2126 ^{10}	1.507 1475 ^{10}	1.687 1054 ^{10}
9	7.447 3879	8.511 3005	9.708 2021	1.105 2415 ^{11}	1.255 9562 ^{11}
10	4.617 3805 ^{11}	5.362 1193 ^{11}	6.213 2494 ^{11}	7.184 0696	8.289 3111
11	2.560 5474 ^{12}	3.022 2854 ^{12}	3.558 4974 ^{12}	4.179 8223 ^{12}	4.898 2293 ^{12}
12	1.280 2737 ^{13}	1.536 3284 ^{13}	1.838 5570 ^{13}	2.194 4067 ^{13}	2.612 3889 ^{13}
13	5.810 4729	7.090 7466	8.627 0750	1.046 5632 ^{14}	1.266 0039 ^{14}
14	2.407 1959 ^{14}	2.988 2432 ^{14}	3.697 3179 ^{14}	4.560 0254	5.606 5886
15	9.147 3445	1.155 4540 ^{15}	1.454 2784 ^{15}	1.824 0101 ^{15}	2.280 0127 ^{15}
16	3.201 5706 ^{15}	4.116 3050	5.271 7591	6.726 0374	8.550 0476
17	1.035 8022 ^{16}	1.355 9593 ^{16}	1.767 5898 ^{16}	2.294 7657 ^{16}	2.967 3695 ^{16}
18	3.107 4067	4.143 2090	5.499 1683	7.266 7581	9.561 5238
19	8.668 0293	1.177 5436 ^{17}	1.591 8645 ^{17}	2.141 7813 ^{17}	2.868 4571 ^{17}
20	2.253 6876 ^{17}	3.120 4906	4.298 0342	5.889 8987	8.031 6800
21	5.473 2414	7.726 9290	1.084 7420 ^{18}	1.514 5454 ^{18}	2.103 5352 ^{18}
22	1.243 9185 ^{18}	1.791 2426 ^{18}	2.563 9355	3.648 6775	5.163 2228
23	2.650 0872	3.894 0057	5.685 2483	8.249 1839	1.189 7861 ^{19}
24	5.300 1744	7.950 2617	1.184 4267 ^{19}	1.752 9516 ^{19}	2.577 8700
25	9.964 3279	1.526 4502 ^{19}	2.321 4764	3.505 9031	5.258 8547
26	1.762 9196 ^{19}	2.759 3524	4.285 8026	6.607 2790	1.011 3182 ^{20}
27	2.938 1993	4.701 1188	7.460 4712	1.174 6274 ^{20}	1.835 3553
28	4.617 1703	7.555 3695	1.225 6488 ^{20}	1.971 6960	3.146 3233
29	6.846 1490	1.146 3319 ^{20}	1.901 8689	3.127 5177	5.099 2137
30	9.584 6086	1.643 0758	2.789 4077	4.691 2766	7.818 7943

n	$m = 71$	$m = 72$	$m = 73$	$m = 74$	$m = 75$
31	$1.267\ 6418^{20}$	$2.226\ 1027^{20}$	$3.869\ 1784^{20}$	$6.658\ 5861^{20}$	$1.134\ 9863^{21}$
32	$1.584\ 5522$	$2.852\ 1940$	$5.078\ 2967$	$8.947\ 4751$	$1.560\ 6061$
33	$1.872\ 6526$	$3.457\ 2049$	$6.309\ 3989$	$1.138\ 7696^{21}$	$2.033\ 5171$
34	$2.092\ 9647$	$3.965\ 6174$	$7.422\ 8222$	$1.373\ 2221$	$2.511\ 9917$
35	$2.212\ 5627$	$4.305\ 5274$	$8.271\ 1448$	$1.569\ 3967$	$2.942\ 6188$
36	$2.212\ 5627$	$4.425\ 1254$	$8.730\ 6528$	$1.700\ 1798$	$3.269\ 5765$
37			$8.730\ 6528$	$1.746\ 1306$	$3.446\ 3103$
38					$3.446\ 3103$

n	$m = 76$	$m = 77$	$m = 78$	$m = 79$	$m = 80$
1	7.6^{1}	7.7^{1}	7.8^{1}	7.9^{1}	8.0^{1}
2	2.850^{3}	2.926^{3}	3.003^{3}	3.081^{3}	3.160^{3}
3	$7.030\ 0^{4}$	$7.315\ 0^{4}$	$7.607\ 6^{4}$	$7.907\ 9^{4}$	$8.216\ 0^{4}$
4	$1.282\ 975^{6}$	$1.353\ 275^{6}$	$1.426\ 425^{6}$	$1.502\ 501^{6}$	$1.581\ 580^{6}$
5	$1.847\ 4840^{7}$	$1.975\ 7815^{7}$	$2.111\ 1090^{7}$	$2.253\ 7515^{7}$	$2.404\ 0016^{7}$
6	$2.186\ 1894^{8}$	$2.370\ 9378^{8}$	$2.568\ 5160^{8}$	$2.779\ 6268^{8}$	$3.005\ 0020^{8}$
7	$2.186\ 1894^{9}$	$2.404\ 8083^{9}$	$2.641\ 9021^{9}$	$2.898\ 7537^{9}$	$3.176\ 7164^{9}$
8	$1.885\ 5884^{10}$	$2.104\ 2073^{10}$	$2.344\ 6881^{10}$	$2.608\ 8783^{10}$	$2.898\ 7537^{10}$
9	$1.424\ 6668^{11}$	$1.613\ 2256^{11}$	$1.823\ 6463^{11}$	$2.058\ 1151^{11}$	$2.319\ 0030^{11}$
10	$9.545\ 2673$	$1.096\ 9934^{12}$	$1.258\ 3160^{12}$	$1.440\ 6806^{12}$	$1.646\ 4921^{12}$
11	$5.727\ 1604^{12}$	$6.681\ 6871$	$7.778\ 6805$	$9.036\ 9965$	$1.047\ 7677^{13}$
12	$3.102\ 2119^{13}$	$3.674\ 9279^{13}$	$4.343\ 0966^{13}$	$5.120\ 9647^{13}$	$6.024\ 6643$
13	$1.527\ 2428^{14}$	$1.837\ 4640^{14}$	$2.204\ 9567^{14}$	$2.639\ 2664^{14}$	$3.151\ 3629^{14}$
14	$6.872\ 5924$	$8.399\ 8352$	$1.023\ 7299^{15}$	$1.244\ 2256^{15}$	$1.508\ 1522^{15}$
15	$2.840\ 6715^{15}$	$3.527\ 9308^{15}$	$4.367\ 9143$	$5.391\ 6442$	$6.635\ 8698$
16	$1.083\ 0060^{16}$	$1.367\ 0732^{16}$	$1.719\ 8663^{16}$	$2.156\ 6577^{16}$	$2.695\ 8221^{16}$
17	$3.822\ 3742$	$4.905\ 3802$	$6.272\ 4534$	$7.992\ 3197$	$1.014\ 8977^{17}$
18	$1.252\ 8893^{17}$	$1.635\ 1267^{17}$	$2.125\ 6648^{17}$	$2.752\ 9101^{17}$	$3.552\ 1421$
19	$3.824\ 6095$	$5.077\ 4988$	$6.712\ 6256$	$8.838\ 2904$	$1.159\ 1200^{18}$
20	$1.090\ 0137^{18}$	$1.472\ 4747^{18}$	$1.980\ 2245^{18}$	$2.651\ 4871^{18}$	$3.535\ 3161$
21	$2.906\ 7032$	$3.996\ 7169$	$5.469\ 1916$	$7.449\ 4162$	$1.010\ 0903^{19}$
22	$7.266\ 7581$	$1.017\ 3461^{19}$	$1.417\ 0178^{19}$	$1.963\ 9370^{19}$	$2.708\ 8786$
23	$1.706\ 1084^{19}$	$2.432\ 7842$	$3.450\ 1304$	$4.867\ 1482$	$6.831\ 0852$
24	$3.767\ 6561$	$5.473\ 7645$	$7.906\ 5487$	$1.135\ 6679^{20}$	$1.622\ 3827^{20}$
25	$7.836\ 7247$	$1.160\ 4381^{20}$	$1.707\ 8145^{20}$	$2.498\ 4694$	$3.634\ 1373$
26	$1.537\ 2037^{20}$	$2.320\ 8762$	$3.481\ 3142$	$5.189\ 1288$	$7.687\ 5982$
27	$2.846\ 6735$	$4.383\ 8772$	$6.704\ 7533$	$1.018\ 6068^{21}$	$1.537\ 5196^{21}$
28	$4.981\ 6786$	$7.828\ 3521$	$1.221\ 2229^{21}$	$1.891\ 6983$	$2.910\ 3050$
29	$8.245\ 5370$	$1.322\ 7216^{21}$	$2.105\ 5568$	$3.326\ 7797$	$5.218\ 4780$
30	$1.291\ 8008^{21}$	$2.116\ 3545$	$3.439\ 0761$	$5.544\ 6328$	$8.871\ 4125$

n	$m = 76$	$m = 77$	$m = 78$	$m = 79$	$m = 80$
31	$1.916\ 8657^{21}$	$3.208\ 6665^{21}$	$5.325\ 0210^{21}$	$8.764\ 0971^{21}$	$1.430\ 8730^{22}$
32	$2.695\ 5924$	$4.612\ 4581$	$7.821\ 1246$	$1.314\ 6146^{22}$	$2.191\ 0243$
33	$3.594\ 1232$	$6.289\ 7156$	$1.090\ 2174^{22}$	$1.872\ 3298$	$3.186\ 9444$
34	$4.545\ 5087$	$8.139\ 6319$	$1.442\ 9348$	$2.533\ 1521$	$4.405\ 4819$
35	$5.454\ 6195$	$1.000\ 0119^{22}$	$1.813\ 9751$	$3.256\ 9099$	$5.790\ 0620$
36	$6.212\ 1953$	$1.166\ 6806$	$2.166\ 6925$	$3.980\ 6676$	$7.237\ 5775$
37	$6.715\ 8868$	$1.292\ 8082$	$2.459\ 4888$	$4.626\ 1813$	$8.606\ 8489$
38	$6.892\ 6206$	$1.360\ 8507$	$2.653\ 6589$	$5.113\ 1477$	$9.739\ 3290$
39		$1.360\ 8507$	$2.721\ 7015$	$5.375\ 3604$	$1.048\ 8508^{23}$
40				$5.375\ 3604$	$1.075\ 0721$

n	$m = 81$	$m = 82$	$m = 83$	$m = 84$	$m = 85$
1	8.1^{1}	8.2^{1}	8.3^{1}	8.4^{1}	8.5^{1}
2	3.240^{3}	3.321^{3}	3.403^{3}	3.486^{3}	3.570^{3}
3	$8.532\ 0^{4}$	$8.856\ 0^{4}$	$9.188\ 1^{4}$	$9.528\ 4^{4}$	$9.877\ 0^{4}$
4	$1.663\ 7406^{6}$	$1.749\ 060^{6}$	$1.837\ 620^{6}$	$1.929\ 501^{6}$	$2.024\ 785^{6}$
5	$2.562\ 1596^{7}$	$2.728\ 5336^{7}$	$2.903\ 4396^{7}$	$3.087\ 2016^{7}$	$3.280\ 1517^{7}$
6	$3.245\ 4022^{8}$	$3.501\ 6181^{8}$	$3.774\ 4715^{8}$	$4.064\ 8154^{8}$	$4.373\ 5356^{8}$
7	$3.477\ 2166^{9}$	$3.801\ 7568^{9}$	$4.151\ 9186^{9}$	$4.529\ 3658^{9}$	$4.935\ 8473^{9}$
8	$3.216\ 4254^{10}$	$3.564\ 1470^{10}$	$3.944\ 3227^{10}$	$4.359\ 5146^{10}$	$4.812\ 4511^{10}$
9	$2.608\ 8783^{11}$	$2.930\ 5209^{11}$	$3.286\ 9356^{11}$	$3.681\ 3679^{11}$	$4.117\ 3193^{11}$
10	$1.878\ 3924^{12}$	$2.139\ 2802^{12}$	$2.432\ 3323^{12}$	$2.761\ 0259^{12}$	$3.129\ 1627^{12}$
11	$1.212\ 4169^{13}$	$1.400\ 2562^{13}$	$1.614\ 1842^{13}$	$1.857\ 4174^{13}$	$2.133\ 5200^{13}$
12	$7.072\ 4320$	$8.284\ 8489$	$9.685\ 1051$	$1.129\ 9289^{14}$	$1.315\ 6707^{14}$
13	$3.753\ 8293^{14}$	$4.461\ 0725^{14}$	$5.289\ 5574^{14}$	$6.258\ 0679$	$7.387\ 9968$
14	$1.823\ 2885^{15}$	$2.198\ 6714^{15}$	$2.644\ 7787^{15}$	$3.173\ 7344^{15}$	$3.799\ 5412^{15}$
15	$8.144\ 0220$	$9.967\ 3106$	$1.216\ 5982^{16}$	$1.481\ 0761^{16}$	$1.798\ 4495^{16}$
16	$3.359\ 4091^{16}$	$4.173\ 8113^{16}$	$5.170\ 5424$	$6.387\ 1406$	$7.868\ 2166$
17	$1.284\ 4799^{17}$	$1.620\ 4209^{17}$	$2.037\ 8020^{17}$	$2.554\ 8562^{17}$	$3.193\ 5703^{17}$
18	$4.567\ 0398$	$5.851\ 5198$	$7.471\ 9406$	$9.509\ 7426$	$1.206\ 4599^{18}$
19	$1.514\ 3343^{18}$	$1.971\ 0382^{18}$	$2.556\ 1902^{18}$	$3.303\ 3843^{18}$	$4.254\ 3585$
20	$4.694\ 4362$	$6.268\ 7704$	$8.179\ 8087$	$1.073\ 5999^{19}$	$1.403\ 9383^{19}$
21	$1.363\ 6219^{19}$	$1.833\ 0656^{19}$	$2.453\ 9426^{19}$	$3.271\ 9235$	$4.345\ 5234$
22	$3.718\ 9689$	$5.082\ 5909$	$6.915\ 6564$	$9.369\ 5990$	$1.264\ 1523^{20}$
23	$9.539\ 9638$	$1.325\ 8933^{20}$	$1.834\ 1524^{20}$	$2.525\ 7180^{20}$	$3.462\ 6779$
24	$2.305\ 4912^{20}$	$3.259\ 4876$	$4.585\ 3809$	$6.419\ 5333$	$8.945\ 2513$
25	$5.256\ 5200$	$7.562\ 0113$	$1.082\ 1499^{21}$	$1.540\ 6880^{21}$	$2.182\ 6413^{21}$
26	$1.132\ 1735^{21}$	$1.657\ 8256^{21}$	$2.414\ 0267$	$3.496\ 1766$	$5.036\ 8646$
27	$2.306\ 2794$	$3.438\ 4530$	$5.096\ 2785$	$7.510\ 3052$	$1.100\ 6482^{22}$
28	$4.447\ 8246$	$6.754\ 1041$	$1.019\ 2557^{22}$	$1.528\ 8836^{22}$	$2.279\ 9141$
29	$8.128\ 7830$	$1.257\ 6608^{22}$	$1.933\ 0712$	$2.952\ 3269$	$4.481\ 2104$
30	$1.408\ 9890^{22}$	$2.221\ 8673$	$3.479\ 5281$	$5.412\ 5993$	$8.364\ 9262$

n	$m = 81$	$m = 82$	$m = 83$	$m = 84$	$m = 85$
31	$2.318\ 0142^{22}$	$3.727\ 0033^{22}$	$5.948\ 8706^{22}$	$9.428\ 3988^{22}$	$1.484\ 0998^{23}$
32	$3.621\ 8973$	$5.939\ 9115$	$9.666\ 9148$	$1.561\ 5785^{23}$	$2.504\ 4184$
33	$5.377\ 9687$	$8.999\ 8659$	$1.493\ 9777^{23}$	$2.460\ 6692$	$4.022\ 2478$
34	$7.592\ 4263$	$1.297\ 0395^{23}$	$2.197\ 0261$	$3.691\ 0038$	$6.151\ 6730$
35	$1.019\ 5544^{23}$	$1.778\ 7970$	$3.075\ 8365$	$5.272\ 8626$	$8.963\ 8664$
36	$1.302\ 7639$	$2.322\ 3183$	$4.101\ 1154$	$7.176\ 9519$	$1.244\ 9815^{24}$
37	$1.584\ 4426$	$2.887\ 2066$	$5.209\ 5249$	$9.310\ 6403$	$1.648\ 7592$
38	$1.834\ 6178$	$3.419\ 0604$	$6.306\ 2670$	$1.151\ 5792^{24}$	$2.082\ 6432$
39	$2.022\ 7837$	$3.857\ 4015$	$7.276\ 4619$	$1.358\ 2729$	$2.509\ 8521$
40	$2.123\ 9229$	$4.146\ 7066$	$8.004\ 1081$	$1.528\ 0570$	$2.886\ 3299$
41	$2.123\ 9229$	$4.247\ 8458$	$8.394\ 5524$	$1.639\ 8661$	$3.167\ 9231$
42			$8.394\ 5524$	$1.678\ 9105$	$3.318\ 7765$
43					$3\ 318\ 7765$

n	$m = 86$	$m = 87$	$m = 88$	$m = 89$	$m = 90$
1	8.6^{1}	8.7^{1}	8.8^{1}	8.9^{1}	9.0^{1}
2	3.655^{3}	3.741^{3}	3.828^{3}	3.916^{3}	4.005^{3}
3	$1.023\ 40^{5}$	$1.059\ 95^{5}$	$1.097\ 36^{5}$	$1.135\ 64^{5}$	$1.174\ 80^{5}$
4	$2.123\ 555^{6}$	$2.225\ 895^{6}$	$2.331\ 890^{6}$	$2.441\ 626^{6}$	$2.555\ 190^{6}$
5	$3.482\ 6302^{7}$	$3.694\ 9857^{7}$	$3.917\ 5752^{7}$	$4.150\ 7642^{7}$	$4.394\ 9268^{7}$
6	$4.701\ 5508^{8}$	$5.049\ 8138^{8}$	$5.419\ 3124^{8}$	$5.811\ 0699^{8}$	$6.226\ 1463^{8}$
7	$5.373\ 2009^{9}$	$5.843\ 3560^{9}$	$6.348\ 3373^{9}$	$6.890\ 2686^{9}$	$7.471\ 3756^{9}$
8	$5.306\ 0359^{10}$	$5.843\ 3560^{10}$	$6.427\ 6916^{10}$	$7.062\ 5253^{10}$	$7.751\ 5521^{10}$
9	$4.598\ 5644^{11}$	$5.129\ 1680^{11}$	$5.713\ 5036^{11}$	$6.356\ 2728^{11}$	$7.062\ 5253^{11}$
10	$3.540\ 8946^{12}$	$4.000\ 7510^{12}$	$4.513\ 6678^{12}$	$5.085\ 0182^{12}$	$5.720\ 6455^{12}$
11	$2.446\ 4363^{13}$	$2.800\ 5257^{13}$	$3.200\ 6008^{13}$	$3.651\ 9676^{13}$	$4.160\ 4694^{13}$
12	$1.529\ 0227^{14}$	$1.773\ 6663^{14}$	$2.053\ 7189^{14}$	$2.373\ 7790^{14}$	$2.738\ 9757^{14}$
13	$8.703\ 6675$	$1.023\ 2690^{15}$	$1.200\ 6356^{15}$	$1.406\ 0075^{15}$	$1.643\ 3854^{15}$
14	$4.538\ 3409^{15}$	$5.408\ 7077$	$6.431\ 9767$	$7.632\ 6123$	$9.038\ 6199$
15	$2.178\ 4036^{16}$	$2.632\ 2377^{16}$	$3.173\ 1085^{16}$	$3.816\ 3062^{16}$	$4.579\ 5674^{16}$
16	$9.666\ 6661$	$1.184\ 5070^{17}$	$1.447\ 7308^{17}$	$1.765\ 0416^{17}$	$2.146\ 6722^{17}$
17	$3.980\ 3919^{17}$	$4.947\ 0586$	$6.131\ 5655$	$7.579\ 2963$	$9.344\ 3379$
18	$1.525\ 8169^{18}$	$1.923\ 8561^{18}$	$2.418\ 5620^{18}$	$3.031\ 7185^{18}$	$3.789\ 6481^{18}$
19	$5.460\ 8184$	$6.986\ 6353$	$8.910\ 4914$	$1.132\ 9053^{19}$	$1.436\ 0772^{19}$
20	$1.829\ 3742^{19}$	$2.375\ 4560^{19}$	$3.074\ 1195^{19}$	$3.965\ 1687$	$5.098\ 0740$
21	$5.749\ 4617$	$7.578\ 8358$	$9.954\ 2919$	$1.302\ 8411^{20}$	$1.699\ 3580^{20}$
22	$1.698\ 7046^{20}$	$2.273\ 6508^{20}$	$3.031\ 5343^{20}$	$4.026\ 9635$	$5.329\ 8047$
23	$4.726\ 8302$	$6.425\ 5347$	$8.699\ 1855$	$1.173\ 0720^{21}$	$1.575\ 7683^{21}$
24	$1.240\ 7929^{21}$	$1.713\ 4759^{21}$	$2.356\ 0294^{21}$	$3.225\ 9480$	$4.399\ 0199$
25	$3.077\ 1664$	$4.317\ 9593$	$6.031\ 4353$	$8.387\ 4647$	$1.161\ 3413^{22}$

n	$m = 86$	$m = 87$	$m = 88$	$m = 89$	$m = 90$
26	7.219 5059 ^{21}	1.029 6672 ^{22}	1.461 4632 ^{22}	2.064 6067 ^{22}	2.903 3532 ^{22}
27	1.604 3346 ^{22}	2.326 2852	3.355 9524	4.817 4156	6.882 0223
28	3.380 5623	4.984 8969	7.311 1821	1.066 7135 ^{23}	1.548 4550 ^{23}
29	6.761 1245	1.014 1687 ^{23}	1.512 6584 ^{23}	2.243 7766	3.310 4900
30	1.284 6137 ^{23}	1.960 7261	2.974 8948	4.487 5532	6.731 3297
31	2.320 5924	3.605 2061	5.565 9322	8.540 8270	1.302 8380 ^{24}
32	3.988 5182	6.309 1106	9.914 3167	1.548 0249 ^{24}	2.402 1076
33	6.526 6662	1.051 5184 ^{24}	1.682 4295 ^{24}	2.673 8612	4.221 8861
34	1.017 3921 ^{24}	1.670 0587	2.721 5771	4.404 0066	7.077 8678
35	1.511 5539	2.528 9460	4.199 0047	6.920 5819	1.132 4589 ^{25}
36	2.141 3681	3.652 9220	6.181 8681	1.038 0873 ^{25}	1.730 1455
37	2.893 7407	5.035 1088	8.688 0308	1.486 9899	2.525 0772
38	3.731 4024	6.625 1431	1.166 0252 ^{25}	2.034 8283	3.521 8182
39	4.592 4953	8.323 8978	1.494 9041	2.660 9293	4.695 7575
40	5.396 1820	9.988 6773	1.831 2575	3.326 1616	5.987 0909
41	6.054 2530	1.145 0435 ^{25}	2.143 9112	3.975 1687	7.301 3303
42	6.486 6996	1.254 0953	2.399 1388	4.543 0499	8.518 2187
43	6.637 5531	1.312 4253	2.566 5205	4.965 6593	9.508 7093
44		1.312 4253	2.624 8505	5.191 3711	1.015 7030 ^{26}
45				5.191 3711	1.038 2742

n	$m = 91$	$m = 92$	$m = 93$	$m = 94$	$m = 95$
1	9.1 ^{1}	9.2 ^{1}	9.3 ^{1}	9.4 ^{1}	9.5 ^{1}
2	4.095 ^{3}	4.186 ^{3}	4.278 ^{3}	4.371 ^{3}	4.465 ^{3}
3	1.214 85 ^{5}	1.255 80 ^{5}	1.297 66 ^{5}	1.340 44 ^{5}	1.384 15 ^{5}
4	2.672 670 ^{6}	2.794 155 ^{6}	2.919 735 ^{6}	3.049 501 ^{6}	3.183 545 ^{6}
5	4.650 4458 ^{7}	4.917 7128 ^{7}	5.197 1283 ^{7}	5.489 1018 ^{7}	5.794 0519 ^{7}
6	6.665 6390 ^{8}	7.130 6836 ^{8}	7.622 4548 ^{8}	8.142 1677 ^{8}	8.691 0778 ^{8}
7	8.093 9902 ^{9}	8.760 5541 ^{9}	9.473 6224 ^{9}	1.023 5868 ^{10}	1.105 0085 ^{10}
8	8.498 6897 ^{10}	9.308 0887 ^{10}	1.018 4144 ^{11}	1.113 1506 ^{11}	1.215 5093 ^{11}
9	7.837 6805 ^{11}	8.687 5495 ^{11}	9.618 3583	1.063 6773 ^{12}	1.174 9923 ^{12}
10	6.426 8980 ^{12}	7.210 6661 ^{12}	8.079 4210 ^{12}	9.041 2568	1.010 4934 ^{13}
11	4.732 5340 ^{13}	5.375 2238 ^{13}	6.096 2904 ^{13}	6.904 2325 ^{13}	7.808 3582
12	3.155 0227 ^{14}	3.628 2761 ^{14}	4.165 7984 ^{14}	4.775 4275 ^{14}	5.465 8507 ^{14}
13	1.917 2830 ^{15}	2.232 7853 ^{15}	2.595 6129 ^{15}	3.012 1927 ^{15}	3.489 7355 ^{15}
14	1.068 2005 ^{16}	1.259 9288 ^{16}	1.483 2074 ^{16}	1.742 7686 ^{16}	2.043 9879 ^{16}
15	5.483 4294	6.551 6299	7.811 5587	9.294 7661	1.103 7535 ^{17}
16	2.604 6290 ^{17}	3.152 9719 ^{17}	3.808 1349 ^{17}	4.589 2908 ^{17}	5.518 7674
17	1.149 1010 ^{18}	1.409 5639 ^{18}	1.724 8611 ^{18}	2.105 6746 ^{18}	2.564 6037 ^{18}
18	4.724 0819	5.873 1829	7.282 7468	9.007 6079	1.111 3283 ^{19}
19	1.815 0420 ^{19}	2.287 4502 ^{19}	2.874 7685 ^{19}	3.603 0432 ^{19}	4.503 8040
20	6.534 1512	8.349 1932	1.063 6643 ^{20}	1.351 1412 ^{20}	1.711 4455 ^{20}

n	$m = 91$	$m = 92$	$m = 93$	$m = 94$	$m = 95$
21	$2.209\ 1654^{20}$	$2.862\ 5805^{20}$	$3.697\ 4999^{20}$	$4.761\ 1642^{20}$	$6.112\ 3054^{20}$
22	$7.029\ 1627$	$9.238\ 3281$	$1.210\ 0909^{21}$	$1.579\ 8408^{21}$	$2.055\ 9573^{21}$
23	$2.108\ 7488^{21}$	$2.811\ 6651^{21}$	$3.735\ 4979$	$4.945\ 5887$	$6.525\ 4296$
24	$5.974\ 7883$	$8.083\ 5371$	$1.089\ 5202^{22}$	$1.463\ 0700^{22}$	$1.957\ 6289^{22}$
25	$1.601\ 2433^{22}$	$2.198\ 7221^{22}$	$3.007\ 0758$	$4.096\ 5960$	$5.559\ 6660$
26	$4.064\ 6944$	$5.665\ 9377$	$7.864\ 6598$	$1.087\ 1736^{23}$	$1.496\ 8332^{23}$
27	$9.785\ 3755$	$1.385\ 0070^{23}$	$1.951\ 6008^{23}$	$2.738\ 0667$	$3.825\ 2403$
28	$2.236\ 6572^{23}$	$3.215\ 1948$	$4.600\ 2018$	$6.551\ 8025$	$9.289\ 8693$
29	$4.858\ 9451$	$7.095\ 6023$	$1.031\ 0797^{24}$	$1.491\ 0999^{24}$	$2.146\ 2801^{24}$
30	$1.004\ 1820^{24}$	$1.490\ 0765^{24}$	$2.199\ 6367$	$3.230\ 7164$	$4.721\ 8163$
31	$1.975\ 9710$	$2.980\ 1530$	$4.470\ 2295$	$6.669\ 8662$	$9.900\ 5826$
32	$3.704\ 9456$	$5.680\ 9166$	$8.661\ 0696$	$1.313\ 1299^{25}$	$1.980\ 1165^{25}$
33	$6.623\ 9937$	$1.032\ 8939^{25}$	$1.600\ 9856^{25}$	$2.467\ 0925$	$3.780\ 2224$
34	$1.129\ 9754^{25}$	$1.792\ 3748$	$2.825\ 2687$	$4.426\ 2543$	$6.893\ 3468$
35	$1.840\ 2456$	$2.970\ 2210$	$4.762\ 5958$	$7.587\ 8645$	$1.201\ 4119^{26}$
36	$2.862\ 6043$	$4.702\ 8500$	$7.673\ 0710$	$1.243\ 5667^{26}$	$2.002\ 3531$
37	$4.255\ 2226$	$7.117\ 8270$	$1.182\ 0677^{26}$	$1.949\ 3748$	$3.192\ 9415$
38	$6.046\ 8953$	$1.030\ 2118^{26}$	$1.741\ 9945$	$2.924\ 0622$	$4.873\ 4370$
39	$8.217\ 5757$	$1.426\ 4471$	$2.456\ 6589$	$4.198\ 6534$	$7.122\ 7156$
40	$1.068\ 2848^{26}$	$1.890\ 0424$	$3.316\ 4895$	$5.773\ 1484$	$9.971\ 8018$
41	$1.328\ 8421$	$2.397\ 1270$	$4.287\ 1694$	$7.603\ 6589$	$1.337\ 6807^{27}$
42	$1.581\ 9549$	$2.910\ 7970$	$5.307\ 9240$	$9.595\ 0934$	$1.719\ 8752$
43	$1.802\ 6928$	$3.384\ 6477$	$6.295\ 4447$	$1.160\ 3369^{27}$	$2.119\ 8462$
44	$1.966\ 5740$	$3.769\ 2668$	$7.153\ 9145$	$1.344\ 9359$	$2.505\ 2728$
45	$2.053\ 9772$	$4.020\ 5512$	$7.789\ 8180$	$1.494\ 3732$	$2.839\ 3092$
46	$2.053\ 9772$	$4.107\ 9545$	$8.128\ 5057$	$1.591\ 8324$	$3.086\ 2056$
47			$8.128\ 5057$	$1.625\ 7011$	$3.217\ 5335$
48					$3.217\ 5335$

n	$m = 96$	$m = 97$	$m = 98$	$m = 99$	$m = 100$
1	9.6^{1}	9.7^{1}	9.8^{1}	9.9^{1}	1.00^{2}
2	4.560^{3}	4.656^{3}	4.753^{3}	4.851^{3}	4.950^{3}
3	$1.428\ 80^{5}$	$1.474\ 40^{5}$	$1.520\ 96^{5}$	$1.568\ 49^{5}$	$1.617\ 00^{5}$
4	$3.321\ 960^{6}$	$3.464\ 840^{6}$	$3.612\ 280^{6}$	$3.764\ 376^{6}$	$3.921\ 225^{6}$
5	$6.112\ 4064^{7}$	$6.444\ 6024^{7}$	$6.791\ 0864^{7}$	$7.152\ 3144^{7}$	$7.528\ 7520^{7}$
6	$9.270\ 4830^{8}$	$9.881\ 7237^{8}$	$1.052\ 6184^{9}$	$1.120\ 5293^{9}$	$1.192\ 0524^{9}$
7	$1.191\ 9192^{10}$	$1.284\ 6241^{10}$	$1.383\ 4413^{10}$	$1.488\ 7032^{10}$	$1.600\ 7561^{10}$
8	$1.326\ 0102^{11}$	$1.445\ 2021^{11}$	$1.573\ 6645^{11}$	$1.712\ 0086^{11}$	$1.860\ 8789^{11}$
9	$1.296\ 5433^{12}$	$1.429\ 1443^{12}$	$1.573\ 6645^{12}$	$1.731\ 0309^{12}$	$1.902\ 2318^{12}$
10	$1.127\ 9926^{13}$	$1.257\ 6470^{13}$	$1.400\ 5614^{13}$	$1.557\ 9279^{13}$	$1.731\ 0309^{13}$

n	$m = 96$	$m = 97$	$m = 98$	$m = 99$	$m = 100$
11	$8.818\ 8516^{13}$	$9.946\ 8442^{13}$	$1.120\ 4491^{14}$	$1.260\ 5053^{14}$	$1.416\ 2980^{14}$
12	$6.246\ 6865^{14}$	$7.128\ 5717^{14}$	$8.123\ 2561$	$9.243\ 7052$	$1.050\ 4211^{15}$
13	$4.036\ 3205^{15}$	$4.660\ 9892^{15}$	$5.373\ 8464^{15}$	$6.186\ 1720^{15}$	$7.110\ 5425$
14	$2.392\ 9615^{16}$	$2.796\ 5935^{16}$	$3.262\ 6924^{16}$	$3.800\ 0771^{16}$	$4.418\ 6943^{16}$
15	$1.308\ 1523^{17}$	$1.547\ 4484^{17}$	$1.827\ 1078^{17}$	$2.153\ 3770^{17}$	$2.533\ 3847^{17}$
16	$6.622\ 5208$	$7.930\ 6731$	$9.478\ 1215$	$1.130\ 5229^{18}$	$1.345\ 8606^{18}$
17	$3.116\ 4804^{18}$	$3.778\ 7325^{18}$	$4.571\ 7998^{18}$	$5.519\ 6119$	$6.650\ 1349$
18	$1.367\ 7886^{19}$	$1.679\ 4367^{19}$	$2.057\ 3099^{19}$	$2.514\ 4899^{19}$	$3.066\ 4511^{19}$
19	$5.615\ 1322$	$6.982\ 9208$	$8.662\ 3575$	$1.071\ 9667^{20}$	$1.323\ 4157^{20}$
20	$2.161\ 8259^{20}$	$2.723\ 3391^{20}$	$3.421\ 6312^{20}$	$4.287\ 8670$	$5.359\ 8337$
21	$7.823\ 7509$	$9.985\ 5768$	$1.270\ 8916^{21}$	$1.613\ 0547^{21}$	$2.041\ 8414^{21}$
22	$2.667\ 1878^{21}$	$3.449\ 5629^{21}$	$4.448\ 1206$	$5.719\ 0122$	$7.332\ 0669$
23	$8.581\ 3869$	$1.124\ 8575^{22}$	$1.469\ 8138^{22}$	$1.914\ 6258^{22}$	$2.486\ 5270^{22}$
24	$2.610\ 1718^{22}$	$3.468\ 3105$	$4.593\ 1680$	$6.062\ 9817$	$7.977\ 6076$
25	$7.517\ 2949$	$1.012\ 7467^{23}$	$1.359\ 5777^{23}$	$1.818\ 8945^{23}$	$2.425\ 1927^{23}$
26	$2.052\ 7998^{23}$	$2.804\ 5292$	$3.817\ 2759$	$5.176\ 8536$	$6.995\ 7482$
27	$5.322\ 0734$	$7.374\ 8732$	$1.017\ 9402^{24}$	$1.399\ 6678^{24}$	$1.917\ 3532^{24}$
28	$1.311\ 5110^{24}$	$1.843\ 7183^{24}$	$2.581\ 2056$	$3.599\ 1459$	$4.998\ 8137$
29	$3.075\ 2671$	$4.386\ 7780$	$6.230\ 4963$	$8.811\ 7019$	$1.241\ 0848^{25}$
30	$6.868\ 0965$	$9.943\ 3635$	$1.433\ 0142^{25}$	$2.056\ 0638^{25}$	$2.937\ 2340$
31	$1.462\ 2399^{25}$	$2.149\ 0495^{25}$	$3.143\ 3859$	$4.576\ 4000$	$6.632\ 4638$
32	$2.970\ 1748$	$4.432\ 4147$	$6.581\ 4642$	$9.724\ 8501$	$1.430\ 1250^{26}$
33	$5.760\ 3390$	$8.730\ 5137$	$1.316\ 2928^{26}$	$1.974\ 4393^{26}$	$2.946\ 9243$
34	$1.067\ 3569^{26}$	$1.643\ 3908^{26}$	$2.516\ 4422$	$3.832\ 7350$	$5.807\ 1743$
35	$1.890\ 7466$	$2.958\ 1035$	$4.601\ 4943$	$7.117\ 9365$	$1.095\ 0672^{27}$
36	$3.203\ 7650$	$5.094\ 5115$	$8.052\ 6150$	$1.265\ 4109^{27}$	$1.977\ 2046$
37	$5.195\ 2946$	$8.399\ 0596$	$1.349\ 3571^{27}$	$2.154\ 6186$	$3.420\ 0295$
38	$8.066\ 3784$	$1.326\ 1673^{27}$	$2.166\ 0733$	$3.515\ 4304$	$5.670\ 0490$
39	$1.199\ 6153^{27}$	$2.006\ 2531$	$3.332\ 4204$	$5.498\ 4937$	$9.013\ 9240$
40	$1.709\ 4517$	$2.909\ 0670$	$4.915\ 3201$	$8.247\ 7405$	$1.374\ 6234^{28}$
41	$2.334\ 8609$	$4.044\ 3126$	$6.953\ 3796$	$1.186\ 8700^{28}$	$2.011\ 6440$
42	$3.057\ 5560$	$5.392\ 4169$	$9.436\ 7295$	$1.639\ 0109$	$2.825\ 8809$
43	$3.839\ 7214$	$6.897\ 2774$	$1.228\ 9694^{28}$	$2.172\ 6424$	$3.811\ 6533$
44	$4.625\ 1190$	$8.464\ 8404$	$1.536\ 2118$	$2.765\ 1812$	$4.937\ 8236$
45	$5.344\ 5819$	$9.969\ 7009$	$1.843\ 4541$	$3.379\ 6659$	$6.144\ 8471$
46	$5.925\ 5148$	$1.127\ 0097^{28}$	$2.123\ 9798$	$3.967\ 4339$	$7.347\ 0998$
47	$6.303\ 7391$	$1.222\ 9254$	$2.349\ 9351$	$4.473\ 9148$	$8.441\ 3487$
48	$6.435\ 0670$	$1.273\ 8806$	$2.496\ 8060$	$4.846\ 7411$	$9.320\ 6559$
49		$1.273\ 8806$	$2.547\ 7612$	$5.044\ 5672$	$9.891\ 3083$
50				$5.044\ 5672$	$1.008\ 9134^{29}$

y	$\Phi(y)$	y	$\Phi(y)$	y	$\Phi(y)$
0.00	1.0000	0.40	0.6892	0.80	0.4237
.01	.9920	.41	.6818	.81	.4179
.02	.9840	.42	.6745	.82	.4122
.03	.9761	.43	.6672	.83	.4065
.04	.9681	.44	.6599	.84	.4009
0.05	0.9601	0.45	0.6527	0.85	0.3953
.06	.9522	.46	.6455	.86	.3898
.07	.9442	.47	.6384	.87	.3843
.08	.9362	.48	.6312	.88	.3789
.09	.9283	.49	.6241	.89	.3735
0.10	0.9203	0.50	0.6171	0.90	0.3681
.11	.9124	.51	.6101	.91	.3628
.12	.9045	.52	.6031	.92	.3576
.13	.8966	.53	.5961	.93	.3524
.14	.8887	.54	.5892	•.94	.3472
0.15	0.8808	0.55	0.5823	0.95	0.3421
.16	.8729	.56	.5755	.96	.3371
.17	.8650	.57	.5687	.97	.3320
.18	.8572	.58	.5619	.98	.3271
.19	.8493	.59	.5552	.99	.3222
0.20	0.8415	0.60	0.5485	1.00	0.3173
.21	.8337	.61	.5419	.01	.3125
.22	.8259	.62	.5353	.02	.3077
.23	.8181	.63	.5287	.03	.3030
.24	.8103	.64	.5222	.04	.2983
0.25	0.8026	0.65	0.5157	1.05	0.2937
.26	.7949	.66	.5093	.06	.2891
.27	.7872	.67	.5029	.07	.2846
.28	.7795	.68	.4965	.08	.2801
.29	.7718	.69	.4902	.09	.2757
0.30	0.7642	0.70	0.4839	1.10	0.2713
.31	.7566	.71	.4777	.11	.2670
.32	.7490	.72	.4715	.12	.2627
.33	.7414	.73	.4654	.13	.2585
.34	.7339	.74	.4593	.14	.2543
0.35	0.7263	0.75	0.4533	1.15	0.2501
.36	.7188	.76	.4473	.16	.2460
.37	.7114	.77	.4413	.17	.2420
.38	.7039	.78	.4354	.18	.2380
.39	.6965	.79	.4295	.19	.2340

The definition of the Error Function is $\Phi(y) = \sqrt{\frac{2}{\pi}} \int_y^\infty e^{\frac{-v^2}{2}} \, dy$

y	$\Phi(y)$	y	$\Phi(y)$	y	$\Phi(y)$
1.20	0.2301	1.60	0.1096	2.00	0.0455
.21	.2263	.61	.1074	.01	.0444
.22	.2225	.62	.1052	.02	.0434
.23	.2187	.63	.1031	.03	.0424
.24	.2150	.64	.1010	.04	.0414
1.25	0.2113	1.65	0.0989	2.05	0.0404
.26	.2077	.66	.0969	.06	.0394
.27	.2041	.67	.0949	.07	.0385
.28	.2005	.68	.0930	.08	.0375
.29	.1971	.69	.0910	.09	.0366
1.30	0.1936	1.70	0.0891	2.10	0.0357
.31	.1902	.71	.0873	.11	.0349
.32	.1868	.72	.0854	.12	.0340
.33	.1835	.73	.0836	.13	.0332
.34	.1802	.74	.0819	.14	.0324
1.35	0.1770	1.75	0.0801	2.15	0.0316
.36	.1738	.76	.0784	.16	.0308
.37	.1707	.77	.0767	.17	.0300
.38	.1676	.78	.0751	.18	.0293
.39	.1645	.79	.0735	.19	.0285
1.40	0.1615	1.80	0.0719	2.20	0.0278
.41	.1585	.81	.0703	.21	.0271
.42	.1556	.82	.0688	.22	.0264
.43	.1527	.83	.0672	.23	.0257
.44	.1499	.84	.0658	.24	.0251
1.45	0.1471	1.85	0.0643	2.25	0.0244
.46	.1443	.86	.0629	.26	.0238
.47	.1416	.87	.0615	.27	.0232
.48	.1389	.88	.0601	.28	.0226
.49	.1362	.89	.0588	.29	.0220
1.50	0.1336	1.90	0.0574	2.30	0.0214
.51	.1310	.91	.0561	.31	.0209
.52	.1285	.92	.0549	.32	.0203
.53	.1260	.93	.0536	.33	.0198
.54	.1236	.94	.0524	.34	.0193
1.55	0.1211	1.95	0.0512	2.35	0.0188
.56	.1188	.96	.0500	.36	.0183
.57	.1164	.97	.0488	.37	.0178
.58	.1141	.98	.0477	.38	.0173
.59	.1118	.99	.0466	.39	.0168

y	$\Phi(y)$	y	$\Phi(y)$	y	$\Phi(y)$
2.40	0.0164	2.70	0.0069	3.00	0.0027
.41	.0160	.71	.0067	.10	.0019
.42	.0155	.72	.0065	.20	.0014
.43	.0151	.73	.0063	.30	.0010
.44	.0147	.74	.0061	.40	.0007
2.45	0.0143	2.75	0.0060	.50	0.0005
.46	.0139	.76	.0058	.60	.0003
.47	.0135	.77	.0056	.70	.0002
.48	.0131	.78	.0054	.80	.0001
.49	.0128	.79	.0053	.90	.0001
2.50	0.0124	2.80	0.0051	4.00	0.0001
.51	.0121	.81	.0050		
.52	.0117	.82	.0048		
.53	.0114	.83	.0047		
.54	.0111	.84	.0045		
2.55	0.0108	2.85	0.0044		
.56	.0105	.86	.0042		
.57	.0102	.87	.0041		
.58	.0099	.88	.0040		
.59	.0096	.89	.0039		
2.60	0.0093	2.90	0.0037		
.61	.0091	.91	.0036		
.62	.0088	.92	.0035		
.63	.0085	.93	.0034		
.64	.0083	.94	.0033		
				1.645	0.1
2.65	0.0080	2.95	0.0032	2.576	.01
.66	.0078	.96	.0031	3.291	.001
.67	.0076	.97	.0030	3.891	.0001
.68	.0074	.98	.0029	4.417	.00001
.69	.0071	.99	.0028	4.892	.000001

y	$\phi_{-1}(y)$	$\phi(y)$	$\phi'(y)$	$\phi''(y)$
0.0	+0.50000	+0.39894	−0.00000	−0.39894
0.1	0.53983	0.39695	0.03970	0.39298
0.2	0.57926	0.39104	0.07821	0.37540
0.3	0.61791	0.38139	0.11442	0.34706
0.4	0.65542	0.36827	0.14731	0.30935
0.5	+0.69146	+0.35207	−0.17603	−0.26405
0.6	0.72575	0.33322	0.19993	0.21326
0.7	0.75804	0.31225	0.21858	0.15925
0.8	0.78814	0.28969	0.23175	0.10429
0.9	0.81594	0.26609	0.23948	−0.05056
1.0	+0.84134	+0.24197	−0.24197	+0.00000
1.1	0.86433	0.21785	0.23964	0.04575
1.2	0.88493	0.19419	0.23302	0.08544
1.3	0.90320	0.17137	0.22278	0.11824
1.4	0.91924	0.14973	0.20962	0.14374
1.5	+0.93319	+0.12952	−0.19428	+0.16190
1.6	0.94520	0.11092	0.17747	0.17304
1.7	0.95543	0.09405	0.15988	0.17775
1.8	0.96407	0.07895	0.14211	0.17685
1.9	0.97128	0.06562	0.12467	0.17126
2.0	+0.97725	+0.05399	−0.10798	+0.16197
2.1	0.98214	0.04398	0.09237	0.14998
2.2	0.98610	0.03547	0.07804	0.13622
2.3	0.98928	0.02833	0.06515	0.12152
2.4	0.99180	0.02239	0.05375	0.10660
2.5	+0.99379	+0.01753	−0.04382	+0.09202
2.6	0.99534	0.01358	0.03532	0.07824
2.7	0.99653	0.01042	0.02814	0.06555
2.8	0.99744	0.00792	0.02216	0.05414
2.9	0.99813	0.00595	0.01726	0.04411
3.0	+0.99865	+0.00443	−0.01330	+0.03545
3.1	0.99903	0.00327	0.01013	0.02813
3.2	0.99931	0.00238	0.00763	0.02203
3.3	0.99952	0.00172	0.00568	0.01704
3.4	0.99966	0.00123	0.00419	0.01301
3.5	+0.99977	+0.00087	−0.00305	+0.00982
3.6	0.99984	0.00061	0.00220	0.00732
3.7	0.99989	0.00042	0.00157	0.00539
3.8	0.99993	0.00029	0.00111	0.00392
3.9	0.99995	0.00020	0.00077	0.00282
4.0	+0.99997	+0.00013	−0.00054	+0.00201

The notation is: $\phi(y) = \dfrac{1}{\sqrt{2\pi}} e^{\frac{-y^2}{2}}$,

y	$\phi'''(y)$	$\phi^{iv}(y)$	$\phi^{v}(y)$	$\phi^{vi}(y)$
0.0	+0.00000	+1.19683	−0.00000	−5.98413
0.1	0.11869	1.16708	0.59146	5.77625
0.2	0.23150	1.07990	1.14197	5.17112
0.3	0.33295	0.94130	1.61420	4.22226
0.4	0.41835	0.76070	1.97770	3.01221
0.5	+0.48409	+0.55010	−2.21141	−1.64481
0.6	0.52783	0.32309	2.30517	−0.23237
0.7	0.54863	+0.09371	2.26012	+1.11354
0.8	0.54694	−0.12468	2.08800	2.29382
0 9	0.52445	0.32034	1.80951	3.23026
1.0	+0.48394	−0.48394	−1.45182	+3.87153
1.1	0.42895	0.60909	1.04580	4.19585
1.2	0.36352	0.69255	0.62301	4.21034
1.3	0.29184	0.73413	−0.21300	3.94753
1.4	0.21800	0.73642	+0.15897	3.45953
1.5	+0.14571	−0.70425	+0.47355	+2.81094
1.6	0.07809	0.64405	0.71813	2.07125
1.7	+0.01759	0.56316	0.88702	1.30785
1.8	−0.03411	0.46915	0.98090	+0.58014
1.9	0.07605	0.36928	1.00583	−0.06467
2.0	−0.10798	−0.26996	+0.97184	−0.59390
2.1	0.13024	0.17646	0.89150	0.98987
2.2	0.14360	0.09274	0.77844	1.24885
2.3	0.14920	−0.02141	0.64604	1.37883
2.4	0.14834	+0.03623	0.50642	1.39654
2.5	−0.14242	+0.07997	+0.36974	−1.32421
2.6	0.13279	0.11053	0.24376	1.18645
2.7	0.12071	0.12926	0.13381	1.00761
2.8	0.10727	0.13793	+0.04287	0.80970
2.9	0.09339	0.13850	−0.02810	0.61102
3.0	−0.07977	+0.13296	−0.07977	−0.42546
3.1	0.06694	0.12313	0.11395	0.26242
3.2	0.05523	0.11066	0.13319	0.12712
3.3	0.04485	0.09690	0.14036	−0.02130
3.4	0.03586	0.08290	0.13840	+0.05607
3.5	−0.02825	+0.06943	−0.13000	+0.10784
3.6	0.02194	0.05703	0.11755	0.13802
3.7	0.01680	0.04599	0.10297	0.15102
3.8	0.01269	0.03646	0.08777	0.15124
3.9	0.00946	0.02842	0.07302	0.14264
4.0	−0.00696	+0.02181	−0.05942	+0.12861

$$\phi_{-1}(y) = \int_{-\infty}^{y} \phi(y)\,dy, \qquad \phi^{i}(y) = \frac{d^{i}\phi(y)}{dy^{i}}.$$

j	$\epsilon = 0.1$	$\epsilon = 0.2$	$\epsilon = 0.3$	$\epsilon = 0.4$	$\epsilon = 0.5$
0	9.0484^{-1}	8.1873^{-1}	7.4082^{-1}	6.7032^{-1}	6.0653^{-1}
1	9.0484^{-2}	1.6375	2.2225	2.6813	3.0327
2	4.5242^{-3}	1.6375^{-2}	3.3337^{-2}	5.3626^{-2}	7.5816^{-2}
3	1.5081^{-4}	1.0916^{-3}	3.3337^{-3}	7.1501^{-3}	1.2636
4	3.7702^{-6}	5.4582^{-5}	2.5003^{-4}	7.1501^{-4}	1.5795^{-3}
5		2.1833^{-6}	1.5002^{-5}	5.7201^{-5}	1.5795^{-4}
6				3.8134^{-6}	1.3163^{-5}

j	$\epsilon = 0.6$	$\epsilon = 0.7$	$\epsilon = 0.8$	$\epsilon = 0.9$
0	5.4881^{-1}	4.9659^{-1}	4.4933^{-1}	4.0657^{-1}
1	3.2929	3.4761	3.5946	3.6591
2	9.8786^{-2}	1.2166	1.4379	1.6466
3	1.9757	2.8388^{-2}	3.8343^{-2}	4.9398^{-2}
4	2.9636^{-3}	4.9679^{-3}	7.6685^{-3}	1.1115
5	3.5563^{-4}	6.9551^{-4}	1.2270	2.0006^{-3}
6	3.5563^{-5}	8.1143^{-5}	1.6360^{-4}	3.0009^{-4}
7	3.0483^{-6}	8.1143^{-6}	1.8697^{-5}	3.8584^{-5}
8			1.8697^{-6}	4.3406^{-6}

j	$\epsilon = 1$	$\epsilon = 2$	$\epsilon = 3$	$\epsilon = 4$	$\epsilon = 5$
0	3.6788^{-1}	1.3534^{-1}	4.9787^{-2}	1.8316^{-2}	6.7379^{-3}
1	3.6788	2.7067	1.4936^{-1}	7.3263	3.3690^{-2}
2	1.8394	2.7067	2.2404	1.4653^{-1}	8.4224
3	6.1313^{-2}	1.8045	2.2404	1.9537	1.4037^{-1}
4	1.5328	9.0224^{-2}	1.6803	1.9537	1.7547

j	$\epsilon = 1$	$\epsilon = 2$	$\epsilon = 3$	$\epsilon = 4$	$\epsilon = 5$
5	3.0657^{-3}	3.6089^{-2}	1.0082^{-1}	1.5629^{-1}	1.7547^{-1}
6	5.1094^{-4}	1.2030	5.0409^{-2}	1.0420	1.4622
7	7.2992^{-5}	3.4371^{-3}	2.1604	5.9540^{-2}	1.0444
8	9.1240^{-6}	8.5927^{-4}	8.1015^{-3}	2.9770	6.5278^{-2}
9	1.0138	1.9095	2.7005	1.3231	3.6266
10		3.8190^{-5}	8.1015^{-4}	5.2925^{-3}	1.8133
11		6.9436^{-6}	2.2095	1.9245	8.2422^{-3}
12		1.1573	5.5238^{-5}	6.4151^{-4}	3.4342
13			1.2747	1.9739	1.3209
14			2.7315^{-6}	5.6397^{-5}	4.7174^{-4}
15				1.5039	1.5725
16				3.7598^{-6}	4.9139^{-5}
17					1.4453
18					4.0146^{-6}
19					1.0565

j	$\epsilon = 6$	$\epsilon = 7$	$\epsilon = 8$	$\epsilon = 9$	$\epsilon = 10$
0	2.4788^{-3}	9.1188^{-4}	3.3546^{-4}	1.2341^{-4}	4.5400^{-5}
1	1.4873^{-2}	6.3832^{-3}	2.6837^{-3}	1.1107^{-3}	4.5400^{-4}
2	4.4618	2.2341^{-2}	1.0735^{-2}	4.9981	2.2700^{-3}
3	8.9235	5.2129	2.8626	1.4994^{-2}	7.5667
4	1.3385^{-1}	9.1226	5.7252	3.3737	1.8917^{-2}
5	1.6062	1.2772^{-1}	9.1604	6.0727	3.7833
6	1.6062	1.4900	1.2214^{-1}	9.1090	6.3055
7	1.3768	1.4900	1.3959	1.1712^{-1}	9.0079
8	1.0326	1.3038	1.3959	1.3176	1.1260^{-1}
9	6.8838^{-2}	1.0140	1.2408	1.3176	1.2511
10	4.1303	7.0983^{-2}	9.9262^{-2}	1.1858	1.2511
11	2.2529	4.5171	7.2190	9.7020^{-2}	1.1374
12	1.1264	2.6350	4.8127	7.2765	9.4780^{-2}
13	5.1990^{-3}	1.4188	2.9616	5.0376	7.2908
14	2.2281	7.0942^{-3}	1.6924	3.2384	5.2077
15	8.9126^{-4}	3.3106	9.0260^{-3}	1.9431	3.4718
16	3.3422	1.4484	4.5130	1.0930	2.1699
17	1.1796	5.9640^{-4}	2.1238	5.7863^{-3}	1.2764
18	3.9320^{-5}	2.3193	9.4389^{-4}	2.8932	7.0911^{-3}
19	1.2417	8.5449^{-5}	3.9743	1.3704	3.7322

j	$\epsilon = 6$	$\epsilon = 7$	$\epsilon = 8$	$\epsilon = 9$	$\epsilon = 10$
20	3.7251^{-6}	2.9907^{-5}	1.5897^{-4}	6.1670^{-4}	1.8661^{-3}
21	1.0643	9.9690^{-6}	6.0561^{-5}	2.6430	8.8861^{-4}
22		3.1720	2.2022	1.0812	4.0391
23			7.6598^{-6}	4.2309^{-5}	1.7561
24			2.5533	1.5866	7.3173^{-5}
25				5.7117^{-6}	2.9269
26				1.9771	1.1257
27					4.1694^{-6}
28					1.4891

j	$\epsilon = 11$	$\epsilon = 12$	$\epsilon = 13$	$\epsilon = 14$	$\epsilon = 15$
0	1.6702^{-5}	6.1442^{-6}	2.2603^{-6}		
1	1.8372^{-4}	7.3731^{-5}	2.9384^{-5}	1.1641^{-5}	4.5885^{-6}
2	1.0105^{-3}	4.4238^{-4}	1.9100^{-4}	8.1490	3.4414^{-5}
3	3.7050	1.7695^{-3}	8.2766	3.8029^{-4}	1.7207^{-4}
4	1.0189^{-2}	5.3086	2.6899^{-3}	1.3310^{-3}	6.4526
5	2.2415	1.2741^{-2}	6.9937	3.7268	1.9358^{-3}
6	4.1095	2.5481	1.5153^{-2}	8.6959	4.8395
7	6.4577	4.3682	2.8141	1.7392^{-2}	1.0370^{-2}
8	8.8794	6.5523	4.5730	3.0436	1.9444
9	1.0853^{-1}	8.7364	6.6054	4.7344	3.2407
10	1.1938	1.0484^{-1}	8.5870	6.6282	4.8611
11	1.1938	1.1437	1.0148^{-1}	8.4359	6.6287
12	1.0943	1.1437	1.0994	9.8418	8.2859
13	9.2595^{-2}	1.0557	1.0994	1.0599^{-1}	9.5607
14	7.2753	9.0489^{-2}	1.0209	1.0599	1.0244^{-1}
15	5.3352	7.2391	8.8475^{-2}	9.8923^{-2}	1.0244
16	3.6680	5.4293	7.1886	8.6558	9.6034^{-2}
17	2.3734	3.8325	5.4972	7.1283	8.4736
18	1.4504	2.5550	3.9702	5.5442	7.0613
19	8.3971^{-3}	1.6137	2.7164	4.0852	5.5747
20	4.6184	9.6820^{-3}	1.7657	2.8597	4.1810
21	2.4192	5.5326	1.0930	1.9064	2.9865
22	1.2096	3.0178	6.4589^{-3}	1.2132	2.0362
23	5.7849^{-4}	1.5745	3.6507	7.3846^{-3}	1.3280
24	2.6514	7.8725^{-4}	1.9775	4.3077	8.2998^{-3}

j	$\epsilon = 11$	$\epsilon = 12$	$\epsilon = 13$	$\epsilon = 14$	$\epsilon = 15$
25	1.1666^{-4}	3.7788^{-4}	1.0283^{-3}	2.4123^{-3}	4.9799^{-3}
26	4.9357^{-5}	1.7441	5.1414^{-4}	1.2989	2.8730
27	2.0109	7.7513^{-5}	2.4755	6.7352^{-4}	1.5961
28	7.8998^{-6}	3.3220	1.1493	3.3676	8.5506^{-4}
29	2.9965	1.3746	5.1522^{-5}	1.6257	4.4227
30	1.0987	5.4985^{-6}	2.2326	7.5868^{-5}	2.2114
31		2.1284	9.3625^{-6}	3.4263	1.0700
32			3.8035	1.4990	5.0157^{-5}
33			1.4984	6.3594^{-6}	2.2799
34				2.6186	1.0058
35				1.0474	4.3107^{-6}
36					1.7961

j	$\epsilon = 16$	$\epsilon = 17$	$\epsilon = 18$	$\epsilon = 19$	$\epsilon = 20$
0					
1	1.8006^{-6}				
2	1.4405^{-5}	5.9822^{-6}	2.4673^{-6}	1.0113^{-6}	
3	7.6824	3.3899^{-5}	1.4804^{-5}	6.4049	2.7482^{-6}
4	3.0730^{-4}	1.4407^{-4}	6.6616	3.0423^{-5}	1.3741^{-5}
5	9.8335	4.8984	2.3982^{-4}	1.1561^{-4}	5.4964
6	2.6223^{-3}	1.3879^{-3}	7.1945	3.6610	1.8321^{-4}
7	5.9937	3.3706	1.8500^{-3}	9.9369	5.2347
8	1.1987^{-2}	7.1625	4.1625	2.3600^{-3}	1.3087^{-3}
9	2.1311	1.3529^{-2}	8.3251	4.9822	2.9082
10	3.4098	2.3000	1.4985^{-2}	9.4662	5.8163
11	4.9597	3.5545	2.4521	1.6351^{-2}	1.0575^{-2}
12	6.6129	5.0355	3.6782	2.5889	1.7625
13	8.1389	6.5849	5.0929	3.7837	2.7116
14	9.3016	7.9960	6.5480	5.1351	3.8737
15	9.9218	9.0621	7.8576	6.5044	5.1649
16	9.9218	9.6285	8.8397	7.7240	6.4561
17	9.3381	9.6285	9.3597	8.6327	7.5954
18	8.3006	9.0935	9.3597	9.1123	8.4394
19	6.9899	8.1363	8.8671	9.1123	8.8835

j	$\epsilon = 16$	$\epsilon = 17$	$\epsilon = 18$	$\epsilon = 19$	$\epsilon = 20$
20	5.5920^{-2}	6.9159^{-2}	7.9804^{-2}	8.6567^{-2}	8.8835^{-2}
21	4.2605	5.5986	6.8403	7.8323	8.4605
22	3.0986	4.3262	5.5966	6.7642	7.6914
23	2.1555	3.1976	4.3800	5.5878	6.6881
24	1.4370	2.2650	3.2850	4.4237	5.5735
25	9.1969^{-3}	1.5402	2.3652	3.3620	4.4588
26	5.6596	1.0070	1.6374	2.4569	3.4298
27	3.3539	6.3406^{-3}	1.0916	1.7289	2.5406
28	1.9165	3.8497	7.0176^{-3}	1.1732	1.8147
29	1.0574	2.2567	4.3558	7.6864^{-3}	1.2515
30	5.6393^{-4}	1.2788	2.6135	4.8680	8.3435^{-3}
31	2.9106	7.0128^{-4}	1.5175	2.9836	5.3829
32	1.4553	3.7255	8.5359^{-4}	1.7715	3.3643
33	7.0561^{-5}	1.9192	4.6559	1.0200	2.0390
34	3.3205	9.5961^{-5}	2.4649	5.6998^{-4}	1.1994
35	1.5179	4.6609	1.2677	3.0942	6.8537^{-4}
36	6.7464^{-6}	2.2010	6.3383^{-5}	1.6330	3.8076
37	2.9174	1.0113	3.0835	8.3859^{-5}	2.0582
38	1.2284	4.5241^{-6}	1.4606	4.1930	1.0833
39		1.9720	6.7413^{-6}	2.0427	5.5551^{-5}
40			3.0336	9.7030^{-6}	2.7776
41			1.3318	4.4965	1.3549
42				2.0341	6.4520^{-6}
43					3.0009
44					1.3641

ν	$\epsilon = 0.1$	$\epsilon = 0.2$	$\epsilon = 0.3$	$\epsilon = 0.4$	$\epsilon = 0.5$
0	1.0000	1.0000	1.0000	1.0000	1.0000
1	9.5163^{-2}	1.8127^{-1}	2.5918^{-1}	3.2968^{-1}	3.9347^{-1}
2	4.6788^{-3}	1.7523^{-2}	3.6936^{-2}	6.1552^{-2}	9.0204^{-2}
3	1.5465^{-4}	1.1485^{-3}	3.5995^{-3}	7.9263^{-3}	1.4388
4	3.8468^{-6}	5.6840^{-5}	2.6581^{-4}	7.7625^{-4}	1.7516^{-3}
5		2.2582^{-6}	1.5785^{-5}	6.1243^{-5}	1.7212^{-4}
6				4.0427^{-6}	1.4165^{-5}
7					1.0024^{-6}

ν	$\epsilon = 0.6$	$\epsilon = 0.7$	$\epsilon = 0.8$	$\epsilon = 0.9$
0	1.0000	1.0000	1.0000	1.0000
1	4.5119^{-1}	5.0341^{-1}	5.5067^{-1}	5.9343^{-1}
2	1.2190	1.5580	1.9121	2.2752
3	2.3115^{-2}	3.4142^{-2}	4.7423^{-2}	6.2857^{-2}
4	3.3581^{-3}	5.7535^{-3}	9.0799^{-3}	1.3459
5	3.9449^{-4}	7.8554^{-4}	1.4113	2.3441^{-3}
6	3.8856^{-5}	9.0026^{-5}	1.8434^{-4}	3.4349^{-4}
7	3.2931^{-6}	8.8836^{-6}	2.0747^{-5}	4.3401^{-5}
8			2.0502^{-6}	4.8172^{-6}

ν	$\epsilon = 1$	$\epsilon = 2$	$\epsilon = 3$	$\epsilon = 4$	$\epsilon = 5$
0	1.0000	1.0000	1.0000	1.0000	1.0000
1	6.3212^{-1}	8.6466^{-1}	9.5021^{-1}	9.8168^{-1}	9.9326^{-1}
2	2.6424	5.9399	8.0085	9.0842	9.5957
3	8.0301^{-2}	3.2332	5.7681	7.6190	8.7535
4	1.8988	1.4288	3.5277	5.6653	7.3497

ν	$\epsilon = 1$	$\epsilon = 2$	$\epsilon = 3$	$\epsilon = 4$	$\epsilon = 5$
5	3.6598^{-3}	5.2653^{-2}	1.8474^{-1}	3.7116^{-1}	5.5951^{-1}
6	5.9418^{-4}	1.6564	8.3918^{-2}	2.1487	3.8404
7	8.3241^{-5}	4.5338^{-3}	3.3509	1.1067	2.3782
8	1.0249	1.0967	1.1905	5.1134^{-2}	1.3337
9	1.1252^{-6}	2.3745^{-4}	3.8030^{-3} ·	2.1363	6.8094^{-2}
10		4.6498^{-5}	1.1025	8.1322^{-3}	3.1828
11		8.3082^{-6}	2.9234^{-4}	2.8398	1.3695
12		1.3646	7.1387^{-5}	9.1523^{-4}	5.4531^{-3}
13			1.6149	2.7372	2.0189
14			3.4019^{-6}	7.6328^{-5}	6.9799^{-4}
15				1.9932	2.2625
16				4.8926^{-6}	6.9008^{-5}
17				1.1328	1.9869
18					5.4163^{-6}
19					1.4017

ν	$\epsilon = 6$	$\epsilon = 7$	$\epsilon = 8$	$\epsilon = 9$	$\epsilon = 10$
0	1.0000	1.0000	1.0000	1.0000	1.0000
1	9.9752^{-1}	9.9909^{-1}	9.9966^{-1}	9.9988^{-1}	9.9995^{-1}
2	9.8265	9.9270	9.9698	9.9877	9.9950
3	9.3803	9.7036	9.8625	9.9377	9.9723
4	8.4880	9.1823	9.5762	9.7877	9.8966
5	7.1494	8.2701	9.0037	9.4504	9.7075
6	5.5432	6.9929	8.0876	8.8431	9.3291
7	3.9370	5.5029	6.8663	7.9322	8.6986
8	2.5602	4.0129	5.4704	6.7610	7.7978
9	1.5276	2.7091	4.0745	5.4435	6.6718
10	8.3924^{-2}	1.6950	2.8338	4.1259	5.4207
11	4.2621	9.8521^{-2}	1.8411	2.9401	4.1696
12	2.0092	5.3350	1.1192	1.9699	3.0322
13	8.8275^{-3}	2.7000	6.3797^{-2}	1.2423	2.0844
14	3.6285	1.2811	3.4181	7.3851^{-2}	1.3554
15	1.4004	5.7172^{-3}	1.7257	4.1466	8.3458^{-2}
16	5.0910^{-4}	2.4066	8.2310^{-3}	2.2036	4.8740
17	1.7488	9.5818^{-4}	3.7180	1.1106	2.7042
18	5.6917^{-5}	3.6178	1.5943	5.3196^{-3}	1.4278
19	1.7597	1.2985	6.5037^{-4}	2.4264	7.1865^{-3}

ν	$\epsilon = 6$	$\epsilon = 7$	$\epsilon = 8$	$\epsilon = 9$	$\epsilon = 10$
20	5.1802^{-6}	4.4402^{-5}	2.5294^{-3}	1.0560^{-3}	3.4543^{-4}
21	1.4551	1.4495	9.3968^{-5}	4.3925^{-4}	1.5883
22		4.5263^{-6}	3.3407	1.7495	6.9965^{-4}
23		1.3543	1.1385	6.6828^{-5}	2.9574
24			3.7255^{-6}	2.4519	1.2012
25			1.1722	8.6531^{-6}	4.6949^{-5}
26				2.9414	1.7680
27					6.4229^{-6}
28					2.2535

ν	$\epsilon = 11$	$\epsilon = 12$	$\epsilon = 13$	$\epsilon = 14$	$\epsilon = 15$
0	1.0000	1.0000			
1	9.9998^{-1}	9.9999^{-1}	1.0000	1.0000	
2	9.9980	9.9992	9.9997^{-1}	9.9999^{-1}	1.0000
3	9.9879	9.9948	9.9978	9.9991	9.9996^{-1}
4	9.9508	9.9771	9.9895	9.9953	9.9979
5	9.8490	9.9240	9.9626	9.9819	9.9914
6	9.6248	9.7966	9.8927	9.9447	9.9721
7	9.2139	9.5418	9.7411	9.8577	9.9237
8	8.5681	9.1050	9.4597	9.6838	9.8200
9	7.6801	8.4497	9.0024	9.3794	9.6255
10	6.5949	7.5761	8.3419	8.9060	9.3015
11	5.4011	6.5277	7.4832	8.2432	8.8154
12	4.2073	5.3840	6.4684	7.3996	8.1525
13	3.1130	4.2403	5.3690	6.4154	7.3239
14	2.1871	3.1846	4.2696	5.3555	6.3678
15	1.4596	2.2798	3.2487	4.2956	5.3435
16	9.2604^{-2}	1.5558	2.3639	3.3064	4.3191
17	5.5924	1.0129	1.6451	2.4408	3.3588
18	3.2191	6.2966^{-2}	1.0954	1.7280	2.5114
19	1.7687	3.7416	6.9833^{-2}	1.1736	1.8053
20	9.2895^{-3}	2.1280	4.2669	7.6505^{-2}	1.2478
21	4.6711	1.1598	2.5012	4.7908	8.2972^{-2}
22	2.2519	6.0651^{-3}	1.4081	2.8844	5.3106
23	1.0423	3.0474	7.6225^{-3}	1.6712	3.2744
24	4.6386^{-4}	1.4729	3.9718	9.3276^{-3}	1.9465

ν	$\epsilon = 11$	$\epsilon = 12$	$\epsilon = 13$	$\epsilon = 14$	$\epsilon = 15$
25	1.9871^{-4}	6.8563^{-4}	1.9943^{-3}	5.0199^{-3}	1.1165^{-2}
26	8.2050^{-5}	3.0776	9.6603^{-4}	2.6076	6.1849^{-3}
27	3.2693	1.3335	4.5190	1.3087	3.3119
28	1.2584	5.5836^{-5}	2.0435	6.3513^{-4}	1.7158
29	4.6847^{-6}	2.2616	8.9416^{-5}	2.9837	8.6072^{-4}
30	1.6882	8.8701^{-6}	3.7894	1.3580	4.1845
31		3.3716	1.5568	5.9928^{-5}	1.9731
32		1.2432	6.2052^{-6}	2.5665	9.0312^{-5}
33			2.4017	1.0675	4.0155
34				4.3154^{-6}	1.7356
35				1.6968	7.2978^{-6}
36					2.9871
37					1.1910

ν	$\epsilon = 16$	$\epsilon = 17$	$\epsilon = 18$	$\epsilon = 19$	$\epsilon = 20$
0					
1					
2	1.0000	1.0000			
3	9.9998^{-1}	9.9999^{-1}	1.0000	1.0000	
4	9.9991	9.9996	9.9998^{-1}	9.9999^{-1}	1.0000
5	9.9960	9.9982	9.9992	9.9996	9.9998^{-1}
6	9.9862	9.9933	9.9968	9.9985	9.9993
7	9.9599	9.9794	9.9896	9.9948	9.9974
8	9.9000	9.9457	9.9711	9.9849	9.9922
9	9.7801	9.8740	9.9294	9.9613	9.9791
10	9.5670	9.7388	9.8462	9.9114	9.9500
11	9.2260	9.5088	9.6963	9.8168	9.8919
12	8.7301	9.1533	9.4511	9.6533	9.7861
13	8.0688	8.6498	9.0833	9.3944	9.6099
14	7.2545	7.9913	8.5740	9.0160	9.3387
15	6.3247	7.1917	7.9192	8.5025	8.9514
16	5.3326	6.2855	7.1335	7.8521	8.4349
17	4.3404	5.3226	6.2495	7.0797	7.7893
18	3.4066	4.3598	5.3135	6.2164	7.0297
19	2.5765	3.4504	4.3776	5.3052	6.1858

ν	$\epsilon = 16$	$\epsilon = 17$	$\epsilon = 18$	$\epsilon = 19$	$\epsilon = 20$
20	1.8775^{-1}	2.6368^{-1}	3.4908^{-1}	4.3939^{-1}	5.2974^{-1}
21	1.3183	1.9452	2.6928	3.5283	4.4091
22	8.9227^{-2}	1.3853	2.0088	2.7450	3.5630
23	5.8241	9.5272^{-2}	1.4491	2.0687	2.7939
24	3.6686	6.3296	1.0111	1.5098	2.1251
25	2.2315	4.0646	6.8260^{-2}	1.0675	1.5677
26	1.3119	2.5245	4.4608	7.3126^{-2}	1.1218
27	7.4589^{-3}	1.5174	2.8234	4.8557	7.7887^{-2}
28	4.1051	8.8335^{-3}	1.7318	3.1268	5.2481
29	2.1886	4.9838	1.0300	1.9536	4.3334
30	1.1312	2.7272	5.9443^{-3}	1.1850	2.1818
31	5.6726^{-4}	1.4484	3.3308	6.9819^{-3}	1.3475
32	2.7620	7.4708^{-4}	1.8133	3.9982	8.0918^{-3}
33	1.3067	3.7453	9.5975^{-4}	2.2267	4.7274
34	6.0108^{-5}	1.8260	4.9416	1.2067	2.6884
35	2.6903	8.6644^{-5}	2.4767	6.3674^{-4}	1.4890
36	1.1724	4.0035	1.2090	3.2732	8.0366^{-4}
37	4.9772^{-6}	1.8025	5.7519^{-5}	1.6401	4.2290
38	2.0599	7.9123^{-6}	2.6684	8.0154^{-5}	2.1708
39		3.3882	1.2078	3.8224	1.0875
40		1.4162	5.3365^{-6}	1.7797	5.3202^{-5}
41			2.3030	8.0940^{-6}	2.5426
42				3.5975	1.1877
43				1.5634	5.4252^{-6}
44					2.4243
45					1.0603

VIII. PEARSON'S CRITERION

s'	$P = .99$	$P = .98$	$P = .95$	$P = .90$	$P = .80$	$P = .70$
I	0.000157	0.000628	0.00393	0.0158	0.0642	0.148
2	0.0201	0.0404	0.103	0.211	0.446	0.713
3	0.115	0.185	0.352	0.584	1.005	1.424
4	0.297	0.429	0.711	1.064	1.649	2.195
5	0.554	0.752	1.145	1.610	2.343	3.000
6	0.872	1.134	1.635	2.204	3.070	3.828
7	1.239	1.564	2.167	2.833	3.822	4.671
8	1.646	2.032	2.733	3.490	4.594	5.527
9	2.088	2.532	3.325	4.168	5.380	6.393
10	2.558	3.059	3.940	4.865	6.179	7.267
11	3.053	3.609	4.575	5.578	6.989	8.148
12	3.571	4.178	5.226	6.304	7.807	9.034
13	4.107	4.765	5.892	7.042	8.634	9.926
14	4.660	5.368	6.571	7.790	9.467	10.821
15	5.229	5.985	7.261	8.547	10.307	11.721
16	5.812	6.614	7.962	9.312	11.152	12.624
17	6.408	7.255	8.672	10.085	12.002	13.531
18	7.015	7.906	9.390	10.865	12.857	14.440
19	7.633	8.567	10.117	11.651	13.716	15.352
20	8.260	9.237	10.851	12.443	14.578	16.266
21	8.897	9.915	11.591	13.240	15.445	17.182
22	9.542	10.600	12.338	14.041	16.314	18.101
23	10.196	11.293	13.091	14.848	17.187	19.021
24	10.856	11.992	13.848	15.659	18.062	19.943
25	11.524	12.697	14.611	16.473	18.940	20.867
26	12.198	13.409	15.379	17.292	19.820	21.792
27	12.879	14.125	16.151	18.114	20.703	22.719
28	13.565	14.847	16.928	18.939	21.588	23.647
29	14.256	15.574	17.708	19.768	22.475	24.577
30	14.953	16.306	18.493	20.599	23.364	25.508

Taken from *Statistical Methods for Research Workers*, by R. A. Fisher. Published by Oliver & Boyd, Edinburgh.

s'	$P = .50$	$P = .30$	$P = .20$	$P = .10$	$P = .05$	$P = .02$	$P = .01$
1	0.455	1.074	1.642	2.706	3.841	5.412	6.635
2	1.386	2.408	3.219	4.605	5.991	7.824	9.210
3	2.366	3.665	4.642	6.251	7.815	9.837	11.341
4	3.357	4.878	5.989	7.779	9.488	11.668	13.277
5	4.351	6.064	7.289	9.236	11.070	13.388	15.086
6	5.348	7.231	8.558	10.645	12.592	15.033	16.812
7	6.346	8.383	9.803	12.017	14.067	16.622	18.475
8	7.344	9.524	11.030	13.362	15.507	18.168	20.090
9	8.343	10.656	12.242	14.684	16.919	19.679	21.666
10	9.342	11.781	13.442	15.987	18.307	21.161	23.209
11	10.341	12.899	14.631	17.275	19.675	22.618	24.725
12	11.340	14.011	15.812	18.549	21.026	24.054	26.217
13	12.340	15.119	16.985	19.812	22.362	25.472	27.688
14	13.339	16.222	18.151	21.064	23.685	26.873	29.141
15	14.339	17.322	19.311	22.307	24.996	28.259	30.578
16	15.338	18.418	20.465	23.542	26.296	29.633	32.000
17	16.338	19.511	21.615	24.769	27.587	30.995	33.409
18	17.338	20.601	22.760	25.989	28.869	32.346	34.805
19	18.338	21.689	23.900	27.204	30.144	33.687	36.191
20	19.337	22.775	25.038	28.412	31.410	35.020	37.566
21	20.337	23.858	26.171	29.615	32.671	36.343	38.932
22	21.337	24.939	27.301	30.813	33.924	37.659	40.289
23	22.337	26.018	28.429	32.007	35.172	38.968	41.638
24	23.337	27.096	29.553	33.196	36.415	40.270	42.980
25	24.337	28.172	30.675	34.382	37.652	41.566	44.314
26	25.336	29.246	31.795	35.563	38.885	42.856	45.642
27	26.336	30.319	32.912	36.741	40.113	44.140	46.963
28	27.336	31.391	34.027	37.916	41.337	45.419	48.278
29	28.336	32.461	35.139	39.087	42.557	46.693	49.588
30	29.336	33.530	36.250	40.256	43.773	47.962	50.892

For larger values of s' use Appendix V, with $y = \sqrt{2s' - 1} - \sqrt{2\chi^2}$ and $P = \phi_{-1}(y)$.

IX. STUDENT'S TEST OF SIGNIFICANCE $2P$ ($> |t|$)

n'	$P = 0.9$	0.8	0.7	0.6	0.5	0.4	0.3	0.2	0.1	0.05	0.02	0.01
1	0.158	0.325	0.510	0.727	1.000	1.376	1.963	3.078	6.314	12.706	31.821	63.657
2	0.142	0.289	0.445	0.617	0.816	1.061	1.386	1.886	2.920	4.303	6.965	9.925
3	0.137	0.277	0.424	0.584	0.765	0.978	1.250	1.638	2.353	3.182	4.541	5.841
4	0.134	0.271	0.414	0.569	0.741	0.941	1.190	1.533	2.132	2.776	3.747	4.604
5	0.132	0.267	0.408	0.559	0.727	0.920	1.156	1.476	2.015	2.571	3.365	4.032
6	0.131	0.265	0.404	0.553	0.718	0.906	1.134	1.440	1.943	2.447	3.143	3.707
7	0.130	0.263	0.402	0.549	0.711	0.896	1.119	1.415	1.895	2.365	2.998	3.499
8	0.130	0.262	0.399	0.546	0.706	0.889	1.108	1.397	1.860	2.306	2.896	3.355
9	0.129	0.261	0.398	0.543	0.703	0.883	1.100	1.383	1.833	2.262	2.821	3.250
10	0.129	0.260	0.397	0.542	0.700	0.879	1.093	1.372	1.812	2.228	2.764	3.169
11	0.129	0.260	0.396	0.540	0.697	0.876	1.088	1.363	1.796	2.201	2.718	3.106
12	0.128	0.259	0.395	0.539	0.695	0.873	1.083	1.356	1.782	2.179	2.681	3.055
13	0.128	0.259	0.394	0.538	0.694	0.870	1.079	1.350	1.771	2.160	2.650	3.012
14	0.128	0.258	0.393	0.537	0.692	0.868	1.076	1.345	1.761	2.145	2.624	2.977
15	0.128	0.258	0.393	0.536	0.691	0.866	1.074	1.341	1.753	2.131	2.602	2.947
16	0.128	0.258	0.392	0.535	0.690	0.865	1.071	1.337	1.746	2.120	2.583	2.921
17	0.128	0.257	0.392	0.534	0.689	0.863	1.069	1.333	1.740	2.110	2.567	2.898
18	0.127	0.257	0.392	0.534	0.688	0.862	1.067	1.330	1.734	2.101	2.552	2.878
19	0.127	0.257	0.391	0.533	0.688	0.861	1.066	1.328	1.729	2.093	2.539	2.861
20	0.127	0.257	0.391	0.533	0.687	0.860	1.064	1.325	1.725	2.086	2.528	2.845
21	0.127	0.257	0.391	0.532	0.686	0.859	1.063	1.323	1.721	2.080	2.518	2.831
22	0.127	0.256	0.390	0.532	0.686	0.858	1.061	1.321	1.717	2.074	2.508	2.819
23	0.127	0.256	0.390	0.532	0.685	0.858	1.060	1.319	1.714	2.069	2.500	2.807
24	0.127	0.256	0.390	0.531	0.685	0.857	1.059	1.318	1.711	2.064	2.492	2.797
25	0.127	0.256	0.390	0.531	0.684	0.856	1.058	1.316	1.708	2.060	2.485	2.787
26	0.127	0.256	0.390	0.531	0.684	0.856	1.058	1.315	1.706	2.056	2.479	2.779
27	0.127	0.256	0.389	0.531	0.684	0.855	1.057	1.314	1.703	2.052	2.473	2.771
28	0.127	0.256	0.389	0.530	0.683	0.855	1.056	1.313	1.701	2.048	2.467	2.763
29	0.127	0.256	0.389	0.530	0.683	0.854	1.055	1.311	1.699	2.045	2.462	2.756
30	0.127	0.256	0.389	0.530	0.683	0.854	1.055	1.310	1.697	2.042	2.457	2.750
∞	0.12566	0.25335	0.38532	0.52440	0.67449	0.84162	1.03643	1.28155	1.64485	1.95996	2.32634	2.57582

Taken from *Statistical Methods for Research Workers*, by R. A. Fisher. Thirteenth Edition published by Oliver & Boyd, Edinburgh.

Index of Notation

$[a_{j,k}]$	278	r_{xy}	333
$\downarrow a_{j,\cdot} \downarrow$	278	$r \downarrow$	137
$[a_{\cdot,k}]$	278	s	198
C_n^m	35	$^aS_{j_1, j_2 \ldots j_a}$	46
covar (xy)	201	^aS_n	46
d	197	var x	199
$g(u)$	211	δ	198
$G(u)$	211	$\hat{\epsilon}$	302
$H_i(y)$	258	$\epsilon_i(x)$	189, 192
$p(>|t|)$	344	$\mu_i(x)$	192
P_n^m	34	$\nu_x(y,r)$	96
$P_{m_1, m_2, \ldots, m_a}^{m_1, m_2, \ldots, m_a}$	35	σ	199
$P(j)$	245, 356	$\hat{\sigma}$	302
$P_x(y,r)$	132	$\hat{\Sigma}$	46
$P(n_1, n_2, \ldots, n_a)$	253	Σ^*	201
$P(x_1, x_2, \ldots, x_a)$	255	$\phi(y)$	227
$P(A)$	59	$\phi_{-1}(y)$	235
$P(A,B)$	72	$\phi(y)$	260
$P(A \cap B)$	72	χ^2	316
$P(B|A)$	66	$\cap$	16
$P_{a'}(> \chi^2)$	318	$\cup$	16

Index

Except where otherwise noted, numbers refer to pages.

At random (*see also* Random), 65
  collectively, 239–240
  individually, 239
Averages, Chapter VIII
  definition of, 188
  of continuous variable, 193–195

Bayes' theorem, Chapter VI
  application to sampling theory, 154–155
  for continuous variables, 167–169
  limitations on use of, 152–153
  statement of, 147
Bernoulli's theorem, Chapter V
  First half of Theorem, 114
  Second half of Theorem, 118
  Proof of first half, 125–127
  Proof of second half, 127–128
Beta function, 40
Beta-ray emission, distribution of, 249–251
Biased die, 309–316, 319–323
Binomial coefficients, 35–42
  Pascal's triangle, 37–39
  relations among, 38, 40–42, 53–55, 100, 102, 140–141
  table of, Appendix III
  with fractional indices, 41
  with negative indices, 41
Binomial distribution, 81–83, 111–121, 229–236
  expectation of, 204–205
  for beta-ray emission, 249–250
  for traffic congestion, 365
  generating function for, 224
  Gram-Charlier approximation to, 261–264
  limiting forms of, 113–116, 229–234, 236–238
  Poisson approximation to, 236–238
  normal approximation to, 229–234
  standard deviation of, 222
  sums of terms of, 234–236
  variance of, 222

Binomial theorem, 39–40
Bose-Einstein distribution, 89

Cauchy distribution, 221, 224
Central limit theorem, 264–273
Chance, 10–11
  event, 10
  function, 21–22
  integer, 218–220
  non-numerical chance functions, 22
  paths (*see* Chance paths)
  probability as a chance function, 22
  sums of chance integers, 218–220
Chance paths, 92–102, 131–134
  of given length, 94–102, 132–134
  loop of length L, 142
  with given end points, 94–102
Chi-square distribution, 318
  table of, Appendix VIII
Chi-square test, 312–321
  of independence, 327–328
Combinations, Chapter III
  definition, 27
  including like objects, 42–44
  of m things n at a time, 36
Conditional probabilities, 66–72, 166–169
  defined, 66
  generating functions for, 214–216
  provisos which alter, 66–67, 72
  representation in sample space, 71–72
Confidence, 20–21, 305–306
  interval, 21, 306
  level of, 21, 306
  limit, 21
Congestion (*see also* Double connections; Hunting problems; Traffic)
  degree of, 365–384
  problems of, Chapter XII
Convolution, 220–221
Correlation, 325–339
  coefficient of, 333

Correlation (*continued*)
  relation to regression, 333–335
  rotation of axes, 337–339
Covariance:
  defined, 201
  of independent variables, 201

Delays in awaiting service (*see* Traffic, delayed)
Dependence:
  tests of, 325–339
  the χ^2 test, 327–328
Deviation:
  from expectation, 198
  from the mean, 197
  mean square, 197
  standard (*see* Standard deviation)
Dichotomy, 13, Chapter V
Distribution function, Chapter X
  Binomial (*see* Binomial distribution)
  Bose-Einstein, 89
  Cauchey, 221, 224
  change of variable in, 169–177, 179–186
  defined, 14
  derived empirically, 165–166
  F-distribution, 344–346
  Fermi-Dirac, 88
  hypergeometric, 87, 205
  Maxwell-Boltzmann, 88
  Multinomial (*see* Multinomial distribution)
  non-random, 164–165
  normal (*see* Normal distribution)
  normalized, 199
  of beta-rays, 249–251
  of continuous variable, Chapter VII
  of $\bar{s}^2$, 343–344
  of the mean, 272, 341
  of the ratio of two variances, 344–346
  of the variance, 306, 342
  Poisson (*see* Poisson distribution)
  random, 157–162
  standard form of, 199
  t-distribution, 343–344
Double connections, 395–397

Equilibrium, statistical, 288, 362
Estimation of parameters, 301 303
  best estimate, 302
  efficient statistic, 303

Events, 1, 12–13
  complementary, 12
  composite, 13, 24
  composition of, 24–26
  compound, 25
  equally likely, 4–5
  independent, 26, 325–339, Chapter V
  random association of, 64–65
Expectation, 188–197, 209–211
  definition of, 188
  mathematical, 188
  of a continuous variable, 193–195
  of a function, 194–195
  of a probability, 209–211
  of a sum, 200
  relation to fair games, 190–192
Experiment, 11

Factorials, 32–34
  of negative integers, 32
  of non-integers, 33
  Stirling's approximation, 121–124
  tables of, Appendices I and II
F-distribution, 334–346
Fermi-Dirac distribution, 89
Fit (*see* Goodness of fit)

Game, fair, 190–192, 206–209
Gamma function, 34
Gas theory:
  escape velocities, 181–183
  Maxwell's equation, 177–179
  molecular energy, 194–195
  molecular speeds, 181
  molecular velocities, 179–180
Generating function, 212–220
  definition of, 212
  for continuous variables, 221–222
  for sums of chance integers, 218–220
  moment, 212
  of conditional probabilities, 212–216
  of incomplete sets, 212–216
  of Poisson distribution, 217
Goodness of fit, 307–325
Gram-Charlier series, 257–270
  for binomial distribution, 261–263
  for Poisson distribution, 263–264

Hermite polynomials, 257–258
Hunting problems, 384–395

Hypergeometric distribution:
  definition of, 87
  expectation of, 205
Hyperspherical coordinates, 183
Hypotheses, tests of:
  Chi-square test, 312–321
  criterion, 308
  examples of, 309–328, 346–350
  null hypotheses, 322
  type I and type II errors, 323

Independence, tests of (*see* Dependence, tests of)
Independent trials, Chapter V
  distribution of successes, dichotomy, 81–83, 111–113
  distribution of successes, general case, 83–84, 88
  limiting form of distribution, 113–120, 229–238, 253–255
  sums of, 264–273
Inference, statistical, 19–21, Chapter XI

Jacobian, 169–175

Kollektiv, 110

Limit, definition of, 107

Marginal probability, 168
Markov processes (*see* Processes)
Matching, 90–92, 100 (*see also* Psychic research)
Mathematical expectation (*see* Expectation)
Mathematical model, 11
Matrices, 277–289
  as operators, 280–281
  contingency, 78–79, 327–328
  defined, 277
  distribution, 278
  multiplication of, 279
  transition, 69, 281
Maxwell-Boltzmann distribution, 89
Maxwell's equation, 179
Mean:
  definition of, 188
  distribution of, 224, 272, 342
  square, 192
Measurement, precision of, 298–305
Measuring probability, Chapter I
  by experiment, 109–111, 128–129, 309–316

Measuring probability (*continued*)
  by sets and subsets, 6–7, 14–15, 63–64
  need for more than one method, 7–8
  primary method, 2–9
  shortcomings of primary method, 7–8
Median:
  definition of, 195
  expected, 196
Moments:
  definition of, 195
  distribution of, 196
Monte Carlo method, 12
Multinomial distribution, 84–88
  normal approximation to, 253–255
Multiplication theorem, 73, 129–131, 166–169

Normal distribution:
  approximation to binomial, 229–236
  approximation to multinomial, 253–255
  approximation to Poisson, 251–253
  derivatives of, 257–258, Appendix V
  error function, 260, 304, Appendix IV
  expectation of, 222
  importance of, 227–229, 257
  in more than one variable, 179, 253–255, 316
  of velocities of gas molecules, 181
  standard deviations of, 222
  table of, Appendix V
  use in calculating sums of binomial terms, 234–236

Paradox:
  Bertrand's box, 148
  life on Mars, 144–146
  St. Petersburg, 206–209
  zero, 161–162
Particle physics, 88–89
Partition, 28, 50–51, 54
Permutations, Chapter III
  definition of, 27
  including like objects, 30–31, 35, 49–50, 55
  of m things m at a time, 30, 35
  of m things n at a time, 30, 32, 35
Poisson distribution:
  as limit of binomial, 236–238
  derivation of, 217, 240–243
  distribution of sums, 224
  expectation of, 224

Poisson distribution (*continued*)
  for traffic congestion, 366–367
  generating functions for, 224, 248
  Gram-Charlier approximation to, 263–264
  normal approximation to, 251–253
  sums of terms of, 366, Appendix VII
  table of, Appendix VI
  uses of, 243–248
  with variable density, 246–248
Population, 18–19
Precision of measurement (*see* Measurement, precision of)
Processes, Chapter X
  Bernoulli, 293
  Markov, 281–290
  non-Markovian, 291–293
  stationary, 290, 293
Psychic research, 60–62, 67–68, 70, 74–75, 79–81, 99

Queueing problems (*see* Problems of congestion)

Random (*see also* At random)
  association of events, 64–65
  distribution, 14, 160, 162
  event, 10
  paths (*see* Random paths)
  variable, 21
Random paths (*see also* Chance paths) 134–142
  first and subsequent passage, 137–142
  first and subsequent return, 139–141
  loop of length L, 135–137
  with given end points, 134
Regression, 328–335
  curve of, 329–336
  line of, 331
  point of, 329
  relation to correlation, 333
Root mean square, 192

Sample space;
  continuous, 11
  defined, 11
  examples of, 63–64

Sample space (*continued*)
  representation of conditional probabilities in, 71–72
Sampling theory, 19–21, 346–347
  application of Bayes' theorem to, 154–155
Sets, 15–18
  upper bound of, 107–109
Standard deviation:
  defined, 199
  distribution of, 342
  sample, 198
Statistical equilibrium (*see* Equilibrium, statistical)
Statistical inference (*see* Inference, statistical)
Statistics, 13 (*see also* Goodness of fit; Hypotheses, tests of; Sampling theory)
  Bose-Einstein, 89, 283–285
  distribution of, 339–346
  efficient, 303
  estimation of parameters, 301–303
  Fermi-Dirac, 89
  foundations of, Chapter XI
  Maxwell-Boltzmann, 89
  precision of measurement, 298–305
Stirling's formula, 121–124
Stochastic, 10
Symmetric functions, 44–47

Taylor series, 41
t-distribution, 344
  table of, Appendix IX
Traffic:
  allowable, 378–383
  delayed, 286–289, 397–409
  lost, 358–384

Variable:
  chance, 21
  change of, 169–177, 179, 180, 183–186
  random, 21
Variance:
  defined, 199
  distribution of, 306, 342
  of a sum, 201
  sample, 198

Weldon's dice data (*see* Biased die)